# JUSTICE FOR ALL

# JUSTICE FOR ALL

Earl Warren and the Nation He Made

## JIM NEWTON

RIVERHEAD BOOKS

*a member of Penguin Group (USA) Inc.*

*New York*

*2006*

RIVERHEAD BOOKS
Published by the Penguin Group
Penguin Group (USA) Inc., 375 Hudson Street, New York, New York 10014, USA ·
Penguin Group (Canada), 90 Eglinton Avenue East, Suite 700, Toronto, Ontario
M4P 2Y3, Canada (a division of Pearson Penguin Canada Inc.) · Penguin Books Ltd,
80 Strand, London WC2R 0RL, England · Penguin Ireland, 25 St Stephen's Green,
Dublin 2, Ireland (a division of Penguin Books Ltd) · Penguin Group (Australia),
250 Camberwell Road, Camberwell, Victoria 3124, Australia (a division of
Pearson Australia Group Pty Ltd) · Penguin Books India Pvt Ltd, 11 Community
Centre, Panchsheel Park, New Delhi–110 017, India · Penguin Group (NZ),
Cnr Airborne and Rosedale Roads, Albany, Auckland 1310, New Zealand (a division
of Pearson New Zealand Ltd) · Penguin Books (South Africa) (Pty) Ltd,
24 Sturdee Avenue, Rosebank, Johannesburg 2196, South Africa

Penguin Books Ltd, Registered Offices:
80 Strand, London WC2R 0RL, England

The author gratefully acknowledges permission to quote from the following:
Excerpts from the Earl Warren Oral History Project. Courtesy The Bancroft Library, University of California, Berkeley.
"The Gift Outright" from *The Poetry of Robert Frost*, edited by Edward Connery Lathem. Copyright 1969 by Henry Holt and Company. Copyright 1942 by Robert Frost, copyright 1970 by Lesley Frost Ballantine. Reprinted by permission of Henry Holt and Company, LLC.

Library of Congress Cataloging-in-Publication Data

Newton, Jim, date.
Justice for all : Earl Warren and the nation he made / by Jim Newton.
p.        cm.
Includes bibliographical references and index.
ISBN 1-59448-928-9
1. Warren, Earl, 1891–1974.    2. Judges—United States—Biography.
3. United States. Supreme Court—Biography.    I. Title.
KF8745.W3N49        2006                    2006046464
347.73'2634—dc22
[B]

Printed in the United States of America
1   3   5   7   9   10   8   6   4   2

BOOK DESIGN BY AMANDA DEWEY
PHOTO INSERT BY NICOLE LAROCHE

*To Karlene and Jack*

# Contents

PART THREE

# AMERICAN JUSTICE

# JUSTICE FOR ALL

Prologue

# FIRST VACANCY

T HE GOVERNOR WAS ASLEEP, and those who knew him knew he did not
like interruption. So when California's First Lady snatched the receiver
from its cradle at dawn on September 8, 1953, she assumed it was urgent.
"I'd like to talk to the boss and it's really important," Bartley Cavanaugh said as
she answered. Nina Warren was a gentle woman but a tough guardian, protective of
her husband and children. She did not put callers through casually. This time, she
heard the tightness in Cavanaugh's voice and relented. "I'll wake him up."[1]

Cavanaugh had known Earl Warren for more than thirty years. They'd been
acquaintances first, their lives crossing occasionally in the years just after World
War I, when they both worked in the hustle and grab of California's legislature,
Warren as a young prosecutor with occasional business in Sacramento, and
Cavanaugh as the district manager for a cement company with government work.
In 1939, when Warren's career was just taking off and he was confronted with a
tough first test of his new position as California attorney general, he'd hauled Cavanaugh before a grand jury to make him testify about political contributions to
Frank Merriam, who had left the California governorship just weeks earlier and
whom Cavanaugh had served as a campaign manager.[2] Time had papered over that
indignity, and suffering had fused their lives—in late 1950, both had children fall
victim to polio. Their youngsters recovered slowly, and the two men had leaned on
each other for comfort in those difficult weeks.[3]

Now they were close, unusual for Warren, who was friendly with many people but intimate with few. Warren had an extraordinary capacity for names and personal details—a self-taught and much-practiced politician's skill for recalling a constituent's alma mater or the name of his oldest son, for absorbing the interest and attention of the person with whom he was speaking, and, for that moment, drawing that person to his intense attention. But for all that bluffness, Warren was a private man with few ardent associations outside his family. He was formal and reserved—he stood whenever his wife entered a room, looked good in a tux, held up his end of a receiving line—but he shared little of his inner self. He rarely sought or accepted help. Cavanaugh was one of those few who could so presume.

When Warren's voice, a voice known to every Californian of his generation, came sleepily on the line, Cavanaugh blurted out the news: "Did you know that the chief justice has just died?" he asked.

"No, I didn't," Warren responded. "That's too bad."

"Well," Cavanaugh asked, "would you mind if I got my nose into this thing?"

Warren was skeptical. "This is a field," the governor offered cautiously, "that you shouldn't do too much in."[4]

If reserve was one of Warren's identifying characteristics, caution was another. Warren's ascent through California politics had been deliberate—he spent more than a decade as Alameda County's district attorney before an opening convinced him to run for attorney general. Once there, he had been inclined to stay, but the state's then governor slighted Warren, and Warren did not take insult lightly. At the next opportunity, he ran for the job of governor and pushed his adversary aside. Still, that had taken provocation. Warren did not make snap decisions, and Cavanaugh knew it. Moreover, this was a spot on the Supreme Court, and the audience for it was not the electorate but a president.

One does not run for the Court, precisely. One pursues it by indirection. Friends lobby and beseech. The candidate himself is expected not to covet the job too openly. Warren knew that, and though he wanted a seat on the Court—wanted it badly, in fact—he knew better than to advertise his interest.

Still, Cavanaugh dared to persist. The early commentaries announcing the death of Chief Justice Fred Vinson included remarks from leading American Catholics that the Court had no Catholic members and that Vinson's death represented a chance for the nation's new president, Dwight Eisenhower, to fill that void. As both Cavanaugh and Warren recognized, political calculations also might have inclined Eisenhower in that direction: Although he had been elected a year earlier to overwhelming national acclaim, Eisenhower's one political weak spot was the Northeast, where Catholics held substantial influence. The East Coast was three hours ahead of California, and those who wanted a Catholic nominee already were at work. For Warren to have a place in the running, his supporters would have to work fast to keep the nomination from being wrapped up.

Warren saw Cavanaugh's point and, after first hesitating, now agreed to set his candidacy in motion. Cavanaugh went to work. He called the bishop of Sacramento, who called another cardinal, who called Cardinal Spellman in New York, and "by noontime the White House was aware that those men in the church at least, and they were pretty ranking, would look with favor on Warren."[5] Warren's campaign for chief justice had begun.

While Cavanaugh put Warren's hat in the ring, Eisenhower and his men set about their work as well. This was not a vacancy that Eisenhower had expected, but he welcomed it—as a chance to extend his own influence and as an opportunity to bring cohesion to a Court whose struggles had become a source of distraction and even embarrassment. Fred Vinson labored from 1946 to 1953 against smarter, more determined colleagues to bring order to the Supreme Court and stability to the nation whose laws it oversaw. By the time his heart gave out in the hours after midnight of September 8, 1953, it was painfully clear that he had failed as chief justice.

As word of Vinson's death crackled across the nation's radios, his fellow justices generally praised Vinson as a friend and leader, as a gentleman, as a jurist, and as a "lovable man who had devoted his life to the public good."[6] Two of the Court's great minds, Justices Hugo Black and Robert Jackson, had feuded for years but held in common a mild disrespect for the now dead chief; they each offered gracious but restrained praise. By contrast, Associate Justice Felix Frankfurter was never one to disguise his contempt for a colleague, even a dead one. He released a terse one-sentence statement: "Chief Justice Vinson's death comes as a great shock to me."[7] In private, he told a clerk that it provided him with his first solid evidence of the existence of God.[8]

Those deep and personal divisions among the justices made the job of replacing Vinson an urgent one. The next chief justice would be charged with bringing unity to a fractured Court even as it turned to face some of the nation's most pressing questions. War and renewed prosperity had brought America to the forefront of the world's nations, but in 1953 it remained an immature country in many respects. Institutionally sanctioned racism eroded America's moral authority. The Cold War and internal debate over Communism ran rivulets of fear and divisiveness through the body politic. Spotty respect for the human rights promised to its citizens in the Declaration of Independence but withheld from them by its courts undermined America's desire to lead the world by example. Under Vinson, the Court's divisions had underscored intellectual disagreement over how far it could or should go in protecting the civil and economic rights of Americans. Now, with the center chair open, nothing less than the place of the Supreme Court in American life and of America in the world was at stake.

James Reston of the *New York Times*—the most influential reporter of his day—informed America the following morning of the circumstances of the chief justice's death, then turned coolly to the business at hand. He ticked off the list of possible successors. Among them: Thomas Dewey, the governor of New York, once nearly president himself, now the "leader of the Republican liberal wing"; John J. McCloy, former U.S. high commissioner in Germany; New Jersey Supreme Court chief justice Arthur Vanderbilt; and John Foster Dulles, brilliant and pompous and recently selected by Eisenhower as his secretary of state. While offering up those possibilities, Reston cautioned "there was no hard evidence to suggest . . . that [they] were anything except guesses." One name, however, Reston elevated to special importance. "Gov. Earl Warren of California," Reston wrote, "was being prominently mentioned as a likely successor to the Kentuckian."[9]

The president liked to delegate, and he entrusted the task of identifying candidates to Herbert Brownell, his attorney general and political adviser, one of his closest friends in politics and one of the few in his cabinet to whom Eisenhower felt personally attached. Brownell went to work. He shuffled name after name, guided by Eisenhower's loose criteria. The president wanted the next justice to be a capable administrator and young enough to wield influence over many years; the age cutoff, Eisenhower said, was sixty-two. More generally, Eisenhower told the dean of Columbia Law School, he was seeking a "man of broad experience, professional competence, and with an unimpeachable record and reputation for integrity."[10]

Orie Phillips and John Parker, two well-regarded federal judges, made Brownell's first cut. So, as Reston predicted, did Vanderbilt, though Brownell uncovered a concern about his health—the justice had "suffered a heart attack, although that was not generally known."[11] Brownell considered proposing the elevation of Associate Justice Jackson, but Jackson, the chief prosecutor at the Nuremberg trials, had publicly and intemperately blamed Black when passed over in favor of Vinson, an ugly episode that critics remembered well.[12] In addition, Jackson's support for FDR's court-packing plan years earlier had made him controversial in Congress. Jackson would not get the nod.

Promoting another justice also received some thought, but by then the Supreme Court had eight Democrats and a single Republican, Harold Burton. Few considered Burton worthy of the chief justiceship; the Eisenhower administration never seriously considered elevating him. With Jackson and Burton eliminated from contention and the rest of the justices of little appeal to a newly elected Republican president, the search returned to candidates not then serving on the Court. Reflecting his deep conservatism and discomfort with the rumbling of racial equality, Eisenhower for a time considered John Davis, a distinguished lawyer and onetime Democratic presidential candidate then representing the Southern states in a case pending before the Court. Within a year, its caption alone would become a hallmark of American history—*Brown v. Board of Education*. As counsel in that case, Davis was arguing on behalf of the proposition that white and black children should not be required to attend the same public schools. Although he was dropped from the list of candidates—largely, it seemed, because of his age, not his politics—Davis's initial place among the contenders foreshadowed Eisenhower's tragic ambivalence about the opening of American institutions to blacks.

As other names came and went, Warren remained. In one sense, he was a stretch—he had, after all, never served a day as a judge. But neither had a number of the Court's dominant figures of the period; Frankfurter, Jackson, and William O. Douglas all came to the high court without any judicial background, and Black had served as a night police court judge only briefly. Warren, meanwhile, had other credentials to commend him. He was a towering figure in the West and in American politics at mid-century. Philosophically, he was a Progressive Republican, a rare species nationally but part of a potent political tradition in California and seemingly one not unlike Eisenhower's centrist Republicanism. Warren's long and complicated record—as a former Alameda County district attorney and state attorney general—included vigorous prosecutions of Communists and labor activists, support for tax hikes and universal health insurance, and outspoken support for the internment of Japanese-Americans during World War II. Through all that, Warren, far more than any contemporary or successor, mastered California's complex and sometimes vicious politics. He counted among his allies the conservative publishers of the *Los Angeles Times* and the *Oakland Tribune*, but also was accused of betraying the Republican Party's candidates and even, with his efforts on behalf of health care reform, of socialism. And yet Warren had been elected three times as governor of California, carrying Democrats along with Republicans. His most recent campaign, in 1950, ended with his smashing defeat of none other than James Roosevelt, son of the revered former president. Warren beat him by more than a million votes.

Warren's broad political appeal in California made him unique in American politics, but he was easy to misjudge. On one hand, he was a lifelong Republican and a determined anti-Communist who had passionately denounced the New Deal. That seemed to cast him as a type—one familiar to Eisenhower and to Republicans nationwide. But what was harder to see was that Warren's record was not an expression of a personal philosophy so much as it was an accumulation of his experience; he learned as he went, and built up his profile as he adjusted his politics to suit the problems before him. The result is that he confused political stereotypes, and his upbringing confounded them further. California's Progressive-era election rules favored a different type of politician, and they stunted political organizing and tactics that were popular elsewhere. Among other things, California was governed by the referendum and the recall—two measures that encouraged direct democracy and wrested power away from political parties and bosses—and the right to "cross-file," meaning that candidates could run as Republicans, Democrats, or both. Faced with a Democratic electorate in California, Warren had adopted a commitment to bipartisanship that suited his state as well as his temperament. With this commitment as his guide, Warren led California through a period of historic growth, of breakneck expansion placidly and professionally managed. The California he inherited in 1942 was politically divided, bereft by the Depression, terrified by war. By 1953, its people were prosperous, its budget balanced, its universities envied, its politics tranquil and Republican.[13]

There was no arguing, then, with Warren's record. But he was a hard man to read. His politics were idiosyncratic, and his temperament offered a bland exterior surrounding a web of gently opposing forces. Warren was a man of order, raised in a strict Scandinavian home, taught to distrust the rowdy Western antics of his boyhood town, Bakersfield. And yet he liked a little looseness in the joints, too. As a boy, he nosed his way through Bakersfield's saloons and whorehouses, took up the clarinet, and explored the surrounding brushland on his pet donkey. In public, Governor Warren was invariably under tight self-control, and he rarely put a revealing thought on paper. But he could lay into an aide. He enjoyed a nightly nip all through Prohibition and he nursed a lifelong love of poetry. Warren could appear simple—he favored straight prose, uncomplicated language—but he was not dumb. He was canny and insightful, and he was big. Though only just over six feet tall, Warren, with his bear chest and booming voice, commanded a room before speaking a word, even though he was in some ways shy. He could be cranky when taken by surprise.

And just as Warren was himself big, so was the canvas upon which he had painted his life and career. For Warren, no struggle was as personally or professionally defining as his labor for balance—between workers and employers; plain talk and poetry; politics and service; sobriety and good cheer; government power and individual rights; decency and self-expression; and, most momentously, the freedom of America's people and the security of its borders and institutions.

Preoccupied with such issues and convinced that he was better suited than most to address them, Warren naturally aspired to national office, and it was in that arena that he and Eisenhower first came to know each other. Warren ran unsuccessfully for vice president in 1948, and competed for the Republican presidential nomination in 1952, losing to Eisenhower himself. The campaign was shadowed and influenced at a key juncture by a young California congressman, Richard Nixon, whose own place in history was quickly taking shape and whose legacy would develop as a counterpoint to Warren's—Nixon the incisive, calculating political operator, haunted by his struggles; Warren the intuitive and congenial spirit, austere at times, blessed by his triumphs. By 1953, their rivalry was well on its way to becoming a Herculean political fact of the late twentieth century.

Eisenhower chose Nixon as his running mate in 1952, but that was to achieve balance on his ticket; Nixon's youth was a prime consideration. In Warren, the president thought he saw more of himself. They were big men with heavy hand-shakes and open faces, comfortable outdoors and at ease with themselves, capable extroverts who liked to lead. They did not know each other well, but they appreci-ated each other. So it was natural that the new president should seek a place in pub-lic life for Warren. In the months of early 1953, the two discussed in person and over the phone Warren's possible place in the administration. The president came away impressed, he wrote later, "that [Warren's] views seemed to reflect high ideals and a great deal of common sense."[14] Eisenhower passed over Warren for his cabi-net but instead proposed finding a spot for him on the Court—the first vacancy, both recalled, and Warren remembered Eisenhower offering that as "my personal commitment to you."[15] But the president also suggested the idea of Warren serving as solicitor general until a vacancy arose. During the second of two visits to the White House in 1953, Warren explored the solicitor generalship with Brownell and Eisenhower, and was offered the job. The position was appealing in some respects: It gave Warren the chance to return to the courtroom and would groom him for a Supreme Court appointment when one arose. And yet it would be, by most meas-ures, at least a temporary step down. Warren had twice sought the presidency, and had come within a hair of winning the vice presidency on the ticket with Dewey in 1948. Serving as solicitor general would take Warren well away from a limelight to which he had grown accustomed. Then there was the money: Although the solici-tor generalship paid $25,000 a year, the same salary he was earning as governor, the governorship came with a house and car, neither of which was provided to the na-tion's chief lawyer. In effect, this would be a pay cut. Warren had spent virtually his whole life working in government. Since he had six children and no real savings, the issue of money weighed heavily on the governor.

But Warren had to wonder about his options. He was already in his third term as governor, and his ambitions for the presidency had been thwarted. A Republican was in the White House, and it was not Warren. A seat in Congress had little appeal to the longtime chief executive, private practice no draw for a man who believed im-plicitly in the value of service to others. As Earl and Nina traveled through Europe that summer, the two grabbed moments alone to discuss the offer and the future of their family. In the end, they realized they could not refuse, and Warren wired Brownell in the code the two had devised: "Thanks for message. Stop. Have been re-freshed by trip. Stop. Looking forward to my return to work." Brownell consulted with Eisenhower, then responded, "We are both gratified to receive your cable."[16]

Warren then returned to California and, knowing that he had an offer in his pocket, announced that he would not seek another term as governor. "I will not be a candidate for the governorship next year, and the people of California should be the first to know that fact in order to have ample time for the selection of my successor,"[17] Warren told reporters. He did not say that he had accepted the job of solicitor general, leaving that for the Eisenhower administration to announce.

And then, before that announcement could be made, Vinson died. Just as suddenly, the equation changed, for while Eisenhower had seen Warren as a solid replacement for a New Deal liberal, as one of nine justices, he had not considered him for the Court's lead role, especially so soon. The machinations began again. In their earlier conversations, Eisenhower had seen Warren's gentler attributes; now he would learn another aspect of Warren's character. Warren was a stubborn man.

When Vinson died, Warren struck a pose of public reserve, while at the same time moving to claim the promise he felt was his. The governor typically met with reporters on Tuesdays, but Warren canceled the event that week. He had no desire to field questions about the death and its implications for him.[18] Instead, he publicly released a statement lamenting Vinson's death but never mentioning himself as a possible successor. That allowed Warren to proceed with dignity, and it disguised, as it often had before and would in the future, his keen determination. For while Warren maintained public silence, he bluntly pressed the White House behind the scenes.

Roused by Cavanaugh that morning, Warren turned his friend loose to contain momentum for a Catholic candidate. Warren then began to work the phones. He called California's chief justice, Phil Gibson; the state's attorney general, Pat Brown; and its junior senator, Tom Kuchel. He conferred with one of his most trusted political advisers, an elegant and insightful San Francisco lawyer named Jesse Steinhart. And all through that day and the next and the next, Warren placed calls to judges, law professors, and politically connected men—Judge John Gabbert in Southern California, Professor Arthur Sherry in Oakland, Judge Paul Vallee in Los Angeles, Judge Murray Draper in San Mateo, kingmaker Asa Call in Los Angeles. These were men who knew politics and the law, men with reach to Washington. In those crucial days, as Brownell and Eisenhower contemplated their pick, Warren called in chits.

Warren was right to recognize that he needed to bring pressure on Eisenhower. Despite his promise, Eisenhower felt no obligation to Warren. The pledge, Eisenhower told Brownell, was offered for an associate justice's seat, not for the chief justice's slot. As such, Eisenhower did not feel bound by it. Indeed, unbeknownst to Brownell, the president offered the position to Secretary of State Dulles, who said he was "highly complimented by the implication that I might be suited to the position of chief justice, but I assure you that my interests lie with the duties of my present post."[19]

Eisenhower may have counted on Warren's affability in trying to renegotiate the terms of their understanding. If so, he made the mistake that many others had: confusing the governor's congeniality with a lack of purpose. Warren would not release Eisenhower from his promise, continuing to maintain that he had an offer and he intended to accept. So while his friends made their calls and advanced Warren with the press and the president, Warren himself deliberately cut off communications, taking two of his sons hunting on an island off the coast of Southern California, out of reach of reporters and of White House aides interested in cutting a deal. That left Eisenhower to ponder the reaction to passing over the candidate by now seen as the leading contender. And it gave Warren time to prepare for a final round of talks with the White House.

"It was kind of a hideout," Warren explained years later. "I didn't want to be in on the middle of all that speculation and answering questions and so forth."[20]

Hurrying now, Brownell checked out the possible nominees. He peppered Warren's friends and associates with questions. "The particular question that they were asking me was whether he had really had any amount of trial work," recalled long-time associate Warren Olney III, another of those very few who cracked Warren's public façade and grew to know him up close.[21] Olney was never asked whether Warren would make a good chief justice; he figured Brownell already knew how he would respond.

On Friday, September 25, the Coast Guard tracked down Warren and his sons on their deer hunt and delivered word that the governor was urgently being sought by officials from the White House. The Warrens were eating breakfast when the Coast Guard arrived. They boarded a PT boat and raced to shore, where they were escorted to a beach house belonging to a friend and hunting partner of the governor's. There, with Earl Warren, Jr., listening in, Warren spoke with Brownell. Again, the attorney general raised the possibility of Warren's accepting another appointment. Again, Warren refused. "The first vacancy," Earl Jr. recalled his father saying emphatically, "means the first vacancy."[22]

Unable to persuade Warren by phone, Brownell flew to McClellan Air Force Base in Sacramento that Sunday, the sole passenger on the military plane. Warren arrived without fanfare, still dressed in his hunting clothes. And there Brownell tried one last time to talk Warren out of the chief justiceship. Finally and insistently, Warren held his ground, repeating his position in almost the same words that he had used in their telephone call. "Warren made it plain that he regarded the present vacancy as 'the next vacancy,'" Brownell said later.

"So after a couple hours out at McClellan Field in one of the offices out there," Merrell F. Small, the governor's administrative secretary, said, "Brownell went back and told Ike, 'We're stuck with him, I guess.'"[23]

The governor emerged smiling.

The announcement was Eisenhower's to make, not Warren's, so the governor kept his peace for the next day or two. With one exception. Early on the morning that his nomination was to be announced, Warren this time sought out Cavanaugh. "We made it," Warren said. "On the bench?" Cavanaugh asked. "No," Warren responded. "The top job." Delighted, Cavanaugh said he'd call up the Carmelites and get them off their knees. "They've been praying for five days."[24] Warren made them wait a few hours longer, until Eisenhower made it official.

Eisenhower did so later the same day, September 30, as he told reporters of his intention to appoint Warren, confirming widespread reports by then that the nomination was assured. That Friday evening, Earl Warren addressed the state of California as its governor for the final time; he was sworn in as chief justice on Monday morning. Eisenhower and Nixon shared the front row.[25]

The early response was positive, though notably cautious. The *New York Times* praised Warren's intelligence, tact, and qualifications, and noted, "Nobody can know in advance what will happen when a first-class mind, of whatever previous experience, is applied to our highest constitutional problems."[26] At the *Los Angeles Times*, Warren was seen as one of that paper's own, and his appointment was cheered as "A Great Honor for California." The staunchly Republican paper welcomed the first nominee placed on the bench by a Republican since 1932 and hoped it would begin "an upgrading of the quality of the court, which it much needs."[27]

It would not be long before Republicans—at the *Los Angeles Times*, in the Eisenhower administration, and elsewhere—would learn how elementally they had misjudged Warren. Eisenhower would later harbor second thoughts about this early appointment, one that would make him responsible, at least indirectly, for some of the most revolutionary social and legal change in American history. Indeed, soon after appointing Warren, Eisenhower would instruct Brownell never again to recommend a Supreme Court nominee who did not have a judicial record upon which to predict how he might perform as a justice.[28]

Some would furiously denounce what would become known as the "Warren Court." Billboards proclaiming, "Impeach Earl Warren" would dot the nation's highways, Joseph McCarthy would sneer at Warren's politics, and Congress periodically would explore ways to curb the Court's power. Others would welcome Warren and his assertive brethren as little short of salvation. John Lewis, who would go on to a distinguished career in Congress after a youth defined by civil rights protest, never forgot the day that Warren and his colleagues opened the doors of schoolhouses to young black children; Lewis, like so many others, felt on that momentous morning that promise long denied was now possible.

"Everything," the fourteen-year-old boy believed that day, "was going to change now."[29]

And that was merely the beginning of Warren's historic role in transforming American legal and social institutions. By the time he was through, Warren influenced his times more than any president with whom he served and became more responsible for America's sense of itself than any but a small handful of twentieth-century figures. The smiling governor of California, a mild Republican who, at sixty-two, joined the nation's high court unencumbered by a guiding ideology, would, over the next sixteen years, remake the nation's voting rights, empower criminal defendants, break down racial segregation, halt the demagogic pursuit of Communists, expand the rights of protest and dissent, embolden newspapers to challenge public leaders, and reimagine the relationship between liberty and security in a free society. Under Warren's leadership and in the face of bitter opposition, the Warren Court imported the great values of America's Declaration of Independence and the promises of its Bill of Rights into the working life of the nation. Those changes came to be regarded as a liberal high-water mark in American history, and the "Warren Court" became a deceptively simplistic moniker for a complex series of compromises that created the foundations of contemporary American society. Warren led the Court through those changes, its undisputed chief.

Today, Warren's legacy stretches across countless courthouses and interrogation rooms, city desks, classrooms, and hospital corridors. It sets the parameters of American politics and extends into the most intimate and personal moments of private life—the pained deliberations of women as they contemplate abortions, the anguished choices given to parents worrying about the education of their children, the whispered confidences of clients to their lawyers, the prayers of children, the protests of young people, the last meditations of the dying. Today's America is in many ways the America that Earl Warren made.

PART ONE

# MADE BY CALIFORNIA

Chapter 1

# YOUNG MAN
# OF CALIFORNIA

*Life in California is a little fresher, a little freer, a good deal richer, in its physical*
*aspects, and for these reasons, more intensely and characteristically American.*

DAVID STARR JORDAN, 1898[1]

EARL WARREN could not have become the man he was had he been raised anywhere but in the time and place of his upbringing. He was a man for whom experience mattered—philosophy and reading influenced him less than the scratch of life—so geography left its mark. And he grew up in California, a state defined by its cultural and geographic extremism, where one's association with the industrious cities of Los Angeles and San Francisco or its vast agricultural valleys determined who one was. Warren embodied a bit of each. He was born in Southern California, raised in its San Joaquin Valley, and educated in the north. By the time he was a young man, Warren was a Republican in the fashion of Los Angeles's leadership, a second-generation union man as one might expect of a San Franciscan, and a bit of Bakersfield rube.

Earl's parents, Methias and Chrystal Warren, came to California the way so many did—poor, drawn by the promise of work, eager to settle amid storied abundance. Methias was a broad-shouldered man with thin features, clipped with words and parsimonious. Born in Haugesund, Norway, he emigrated to the United States as an infant, carried by his parents along with his brother, Ole, two years older. They settled first in Illinois and then moved to Iowa, bypassing America's cities, changing their name from Varran, and finding their way, as Earl Warren later would relate, "to the open spaces of the Middle West."[2] Their mother gave birth to two more sons, one dying in infancy, before she herself died when Methias was four years old. Methias's father remarried and had eight more children by his second wife, but then his health entered a decline, and the three older boys took up too much room in the crowded house. Without their mother there to advocate for them, they were sent away, the youngest to relatives, Methias and Ole to farmers who lived nearby. Methias and Ole worked for their keep, and though separated from the rest of their family, they remained paired with each other for several years until Ole, stricken with tuberculosis and too poor to pay for good medical care, died in his brother's arms one sad Christmas Eve. Clutching his dying sibling, Methias swore to himself he would never, as an adult, allow himself to be poor.[3] Methias then moved to Minneapolis in search of work and there met another Scandinavian immigrant, Chrystal Hernlund. She was Swedish and pretty and particular—her real name was Christine, but she didn't like it, and instead adopted Chrystal. Chrystal's family had settled in Chicago after emigrating from Sweden, but had left after the city's 1871 fire, and, like Methias, had come to roost in Minneapolis. On Valentine's Day in 1886, they were married.

Their first child, Ethel, was born a year later, and the young family came to California soon after, settling eventually in a five-room rented cottage on Turner Street, near the Los Angeles train depot. Methias found work with the Southern Pacific Railroad. There, on March 19, 1891, Earl Warren—too poor to have a middle name, his father later would joke—was born.

Those were hard days in Los Angeles. It was known formally as El Pueblo de Nuestra Señora la Reina de los Angeles de Porciuncula, and as the name suggested, its emotional and cultural ties were with Mexico. As an American city after 1850, however, Los Angeles grew under the grim guidance of an oligarchy determined to build a great city and to profit by its growth. Their city was struck in their image, one startlingly in contrast to San Francisco's. The City, as San Francisco would forever be known to Californians, was liberal, Catholic, and organized around the sea and its workforce. Los Angeles was Protestant, conservative, oriented toward its dry valleys, and staggeringly effective at keeping labor in its place. Methias would soon learn, as would many others, what it meant to be a union man in nineteenth-century Los Angeles.

In the time of Warren's youth, Los Angeles's leaders included land barons and water pirates, engineers, rail men, and an extraordinary newspaper publisher. Henry Huntington was among those pioneers. He lived in the hills above Los Angeles in an unorthodox cohabitation with his aunt. His uncle, her husband, San Francisco railroad baron Collis Huntington, had died and left his fortune to his wife and nephew. They consolidated it by marrying each other and then multiplied that fortune by investing in land and streetcars. It was brilliantly simple—new plots with new homes would open on Huntington land; they would be served by a Huntington streetcar service. The arrivals came and the Huntingtons prospered. So did George Chaffey, a clever engineer and master irrigationist, who built an empire of water beginning on Thanksgiving Day of 1881, when he purchased the land for what became the farming community of Etiwanda.[4] From it he spiraled towns and projects that made him rich and drew immigrants into new homes stretching through once-arid valleys, watered by Chaffey.

The region's true general, however, was Harrison Gray Otis, a Civil War colonel, Spanish-American War general, land baron, and founder of the *Los Angeles Times*. He was brusque, determined, and vicious. To advance his vision of Los Angeles as a place of salvation, he hired a singularly energetic, eclectic city editor, Charles Fletcher Lummis, who tried to save his shaky health by walking from Ohio to Los Angeles. He filed dispatches for the *Times* along the 143-day journey, and, reaching the outskirts of the city, was met there in person by Otis. The two conferred beneath an oak tree outside the city, and Otis offered him a job on the spot. For decades thereafter, Lummis would survive bouts of exhaustion, drinking, and depletion to join with Otis in trumpeting the virtues of their region. They sold Los Angeles as a Mediterranean paradise, as a destination that would cure the sick and make the poor rich, as a business center unfettered by the government. And they built a giant and influential newspaper.

Together, Otis and Lummis—the general and his deputy—refashioned Los Angeles into an extension of its paper. "From the 'wide-open,' saloon-ridden, raw frontier town I first knew, to the Los Angeles of today," Lummis wrote in 1900, "is not only a long-distance march but a long war—with more picket-firing, skirmishes and pitched battles than most of us realize today. . . . But our army of lions has had a lion for a leader. Now this is a large thing to say, but a true one: I cannot recall a single considerable reform or forward movement in Los Angeles in 15 years of which the *Times* was not the standard-bearer."[5]

True enough, though that influence cut many ways. While Lummis and Otis touted Los Angeles to the East, they also struck hard against labor. For decades, the *Times* carried in its banner the slogan "True Industrial Freedom," advertising its commitment to the fight against union representation. As fierce as he was determined, Otis enforced that precept vigorously. When typographers balked at a twenty-percent pay cut in 1890, Otis refused to negotiate. The unions struck, and Otis responded by hiring scabs and vowing to remake Los Angeles as an open shop.[6] Otis won, as he usually did. And in winning, he gave his city a platform from which to compete with San Francisco—lower wages combined with the climate as two of Los Angeles's chief selling points to new business.

As the century turned, a deep national depression dampened life across the nation and reached the town of Earl Warren's birth. In rail yards from Chicago to the Pacific, the American Railway Union, headed by Eugene V. Debs, gained strength among white workers (blacks and Chinese were not permitted to join). One new member was Methias Warren, who joined the union in early 1894. When a strike was called later that year, Methias Warren struck.

The Pullman strike of 1894 was reluctantly launched but then stirringly engaged. The Pullman car company was notorious for its abuse of its nearly captive workforce, and when the company cut wages in the midst of the Depression, its workers, already stretched to their limits, walked out in protest. Debs had not asked for this strike, but when he visited the Pullman yards, he endorsed it. He tried to lure Pullman officials into negotiations, but they refused. At noon on June 26, 1894, Debs ordered railway union members to pull the sleeping cars from trains and sidetrack them. The railroads refused to move trains without sleeping cars, and so the strike was joined. Within days, it had escalated into a historic confrontation of national scope. More than 100,000 men walked off their jobs; railroad service between Chicago and the West Coast was all but ended.[7] The strike was particularly effective in the West, as strikers there took to the ramparts with enthusiasm and resolve. They were, however, met by a powerful adversary, General Otis. "In the great railroad strike of '94, the *Times* was the only daily on the Pacific Coast which 'stood fast, stood firm, stood true' . . . for law and order," Lummis wrote in 1900.[8]

With the *Times*'s encouragement, the federal government moved against the union. Debs was imprisoned (the Supreme Court would later uphold his jailing), and after riveting the nation and paralyzing its transportation, the strike was crushed. Methias Warren had made a hard choice to walk off his job—he was no activist, just a man loyal to his colleagues. Now he paid the price for that. He was fired and blacklisted by the railroad. He had brought his family to Los Angeles for work, but had butted up against its leadership code. He risked poverty again, the poverty he had vowed since boyhood to avoid. Methias was unable to find other work in Los Angeles, so he set out in search. He was successful, in a fashion. He was hired by the Santa Fe railroad to work its yards in the blinding-hot desert east of Los Angeles. That restored Methias to a payroll, but those little yards were no place for a family, so he sent back money as he searched for something better, permanent. Eventually, he settled outside Bakersfield—a hundred hard, hot, dusty miles north and inland from Los Angeles, but a real town, not a mere desert depot. Methias then sent for his family.[9]

Earl Warren carried more impressions than memories of his early childhood in Los Angeles. He vaguely absorbed the colors and sounds of its Mexican culture, of flowers and sonorous music drifting in the city's flat light. Mexico would always retain a romantic place in Warren's heart—he was an annual guest at Santa Barbara's summer fiesta, a celebration of its Californian and Mexican heritage, and one of Warren's lasting Army friendships would be with Leo Carrillo, who would have a successful acting career as the sidekick to the Cisco Kid and thus be one of Hollywood's first Mexican-American stars, and who would campaign for Warren among Mexican-Americans. Though Warren would, of course, go on to great fame for his role in ending school segregation against blacks, his quieter first act of that mission would be in the liberation of Mexican-American children in California.

But while Mexico supplied a warm backdrop to Warren's youth, two sharper Los Angeles memories stabbed through his gauzy recollections of those early years. They both would echo through his consciousness for three-quarters of a century, haunting him as he sat to write his memoirs in the early 1970s. One was the sound of a young neighbor, stricken by polio or meningitis—Warren could not remember which—crying and sobbing in pain as she died a few feet away, her family unable to comfort or cure her. The other was of the railroad strike, and of a raucous evening when strikers set a bonfire and burned an effigy above it. That night, Warren recalled, "gave me a horror of mob action which has remained with me to this day."[10] Indeed, those two memories stand for the most enduring lesson of Warren's youth—his abhorrence of disorder. No matter how much Warren would grow as a boy, no matter how hard he would tug at his parents or school administrators or teachers, he always found security in structure.

Bakersfield hardly seemed the place to find it. In Bakersfield, the Warrens—and particularly their young son—would discover a frontier town in California clothing, romantic and dangerous, tantalizing to a young boy but frightening as well. Bakersfield had no business titans to impose order. It was chaotic and freewheeling. Its streets, one visitor recorded in 1882, were "generally full of horses, caparisoned in the Spanish style, tied to the hitching posts and awaiting their owners in the stores and taverns. The sheep-herders are a lonely class, who become morose and melancholy through long wanderings with their flocks far from the habitations of men and human speech." The city's shops, the writer noted, were "kept by Jews," while Chinatown stood apart, separated by an irrigation ditch "like a moat." Gypsies lived on the edge of town, while the great ranches of the era were located just outside.[11]

Upon arriving in 1895, Methias Warren went to work inspecting cars for the Southern Pacific. So eager was the company to attract workers to its new facilities that the blacklist was forgotten. He was based in Kern, a small knot of homes and railroad buildings erected two miles from the center of Bakersfield after Bakersfield refused concessions to bring the rail into the city center (Kern later was annexed by Bakersfield). The young family at first moved into a small rented house near the railroad tracks. Methias walked to work.

The Warren family settled into Kern and Bakersfield just as the area burst to life. The city opened the twentieth century with $4,347.24 in its treasury, and oil was bringing in plenty more. Sidewalks were being paved, and roads were under construction. Respectable establishments were taking root—three major land companies produced cattle, grain, and hay, while growers harvested peaches and apricots.[12] One visiting editorial writer noted, "[S]ubstantial business buildings, an atmosphere of business thrift and engagement, a satisfied and unconcealed air of content, activity, briskness, good order on the streets and general observance of the dignity of the peace left upon the minds of the visitors . . . the impression that Bakersfield is a steady, growing, pushing and successful city."[13]

Still, disorder and vice were among the hallmarks of the young town. The city boasted roughly a hundred saloons—they were, the same editorial writer observed, "as thick as the leaves of autumn forest glades"—and the city's 7,000 residents were said to include 500 prostitutes. Crime was commonplace and widely reported in the *Daily Californian*, where coverage was splashy and at times revealing. A Wednesday evening knife battle was detailed under the headline "Mexican Stabbed in Leg Muscles." When three Indian men were arrested for public drunkenness, the paper cited the law against supplying Indians with liquor and asked the question in its headline "Who Gave Them Whiskey?"[14]

More serious was a fatal Chinatown shooting that captured local attention as the century turned. Jee Sheok, a Chinese resident of that Bakersfield quarter, shot and killed Jee Duck in the fall of 1899 over what witnesses reported was a disputed business deal. The following January, Sheok came to trial, drawing a large and curious crowd, including many native Chinese—an assembly the *Californian* described as "this outpouring of heathendom."[15] The defendant, a "villainous-faced Chinaman," sat without comment through the early days of the proceeding, which moved slowly in part because of the difficulty of finding twelve jurors in the county willing to give equal credence to the testimony of an Asian as that of a Caucasian. Once a jury was seated, Sheok was convicted largely on the account of a nine-year-old white boy, Percy Baker, who saw the shots fired and told the jury that the dead man carried no gun, rebutting the defendant's argument that he fired in self-defense. "This was the little fellow's story and no amount of questioning by the defendant's attorney Mr. Emmons could shake it," the *Californian* reported. "The boy knew what he knew, he showed that he understood the oath, and his manner carried conviction to the listener."[16] Sheok was sentenced to life in prison.

Like young Percy Baker, Earl Warren was nine years old when Jee Sheok was sent away to San Quentin, California's maximum-security prison. As a young boy, Warren was quiet and mannerly, and by the time he was ready to enter school, Methias was sufficiently established to be able to let Chrystal dress her little boy in dapper, if slightly prettified, outfits. Earl was first enrolled in the local elementary school at age five—technically, children were supposed to be six to begin school, but the principal allowed Warren to begin early, perhaps because he already had some reading and writing skills. He was taught in the rough style of the day: When teachers found him favoring his left hand, they tied it to his body and forced him to write with his right. For the rest of his life, Warren would write and eat right-handed but play sports left-handed.[17]

Even right-handed, he mastered penmanship. His schoolbooks from those days are lined with the careful notations of a young boy with precise handwriting, marking in the margins his questions and definitions of difficult words. Although the family was striving, the children did not suffer. Books, in particular, were never hard to come by, as Methias Warren made sure to set aside enough money to buy his children anything they cared to read. Earl received *Peck's Bad Boy* for Christmas in 1901 and a sequel the following Christmas.[18] A library, meanwhile, was built just two blocks away, its wide Victorian eaves providing shade to the cool interior on Bakersfield's hot days. Earl Warren, already young for his class, progressed well enough to be allowed to skip the second grade.[19]

Away from school, Earl Warren lent his father a hand on the first of many houses that Methias Warren constructed in his off-hours from the Southern Pacific. Or rather, Earl tried to help. He was not much good at construction, and though he admired those who could work with their hands, he had trouble emulating them. Beyond his work with his father, Earl took odd jobs for spending money and his own savings. He delivered the *Daily Californian*, and was a success at selling ice; it would have been hard to fail in Bakersfield's 100-degree summers before the days of air-conditioning. But he had his setbacks, too. Young Earl became fascinated by the assassination of President McKinley and the Boer War, two subjects heavily covered in the local papers. Earl rooted for the Boers to rout the English and lamented McKinley's death at the hands of an assassin. So when a biography of McKinley and another book on the Boer War appeared in the early 1900s, Earl saw an advertisement for them in the paper and believed his enthusiasm for the subjects would make him a natural salesman for the books. But he was too little and too softspoken to be taken seriously; neighbors simply turned him away. When he could not convince his father to buy a copy, Earl realized he was through as a salesman.[20] He dropped the effort.[21]

The Warrens were never wealthy, but Methias was a frugal man with a steady income, and the family gradually improved its living standards. Although the family lived in a rented house when they first arrived, Methias managed to save enough to buy a house a few years later, and he moved his wife and children, Ethel and Earl, into it. Over time, Methias would acquire other small homes and rent them out, supplementing his railroad income and eventually giving him the means to retire from the Southern Pacific.

Earl's mother and father both raised him, but his lasting memories and deepest impressions were connected with his father. In a reckless town, Methias was a stable, if somewhat grim, source of constancy. He valued work and careful handling of money. There was no drinking or smoking in the Warren home, a gesture of seriousness as well as frugality. There was music—the Warrens owned a Victrola, and Earl enjoyed the music of John Philip Sousa. But there was little laughter or hugging. When there was punishment to be administered, Methias doled it out, sometimes with a birch rod.[22] Methias insisted on education for his children, and he demanded honesty, a lesson that found deep purchase in his son. To his own grand-children, Earl Warren would insist that the measure of a man lay in his refusal to tell a lie.[23] Those were Methias's words echoing across three generations.

For all its emphasis on virtue, the Warren home was not deeply concerned with religion. Earl and Ethel were raised as Methodists, and the family kept a Bible, but they did not attend services diligently, and Earl absorbed religion in a general way—his was a moral upbringing but not a devout one. Methias was far more ve-hement about education than he was about God. He supported Earl's desire to go to college, and he occasionally would take his son to hear speakers as they traveled through the area. One afternoon, the two traveled together to hear an address in town. Earl never forgot it.

The speaker was Russell H. Conwell, and his talk, "Acres of Diamonds," was one of the most acclaimed pieces of oratory of its day. Conwell, the founder of Temple University, traveled across America delivering versions of his talk thousands of times in the early twentieth century. He would arrive in a small town, talk to resi-dents, and hear the story of their hamlet. When he rose to speak that afternoon, he would weave their stories into his speech, identifying for the crowd the "diamonds" in their town or village and reminding them to treasure those aspects of their lives and community. One day, Conwell's journey brought him to Bakersfield.[24]

Religious in fervor, moral in tone, and yet practical in its advice, the speech foreshadowed much of what Warren would become. "Greatness consists not in the holding of some future office, but really consists in doing great deeds with little means and the accomplishment of vast purposes from the private ranks of life," Conwell said. "He who can give to this city better streets and better sidewalks, bet-ter schools and more colleges, more happiness and more civilization, more of God, he will be great anywhere."[25]

Sitting in front of the stage, looking up at the orator, Earl Warren was spell-bound. "I can still see his towering form and hear his powerful voice as he told his never-to-be-forgotten story," Warren recalled a half century later. "Of all the lec-tures I heard in my youth, this one made the greatest impression on my young mind."[26]

If Warren's early life featured exposure to learning and inculcation of values, it also came in a notably narrow home—while Bakersfield had its Mexicans, its Jews, its Chinese, and even a few blacks, they were not guests of the Warrens. Moreover, home was not a place of debate and discussion; it was one where children did as they were told by strict, conventional parents. Its stability appealed to Warren, but it lacked intellectual energy; it was a place of reading but not of sophistication; it was Scandinavian and Protestant, and young Earl had little exposure to the vitality of urban America, or to those raised in families more accustomed to disputatious-ness. As he grew older, Warren would sometimes be confounded by those who enjoyed the clamor of clashing views, of debate as intellectual exercise. His uneasiness with that style of argument would cause some to conclude he was less intelligent than he actually was.[27] They were wrong to underestimate him. Had they appreciated Warren's Bakersfield, they would have better understood that he was taught to live by simple values and formed in the crux between the attraction of a stable home and the appeal of a loose little town.

His companions in his ramblings through the city were Earl's many animals. A rare surviving photograph of Earl as a boy shows a handsome youngster, blond hair tousled, a straight nose and finely drawn bones, a half grin across his eleven-year-old face as he stares directly at the camera. Behind him are fallen leaves, a crate, and a shovel leaned against some brush. Earl's left arm is draped around the neck of a cheerful, bright-eyed hound. His animals—others included more dogs, a sheep, an eagle, and chickens—kept Earl company, but his stalwart was a burro named Jack, "my friend and constant companion for years," Warren wrote later.[28] The two would hunt together, and chase rabbits in the dry fields that extended from the edge of town to the looming Tehachapis at the horizon. When news broke in Bakersfield, as it did on April 19, 1903, Jack and his twelve-year-old master, Earl, clopped curiously to the scene.

The events of that day capped a wild winter and spring in the life of Bakersfield. A new sheriff, John Kelly, had taken office and set out to shut down the city's gambling houses. Kelly informed the owners that he intended to enforce the law—a view novel only by the standards of Bakersfield, where gambling had been allowed for virtually all of its history. Kelly's actions were cheered by the Bakersfield establishment, but the gamblers struck back, hiring as their lawyer E. J. Emmons, the same man who had represented Sheok at his murder trial. Emmons persuaded a judge that Kelly had exceeded his authority in closing down the houses. Instead of the gamblers going out of business, Kelly himself was placed under arrest. And then, with the town divided and unprotected, it came under attack.

Jim McKinney was a Western bandit, a thief and a murderer who lay in wait by the side of a trail in order to kill two men, then held up a rancher, forced him to shoe two horses, and disappeared into the badlands of Southern California and Arizona. Newspapers followed his exploits, posses were gathered to capture him, and rewards were posted for his return, "Dead or Alive." The gambling dispute suddenly seemed less urgent, and Kelly won his release from jail to lead his men in pursuit of the outlaw. At four P.M. on April 12, they found him. Shots were fired, and deputies believed they had hit McKinney, but the bandit got away, fleeing on the speedy horses he had stolen a few days before. A second battle, the following morning, deprived McKinney of his horses, but he continued to elude capture, and now turned toward Bakersfield. "Fugitive May Attempt to Come Down Kern River," the *Californian* warned.[29]

And so he did. On the morning of Sunday, April 19, deputies closed in. They found him at the Duvall Hotel, a local Chinese gambling house. One of the deputies, Bert Tibbet, staked out a spot in back and, when shots rang from inside the building, burst through a gate on the heels of a colleague. Inside, another deputy, Jeff Packard, was bleeding from a shattered arm. "Look out, look out for God's sake, he'll get you," Packard called. Tibbet wheeled and fired his shotgun. It struck McKinney in the neck, but he raised himself. Tibbet shot him a second time, killing him. "M'Kinney's Head Shattered with a Load of Buckshot," the *Californian* proclaimed the next morning.[30]

Earl Warren was twelve years old when the McKinney shootout occurred in his hometown. The gunshots had barely stopped ringing that morning when Earl and his donkey came trotting up. In the days after the shooting, Earl stayed rapt with interest as it morphed into a legal drama. It turned out that McKinney had had an accomplice, and not just anyone, but a sheriff's deputy named Al Hulse. Earl had met Hulse a few months earlier at a turkey-shooting contest. There, Earl had admired Hulse's marksmanship, and the deputy gave Earl a turkey. Now Hulse was accused of aiding the bandit and of firing the shot that killed Tibbet's brother, Will. The cornered Hulse first offered unconvincing explanations of his whereabouts, then gave a halting statement to town leaders, including a reporter from the paper, from his cell.

Hulse claimed innocence and went to trial. Earl went, too, sitting in the back with other boys from town. From that seat, surrounded by friends and neighbors, Earl watched the drama unfold, and a surprising idea took root. Earl decided to become a lawyer. That was odd in some respects. He was still a shy youngster, small for his age and unassuming. How, he might have wondered, could a boy who could not convince his neighbors to buy books on McKinley persuade a jury to believe his client? Other boys his age gravitated toward oil exploration and mining. But as Earl watched the town grapple with its gamblers and its outlaws, he allowed himself to appreciate the dazzle of the lawyers as well as their importance. They restored order when gamblers threatened it, but they were not stark or repressive. Denied much fun at home, he found excitement in the law, in the tale of Hulse and McKinney, which ended on a shocking note: Hulse was convicted of second-degree murder, and as he awaited transfer to state prison, he asked for a razor to shave. He used it to slit his throat.

Improbably, then, the shy boy who spent his afternoons with his animals and whose mother liked to dress him in curls and shorts began to imagine a career as a great trial lawyer. It would not turn out quite the way he expected, but the seed of Warren's career took hold that spring, when he was just twelve years old.

It was one thing to daydream of such a life. It was another to work toward it. Methias urged his son to work hard for grades, but that was one admonition that did not register with Earl. He squeaked by in high school with admittedly mediocre study habits—when the final class bell would ring, Warren was the first out the door, classmates recalled. Reflecting on his high school days in 1969, one former classmate called him "the bunk" in physics and described him, simply, as "never outstanding."[31]

His high school transcripts are a study in mediocrity. Latin was a particular struggle; in his two years of Latin, he never managed to top a 77. French was similarly disappointing, and his classmate's recollection of his work in physics was accurate. He received a 75, the second-worst grade of his high school career, exceeded only by junior-year algebra (a 70). One telling mark, however: Warren's best grade for all four years of high school came in his last, when he scored a 94 in American history.[32] At the same time, school introduced him to poetry, and Warren took to it. In 1904, he received his copy of a collection of English poetry masterpieces; he dutifully inscribed his name and kept the book his entire life.[33]

Warren's reputation as a lazy student was a shared joke between him and his classmates. In the commencement issue of their school publication, *The Oracle*, the annual "prophecy" for the graduates of 1908 lauded each of the school's sixteen graduating seniors. It remarked of one classmate, "The world ne'er had a wiser man before," and of another that "greater orator ne'er did audience command." Of Warren, the description was more modest and the prediction for the future limited indeed:

> On the corner an old street faker stands
> And the attention of the passing crowd commands.
> His specialty is "Warren's New Hair Dope."
> Put up in form of tonic and of soap.
> He says his motto is "My goods are not bush."
> Good luck, Earl, in your business is our wish.[34]

Warren did not argue much more for himself. In the class "will," he bequeathed to Lorraine K. Stoner "my ability to slide through, doing as little work as possible, hoping that in so doing, he may gain laurels on the Track Team." His final word on high school: "I know many things, but nothing distinctly."[35]

High school thus did not do much to shape the man that Earl Warren was to become, but it did in one sense augur his future. Starting in those early years, Earl would succeed best at what he felt most intimately. He was drawn to the law by sitting in a courtroom, not by the consideration of its structure or principles. Earl drifted in the face of abstraction—Latin, say, or physics. Poetry was the exception that proved the rule. He loved it, but for its stories, not for rhyme or meter.

Earl was, however, learning, if not always in the classroom and sometimes despite himself. Through his high school years, Earl spent some summers working for the Southern Pacific after securing his father's permission—which was granted only on the condition that Earl return to school at the end of his summer employment. Earl's job as a "call boy" was to run through town and gather up crews for departing trains. It was eye-opening work for a teenaged boy. He tramped through the city's underside in order to round up crews, sober them up, and deliver them to their posts. He watched men gamble away their earnings and saw the Southern Pacific strip poor workers of much of their paychecks by luring them to the company store. And he saw some blacklisted because of their union membership, the fate his own father had suffered before escaping to Bakersfield.[36]

Most shocking to Warren were the injuries he witnessed. Still just a teenager, he watched in horror as men were crushed between cars and carried in agony to the workplace lathe. There, held tightly by their fellow workers, the railroad men had their arm or leg cut clean off with the workplace blade. "My nature," he remembered years later, "always recoiled against these inequities. All my life, I wanted to see them wiped out."[37] Many years later, even some of Warren's liberal colleagues on the United States Supreme Court would wonder at his insistence that the Court take up seemingly minuscule cases involving workers seeking compensation for injuries; only when they grasped it as an extension of his youth did they understand.[38] Earl never did delay a train, and the friends he made with trainmen would help him later in life, when he toed the difficult line in California as a Republican in search of labor support.[39] As a boy in Bakersfield, he took his first, modest step in that complicated, lifelong relationship with organized labor: On April 1, 1906, Earl, who learned to play the clarinet and to play it well, joined the local chapter of the American Federation of Musicians.[40]

In time, Warren's love of practical learning and reliance on his personal experience over academic diligence came to help him; they grounded his ideology in real life and infused his politics and jurisprudence with a common, practical touch. But when he was a high school student, that bias nearly sank him. His grades were bad enough, his attitude toward schoolwork worse. Indeed, Warren almost did not graduate at all. During the week of the ceremony, he and several classmates stayed up late rehearsing their end-of-the-year play. Tired the next morning, several were late to school. Their principal smelled a prank, and abruptly expelled the three when they arrived on campus. After a debate in which Warren recalled delicately that the "rhetoric became somewhat heady," the three were sent home and news of their expulsion ran through the school and community. That night, after a special hearing before the local education board, they were reinstated, the play went on, and they graduated with their class the day after that. Writing of the flap nearly seventy years later, Warren remained revealingly bitter. The principal, whom he did not name, "did not return to the school the next term, but I do not know whether the foregoing incident had anything to do with it."[41] And though Warren took pains to emphasize that he sought out and befriended the principal years later, the near-expulsion remained a burr in the hide of a man who by then had risen to international renown.

For now, however, Warren was headed away, to Berkeley. In the sweltering heat of Bakersfield in August, Warren boarded the train north, riding on the free pass that the Southern Pacific gave its employees. He had $800 saved up for college, plenty in those days to live well as a student. Once he had gone, Warren largely shut the door on his youth. Though he was tragically summoned back to his hometown in 1938 and though he appeared for high school class reunions in 1958 and 1973, life would rarely bring Warren back to Bakersfield. It remained a part of his past, and Warren was not inclined to dwell there. He preferred to move ahead.

THE FRESH dash of a new start would always brighten Earl Warren's memory of his arrival in San Francisco on an August evening in 1908, when The City's political tribulations were in full swing. Warren never forgot the cool air, the sense of life unfolding, of promise reaching out to him and finding his comfortable grasp. No other place would ever again feel quite like home.

Warren's arrival in the north placed him in the center of social and political traditions vastly different from those of either Los Angeles or Bakersfield. Where Southern California had grown from the Mexican land grants and the steely businessmen who snapped them up—and where the San Joaquin Valley of Warren's youth was built on oil, agriculture, and ranching—San Francisco was made by gold. Gold was discovered in 1848, and extensive lodes eventually were uncovered throughout the Western Sierra Nevada Mountains east of Sacramento. Gold brought people, arriving frantically at mid-century, and gold gave California its first and most enduring identity. In 1849, California's population stood at just over 100,000; by 1852, it was 255,122[42] and characterized by what Hubert Howe Bancroft, the state's first great historian, called its "two remarkable features . . . youthfulness and paucity of women."[43] In 1850, under the full flood of the Gold Rush, California was more than 92 percent male, an imbalance that subsided slowly. Females made up just over 10 percent of the state's population in 1860 and about one-third by 1880.[44] Few of those who came to California—of the many men or few women—made their fortune in gold, but they stayed to trade; to farm; to hunt for bear; to trap beaver and otter; to fish; to work the railroads then under furious construction; or to man the docks of one of the world's great natural ports in San Francisco. In 1887, before earthquake and fire would remake the city—not for the last time—it was home to 290,000 raucous residents.

Built up by the influx of young men, San Francisco was, from the outset, an undisciplined city. It was California's first great metropolis and a happily decadent one. Leland Stanford, Charles Crocker, Collis Huntington (uncle of Southern California's Henry), and Mark Hopkins maintained opulent residences on Nob Hill, from which they oversaw their intertwined railroad and trading businesses. Beneath and behind them lay the Chinese ghetto and the teeming red-light district. In the city's twenty central blocks were whole streets given over to brothels and saloons, with room for just one school and three churches[45]—scant refuge for a growing middle class, devout and serious. Northern California life centered around The City, as generations of Californians would know it, with its bustle, its docks, its powerful unions, and its austere political bosses, dressed in high collars and stiff suits. Horses clattered across glass-cobbled streets, and a battle-tested working class—Catholic and liberal—engaged in escalating conflict with corrupt politicians and their vigilante allies.

*The Communist Manifesto*, published in 1848, had given new structure to working-class grievances, and Germany, France, and England thereafter were gripped by Communism and the rise of the First International. So, too, did San Francisco ebb and wrestle beneath the firm tug of radical politics. In the winter of 1849, carpenters and joiners in San Francisco waged what is believed to be the first strike in the state's history (actually, prehistory, since California's formal admission came in 1850).[46] With that, San Francisco embarked on a long drama of organization, strike, resistance, and violence that waxed and waned with its tumultuous economy.

When Warren arrived, San Francisco still was struggling to right itself from its greatest crisis and was in the midst of confronting yet another. At 5:12 A.M. on April 18, 1906, California's preeminent city, its cultural and economic jewel, had fallen into a heap. Some locals called it the "ground shake," forty-seven seconds of earthquake.[47] South of Market Street, San Francisco's main thoroughfare, cheaply built tenements fell like cards; hundreds died in the first wave alone. Gazing out on the wreckage in the minutes immediately after the first blow, John Barrett, the city-desk news editor of the *San Francisco Examiner*, described the "earth . . . slipping quietly away from under our feet. There was a sickening sway, and we were all flat on our faces." Outside was pandemonium. "Trolley tracks were twisted, their wires down, wriggling like serpents, flashing blue sparks all the time. The street was gashed in any number of places. From some of the holes water was spurting; from others, gas." Barrett turned to two reporters for the paper and remarked, "This is going to be a hell of a day."[48]

It was, in fact, a hell of a week. Fires were the second act of California earthquakes. In San Francisco, city fire crews, hindered by the death of their chief, were overwhelmed and resorted to dynamiting buildings in order to deny the fire fuel. Block after block of The City fell.

The damage to San Francisco was overwhelming, and the reconstruction was protracted. For more than a year, the grand clock above the city's Ferry Building, one of few prominent edifices to survive, stood hauntingly stuck at 5:16, the moment at which the trembling of the earth threw its works apart. Even in 1908, when Warren arrived, the city remained in tatters. It was, he said, a "sad sight to behold. . . . Downtown, the place was a mass of rubble, with the frames of a few buildings, gutted by fire, standing skeleton-like in the midst."[49]

Then, from the rubble of the earthquake and the detritus of the fire, came the great reckoning of San Francisco politics. It was to be the catapult by which Progressivism was heaved into the history of California—and the life of Earl Warren.

By the early twentieth century, San Francisco was among the most nakedly corrupt cities in America, a place where bribery was institutionalized and where candidates sought office for the explicit purpose of enrichment at the public's expense. Behind the government's elaborately constructed municipal scam were an erudite, dapper lawyer, Abraham Ruef, and his handpicked mayor, Eugene "Handsome Gene" Schmitz. Under their simple scheme, those seeking franchises or other business with the city hired Ruef, who divided up his "earnings" among himself, the mayor, and the city supervisors, also under Ruef's control after the elections in 1905, when Ruef's slate won the entire membership of the supervisory board. As a general rule, Ruef took about twenty-five percent, as did Schmitz. The supervisors then divided the other half among themselves. Telephone companies, rail service agencies, fight promoters, gas companies, and others paid their bribes and got their business. At the height of their power, Schmitz and Ruef even arranged for the construction of a city-supported brothel—the Municipal Crib, it was called.

Their system grew increasingly brazen. In one case, Charles Boxton, the chairman of the city's public works committee, minced few words in putting the grip on the president of the Parkside Realty Company, then seeking approval for trolley service to reach its development project along San Francisco's western dunes. After a tour of the property and a lavish lunch with much wine, Boxton rose before the developers and his colleagues. The Parkside president, he said,

> should bear in mind that we are the city fathers; that from the city fathers all blessings flow; that we, the city fathers, are moved in all our public acts by a desire to benefit the city, and that our motives are pure and unselfish. . . . But it must be borne in mind that without the city fathers there can be no public service corporations. The street cars cannot run, lights cannot be furnished, telephones cannot exist. And all the public service corporations want to understand that we, the city fathers, enjoy the best health and that we are not in business for our health. The question at this banquet board is: "How much money is in it for us?"[50]

As its rapaciousness grew, so did public uneasiness, particularly among the city's reform-minded elites. One of San Francisco's wealthiest businessmen, the young and charismatic Rudolph Spreckels, soon to become a stalwart of the California

Progressives, struck a deal with the city's district attorney, W. H. Langdon, who was not part of the bribery web. Spreckels agreed to put up $100,000 to pay for a corruption inquiry, while Langdon pledged to wage it. Trust-busting, corruption-battling President Roosevelt supported their efforts from offstage by dispatching two special investigators to help conduct the inquiry. Closer up, the investigation was promoted and driven by Fremont Older, a rampaging San Francisco newspaper editor who once had accepted stipends from the Southern Pacific but who now leapt to the head of the attack on San Francisco corruption.[51]

Older, Spreckels, and their allies conferred quietly in early 1906 and concluded that they had enough evidence to warrant a full investigation. Although they did not know how far their inquiry would lead, all were confident that Ruef and Schmitz would be targets, and Spreckels in particular wanted to go even further: He had in mind the Southern Pacific railroad and its emissaries as the ultimate targets.[52] Although they did not yet call themselves Progressives, their effort was a clear predecessor of that movement, with its corporate targets, aversion to public corruption, and reformist zeal.

The earthquake postponed the investigations as all attention naturally shifted to the recovery effort, a monumental task that seemed to bring out the best in Schmitz. He would often remark in later years that he felt reborn by the earthquake, and his actions in the hours and days after the quake suggested new energy and honesty. For months, the investigation went underground as San Francisco struggled to its feet.[53]

Even the earthquake, however, could not stop the gathering determination to topple San Francisco's leadership. After the admirable recovery interlude, Ruef and Schmitz resumed their work, and Ruef extended his reach to state politics. In return for $20,000, he delivered San Francisco's nominating votes in the 1906 Republican state convention to James Gillett, Southern Pacific's choice for governor.[54] And in his crowning arrogance, Ruef gathered with California's boss leadership for a photograph, memorializing the deal. In the picture, Gillet stands behind Ruef, his arm on Ruef's shoulder. They are surrounded by state Republican leaders, cigars and drinks in hand. When the photograph was made public and reprinted in reform papers under the headline "Shame of California," it stood as an icon of smug Southern Pacific manipulation of California politics.[55] Kevin Starr's description of the photograph is itself worthy of reproduction: "Perusing it today—the walrus mustaches, the amply distended vests, the high starched collars, the smiles of men at their ease after wine and dinner, so pleased with themselves after having insured the election of the next governor of California—one can almost hear a background of Scott Joplin music."[56] The photograph captured the high-water mark of Southern Pacific domination. After it, the public's anger hardened to resolve, and Ruef turned increasingly desperate to hold on to power, attempting even to remove Langdon from the case.

On November 15, 1906, the grand jury in San Francisco handed up the first of many indictments, charging Schmitz, Ruef, and the city's police chief. Ruef eventually pleaded guilty and agreed to testify against his former friend and ally. Convicted and cast aside by his sponsor, Schmitz fought on.

Schmitz's efforts took place against a deepening backdrop of public crisis in San Francisco. In May 1907, a sick man was brought to the hospital and died soon after, the cause at first undetermined. As more and more victims straggled in, it became clear that San Francisco was in the grip of a public health emergency: the earthquake had ripped apart sewer hookups and unleashed a wave of rats upon the streets, scattering them to neighborhoods rich and poor. The rats carried the plague. Now, in addition to burned and devastated buildings, The City was confronted with a deadly disease and a dithering administration. "In San Francisco," the Citizens' Health Committee wrote in an extraordinary report on the period, "plague met politics. Instead of being confronted by a united authority with intelligent plans for defense, it found divided forces among which the question of its presence became the subject of factional dispute. There was open popular hostility to the work of the sanitarians, and war among the City, State, and Federal health authorities."[57]

Schmitz was eager to suppress news of the epidemic. (He was, incidentally, remarkably successful; even today, few accounts of it survive.) To squelch coverage and fallout, he refused, among other things, to allow health reports to be printed; his administration fired a federal health officer who raised alarms. By his actions, Schmitz allied the enemies of reform with the threat not just to public morals but to public health as well. The efforts of their opponents, the nascent Progressives, thus acquired additional respectability. Only Schmitz's removal from office by the corruption probe eventually cleared the way for an aggressive health effort. Cases peaked in September 1907 and continued through the fall until the Citizens' Committee took command; seventy-seven people would die before the committee succeeded in halting the spread of the disease, but it did succeed and did so in spite of the city's politics. That triumph of the Citizens' Committee made a deep impression on Warren, demonstrating vividly the potential for enlightened public participation. Warren would adopt a similar model in later years, as he crafted policy for California. In the meantime, the enlightened citizens of San Francisco hunted rats and dipped their dead bodies in flea-killing poison.[58]

After protracted delaying tactics by the defense, the trials of the San Francisco political elite reached their critical stage at precisely the moment that Warren arrived to begin college. The young would-be lawyer who had so enjoyed the Tibbet case in Bakersfield now was treated to an even grander act of civic moralism in the hands of a trial lawyer.

Up until that point, Hiram Johnson, still a relatively obscure young prosecutor, occupied the second chair at the graft prosecution table, toiling away behind Francis Heney as the senior lawyer took the lead in prosecuting businessmen said to have paid bribes to Schmitz, Ruef, and their cohorts. As lead prosecutor, Heney had responsibility for jury selection, and in the spring of 1908, one San Francisco man, Morris Haas, had been dismissed from jury service after an ugly courtroom joust with Heney. Heney had allowed Haas to be seated as a juror, but then discovered evidence that Haas had served time in prison. Heney confronted him with evidence of his criminal record and accused him of covering it up in order to land a seat on the jury and then parlay his influence in order to help Ruef. Haas was dismissed, and he stewed over it for months. He then arrived in court on November 13, while Warren was in his first semester at the University of California, Berkeley, pulled a revolver, and shot Heney in the head. Heney was rushed to the hospital and feared dead. The mantle then fell to Johnson. Blustery and truculent, Johnson performed with the panache that was to become his trademark. His closing appeal to the jury, including four members thought to be in Ruef's pocket, was stunningly effective. Naming each juror and pointing at him, Johnson boomed, "You, you dare not, acquit this man!"[59] Ruef was convicted. Johnson was on his way to a historic career in law and politics.

All of this made for sensational coverage, and it left its mark on Warren, who saw in Johnson a people's champion—not a demagogue but a lawyer, a man of California's middle class empowered by the law to restore order and health to one of its great cities. Warren had set out to become the lawyer that Johnson was. The following year, Warren volunteered for service as an election monitor to help guarantee a clean vote for the Lincoln-Roosevelt League, the reform party of which Johnson was then secretary. Heney, who miraculously recovered from his wounds, was running for district attorney that year, asking voters to put him in office in order to keep the prosecutions alive. Picked to oversee a rough neighborhood south of Market Street on that Election Night, Warren, still too young to vote, admitted that he was not sure how much good he'd done. "No wrongdoing was visible to me," he said, "but throughout the night I wondered what I could have done in those intimidating surroundings even if I had seen any skullduggery."[60]

Warren remembered the reformers' winning, but his memory recorded his hopes, not the true outcome. In fact, Heney lost. He was replaced by a new district attorney, Charles Fickert, who promptly shut down the prosecutions of The City's business elite. The graft trials ended without ever reaching the bribers, a failure that Warren vowed to avoid when his turn came two decades later. In the meantime, the Progressive forces behind the investigation turned instead to statewide office. They launched their first such effort in 1910, with Hiram Johnson as their gubernatorial candidate.

Johnson was a barnstorming, energetic campaigner, and on August 16, 1910, he won the Republican primary. His strongest support came from the areas near Warren's hometown of Bakersfield, and he also carried Alameda County, home of Berkeley. Johnson was a humorless standard-bearer for the movement, but he was tireless and intense, motivated in part by his abiding hatred for his father, Grove Johnson, a member of the legislature and, of all things, a lawyer for the Southern Pacific. When Hiram Johnson joined the graft prosecution, his father contemplated signing on with the defense. Hiram was elected governor that year, and Warren cheered the results. Grove Johnson was less impressed: He resigned from the legislature rather than serve with his son.

Johnson may not have had much to offer young Warren as a personal mentor, but there was much to commend him as a political one. As governor, Johnson would move with extraordinary vigor to upend California politics. Measures such as the recall, the initiative, and the referendum—all trumpeted by Johnson and the Progressives—sharply curtailed the power of the Southern Pacific and other big-business bosses. Moreover, they injected into California politics a seriousness of purpose and a sense of reform as moral calling.[61] Johnson resembled much of what Warren imagined for himself—Johnson was a tough, uncompromising lawyer who had taken on the serious business of the people as his own moral mantle. And Progressivism gave Warren's instincts a political identity—an affirmation of the place in politics for middle-class men and values. As one Progressive journal observed in 1908: "Nearly all the problems which vex society have their sources above or below the middle-class man. From above come the problems of predatory wealth. . . . From below come the problems of poverty and of pigheaded and brutish criminality."[62] The proposition that the middle class was the locus of reform and progress undergirded Johnson's success and spoke directly to Warren. Edward White, a brilliant historian of the Supreme Court who clerked for Warren, understood its mark on him:

> Warren *believed* in the political values of California Progressivism. His own childhood furnished dramatic evidence of the power of the Southern Pacific. He had been brought up in an atmosphere where one's moral values were taken with great seriousness. He had developed a tendency to scrutinize the actions of those in authority, holding them to his own moral or practical standards: He was ideally suited to be a watchdog for the "public interest."[63]

Present at the birth of Hiram Johnson's career, Warren never lost his awe for him. "There ensued an administration of reform measures never equaled in California or probably in any other state before or since," Warren wrote later.[64] In 1934, when Warren, then the state Republican Party chairman, sent off congratulatory notes to his fellow Republicans, most were formal and restrained. Only the note to Johnson, then serving in the United States Senate, could be described as effusive, as Warren congratulated the party's senior Washington representative on the support he had received for a fourth term, "which has been so deservedly voted by the people of the state you have served so well."[65]

Johnson's two gubernatorial terms were California's first serious attempt to fashion a political center after the blisteringly factional politics of the late nineteenth and early twentieth centuries. He ran outside the normal two-party system, and his wide appeal was demonstrated by his reelection in 1914 as well as his long Senate career after that. But Johnson and the Progressives achieved a kind of negative center: They successfully cast off much of what had corrupted and diminished government and installed political reforms intended to democratize the process. They did not, however, create any lasting social system to connect California's polarized classes, economic reforms to bridge its disparities of wealth, or great physical structures to connect its vast landscape. Those accomplishments—the calming of labor-management disputes; the construction of school and transportation networks; the harnessing of northern water for southern agriculture; the construction of a modern, cosmopolitan state—would await the emergence of a politician with Johnson's drive and integrity but with a more complete vision of constructive politics. It would take a generation until that politician finished the work that Johnson and the Progressives left undone.

When he did, when Earl Warren became governor in 1943, he hung just one photograph in his office, that of Hiram Johnson.

Chapter 2

# AWAY FROM HOME

*He matured a little later, I think.*

NEWTON DRURY, ON HIS CLASSMATE EARL WARREN[1]

T HE UNIVERSITY OF CALIFORNIA at Berkeley greeted Earl Warren with a young and growing campus—the monumental neoclassical architecture that today helps convey its grandeur and yet nods to its place in the California that was just then taking shape, financed largely by Phoebe Apperson Hearst, mother of newspaper publisher William Randolph Hearst. Though the university was just a quarter-century old, it already was established as California's foremost center of higher education, and Warren's arrival there signaled his admission into an emerging California elite, more open than the baronages of San Francisco and Los Angeles and yet selectively meritocratic. Beneath the live oaks and redwoods of the East Bay, with its signature view of the then-unbridged Golden Gate, Berkeley represented the early forming point of California culture and intelligentsia. Warren was thrilled to be there. His love of it never diminished.

Warren was a "freshie," and as such was expected to adhere to Berkeley's light-hearted repression of its youngest students. No caps, no pipe smoking, no entering North Hall by the front steps—those were just a handful of the freshman restrictions, violation of which subjected a student to "a much-needed submersion in that slippery, slimy, slushy slough of stagnation . . . Chem Pond."[2] And yet Warren had barely set foot in Berkeley before he was in trouble. On his first Sunday after arriving, Warren joined members of La Junta Club, a local fraternity where he had an introduction, for dinner. Eager to impress, the young incoming freshman boasted of his friction with his high school principal, of the events that nearly saw him expelled on the last day of school, and of cheating on schoolwork to harass the hated administrator. One of the seniors who overheard Warren's story pulled him aside later in the week and warned him that he was out of line. Ethics at Berkeley were important, and grading was on a curve. As a Berkeley student now, Warren was expected to understand and obey its honor code. The lecture sobered Warren. "I was deeply touched by the kind manner in which he talked to me, and promised him I would never violate the honor system," Warren said.[3] The members of La Junta soon invited Warren to join, which he happily did. He moved into the house on College Street, at the edge of the Berkeley campus, and set about discovering the town, nestled between the austerity of the school and the lure of the nearby docks and their longshoreman bars. Not for the first nor the last time would Warren find himself pulled between those poles.

Warren's classmates were to become a storied group of Berkeley students, even today referred to as the Illustrious Class of 1912. Horace Albright and Newton Drury, two early and important environmentalists, were among the members of the class, as was Herman Phleger, a San Francisco lawyer and adviser to President Eisenhower; others, men and women who became judges and lawyers and people of influence, rounded out the class. Warren ended up being the most significant of them all, but in his student days, he gave little indication that he would rank with them in history. Drury went on to California fame as a savior of the state's redwood forests. He admired Warren greatly, but recalled him as a charming but shallow student. "He matured a little later, I think," Drury gently remembered.[4]

Warren tried out for the university baseball team but did not make it. He took classes but didn't study hard. "I'm afraid I didn't have any craving for knowledge," he admitted years later. It was, instead, camaraderie that he enjoyed. "Companionship," he said, "was the greatest thing I found at the university."[5] Warren had barely arrived before he began to make a name for himself as a hearty, boisterous classmate. He ate with gusto that first year, piling on weight. He gained thirty pounds as a freshman and kept growing, eventually reaching his full height of six-foot-one and weight of 200 pounds.[6] As he did, Warren's high school shyness also seemed to melt away. "He was a hail-fellow-well-met," Drury remembered.[7] He was handsome and might have been a natural ladies' man, but still he carried the residue of his awkward youth; he could be clumsy around women. That is not to say he avoided them entirely. His sophomore hop dance card had a few entries—Dorothy P and Miss Eggert each got a spin around the floor—and he socialized now and again.[8] For now, however, his principal relations were with men. He was a welcome fixture in his fraternity, Sigma Phi (Sigma Phi initially was La Junta, but changed its name when it affiliated with the national fraternity). Throughout his life, Warren would enjoy the hearty company of male friendship, of ball games and bars, of male clubs and duck blinds. And he would long retain a trace of awkwardness in the company of women.

Among his growing group of friends, Warren soon acquired a nickname— "Pink," though some preferred "Pinky." It appears to have resulted from an encounter with a young nurse, whom Warren visited for treatment of a bout of pinkeye.[9] "Come on, Pinky, it's time for your medicine," he recalled the nurse calling out to him.[10] It, too, stuck. For the rest of his life, college friends would address Earl Warren, even as Chief Justice of the United States, as "Pink."

Student office might have seemed a natural for Warren, who liked joining and leading, but he ignored the opportunity. He did dabble in the local politics of the area, however, his first participation in active political life. One candidate Warren helped was John Stit Wilson. He was "an avowed Socialist" who sought in 1911 to unseat Beverly Hodgehead, whom Warren characterized as "a conservative corporation lawyer" representing "some of the large public utilities on which the campaign was focused."[11] During the election, Berkeley students took over a political rally and rousted the speakers—an event that Warren participated in. He added that on other occasions, "we stopped traffic on the streets, put streetcars out of commission for hours, overrode the police by disproportionate weight of numbers, made loud tumultuous noises until all hours of the night . . . and even broke up political meetings." Wilson won the election, and Warren wrote, "contrary to dire predictions, the heavens did not fall and tranquility soon returned to the campus and the city. Mayor Wilson was an honest man, a good mayor, and was reelected at the end of his first term."[12]

Warren was an extrovert, hearty and boisterous in his politics and his friendships. And yet Berkeley also deepened his love of poetry. Even there, the intellectualism was subsumed by fellowship, in this case in the membership of a group called the Gun Club. Drury was a member as well. As he recalled it:

> It was called the Gun Club because it had been formed some twenty years before by a group of fellows thinking that if they went to a tavern there on the edge of the city they could borrow some guns and shoot some ducks in the Berkeley marshes. But they never got any further than the tavern, so instead of the hunting expedition, they decided to form the Gun Club. . . . When we were in college, we would have beer and poetry, and we'd get a big porterhouse steak for 50 cents.[13]

Warren favored American and British poets—Robert Service and Rudyard Kipling were two favorites. He liked stories in his poems and shied away from modernists. As his grandson and great admirer Jeffrey Earl Warren once noted, he liked "manly poets."[14] Viewed in the light of the defining tension of his youth—between the romance of Bakersfield's taverns and the order of the Warren home—poetry was a natural amusement for Warren. It balanced creativity and structure, humor and seriousness. He took to it. With several classmates, Warren founded a new poetry society as well and gave it a mischievous name: U.N.X. The initials were un-revealing enough that U.N.X. found its way to official recognition in the university's annual yearbook, the *Blue and Gold*, but in fact the name disguised an etymology from a ribald drinking song.[15] Versions of the song have evolved over the years but they have a common theme. In it, a sultan eyes his harem on Christmas Eve:

> The Sultan said, as he entered
> These lovely spacious halls:
> Boys, what do you want for Christmas?
> And the Eunuchs answered BALLS![16]

U.N.X., unbeknownst to the administration, stood for "eunuchs." Poetry thus also supplied an outlet for Warren's ribald streak, as well as a form of expression for a man who would often admire and even envy those with a greater gift than his own for eloquence. He never lost his love for it. Many years later, when he had reached one of the pinnacles of his professional life, a friend and aide named Bill Sweigert chose to memorialize the occasion with a poem, and he began it with Warren's days at Berkeley.

> Now listen to my story
> About a man of fame,
> The mighty Earl of Warren
> Who well enriched that name.
>
> Upon the shores of Oakland,
> Bedecked in blue and gold,
> He vowed he'd ring the welkin
> As ne'er in days of old.[17]

His literary interests stirred by poetry, Warren became a member of the college literary society, Skull and Keys, as well as the Gun Club, his fraternity, and an es-teemed honorary society known as the Order of the Golden Bear. That order, which continues today, honors Berkeley's most admired students, not for their ac-ademic work but rather for their contribution to the campus and society. Warren was a natural member.

Inside the classroom, meanwhile, Warren survived but without distinction. He fared decently in subjects he liked, less well in those in which he saw little relevance. And yet despite his lackluster academic performance, Warren did in fact expand in-tellectually. Interviewed by biographer John Weaver, Warren could not cite a single book or author that influenced him,[18] but by the time he sat down to write his memoirs, the names of three came back to him: Upton Sinclair, Jack London, and Frank Norris. Significantly, all three struck a personal chord with Warren.

Consider, for example, Warren's appreciation of Norris. Like Warren, Norris attended Berkeley and was a founder of Skull and Keys. That may be what first drew Warren to Norris's work, and once there, Warren found himself and his life contained within it. *The Octopus*, Norris's great novel, is the only book mentioned by name in the section of Warren's memoirs devoted to his college years. Thus, while its precise impact on Warren is difficult to assess, the novel stayed with him for more than fifty years, earning it an exclusive place in the college memories of the retired chief justice.

*The Octopus* tells the intertwined stories of California wheat farmers and their war with a terrifyingly powerful railroad, called, in the novel, the Pacific and Southwestern Railroad but conspicuously meant to be the Southern Pacific. Modeled after an actual violent battle between the Southern Pacific and California wheat farmers in 1877,[19] *The Octopus* helped gird the California public for its showdown with the Southern Pacific. In *The Octopus*, subtitled *A California Story*, Norris encouraged just such a campaign, portraying the railroad as a ruthless exploiter of land and wealth, immune to the pleas of farmers and others dependent on its services. When Magnus Derrick, an imposing central character of the novel, contemplates an attempt to buy the elections of railroad commissioners in order to even the fight against the railroad, his wife despairs:

> Annie Derrick feared the railroad. At night, when everything else was still, the distant roar of passing trains echoed across Los Muertos, from Guadalajara, from Bonneville, or from the Long Trestle, straight into her heart. At such moments she saw very plainly the galloping terror of steam and steel, with its single eye, cyclopean, red, shooting from horizon to horizon, symbol of a vast power, huge and terrible; the leviathan with tentacles of steel, to oppose which meant to be ground to instant destruction beneath the clashing wheels. No, it was better to submit, to resign oneself to the inevitable.[20]

How could such a description not hold Warren's attention? It described the company that employed him and his father—after having first fired and then blacklisted him—and that abused the men Earl was responsible for as a teenager. The novel thus tapped his personal experience and provided a literary underpinning for the politics he was then developing: anticorporate, anticorruption, rudimentarily populist. The novel also gave voice to a darker side of Warren's youth. As with much popular fiction of the time, Norris's attack on the railroad was woven together with the subtle lacings of racism, and in Norris's case that racism was consistent with the dominant culture of California and its nascent reform movement. In his novel, Norris more than once describes an act of cheapness as "Hebraic," and as California's great modern historian Kevin Starr notes, Norris's active characters invariably are white and of European descent. The Mexican and other Latin characters in the novel exist mainly to provide color for a barn dance and to take the lead in a slaughter of rabbits too repulsive for whites to join: "Blindly, furiously, they struck and struck. The Anglo-Saxon spectators drew back in disgust, but the hot, degenerated blood of Portuguese, Mexican and mixed Spaniard boiled up in excitement at this wholesale slaughter."[21]

As for London and Sinclair—Warren's other remarked-upon California authors—the most striking aspects of each, insofar as they made and retained a positive impression on Warren, are that both were plainspoken tellers of narrative stories, that both were socialists, and that both were or would become personally known to Warren. During his Berkeley years, Warren and friends would tromp down to the dive bars along the Oakland waterfront. There, with the fog and mist outside and with pipe smoke curling through the wood-paneled rooms, they would sit, spellbound, as London told the tales of his adventures, as only London could.

Though Warren appears to have been drawn to London's exploits more than his politics, London's legacy is an inextricable mix of the two. In later years, London would back Warren's opponents politically, but Warren retained affection for London's work. Similarly, Sinclair was a better writer than a politician, but his career in California makes it impossible to consider one without the other. In the 1930s, Sinclair made a quixotic but nearly successful run for governor. That campaign included many participants, and one notable one was the newly appointed state Republican Party chief, Earl Warren.

Warren focused sufficiently on his studies to be awarded a bachelor of letters in jurisprudence on May 15, 1912. Newton Drury delivered the commencement address, "What the Public Wants." The less illustrious Earl Warren sat in the audience.[22]

Having completed his undergraduate courses, Warren slid without much effort into Berkeley's law school. There again, he displayed modest academic interest, though he also evidenced a solidifying character marked by his sensitivity to challenge. Law school rules of the day prohibited students from working with law firms while full-time students. Warren ignored the rule at considerable peril. Discovery could well have resulted in expulsion. Still, he believed that the value of practical experience outweighed his chances of being caught, and he set his mind to it. He persuaded a local law office to hire him, then sneaked off campus to go to work. He managed to avoid detection or consequence.

Later, as his days in Berkeley were drawing to a close, Warren was warned by a law school dean that he was in danger of failing courses because he spoke up so infrequently in class. Rather than simply start contributing, Warren struck a stand on principle: Where, he demanded, was it written that he was required to volunteer in class? The dean, apparently taken aback, conceded that there was no such written rule, but warned Warren that if he failed any of his exams, he would not receive a degree. Warren passed.[23]

Once Warren's career took him to the pinnacle of the legal profession, his modest accomplishments as a law student would become a source of amusement to himself and to friends. When Jim Gaither, one of the many gifted students who clerked for Warren during his chief justiceship, was first interviewed for the job, he talked about the law and his shiny academic accomplishments—Gaither was a Princeton undergraduate and an outstanding law student at Stanford. Gaither was invited back a second time, and he studied rigorously for the interview, reading cases, examining the jurisprudence of the Warren Court. He showed up for the session with Warren's two-man interviewing team, and instead of grilling him about the law, the interviewers asked Gaither questions about baseball and football. "Three hours," he recalls, "not one question of substance." Once Gaither got the job, he asked what that had all been about. "We wanted you the first time," one of his interviewers replied. "But we thought you were so serious you would drive the Chief crazy."[24]

Warren may have taken law school lightly, but he put in enough work to graduate. A thesis was required, so he wrote one. Titled "The Personal Liability of Corporation Directors in the State of California," it was just thirty-one pages long and a work of neither great originality nor great scholarship. It was serviceable, however, and on May 6, 1914, it was approved by the dean—the same dean who had warned Warren about his failure to speak up more often in class.[25] Warren graduated with his class that month. The entire group of students was admitted to the practice of law without the need of a bar exam.

Warren now was a lawyer but one in search of work. He first accepted a job with the Associated Oil Company in San Francisco. It was not a happy experience. The company's chief counsel, Edmund Tauske, was brusque and unappreciative. Warren had worked to become a lawyer, and now that he was one, Tauske used him to fetch cigars. Warren described Tauske as "an irascible old man," and determined to quit. When the time came, Warren took great delight in telling his boss of his discontent:

> I told him . . . I was not happy there; that there was no human dignity recognized in the office, and that I wanted to make another start in more congenial surroundings. He seemed hurt by my frank statement, and said, "I have had probably fifty young men work for me, and none of them ever expressed such dissatisfaction." I was bold enough to tell him that if he had treated them differently perhaps he would have needed only one instead of the fifty.[26]

Warren stayed long enough to find a replacement for himself, and as he considered his own options, he debated leaving the law altogether. A respectful audience with the chief justice of the state Supreme Court turned him back around. Warren arrived one day to pick up an order, and the chief justice invited him to sit down and talk. Warren was flattered by the justice's interest in him, and it revived his enthusiasm for the law. He relocated to Oakland, joined the law firm of Robinson and Robinson, and took an active role in starting up a young lawyers' association—one of many such instances in which Warren found satisfaction in organizing professional or social clubs. The time passed quickly, and in 1917 Warren and two classmates were preparing to form their own firm, only to be interrupted by the Great War.

Warren wanted badly to fight. He tried several times to enlist, but he was turned away first in the flood of applicants, then because of hemorrhoids and a case of ether pneumonia contracted while having his hemorrhoids operated on. Once finally cleared for enlistment, he entered the service on September 7, 1917, and was promoted to sergeant less than two months later.[27] He was sent first to Camp Lewis, Washington, and later Camp Lee, Virginia.

Warren was a good soldier and a capable supervisor. He was fair and patient, and his men regarded him as a good listener.[28] At Camp Lewis, he met Leo Carrillo. They struck up a friendship, and Carrillo described Sergeant Warren as a "big man mentally and physically, a great hulking, strong, sturdy soldier without any pettiness."[29] Accepted into the officer program, Warren received his commission as a second lieutenant on June 1, 1918, and was shipped to Camp Lee, where he was assigned to the bayonet program. His rigorous preparation at Camp Lewis was welcome—Warren was one of only two students to survive the bayonet training without needing a stay in the hospital.[30]

Although Warren rarely had time to leave the bases to which he was assigned, he did manage, while in the service, to maintain a playful romance with a California girl living in New York—the first recorded romantic relationship of Warren's life. Earl had met Ina Perham back in California; she was a student at Oakland's Academy of Fine Arts while Earl was attending nearby Berkeley. Ina was a smart and adventurous young artist, as vivacious as he was staid. She seemed to bring out the mischief in Warren.

"I do wish I could get away from this camp for a few days," Warren wrote Ina from Camp Lee. "And by the way, don't you *dare* to leave N.Y. before I get up there to see you. . . . The first chance I get I am coming to N.Y. and you must be there to celebrate with me."

In his letter, Warren allowed himself to complain, something he rarely would do as he became a more public figure. Writing to Ina without such inhibitions, he grumbled about not liking the people of Virginia and about his confinement to the camp: "Just think, I have been here nearly five months, and have only slept outside of camp two nights in all that time." He worried the war would end before he could fight, and envied another young man who had recently shipped out. "If he ever gets a chance to cut loose at the Huns with machine guns, he can be positive that he has 'done his bit,'" Warren wrote, adding that he hoped his own bayonet work, once employed in battle, "would kill enough Germans to keep the rest of their army busy." More personally, Warren encouraged Ina to fend off the advances of an older man, and he attempted humor along with charm. But Warren's naïveté is the letter's dominant undercurrent. He tried, for instance, lamely to joke about Ina's recent weight gains: "So you have gained nine pounds on your trip," he wrote. "Just you look out or you will be in the heavyweight class, and that isn't the style now, is it?"

Closing his note, Warren added, "Well, 'Fatty,' I guess I will say 'olive oil.'"[31]

Warren did not make it to New York for his hoped-for celebration with Ina Perham and the romance fizzled out, though they maintained a formal friendship through the years. Promoted to first lieutenant on November 4, 1918, he was transferred just a few weeks later to Camp MacArthur in Waco, Texas. And then, quickly, the war ended. Warren was discharged from the Army on December 9, 1918, and returned home to Bakersfield for Christmas. He arrived in uniform and continued to wear it during his job search. Partly the reason was financial: Warren left the service with only $60 in muster pay, and spent much of that on Christmas presents for his family.[32] His old suits no longer fit the more muscular veteran, so he did not have much to wear. That said, it did not hurt in 1919 to be identifiable as a veteran while looking for a job.

After a month in Bakersfield, Warren picked up his life again. His old partners had moved on, so he dropped thoughts of starting up the law firm. And he certainly had no interest in staying in Bakersfield, which he already had left once. His sister provided him with an option. Ethel, who had dropped out of high school before graduating, had by then married Vernon Plank, a Southern Pacific man just like Methias, and the couple had moved north.[33] Theirs would prove a sad life— Vernon Plank died one day on the golf course before his fiftieth birthday, and their daughter, Dorothy, would die of tuberculosis after a long and unsuccessful attempt at recovery in a sanatorium. But now they offered Earl a base in Northern California, and Earl was by then far more a man of Berkeley than of Bakersfield. He accepted, and headed back to Oakland, by the Bay where he had spent his college years.

Warren stayed for a time with Ethel and Vernon before a chance encounter with old classmates sent him to Sacramento. Leon Gray, a former colleague from Robinson and Robinson, had just been elected to the state legislature from Oakland, and he offered Warren a job as a legislative analyst, a post that paid $5 a day. Warren agreed, but hoped he could find something to supplement that when he got to Sacramento. Soon after arriving, he sought out another classmate, Assemblyman Charlie Kasch. Warren, still in uniform, found Kasch in the legislature and asked him if he would check around for openings. Kasch promised he would. The next morning, Kasch was back at his desk when Warren strode up again, pleased with himself. With the help of still another classmate—Berkeley supplied more than its share of the California state legislature in those years—he had recently landed a job as clerk to the Judiciary Committee, earning $7 a day. "It was a very good [job], even better than he expected," a friend recalled.[34] Warren held the position for the length of that year's legislative session, commencing a career of public service that stretched across more than fifty years with barely an interruption.

Sacramento, this time, was a brief stop—the session ran from January through the spring—and Warren returned to Oakland. Associates had tried to use leverage to force the Alameda district attorney, Ezra Decoto, to hire Warren, but Warren demurred, uncomfortable with the notion of strong-arming his place onto the prosecutor's staff. Instead, he made one last attempt at a private career, hanging out a shingle with Leon Gray. But before Warren could land a single client, the Oakland city attorney, H. L. Hagan, offered Warren a job in his office. Warren would have the chance to advise city officials and defend them from legal action, and he would have access to policy decisions and help guide the public interest. Sensing that his meandering search for a career was over, Warren accepted. "[A]t last," he said, "the heavy gate was opening for me."[35]

Chapter 3

# PROSECUTOR, FATHER

*He was always known to us as "the Chief," and he still is.*

CLARENCE A. SEVERIN[1]

*I've always had a father, and I never called him anything but Dad.*

JIM WARREN, ADOPTED SON OF EARL WARREN[2]

W ARREN TURNED DOWN his first chance to become a prosecutor, when he was considered for the job only because his political friends were willing to put pressure on District Attorney Ezra Decoto to hire him. But the alternative, his job in the city attorney's office, though an entry into public service, was never what Warren had in mind for a career. Ever since Bakersfield, he'd dreamed of the ordered romance of trial lawyering. His chance came in early 1920, when Decoto, impressed by the young man who had refused to apply pressure at his disposal, offered to let Warren try cases on behalf of the People of the State of California for $150 a month. That meant taking a pay cut—the job as city attorney paid $200 a month—and it required moving from the modern offices of the city attorney to the county's rickety courthouse, where the district attorney's office was up an old flight of wobbly stairs. None of that mattered to Warren. He was being offered the career he had imagined since he was twelve years old. He accepted, and on May 20, 1920, he became a deputy district attorney for the county of Alameda.[3]

It was not a placid time to accept responsibility for enforcing the laws of California, particularly not for an idealistic, moderate young man. The state was divided into opposing camps, moving further apart with each passing year. On one side were the state's business leaders, largely Republican, consolidating their fortunes and trying to build a modern economy; on the other was organized labor, powerful but confused in San Francisco, suppressed in Los Angeles. Neither side had much patience for compromise; both were all too willing to reach for the bludgeon or the dirk.

There was no single event that caused that fissure; indeed, the state's history seemed to ordain it. But the particular set of calamities that set the temper in 1920 began a decade earlier, with the bombing of the *Los Angeles Times* by three union activists. They first denied their crime, and labor furiously rose to their support. Then two confessed, humiliating those who had championed them, setting back labor's campaign in Los Angeles and sealing the paper's violent antipathy toward labor; even in the 1950s, Norman Chandler, grandson of General Otis, could boast, "I have never bargained with a labor organizer or negotiator in my life."[4] Six years after the *Times*'s bombing in Los Angeles, another explosion, in San Francisco, scattered more victims across more pavement. This time, a belligerent union tough named Tom Mooney was arrested, along with Warren Billings, another Socialist.

They were prosecuted by San Francisco DA Charles Fickert—the same district attorney who had beaten the Progressive candidate in the election that Warren monitored as a student. On February 9, 1917, the jury in the Mooney case filed back. Its foreman caught the eye of one of the prosecutors and drew a finger across his throat. Mooney was convicted, and on February 24, sentenced to hang. Barely had the case concluded, however, before problems began to appear regarding the witnesses against Mooney and his codefendant. Some admitted to having concocted their accounts, others to embellishment. Strong evidence suggested that Fickert and his staff had offered bribes and doctored physical evidence. One witness, confronted with a contradiction in her testimony that put her in two places nearly a mile apart at the same instant, insisted that her flesh was in one location but that she had witnessed the bombing with her "astral eyes."[5] Eventually, even the trial judge became convinced that the case against Mooney had been unfair.

Sentenced to hang, Mooney went to San Quentin and there became an international labor martyr. From his cell, he demanded his release and rejected attempts to cut a compromise under which he would accept parole.[6] Mooney became, as historian Starr notes, both the "most revered martyr of the labor movement" and, after Douglas Fairbanks and Mary Pickford, the "best-known Californian in the world."[7] As the 1920s began, Tom Mooney was alive, angry, and in prison—a spark in California's superheated politics.

At about the same time, another player added fuel. The International Workers of the World, formed in Chicago in 1905, came to California to organize its poorest workers, including migrants and minorities—groups beyond the interest of most of the state's labor organizers. The IWW was ramshackle and its aims were at times incoherent, but it was ambitious as well. It embraced revolutionary rhetoric. Its organizing campaigns cut across industries and racial groups—unlike Debs's

American Railway Union, the IWW welcomed black and Asian members. That was enough to enrage California's elites. The IWW's loose-knit leaders—the *Times* was apparently the first to call them "Wobblies"[8]—were demonized and persecuted. They were subjected to sadistic assaults in Fresno (1910 to 1911), San Diego (1912), and Wheatland (1913), among other places, and vilified in the California legislature, a reliable engine of repression. It was during Warren's brief service there in 1919 that the legislature passed the Criminal Syndicalism Act, intended specifically to give law enforcement additional power to suppress the IWW. The act prohibited advocacy of "any doctrine or precept advocating, teaching or aiding and abetting the commission of crime, sabotage . . . or unlawful acts of force and violence or unlawful methods of terrorism as a means of accomplishing a change in industrial ownership or control or effecting any political change."[9] By allowing prosecutions for advocacy, rather than action, the Criminal Syndicalism Act vastly broadened the scope of illegal activity related to union organizing, at least as practiced by the IWW. Within months, scores of IWW members across the state were under arrest, charged with violating the act not by committing violence but for giving speeches or otherwise expressing the belief that force was justified in changing "industrial ownership or control."

Under those circumstances, moderation was a hard value to practice, especially for a young lawyer in his first courtroom job. Earl Warren was assigned his first case less than a month after he joined the office, and he was paired with a senior prosecutor, A. A. Rogers. Warren's assignment was to secure a conviction of John Taylor, a union leader and onetime Socialist candidate for mayor of Oakland whose affiliation with the Communist Labor Party brought him afoul of California's Criminal Syndicalism law. With less than a month on the job, Warren entered California's fast currents of labor, violence, and repression.

Taylor's offense was not that he had committed acts of violence but rather that he believed in the principles of the Communist Labor Party and that he had admitted to once being a member of the IWW. Taylor represented himself at trial. He maintained that his beliefs might be radical but they were not violent, and he contended that police and police informers tilted their testimony against him and paid money to secure damning evidence. Warren rose on June 16, 1920, to deliver the prosecution's response to those charges in the form of a closing argument. He accused Taylor of slander and demeaned Taylor's attempts to introduce nonviolent socialist teachings into the case. Those writings were irrelevant, Warren told jurors, because Taylor had stayed with the Communist Labor Party when that party broke from the less violent socialists.[10] Warren condemned Taylor's attacks on prosecution witnesses, though in fact the prosecution had relied on a number of shady informers to make its case that the IWW was a violent organization. Labor fiercely resented those informers, describing one as a "self-confessed burglar convict, a stick-up man and trench dodger," and another as "a twelve-time deserter from military and naval service . . . identified by hospital officials as evilly diseased and paretic."[11] Later, Warren too would express reservations about the witnesses used in that and other syndicalism cases. In his memoirs, Warren described the witnesses as "repulsive" and confessed to having felt "squeamish about them."[12] The jury in Taylor's trial did not hear any of that, at least from the prosecution. Instead, Warren reminded jurors of the law and accused Taylor first of breaking it, then of lying to save himself from the consequences.

On June 18, 1920, Taylor was convicted of two counts of violating the Criminal Syndicalism Act. He was sentenced to one to fourteen years in the state penitentiary. His was one of the early convictions under the law, which would eventually see 531 men and women charged with criminal syndicalism and would send 128 of those to California prisons.[13]

Although Warren later would insist defensively that he had never initiated a syndicalism prosecution as Alameda's district attorney, the law had run its course by 1925, when Warren took that office. In fact, no prosecution anywhere in California was brought under the act after August 15, 1924.[14] Moreover, while Warren did not bring new cases, his office, even after he headed it, played an important role in defending syndicalism nationally. Anita Whitney was among the first defendants convicted under California's law, and she, like Taylor, was prosecuted in Alameda County. She appealed her conviction all the way to the United States Supreme Court during the years that Warren was rising through that office. The decision, in 1927, was most notable for the concurring opinion of Justice Louis Brandeis, who defended speech over fear—"Men," he wrote, "feared witches and burnt women. It is the function of speech to free men from the bondage of irrational fears"[15]—but the Court upheld Whitney's conviction, vindicating Alameda's prosecution of her. The decision in *Whitney* stood for forty-two years. When it fell, it was by the hand of Warren's Court.

In the meantime, young Earl Warren's pursuit of Taylor won him friends in the office. On the final day of closing arguments in the Taylor case, Warren's senior colleague, Rogers, praised his associate for his work on the case, predicting "a brilliant career for Warren as a prosecutor."[16] The defendant's supporters were less impressed. "When future generations read these trials, children of that day will blush and hide because of descent from such brutes," the IWW wrote.[17]

Most of Warren's early cases were not so emotional, and he settled well into the requirements of trial work. He admired Hiram Johnson, but did not emulate him as a lawyer. Johnson was theatrically big. Warren, by contrast, was an understated advocate for the most part, restrained and meticulous—no bombast or tricks, no diversions. Helen MacGregor was a young law school graduate who spotted Warren one day in court. The county was a party to a lawsuit, the case turning on an interpretation of the interstate commerce clause. Warren's questioning, she remembered half a century later, was thoughtfully constructed—every question yielded an answer that bore directly on the matter before the court. There was, she said, "no wasted motion. The case was like an architectural structure."[18] Moreover, it was delivered by an attractive and sober young man. When, years later, MacGregor got the chance to work for Warren, she took it and then followed him through his rise in California politics.

As Warren honed his courtroom skills, he also expanded his influence in the office, where Decoto learned to rely ever more heavily on his deputy. Often, when a prosecutor would leave the office, and someone would need to pick up his cases, the job would fall to Warren, who already had researched the underlying law. Decoto recalled later that when he would broach a legal question on a Friday, Warren would produce the answer on Monday morning.[19] So Decoto moved the ambitious young man through a variety of administrative posts. One of those jobs took Warren out of the courtroom but introduced him to a new arena, as he was assigned the job of giving legal counsel to the county Board of Supervisors. In that position, Warren not only wielded policy influence, he befriended the county's leaders and found time to frequent local newspaper offices. "He used to make it a practice to cultivate every important person on the [Oakland] paper," remembered Mary Shaw, a member of the Bay Area press corps in those days. "I always had a feeling that his sticking around the city editors was just a part of the job to get where he wanted to go."[20]

Warren was almost all business, but not quite. Although his wartime correspondence with Ina Perham revealed his clumsiness as a suitor, he was a serious and handsome man with a bright future. Women could not fail to notice him. One sunny Sunday morning, one did. Nina Palmquist Meyers was a lovely young woman, mannered and graceful, energetic, intelligent, serious, generous. Born in Sweden in 1893, she had arrived in the United States six months to the day later and then was raised in Oakland.[21]

She had her quirks: Cats terrified her, the result of a frightening childhood moment when Nina, her arms immobilized in a cast, was attacked by a house cat that scratched and bit her. She never got over it; in fact, her hatred of cats was so intense that she could not even abide fur coats.[22] Mostly, though, in 1921, Nina Palmquist was lonely, the consequence of a life too draped, in its early years, with loss. Nina's mother died at age twenty-nine, leaving five young children, including three-year-old Nina. Her father, a Baptist minister, remarried a hard woman, Sophia Rosenberg. Reflecting on her youth decades later, Nina recalled the year she saved up a dime to buy her older brother, whom she adored, a toy lamb for his birthday. When her stepmother discovered the present, she was outraged at the waste of money. She ordered Nina to return the gift. Sobbing, Nina did.[23] As an adult, Nina never made much out of birthdays. She adamantly refused to celebrate her own.[24]

Nina's difficulties followed her throughout her young life. Her father died in 1907, and two of her brothers after that. On September 26, 1914, at the age of twenty-one, she married a promising young pianist, Grover Cleveland Meyers.[25] In 1919 they had a son, Jim. While Jim was still an infant, his father died of tuberculosis. Nina, her modest savings depleted by Grover's illness, was now a widow with a baby. Having nowhere else to turn, Nina Meyers moved back home, joining her stepmother in an Oakland flat and taking a job in her specialty shop.[26] There the two widows and the young boy lived together.[27]

One Sunday morning in 1921, Jim, then just two years old, was home while Nina enjoyed a leisurely weekend morning. She went with friends to the Piedmont Baths in Oakland, a popular spot among young people in those days, and she was swimming when Earl Warren spotted her across the pool. "She was in the water, and I could only see her head," he remembered. "But she looked wonderful to me."[28] He asked a friend to introduce them, and Earl and Nina struck up a conversation; when it came time for breakfast, Warren arranged to be seated next to her, and the following weekend, he took her on their first date. They saw a play, *Smilin' Through*.[29] They were attracted to each other right away, but both proceeded slowly. Neither would ever be called impulsive. Earl, then thirty years old, was by nature cautious, and twenty-eight-year-old Nina was afraid of chasing off such a promising suitor. Yet slowly they moved together. Their early conversations gave way to a regular Saturday date, the two meeting after she closed up the shop and he put away his legal research for the evening.

At first glance, they might have struck one as an unusual couple: Earl towered over the five-foot-two Nina. He was booming and hearty; she was softer, gentler. But that surface difference obscured deeper commonalities. They were deliberate, efficient people, intelligent and modest. Each was eager for a family, each capable of great affection and appreciative of the other; he was protective, she was wounded. Over the months, their relationship deepened, and Earl grew close to Nina's son. On nights when Earl was scheduled to come to the apartment, Jim would grow restless as he awaited Earl's arrival. When Earl came inside and sat down, Jim would clamber up into the big man's lap.[30] Nina, so protective of her only son, would only have allowed that attachment to grow had she been confident that Earl was destined to be her husband. Still, their romance stretched forward with no wedding date in sight. The reason was practical: Warren had no intention of letting his wife work, and his income in the early 1920s would not support a family. So they waited—patience was another of their common traits—for the break that would push Warren ahead and allow their lives to take the next step.

Warren's attention to the details of political advancement paid off in 1925, when Decoto was being touted for a position on the state Railroad Commission.

The rumors of his pending appointment swirled for weeks, creating a tussle among his deputies over who would succeed him. Although the district attorney's job was an elected position, the five supervisors had the power to fill midterm vacancies, such as those caused by resignation of the incumbent. For Warren, this was opportunity, but also a moment of self-evaluation. The Board of Supervisors was dominated by a local machine boss, Mike Kelly, whose political inclinations were Progressive but whose preference for DA was Frank Shay, a Warren rival in the office. To fight Shay for the position was to challenge the Progressive-backed candidate and to join forces with the traditional Republicans of Alameda County, whose most prominent voice was the *Oakland Tribune*. To win, Warren would need to tack right ideologically, moving away from the Progressive tradition that had guided him since college and reaching for a more traditional, conservative Republican base. The alternative for Warren would have been to defer to the Progressive candidate and wait his turn.

Warren chose to run. He sought out the backing of the *Tribune* and its conservative Republican publisher, Joe Knowland. Born in 1873, less than a quarter century after California achieved statehood, Knowland was struck in the state's early image. He had started in the lumber business and expanded, as the state grew, into banking. He held state and federal offices around the turn of the century—he was featured just at the edge of the infamous "Shame of California" photograph, a young man among much older and established ones, but there nonetheless. In 1914, Joe Knowland left his seat in the House of Representatives to run for the United States Senate. He lost, and that ended his elective career but by no means his life in politics. Instead, Knowland expressed his deeply conservative views through his influential place in the state Republican Party and through his ownership of the *Oakland Tribune*, the leading paper in Alameda County.

When Warren appealed to Knowland for help in his first effort to secure an office, Knowland gave it. It came in two forms: He backed Warren directly with the paper, and he reined in one of his reporters, a Shay supporter who was using his news stories to promote Shay.[31] The contest was close. Shay enjoyed the support of two supervisors, and Warren had the backing of two others. The deciding vote belonged to John Mullins, who had been elected with Kelly's help but who liked Warren and who decided to vote his conscience, not his interests. Discussing his decision in 1970, Mullins remembered walking with Warren in the Oakland estuary during the days when Decoto's resignation appeared imminent:

> I turned to Warren and I said, "Kid . . . you're the next District Attorney of Alameda County."
>
> Earl said, "Well, Johnny, that's only one vote."

I said, "Earl, you're going to be the next District Attorney of this county."

And from that minute on I figured it out that I could put it over, even though Mike Kelly, the political boss and power at that time, was for Frank Shay, which was equivalent to election. He wanted Shay. I wanted Warren.[32]

Mullins won. In his memory, Mullins not only tipped the vote to Warren but also led the move to draft him. Others recalled it differently, noting that Warren had by then already begun to cultivate backers, some of whom weighed in on his behalf, helping to lobby Mullins. What is clear is that Mullins was the swing vote, and without him Warren's plans would have ended there. Instead, on January 12, 1925, Decoto resigned his position, and Mullins backed Warren. Faced with a 3–2 vote to confirm the new district attorney, the other supervisors folded and made it unanimous.[33]

Mike Kelly did not bear a grudge against Warren, but he did extract his vengeance on Mullins, defeating him with a candidate of his own in the next election. Mullins never regretted the role he played in launching Earl Warren's political career. It was, he would say as he grew old, his greatest political achievement.[34] Frank Shay, Warren's defeated colleague, did not take it so well. As soon as the vote was taken, Shay walked out of the district attorney's office and never returned.[35]

Decoto, by contrast, remained a friend of Warren's for the rest of his life, and Warren reciprocated. Their correspondence through the 1930s was affectionate and thoughtful, Decoto breezily thanking Warren for the loan of five dollars, advising him on his political options, and movingly expressing gratitude in 1930 when Warren offered to look after his business affairs when he was scheduled for a hernia operation.[36]

Warren's elevation to the district attorney's job gave him his first taste of politics, made him a ranking county official, and opened new professional and political opportunities that ultimately would set him on a path to the governor's office. He was now a prosecutor, yes, but also an administrator, and he would develop a talent for selecting gifted associates and supervising their work in a plain, direct manner that made an impression on subordinates and cultivated loyalty. Warren was a good boss—not an effusive one and not without his flare-ups, but greatly admired by those he worked with.

For the moment, however, the implications of his victory were more personal. He and Nina could finally marry. Their initial planned date had to be reset when Warren's mother took ill—a severe abdominal ailment required surgery—but she recovered and was in attendance when, on October 14, 1925, Alameda County's district attorney and his bride were united. Earl was a Methodist and Nina a Baptist, but she felt more strongly about her faith than he did, so the wedding took place at the First Baptist Church in Oakland. They were accompanied by a thrilled six-year-old Jim, whom Warren now adopted. Warren had hoped to have a quiet wedding with little fanfare, but two friends—an associate from the district attorney's office and the manager of the Alameda County garage—got wind of the event and showed up with the local contingent of the highway patrol. Warren then invited them to join the wedding party, and the highway patrol escorted the newlyweds through town, sirens blaring.[37]

Once married and back from a short honeymoon in Vancouver, the Warrens set about fulfilling their family plan—three sons for her, three daughters for him, they liked to say in later years. And so the children came. Jim, of course, was there first, and he was so thoroughly integrated into the growing Warren family that not until 1948, when Warren was a candidate for the vice presidency, did the other children learn that their brother had a different father from the rest of them (Earl Jr. recalls suspecting it after rummaging through some old family records one day, but none of the children knew it officially until later).[38] Virginia was born in 1928 and named for the sister of one of Jim's friends. Two years later, Earl and Nina had their first son together, and chose to name him Earl Jr.—Ju Ju, he would be called later. Dorothy was born in 1931; Nina Elizabeth, named for her mother and the first Warren child to have a middle name but known to her siblings and to a generation of Californians as "Honey Bear," in 1933; and, finally, Robert, forever known as Bobby, in 1935.

Sundays were Nina Warren's day off, and Earl's to tend to the children. He often took them on weekend outings, which became part of the Warren lore. On those outings, the children would be allowed to vote on where they wanted to go, and their father would transport them according to the majority's will.[39] So cherished were those outings, and so central were they to the Warren family, that Warren overcame his reluctance to put down personal thoughts in writing in order to memorialize them years later. His recollection is undated, though references to himself as governor place it between 1943 and 1953, and the form is unusual: It was written for Nina to deliver, and thus in it, Warren describes himself in the third person, but the note is in his hand and clearly reflects his memory. It was filed among his family papers at the Library of Congress, but it is marked "unused." Warren wrote:

> The trips were almost a ritual. They would leave directly from Sunday school, he bringing those that were too young because five of them were born between September 1928 and January 1935 and there was always at least one who had to be in in [sic] one of those little seats that clamp on the top of the front seat. His equipment would consist of a few toys, one bag of bottles of milk, another of cookies and a third of diapers; simple equipment but all necessary. Sometimes they would come home at ten o'clock at night, but you could always tell that they had been having fun. And they all slept like logs until morning.[40]

In interviews more than sixty years later, the faces of Warren's children brightened at the memory of those Sunday afternoons, recalling trips to swim at the Athens Club or the Piedmont Club, where the Warrens were members, or to the Oakland Zoo or to the park for an afternoon picnic. "I've ridden thousands of miles on merry-go-rounds," Warren remembered later, and visited the zoo "so many times I've forgotten."[41] Often, they recalled, the day would end with their reuniting with their mother, either at the Athens Club or at a local restaurant—the children especially enjoyed the Four Seas in San Francisco's Chinatown. When she joined the rest of the family for those dinners, the children regaled her with stories of their day. Nina would sometimes skip dinner, though, particularly if the family was heading out for Chinese—Nina never did like Chinese food. On those nights, she'd stay home, and when the children piled back inside, they'd find her at the table snacking on toast, jam, and cheese—Swedish fare was more to Nina's taste.[42]

"It was a great period in the lives of the children," Warren wrote in that personal reflection of those years and those Sundays. "They came to really know their father, and they remember with fondness every place they went in those days. The governor also remembers those wonderful days and places and attributes his understanding and appreciation of his children to the things he learned about them on these occasions."[43]

Earl Warren was not a demonstrative father, but as that reflection attests, he was not remote, either. He liked to engage his children in conversation, and would encourage them to discuss issues with him in the evenings. At home, dinner featured Information, Please, a Warren-family game that revolved around the day's news quiz in the local paper. Earl Warren would ask one of his children to read the quiz and then the others would, one at a time, offer their answers. The child reading the quiz would then proclaim the day's winner.[44]

Nina and Earl learned from their children and determined to let each grow up his or her own way. Jim expressed an interest in art, and eventually took over the task of producing the family's annual Christmas card, which featured carefree likenesses of each family member (including pets), often overlaid across a California landscape; his works remain, decades later, icons of the Warren era. Earl Jr., shy as a young boy, pursued taxidermy and chemistry. Virginia took up pottery. Dorothy dreamed of babies, though she, sadly, would be the only Warren sibling never to have a child of her own. Honey Bear and Bobby, too young in those days to have much in the way of hobbies, would discover horses after the family move to Sacramento; once they did, they were fixtures at the local stables.[45]

At bedtime each night, the boys and girls would stall, improvising ways to stretch the day out a little longer. Nina lit upon the solution to that. She told the children they could stay up until the radio signed off, then invited them into the room and lined them up before the receiver. As the station ended its day with Kate Smith's rendition of "God Bless America," the Warren children, shoulder to shoulder and ready for bed, belted out the song with Smith. Then, spent, they tottered into their rooms and to sleep.[46]

Earl and Nina Warren lived a long and public life, but they created a family in which the children loved and respected one another, a safe place away from the distractions of their father's public life. To Jim Warren, Earl Warren was, quite simply and completely, his dad. "I've always had a father," Jim Warren said, "and I never called him anything but Dad."[47]

Warren's instinct toward moderation was evident in those days in his approach to the tricky question of how to respond to Prohibition. Ratified in 1919 and put in effect the following year, Prohibition banned the sale, manufacture, and transportation of intoxicating beverages. As a prosecutor, it was Warren's job to enforce Prohibition, though he himself had no qualms about social drinking. For Nina, there was no conflict. She never took a drop of drink in her life; later, when she christened ships built during the war, Nina would use fruit juice. For Earl, Prohibition provided an excuse to cut down on socializing—he felt it would be unseemly to appear at social functions where alcohol was served. But it did not cause him to give up drinking altogether. Instead, he would take a drink or two each evening after arriving home. It was, he and Nina told the children, his "medicine," and he sipped his bourbon while changing for dinner.[48]

While the Warrens built and nurtured their growing family, Earl settled in at work, where his style as a supervisor was not so different from his approach to parenting. There, too, he presided. He was a formal and sometimes forbidding guardian, who set strict rules and expected quality. He struck some as unappreciative, but his stern insistence on professionalism was infectious. He also gave latitude to his subordinates, and those who worked for him almost invariably recall the sense of mission and significance that they had in his presence. Warren tightened ethics policies—restricting the amount of outside work that prosecutors were allowed to take on—and took personal command of his staff. He encouraged discussion but not dissent.[49] He initiated a series of weekly meetings, convening with his criminal division members one day a week, civil prosecutors another day, and the entire legal staff every Saturday morning. Lawyers were urged to raise issues, and those who were afraid to state their opinions were viewed unfavorably. Once Warren had decided a question, though, he insisted on loyalty. Prosecutors were not to build their own relationships with reporters—a restriction that Warren later would impose on his Supreme Court clerks as well. Moreover, mistakes, while rarely fatal, were the occasion for a public dressing-down. "If a complaint had been lodged with the Chief about something, why we would explore it right there,"

Arthur Sherry, who came to the DA's office in 1933, remembered. "Boy, if you hadn't handled that problem right, he'd just get so mad. He'd pound on the desk. . . . 'Harry, you should know better than to do that!'"[50]

As district attorney, Warren surrounded himself with lawyers—almost all men, though eventually a few women—who were eclectic in their politics and personal behavior but shared an intense devotion to their boss. He was a careful, skillful judge of character. Warren looked for men from good families, willing to work for a time for free before signing on to the paid staff. Some spent a year or even more before getting their first paycheck. Once they joined Warren's staff, he insisted that they show him the respect of his office. None were ever to refer to him in public as Earl; those who slipped up and did so were reminded never to do so again. "He was always known to us as 'the Chief,' and he still is," Clarence A. Severin, Warren's chief clerk in the district attorney's office, said in 1972.[51]

Warren's staff took shape around him over time. Oscar Jahnsen was an Internal Revenue Service Prohibition enforcer of Norwegian descent who dropped out of school after the eighth grade and seemed destined to follow his father's lead as a sailor; instead, he rejected the sea and became a stalwart of Warren's investigative efforts, heading up the new DA's investigative staff. Chester Flint, quiet, secretive, and relentless in his intelligence-gathering, was so committed to that work that even decades later, long after Warren was gone, he remained protective of his files, which were housed in a special office off Warren's. (Though Warren later would express apprehension about government surveillance of suspected radicals, he harbored no evident qualms about the practice in his early years.) Charlie Wehr was a big German-American man whose intellect made him a powerful opponent and a bear of a colleague, and whose appetites for women and food made him the object of tittering among the office secretaries. Nathan Harry Miller, one of few Jews on the staff, was hired early in Warren's term, in part to firm up Warren's relationship with labor, then tenuous in part because of the office's aggressive pursuit of the IWW; Miller became a close confidant of the chief, who turned to him in 1938 during a wrenching hour.

The office was overwhelmingly male—hardly unusual in those years—but two women also enjoyed positions of prominence on the Warren team. Helen MacGregor served Warren in the district attorney's office, the attorney general's office, and up to the final days of his governorship. Precise, guarded, and utterly committed to Warren, MacGregor, though trained as a lawyer, acted as private secretary and protector. Even in his retirement, she continued to gently shadow him, accompanying the retired chief justice to occasional interviews and nudging his memory.[52] The other woman standout of the DA years was Cecil Mosbacher, who began as an unpaid deputy but developed a specialty in prosecuting fraud, aided by her meticulous trial preparation, which included grilling potential witnesses well into the night. For both women, the rewards of working with Warren were real, though both also suffered from his unwillingness to treat them entirely as equals to their male colleagues. MacGregor's legal skills were never called upon in the courtroom, and Mosbacher, later to become a distinguished California Superior Court judge, spent much of her trial time in support of male colleagues.[53] If she resented that, she never let on. When Warren, as governor, placed her on the bench in 1951, making her the first woman ever to serve as a Superior Court judge in Alameda County, Mosbacher expressed her "everlasting appreciation for the privilege he gave me 16 years ago when I was first admitted to the practice of law, to become a member of the district attorney's staff."[54]

Still another woman destined to become an icon of the California judiciary had to make her way by Warren's befuddlement in the presence of women as colleagues. Mildred Lillie was on the verge of graduating from law school when she came to visit Warren in Alameda, hopeful of lining up a job. Warren was kindly and gracious, welcoming her to his office. But he seem perplexed that Lillie would presume to work for him. "I don't encourage you very much because I think women probably don't belong in the law," he warned her. Lillie left that day, but her career continued despite Warren's brush-off. Indeed, as he did with Mosbacher, Warren eventually relented and put Lillie on the bench. She took her place in 1947, and that marked the beginning of a judicial career that lasted more than half a century—and that turned the story of her first meeting with Warren into a source of amusement for California judges.[55]

Many contributed to Warren's staff, but two would shape his tenure and legacy. Warren Olney III was from one of California's most distinguished legal families and was a late arrival to Warren's office, coming on board in 1930. Once there, he would become Warren's lifelong aide-de-camp, following Warren to the offices of attorney general, governor, and chief justice. Olney ran the California Crime Commission during Warren's gubernatorial tenure, and he administered the federal courts during Warren's time as chief justice. Other than Warren's wife, no single person spanned so much of Warren's adult life as Olney.[56]

In the meantime, there was J. Frank Coakley. A Catholic and a Democrat, Coakley was something of an alter ego to Warren, as well as one of his successors in the district attorney's office. Six years younger than Warren, Coakley was the son of a San Francisco mother and an Irish-immigrant father who ran a butcher's shop in the East Bay. Coakley studied to be a lawyer while working the docks, and pushed ahead with his interest so quickly that he passed the bar while still in law school, forcing him to finish up school in order to catch up with the legal practice he already was authorized to pursue. He joined the Alameda DA's office in 1923 and got to know Warren right away. When Warren advanced to the top job, Coakley became his principal deputy, prosecuting a number of the office's most high-profile or difficult cases, sometimes alongside Warren himself.

Warren insisted on a high degree of personal integrity. Deputies were forbidden to accept gifts, and were discouraged from representing private clients—a common practice in the years before Warren became district attorney. Warren was similarly tough on himself, often rejecting gifts, though he did make a very occasional exception. In 1933, for instance, the new Oakland Baseball Club sent the district attorney a season pass book. Warren accepted it, then, on the same day, forwarded the gift to his nephew, Buddy Plank.[57]

As DA, Warren, with his deputies, confronted the full array of bad deeds that make up the grist of prosecutorial work. They broke up a corrupt bail bond ring, closed down stills and speakeasies, jailed thugs and murderers. Through it, Warren projected an air of authority and independence—a source of personal pride and, increasingly, of political capital. His record was not unblemished. An early investigation of the Alameda County sheriff, considered a suspect in the murder and mutilation of a young woman named Bessie Ferguson, failed to win indictment. Even there, however, Warren benefited. The notoriety of the case drove the sheriff from office, and his replacement, who came to office in 1926, gave Warren the chance to take on the first big corruption case of his career.

Those who knew him had reason to suspect that Sheriff Burton Becker would disappoint the residents of Alameda County. He was, among other things, a member of the Ku Klux Klan, part of the then-active klavern in the East San Francisco Bay Area. And Becker was more than just a bigot; he was greedy, too. He no sooner occupied the office than he set out to run it for his personal plunder. Becker offered protection for bootleggers, brothel owners, and organized-crime figures in return for cash, and he did so overtly. As he grew more rapacious, Becker also cut himself in on public-works graft. His former undersheriff was elected street commissioner in Oakland, and once in office he initiated a bribery scheme under which contractors paving Oakland's streets banded together in a consortium and rigged their bids for city work. The commissioner received a half-cent for every square foot of paving as a bribe, and Sheriff Becker provided law-enforcement protection for the racket.[58] But what is bad for society sometimes is good for a prosecutor. Warren had long seen himself as a corruption-busting trial lawyer in the mold of Hiram Johnson. In Becker, then, Warren had a target.

Before bringing a case, Warren tried to persuade Becker to stop. He confronted Becker and warned him of the damage he was doing to the community. The sheriff was unmoved. "You take care of your business," Becker replied, "and I will take care of mine." Warren responded, "That is exactly what I will do. I will not mention it to you again."[59] Rather than drop it, however, Warren took his complaint to Becker's political sponsor, the same Mike Kelly who had backed Warren's opponent in his initial bid to win the supervisors' promotion to district attorney. Warren warned Kelly that Becker's conduct was too outrageous and too public to go unchecked, and Warren promised that his interest in Becker was not directed at Kelly. "Politics is not my motive," Warren added. "But if Sheriff Becker doesn't clean up this mess, we'll have to seek the evidence to indict him."[60]

Kelly pledged to do what he could, and Warren then waited, hoping though apparently not expecting to see Becker reform. Indeed, Warren continued to prepare himself and his office for what he believed would be a showdown with the sheriff. He was sifting through the allegations against Becker when he happened to encounter Franklin Hichborn, a Progressive journalist and author who had documented the San Francisco graft cases. Hichborn recommended his own examination of those trials, entitled *The System*, and sent Warren a copy. Warren devoured it, reading it over and over and concluding that it was one of the most important books he had ever read. It is easy to see why. Brightly and forcefully written, *The System* recounts the efforts by leading San Franciscans to derail the investigation and prosecution of corrupt officials and businessmen. The book is sympathetic to Hiram Johnson, Francis Heney, and the prosecution team, and it provides nearly step-by-step instructions to a prosecutor facing similar obstacles. In particular, it warns anyone who undertakes a graft prosecution to be wary of delay, which in San Francisco helped tire the public of the cases and sap political support for the cause.[61] Warned of those hazards, Warren set out to avoid them.

To move the matter quickly, Warren was bold enough to call on the chief justice of the California Supreme Court and tell him what was unfolding. Warren asked only that the courts allow the cases to move quickly and that if judges in Alameda were disqualified from sitting on the cases, that others be brought in right away. The chief justice, William H. Waste, agreed. Facing stubborn witnesses, Warren also minded Hichborn's advice and refused to allow them to obstruct, in this case, even by invoking their rights. Warren put witnesses on the stand, and if they claimed their right not to testify against themselves under the Fifth Amendment, Warren released the transcript of their refusal to the press, making them pay a public relations price for the exercise of a constitutional privilege. That put Warren at the fringe of ethical behavior, and he later counseled against such tactics by future district attorneys. "I would not recommend for today the vigorous cross-examination we gave to those prominent paving company people when they exercised their right against self-incrimination," he noted delicately in his memoirs.[62] But Warren was offended by the efforts to thwart him. He had his first great scandal, and he was eager to succeed.

Warren's later insistence on police and prosecutorial regard for constitutional protections has, over the years, struck many observers and more than a few of his friends as inconsistent, and thus as evidence of a break in his personality—suggesting that something dramatic changed the county prosecutor on his way to becoming chief justice. Certainly it is true that Warren saw his obligations differently in the

1970s than he had in 1930, but the prosecutor and the judge are connected across the decades by an unwavering self-confidence and devotion to principle, albeit a somewhat different principle. Warren believed in 1930 that Sheriff Becker and the paving contractors were harming society and thumbing their noses at law enforcement. "[W]e were sure," he wrote in reflection, "there was an industry-wide conspiracy to squelch by silence any attempts to root out widespread acts of corruption in city government."[63] Confronted many years later with acts of racism and intransigence in cases before the Supreme Court, Warren would prove no less stern.

The Becker prosecution unfolded in stages, and Warren pursued it patiently. The first of the cases to go to trial involved three of Becker's top aides, and Coakley led the prosecution. The case dragged on for six weeks as the jury weighed complex evidence of conspiracy to violate gambling and liquor laws. On the trial's final day, the lawyers gathered for closing arguments, only to wait hour after hour for Judge Engs, who had presided over the case. Eventually, another judge was found to charge the jury, and it returned guilty verdicts the following day. More than a week later, Engs's body was discovered in a nearby quarry. Coakley always believed the judge had gone for a walk and slipped while contemplating his jury instructions. Warren, who worried about the enormous strain on the relatively young and inexperienced judge, considered it more likely that Engs had killed himself.[64]

With Becker's top lieutenants convicted, Warren and Coakley turned to Becker himself. One early obstacle was the Klan. The grand jury, whose eighteen members included seven Klansmen, initially agreed to indict Becker's bag man—a cohort who collected the bribes—but would not indict Becker himself.[65] Warren refused to accept that indictment and moved for its dismissal. He then called Becker before the grand jury and sought to question him. Becker refused, citing the threat of self-incrimination. A sheriff taking the Fifth was too much even for the Klan. Said Warren, "The head of the Ku Klux Klan group came to me and said, 'Well, go ahead and prepare your indictment. If the so-and-so won't take care of himself, well, he can't expect anyone else to.'"[66]

As the trial approached, Warren's investigators continued to chase leads, seeking with particular energy an automobile dealer named Fred Smith, who was alleged to have collected payoffs for Becker. Smith had fled the area when the scandal broke, and Warren's office had been looking for him for more than a year. Then, a newspaper reporter from the *San Francisco Examiner* learned of Smith's whereabouts and shared the information with Warren on the condition that the *Examiner* be allowed to have two reporters present when the arrest was made. Smith was captured, and Warren's investigators brought him to a hotel to meet personally with Warren. "I told him he had a choice to make," Warren said, "that of being a witness for the prosecution in the graft investigation or a defendant in a grand larceny charge." Smith chose to be a witness. He admitted that a lawyer for some local

Chinese lottery houses had paid him $2,700 for protection and that Smith had passed the money along to Becker; he also said he had received similar payoffs from bootleggers.[67] But on the eve of his testimony, he reconsidered. Warren instructed Coakley to have Smith charged with larceny, and then Smith thought again. He testified the following day.[68] From there, Becker was done. He was convicted of "willful and corrupt misconduct" and sent to San Quentin.[69]

Warren was deluged with congratulations. The Merchants' Exchange hosted a testimonial dinner for him, while churches, civic organizations, and citizens sent hundreds of letters thanking him for his work. "Future generations of Alameda County will owe more to your vision and your courage than they will ever know," the Public Welfare League proclaimed. "We are with you," the Oakland Boosters' Club said simply. One pastor must have especially pleased Warren with a note urging him onward and comparing his courtroom success to that of Hiram Johnson. Even the Ku Klux Klan dropped him a line, praising the verdicts while stressing that the defendants were no longer Klansmen, having been forced out of the Invisible Empire "for various reasons."[70]

His corruption victories helped seal Warren's political standing in Alameda. They set the tone for Warren's prosecutorial administration: tough, efficient, incorruptible. After 1930, he never faced a serious challenge to his incumbency. But because the Becker case took years to unfold, Warren had to run in 1926 before he had secured those convictions. That year, he was a new DA, appointed by the board and never tested by the voters. It was arguably Warren's most important election—incumbency tends to start soft and solidify over time as the public grows accustomed to reelecting an official. That makes an early victory especially important and an early loss often devastating. Warren proved a tough fighter. He announced in June 1926 by boasting of convictions in 414 of the 499 felony cases resolved in Superior Court on his watch. He alluded to his military service and deftly sought to ally any opponent with the criminals he was prosecuting as district attorney. His opponents, he said, had accumulated a "slush fund of $25,000 . . . from the underworld" to defeat him.[71]

His rival in the race, a local defense lawyer named Preston Higgins, understandably did not take kindly to being cast as an underworld candidate and responded by writing to local ministers and others. In his letter, Higgins accused Warren of grandstanding in his raids on local bootleggers and others—staging those events for political purposes while doing little to dislodge crime. More stingingly, Higgins argued that Warren was a candidate "of the political bosses which have handled 'politics' in this county for twenty years."[72]

That last charge was meant to associate Warren with the Kelly machine, since Warren had received his appointment from the county supervisors. It was patently unfair, and Warren was not inclined to let the slight go. He wrote to the ministers himself, rebutting Higgins's charges one at a time and defending his allegation that his opponent was tied to the darker forces in local politics. While Warren had been serving as the appointed DA, he noted, his opponent had been working as a defense lawyer, where he "defended more than 250 bootleggers, gamblers and prostitutes, of which more than 90% were convicted."[73] Not only was Higgins associated with criminals, Warren stressed, he wasn't even particularly good at it. If anything, Warren's response was overkill, though it was understandable from a political novice whose standing with voters in that first election was tentative. Warren won the election going away. He never again faced a serious challenge to keep the job of Alameda DA.

Warren's secure place as county district attorney allowed him the luxury of buying a house big enough for the family. He had not saved much, and needed a large house for such a brood of children, but it was the Depression, and banks were eager for buyers. He and Nina picked a large, gray house on a quiet street and moved their family in. Bobby was still a baby when the Warrens moved to 88 Vernon Street. Eighty-eight, as it became known in the Warren household, was a tall, severe structure in the hills above Oakland, with big yards front and back. It had three stories, with kitchen and living spaces on the first, four bedrooms on the second, and Warren's office and two more bedrooms on the third. Beneath sat a large basement, where the Warrens' Christmas celebration was centered each year. The house sat across from an empty lot that the Warren children would often play in during the afternoons. It was the last house that Earl and Nina Warren would own.

The Warrens were a public family but a guarded one. The graft trials had exposed them to anger and threats, and though they were listed in the local phone book, they did not draw attention to their home. When Jim Warren arranged one day to have the curb freshly painted with the address, his mother pulled him aside and warned him against such attention-getting in the future.[74]

The clear roles that Earl and Nina played in their family—he as its presiding officer, she as its functional manager—were reflected in the home itself. Warren's office sat atop the house, a place where he could read or work while still being close to his children. Nina, meanwhile, was a near-constant presence in the kitchen. She produced angel food and devil's food cakes for family and friends, and seemed constantly to be working thick sheets of batter across the flat, clay platter she used for mixing. Always shy and occupied with the children, Nina asked to be excused from the political obligations of marriage to an elected official; not once did she deliver a speech on behalf of her husband. Earl, she said, understood and approved.[75] Indeed, with such a large family, Nina seemed to her children always to be busy; there were times, she said many years later, that she actually was glad when Earl got home too late for supper. "She couldn't have made it with one more meal to prepare," their friend, journalist Drew Pearson, recalled.[76]

Warren's work was paying off. He had become a formidable political figure, and the graft cases established him in the image he sought for himself—the stalwart, corruption-fighting prosecutor undeterred by political powers in his quest for clean government. By 1931, he was attracting attention well beyond Alameda County. Raymond Moley, then a professor of public law and jurisprudence at Columbia University, contrasted Warren's success with San Francisco's "traditionally inefficient system of prosecution," and concluded that Warren was "to my mind, the most intelligent and politically independent District Attorney in the United States."[77] That was gratifying praise, but more significant was the approval that Warren sought and received during the early 1930s from a man whose life would overlap with Warren's from then on: J. Edgar Hoover.

Warren first enlisted Hoover's help when Warren was a prosecutor of growing renown and Hoover was the head of the Justice Department's Division of Investigations, forerunner of the FBI. The subject was one of Warren's regular efforts to combat organized crime, in this case by creating an Anti-Racket Council for Alameda County, whose members included, among others, Joseph Knowland. Hoover provided assistance, and in 1934 sent a top official to consult with Warren about the developing council. Those contacts took place in the context of the hierarchy of their early relationship—Warren was beseeching, even obsequious, while Hoover took the pose of a grand Washington official, in position to grant or withhold favors and approbation. When, for instance, an agent visited Warren at Hoover's suggestion in 1934, the agent reported back to Hoover that Warren "asked me to extend to you his personal regards, and to state that he was extremely sorry that he had missed you on his last trip back East."[78] Through the 1930s, that pattern would continue: Warren would ask favors of Hoover, would invite him to attend events, would pass along praise of his agents and would, after seeking an audience, visit him in Washington. That relationship would undergo two significant transformations in the years ahead, but by the mid-1930s, Hoover's special agent in charge of the San Francisco office, through which much of Warren's communication was handled, was able to report accurately a "very close spirit of cooperation . . . between Earl Warren's office and the San Francisco office of the Bureau."[79]

The Becker case was a clean victory for Warren, satisfying both substantively and politically. The other defining case of Warren's prosecutorial tenure carried other implications, however, far more complex ones. It, too, would help cast his image in the minds of many Californians, but this time with darker shades.

The case began in the early morning hours of Sunday, March 22, 1936.[80] There, in a cabin of the *Point Lobos*, a steamship docked in the Alameda harbor and preparing to sail the following day, Chief Engineer George Alberts was beaten to death. Alberts was not a likable man, and there was no shortage of suspects, since he had antagonized his crew with his bullying and undisguised contempt for their unions.

Earl Warren and his principal homicide deputy, Charlie Wehr, learned of the killing within hours, and Wehr was on board the *Point Lobos* that night, questioning people and dispatching police in search of suspects. The search was a long one, but five months later, Warren announced the arrests of four men: Earl King, Ernest Ramsay, Frank Conner, and George Wallace. A fifth suspect, Ben Sakovitz, was said to be at large. All five were members of the Marine Firemen, Oilers, Watertenders and Wipers Association, an influential local union believed to harbor Communists or other radicals. Warren and his prosecutors alleged that the attack was ordered up by King and Ramsay, who sent Wallace and Sakovitz to rough up the chief engineer in retaliation for his mistreatment of union workers. In administering the beating, Warren's office charged, the defendants went too far and killed Alberts. The murder, Warren said when he announced the indictments, was a "paid assassin's job, and the basis of the plot was communistic."[81]

To label the case "communistic" was a singularly provocative act in the circumstances under which the *Point Lobos* defendants would come to trial. The West Coast was then preparing for the latest act in its long-running drama between labor and management. Maritime workers from San Diego to Seattle were threatening to strike, and employers were girding for a protracted confrontation. So when Warren elected to prosecute the *Point Lobos* murder as a labor conspiracy—and to link that conspiracy to Communism—he gave strong moral support to employers.

The result: Earl Warren, who loved to brag of his Musicians' Union membership, now became the enemy of Bay Area unions, which saw him as a tool of Knowland, the *Oakland Tribune*, and employers in general. Warren plowed ahead, indulging in tactics that bordered on improper. His deputies traveled to Seattle and arrested Conner, a dim man with little ability to hold his own in an interrogation. Back in Alameda, they took Conner to the Hotel Whitecotton rather than to jail, where he would have had access to a lawyer. While in DA custody and out of public view, Conner confessed to his role in the murder, saying that he and Sakovitz had been sent to "tamp up" Alberts and that Sakovitz had administered the fatal blows. Once finally allowed to see a lawyer, Conner recanted that confession, and the defense protested vigorously that it had been coerced.

The composition of the grand jury that delivered indictments in the case reinforced doubts about the fairness of the case against the defendants. In selecting citizens to serve on the county grand jury, Warren and his staff scoured the community for respectable citizens—seeking, for instance, the recommendations of local bankers, lawyers, and other businessmen. Although the practice of relying on leading citizens for grand juries was not limited to Warren in those days, it had particular implications when that group of citizens took the measure of the evidence in the *Point Lobos* case, with its overtones of Communism and violence. The *Point Lobos* defense lawyers were convinced that jurors had been picked for their loyalties, if not to Warren directly then at least to a status quo unfriendly to labor. "The ordinary worker or the ordinary person didn't have much of a chance to make it," one of the defense lawyers, Aubrey Grossman, said later.[82]

Finally, Warren intervened personally in the selection of the judge to hear the case. Both sides agreed that the first judge assigned to the case, Edward Tyrrell, was not up to such a complicated and important trial. But Warren managed to have Tyrrell replaced by Frank Ogden, who had worked with and for Warren in the district attorney's office. Ogden's association with Warren made defense lawyers suspicious, and his sympathetic treatment of the prosecution case reinforced those suspicions.

The *Point Lobos* trial opened on October 26, 1936. That same week, maritime unions called a strike. On October 31, at midnight, 15,000 longshoremen, 7,000 sailors, 4,000 cooks and stewards, 3,000 firemen, 3,000 engineers, 2,000 radio operators, 2,000 warehouse men, and thousands of mates, masters, and pilots walked off their jobs and joined picket lines along the entire Pacific Coast of the United States.[83] Violence followed swiftly. The lead photograph in that morning's *Los Angeles Times* was of a bandaged man, above the predictable headline "Injured in Attack by Unionists."[84] With tensions high and thousands engaged on both sides, Warren and his prosecution team entered the courthouse through cordons of protesters. The protesters would stay for the entire case, badgering lawyers and witnesses for the government and forcing the jury to be sequestered. Threats were directed toward the Warren family as well, and pickets occasionally massed in front of their home on Vernon Street. A member of Warren's staff was given the job of shuttling the children to and from school.

At trial, Wallace broke from the other defendants and testified against them, earning him the lifelong enmity of organized labor and forcing him out of the defense pact that enveloped King, Ramsay, and Conner (once Conner had recanted his confession, he had been welcomed back).

Warren personally led the prosecution of the *Point Lobos* defendants and even took the stand twice as defense lawyers turned him into a witness regarding the facts surrounding Conner's contested confession. As a lawyer and even as a witness, Warren was even and unflappable, righteous, and, to the defendants, infuriating.

Warren delivered the prosecution's closing statement himself, and he used it to try to separate the defendants from their union supporters. "This is not," he insisted, "a case against union labor, it is a case against four men." Of those men, Warren was unforgiving. "All I want is the law enforced," he said. "All I want to see is life and property safe in this community."[85]

Judge Ogden then did his part. Using a prerogative of California judges during that period—one created by a constitutional amendment that Warren's staff had helped write—Ogden told the jurors that Wallace's confession was persuasive to him and that Conner's confession, despite his attempt to recant it, also was made voluntarily.[86] In effect, Ogden directed the jury to convict the defendants. On January 5, 1937, the jury complied. It deliberated for five hours and forty minutes and then returned guilty verdicts of second-degree murder against all four defendants.[87]

Defense lawyers then and later complained bitterly of Warren's prosecution. In some cases, their charges against Warren were plainly false. Despite defense claims, for instance, no evidence ever surfaced of defendants being physically mistreated while in Warren's custody. Still, the composition of the grand jury, the selection of a clearly proprosecution judge, and the secretive questioning of Conner all undermined Warren's insistence that he ran an exceptionally principled prosecutorial staff, at least in this case. Moreover, unbeknownst to the defendants or their lawyers, Warren's staff also secretly recorded at least one of the defendants while in custody, parking an office secretary nearby to transcribe his conversation with another inmate.[88] And Warren investigators broke into a San Francisco hotel room, installed a hidden microphone, and used it to listen in on conversations involving King and another union official, Albert Murphy.[89] When they confronted Murphy with the evidence of their eavesdropping, he implicated King, Ramsay, Wallace, and Sakovitz in the murder in order to avoid prosecution himself.[90] In later years, Warren would make much of his refusal to use hidden microphones, and it is not clear whether he knew that his deputies had used them in this case.

Warren was pleased by the outcome of the trial and undoubtedly shared his reaction with his friend the judge. Warren's personal calendar shows that he lunched with Judge Ogden three weeks after the defendants were convicted and just seven days after Ogden sentenced them to prison. They remained close afterward, with Warren attending an Elks reception for him in April and meeting again with him for breakfast in May.[91]

That was not the last of the *Point Lobos* case, however. While the trial was under way, some of the defendants spied clues of what they believed was improper contact between Wehr, the lead prosecutor, and a juror named Julia Vickerson. In the screening of prospective jurors, Vickerson had acknowledged a passing relationship with Wehr, who had drawn up a will for Vickerson's aunt. Vickerson denied any more personal contact with the prosecutor, however, and she was seated with the rest of the jury. During trial, Ramsay kept an eye on her and said he noticed exchanges of winks and sly nods between the two. Once the defendants were convicted, their lawyers continued to press their investigation. They concluded that Vickerson and Wehr were romantically involved and that Wehr had urged her to conceal that fact so that he could be assured of her support for a guilty verdict. Their suspicions only seemed confirmed when Wehr died a few years later and Vickerson sought $15,000 from his estate, saying she had lent him the money years earlier and now wanted it repaid. Those issues were piled into the defendants' appeal, and for Warren they formed a potentially lethal political threat. Had a judge accepted the argument of jury tampering in the most prominent case of his prosecutorial career, Warren would have been tainted by a serious charge of misconduct—potentially devastating to a prosecutor whose probity was his chief political asset. It is not too much to think the scandal could have ended Warren's career. But as it turned out, a retired Los Angeles County judge, Hartley Shaw, heard the evidence and decided against the defendants, a ruling based partly on his finding that Vickerson's claim against Wehr's estate was not believable. That ruling was upheld later by the California Supreme Court. The defendants remained in prison. Warren was saved.

Defense lawyer Aubrey Grossman, who helped argue the appeal, believed his failure to win had cleared Warren's political path, and for the rest of his life, that irony haunted him. Grossman firmly believed that Warren and his staff had broken the law in securing the *Point Lobos* convictions. As chief justice, Warren would invalidate some of the same practices that had infuriated Grossman during the *Point Lobos* case. As a result, the failure of Grossman's appeal can credibly be said to have made possible the enshrinement of the principles upon which that appeal was based. The steely leftist lawyer wrestled for decades with the question of whether right had been served in that appeal. "Was I right or wrong?" he mused a half century later. "Was it good or bad? Was it good for society . . . ? It's a difficult thing to determine."[92]

Many lives turned on the trial. King, Ramsay, and Conner—as well as Wallace—went to San Quentin. They remained there until a few days before Pearl Harbor, paroled in November 1941 by Governor Culbert Olson, over then Attorney General Earl Warren's loud objections.[93] King went to work as a janitor and eventually made his way back to the sea. Conner did not handle freedom as well. He suffered a nervous breakdown and ended his days in a New York mental hospital, gazing at the ocean and convinced that he owned the fleet. Ramsay found work and fought deportation proceedings that were the result of his conviction, a fight that eventually would reunite him with Warren.

Some of those who criticized Warren's handling of *Point Lobos* ultimately forgave his excesses, writing them off as a small blot against an otherwise impressive record. "During the 13 years that he was District Attorney of Alameda County, no case that Warren tried was reversed by a higher court," Irving Stone, his admiring biographer, wrote of Warren in 1948. "No complaint was ever lodged against his methods by the vigilant American Civil Liberties Union. He prosecuted only when he had to and when the evidence was complete."[94]

Edward White, in his more balanced accounting, concludes that Warren's critics exaggerated in some respects—the trial, he finds, was largely conducted according to the legal standards and norms of the period. Still, he notes, "Under Warren Court standards of criminal procedure, King, Ramsay, Conner, and possibly Wallace would never have been convicted."[95] That, White argues, is because Conner's confession was coerced under Warren Court standards, King and Ramsay were convicted partly on the basis of eavesdropping devices that the Warren Court disallowed, and Wallace might have argued that his conviction was tainted by the pretrial publicity that Warren generated. Those are provocative reminders of how Warren's jurisprudence would evolve from his days as a prosecutor to his tenure as a justice. His character may not have changed—he remained principled and devoted to the rules of his job—but as his job changed, so did the scope of his thinking. And yet none of those rules were in effect until Earl Warren, much later, helped put them there, so the defendants could not reasonably claim them at the time. The forty-five-year-old Warren can hardly be blamed for failing to adhere to the rules that the seventy-four-year-old Warren would write.

For the survivors of the *Point Lobos* case, Warren's zeal was harder to rationalize. Myron Harris, a sharp-witted defense lawyer who had worked with Warren in the DA's office but who was part of the *Point Lobos* defense team, stewed in his anger to the end of his life. On June 14, 1972, he lay in bed in his Piedmont Hills home, watched over by a nurse, less than a year from death. By then, Earl Warren had served and retired from the United States Supreme Court, leaving to the acclaim of liberals and civil libertarians across the nation. He was a hero to many Americans whose politics were shared by Harris. But Earl Warren had no friend that day in Piedmont.

"Tears as big as apples will roll down [liberals'] cheeks when Earl Warren dies," Harris said. "You won't see tears on my cheeks."[96]

Chapter 4

# POLITICIAN

*Friends are friends, however attained.*

EARL WARREN[1]

As DISTRICT ATTORNEY of Alameda County, Earl Warren was the chief law-enforcement officer for California's third-largest county. The job was defined principally in terms of crime fighting, but because it was an elected office, it also represented his move into politics, and Warren's early approach to the challenges of winning and holding office paralleled his personal maturation.

At Berkeley, he had joined clubs and a fraternity, and from them extracted companionship. As a politician, he followed the same pattern. He joined groups, then drew upon those friends for political ideas and for support. And in that company, he developed without much consideration an ideological centrism that naturally expressed his personal moderation. He tended to trust majorities and to express skepticism for extremist or radical thought. And just as he was moderate ideologically, he was also cautious temperamentally. Warren never took an opponent for granted. He picked his races with care. He built his record one trial at a time, always with an eye toward accomplishment that he could demonstrate to voters. Later, as a justice freed of the restraints of politics, Warren would show a more daring willingness to challenge social norms. In the meantime, there were elections to win.

The first of Warren's political affiliations—an attachment he made before ever entering politics—was the Republican Party. But he joined the party without much thought and certainly without embracing the entirety of its program for California. In those years, the ideological banner of the Republicans stretched all the way from the early Progressives to the hard, anti-Communist right of organizations such as the Associated Farmers, the lobbying organization for California's notoriously right-wing agricultural interests. Warren was a Progressive, but that placed him in the company of more conservative forces, whom he neither renounced nor fully embraced. Given that he was not inclined to close ideological self-examination, his Republicanism was loosely adhered to; he embraced the party's general values and sought its support without finely tuning his own beliefs toward hard-line loyalty.

California's novel politics augmented the looseness of Warren's party affiliation. Among the reforms that distinguished the tenure of Hiram Johnson was the so-called cross-file, under which a candidate could seek the nomination of more than one political party at a time. Cross-filing was intended to liberate candidates from the strict dictates of party domination and thus to wean them from the Southern Pacific and its domination over the party machinery in the early twentieth century. In Warren's hands, it would become that and more, as he used his centrism and pragmatism to carve out a viable California center, between California's mean right wing and its loopy left. Democrats would join Republicans in supporting him, and thus Warren could and did assemble enough votes to win without the enthusiastic support of ideologues in either party.

At the outset, however, Warren gave every indication of following a more traditional Republican path. Although Warren joined the Republican Party casually, he came to affiliate with it more strongly during his years as a prosecutor. He genuinely disliked criminals. He had from his boyhood, and his offense at vice only grew during his years as a prosecutor.[2] As a result, he prosecuted vigorously and found much support for his approach from conservative Republicans, notably Joseph Knowland and his *Oakland Tribune*. Since Republicans held sway in Sacramento, a law-enforcement agent in those years—as Warren was—also tended to enforce Republican will. His courtroom victories therefore reinforced his party identification.

Moreover, Warren attempted through his entire political life in California to draw a distinction between himself as a local official and as a national advocate. When he ran for Alameda County or later statewide offices, Warren presented himself to voters as a nonpartisan, but in alternating election cycles, when the presidential race appeared on the ballot, he affiliated with the Republican Party and backed its nominees. That embrace of partisanship at the national level extended to his views of national affairs, where he hewed a more traditionally Republican line. Nowhere was that more evident than in his curt rejection of FDR and the New Deal.

To Warren—at least the Warren of the early 1930s—the New Deal was worse than impractical. It was immoral. Its fluid experimentation offended his sense of stability, and its challenge to the established rules of business and regulation up-ended the order to which Warren was committed, even in the crisis of the Depression. As FDR improvised with the economic engines of American society, searching for ways to stimulate consumer spending and production, Warren fumed. When, for instance, the Supreme Court upheld the federal government's abandonment of the gold standard, Warren stormed around the district attorney's office, slamming shut law books. "Throw them away, forget them," he complained. "They're no good now, contracts don't mean anything anymore."[3]

The machinations of the New Deal offended Warren all the more because they were drafted in Washington. Once he himself governed from the nation's capital, Warren would view centralized authority with less suspicion and would see states more as obstacles to freedom than protectors of it—as indeed they were during much of the long struggle for civil rights that Warren helped to lead. For now, however, Warren viewed politics from California, and saw Washington as a somewhat foreign power, capable of great action but also of roughshod tactics. "The doctrines of individual freedom and personal property rights," he warned in 1934, "as laid down by our forefathers in the Constitution of the United States [are] under dangerous attack. These attackers must be repulsed."[4]

And yet Warren was more complex than that rhetoric implied. In August 1933, apparently at the request of Raymond Moley, Warren submitted to the Roosevelt administration a detailed memo proposing ways to overcome what he termed the "three great factors which are largely responsible for our failure to suppress crime in this country."[5] The memo captures Warren at that interesting juncture in his life. Warren's "three factors"—decentralization of enforcement, ignorance on the part of local police and prosecutors, and politics—summed up his blend of pragmatism and Progressivism. His more specific suggestions, however, went beyond those areas. Warren proposed expanded congressional authority in controlling crime and increased federal presence in investigating certain crimes. He also recommended that the government deport "every alien convicted of a felony or any crime involving moral turpitude," an idea he would disavow as chief justice, when his commitment to citizenship would deepen. He also recommended universal fingerprinting, if not of all Americans, then at least of all children in public schools "for their own protection," and for all adults on a voluntary basis. Finally, he proposed a national ban on the manufacture and sale of machine guns, which, he said, serve "no good purpose and should be prohibited."[6]

Those proposals suggested that while Warren might still harbor objections regarding federal interference in local affairs, he recognized the importance of national values and rules—in effect of the federalizing of certain offices and offenses in order to establish minimum national standards. "In view of the changes in recent years of economic conditions, modes of transportation, and population factors, it would seem as though the time has arrived when both Congress and the Courts could agree that the United States Government must enlarge upon its concept of the obligations due from it," Warren wrote. His willingness to accept national standards in those areas resembled, on a smaller scale, the view of national rights Warren would express as chief justice, when he found intolerable the actions of states to subvert what he saw as basic human and constitutional principles. In 1933, those ideas were still undeveloped—and to the extent that they were developing, they remained limited to law enforcement. So although the memo expresses Warren's 1930s federalism, it also hints at his later reconsideration of that idea, once he was wielding federal authority and state officials were those standing in his way.

In later years, as Warren's politics expanded and to some degree moved to the left, his friendship with his early supporters would be tested, but the personal bonds usually held—Knowland, for instance, never wavered in his admiration of Warren. With Knowland's help, Warren rose to more prominent office and eventually became, as governor, the leading Republican in a state dominated by Democratic voters. In that position, he acquired the additional value to the state's Republican old guard of being able to win and hold office against political odds, protecting them against Democratic landslides. It endeared him to such leading members of the party as Harry and Norman Chandler, scions of the *Los Angeles Times*.

With such strong conservative backing, Warren was protected from right-wing criticism even when he embraced issues that conservatives did not like, as would become common during his gubernatorial years. In the parlance of today's politics, Warren shored up his base before moving to the middle. And yet his early moves seem more reflexive than calculated, more the result of a law-enforcement focus and allegiance to Knowland than of a deliberate attempt to fashion a political base. As late as 1930, Warren still did not think of himself as a lifelong politician. He seriously considered leaving politics that year, and was counseled to do so by one of his mentors, Ezra Decoto, who believed the time was right to pass the office to a subordinate and for Warren to embark on a more lucrative private legal practice.[7] After giving the idea thought, Warren rejected it—he was in the middle of the graft cases, and public service, he concluded, was simply too fulfilling to give up. Private practice offered money but neither fulfillment nor prestige.

If the Republican Party was Warren's somewhat by happenstance, his community affiliations were more deliberately developed, though initially as an outgrowth of his personality and only later as a device to expand his political reach. Starting in 1918 and 1919, Warren, already active in University of California alumni affairs, joined the American Legion, the Elks, and the Masons. Each of those groups brought Warren acquaintances and friends, though also entanglements. The American Legion in those years was distinguished by its virulent, sometimes extralegal, anti-Communism—its attacks on the Wobblies were vicious. But Warren, while seconding the Legion's views on Communism, never supported violence; indeed, he explicitly urged fellow Legionnaires to respect the rights of citizens and to leave law enforcement in the hands of the government.[8]

Warren also took care to soften the edges of his Masonry, whose quasi-religious order and reliance on ancient rites subjected it to charges that it was anti-Catholic. John Mullins, whose vote as a county supervisor had given Warren the position of district attorney, was Catholic, and some friends warned him about associating with Warren. "They said to me, 'Earl Warren is a Mason and you know what that means,'" Mullins told Warren biographer Leo Katcher in the mid-1960s. "I answered I knew what it meant. It meant each year when the Shrine entertained Earl Warren as a Past Potentate, he had the band play 'My Wild Irish Rose' for me."[9]

The draw of the Masons for Warren took the same form as the attraction of the Progressives. Both were bourgeois, professional, and gently elitist—sufficiently selective to appeal to Warren's clubbiness but not so selective as to prevent a young man from a working-class Bakersfield background from joining. The Masons, like the Progressives, took themselves and their moral mission seriously, believing in their responsibility as professionals to lead and to improve society. Moreover, the Masons drew upon an ancient history of service, and Warren enjoyed that sense of attachment to a larger tradition—it bound him to the Masons as it did to Berkeley and the Order of the Golden Bear. Warren's attachments in each instance worked in two directions: He thrived in the Masons because he shared their ideals, but those ideals also helped to shape him, nurturing his commitment to service, deepening his conviction that society's problems were best addressed by small groups of enlightened, well-meaning citizens. Those ideals knitted together Warren's Progressivism, his Republicanism, and his Masonry.

Warren was, in the vernacular of the Masonic order, "raised to the sublime degree of Master Mason" on November 1, 1919, in Sequoia Lodge No. 349 at Oakland. Year after year, he advanced, becoming a steward (1922 and 1923), then a junior deacon (1924), then senior deacon (1925), junior warden (1926), senior warden (1927), and master (1928). His schedules through those years show his active participation; rarely did a month go by without his attending some meeting or event put on by the Masons. After five years of committee work for the "Grand Lodge," he won a series of senior positions that culminated in 1935 with his election as grand master of the Masons for California.

"The foregoing Masonic record closely indicates that, from the beginning of his Masonic career, Brother Warren has shown a keen interest in our ancient and honorable fraternity," according to the Masons' official record.[10] Not coincidentally, Warren's Masonic ties also helped bolster his growing political aspirations, and he recognized and appreciated that fact as well. "While the Masonic Order is strictly nonpolitical,

friends are friends, however attained, and I have no doubt that these friendships contributed substantially to the success of many of my campaigns," he wrote.[11]

Still, friends come with their own ideas, and each of Warren's affiliations came
with attachments, none more troubling than those associated with an organization
little known outside California but well established within it. Called the Native Sons
of the Golden West, the group extolled California history and its pioneers. The organization was divided into "parlors," and the Native Sons grew rapidly around the
turn of the century, establishing major centers in San Francisco and Los Angeles,
forming dozens of groups in a swarm of parlors that covered the state from border
to border. Only native-born Californians were allowed to join, which in part ac-
counted for a large of number of politician members; for politicians or aspiring
politicians, membership was proof of their California roots. So Warren's decision to
affiliate with the Native Sons was not surprising. Membership accomplished two
valuable political objectives: it advertised his heritage as well as his devotion to California. But as Warren well knew, the Native Sons did more than put up plaques and
hold their signature Admission Day memorials—two functions that the organization still performs today. In early-twentieth-century California, the Native Sons
served as an aggressive proponent of white supremacy.

And yet, on July 24, 1919, soon after becoming a member of the city attorney's
office in Oakland and just a few months before joining the Masons, Earl Warren
was initiated into the Native Sons of the Golden West. He joined the Fruitvale Parlor in Oakland, known within the Native Sons as Parlor 252.[12] Within months of
Warren's decision to join, United States senator James D. Phelan—another of the
Progressives for whom racism and political reform existed as complementary
values[13]—appealed to the Native Sons' membership by writing in their monthly
magazine a screed against miscegenation: "Imagine a Japanese seeking the hand of
an American woman in marriage!" he exclaimed. "If you knew how these people
raise their garden truck, you would never let a bite of it pass your lips."[14] Soon after, when Governor William Stephens refused to call a special session of the legislature to consider anti-Japanese bills, the Native Sons called for his recall, urging
their followers to preserve California as "the White Man's Paradise."[15]

"We have taken an active interest in the conservation of our natural resources,"
Fletcher A. Cutler, grand president of the Native Sons of the Golden West, wrote in
1926, "the preservation of our scenic wonders and making them accessible to all;
the retention of the State and its soil for the White race; all legislation, Federal and
State, affecting the State and its interests."[16]

By 1942, when Warren was running for governor and Pearl Harbor had stoked
anti-Japanese sentiment in California and across the nation, the Native Sons were
bursting with indignation. The May issue of the organization's newsletter, *The
Grizzly Bear*, approvingly published the remarks of Mississippi senator John

Rankin, a man with few peers in race-baiting. "This is a race war, as far as the Pacific side of this conflict is concerned," Rankin wrote. "This is a question we have to settle now, and we might as well understand it. I am for catching every Japanese in America, Alaska and Hawaii now and putting him in concentration camps and shipping them back to Asia as soon as possible."[17]

Warren's own parlor, in Alameda, took the lead in persecuting the state's Japanese residents during the crisis months of early World War II, and Warren participated. "The Order of Native Sons of the Golden West has for the past quarter-century warned against the very dangers which have now come upon us," began a resolution introduced by the president of Warren's parlor. Approved by the Grand Parlor during its sixty-fifth meeting, held over three days in May 1942, the resolution called for the Sons to file a lawsuit challenging the right of Japanese to hold American citizenship and for the organization to draft a constitutional amendment to exclude all "persons of Japanese ancestry" from citizenship.[18] The same resolution called on parlors to raise money for those efforts, and every Native Son was asked to give at least $1. Warren endorsed the resolution.[19]

Warren's embrace of the Native Sons' agenda was ambivalent in some respects. His prepared remarks for the convention that year included no reference to the citizenship debate. But he must have added them at the last minute, and then William Knowland, son of Joseph Knowland, made sure that they would receive attention. After the conference was over for the day, Knowland returned to his office at the *Oakland Tribune* and read the Associated Press account of the meeting. That story did not quote Warren, so Knowland took it upon himself to edit in the comments of his friend, the attorney general and gubernatorial candidate. "I took off the A.P. dateline and re-arranged the story, putting you in with a few quotes which I remembered which I think were perfectly safe," Knowland explained in a letter to Warren.[20]

In its revised form, the story began, "Vigorous prosecution of suits pending in the Federal courts to prevent land holding and citizenship rights to Japanese was advocated here last night by Atty. Gen. Earl Warren."[21]

Two months after Warren and the Native Sons endorsed the exclusion of Japanese from citizenship, Warren advertised his gubernatorial candidacy in *The Grizzly Bear*. To his fellow members, Warren billed himself as "A Californian for California," a message sure to appeal to the Native Sons and one that slyly alluded to the Utah birth of his opponent, Culbert Olson. His second ad, which appeared in the October issue of the magazine, similarly identified him as "a true Californian" and appeared just above a letter from a "Native Daughter of Pioneer Parents." Of the Japanese, she wrote, "If they are allowed to continue their citizenship and their ownership of land, they will always be thorns in the flesh of our democracy."[22]

Though he had little involvement with the organization after joining the United States Supreme Court, Earl Warren never resigned from the Native Sons or renounced his membership. As with the Legionnaires, he skirted the edges of the Native Sons' most objectionable positions, but his association with it highlights a weakness of his early, club-based politics: by making philosophy an extension of his affiliations, Warren placed himself in uncomfortable company, and it was difficult for others to assess his true beliefs. To critics, the American Legion was anti-Communist, the Masons anti-Catholic, and the Native Sons anti-Japanese. Even though those groups were, for Warren, more about fraternity than ideology, his membership in them contributed to early misappraisals of his values. He seemed, in short, more conservative than he was.

Compounding that misunderstanding was Warren's enduring bond with his first and most important political patron, Joseph Knowland. After backing Warren in his initial bid to become Alameda County district attorney, Knowland stayed with the young prosecutor. Knowland joined the Native Sons in 1891, when he was just eighteen years old, and was an enthusiastic member.[23] More important, he was a highly influential leader of the California Republican Party's conservative wing, and he used his influence to advance his politics and protégés. Warren courted Knowland's favor. Their correspondence through the 1920s and 1930s is replete with favors given and sought by both men. In early 1927, for instance, Knowland inquired about a case involving an Oakland doctor whose wife had died under mysterious circumstances the year before. Warren dispatched one of his investigators, who produced an analysis for Warren on February 14, 1927. Warren forwarded it to Knowland the following day, noting that it was sent "in accordance with your request."[24] That same month, Warren forwarded a divorce file to the publisher, whose newspaper was fascinated by the then-sordid topic of marital breakups and regularly published embarrassing details about husbands and wives who divorced.[25]

Not all the favors were sought by Knowland and granted by Warren. Sometimes, the DA had requests of his own. In 1933, for instance, Warren asked for Knowland's help in securing a commission with the Judge Advocate section of the U.S. Army, acknowledging that such an appointment would be difficult in light of the limited number of spots, but adding that "if you can assist me or offer any suggestions as to a mode of procedure, I will greatly appreciate it."[26]

In general, the two friends reciprocated innocent favors, the publisher getting tips and information from Warren while Warren received political support from Knowland. In some cases, however, the information exchanged could have compromised Warren's office. Having a public official perform an investigation for a newspaper publisher, for instance, was dubious even by the prevailing legal standards of that era. And on March 26, 1935, Warren sent to Knowland "copies of confidential reports concerning the matter we discussed yesterday."[27] Later in life, Warren sought to minimize Knowland's influence on his early political development. He rejected the implication that Knowland was a machine politician and that Warren benefited from his patronage. Interviewed after his retirement from the Supreme Court, Warren said:

> Joe Knowland . . . he was running the newspaper, that's all. He had nothing to do with county government. You know, I think some of the writing people have overemphasized the position of Joe Knowland in the county. He had no political organization. There wasn't any political organization. He was one of the anti's against the Mike Kelly group, but he had no organization of his own, and he was always friendly to me and helpful as far as he could be in his newspaper, but that's all.[28]

True, but misleading. While Knowland did not hand out offices in the manner of Mike Kelly, he looked out for his people. And Warren was, from 1925 on, one of Knowland's people. The *Tribune*'s backing helped Warren win elections in 1926, 1930, and 1934. That helped protect Warren from challenges at home, and allowed him to turn his political attention elsewhere. He was aided there as well by Knowland, who in 1934 supported the district attorney's bid to become chairman of the state Republican Party. Knowland's backing helped Warren land that position, which elevated his stature at a propitious moment, just as California's conservatives felt a threat unlike any they had experienced before.

UPTON SINCLAIR was earnest and occasionally brilliant—his masterwork, *The Jungle*, stands as one of the century's great pieces of journalism—and sometimes painfully naïve. Sharp of tongue and in appearance, Sinclair was a gifted polemicist, an author of novels and journalism, a vegetarian, a teetotaler, and a long-standing member of the Socialist Party. Indeed, Sinclair had run for office as a Socialist, though without success. On September 1, 1933, however, Sinclair paid a quiet visit to Beverly Hills City Hall, where he reregistered, this time as a Democrat, and set out to run again.[29] At first, the only people who seemed bothered by that were Socialists, including Sinclair's son, who saw him as a traitor for abandoning the cause and party with which he had long been associated.[30]

But Sinclair, operating out of his Sunset Avenue bungalow in Pasadena, campaigned with the manic energy that had allowed him to produce more than forty books. Characteristically, when he launched his campaign for governor, he did it with a pamphlet. It was released in October 1933, just over a year before the gubernatorial election day. The title of Sinclair's debut work of his first bid for office as a Democrat bore his signature enthusiasm and hubris: *I, Governor of California, and How I Ended Poverty: A True Story of the Future*.

"This is not just a pamphlet," the cover declared. "This is the beginning of a

Crusade. A Two-Year Plan to make over a State. To capture the Democratic primaries and use an old party for a new job. The EPIC plan: (E)nd (P)overty (I)n (C)alifornia!"[31] The sixty-four-page document sold for twenty cents a copy. It raced out of its author's hands. Within months, it was the biggest-selling "book" in the history of California. In it, Sinclair outlined a twelve-point program for eliminating poverty and doing it so quickly that he envisioned having time to spare in his four-year term before then bowing back out of office and returning to life as a writer. The EPIC plan called for the creation of state-owned land colonies and factories, which would trade with one another in a special California-issued scrip, to be monitored by a new state agency known as the California Authority for Money. It represented a staggering assault on free-market capitalism.

EPIC's promises can strike a modern ear as naïve or outlandish, but they were directed toward a society perched at the edge of ruin. The Depression in those years painfully gripped the American economy, shadowing millions of its souls, stripping them of homes, sustenance, income, and at times even the will to live. California's suffering was particularly acute. By 1932, an estimated 28 percent of Californians were out of work, and by 1934, more than 1.25 million Californians were receiving public relief, along with millions more scraping by on reduced wages.[32]

So when Sinclair complained that the state and national economies were in shambles, his appeal reached despairing workers in fields and cities, in relief lines and outside shuttered factories. It struck a chord with intellectuals as well, as it tapped a growing effort to comprehend the depth of the California crisis. Dorothea Lange, Horace Bristol, and others vividly captured the woefulness of California's Depression in their haunting photographs; economist Paul Taylor documented the depth and breadth of the crisis. "There is," John Steinbeck would write in 1939, "a sorrow here that weeping cannot symbolize. There is a failure here that topples all our success."[33]

The woe of poverty was joined by a burning, building anger, cresting just as Sinclair began his campaign for the governorship. San Francisco's docks in 1934 were busy, prosperous, and ready to explode. Labor was itching to reclaim ground lost to employers during the 1920s and to eliminate a humiliating employment practice known as the "shape-up," a daily dock call in which workers were forced to gather and be picked for work. The practice led to corruption—a man in charge of picking workers often could be induced to pick the right ones for a share of their wage—and even at its best it demeaned those forced to plead for work day after day.

If labor had its grievances, employers felt the press of battle, too. They had fought to a tie in the previous decade, but now set their jaw in opposition to labor's effort to unify the dockworkers of the West Coast under a single union, the International Longshoremen's Association. Just as Eugene Debs had hoped to bring railway workers under the unifying banner of the American Railway Union—and had confronted the talons of business when he did—so now did longshoremen seek common representation. Employers and their allies showed no less restraint in response to dockworker power than they did when faced with railroad workers. Warren, whose Alameda County was home to the docks of the East Bay, warned against the rising agitation, calling for law enforcement across the state to band together to resist encroaching Communism.[34] Police prepared to lay siege.

Through the spring, the two sides engaged in a series of preliminary skirmishes, until, on May 9, 1934, the longshoremen walked out and the locus of their strike settled on San Francisco. May and June of 1934 were violent months in The City, as labor staged a series of protests, provoking police, who responded with escalating violence and weaponry—tear gas in some cases, specially made clubs in others. Complicating the matter politically, Governor James Rolph, a likable if unimpressive Republican whose single noteworthy contribution to California politics was his tragic endorsement of a 1933 lynching in San Jose, died on June 2, just as the conflict was gathering in danger. Rolph was replaced by Lieutenant Governor Frank Merriam, a Long Beach real estate salesman who was neither likable nor moderate. Merriam unabashedly sided with employers. His embrace of their cause—typical of the state's Republican leadership—emboldened employers, who held fast against labor and counted on Merriam to supply the muscle if conflict erupted.

It did. The crescendo of the Great Maritime Strike occurred in early July 1934, in the form of a series of bloody, spectacular, and theatrical confrontations movingly reconstructed in Kevin Starr's *Endangered Dreams*. On July 3, thousands of longshoremen and 700 policemen faced each other at San Francisco's Pier 38, where police had forced their way in the day before and symbolically restored the port to the employers. The police clanked open the pier doors just after noon. As thousands watched, police escorted five trucks along the waterfront, protecting their cargo from the angry dockworkers outside. The police cordon was intended to agitate, and it succeeded. By midafternoon, the two sides were at war, giving vent to decades of anger and desperation. Longshoremen hurled bricks and pavement, and helmeted police swung clubs and fired gas and bullets. The battle raged and spread for days. Sixty-four people were injured and two strikers died as San Francisco was engulfed in the worst labor violence it had ever experienced.[35] Merriam, meanwhile, declined to declare martial law, but delivered troops to San Francisco to secure state property along the waterfront. At his instruction, the 40th Infantry Division of the California National Guard took up positions in The City, and held the areas around Fisherman's Wharf, while two regiments claimed property along the Embarcadero. By mid-July, more than 4,500 soldiers were ensconced in San Francisco, their guns and bayonets symbols of where the state's sympathies lay.[36]

Labor recognized the force arrayed against it, and opted to shut The City down rather than to challenge the army in combat. At their call, a general strike closed San Francisco from July 16 through July 18. Through those eerie days, San Francisco lay quiet, its normal bustle tamped down by force of labor's will.[37] Finally, on July 18, labor's organizing council narrowly approved a motion to lift the general strike, and order began to return the following day. Streetcars resumed operation, and all workers other than Teamsters returned to their jobs. The *San Francisco Call Bulletin*, its pages sighing with relief, observed a "ground-swell indicating return to work." "Expect S.F. Peace in 24 Hours," the newspaper headlined to an exhausted, tremulous city.[38]

In those fervid days, those who came to California to take the measure of its politics and anxieties were sometimes aghast at what they found. Lorena Hickok was an insightful reporter who had made her mark with the Associated Press but left the agency when her friendship with Eleanor Roosevelt reached the point that she was forced to choose between that relationship and journalism. Picking Roosevelt, Hickok then joined the administration and was given the job of chronicling the living feel of the Depression for the director of FDR's Federal Emergency Relief Administration, Harry Hopkins. Hickok visited some of the nation's most desperate communities, and on June 27, 1934, she came to Los Angeles. She arrived expecting to find "the blackest spot in the United States" in terms of the relief problem.[39] Hickok's initial impression was that conditions in California might actually be improving. It took just days to change her mind. On July 1, 1934, she wrote to Hopkins after a trip to the Imperial Valley, southeast of Los Angeles. "I returned late last night from a three-day trip into the desert," she began. "The impressions I have brought back with me are somewhat confused and not too cheerful. They consist of heat, depression, bitterness, more heat, terrible poverty, confusion, heat again, and a passionate longing for some sort of orderly plan for procedure."[40] Traveling through California's Imperial and San Joaquin Valleys that summer, Hickok winced:

> I believe there is some sort of state law in California compelling growers to provide some sort of decent housing and sanitation for the seasonal workers they employ. If there is, it is disregarded. These laborers move in with their families, thousands and thousands of them, living in colonies of tents or shacks built of cardboard . . . with no sanitation whatever. . . . There was a good deal of sickness in some of the camps last winter. They were fertile territory for the Communists.[41]

In political terms, what Hickok found and what the San Francisco strike proved was the collapse of California's already shaky political and social center. The tensions between labor and management, between farmers and workers, between the rich and the poor had always tugged at California's middle. Hiram Johnson had patched them briefly by chasing out big business on behalf of small business, but his reforms had provided political reform and social respite, not genuine social or economic change. Now the social order was challenged by right and left, and the center gave way.

It was in that moment of collapse that Upton Sinclair pressed his campaign. He capitalized on the listlessness of the Democratic Party and reached around it to engage those same desperate people whose plight Hickok documented. Through those months, no other Democrat declared against Sinclair, and few took seriously a campaign with virtually no institutional support—newspapers belittled his effort, Democratic Party leaders ignored it. It was not until late spring that the official Democratic Party awakened to the Sinclair candidacy. Desperately playing catch-up, the Democratic field closed in July with eight candidates, the most notable among them Sinclair; George Creel, a crusading writer who had managed propaganda efforts for Woodrow Wilson and who had attempted to mediate the San Francisco maritime strike; and hotly anti-Communist Justus Wardell.

The furious politics of that summer culminated on August 28, when Sinclair not only won the Democratic primary but also lapped the field. The same candidate who four years earlier had received 50,000 votes for governor as a Socialist now tallied 436,000 as a Democrat. His finish exceeded that of all other Democrats combined, and represented nearly 100,000 votes more than Merriam, the state's newly ascended but incumbent Republican governor, polled in his primary. By nightfall of the following day, the state Republican Party and some of its Democrats were plotting the end of Upton Sinclair. To accomplish it, they realized, would require a bipartisan effort, one built around fear of Sinclair, since support for his opponent, Merriam, would be hard to muster. It would require new political faces, untainted by Merriam or the politics that Sinclair was challenging. It would require, among others, Earl Warren.

It was a campaign not just to defeat but to destroy Sinclair. It had many tentacles, and Sinclair proved singularly vulnerable. In Hollywood, movie titans were perturbed by his policies—especially his plans for a state-run movie studio—and they also took his challenge personally, in part because of his authorship of *Upton Sinclair Presents William Fox*, which Sinclair self-published in 1933.[42] Although just one entry in Sinclair's extensive list, the book contained much for Hollywood to abhor. It excoriated the financial interests behind the movies, and sneeringly reviewed some of the industry's captains. It also was laced with passage after passage that seemed to reveal in Sinclair a vulgar anti-Semitism. The book opened with a description of Fox's "good Jewish nose" and went on, in "reel" after "reel" (Sinclair's name for the chapters of the book), to suggest that the Jewishness of Hollywood was corrupting, even evil. Sinclair described one figure as "what is known as a

'Kentucky colonel'; he was born in that state, and does not mention that he is a Jew unless you cross-examine him about it."[43]

As Sinclair's candidacy gained momentum, Hollywood, under the leadership of Louis B. Mayer, moved to protect itself, most notably in the form of a mendacious and effective series of "newsreels" that characterized Sinclair supporters as bums and Communists. Movie theaters were then owned by the studios, and the studios in 1934 ordered them to play the newsreels. In those clips, an interviewer purported to survey Californians on their political views. An elderly woman in one complained that she was voting for Merriam because she could not afford to lose her house. A threadbare man speaking in a distinctly foreign accent, by contrast, said he was for Sinclair. "Vell, his system worked vell in Russia, vy can't it vork here?" he asked.[44] One piece of footage showed derelicts disembarking trains as they arrived in California, flocking in search of Sinclair's Utopia. The ruse was exposed when viewers recognized some of the bums as Hollywood actors and figured out that the "newsreel" was in fact a discarded piece of footage from a Hollywood picture. The state's major newspapers were united in their opposition to Sinclair, however, so the truth got little attention.

In the pages of the *San Francisco Chronicle* and the *Oakland Tribune*, the assault on Sinclair was daily and unyielding. In the *Los Angeles Times*, it was spiteful. Particularly effective was a series of front-page boxes, each excerpting some offensive piece of Sinclair's work, though often glaringly out of context. The excerpts ran a few sentences each, beneath a common headline announcing "Sinclair on" the day's topic—Education, say, or Marriage or Religion or any of his various targets in his many books. Those excerpts were backed up by scathing coverage of his plans and merry attacks on his missteps. On September 26, for instance, Sinclair responded to a question about whether his plan would attract the unemployed to California. "I told Harry Hopkins, the Federal Emergency Relief Administrator, that if I am elected, half the unemployed of the United States will come to California, and he will have to make plans to take care of them," Sinclair responded.[45] He recalled saying it with a laugh. Reported as serious, it became an anvil around his candidacy. The *Times* ran it on page 1, under the headline "Heavy Rush of Idle Seen by Sinclair," and reproduced the quote as: "If I'm elected Governor, I expect one-half the unemployed in the United States will hop the first freights for California."[46] Only that day's other major news story, the pending arraignment of Bruno Hauptmann for the kidnapping and murder of the Lindbergh baby, kept Sinclair's comments from getting even bigger play. The *Times* and the rest of the anti-Sinclair camp made up for that over the next weeks, as they returned to that remark again and again. Billboards and mailers repeated it, and the newsreel shots that featured bums flocking to California were specifically intended to remind viewers of Sinclair's ill-considered prediction.

Sinclair was a fat target for political attack, but Republicans, in order to wage their campaign well, needed a more presentable front man than Merriam provided. As the campaign reached its critical point, they found him. On September 24, Joe Knowland wrote to a longtime friend in Southern California, C. C. Teague, to compare notes on the effort to put down the EPIC and its standard-bearer. In his letter, Knowland remarked that he and other Republican leaders, without the consent of Merriam, had settled on a new leader. Earl Warren would now run the party—specifically because he was just what Republicans needed to answer Sinclair. "Earl represents the younger group, and is a man of splendid character," Knowland wrote, adding that he was "the kind of leader we could well put to the front this year."[47]

Warren needed no persuading. Though he bore no personal grudge against Sinclair, the novelist's candidacy struck deeply at Warren's sense of order. Sinclair belittled marriage and religion and the clubby gatherings of the well-connected. Those were Warren's friends. Sinclair spoke to desperate working people and offered to upend society on their behalf; Warren came from people invested in society and appalled by upheaval. Yes, Warren was a Republican and Sinclair a Democrat, but that was not their fundamental difference. Sinclair had been a Democrat for less than a year, and Warren was a Republican mostly by chance. What separated them was their regard for order: Sinclair mocked it; Warren protected it. So Warren assumed the leadership of the California Republican Party and served precisely the function that Knowland had envisioned: He gave the Republican campaign a solid, credible spokesman, a new and persuasive voice.

Arriving in Los Angeles on October 5, Warren warned that Sinclair's election would represent the end of civilized democracy in California. And he pounced on Sinclair's prediction that the unemployed would flock to California. "Without waiting for his election, the unemployed and penniless are coming in droves now, and if the movement gains proportion it can't be stopped," Warren said. "They will keep on coming without rhyme or reason. I regard that as the great menace of the situation."[48]

Thus engaged, Warren stumped hard for Sinclair's defeat. He gave regular press conferences and issued a stream of statements predicting doom for the state if Sinclair took office. He managed, however, to keep his head. As the election grew nearer, Warren's statements became more hyperbolic, but he took great care to avoid any appeal to partisanship. "This is no longer a campaign between the Republican Party and the Democratic Party of California," he said on October 15. "It is a crusade of Americans and Californians against Radicalism and Socialism."[49] A week later, in his first-ever statewide radio address, Warren again reached out to Democrats, acknowledging as he did the oddity of his message:

I am by a strange twist of fate appealing with equal force to Democrats and Republicans to join in the common cause of rescuing our state from the most freakish onslaught that has ever been made upon our long established and revered American institutions of government in the history of our country . . .

    This is not a partisan campaign. It is not a contest between Democrats and Republicans. . . . [It] is a simple issue between those who believe in the Constitution of the United States and in our Democratic institutions on the one hand and those who would destroy both in favor of a foreign philosophy of government, half socialistic and half communistic. . . . The battle is between two conflicting philosophies of government—one that is proud of our flag, our governmental institutions and our honored history, the other that glorifies the Red Flag of Russia and hopes to establish on American soil a despotism based upon class hatred and tyranny.[50]

Nor were Warren's efforts confined to public appeals. Seeking to build Democratic opposition to Sinclair, Warren arranged for a series of secret payments from the state Republican organization to a Democratic front group, whose headquarters happened to be just down the hall from the GOP offices at San Francisco's Palace Hotel. The full extent of Warren's support for the Merriam-Hatfield Democratic Club is not recorded, but the general chairman of that group wrote to Warren on October 31, 1934, thanking the Republican chairman for the latest weekly check and expressing confidence that, because of his support, the club was sufficiently funded to make it through election day. At the conclusion of the campaign, the chairman, J. Pendleton Wilson, cabled Warren his appreciation: "The Democrats of California have been proud of the privilege of serving with you in accomplishing a patriotic duty."[51]

Warren also lent his support to voter-suppression measures intended to intimidate Sinclair supporters. Through late October and early November, Warren received house-by-house tallies of Alameda voters whom Merriam alleged were illegally registered, and in his capacity as Republican chairman, Warren chastised Sinclair for relying on what Warren described as illegal voters. "My personal respect for Upton Sinclair has abated since he has denounced efforts to purge the rolls," Warren said. On October 25, Warren, who still held the elected position of Alameda County district attorney, called on all state and county political leaders to join in the effort to "strike the spurious registrations from the records" and suggested that evidence of such fraud be submitted to district attorneys, himself included.[52] The following day, Warren proposed for a statewide conference to purge voting rolls "so that these frauds could be stamped out and that voters not properly qualified shall be kept from the polls."[53]

For Warren, aggressiveness was not to be confused with partisanship. He understood that asking voters to reject Sinclair because he was a Democrat could easily backfire, so Warren fended off attempts to rally Republicans as Republicans. On October 29, with National Republican Chairman Henry P. Fletcher preparing to go

on nationwide radio, Warren telegrammed to warn him against invoking partisanship in the California governor's race. "The gubernatorial campaign in California
has been organized along non-partisan lines and large number of Democrats have
joined with us in support of Gov. Merriam," Warren wrote. "Our campaign is now
in satisfactory condition. We hope that no partisan mention will be made of California's situation in your broadcasts."[54]

On Election Day, Merriam tallied just over 1.1 million votes, outpolling Sinclair's 879,000. A third candidate, Raymond Haight, received 300,000 votes, enough
to keep Merriam from being able to claim a majority for his candidacy. Sinclair was
exhausted and now rejected. On Election Night, he arrived at a Beverly Hills radio
station as the ballots still were being counted, and angrily discovered that Merriam
already was there. Sinclair refused to join his rival on the radio, but spoke after
Merriam finished. "My face burns when I think of the lies and forgeries circulated
by men with millions to spend to defeat me," he told that night's audience. "But it
won't go on. Be of good cheer. We're not going to stop. This is only one skirmish,
and we're enlisted for the war."[55] Warren, his work completed, was more restrained.
He wired his congratulations to Merriam and then went quietly back to work.

Sinclair's strong showing and the respectable turnout for Haight helped doom
Merriam to a short life at the top of California politics. Republican strategists recognized that he could not carry the party forward and began to search for a new
leader. The victory was, as Warren noted the day after the election, "a progressive
victory . . . non-partisan in character and . . . consistent in every respect with
the highest ideals of our American form of government."[56] Merriam was no
Progressive—he never would be. Earl Warren was.

Warren's role in the Sinclair campaign seemed consistent with his prosecution
of the IWW, his membership in the Native Sons, and his friendship with Joseph
Knowland. To friends as well as critics, Warren appeared firmly set on the much-
traveled path to Republican leadership in California, one vested in the state's business and propertied interests. In fact, however, Warren was subtly creating his own
way, under the aegis of the Republican Party but not in its thrall. Warren's actions
were taken not so much in defense of the Republican Party as in defense of what he
saw as California's faltering political center. Since Sinclair offended not Warren's
sense of partisanship but rather his belief in order and reason, Warren struck back
in alliance with the state's right wing. Still, Warren did not oppose Sinclair because
he was a Democrat; he did so because he believed—and his friends believed—that
Sinclair was a radical.

ONCE SINCLAIR was finished, the new state Republican chairman turned at home
to the *Point Lobos* prosecution, still then under way, and within state political cir-

cles to the effort to defeat Roosevelt's reelection. Both undertakings helped affirm for California's Republican leadership, principally the Chandlers and Knowlands, that Warren was trustworthy. In 1936, as Republican chairman, Warren sealed their loyalty by leading the California Republican Party through a duel between former President Herbert Hoover and self-appointed Republican newspaper baron William Randolph Hearst.

Since his defeat in 1932, Hoover had sulkily returned to Palo Alto, where he plotted a return to national politics. As the party's nominal leader, Hoover was hard to ignore, but more astute observers realized that his smashing by Roosevelt and association with the Depression made Hoover a sure loser. When he began campaigning to head the California delegation to the 1936 Republican National Convention, party insiders did their best to cut him off.

Hearst, meanwhile, was a latecomer to California politics and to the Republican Party. He had supported FDR in 1932 but quickly lost patience with the president, and now, four years later, schemed to defeat him. Hearst, whose newspaper empire had major outlets in Los Angeles and San Francisco, realized he would have a difficult time winning for himself, but signed up Governor Merriam to head his delegation, reasoning that Merriam would give him a figurehead through which to control the California delegation. Those two camps—Hoover's and Hearst's—united the opposition, especially the balance of California's Republican newspaper baronage. The Chandlers and the Knowlands, as well as their counterparts at the *San Francisco Chronicle*, could not stomach the ascent of their rival, Hearst, nor could they sanction defeat of the party in order to gratify Hoover. Together with a new moderate group of Republicans known as the California Republican Assembly, they backed a proposal to send an uninstructed delegation to the convention—that is, one that could vote its will, without allegiance either to Merriam or Hearst. The threshold question of who should run that delegation was answered easily enough. They chose Warren.

Warren hesitated at first. He was the chairman of the party, and accepting the leadership of the delegation risked antagonizing both Hoover and Merriam, a Republican ex-president and a sitting Republican governor. Moderate friends pressed him to do it anyway. "A number of us visited Warren and urged him to keep up the fight for an uninstructed delegation," said Ed Shattuck, a longtime leader of the state party. "We felt that this was the way to clean house in the party."[57]

Warren agreed, then faced the challenge of convincing voters that he was not merely fronting for Hoover, just as Merriam was for Hearst. Over lunch at the *San Francisco Chronicle* in the days leading up to the election, Warren advised Hoover to squelch those rumors by announcing that he had no intention of running. Hoover, Warren later remembered, "hit the ceiling. I have never seen anyone so sore."[58] Hoover never forgave Warren the impertinence.[59] Soon after, Warren spoke out brashly against Hearst, charging in a radio address that a man who kept an official residence in New York in order to avoid paying California taxes should not be allowed to play a meaningful role in its politics. Hearst's reaction is not recorded, but it is not difficult to imagine his rage.

Warren and the delegation he headed ran under the slogan "Are You Handcuffed by Hearst? And Muzzled by Merriam? Or Are You Independent, Progressive California Republicans?"[60] Warren's delegation won, and his victory marked a generational as well as an ideological transition. In just two years, Warren had defended Merriam against a serious challenge from his left by appealing to the voters' nonpartisanship; now he had vanquished Merriam with a new variant of that theme—that "independent, Progressive" Republicanism was needed even within the Republican Party. Hoover and Merriam, leaders of California's traditional conservative Republicans, were being consigned to the status of elder statesmen. Warren's string of victories was growing longer.

Warren already enjoyed Knowland's unqualified support, and his actions through 1934, 1935, and 1936 brought the Chandlers on board as well. Although he was never theirs—and though they would eventually bring their own champion, Richard Nixon, to the contest—for the present, Warren sufficed. He was tough, young, unblemished, and able to carry votes in a state dominated by Democrats. His handling of Hoover and Hearst proved he did not shrink before power. The *Los Angeles Times* became a supporter in those years, and would give him vital backing in Southern California for the rest of his state political career.

With his newspaper support lined up and his conservative base solid, all Warren needed was an opening. Given his background, the obvious next step was the California attorney general's office, a job that would make use of Warren's prosecutorial credentials but expand his reach beyond Alameda County. Warren had eyed the office for several years. Indeed, even as he had helped defeat Sinclair, Warren and his staff first drafted and then advocated passage of a set of amendments to the California Constitution to invigorate the office of the state attorney general. Until then, the attorney general had acted as lawyer for the government and little else. Under the amendments, the attorney general's duties and office would be expanded and he would be turned into the foremost law-enforcement officer of the state, with the power to initiate investigations anywhere in California and with supervisory authority over the state's police and sheriffs. The attorney general also would receive a raise to $11,000 a year. Warren stumped for the changes and took advantage of a spate of crime to convince voters to agree with him. A series of bank robberies tested law-enforcement coordination in the state, and then an appalling mob lynching of two men who had been arrested for the kidnapping of a young man named Brooke Hart helped persuade voters that local authorities could not handle certain types of violence. Convinced that new authority was needed at the state level, voters approved the Warren-backed changes in 1934, making the attorney general's office into one that Warren might now like to hold.[61]

The office was good for Warren, and Warren was ready for the office, but impeding that path was U. S. Webb, the wizened incumbent attorney general who had been in office since 1902 and whose tenure was marked more by longevity than accomplishment. Warren knew better than to challenge Webb directly, but Warren did ask Webb to let him know should he ever prepare to retire.

In 1937, the call came. The seventy-year-old Webb told Warren that he would not stand for reelection. Warren announced his candidacy on February 17, 1937: "[T]he future of our democracy depends on the quality of our local and state governments and on whether or not we have an honest, fearless and uniform enforcement of the law."[62] Backed by Republicans and their newspapers and unchallenged by united Democratic opposition, Warren appeared in the early months of the campaign to be coasting toward victory.

It was an exhilarating moment. Warren's diligence had created a coveted office, and his attention to politics had made him the presumptive holder of it. Warren was forty-seven years old, the head of a large and healthy family. His youngest was still just a toddler, but college loomed for the Warren brood, and the pay hike— from $7,200 a year to $11,000 a year—boded well for the family's future.

But before Warren could move to Sacramento to assume the spot that seemed destined to be his, he was jolted. On a Sunday morning in May 1938, Warren was speaking at the Claremont Hotel in Berkeley to a Masonic gathering when he was handed a telegram. It informed him of a murder the night before in Bakersfield. The blood-soaked body had been found that morning at 9:10 A.M. The victim was Methias Warren.

Chapter 5

# MURDER

*Come quickly. Father needs you.*

WILLIAM REED TELEGRAM TO EARL WARREN[1]

EARL WARREN HAD PLANNED an average day for Sunday, May 15, 1938, at least by the standards of a politician in the middle of his first campaign for statewide office. After addressing the Masters' and Wardens' Breakfast of the Masons at 8:30 A.M. in Berkeley, he was planning to take his son, Earl Jr., to a barbecue lunch at the Golden Gate Gun Club in West Alameda. Like much of his schedule in those days, Warren's stops were partly social and partly political. They involved meeting old friends and sometimes even included family, but they also were chances to talk about crime in California and what he, if elected attorney general, intended to do about it.[2]

The breakfast was already under way when an aide pulled Warren aside and told him the news from Bakersfield. Methias Warren had been beaten with an iron pipe. The assailant had entered through the back door of Warren's tiny childhood home on Niles Street. Methias had been sitting in a kitchen chair when the killer struck and cracked apart his skull. Initial police speculation suggested a left-handed killer swinging from behind. Later, investigators adopted a more provocative theory: that the blows were delivered by a killer face-to-face with the seventy-one-year-old man—implying that the victim knew his murderer. Once beaten and bleeding, Methias either dragged himself or was dragged across the room, from the area near his chair onto his bed, and the killer then rifled the house. Warren's watch lay near the body, undiscovered or ignored by his assailant.[3] Methias Warren died in his bed.[4]

William Reed, who worked for Methias, found the body when he came to call on his boss on Sunday morning regarding some business. A trail of blood led from the kitchen to the bedroom. Bloody handprints were on the doors and oven. Reed immediately called police and fired off the enigmatic telegram.[5] Within minutes, Alameda's district attorney had dispatched senior members of his staff to Bakersfield, one group by car, the other in a plane carrying Warren as well. Warren asked Oscar Jahnsen, the lead investigator for the Alameda County DA's office, to monitor the unfolding inquiry; Nathan Miller, another trusted aide, went to act as Warren's lawyer and to investigate the estate of Methias Warren. Warren's actions were taken quickly, but those close to him could see how rattled he was. "I knew he was fighting to keep control of himself," Jahnsen recalled.[6]

In the coming days, newspaper readers across California would learn details of Methias Warren's murder and the intense police effort to find the killer or killers. It was, after all, a sensational story—the father of a leading candidate for attorney general clubbed to death in the middle of the night. Many of California's prison cells held men put there by Earl Warren. He had enemies, and the press jumped at the possibilities, along with their political ramifications. In that mountain of coverage, however, reporters would say next to nothing of how it was that Methias Warren came to be alone that Saturday night. Although the *Bakersfield Californian* noted that he lived by himself in the house, it did not ask why. The answer was that Methias Warren, always careful with money, had grown increasingly penurious as he aged. Isolation had turned to reclusiveness, as Warren retreated into his modest rental-property business. Gradually, he transformed his home into a ramshackle workshop. Spare furniture was piled into some rooms; the backyard teemed with plumbing fixtures, lumber, and other supplies. Even his eating habits changed, as he watched each penny. On the night of his murder, the dinner he left was a half-eaten grapefruit.

As Methias Warren squirreled away his cash, he left room for little else. His wife, Chrystal, had moved out during the late 1920s, settling in Oakland in an apartment near their daughter Ethel. By the time Methias was killed, he and his wife had been separated for more than a decade.[7] The facts were painful to Warren—as well as a potential liability for a candidate whose public image centered in some measure on his sturdy family. For decades, he covered up the truth, telling biographer John Weaver that his mother was visiting Oakland at the time of the murder in order to undergo surgery for cataracts. Although that was partly true—Chrystal Warren did have the surgery—it concealed the less pleasant fact of his parents' long separation. So committed was Warren to that version of events that he recorded it in his memoirs as well, long after it could have had political ramifications for him.[8]

Warren was aided in the protection of his secret by a press markedly more reticent than today's to reveal embarrassing personal details about its public officials and by his own solid reputation among reporters. They liked him, and when the murder occurred, they treated Warren as a victim first and only after that as a story. Still, the murder of Methias Warren ricocheted through the state political campaign. Early speculation naturally focused on whether Methias might have been killed by someone trying to get even with his famous son. Speaking to reporters before leaving for Bakersfield, Warren discounted vengeance as a motive, even as he reminded voters of his long record protecting the public from criminals:

> True, in the 13 or more years I have been a prosecutor, I have sent an average of 15 killers to death or to prison. I have sent countless other prisoners up, but I have never heard expressed toward me the threat of vengeance, either openly or indirectly. I have received no threatening letters. I know of no one who could have killed my father to strike at me.[9]

Arriving in his hometown, Warren was met by Jahnsen and the other members of his staff who had driven or flown to the scene. Warren and his retinue drove to his old home, and there he stepped inside, through the yard where his burro Jack had been tethered and where he had played with his dog, into the kitchen where he had done his homework and returned after hauling ice through the city's sweltering summers, through the living room with the old Victrola and the books read so long ago. Now that same lot was covered in debris. The kitchen was drenched in the dirt-brown of dried blood. Police scoured the area for clues, while at police headquarters detectives questioned suspects. One, an out-of-work sixty-three-year-old laborer, Hulet Bell, had been arrested early Sunday morning for public drunkenness. As police took him into custody, Bell blurted out, "I didn't kill him. I didn't kill him."[10] Since Warren's murder had not been publicized at that point, police were questioning the now sober Bell in connection with the murder. Ernest Wearne, who lived in one of Warren's rental homes, also was in police hands, said to have threatened Warren and a local judge after a drunk-driving conviction. He too was being questioned.[11]

In addition to Warren's men, police arrived from Los Angeles to help with the investigation, and the FBI (after a period in which it was known as the Division of Investigation, the formal FBI was born in 1935) supplied assistance as well. Hoover wrote personally to Warren to express his condolences, and the Bureau would assist from offstage in the investigation for years.[12]

That day, Earl Warren surveyed the progress of the case, braced for the onslaught of coverage, and then retreated briefly to his hotel room. There, the events of the past twenty-four hours overtook him. Yes, his father had receded from the family in recent years, but Warren was suddenly immersed in the town of his youth, thrust back into the memories of childhood and growing up, of his father's tutelage and care. That they had not been close in recent years only added to the tragedy— their separation was now permanent, their differences forever irreconcilable. Warren broke down and cried in front of the press.

A photographer took a picture. But Earl Warren's popularity protected him from more than the exposure of his parents' separation. When the bulb went off, the rest of the press corps turned on the photographer and demanded that he pull the film from his camera. "There was a concerted effort in that room by the rest of us to see that that picture would never be used," said Ralph Kreiser, the police reporter for the *Bakersfield Californian*. "No picture appeared."[13]

One witness to that strange scene was Bakersfield's unconventional police chief, Robert Powers. An almost entirely self-educated man (he dropped out of school before reaching sixth grade), Powers was curious, witty, and quietly forceful. He described himself as "an extremely devious person."[14] He had been chief since 1933, and had little use for the wave of law-enforcement agents now descending on his department, offering their help solving the murder of Methias Warren. Powers affected graciousness but pushed back at those who would take over his investigation, including the well-meaning aides of Earl Warren.

Powers's resistance to interference did not translate into hostility toward Warren, however. Indeed, like the reporters covering the case, Powers wanted to protect the district attorney, whom he knew from conferences and supported in his bid for attorney general.[15] His initial impulse, on arriving at the scene of the crime, was to consider whether the image of Methias Warren's disheveled home would hurt Earl Warren's candidacy, as reporters would question why a well-off son would let his father sink to such depths. Only after Powers discovered that Methias Warren was in fact reasonably well off and lived that way because he chose to did Powers's concern for Earl Warren subside.[16] And Powers's admiration only grew as he witnessed the esteem that others held for Warren. When the press corps convinced the photographer to destroy his picture of the grieving district attorney, Powers cocked an eyebrow. "It's a very strange thing that a man like him, as good a man as he was," Powers recalled, "could get so much genuine affection from a bunch of bastards."[17]

In the days that followed, Powers's staff and Warren's would come to see the murder differently. Powers, who took personal control of the investigation and assigned more than two dozen officers and civilians to it, believed a transient had committed the crime—that a passing vagabond spied Methias Warren counting the receipts from his rental properties and sneaked up from behind the house. As he approached, Powers believed, the assailant grabbed a section of pipe from the cluttered backyard and stole inside the house, which had been left open in Bakersfield's gathering summer heat. The killer, according to Powers's theory, bashed in Warren's head, then rifled through his papers, scattering unimportant documents and pulling out cash.

Jahnsen, Warren's lead investigator, arrived at a different conclusion. Jahnsen strongly believed that Methias Warren knew his killer and that the motive was more complicated than robbery. Jahnsen reached that conviction first from his belief that forensic evidence showed Warren was facing the assailant when struck. His conclusion seemed bolstered, Jahnsen believed, by evidence that Warren would have been too weak from the injury to drag himself into bed and that his assailant thus helped place him there. Under that theory, the killer hit Warren, then helped him to bed, where he died. The murderer, Jahnsen believed, covered the body with a sheet.

Kindness to the dying Warren did not square with a transient killing. They suggested a friend, and Jahnsen was convinced that they pointed to a man named Ed Regan, who helped Warren manage his Bakersfield rental properties.[18] Jahnsen took a bead on Regan at Methias's funeral. There, with family and reporters present, Regan swooned with grief. He fell to the ground, but seemed, to Jahnsen anyway, to take care not to hurt himself. The newspapers reported him as having fainted; Jahnsen thought he'd faked it. In addition, some of Warren's papers were missing, and a small pile of them appeared to have been burned not far from Regan's house. Nathan Miller, hunting through Methias Warren's extensive financial records, looked for irregularities and poured over Regan's documents as well, searching for an unpaid loan or other transaction that might have given him a motive to kill his business partner and friend. Nothing turned up. Trying to increase pressure on Regan, Jahnsen asked him to provide fingerprint samples, ostensibly to eliminate any of those in the house that might match his, since Regan had reason to be there. Jahnsen's real motive, however, was to sweat Regan, to see how he reacted to the pressure of being a suspect. At first, Regan and his wife objected. Then he agreed, but broke into what seemed a nervous sweat. Jahnsen was convinced he had nailed Regan and that he was on the verge of confessing. Just at that moment, however, Los Angeles sheriff's deputies, who were assisting in the investigation, interrupted and began badgering him. Regan was confused, and Jahnsen halted the interrogation, convinced that even if Regan confessed, it would not stand up in court. Jahnsen forever believed the one chance of solving the crime had slipped away.[19]

Another lead passed for different reasons, ones that spoke to the emerging Earl Warren. As officers conducted scores of interviews, they learned of a man who had been in Bakersfield about the time of the murder and had subsequently been arrested, convicted, and sent to San Quentin on an unrelated charge. Powers proposed putting another inmate in the cell with him, planting a microphone in the cell, and urging the inmate to question that man about his possible involvement in the Warren murder. Earl Warren's permission was not required—he was, after all, merely the son of the victim; he had no jurisdiction over the criminal case—but Powers thought it would be easier to get the approval of prison authorities if he could forward the request with Warren's imprimatur. Powers asked Jahnsen to raise the matter with Warren, and Jahnsen soon reported back. "Warren's answer was 'I don't believe in Dictaphones,'" Powers recalled.

Few would have blamed Warren for acceding to a common, if marginal, practice in this pursuit of his father's murderer. But once Warren discovered a position of principle, he held it, as he did here. Powers was struck by his adamancy: "It was a new idea to find this quality of integrity," he said.[20] There was no microphone planted in the cell. That criminal defendant was not the last to receive a break from Earl Warren, but he surely was the one whom Warren must have been most tempted to lean on.

After the first round of suspects were investigated and dismissed, progress on the case slowed and hope faded. "While I shall never be satisfied until this case is cleared," Powers wrote to Warren as leads were beginning to dry up, "still I feel that everything possible has been done up to the present time."[21] Weeks turned to years, and though Powers stayed in touch with Warren, he was never able to report a breakthrough. In 1944, Warren would express his appreciation to Powers by naming him Coordinator of Law Enforcement Agencies for the State of California. The murder of Methias Warren, however, would drift into history, unsolved and theoretically still an open murder investigation of the Bakersfield police department.

In the meantime, Warren trudged on. He pulled his personal date book from his coat pocket and lightly wrote "Cancelled" across each of fourteen consecutive days, starting on the Monday after his father's murder and not ending until Monday, May 30, 1938. He then methodically made a list of all those officers and investigators who had participated in the search for the killer and made sure that each one received a note from him expressing his gratitude.[22]

When he returned home from Bakersfield, Warren talked to his children about their grandfather's death. As he listened, Earl Warren, Jr., sensed in his father a grim resolve, not sadness so much as resignation. After that, Earl Jr. said, "he never made reference to it again."[23] Nina was left to field the children's questions.

What is perhaps most striking about Warren after his father's murder is what did not happen next. Warren did not harden or coarsen. He did not transform the violent death of his father into a campaign of vengeance. He was a prosecutor, and committed to combating crime, and he could easily at this moment have fallen into the angry energy of retribution. Voters would have sympathized. In personal terms as well as political ones, it also must have tempted Warren to succumb to his anger, as so many crime victims do. A conservative, the old saw goes, is a liberal who's been mugged. In Warren's case, however, he showed no such response to his father's murder. He continued to campaign as a law-and-order candidate, but that had been his message prior to the attack on Methias Warren. To the contrary, Warren after the murder flickered with new compassion.

Rather than retreat into the familiar politics of crime fighting, Warren at just this moment evolved a larger self. The impetus was a liberal Los Angeles judge, Robert Kenny. A leading Democrat, a candidate for state senate and the treasurer of

Culbert Olson's gubernatorial campaign, Kenny seemed an unlikely supporter of Warren, the Republican candidate for attorney general. But Fletcher Bowron, a colleague of Kenny's on the Superior Court bench, drove Kenny home one night and on the way urged him to consider backing Warren. Kenny liked Warren and was willing to consider it, but Warren's *Point Lobos* prosecution troubled Kenny. On June 12, less than a month after Methias's murder, Kenny told Warren his support would depend on Warren's views of civil rights. Kenny asked if Warren would be willing to put down in writing his views in that area, and Kenny said that if he liked it, he would consider an endorsement.[24] Warren agreed to write the statement and then submitted it to Kenny. It read, in part:

> I believe the preservation of our civil liberties to be the most fundamental and important of all our governmental problems because . . . if we ever permit these liberties to be destroyed, there will be nothing left in our system worthy of preservation. They constitute the soul of democracy . . .
>
> As Attorney General, I would do my best to prevent Hagueism [Mayor Frank Hague, in New Jersey, had violently turned on protesters there] from gaining a foothold in California. I am unalterably opposed to any species of vigilantes or to any other extra-legal means of a majority exercising its will over a minority. . . . I believe that if majorities are entitled to have their civil rights protected they should be willing to fight for the same rights to minorities no matter how violently they disagree with their views.
>
> I believe that the American concept of civil rights should include not only an observance of our Constitutional Bill of Rights, but also absence of arbitrary action by government in every field.[25]

Those were significantly liberal views coming from a California Republican in the 1930s. The protection of "minority" rights did not much enter into that party's prewar lexicon, and a public willingness to defend protesters and picketers was certainly not part of Governor Merriam's response to the waterfront disturbances of that decade. Warren himself had never shown much public interest in those protections—he had, after all, seemed a dedicated protector of the status quo and a prosecutor of labor. Kenny was delighted, and announced his endorsement as promised. The Hollywood Central Young Democrats condemned him, saying, "Every loyal Democrat should know that Earl Warren is a reactionary Republican."[26] Tom Mooney, still politicking for his pardon from his jail cell in San Quentin, warned Kenny that he would withdraw his support for Kenny's senate candidacy unless Kenny reconsidered his support for Warren.

Kenny held his ground. His endorsement was brave and influential, as the election returns were soon to show. But his real contribution to Warren was putting the Alameda district attorney to the exercise of the statement. It forced Warren out of his natural tendency toward problem solving and required of him a rare trip into philosophy. As a result, the statement, along with subsequent remarks elucidating it, marked an unusually expansive public reflection by the still-developing politician. Having put his views into words, Warren now set out to live up to them. The statement that Kenny extracted from Warren in the summer of 1938 was delivered for political purposes, but its commitments would be fulfilled many times over by a man destined to leave a deep imprint in the fabric of American civil liberties. Remarkably, it flickered first in the summer of 1938, with Warren's father's murder still fresh in his mind.

As Warren campaigned through the summer of 1938, his effort was largely overshadowed by the gubernatorial contest of that year, one that saw Sinclair's failed efforts from 1934 resurrected in milder form by Culbert Olson. Olson undeniably looked like a governor. He had a lean, handsome face, set off by a shock of white hair. His life was devoted to liberal causes and to firm principles. Raised in Utah as a Mormon by a mother committed to women's suffrage, Olson rejected his faith and successfully secured office in Utah as a Democrat. He worked for child labor laws and other Progressive legislation but became frustrated by Utah's conservative politics. In 1920, Olson made his way to California. Then, in 1934, he naturally endorsed Sinclair's EPIC campaign, and while Sinclair's defeat ended his own political career, Olson survived the contest, becoming Democratic Party chairman and winning a seat in the state legislature along with a number of other EPIC candidates who rose even as Sinclair fell. In 1938, Olson attempted to pick up the EPIC banner and carry it forward without the distracting presence of Sinclair. Although Olson would never electrify California the way Sinclair had, nor would he terrify it. He was blessed with a weak opponent in Governor Merriam, whose pointy-elbowed politics seemed more tiresome in 1938 than in 1934, when they were contrasted with the grandiose alternatives offered by Sinclair. That fall, Olson became the first Democrat of the twentieth century to win the governorship of California.

Warren cross-filed on the Republican, Progressive, and Democratic tickets (the Progressives had, by 1938, split from the main guard of the Republican Party). He easily won the Republican and Progressive party nominations for attorney general. More surprising, he edged out his closest Democratic contender, though by a margin so small that he might have lost without Kenny's endorsement. A write-in campaign for a dark-horse candidate buzzed Warren until November, but he overcame it without much trouble, and on November 8, the same Californians who picked Culbert Olson to be their governor overwhelmingly elected Earl Warren as the state's attorney general.

In time, Warren would put his father's murder behind him. Back came the reserve that characterized so much of Warren's public image. Never again would he cry in public over the murder. Never again would his children see him mourn their grandfather. What were left were lessons and a more nuanced politician and man than the one who began the year: To Warren's abhorrence of crime was added a new appreciation for civil liberties, an appreciation tested by the murder and found stronger. That commitment would waver in the coming war, as it would for many of America's great civil libertarians, but civil liberties were now part of Warren's quiver. By the time he sat to write his memoirs, Warren, back under control again, had transformed the murder of his father from a personal tragedy into an object of cool reflection.

"My father's death," he wrote, "must go down in history as one of the thousands of unsolved murder cases that plague our nation each year and cause such general apprehension for the security of our loved ones, ourselves, and our homes."[27]

Chapter 6

# PROGRESSIVE

*His tasks of early manhood*
*Were never known to fail;*
*He chased all lawless villains*
*And locked them up in jail.*

*And when his neighbors bade him*
*Their pirate foes to vex,*
*Forthwith he cracked the masthead*
*Of the gambling schooner "Rex."*

WILLIAM SWEIGERT ON WARREN[1]

ARL WARREN'S first sixty days as California's attorney general in 1939 exhumed his past and foretold his future. In those two months, Warren unveiled the modern attorney general's office as he had recast it with the constitutional amendments of 1934. He reprised his corruption-busting days as a prosecutor in the tradition of Hiram Johnson, using the new powers that he had written for himself. And even as he did so, he tiptoed through the astonishing collapse of his chief Democratic rival for power. Earl Warren took the oath of office on January 2; by the end of February, he was the only consequential politician left standing in California.

Warren arrived early for his first day of work on January 2, 1939. He found two phone messages, one from Walter Jones, the editor of the McClatchy newspapers in California, the other from Joseph Stephans, president of the State Prison Board.[2] Warren assumed them to be social calls welcoming him to his new job, and he happily sat down to return them. It was not yet nine A.M.

Within minutes, Warren was being briefed. Stephans and Jones had heard rumors that an extraordinary sale accompanied the final hours of the administration of Governor Merriam. As of that morning, Merriam had only been gone for a few hours, but according to the reports that Stephans and Jones were hearing, Merriam's private secretary, a cocky young lawyer named Mark Lee Megladdery, who also was Merriam's nephew, had spent those waning moments selling gubernatorial pardons. Prisoners who had access to cash allegedly paid Megladdery, who in turn secured them release from custody by convincing Merriam to sign orders freeing them. Warren called Megladdery, who confirmed that he'd been paid $500 by a San Francisco tavern owner named Clarence Bent, but said the money was a contribution to Merriam's campaign fund and not given in return for a pardon. Megladdery also boasted that he was now out of reach, as Merriam had awarded his aide with a Superior Court judgeship in those same final hours of his administration. Warren, who insisted on modesty in his staff, was unimpressed by Megladdery's swagger—he answered Warren's questions "glibly but not truthfully," Warren recalled later.[3] He ended their conversation convinced that there was more to the story than Megladdery was admitting.

Faced with an investigation that threatened to implicate the outgoing Republican governor, Warren conferred with Culbert Olson. The two met in Olson's suite, as new to Olson as Warren's was to him. If Olson had reservations about entrusting such a task to a Republican, he did not share them; instead, he directed Warren to press ahead. "I am going to continue this investigation to develop the facts," Warren told reporters after his conversation with Olson.[4] Amazingly, that would be the last face-to-face meeting that Olson and Warren would ever have alone.[5]

Within a day, Warren's doubts about Megladdery were deepening. After preliminary inquiries, Warren determined that the money Bent paid was made on behalf of a convicted murderer, Clarence A. Leddy, and witnesses now put the amount at $1,250.[6] In addition, a retired member of the California Assembly, C. C. Cottrell, told Warren's staff that when he had raised the possibility of a pardon for a constituent, a member of Merriam's staff—unnamed by Warren—had offered to secure it in return for a deal to "split the fee" with the assemblyman. Cottrell said he told the governor's aide to "go to hell."[7]

Warren was in a familiar, if risky, position. He was at home prosecuting political corruption, but such cases always involved some hazard—in this case, Warren proposed to take on the outgoing governor and standard-bearer for the state's Republican Party, which was, after all, Warren's party, too. And Warren had only barely moved into office. Still, there was the upside. How better to prove one's nonpartisanship than to prosecute a fellow Republican? Besides, there was his deep offense at graft. If Warren felt conflicted, he did not show it. There is only scant suggestion that he altered his routine at all in those early days of 1939. His calendar, compiled daily by Helen MacGregor, was filled with the customary club and group meetings. Warren supplemented her entries in his handwriting, adding, for instance, an eleven A.M. meeting with Cottrell during that first week.[8] That Friday night was the governor's Inaugural Ball. Unlike his other responsibilities, this one was easily missed. His handwritten note dismissed it. "Not attended," he wrote.[9]

As Warren hunted for witnesses in the pardon-sale investigation, Olson took command of the state government—and for one brief moment it seemed he might succeed. His inaugural speech urged that both sides put the election behind them, and he promised to work with a skeptical business community long accustomed to Republican governors. For the most part, the message was well received. The *Stockton Record* called the message "conciliatory and conservative." The *Los Angeles Times* was more guarded. Although the *Times* allowed that the speech was "restrained, dignified, conciliatory and considerably less leftward than many had expected," the paper added that it was "less informative than might be desired and self-contradictory on some important points."[10]

By week's end, Olson had confirmed the worst fears of the *Times* and its business allies. During the campaign, Olson had said he would, if elected, consider pardoning Tom Mooney, the long-imprisoned labor activist convicted in the San Francisco Preparedness Day bombing of 1916. On Saturday, January 7, Culbert Olson gave Tom Mooney his chance to go free.

Mooney had been incarcerated at San Quentin ever since his conviction. But after the trial, questions were raised about the evidence against him. Eventually, even the trial judge lost faith in the verdict, and President Woodrow Wilson intervened, concerned that the execution of a man regarded around the world as a labor victim of capitalist brutality would embarrass the United States. Governor William D. Stephens refused to pardon Mooney, but he did agree to commute Mooney's sentence to life in prison.[11] That avoided an international incident but prolonged the issue. The longer Mooney and his codefendant, Warren Billings, sat in prison, the more their case became a divining rod in California politics. Conservatives believed them radicals and rightly placed behind bars. Liberals saw them as wrongly convicted and sentenced by a stiffly right-wing government warped by its pursuit of "reds." Conservatives drew strength from the *Times*'s bombing case, when labor's frame-up cries had proved so humiliatingly false; liberals pored over the Mooney trial record and exposed its many inconsistencies. Undecideds were few, the center invisible for so long that it had effectively ceased to exist.

Warren held few illusions about the Mooney case. He opposed a pardon for a man whom he believed guilty, and Mooney had done nothing to court Warren's favor. It had only been a few months since Mooney had threatened to pull his support from Robert Kenny when Kenny had endorsed Warren for attorney general, a meaningful threat given Mooney's international standing. Still, Warren knew he was unlikely to persuade Olson to keep Mooney in prison—the political gap was too wide. Instead, Warren urged only that Olson refrain from denigrating the po-lice, prosecutors, and judges who had supported the conviction. In an open letter to Olson, Warren wrote,

> I realize that an application for pardon is addressed to the conscience of the Governor and that there is no requirement in the law that he give consideration to any particular fact or to any legal decision involving the applicant. I trust, however, that in any action you may take on Mooney's application for a pardon you will bear in mind that today law enforcement is, at best, difficult of accomplishment and that you will neither cast any un-warranted reflection upon the agencies charged therewith, nor lend any encouragement to those forces that are opposed to the enforcement of our laws and to the maintenance of security of life and property.[12]

Others were far less temperate. Ben F. Lamborn, the brother of one bombing victim, warned Olson that if he freed Mooney, that act would "form the basis for an impeachment or recall movement."[13]

On that Saturday morning, the fifth day of the Olson administration, Mooney was brought to the California legislature's Assembly chamber. He arrived in mana-cles as the governor addressed a packed audience. Olson asked anyone with objec-tions to his pardon to stand and make his case. Five hundred people sat without moving. None rose. None asked to speak. Olson then noted for the record Warren's wish that law enforcement not be blamed for the conviction. But Olson did just what Warren had urged him not to do. Mooney was convicted, Olson said, by "false testimony."[14] That testimony, he added, was "presented by representatives of the State of California."[15] Olson asked Mooney to stand, which the graying inmate did, "his features twisting with emotion," the *Times* recorded.[16] Olson signed the full and unconditional pardon for Mooney and handed the document to him, instruct-ing the warden "to now release you to the freedom which I expect you to exercise with the high ideals I have tried to indicate." Mooney took the document and beamed while the audience rose and applauded for a full two minutes until he si-lenced the room with his hand. Then he spoke:

> Your Excellency, I am not unmindful of the significance of this gathering and the forces behind it. They are the signs of democratic expression of the people of California. I am fully conscious of the fact that new political and economic powers are at work.
>
> This is a far cry from the time when the state was controlled by a reactionary corpo-rate machine which turned thumbs down every time through the years when Tom Mooney sought justice.
>
> I recall the night of my conviction, when the jury filed in with its verdict and one of them, facing the prosecutor, drew his finger across his throat. . . .

The present system is in a state of decay, not just here but throughout the world. It will be replaced, I hope, by a new and better social order. Governor Olson, to that cause I dedicate my life. . . .[17]

With that, Mooney was free. The pardon was a moment of high triumph for Olson, a symbolic recognition of labor's restoration in California politics, with a new governor at its head. One can imagine the rumblings in American Legion halls and at gatherings of the Masons. For as surely as Olson's gesture was meant to encourage labor, it was just as obviously guaranteed to antagonize labor's opponents—the employers, Republicans, and newspaper bosses who were Warren's core supporters.

In addition to being divisive, the moment was short-lived. Mooney proved a far more effective martyr than spokesman, as the coming months would reveal more of his difficult personality than was apparent during his decades behind bars. His bitter assaults on capitalism, and his contention that Hitler and Mussolini were of the same cloth as American industrialists, would become increasingly hard for moderates to accept as the nation geared for war against fascism. He campaigned for the release of his codefendant, Billings, who could not be pardoned because of a previous offense; that campaign fell short when the State Pardon Advisory Board voted 3–2 against it. The deciding vote was Earl Warren's. With the hyperbole and bombast that would soon wear out his welcome among many Californians, Mooney charged that Warren was a "virtual personification of the rotten, reactionary, corporate-banker-controlled, Republican machine."[18] Billings's sentence was then commuted by Governor Olson, and he was freed.

Olson's victory was even briefer. Mooney was freed before noon on Saturday, January 7. For a few hours, Olson relished the acclaim as news of the pardon rocketed around the world. But late that afternoon, the new governor visited the state fairgrounds in Sacramento, where he attended a barbecue with more than 130,000 others. As he took the microphone and began to speak, the governor swayed and stumbled, his speech faltering.[19] His son, Richard Olson, grabbed the microphone from his stricken, silent father and apologized to the crowd, explaining that the governor "has not had any sleep for 48 hours and hasn't been feeling well all day."[20] Culbert Olson was helped to a car by friends and from there rushed to a hospital. He spent the next month in bed. Olson then recovered from exhaustion just in time for his wife to die suddenly in April. He was stricken a second time, so devastated that he could not bring himself to continue living at the governor's mansion, where his wife had died. Olson's administration never regained its footing.

Warren did not approve of Olson's decision to pardon Mooney, but he held his tongue publicly. He returned instead to the pardon-sale scandal. On Monday, January 9, with Olson still hospitalized, Warren arrived in his office for a scheduled interview with Megladdery. Megladdery stood him up. Instead of appearing as promised, he sent along a statement to an angry Warren, announcing his refusal to cooperate after a week in which he had "been harassed by unjust accusations and rumors." Warren brusquely responded that Megladdery's refusal to be interviewed was "not an indication of a free conscience, in my opinion."[21] Warren called on old friends in Alameda, where the presiding judge of the Superior Court refused to let Megladdery hear cases until the accusations against him were resolved. Megladdery was increasingly defensive; now he also was isolated, unemployed, and unprotected by his judgeship—just as Warren wanted him.

Even the Republican press gathered around Warren, notwithstanding the potential implications for ex-governor Merriam. The *Times*, after skeptically reviewing Megladdery's public statements defending himself, found that the allegations added up to "an astonishing mess" and concluded, "About the only bright spot in the whole affair is the determined effort of Atty. Gen. Warren to get to the bottom of it, regardless of politics."[22]

All that remained was for Warren to administer the coup de grâce. After a bruising grand jury proceeding in which Merriam himself was summoned twice and Megladdery took the Fifth rather than answer questions about his actions, support for him disintegrated. Warren's deputies uncovered bank accounts with far more deposits than Megladdery's salary warranted, and witnesses insisted that money he claimed to have accepted for Merriam's campaign never reached the governor's political offices. On January 23, Merriam dumped Megladdery over the side, conceding that he would not have given him a judgeship "if I knew last month what I know now about him."[23] Megladdery resigned from the bench on January 25, having never heard a single case. Clarence Leddy, whose last-minute pardon had caught Warren's eye in the first week of the investigation, was indicted on February 3 for lying to the grand jury about his meetings with Megladdery. Then, on February 11, Megladdery and his law partner were charged with bribery and grand theft. Instead of a judgeship, Megladdery would be convicted and sentenced to San Quentin. Merriam, though not directly implicated in the case, was tarred by it beyond redemption. Though some, including Mooney, would fault Warren for not seeking an indictment against the governor, the damage was done: Merriam never again won elected office.

By the end of February 1939, barely two months into the new terms of office, much of California's established political leadership had collapsed: Olson literally and Merriam figuratively. The state's political landscape now suddenly was far more open than it had been when the year began, as the champions of both poles of California's polarized politics were now vastly reduced in stature. Warren's standing, meanwhile, had only grown. He had moved with smart, nonpartisan professionalism—the hallmarks of his candidacy and now of his record. Warren's future was brighter than ever in the spring of 1939.

His position was strengthened as well by a key addition to his staff. Warren Olney III had been a vital aide to Warren in his Alameda County days, but Warren had reluctantly let him go when Olney's father beseeched the district attorney to persuade his son to return to the family law firm. Olney left, but when his father died two years later, Warren immediately asked Olney to rejoin him, now in the office of the state attorney general. Olney buried his father and returned to Warren the following Monday.[24] Many good men and a few women enjoyed Warren's trust over the years, but none ever commanded his respect in quite the same way as Olney, with his apolitical devotion to service and family and his strict, unbending principles. When Olney returned in May 1939, he became chief of Warren's criminal division.

As Warren surveyed his personal options during those months, it was at the outset of a momentous time in California and the world. Nineteen thirty-nine was a signature year, one of those bursts of creativity and passion and violence that occur every few decades, and are dazzling in retrospect. In 1939's twelve months, Hollywood released *Gone With the Wind, The Wizard of Oz, Stagecoach, Mr. Smith Goes to Washington, Of Mice and Men, Wuthering Heights,* and *Dark Victory.* In Europe, James Joyce completed *Finnegans Wake.* In California, Steinbeck published *The Grapes of Wrath* to wide acclaim and furious banishment: Warren's hometown of Bakersfield was one of many in California that barred its children from reading the book.

Steinbeck's fictional account paralleled that same year's publication of Carey McWilliams's *Factories in the Field,* which documented those conditions with precise and moving journalism. The appearance of *Factories in the Field* and *The Grapes of Wrath* in the same year was a coincidence; Steinbeck and McWilliams did not even know each other. But together, their two books supplied much of the public with its first sympathetic looks at California's farmworkers. The farmers who employed those workers were accustomed to power and not to questions, and the books convinced them they needed a champion to argue their case. They turned to Warren.

If the arts were prodigious, politics was perilous and growing more so. On April 1, 1939, Franco completed his rout of Spain's Republican forces and imposed his vengeful dictatorship on that nation's people. FDR opened the New York World's Fair twenty-nine days later, proclaiming that "the eyes of the United States are fixed on the future." The nation's wagon, he said with a firm voice and confident chuckle, was hitched to "a star of peace."[25] Even as FDR spoke, Hitler restlessly extended the reach of his Reich, and Japan's generals stirred in anticipation of their own coup.

Warren thus came to prominence on a stage of local and international tumult. His first targets were familiar—corruption and vice would always be reliable foes for him. Gambling was a particular peeve, as he had long before watched railroad men gamble away their salaries and had joined the Progressives in part because they tapped his abhorrence of vice. That mandate was reinforced in 1939 by the persistent hold of the Depression, then in its tenth year and stubbornly oppressing the lives of Californians. Faced with widespread poverty and empowered as California's top law-enforcement official, Warren took aim at those who would take advantage of the poor.

"Professional gamblers," Warren wrote to police and prosecutors in 1939, "are the most persistent of law violators. They have no scruples as to how they secure immunity for their illegal operations and their large profits make them a power in any community where they obtain a foothold."[26] In addition, as he once wrote a lawyer with a client inquiring as to whether Warren enjoyed the support of gambling interests, the men who backed wagering were "the most corruptive influence in local government." To the lawyer, Warren added, "you may assure [your client] that it will meet with no sympathy from my office."[27]

Good to his word, Warren moved first against California's dog tracks. John "Black Jack" Jerome was at the top of the list. Warren summoned the tough track owner to a meeting in early 1939, informed him that his business was illegal, and told him he would soon be shut down, by force if necessary. Jerome briefly protested and asked for time to consult with a lawyer. Warren agreed, and Jerome made a call. The three then discussed the matter further, and Warren promised that he was not singling Jerome out but rather launching a larger effort against dog tracks in general. Warren's record of that conversation illustrates the depth of his loathing for gambling and its social consequences, as well as his compassion for those affected by it. "You are employing a number of men to assist you in these operations and are thereby directly causing each of them to commit felonies in the course of their daily employment. I do not believe that these men, if left to their own devices, would thus be violating the law," Warren wrote to Jerome.[28] If the track was closed down immediately, Warren added, the employees would not be arrested or prosecuted, sparing them "the resulting hardship and suffering to their wives and children." Jerome agreed, and closed his track that weekend.

Over the coming months, Warren shut down the rest of California's dog tracks, and every time the owner of one threatened to defy him, Warren's deputy, Oscar Jahnsen, asked, "Do you think you are tougher than Black Jack Jerome?" Warren's efforts wiped dog racing out of California; it has never returned.[29]

While the dog track owners went quietly, the operators of a fleet of gambling ships in Southern California put up more colorful resistance. There, Warren and

Olney set out to clean the seas of four ships that had taken up anchorages off the coast of San Pedro and Santa Monica, two small cities south and west of Los Angeles. The planning for the raids involved extensive legal maneuvering, as Warren built the case for his authority to act against the vessels by arguing the theory that bays encompassed by headlands fell within the state's jurisdiction, even when the closest point to shore was more than three miles away. Olney and Helen MacGregor supplied research arguing the attorney general's right to abate the nuisance of the ships, in part on the headland-to-headland theory and also by maintaining that the nuisance extended to shore, since servicing the ships with customers required a fleet of water taxis. Satisfied that he could win in court, Warren then directed a careful operation for the raids—one that required restraint and a dash of high-seas swashbuckling.

One option never discussed was that of simply leaving the ships alone. Their presence off the coast, and their water taxis delivering gamblers to them at all hours, seemed to mock law enforcement. "With things like this going on, nobody can take us seriously," Warren told Olney. "We have to find some practical way of bringing these operations to a stop."[30]

On July 28, 1939, Warren and law-enforcement executives in Southern California warned the gamblers to close immediately or "we will take all necessary steps to compel them to cease their activity."[31] They refused, claiming a legal right to operate off the coast, and on August 1, Olney, assisted by Oscar Jahnsen, took command of his armada. "When the time came, I found myself, to my great surprise, the commander for all practical purposes of a fleet of four patrol boats, sixteen water taxis and seventy-five or 100 men," Olney recalled later. "We were to board and take possession of four large ships located in two widely separated bays and manned by hostile crews and all in the presence of unfriendly and excitable public participants. Quite an assignment for a young man who had never commanded so much as a corporal's guard."[32]

Olney may have been new to the business of admiralty, but he was no stranger to detail. The officers involved were carefully briefed, and Olney even thought to bring along Price Waterhouse accountants to vouch for the disposition of the money that the raiders knew they would find on board the casinos (a few photographers went along as well; Warren was not immune to the lure of publicity). As the spectacle unfolded in Santa Monica Bay, Warren played the role of theater commander. He watched through binoculars from a beach headquarters and sent in directions via shortwave radio.

The little fleet under Olney and Jahnsen's command shoved off early that morning, and three of the ships—the *Texas*, the *Showboat*, and the *Tango*—surrendered without a fight. Boarding, the investigators tossed gambling equipment overboard from one ship, causing the owner later to threaten a lawsuit for piracy. But for the most part, captains allowed their vessels to be raided, and passengers were moved back to shore without incident. The exception, and the case that made the raids a running state story for days, was that of a daring gambler named Tony Cornero and his vessel, the *Rex*. Cornero was a smuggler and rumrunner from Prohibition days whose exploits had made him a minor celebrity and longtime irritant to federal and California law enforcement. He'd once commanded a fleet of speedboats used to ferry liquor into California after dark, and rumor was that Al Capone supplied the cash that got him into the gambling business. Cornero believed he'd outfoxed local authorities with his offshore gambling ships, reasoning that California could not regulate activity beyond its waters. Indeed, by 1939, Cornero's operations were so public that they advertised in Southern California newspapers.[33] (At Warren's request, the attorney general's staff analyzed those advertisements and in June 1939 concluded that $24,375 was spent on advertising for the *Rex* in the *Times* during May and early June, another $27,075 in the *Examiner*, and $15,750 in the *Herald-Express*. Lesser sums were spent on advertising for other ships in those and other local papers.[34])

Having operated within sight of police for years, the gambler may have assumed Warren was bluffing when he threatened raids in late July. If so, that was a misreading of the new attorney general, for Warren was not inclined to bluff. Nor, however, was Cornero one to surrender easily. When the attorney general's navy arrived at the *Rex*, Cornero's crew refused to let the *Rex* be boarded: "Either leave quietly or be thrown overboard," the boarding party was told as it tried to step aboard the *Rex*. The officers retreated to their boats, and then the crew of the *Rex* opened fire on them with hoses.

Rather than try to force their way on board, the raiders, at Warren's direction, backed off and encircled the ship. "It's their next move," Warren announced with studied indifference. "We are satisfied that the *Rex* is not doing business, and if he and his crew want to remain in seclusion three miles out in the ocean indefinitely, we can wait longer than they can."[35]

Warren surmised correctly that Cornero could not hold out long. His ship was full of passengers, many of whom had hoped to duck out for a quick afternoon of gambling and who were expected back at jobs and homes. The longer the standoff went on, the more Cornero's customers would grow impatient for a resolution. Since they could not take it out on Warren, they would inevitably demand that Cornero surrender. Cornero briefly fought for time, and Warren agreed to remove his increasingly restless passengers, leaving the captain and crew alone on the ship. That ended the gambling, but not the standoff, which dragged on through the week. After five days, during which time Cornero at one point threatened to seek Japanese registry for his ship—a gambit intended to raise the specter of accusing Warren's agents of attempting to board a foreign vessel—the gambler folded and allowed the raiders on board. He would continue to fight in court until, in November 1939, the California Supreme Court upheld Warren's view of the headland-to-headland definition of California waters. With that, Cornero realized he was finished, and he accepted a fine as well as the destruction of his gambling equipment, in return for the right to keep the *Rex*, so long as it left California waters. Warren was deeply satisfied, both by the smooth work of his little navy and by the now-clear waters of San Pedro and Santa Monica Bays. "Our ultimate objective of closing all the gambling ships was achieved, and I must say that, of all the raids on law violators I have known, these, as organized and executed by Warren Olney with the help of my investigators under Oscar Jahnsen, were by far the most intelligently planned and successfully carried out," Warren wrote thirty years later.[36]

The standoff with the *Rex* did more than close down a gambling ship. It established the new power of the attorney general's office under the amendments voters had approved in 1934. And as proof that good government can be good politics, too, the raids gave stolid Earl Warren a tough-guy glamour. He liked it, and kept at it. In the coming months, investigators from Warren's office would travel the state and report back on gambling from Orange County to the Oregon border. Olney would review their work and recommend actions to Warren, who would then determine where to concentrate his efforts. Sometimes that merely involved a call to the local sheriff or district attorney; at other times, Warren could be brusque, even threatening. In Riverside County, for instance, the local sheriff resisted Warren's efforts to shut down gambling in the hotels of Palm Springs. On January 3, 1941, he got an abrupt reminder of his duties from the attorney general:

> Reliable information received this office that large-scale public gambling operations carried on on New Year's Eve . . . that all of these establishments are intending to continue gambling operations tonight and tomorrow night. We understand you were informed by letter from District Attorney Neblett several days in advance that gambling operations in these establishments were contemplated on New Year's Eve and that no action was taken by your office to prevent same.[37]

Warren called the sheriff's attention to his obligations to enforce California laws and then demanded written notice that the gambling had been stopped. There is no record of the sheriff's reply.

Warren's campaign against gambling earned him headlines up and down California, and his determined effectiveness contrasted with the flailing efforts of the Olson administration. While Warren was taking gamblers off the high seas, Olson was beset by one petty argument after another with the legislature. The contrasting images—of a professional administrator charged with enforcing the law and a partisan, beleaguered governor arguing politics with other politicians—gave Warren the upper hand in his building feud with Olson, and that advantage became especially significant as the world lurched toward catastrophe.

On September 1, 1939, Hitler invaded Poland. Roosevelt was sleeping when the invasion began but was awakened by a call at three A.M. from William Bullitt, the American ambassador in Paris. "Well, Bill," the president said. "It has come at last. God help us all."[38]

Chapter 7

# DUEL FOR POWER

*Now deeds like this were many;*
*Great Warren stood alone.*
*And soon he sought to tumble*
*King Cuthbert from his throne.*

WILLIAM SWEIGERT

(CUTHBERT IS CULBERT OLSON)[1]

THROUGH THE WINTER of 1939 and the following spring, Earl Warren's widowed mother, Chrystal, struggled with her health and fortunes. After Methias's death she had settled his estate. Her health, never strong, continued to fail. One of her few remaining pleasures was shopping with her granddaughter, Virginia, Earl and Nina's oldest daughter. The two spent many afternoons picking out gloves or other finery in downtown Oakland.[2]

One Tuesday afternoon in April, Chrystal was heading downtown to meet Nina Warren, where they too planned to spend an afternoon. Chrystal arrived first at the office building where they were to meet, but she then stumbled and collapsed outside a beauty parlor. She was carried inside, while Dr. Hamlin, the family doctor, rushed to the scene. Hamlin sent Chrystal Warren to Providence Hospital, just a few miles away. Earl Warren was at work across the Bay when the phone rang with the news. He rushed to the hospital, where he was met by his sister. Chrystal Warren never regained consciousness, but she died with her children at her side.[3] On May 3, her son presided over her funeral at Grant Miller's chapel in Oakland. Her body was cremated.[4]

With Chrystal Warren gone, her son was severed from Bakersfield and the childhood he now had left behind. He rarely would speak of it in the years to come. And yet his mother's gentle passing seems not to have moved him in the same way that the violent circumstances of his father's murder did. Warren neglected to even mention her death in his memoirs, leaving her to simply drift off the narrative as his life continued. As was so often the case, it was left to others to articulate his loss.

"As you know, the Attorney General and I have been very close personally for so long that there is a personal as well as an official feeling in my mind," his colleague Everett Mattoon wrote to Helen MacGregor after she told him of the news. "Earl has suffered much from bereavement within the past year or so but enjoys the blessings of a glorious family to be thankful for."[5]

Ezra Decoto added, "I know your mother was a fine woman because her children have been fine children, and I know that all through her life you pleased her and that she enjoyed your success in life and was proud of the reputation you built for yourself."[6]

Friends paid their respects: Warren Olney, Bill Knowland, John Mullins, Frank Ogden—all sent their sad farewells. Less personal letters poured in from across the nation, tribute to Warren's rising political position. Prosecutors, police chiefs, Governor Olson, and J. Edgar Hoover ("Dear Earl," his letter began) were among those to send their condolences. The funeral home received 164 floral arrangements for the service honoring Chrystal Warren, an immigrant widow who lived out her final years in a modest Oakland apartment.[7] Then the service was over, the mourners were gone. And Earl Warren was alone.

His mother's death darkened what was in many ways already a sad, stressful period in Warren's life, one that he shouldered with heavy grace. Though he never spoke of it, his parents' long separation undoubtedly weighed on him, and his father's murder had unnerved him to the rare point of displaying public emotion. He had pressed on in the face of that murder and through the continuing investigation, but his new job as attorney general was creating additional pressure on him personally. After years being based in Alameda County, Warren, as the attorney general, was now in the first job that forced him to work away from home. And though he was able to spend most days in the San Francisco office, even that distance meant that he often was not home for dinner and that he often slipped out of the house before dawn.

His children saw less of him, missing their Sunday outings with their father, now in demand across the state. At home, he was still the cheerful center of the family, but even there, he showed signs of wear. It was during those years that Warren developed a lifelong habit: He would nod off in any spare moment. Conversation would lull, and his head would droop. For a few minutes, Warren would sleep, then awake and take up the conversation exactly where he had left off. His children learned simply to wait during those catnaps.[8]

For Warren, whose parents were remote to him but whose wife and children constituted so much of his happiness, the new demands of his work were a burden.

He accepted them as part of the price for a job he loved and responsibilities he enjoyed. He never complained at home. But sparks of his unhappiness flickered, despite himself. Speaking at a memorial service for Justice Louis Brandeis, Warren looked out on the crowd gathered at Oakland's Temple Sinai and lamented, "I have so little opportunity to see my Oakland friends individually." That was partly simple politeness, but he added a note of sorrow: "While my home is still only a very short distance from your Temple, I am rarely in Oakland in the daytime. It seems I have become only a night resident of our city."[9]

And add to this the mounting stress and fear of war. The years 1939 and 1940 were a tense interregnum period in American life. The war destroyed friends and allies abroad, as Germany thundered through Europe, and Britain begged for American help. FDR strained to check American isolationists, including Charles Lindbergh and his America First organization, while still lending Britain enough assistance to keep it in the fight. Domestically, the threat of war sharpened political choices. Those years were good for leaders, bad for politicians. FDR in 1940 became the first president elected to a third term by voters convinced that it was no time to play politics with government. The world had suddenly become too dangerous to entrust to partisans.

Californians were of the same mind, which colored the gathering conflict between Warren and Olson.

The battle between these two stubborn, determined men had roots in their personalities, their politics, and their backgrounds. Its inevitability was assured by the pressures of war, as was its outcome. Olson had ascended through the left wings of Utah and California politics, while Warren's route had taken him through the Native Sons, the American Legion, and California's conservative newspapers. Olson and Warren had different clubs, different friends, different lives. Olson was theoretical and abstract, an atheist raised by Mormons; Warren was simpler and more direct, the son of immigrants, his father a railroad man.

Their fundamental differences were apparent in their choice of friends and advisers. By 1938, Warren's inner circle included Joe and William Knowland, two stalwart conservatives. But Warren also turned with increasing trust to Jesse Steinhart, a gifted, liberal San Francisco lawyer who came, naturally, from Warren's left but whose unerring commitment to good government won his affection and admiration. Also there at the smallest Warren table, at the most delicate moments, was Warren Olney III, heir to the long Olney family tradition—a conservative tradition but principally one of service, not of ideological struggle. And in 1940 Warren brought another adviser to his inner circle. Bill Sweigert was a poet and a man of common sense, a Democrat and a Catholic, a supporter of FDR and the New Deal who was loyal to Warren and yet willing to challenge him on areas from states' rights to the free market. Sweigert thus rounded out an ideologically rich group of intimates—

rare is the politician who can draw upon a friend as conservative as Joe Knowland and another as liberal as Bill Sweigert. As a group, they checked one another's impulses and gave Warren a range of intelligent views.

In contrast, Olson's advisers, though sometimes brilliant, were narrower. Olson's son, Richard, was a problematic source, loyal to his father but self-interested as well. Olson's cabinet comprised Democratic Party loyalists, many chosen to reward them for service, not to provide Olson with advice. Two of Olson's best appointments were that of his executive secretary, the able and intelligent Stanley Mosk, who went on to a remarkable career as a judge, attorney general, and justice of the California Supreme Court, and his commissioner of immigration and housing, the brilliant Carey McWilliams. Those were smart and capable men, and McWilliams was California's great social analyst and champion of its farmworkers. Still, even Mosk and McWilliams largely reinforced Olson's view of Warren—neither was a source of nonpartisan perspective. Indeed, McWilliams was happily a radical, reviled by California's conservatives. The Associated Farmers considered McWilliams the state's "number one agricultural pest," and McWilliams would see their work in the rise of Earl Warren, whom McWilliams derided as "the front-man" for the farmers and their big-business allies.[10]

Over the course of their concurrent terms, Warren and Olson viewed each other with increasing suspicion. Their personal differences were exaggerated by a combination of personal traits and political styles: Olson was a fiercely partisan Democrat, and Warren was sensitive to slight, so when Olson acted politically, Warren took it personally. When Warren followed his instincts, Olson thought he spied political maneuvers. As they fought, their views of each other became self-fulfilling: Olson saw Warren as a schemer, and Warren at times became one in order to fend Olson off. Warren believed Olson to be a stiff partisan, and Olson retreated to partisanship when he felt Warren was maneuvering against him. Once their conflict began, there would be no ending it until a winner was definitively declared and a loser decisively dismissed.

After canceling his appointments for several days to be with his family after Chrystal Warren's death, Earl Warren returned to work. Within weeks, that meant fencing again with California's governor, this time over the state's Supreme Court. On May 23, 1940, California chief justice William Waste, suffering from age and exhaustion, was confined to bed. By the following week, his doctors had given up all hope. He died on June 7.

Olson indicated that he intended to elevate Associate Justice Philip S. Gibson to the position of chief justice, but the governor deliberated for several weeks on his choice to replace Gibson. As Olson ruminated, word spread that one top contender was Max Radin, a beloved Berkeley law professor who had long been considered a prime contender for a seat on the court should a Democrat ever win the governorship. Radin's scholarship was extensive—his writings on Roman law were mandatory reading for Berkeley students—and his participation in liberal causes was legendary. It was no surprise, then, that conservatives attempted to knock Radin out early.

Sam Yorty, once a left-wing Los Angeles assemblyman but now an increasingly assertive conservative, accused Radin of impropriety for writing, on University of California stationery, to a Stockton city attorney to suggest that he urge a judge to impose light sentences on eighteen state employees who were held in contempt after they had refused to testify at a Yorty committee investigating the State Relief Administration. Radin suggested a "nominal fine or suspended sentence" for defendants he believed had suffered enough and whose primary offense was youth, not wickedness.[11] Local farm and business groups passed resolutions urging Olson not to appoint Radin. There were rumblings, picked up by Warren undoubtedly, that Radin had supported the *Point Lobos* defendants and that he questioned Warren's role in prosecuting them. Olson ignored the critics, and on June 26 announced that he was naming Radin to the court.[12]

California law at the time placed confirmation in the hands of a three-member panel, the Judicial Qualifications Commission (also known as the State Qualifications Commission), consisting of the chief justice, the presiding judge of the state's appellate courts, and the attorney general, Warren. The new chief justice, Gibson, was certain to vote for Radin, while the presiding appellate judge, John T. Nourse, was a conservative and expected to oppose the nomination. That left Warren likely to decide the matter, and Radin supporters initially were optimistic. As a proud alumnus of the Berkeley law school, Warren often touted his admiration for professors there, and in 1935 had described Radin as one of several "friends of many years standing."[13] And while some Republicans, notably Yorty, were opposing the nomination, Warren was, after all, a committed nonpartisan fresh from his prosecution of former governor Merriam's aide.

On July 2, less than a week after Olson named Radin, Chief Justice Gibson was sufficiently confident of the outcome that he called Warren in the hopes of moving the matter to a speedy, successful conclusion. Warren's secretary took the call and noted that the chief justice urged Warren to resolve Radin's nomination "before next Tuesday, as he desires a full court."[14]

In light of the partisan opposition to Radin's appointment, however, Warren concluded that an investigation was warranted. For that task, he turned to the president of the California Bar Association, Gerald Hagar. That should have sent a warning sign to Radin supporters. Hagar was an archconservative, a curious man to tap for the job of investigating a liberal judicial nominee. In a letter to Carey McWilliams, Radin later fumed about the bar president: "Hagar, though professing great personal friendship for me, is to my knowledge a bitter Republican partisan . . . and a confirmed witch-hunter."[15] And yet, with attentions diverted, that telling decision by Warren went largely unnoticed for the time being. As the investigation proceeded, Warren seized upon Radin's request for leniency in the Yorty case. That, too, should have signaled Warren's predisposition regarding the Radin appointment. In truth, the request was hardly scandalous. There is no bar on law professors or others expressing opinions about sentencing, and even if Radin had done so on university stationery, it was hardly a serious offense. Warren himself had occasionally urged judges to go easy on a defendant. But Warren was assembling a dossier; the Radin letters went into it.

The committee of the state bar that investigated Radin's background took testimony from many people critical of Radin and from Radin himself. The questioning was probing but not vengeful. In his remarks, Radin denied that he was a Communist or that he had ever been affiliated with any Communist group; he acknowledged that he believed one of the *Point Lobos* defendants, Conner, was innocent, but said he had never done anything to publicize that view. The committee did not express a view of Radin's suitability for office. It urged only that the Qualifications Commission closely inspect its investigative file. But then the board overseeing the state bar took the unusual step of voting on a resolution to spell out the criteria it considered relevant for the Qualifications Commission to consider when assessing a judicial nominee. The resolution suggested that no nominee should be confirmed if he had "given just ground to a substantial number of the public for believing that he is either a member of, or in sympathy with, subversive front party organizations" or if he had "given just cause for a substantial number of the public to believe that he is lacking in financial or intellectual integrity." The board approved those principles by a vote of 10–2, with three members absent, and it stressed that a nominee should be rejected if the public held those opinions, even if the nominee had not done anything to justify those public views.[16]

Those resolutions were sent to the commission, and now there was accumulating evidence that the nomination was in trouble. And yet as the vote approached, Warren's position still was in doubt. Newspapermen called in futile hopes of drawing Warren into a comment. Instead, Warren met out of public view with Knowland and Jesse Steinhart.[17] When the commission convened on July 22, it ended the judicial prospects of Max Radin. "The commission considered all the facts, including a report of the board of governors of the State Bar association and has concluded that the appointment of Max Radin should not be confirmed," Warren announced for the commission.[18] Warren's comments were clipped. He declined to release copies of the evidence considered by the commission, and he would not even tell reporters what the vote had been or how he himself had voted. In fact, the vote had been 2–1 against the nomination. Warren's was the deciding vote.

Warren's handling of the Radin nomination was not his finest hour, and his actions suggest more than met the eye. As Warren had to know, the ethics charges against Radin were thin, and his other credentials were outstanding. Warren's clos- est friends did not believe that Warren would have rejected him because of his pol- itics. "It surely wasn't Radin's so-called liberal views or espousal of liberal causes," Warren Olney said later. "Warren wouldn't have turned him down for that."[19]

After the commission's rejection of Radin, Warren stonewalled all efforts to in- quire about it. One group of liberal activists complained, arguing that the effect of the decision—as well as the secret manner in which it was reached—was to "not only undermine trust in the selective process provided by the Constitution, but to deprive the people of this state of the services of an outstanding and courageous public servant."[20] Warren was unmoved. The Radin vote stood.

Warren's silence was telling. He did not like to admit error, and when he made a mistake, his response often took on a sullen stubbornness, his true feelings re- vealed only to a few close friends and indirectly even to them. A few months after the commission vote, Warren had lunch with U.C. Berkeley President Robert Gor- don Sproul, a friend and supporter of long standing, a man Warren could trust. In language so blunt that Sproul filed it away, Warren chastised Sproul for defending Radin and for making him a member of the Berkeley law school faculty. It was, Sproul recorded, "a vigorous denunciation of Professor Radin, which very evi- dently contained a good deal of personal animus." Intemperately, Warren even ac- cused Sproul of "glorifying" Radin by denying publicly that he was a Communist.[21]

A hint of the source of Warren's "personal animus" comes through in the Sproul memo, as Warren recounted that a friend had told him that Radin believed the *Point Lobos* defendants were "framed." Radin had denied that publicly, but Warren appears not to have believed him. If so, that would suggest to Warren that Radin was a radical, for believing that the defendants were framed, and a liar, for denying it. And, most important, an enemy, for believing that Warren himself had done the framing.

With that, Warren hunkered down. He omitted all mention of the controversy in his memoirs—the only reference to the incident was added by editors after his death.[22] Warren's silence makes his actions unexplained, but the most logical infer- ence is that Warren concluded that Radin was a radical and punished him for it. When others tried to disabuse Warren of that view, he refused and then blotted out the episode from his own history.

A seething Olson resolved to get even. And he did so by striking at Warren's sore point, the *Point Lobos* prosecution. Warren already knew that Olson might attempt to reopen the *Point Lobos* case. The wife of George Alberts had written to Warren to say she was worried that Olson might agree to let her husband's murderers stand for pardon or parole.[23] Warren promptly replied, telling her that "nothing could be more unjust" than to free those killers. "I want you to know," Warren added porten- tously, "that at the proper time I will make it definitely known to the public that I am unalterably opposed to either the parole or the pardon of these men. To release them at this time for the horrible crime they committed would simply be an invitation to others so inclined to deprive other wives of their husbands and children of their fathers."[24]

In early 1940, the Advisory Pardon Board met to consider whether to recommend pardons for the three men, and Lieutenant Governor Ellis Patterson read a statement proclaiming his belief that "King, Ramsay and Conner were innocent and that justice had been miscarried." Warren, already angry that the meeting room had been changed to allow more supporters of the defendants to be present, curtly replied, "There was no question as to the guilt of any of the three men." Warren's side prevailed on a 4–1 vote, with only Patterson recommending pardons.[25]

That settled the matter for the moment, but after Warren rejected the Radin nomination, Olson ventured into *Point Lobos* again. Without consulting Warren, Olson visited the *Point Lobos* defendants at San Quentin in October 1940, an act so sure to provoke Warren's anger that it unquestionably was done with that in mind. At a news conference on October 15, the governor revealed his visit and told reporters that the men he'd met did not strike him as murderers. Olson said he was considering pardons or parole for the three men. (Wallace, also convicted of the murder, was not defended by labor, which resented his testimony against his codefendants, along with his admission of having actually participated in Alberts's beating. California law also barred Olson from pardoning Wallace, because he had a prior conviction. In any event, Olson appears never to have contemplated freeing Wallace.) In a real sense, that announcement cost Culbert Olson his political future, as it roused Warren from private anger to public rage.

Warren called the governor's comments "shocking" and responded, "Every good citizen of California should resent it. Everyone who disbelieves in assassination should protest it. Everyone who is loyal to our country in its present crisis should fight to prevent it."[26] Evidence of Warren's suppressed anger erupted elsewhere in the same statement. "Heretofore, I have never said one word against the Governor or any of his official acts," Warren said, implying that he had had plenty to say but had chosen not to, "but silence on my part in this matter would be cowardice."

The testy exchange between Olson and Warren was extended in letters between the two men over the next several days, as they goaded each other and then shared their correspondence with the press. On the day after Warren's statement was released, Olson wrote to the attorney general, promising to give the case a thorough review and snidely adding, "I hope that your own convictions regarding the guilt of these men in connection with the murder of Mr. Alberts are based upon material, tangible and convincing evidence and not upon the prejudice which seems to be exhibited in this statement of yours." Olson chastised Warren for pointing out that he had not been consulted prior to Olson's remarks, and then closed by deploring "this matter of newspaper controversy between a Governor and an Attorney General." "My decision," Olson wrote, "will finally be reached regardless of whom it pleases."[27]

As the combative tone of his letter makes clear, by this point Olson had concluded that Warren was an implacable rival, and that mollifying him was impossible and arguably counterproductive. Whether or not that was true at the moment, the public exchange of statements made it so from then on—a striking example of the self-fulfilling quality of their rivalry. Warren responded to Olson's letter with one of his own, agreeing that conflict between top political leaders was distasteful but continuing it nonetheless. Olson's letter, Warren said, "does not cause me to change one word of my statement to the effect that it was shocking to me and to everyone who believes in law enforcement."[28]

Warren ended that letter with a pledge to discuss the matter with the governor despite their differences. Months went by without action by the governor. Then, on November 27, 1941, the state parole board, whose members were appointed by Olson, voted to release the three men.[29] Warren excoriated Olson in language that precluded any reconciliation:

> The murderers are free today, not because they are rehabilitated criminals but because they are politically powerful Communistic radicals. Their parole is the culmination of a sinister program of subversive politics, attempted bribery, terrorism and intimidation which has evidenced itself in so many ways during the past three years.[30]

Mooney was the first conflict between Olson and Warren, but they skirted a direct confrontation in that case. The Radin nomination was Warren's most regrettable contribution to their fight, and Olson understandably hit back. The release of the *Point Lobos* defendants, however, was of a different type: It challenged Warren directly and personally, and it hinted that he lacked integrity. Once those defendants walked free, Olson could never again count on support from the state's attorney general.

With their feud now a matter of public record, the two men turned to the state's most pressing concern, its readiness for war. As they did, their antagonisms sharpened, and their genuine dislike for each other ripened.

By January 1941, Warren had already begun moving on his own to establish his place as the leader in preparing California for war. That month, he convened law-enforcement officers, and emerged with a plan to divide the state into nine regions, with systems in place for coordinating any needed response between police agencies. "One thing we have to avoid is the stampeding of highways for places of safety in the suburbs in case of bombing or sabotage in the San Francisco and Los Angeles areas," Warren said at that conference.[31] This type of planning came naturally to Warren: It placed him in a group of police and prosecutors, and it was nonpartisan in nature and dedicated to addressing a specific, urgent problem. Throughout 1940 and 1941, he pursued that effort through his group, named the State Civil Defense Council.

Viewed through Olson's eyes, Warren's moves looked like political base-building by a man bent on higher office. In those months, Warren told friends and family that he relished being attorney general and was inclined to run again for that office, but Olson did not know that and probably would not have believed it in any event. So he set about to check Warren's efforts, treating Warren's civil defense planning as pure politics. Olson created his own State Council of Defense, installed himself as chairman, and picked Richard Graves, an old friend of Warren's, to serve as its executive director.

Had Graves been allowed to function, Warren probably would have acquiesced; he agreed to accept a position with the council, and through much of 1941 Warren and Graves met often. Minutes of their sessions show both men contributing and lending help to each other.[32] But Graves felt hamstrung in the position, and Olson expended political capital in a labored effort to create a state guard—needed, he said, to protect California in the event that the National Guard troops were called up and sent into combat, leaving California defenseless. Olson had some legislative and press support for that idea, but as was often the case during his administration, he became embroiled in a self-defeating struggle with the legislature, in this case over the size and funding of the organization. The debates stretched on, and deals whittled away at the size and composition of the force. The eventual bill to reach Olson's desk authorized a force of only 7,000 men and no infantry units; he signed it reluctantly.[33] Yet again, Warren's effort had the appearance of being professional—an impression reinforced by the Republican media—while Olson came off as compromising and ineffective.

While Olson and Warren jostled for position, Warren was moving elsewhere to extend his reach. One of those moves, in the spring of 1941, catapulted him into new and influential company. Founded in 1872 by journalists at the *San Francisco Examiner*, the Bohemian Club was well established in fact and lore. Herbert Hoover was a member, as was Robert Sproul, Warren's friend and schoolmate from U.C. Berkeley. Its other two thousand or so members included much of the business and political elite of California and the nation. It was staid, solid, moneyed, powerful. And its annual summer camp near the Russian River was already—and soon would become even more—a legend, a conglomeration of the nation's powerful men, hidden in a redwood grove from public view and engaged in the chummy warmth of powerful men at ease. What's more, the Bohemian Club with its Grove appealed to other, less conspicuous but more deeply tended aspects of Warren's personality. It cultivated artists and encouraged song and revelry—indeed, artists were offered special memberships, and they helped enliven its annual summer retreats. As a politician, Earl

Warren naturally was drawn to the contacts that the club supplied, but he was a poet of a sort, too, and the club spoke to him in that way as well. For Warren, the Bohemian represented an apex of his long cultivation of clubs. "I have long had a desire to be a member," he wrote in 1941.[34]

Even though he was the attorney general of California, admittance was not guaranteed. He was required to produce sponsors and demonstrate a personal relationship with at least five members of the applicant committee. That he did. After due consideration, Warren was admitted to the club and, at its Grove, made a member of its so-called Isle of Aves, one of the Grove's encampments. From that day forward, Warren would rarely miss spending a few days each summer at the Grove, to escape the heat of Sacramento. There he was known in the aviary lingo of the Grove as "Snow Owl Warren" (campmates included "Fledgling Fenston," "Bald Eagle Hall," "Grouse Ganter," etc.). In the shade of the Grove's famous redwoods, and with a breeze blowing off the ocean and the nearby river, Warren would relax in the company of California's economic and political and artistic leadership.

Culbert Olson was not Bohemian Club material. So as Warren and Olson were taking the measure of each other in the fall of 1941, they were listening to the advice of two distinctly different groups of friends. That Olson would seek reelection was assumed and urged by his advisers. Meanwhile, William Knowland, after canvassing politicians throughout the state, wrote to Warren in September 1941 to report "unanimity of opinion that you would be by far the strongest potential candidate, and the only one in or out of the Republican party who could defeat Olson."[35] Still, Warren continued to resist, and appears to have been genuinely conflicted. As 1941 drew nearer to a close, Warren remained undecided, torn between his frustration with the governor and his natural caution. He conferred and listened, searching for some definitive sign that would tip him decisively toward seeking reelection or taking on the governor. War provided it.

Chapter 8

# "THE BEST PEOPLE
# OF CALIFORNIA"

*Loyalty is a matter of the heart and mind, not of race, creed or color.*

Justice William Douglas, for the Court, December 18, 1944[1]

*[H]ardships are part of war, and war is an aggregation of hardships.*

Justice Hugo Black, for the Court, December 18, 1944[2]

A FTER THE DIFFICULT WEEKS of late 1941, Earl and Nina Warren looked forward to a languid Sunday on December 7. Earl was home for the weekend, and Oakland was stirring with Christmas. The papers carried news of war in Europe and preparations for war in the Pacific—as well as continued turmoil regarding the King, Ramsay, and Conner pardons, and updates on a municipal strike that loomed for Monday in Berkeley. But there was shopping to be done, trees to buy and decorate. At 88 Vernon, the basement was bare—but not for long. On Christmas Eve, after the children had gone to bed, Earl and Nina would set up a grove of little trees, each matching the height of a child. Beneath that child's tree would sit his or her pile of presents. The children would wake and run to their trees.

With the season came festivities. That night of the sixth, the Claremont Country Club, where the Warrens were members of long standing, was hosting a Christmas gala to benefit West Oakland children. The Warrens passed, preferring to spend the night at home with theirs. All were home that holiday—except for Jim, a student at Harvard Business School, where he was enduring but unhappy, pining for his girlfriend, Maggie, soon to be his wife.[3] The rest of the Warren youngsters, from thirteen-year-old Virginia to six-year-old Robert, were in the Warren nest on the morning of December 7. Earl Warren, Jr., always an early riser, puttered around the yard with the radio on. Bobby was in the kitchen with his mother, watching her cook and licking the spoon.[4] As they worked and chatted in the kitchen, the radio interrupted with the news from Hawaii. Within minutes, the phone began to ring.

The attack on Pearl Harbor propelled Warren to quick action. He put aside his disagreements with Olson long enough to join the governor in urging calm. Olson decried "the sudden and almost unbelievable attack on Hawaii," and the following day suggested that German, Italian, and Japanese residents stay inside their homes to avoid retribution. Warren asked residents and law enforcement to be on the alert for sabotage. Anyone spying suspicious activity, he said, should call his office.[5] Warren then summoned his staff for a rare Sunday meeting. His top aides convened at two P.M. to consider their response to the war. The attack, they realized, placed the attorney general's office at the center of California's protection; Warren asked that civil defense experts be collected for a meeting the following morning. Aides scrambled to round them up.

Home late that night, Warren unwound with a long walk. The night was particularly dark, as he, a colleague, and his son Earl wandered through the Oakland neighborhood, the two men talking in low, pained voices while the boy tagged along, silently keeping pace. As they rounded a corner and headed home, the attorney general was struck hard from behind. He staggered forward, as his son and companion froze momentarily, an anxious day cresting in this darkened attack. Then up bounded Eric, a dim-witted neighborhood boxer dog, tail wagging. Earl Warren burst into laughter, gave the dog a shake, and sent him home.[6]

Over the next few days, California went from jumpy to near-panic, as the state braced for what many believed was an imminent strike or even invasion on the West Coast. The FBI rounded up suspicious aliens—German, Italian, and Japanese. More than a thousand were arrested on December 7 and 8. Newspaper reports detailed seizures of weapons, signaling devices, and radios, all believed to have been planted and readied for just this moment. Japanese fishing boats along the West Coast were beached, and the Treasury Department froze all assets belonging to Japanese.[7] On December 8, the civil defense experts brought together by Warren gathered for an emergency conference in San Francisco. Emerging from the five-hour meeting, Warren warned police chiefs and sheriffs to move quickly to secure their areas, and his comments signaled his early preoccupation with the notion that California's enemies were in its midst, not merely abroad. "We are at war," Warren said, "and are immediately confronted with the most serious law enforcement problem of all time. Sabotage is just as much a part of Axis warfare as are military and naval operations."[8]

Tips poured in to Warren's office. There were reports of weapons caches in the Sacramento Valley, of sabotage attempted or suspected. Sheriffs called, pleading for direction.[9] Planes overhead were mistaken for the enemy, and blackouts suddenly became a regular part of nightly life. Members of Warren's staff struggled along

with the rest of the state beneath the new exigencies of conflict. One night soon after Pearl Harbor, Helen MacGregor tried to make her way home with the help of
Bill Sweigert. They were trapped by the blackout rules, but managed to make it to
his house, where she then had to bunk down for the night.[10] At the Warren house,
life was similarly disrupted. One air-raid warning in early 1942 forced the family
into the basement shelter; for two days, Nina and Earl Warren and their children
slept in sleeping bags and ate sandwiches for dinner, straining for sounds of an
attack.[11]

California's fears only deepened as the Japanese Navy enveloped the Pacific Rim
with a lightning series of strikes. In the hours and days following the destruction of
much of the American Pacific fleet, Japan invaded Malaysia, Burma, Midway, Wake
Island, Hong Kong, the Philippines, and Guam. By Christmas, Guam, Wake Island,
and Hong Kong were under Japanese control. On January 2, Manila fell as well. Sin-
gapore braced for its fate. Off the coast of California, Japanese submarines prowled
and occasionally struck. Although the damage of those attacks would be tragically
exaggerated by Lieutenant General John L. DeWitt in justifying the actions he was
about to recommend, military records do reflect the sinking of at least three
vessels—the tanker *Monte Bello* and two other ships—during the week leading up to
Christmas.[12] The war had been thrust upon America, and in those weeks it appeared
quite possible that America would lose.

But what was most curious in California about the six weeks immediately following Pearl Harbor was what, despite the revisionist recollections of many historians, did not happen: Californians, so long steeped in racism toward their
Japanese neighbors, did not rise up against them, even as fury over Pearl Harbor
spread. In those early weeks, acts of violence against California's Japanese were few,
the vitriol surprisingly contained.[13] California politicians, including Warren, later
blamed the public for what happened next, but that was false. It was not the public
that led this descent. It was the work of leaders.

In the aftermath of Pearl Harbor, the state's newspapers were quiet, even respectful toward California's 93,000 Japanese and Japanese-Americans. Through early
January, the *Santa Barbara News-Press* carried regular stories about the arrests of
Japanese suspected of spying, but it also featured the story of a group of local Japanese who had banded together to contribute $3,000 a month in savings bonds and
stamps to help the war effort: "100% of Japanese families in and about Santa Barbara have agreed to buy at least one $25 savings bond a month," the group's leader
stated and the paper reported.[14] Readers had questions about how to treat Japanese
businesses and employees, and the newspaper delivered civil, careful responses. On
January 3, the *Los Angeles Times* quoted FDR at length as the president expressed his
concern over reports that employers across the country were dismissing workers of
German, Italian, or Japanese descent. FDR called that "as stupid as it is unjust" and

reminded the nation that its fight was against nations convinced of their racial superiority. "We must not forget what we are defending: liberty, decency, justice," the president said. "I urge all private employers to adopt a sane policy regarding aliens and foreign-born citizens."[15] Two days later, with Pacific Asia reeling under the might of the Japanese Navy, the *Sacramento Bee* echoed FDR and editorialized in defense of California's Japanese: "Race against race, religion against religion, prejudice against prejudice—that is the Nazi gospel. The wise and sensible American will avoid any of them as he would a deadly poison or a fatal pestilence."[16]

The gentle, protective tone continued through much of January. The *Sacramento Union* on January 18 editorialized against a proposal to investigate the backgrounds of Americans born in the United States of Japanese descent. After acknowledging the rising panic over the war, the *Union* cautioned, "It is utterly deplorable, however, that this hysteria should be reflected in demands on the part of our elected representatives for legislative investigations of the racial backgrounds of American citizens."[17] Even the *Los Angeles Times*, rarely at the vanguard of civil liberties, continued through late January guardedly to urge readers to consider Americans of Japanese descent with equanimity, if not necessarily benevolence. "Many of our Japanese, whether born here or not," the paper offered cautiously, "are fully loyal and deserve sympathy rather than suspicion." Although the paper added a note of caution—"To be sure it would sometimes stump an expert to tell which is which and mistakes, if made, should be on the side of caution"—its larger point was of restraint.[18]

Not all was calm in those weeks. Indeed, an undercurrent of concern about the presence of so many Italians, Germans, and Japanese in the United States was beginning to gather. Officials in Washington were perplexed by the question of how threatening to view the presence of more than a million immigrants from those nations with which the United States now was at war. Officials contemplated new supervisorial authority over Japanese farmers to ensure that crops were delivered as needed for the war effort. A defense plant in Los Angeles burned, and suspicion quickly focused on sabotage.[19] And a few groups, including two that Warren was a member of, the American Legion and the Native Sons of the Golden West, were all too happy to turn on the state's Japanese population. The Legion approved a resolution calling for internment on January 19, 1942, and that action was followed by strenuous local advocacy; among California Legionnaires, there were early mutterings of "concentration camps."[20] But the dominant mood of those weeks, as captured by the coverage in California's newspapers and the comments of its leading politicians, was of American solidarity—a solidarity that included Japanese-Americans—in defiance of a common enemy.

The last week of January brought a marked change. On January 24, United States Supreme Court justice Owen Roberts issued a much-anticipated analysis of the causes of the catastrophe at Pearl Harbor. Roberts's report made scant reference to the islands' Japanese population, but one short passage from the document received much attention in the days that followed. In it, the commission remarked that spies had helped the Japanese military prepare for the attack. Of those spies, the report noted, "some were Japanese consular agents and others were persons having no open relations with the Japanese foreign service. These spies collected and through various channels transmitted information to the Japanese Empire respecting the military and naval establishments and dispositions on the island."[21]

Though the attack on Pearl Harbor had not unleashed California's racism, the report on the attack did. Although the unnamed "persons having no open relations with the Japanese foreign service" were not identified in any way, much less by their race, those few words stoked the anxieties of well-meaning leaders and opened a line of attack for those long interested in pursuing their campaign against Japanese-Americans. On January 27, Los Angeles mayor Fletcher Bowron convened harbor officials and Navy officers to discuss the city's strategic defenses, and the county Board of Supervisors requested the immediate removal of "enemy aliens" from strategically significant areas. The following day, less than a week after urging sympathy for Japanese-Americans, the *Los Angeles Times* called for their removal. "The time has come," the paper intoned, "to realize that the rigors of war demand proper detention of Japanese and their immediate removal from the most acute danger spots." The *Times* showed no particular relish in that position, admitting it was "not a pleasant task," but endorsed it nonetheless.[22] Henry McLemore, a popular East Coast columnist visiting California, on January 29 called for evacuation in the harshest terms, and the *Times* published an only barely cleaned-up version:

> I am for immediate removal of every Japanese on the West Coast to a point deep in the interior. [I don't mean a nice part of the interior either. Herd 'em up, pack 'em off and give 'em the inside room in the badlands. Let 'em be pinched, hurt, hungry and dead up against it.]
>
> Sure, this would work an unjustified hardship on 80 percent or 90 percent of the California Japanese. But, the remaining 10 or 20 percent have it in their power to do damage—great damage to the American people. They are a serious menace and you can't tell me that an individual's rights have any business being placed above a nation's safety.
>
> If making 1,000,000 innocent Japanese uncomfortable would prevent one scheming Japanese from costing the life of one American boy, then let 1,000,000 innocents suffer . . .
>
> Personally, I hate the Japanese. And that goes for all of them.[23]

Those sentiments rumbled through the public, and exposed old wounds. Calls for evacuation or incarceration of Japanese immigrants multiplied. And as the momentum in favor of removal gathered force, the scope of the debate expanded as well: No longer were merely Japanese immigrants, the so-called Isei, under consideration; now, backers of removal also began to clamor for the exclusion of Nisei, people born in the United States and thus citizens, distinguished from other Americans only by their race and heritage. In Los Angeles, all city and county employees who were of "Japanese parentage" were fired, "as public officials expressed alarm at what they said was a potential fifth column danger," the Associated Press reported on January 28.[24]

Warren's actions in the days after the Roberts report was released were curious, in some respects even contradictory. When California's State Personnel Board moved to prevent Japanese-Americans from taking civil service exams, Warren objected. Such a bar, Warren concluded, would be unconstitutional and would deny Japanese-Americans—Americans, after all, born in this country—rights solely on the basis of their race. Warren's opinion annoyed members of the panel, whose spokesman told reporters that Warren was "totally misinformed" about what the board was attempting to accomplish.[25] The board then disregarded Warren's legal advice and proceeded to investigate state workers. By the end of February, the board's true motives had become apparent, and they were just as Warren suspected. On April 2, the board voted to suspend "all state civil service employees of Japanese ancestry."[26] Warren fought the board on those moves, and though he lost, he won the admiration of some of those who waged the principled effort to defend California's Japanese immigrants and American-born citizens of Japanese descent.

"This," said Dillon Myer, who was to become the chief of the War Relocation Authority, was "Earl Warren at his best."[27]

But even as Warren moved to protect some rights, he swung into action to abrogate other, far more important ones. In those pivotal days after the Roberts report was released, Earl Warren and his staff gathered intelligence on Japanese organizations and land holdings, investigated the state's ability to confiscate property belonging to Japanese, and researched the government's right to remove or detain people based solely on their ethnic and national heritage.[28] Once gathered, that information was shared with military authorities, specifically the commanding officer at the Presidio in San Francisco, General DeWitt. In personal meetings and conferences with subordinates and others, Warren and DeWitt fueled each other's suspicions, each pushing the other to see threats of attack, sabotage, and even invasion. "I was," Warren wrote later, "in constant touch with him."[29] That was Warren's bad luck and poor judgment, as DeWitt proved incapable of the command to which he was entrusted.

Born on a Nebraska army base in 1880, DeWitt was a second-generation general, his father having served in the Army of the Potomac during the Civil War and in various Army posts after that. Two brothers also followed their father into the Army, rising to the rank of brigadier general (all four DeWitts are buried at Arlington National Cemetery).[30] But while John DeWitt was long on military experience, he was short on the skills being asked of him in early 1942. A dropout from Princeton who had never spent an adult day as a civilian, DeWitt was an aging man with little experience in the subtleties of political leadership. He was untested by significant military command, and his upbringing—he had been raised in the Indian Wars and served in the brutal American campaign in the Philippines—led some to conclude that he was indifferent to the suffering of minorities.[31] When DeWitt was told that some of his desperately needed reinforcements after Pearl Harbor were black, he complained. "You're filling too many colored groups up on the West Coast," he told his superiors. "I'd rather have a white regiment."[32] He was at once insecure and arrogant, panicky, prone to outburst and susceptible to paranoia. It was not a healthy mix.

DeWitt did not at first embrace the idea of taking responsibility for the coast's Axis aliens. In Washington, the early weeks after Pearl Harbor had been marked by an intense debate between Attorney General Francis Biddle and Secretary of War Henry Stimson over the fate of the West Coast Japanese. Stimson argued for removal of some or all of the Japanese population. Biddle counseled against any such measure, and was supported by some of his own lawyers, as well as, ironically, FBI chief J. Edgar Hoover, who preferred to handle the threat as a law-enforcement matter. In San Francisco, DeWitt in those weeks struggled to articulate a firm position with respect to the Japanese, but at some points seemed inclined to oppose it on practical and constitutional grounds. "I'd rather go along the way we are now . . . rather than attempt any such wholesale internment," he said in a December 26 phone conversation. "An American citizen, after all, is an American citizen."[33]

Among DeWitt's many character flaws, however, was his tendency to vacillate. As Attorney General Biddle later put it, the general was "apt to waver under popular pressure, a characteristic arising from his tendency to reflect the views of the last man to whom he talked."[34] Now, with public anxiety rising over the Roberts Report, DeWitt came under pressure from leading Californians to act.

On January 27, DeWitt conferred with Governor Olson. Olson already had demonstrated his hair-trigger nerves on the day after Pearl Harbor when he proposed keeping enemy aliens indoors. In the weeks since the attack, he had careened from statements urging restraint toward the Japanese to others suggesting that he was fearful of what they might do. DeWitt was similarly alarmed. He was receiving reports of attacks on American shipping by Japanese submarines and of signaling by onshore spies to Japanese vessels off the coast. "Time," DeWitt wrote later, "was of the essence."[35] While the attacks on shipping were real, the grounds for suspicion of involvement by California's Japanese were far flimsier. One particular area of anxiety was the allegation that Japanese residents of the West Coast were signaling to enemy ships and submarines. Once checked, those tips invariably proved to be false—one neighbor reported on a signaling case in Santa Monica, for instance, but the Office of Naval Intelligence and the FBI concluded that it was merely someone adjusting a stuck window shade.[36] Still, the volume of such reports convinced De-Witt that some were real, and he almost certainly shared his growing anxiety with Olson. Soon after his meeting with DeWitt, Olson announced in a radio speech to the state, "It is known that there are Japanese residents of California who have sought to aid the Japanese enemy by way of communicating information, or have shown indications of preparation for fifth-column activities."[37]

In turn, Olson informed DeWitt that leading Californians were becoming increasingly uncomfortable with the Japanese in their midst. Summing up their meeting, DeWitt told Defense officials in Washington, "There's a tremendous volume of public opinion now developing against the Japanese of all classes, that is aliens and non-aliens, to get them off the land. . . . As a matter of fact, it's not being instigated or developed by people who are not thinking but by the best people of California. Since the publication of the Roberts Report they feel that they are living in the midst of a lot of enemies. They don't trust the Japanese, none of them."[38]

Having reached accommodation with Olson, DeWitt then confronted Warren. As an avowed foe of the governor, Warren was in a position to obstruct the growing sentiment against California's Japanese. Had he announced opposition to removal, the issue might well have become a partisan one, debated in the coming election. That would have taken courage, but it was not out of the question. Ever since his statement to Robert Kenny in the 1938 attorney general's race, Warren was on the record in defense of civil liberties—though his definition of civil liberties in that case turned on rights of protest and organization, not defense of racial minorities. He had shown none of the overt racism that some other Progressive politicians had succumbed to, and though Warren was a member of the American Legion and the Native Sons, he had never been enthusiastic about their anti-Orientalism. All that gave hope. Warren, however, tacked in another direction.

No record exists of his January 29 conversation with DeWitt, but the substance of it can be inferred from what each did next. The same day that he spoke with Warren, DeWitt—the same man who, Biddle archly observed, tended to reflect the last good argument he'd heard—told his superiors in Washington that he now favored evacuation of the West Coast. DeWitt specified that evacuation should include not only Japanese immigrants but also Japanese-American citizens.[39] On the following day, Warren told the Associated Press, "I have come to the conclusion that the Japanese situation as it exists today in this state may well be the Achilles heel of the entire civilian defense effort. Unless something is done it may bring about a repetition of Pearl Harbor."[40]

Warren was not alone in expressing such fear of infiltration and subversion, which stretched from Pearl Harbor to Washington. In January 1942, security was the nation's abiding concern; beneath it, cherished values gave way. And one of those values was the idea of America as a home of immigrants, where race and heritage were characteristics of its citizens but not limiting or defining ones. Instead, race and heritage became barometers of trustworthiness, even in men such as FDR and Warren. "It is difficult," Warren told the Associated Press, "to distinguish between a dangerous enemy alien, of which we are certain there are many here, and citizens who may be relied on to loyally support the United States war effort."[41] Unsaid but implied in the context of that debate was the clear message that it was difficult to make that distinction when it came to Japanese aliens, but not Germans or Italians.

When he convened law-enforcement officials the following week to assess the security situation in the state, Warren urged passage of a resolution asking the federal government to remove at once all *alien Japanese* "from all territories in the State of California within 200 miles of the Pacific Coast for the duration of the war."[42] The motion passed. With that, Warren had joined the cause for removal, but he clung to one shred of moderation. As of the first week of February 1942, Warren still proposed only to remove immigrant Japanese, those who lived in the United States but still held Japanese citizenship and who were prevented by law from becoming American citizens. He separated those Japanese-Americans who were born in the United States of Japanese parents and who were, after all, American citizens. That may have seemed like a small distinction to families threatened by removal, but it passed for a moderate position in those weeks. Indeed, that grasp for a center did not hold. The following day, the board of supervisors in Ventura County, a rural coastal area north of Los Angeles, unanimously voted to demand that the government remove not just immigrants but "all persons of the Japanese race."[43] Explaining why they deliberately went beyond what Warren and his colleagues had requested, the supervisors blandly replied that "it is impossible to know those Japanese who are loyal to the United States."[44]

The resolution requesting federal intervention attracted news coverage at the law-enforcement conference, but its real business was the commissioning of a set of maps. At Warren's charge, prosecutors and sheriffs from across the state agreed to conduct an extensive survey of Japanese landholdings in their counties. In each instance, they were to assemble lists of every rural parcel where a Japanese resident lived, worked, or owned land. The results were to be conveyed as quickly as possible back to Warren's office. Among those close to Warren, there was no doubting his enthusiasm for the project. Warren, Tom Clark told the FBI confidentially, "was making quite a drive on alien Japanese through potential violations of the alien land laws of the State of California."[45] So important did Warren believe the undertaking that he placed his most trusted deputy in charge of it. The conference adjourned on February 3, and Warren Olney went to work.

Over the next two weeks, pressure on the federal government to act mounted almost daily in California. And while well-meaning state leaders weighed constitutional protections against the perceived security threat, more venal interests also saw an opportunity to settle old antagonisms. By 1942, California's Japanese had become a significant part of the state's farm economy, specializing in low-yield, high-profit vegetables, as well as flowers, and managing many of the state's nurseries. Japanese farms were estimated in the early 1940s to be responsible for $35 million a year in agricultural output—roughly 40 percent of California's commercial truck crops—and they dominated certain crops, such as strawberries, spinach, and tomatoes. Japanese cultivated roughly 90 percent of all California strawberry acreage.[46] Their farms served California's large urban areas, and thus tended to be located on the outskirts of its large cities. And inside Los Angeles, San Francisco, San Diego, and elsewhere, they sold much of their produce and flowers through Japanese-owned stores. Carey McWilliams estimated that approximately 1,000 Japanese-operated fruit and vegetable stores existed in Los Angeles before the war, employing about five thousand people, most of them Japanese.[47]

The significant place of the Japanese in California agriculture made them natural adversaries of the state's large farming interests. Even before the release of the Roberts Report, those interests leaned on state officials to push the Japanese out and rid white farmers of their competition. On January 3, F. W. McNabb, an official of the Western Growers Protective Association, wrote to Warren to urge removal of the Japanese—as he put it, to ask that Warren "make a sincere effort to eliminate as many of these undesirable aliens from the land of California as is possible at this time."[48] Two days before the release of the Roberts Report, Western growers and shippers meeting in Florida passed a resolution urging immediate internment—not just removal—of Japanese aliens in California, Washington, Oregon, and Arizona. The resolution also called for impounding all money and property. Farms were the clear targets of that measure. Norman Evans, a Los Angeles man elected to head the United Fresh Fruit and Vegetable Association, said internment would prevent violence from breaking out between Filipino and Japanese workers. The Japanese, he said, were "a menace in this country."[49] Austin E. Anson, a Washington lobbyist employed by the Shipper-Grower Association of Salinas, was even more blunt:

> We're charged with wanting to get rid of the Japs for selfish reasons. We might as well be honest. We do. It's a question of whether the white man lives on the Pacific Coast or the brown men. They came into this valley to work, and they stayed to take over. . . . If the Japs were removed tomorrow, we'd never miss them in two weeks because the white farmers can take over and produce everything the Jap grows. And we don't want them back when the war ends either.[50]

The shippers and growers, along with the Associated Farmers, had long hitched their fortunes to those of California's Republican Party. The effort to defeat Upton Sinclair in 1934 had cemented that alliance, and Olson's election in 1938 had given the farmers new need to seek out friends in Sacramento. As the leading statewide Republican and California's top law-enforcement official, Warren was a natural ally who welcomed his backing by farmers.[51]

Until Pearl Harbor, Warren handled the Associated Farmers as he did his other troublesome supporters—by welcoming their friendship and broad goals at the same time that he abjured their more extreme ideas. In 1940, for instance, he spoke to the association but pointedly withheld his support for the organization's growing prejudice toward Japanese farmers. "Should we be in trouble with the Axis Powers, there will be more than three million of their nationals in this country," Warren said, "but I have enough confidence in human nature to believe that the great majority of them will be loyal to the land of their choice. We must promote this loyalty. We must see to it that no race prejudices develop and that there are no petty persecutions of law-abiding people."[52]

That was 1940, when war was Europe's problem. By 1942, when America was at war, Warren was prepared to join the farmers, if not in their bigotry, at least in its effect. By mid-February, law-enforcement officials and farm representatives had responded to Warren's call for their assessments of the situation in each of their areas, and Warren's staff produced an extraordinarily damaging dossier on the threat of the Japanese to California's security. Thirty-five of California's fifty-eight counties responded to Warren's request for information about Japanese leases and land ownership. Their reports were assimilated by Warren Olney in San Francisco. The result, Warren concluded, "shows a disturbing situation."[53]

Olney and Warren found concentrations of Japanese land along electrical lines, railroads, military bases, oil fields, and coastal areas that could be used for invasion. In the fog of conflict, the colored pins on the maps that Warren hung on the wall of his office seemed to present a pattern: To Warren, at least, it appeared that California's Japanese had acquired land in order to hold it until it was needed to wage sabotage or invasion of the United States. "Such a distribution of the Japanese population appears to manifest something more than coincidence," he declared. And even if it did not, he added, "the Japanese population of California is, as a whole, ideally situated ... to carry into execution a tremendous program of sabotage on a mass scale should any considerable number of them be inclined to do so."[54]

There was another explanation, however. Japanese farmers had purchased coastal land because it offered the right climate for the table vegetables they specialized in growing. Others had picked up scraps of property along railroads and electrical lines because it was cheap and available. Indeed, in some cases they picked up those parcels because they were the victims of racist practices that kept better property out of their hands. In effect, then, the Japanese of 1942 were being accused of conspiracy because the Japanese in the years leading up to that point had been the victims of prejudice.

Despite the flaws of his argument, Warren was persuasive, in part because he enjoyed a reputation for fairness and in part because he was diligent in advancing his argument. In early February, Warren began collecting the maps and sharing them with selective, influential audiences. In one crucial gathering, Warren brought together defense experts and Tom Clark, then the Justice Department's representative in California in charge of evaluating the Japanese situation (and later to be Warren's colleague on the Supreme Court). With them, too, was Walter Lippmann, the premier newspaper columnist in America. Lippmann was beating a particular drum during those weeks. In columns and speeches, he berated leaders for failing to bring America quickly to wartime footing, and he chastised citizens who wanted to protect themselves rather than pursue the enemy abroad. "Pearl Harbor," Lippmann argued, "really was the reflection of America's 20 years of self-indulgent refusal to believe the facts of life." America was faced, Lippmann said, with a long war, one that could be won only if it dedicated its strength to attacking its enemies, not to pulling back in self-defense.[55]

With that in mind, Lippmann came to California to study the civil defense situation, and soon encountered Warren. At a meeting in Montecito, an elegant little community on California's coast, Santa Barbara district attorney Percy Heckendorf presented the map of his area to Warren, Clark, and Lippmann. "Mr. Lippmann," Heckendorf recalled, "showed great interest in the map and the significant things that were shown on it."[56] Having reviewed the map and interviewed Warren about its significance, Lippmann set to work writing his column. Headlined "The Fifth Column on the Coast," Lippmann's piece appeared in the *Los Angeles Times* and other papers on February 13, and it adopted Warren's fear of sabotage and invasion: "Nobody's Constitutional rights include the right to reside and do business on a battlefield," he wrote. "And nobody ought to be on a battlefield who has no good reason for being there."[57]

Attorney General Biddle, then still attempting to head off the internment and the military's support for it, bitterly denounced Lippmann and other advocates as "Armchair Strategists and Junior G-Men."[58] Biddle had no way of knowing it, but one of Lippmann's "armchair strategists" was Earl Warren. For while Lippmann did not directly attribute any argument to Warren, Heckendorf wired Warren to congratulate him for his role in shaping Lippmann's views on the subject and on the column's subsequent influence on the debate.[59]

As Lippmann was writing, Warren stepped up his other efforts to build support for the forced removal of the Japanese. At a meeting with the state's leading anti-Japanese organization on February 7, Warren suggested that its members pressure federal authorities to act against local Japanese residents. Undoubtedly referring to the malleable DeWitt, Warren advised that authorities seemed to him responsive to lobbying: "[I]t is my opinion," he told the members of the California Joint Immigration Committee, "without reference to any individual, that, generally speaking, the military and national authorities here would not be averse to having pressure applied in order to show the rest of the country just what their danger is here."[60]

By February 11, Warren had crossed the final Rubicon in his view of what was needed. That day, he was accompanied by Clark and Los Angeles mayor Fletcher Bowron, as the three met with DeWitt. Before the meeting, Warren, Clark, and Bowron agreed that Bowron would take the lead in presenting their position, which all three shared. And it now had become their view—and thus Warren's view—that removal of *all* Japanese and Japanese-Americans was justified, regardless of citizenship, immigration status, or evidence of wrongdoing. Mere ethnicity, to them, warranted removal. Describing that meeting, Bowron said he and his colleagues advocated removal even though they realized "that many of the Japanese were citizens."[61] Since immigrant Japanese were not citizens, Bowron could only have been referring to the Nisei, those people born in the United States of Japanese parentage. Additionally, Warren's maps were now nearly complete, and they identified all land within their counties "owned, occupied or controlled by persons of the Japanese race."[62] No distinction was made between Japanese immigrants and American citizens of Japanese descent. The maps blended those distinctions, showing in red not only those rural properties occupied by immigrants but also the holdings of Nisei. (Indeed, much of the land owned by Japanese in California was actually owned by Nisei, since California's Alien Land Act, then decades old, prohibited Japanese immigrants from purchasing or owning real estate; the law was widely evaded by the Japanese parents, who later turned over title to their native-born children.)

The logic of Warren's maps, like the rest of his presentation, was difficult to resist by desperate, blindered leaders. In his final report on the internment, DeWitt adopted Warren's research at great length and used it to justify the removal. In fact, large sections of Warren's report were simply lifted verbatim by DeWitt—the description of Japanese land ownership in the Santa Maria Valley, for instance, and Heckendorf's analysis of the land situation in Santa Barbara County. "Whether by design or accident, virtually always their communities were adjacent to very vital shore installations, war plants, etc.," DeWitt wrote later. "While it was believed that some were loyal, it was known that many were not."[63] DeWitt's choice of words illuminated his state of mind. To him, "some" Japanese were "believed" to be loyal, "many" were "known" to be not.

On February 14, after speaking with Clark, Bowron, and Warren, DeWitt made his final recommendation to the secretary of war. He asked that the secretary exclude all Japanese aliens and Japanese-American citizens from the West Coast. Other aliens—Germans and Italians—were only to be removed if found to be enemies. In recommending that course, DeWitt also adopted the looking-glass logic that corrupted clear thinking in those vital weeks. Addressing the question of how to justify a mass deprivation of rights in order to prevent sabotage when no acts of sabotage had been committed, DeWitt wrote, "Along the Pacific Coast over 112,000 potential enemies, of Japanese extraction, are at large today. There are indications that these are organized and ready for concerted action at a favorable opportunity. The very fact that no sabotage has taken place to date is a disturbing and confirming indication that such action will be taken."[64] In short, the absence of sabotage became the basis for believing that serious sabotage was being planned. Law-abiding behavior was evidence of insurrection in the works. Warren subscribed to that view as well. What, he and DeWitt might have asked themselves, would a loyal Japanese-American do under those circumstances to convince authorities of his loyalty, if even doing as they asked would be cited as evidence of subversive intent? Once passions had receded, the absurdity of that argument was plain. By then, it could be viewed only with heartache.

Through those weeks, Warren's views on California's Japanese had marched steadily ahead. Never had he uttered a public word of restraint. Not once had he expressed regret about the ramifications that his course of action would have on a substantial bloc of California's population. Warren's abiding sense of duty—his preoccupation with the need to defend California from its enemies—pressed him grimly forward, over hurdles and past restraints. He first stood in defense of Japanese state workers, only to then support their removal altogether. As that idea attracted support, Warren did not lift a hand to help nearly 100,000 California residents whose safety it was his job to protect under constitutional amendments he helped write and under the oath he took as attorney general. His actions against the Japanese bore his trademark effectiveness. His silence in their defense spoke for itself.

Canada began forcibly moving its Japanese population in January. FDR, who six weeks earlier had criticized private employers for firing immigrant workers, on February 19 authorized the military to do whatever it saw fit to safeguard the Pacific Coast. Executive Order 9066 did not mention the Japanese by name, but Roosevelt knew it would be applied only to them. Similar measures were undertaken throughout Latin America and the Caribbean.

Earl Warren's most comprehensive comments on the removal came two days after FDR's order, when he appeared at the first session of the Tolan Committee, a congressional panel on migration that came to California to discuss the possible movement of its Japanese residents. Because Warren's testimony came after the issuance of FDR's order, some of Warren's defenders have downplayed the significance of his remarks. And it is true that his testimony did not, by itself, shape the order. Still, that ignores Warren's actions leading up to his appearance. For weeks, he had been consulting with the principals—especially DeWitt and Clark. He lobbied them personally and asked others to do so as well. Thus, while the testimony did not influence FDR's decision, the thoughts contained within it did, and the significance of the testimony is that it helps reveal the substance of Warren's communications in the days preceding it.

Warren appeared shortly after nine A.M., hustling into the witness room armed with his maps, as well as testimonials he had solicited from sheriffs, prosecutors, and agricultural representatives. Greeted warmly by the chairman, Warren's Oakland neighbor John Tolan—"I found out 25 years ago that in the trial of a lawsuit you take very good care of yourself," Tolan said as Warren took the stand—Warren settled in quickly to the business of his presentation. He opened with the ominous observation that "there are some things transpiring in our State at the present moment that are rather dangerous, and we believe that there is only one way that they can be prevented, and that is by a speedy solution of the alien problem."[65]

Remarking on the curious absence of sabotage since the outbreak of war with Japan, Warren expressed the tortured logic that he and DeWitt shared: "I believe that we are just being lulled into a false sense of security and that the only reason we haven't had a disaster in California is because it has been timed for a different date. . . . Our day of reckoning is bound to come in that regard. When, nobody knows, of course, but we are approaching an invisible deadline."[66]

In one revealing passage, Warren told the committee that his suspicion was based in part on the lack of cooperation that he and other law-enforcement officers were receiving from Japanese residents. Not one Japanese person, he said, had come forward to help any police agency anywhere in California.[67] That was false. Warren himself had repeated during the February 2 conference what police had reported to him: that "five or six" individuals had come forward offering help. What's more, Warren's own staff had been approached by at least one young man pledging his allegiance to the United States and offering to take on jobs for investigators in order to prove it. Sherrill Halbert, a deputy attorney general working for Warren, wrote to Warren Olney about that contact, saying the young man was "willing to do undercover work or anything else that we might ask him." "Personally," Halbert concluded, "I suspect all Japanese, but as they go this man, who is twenty-five years of age, impressed me as being frank and sincere."[68]

There is no evidence that Warren or his staff followed up on that contact, made less than a week before Warren testified to the Tolan Committee. It offered evidence that should have leavened Warren's assertion that no Japanese were willing to provide information. But Warren was in no mood for equivocation. He pressed on.

In another section of his testimony, Warren revealed the blandly shared racism of the period. "We believe that when we are dealing with the Caucasian race we have methods that will test the loyalty of them, and we believe that we can, in dealing with the Germans and the Italians, arrive at some fairly sound conclusions because of our knowledge of the way they live in the community and have lived for many years," Warren said. "But when we deal with the Japanese we are in an entirely different field and we cannot form any opinion that we believe to be sound."[69] Warren saw the Japanese as "different" and was utterly undisturbed by that belief.

Demonstrating how his views had hardened in the short time since he had endorsed the removal of alien Japanese but not American citizens, Warren noted, "While I do not cast a reflection on every Japanese who is born in this country—of course we will have loyal ones—I do say that the consensus of opinion is that taking the groups by and large there is more potential danger to this State from the group that is born here than from the group that is born in Japan."[70] Warren valued "consensus of opinion." Discerning it was his great strength as a politician devoted to centrism. Here, however, the notion failed him. A majority committed to a wrong is still wrong. That idea eventually would become clear to Warren, whose Supreme Court service was distinguished by respect for minority rights against majority interests. But not in 1942.

The Tolan Committee heard from a long list of witnesses, almost all in support of the removal. But Warren's testimony was singular—argued well, delivered by a smart and respected politician. Warren, McWilliams remarked later, "was, perhaps, the most forceful advocate of mass evacuation."[71]

In his defense, Warren never urged that the Japanese, citizens or noncitizens, be interned. He merely proposed, as Lippmann had, their removal from the coastal zone, where attack and sabotage were most threatening. That testifies to his motives—Warren did not approach the alien problem with venom or greed; it was security that concerned him, not vengeance. But it also reveals his overriding commitment to security and his lapsed judgment in the face of danger and political pressure: Where, he might have asked himself, were these 100,000 people to go once forced from their homes, farms, and businesses? Removal placed people adrift. When the initial order for removal came, many confused Japanese evacuated their home communities and moved just over the line of the coastal restricted zone into California's Central Valley. There they were met with suspicion and alarm. If they were too dangerous to live on the coast, could they really be trusted inland?

Faced with the social turmoil caused by evacuation, DeWitt soon turned to internment. By the end of March, California's Japanese were being removed from their homes and taken first to assembly centers and later to detention areas—in effect, prisons. In all, 110,000 Japanese were transported to desert and mountain camps that were hundreds, sometimes thousands, of miles from their homes. Detainees included men, women, and children. Most were incarcerated behind barbed wire for the balance of the war. Many lost homes, cars, furniture, a lifetime of savings and possessions. Even pets were prohibited from the camps.

The cost was enormous, personal, and capricious. As the orders solidified, family after family, all up and down the West Coast of America, sold what they could in the week to ten days that they were given to report. One young woman, her story preserved by a student project decades later, was married on April 5, 1942, and the following day left for the first stop in what would be a three-and-a-half-year journey of imprisonment:

> Honeymoon in horse stables. Sand. Dust
> Odors of hay. Like animals herded. Here.
> We were Americans, most of us,
> But our skin was yellow, we were quiet.
> We turned ourselves outside in. We showed
> No one ourselves, especially not ourselves.
> I drank imaginary champagne, shook imaginary rice
> From my hair.
> No one sent congratulatory telegrams.[72]

Some puzzled over whether the orders applied to them and desperately attempted to comply without destroying families and children. Elaine Black Yoneda was a white woman, a native of Connecticut. Her husband, Karl, was a Japanese-American, born in the United States and educated in Japan. They had a three-year-old son, Tommy. Karl volunteered to help construct Manzanar when that facility was first commissioned, hoping to build habitable spaces for those destined to go there. Karl was at Manzanar in March when Japanese along the coast were ordered to report for processing. Alone and frantic, Elaine Yoneda desperately sought to learn whether Tommy, who was half-white, would be interned. The answer: Tommy was ordered to camp, and Elaine, his mother, was told she could not accompany the three-year-old boy there because she was white. "You needn't, nor will you be allowed to go," an Army captain told her.[73] Refusing to be separated from her son, Elaine Yoneda forced her way onto the train. After months, she and her son were released, but only after she agreed to submit monthly affidavits to General DeWitt attesting, among other things, that Tommy had not been in fights because of ancestry and had not endangered national security. Once free, Tommy was required to be in the custody only of a Caucasian.

Others tried to soften the impact of the evacuation orders, but to little avail. In Los Angeles, Father Hugh T. Lawery at the Catholic Maryknoll Center questioned whether the order should apply to the center's orphanage, where a number of infants, some of mixed race, were being raised. Colonel Karl Robin Bendesten, a

Stanford-educated lawyer serving on the General Staff, responded, "I am determined that if they have one drop of Japanese blood in them, they must go to camp."[74]

For Hideo Murata of Pismo Beach, a small town on California's central coast, the order to report was too much to bear. Murata was the proud recipient of an Honorary Citizenship Certificate, in which Monterey County formally thanked him for his service to his country in World War I—"Our flag was assaulted, and you gallantly took up its defense," the proclamation read. When the order to evacuate came, Murata presented the certificate to the county sheriff, hoping his military service and honorary citizenship would protect him, wondering if, indeed, this was some sort of joke. He was informed that it was serious and applied to him. So Murata paid for a hotel room and checked in. In his room, alone, he held his certificate in one hand. And then he killed himself.[75]

Not one act of sabotage was ever attributed to a Japanese or Japanese-American resident of the United States.

Warren's support for this mass denial of civil liberties was far from a lonely one. It was ordered by FDR himself and supported by many of America's leading liberals. Culbert Olson tried to soften the removal in some respects, but endorsed it along with the great mass of Californians, liberal and conservative. When Kiyoshi Hirabayashi challenged his arrest for violating a curfew order and failing to turn himself over for removal from his hometown of Seattle, the United States Supreme Court upheld DeWitt's authority to impose restrictions on the West Coast Japanese.[76]

As he did after defeating the nomination of Max Radin to the California Supreme Court, Warren after the internment retreated into churlishness. For decades, he refused to discuss the matter publicly, and though later in life he would sometimes reflect on it with his Supreme Court clerks, he maintained a stubborn public silence. To his friend Drew Pearson, Warren confessed pain at the decision. Typically, it hurt him most as it struck most closely to his own experience. "One man, Tasheto Ogawa, had served with me in World War I and was wounded," Warren told Pearson in 1967. "You can imagine how I felt sending him away."[77] Still, Warren did send him away, without apologies.

Tom Clark, Fletcher Bowron, and others who worked with Warren to support the internment made their amends after the war. Warren refused. Thirty years after the fact, Warren declined an invitation to deliver a commencement speech when protesters questioned his internment actions.

Beginning in 1967, Edison Uno, who spent four and a half years in the Crystal City Internment Camp, asked Earl Warren for the apology he felt was long overdue. Writing to *Life* magazine and to Warren directly, Uno urged the chief justice to "publicly settle any doubts about the loyalty of the Nisei for once and for all."[78] When Uno received a belated reply, it came from Warren's secretary, who informed him that she had not had the chance to speak with Warren about his request but warned him that no response was likely to be forthcoming. "He has stated on many occasions that it is a historical fact of many years ago which under no circumstances could be undone, and that it would serve no good purpose to dredge it up at this time," Margaret McHugh wrote. One can only assume that Warren, who was scrupulous with his mail, approved that unsatisfying language. Still, Uno persisted despite the warnings of others in the Japanese-American community that Warren would never be budged. He and other members of the Japanese American Citizens League continued a persistent campaign to convince Warren to reconsider. Reading those appeals decades later, one cannot help but be struck by their clarity and their immense sense of propriety. The men and women who wrote to Warren gave up some portion of their lives in part because of his mistake, and yet not once in their letters was there blame or anger. Instead, they appealed to his place in history and to his demonstrated belief in civil rights and racial equality. "We of the Japanese American Citizens League sincerely admire and respect your judicial leadership in the area of extending civil liberties to all Americans," one letter read. "It is precisely because we feel this way that we ask your help in dispelling the cloud that still hangs over us."[79]

In April 1969, in his final months as chief justice, Earl Warren returned to Boalt Hall, the law school at U.C. Berkeley, to deliver "Observations on Human Rights and Racial Discrimination." It was a moment of great personal satisfaction for a law student of little note who had risen to the pinnacle of his profession and performed with historic significance. Warren was the toast of the university he cherished, and on that day he basked in its approval. But seated at the front of the auditorium were twenty-five determined Japanese-American students. They sat during the standing ovation. The organizer asked if Warren would take questions, but the chief justice, staring into that knot of unfriendly faces, declined.

Outside, on the patio of the Earl Warren Institute, well-wishers pressed forward, eager for a word with the nation's leading justice and the university's most distinguished graduate. When the Japanese-American students interrupted him, one demanded that he explain his role in the internment. "You will have to ask the federal government about that," Warren said. Students quoted Warren's own words from 1942 back to him, and he again replied, "It was done because of federal law."[80]

Still, they pressed, challenging his view of the law—challenging *him*, the Chief Justice of the United States, these students forty years younger than he—demanding that he apologize, *here*, at his university, on his day. "Is it true," one student called out, "that you, of all the principal figures involved, are the only one who has refused to admit error?"

"Yes," Warren answered, "that is true. I never apologize for a past act. Besides, that is just a matter of history now."[81]

And with that, Earl Warren tucked in his chin, set his jaw, and pressed forward through the line. He never looked up, never took the bait, never apologized to those who could not reconcile the great civil libertarian with the man who had interned their parents and grandparents, without a charge having ever been filed or a suspicion ever verified.[82]

The closest that Warren would come in his lifetime to saying he was sorry for his role in the internment came in the form of a letter endorsing the Japanese American Citizens League's long quest for repeal of Title II of 1950 Internal Security Act. That title gave the government authority to open detention camps during a national emergency, and the JACL had begged Warren, then retired, to join them in seeking its repeal. Receiving no reply from him directly, members of the organization lobbied through his son, Earl Jr., then serving on the bench in Sacramento. Warren's response finally came, in the form of a letter written to Jerry Enomoto of the JACL. In it, Warren supported repeal of the law, which he described as "not in the American tradition." And in a wistful allusion to his own role in just such a violation of the "American tradition," Warren added, "I express these views as the experience of one who as a state officer became involved in the harsh removal of the Japanese from the Pacific Coast in World War II, almost 30 years ago."[83]

With that, Uno and his colleagues accepted the closest thing to an apology they would ever receive from the chief justice during his life. Only in his memoirs, published after his death, did Warren finally and publicly acknowledge how wrong he had been, and even then he fought a rearguard action to circumscribe his responsibility for it. Warren noted the atmosphere in California and the strong support for removal, and emphasized that his position had been "not to intern in concentration camps *all* Japanese, but to require them to move from what was designated as the theater of operations, extending seven hundred and fifty miles inland from the Pacific Ocean [emphasis in original]."[84] Warren must have recognized the limited usefulness of that hedge, for he hastened to add, "Of course, for most of them it was the same as directing their confinement." Having lamely attempted to limit his responsibility to his testimony and to confine his testimony to removal, Warren then finally admitted error:

> I have since deeply regretted the removal order and my own testimony advocating it, because it was not in keeping with our American concept of freedom and the rights of citizens. Whenever I thought of the innocent little children who were torn from home, school friends, and congenial surroundings, I was conscience-stricken. It was wrong to react so impulsively, without positive evidence of disloyalty, even though we felt we had good motive in the security of our state. It demonstrates the cruelty of war when fear, get-tough military psychology, propaganda, and racial antagonism combine with one's responsibility for public security to produce such acts. I have always believed that I had no

prejudice against the Japanese as such except that directly spawned by Pearl Harbor and its aftermath.[85]

That apology was long overdue, and it was given only after excruciating effort. Indeed, some of the apology may not even have been Warren's at all.

In the draft of his memoirs, which Warren felt were sufficiently complete to send to close associates for their review, he did allow that he "regretted" the order, but it was only in his edited reflections, released after his death, that his apology had been scaled up to say that he "deeply regretted" it. Indeed, an advance copy of the text, leaked to the *Washington Post* after Warren died, included this sentence as it appears in Warren's manuscript: "I have since regretted the internment. . . ." Warren's regret somehow deepened only after he had died.

For some of those who had lost homes and property, Warren's expression of regret was welcome, although many resented having had to work for it for so long and to have heard it only after he died. And yet for some who had stood with him, it was unnecessary, even objectionable. Warren Olney was Warren's great ally in that and so many other fights, but he took rare issue with Warren over the apology. Reflecting on the events that led to the internment, Olney correctly noted that Warren was disingenuous to blame the internment on "hysteria" when no such clamor had existed until politicians, including Warren, created it. Olney also emphasized the threat of invasion in those months and concluded of the internment, "It was believed to be necessary in order to meet an immediate and major danger to the safety of the country. I was convinced then and am convinced now that it was motivated by nothing else."[86]

For Warren, the decision to push for exclusion represented a concession to fear, along with a more admirable devotion to security. In one sense, in fact, it reflected his exaggerated and in this case misguided sense of service. Warren was committed to the public interest, and he defined that interest as the general security of California, not the particular protection of its Japanese residents. It is notable, for instance, that in his eventual apology, he took care to remark that he had "always believed" that he was not motivated by racism, leaving open the possibility that he was so motivated but was unaware of it. He advocated internment not to punish the Japanese but to protect the rest of California. Warren was not, then or ever, a racist in the most venal sense of that word. But he embodied the racial callousness of his times. In the debate over the internment, that hardness tragically shielded him from the implications of the policy decision he worked to achieve.

Warren's position on the internment also reflected the peril of allowing his political philosophy to be grounded foremost in associations. As 1942 began, Warren was a member of the Native Sons. His supporters included the American Legion and Associated Farmers, Joseph Knowland and the *Los Angeles Times*. He had tempered those relations, always emerging at the moderate edge of his conservative base. His inclination to seek the center had helped him, keeping him at arm's length from California's reactionaries, even as he managed to take their votes. In 1942, however, those cultural and political leaders lurched to the right. Warren's sponsors and friends abandoned all devotion to the constitutional rights of thousands of their fellow citizens. And when they plunged over that cliff, Warren, whose political philosophy was insufficiently developed to give him a strong personal counterweight, went right with them. "I think he was entrapped to a certain extent by his own political support . . . and a kind of political environment out of which he came in California," McWilliams said of Warren at that juncture.[87]

He never did again. After that episode, a larger Warren—bigger in his appreciation of people, deeper in his commitment to social justice—came to dominate his persona. It did not come about all at once; in his first year as governor, he would sound again the alarm about the West Coast Japanese. But the 1942 campaign would expand Warren's vision, just as the attorney generalship had broadened his reach. By the end of that campaign, Warren, though philosophically not a different person, was a man of more solid beliefs, more sensitive to the vulnerabilities of the minority, less subject to the stampede of the majority.

In that sense, the internment can be seen as the culminating mistake of the first act of Warren's life. From 1891 to 1942, Earl Warren grew up in California and learned from it—he absorbed the best and worst of its Progressivism, and he found a sober center when there was one to find. But he was in 1942 still in some ways a backward leader, one who extracted his views from others. The man whom California was about to discover as governor, and whom the nation would soon come to know as a justice, was still stubborn, still principled, still devoted to service. And yet he was bigger, too. The campaign of 1942 and the governorship it brought him would broaden Warren, and the Court would bring him the power to extend his vision to the nation. By 1953, Earl Warren was a more complete man and a more compassionate politician than the attorney general who lost his reason for long enough to incarcerate an innocent people.

If Warren never quite owned up to his responsibility for that calamity, he accepted his role in it and moved forward, as part of his lifelong, sometimes exasperating, determination not to dwell. "Mistakes are not uncommon to human nature," he wrote many years later on a different subject, though in words resonant with the lessons of his actions in 1942. "[T]he test of character is whether one has done everything in his power to rectify them. If that has been done, and the lesson from it is firmly embedded in one's mind, it should become part of the dead past."[88]

PART TWO

# In Command

Chapter 9

# VICTORY

*Whether I had been elected or not, I would have considered the campaign one of the great experiences of my life.*

EARL WARREN, JANUARY 29, 1943[1]

WHEN 1942 BEGAN, Earl Warren was easily misunderstood for a fully realized man and politician. He was half a century old. His oldest son was in business school, his youngest in first grade. He had lost both his father and his mother, one to murder, the other to age and illness. After more than two decades in public life, Warren had important friends. The state's leading newspapers, the Masons, the Bohemian Club, and the leaders of the Republican Party all formed a broad and significant base of influential support. He also was defined to some degree by his opponents: Organized labor still had not forgotten *Point Lobos,* and the liberal intelligentsia would never forgive his treatment of Max Radin. All of that suggested a type recognizable to most Californians: Warren was, by those outward appearances and ties, a Republican in keeping with California's long, dour tradition of that party.

Warren's political views, background, and predilections all seemed to corroborate that stereotype. He believed in restrained government and strong enforcement of the law. He deplored gambling and other vice, and had built a reputation for prosecuting political corruption. The New Deal offended his sense of propriety, never mind EPIC. He liked steaks and chops and nights out with men. He listened to others but guarded his own feelings. He was a veteran. He even looked the part. He was handsome but stern, his strong face framed in horn-rimmed glasses, his eyes usually hard with resolve, occasionally hinting at sadness. In official appearances, he was rarely photographed with a smile.

And yet Warren was not a fully developed man. Even after decades in politics, his horizons were narrow, confined mainly to public safety and law enforcement. He read often but not widely, history but not philosophy, poetry but with a bent toward the accessible, not the reflective. He rarely traveled outside California. He believed in God and saw to it that his children attended the Sunday school of his wife's faith, but he was not strongly religious. He joined clubs and organizations for the camaraderie, but with the exception of the University of California and the Masons, his participation in those groups was more social than heartfelt. He even had a more complex view of the New Deal than he allowed for publicly—its encroachments on states' rights and the right of contract annoyed him, but Warren recognized the need for centralization in the fields he knew best and was open to the importuning of friends more liberal than himself.

What all that meant was that Earl Warren, in early 1942, was a politician in a sense unallied, rooted in his relationships with people and organizations but still unencumbered or clarified by a guiding philosophy. He thought of himself as a Progressive, but that meant less as the Progressives passed from relevance. He had lit upon nonpartisanship as the way to describe his values, but his nonpartisanship was really the expression of opposition to something he abhorred—destructive adherence to a philosophy—not an affirmative statement of what he believed in. Sometimes, in fact, it felt like a bit of a dodge. As attorney general, Warren had touted nonpartisanship, but in a distinctly episodic fashion. He abjured partisanship in California but seemed comfortable with it elsewhere. Warren continued to represent California at Republican national conventions, and he supported the party's nominees in presidential elections. Moreover, much of his tenure as attorney general had been defined by his increasingly testy squabbles with Democratic governor Culbert Olson. It should not have surprised him that many Democrats, including Olson, thought nonpartisanship was a fraud, donned merely to help Warren politically in a state where Democrats outnumbered Republicans.

Beyond his abiding belief that government should solve problems where they arose, Earl Warren, even at the age of fifty, possessed no articulated theory of how government could best help its citizens across the range of human problems. Nineteen forty-two would change that. When it ended, Earl Warren had made an important move. The war had helped to sharpen and intensify political choices, and Warren had evolved into a new breed of politician by the end of that year. He entered 1942 with friends and principles; he ended it with a philosophy.

Differences on pardons, labor, and civil defense set the tempo of the conflict between Warren and Olson, but it was the outbreak of war that gave their bout significance. Immediately after Pearl Harbor, Olson warned that "this state may at any time become a theater of war" and declared a state of emergency in California.[2] His proclamation was broadcast the following day as an all-points bulletin. It gave the relevant authorities the right to act under that decree. In naming those authorities, however, Olson omitted any mention of Warren, a slight that can only have been intentional in light of Warren's law-enforcement responsibilities and his public statements regarding civil defense. Warren pounced. The governor's authority to declare an emergency, Warren announced, was intended to combat natural disasters—earthquakes, fires, floods, and the like—and did not extend to wartime. In effect, Warren accused Olson of declaring martial law.[3] Olson protested, but Warren's staff scoured the proclamation for flaws, and exhaustively researched the legal history of the emergency powers of the California governor.[4] They eventually prevailed. Olson then sulked, refusing to call the legislature back into special session to deal with wartime matters, because he believed Warren and other Republicans would use the session to attack him. The resulting standoff only deepened the sense that Olson was unable to forge alliances in order to steer California in wartime.

By then, Warren was moving with studied efficiency, cutting off Olson in the areas where the governor most needed to demonstrate leadership. Richard Graves, the governor's choice to head his defense council, had agreed to take the job on the condition that Olson not impose hiring limits on him. Graves, the head of the California League of Cities, well knew Olson's reputation for using appointments to settle political debts, and so he insisted on supervising hiring at his own agency. Olson agreed to that condition, and Graves then accepted. But even though Graves had voted for Olson, he was an old friend of Earl Warren's. He consulted Warren before taking the job, and told his old friend of the condition that he'd placed on it. Warren was wary. "Watch it," the attorney general said. "It'll come. It's only a question of when."[5]

As Warren predicted, the time came. Olson called Graves one day and begged to be released from his pledge, saying he needed to find places for some Democratic allies. Graves again consulted Warren, telling him he was inclined to quit if pressed. "That's what you should do," Warren replied crisply. The next day, Graves resigned and switched his registration from "decline to state" to Republican. Graves that day became a Warren Republican; he was not the first Democrat to do so, and he certainly would not be the last.[6] Despite the deepening crisis in the Pacific, Olson did not convene the council again until April 18.[7] By then, the council was enmeshed in politics, and Olson's days as governor were running out.

In the meantime, Olson tried to check Warren where he could. When Warren set about preparing his civil defense maps depicting Japanese land occupation, for instance, Olson attempted to insert himself into that project. On February 10, the governor wrote to General DeWitt to ask DeWitt to send him a map identifying all the state's military-sensitive installations. Pointedly, Olson also asked for a second copy of that map, which he promised to share with Warren; that, the governor said, was preferable to DeWitt communicating directly with the attorney general, which Olson warned would cause "confusion and duplication of effort."[8]

The same week, Olson lit upon another opportunity to tweak his rival, and this one stung. When Warren's office submitted a supplementary budget request for $214,740 to cover additional expenses brought on by the outbreak of war— Warren's staff was running a 24-hour-a-day operation in early 1942—the legislature readily approved it. Olson then vetoed the bill.

Warren bit his tongue. Out of view, however, the attorney general calculated his response. Through the early months of 1942, Warren met frequently with his top political advisers, considering how to address his frustration with the governor. Was the answer accommodation or challenge? Or was it to confront the matter head on, to use the coming election to run himself and knock away the man who seemed so determined to obstruct him? Warren's choice was not an easy one. He enjoyed the job of attorney general and seemed a prohibitive favorite to win reelection. At $11,000 a year, the pay was good—always a factor in his political calculations. Indeed, Warren in those days was paid more than the governor, who made just $10,000 a year. He chafed at the obligations of his state post and the time it took him away from his family, but he worked mostly from San Francisco, so at least his children were in their own home and schools.

Warren's choice had significant implications for his family. Nina had managed to elude the public eye during Warren's time as attorney general. Asked to be excused from politics, she instead was raising their children, insulating them from the publicity of their father's work. At the beginning of 1942, their oldest, Virginia, was on the precipice of her teenage years (Jim, of course, being nine years older than Virginia, was already out of the home, having graduated in 1941 and now trying to enlist for military service), and Bobby was a kindergartner following his brothers and sisters into California's public schools. They were, to a remarkable degree, allowed to grow up outside the world of politics despite their proximity to it. Warren rarely brought work home; when emergencies occurred after hours, he dressed and went into the office. The Warrens almost never entertained for business purposes at home, relying instead on the many clubs that Warren had joined to supply meeting places. Although the pickets during *Point Lobos* had reminded the Warren family of the passions their father could stir, 88 Vernon in 1942 remained a family refuge, busy and bustling with children but unaffected by the rising influence of its presiding officer. Warren liked it that way. "My father liked his house," Virginia Warren recalls. "He was out so much that when he was home he wanted some quiet."[9] That he was able to achieve that peace at home was a tribute, all the children agree, to Nina Warren. She would see to the children's needs and settle their disputes before Earl returned in the evening. Nina was loving but also effective and, when necessary, cleverly indirect. One week, when all the children but Jim neglected to clean their rooms, Nina pooled their 25-cent allowances, piled the quarters up on a table, and gave the whole kitty to Jim. That was the last of that insubordination.[10] Thus it was almost always a quiet house that greeted Earl when he came home from work, took his nip of bourbon or scotch while dressing for dinner, and then sat to hear the stories of the children's day.

While Nina handled routine disputes, Earl was reserved for more serious matters. He himself occasionally had been on the wrong end of a birch rod as a child, but he did not strike his own children. They were instead subjected to his disappointment, which was withering enough. A child who came home with a bad grade would be asked to take a walk around the block with Earl, who would ask for an explanation and then listen, his silence conveying his disapproval.[11] Sometimes his discipline was more punitive. When Jim Warren skipped Sunday school one day, Earl took away movies for a month.[12] But while Earl could be stern, there was no pressure added on the children because of his position. They were expected to try hard and complete what they started, to tell the truth, and to find their own interests—not because of their father's fame but rather because that was what Earl and Nina required of their children. Remarkably, and largely thanks to Nina, they did. "As a child," Earl Jr. recalls, "I never thought of my father in political terms."[13]

To run for governor was to risk upending that hard-earned balance at home, to take a cut in pay, and to move to Sacramento. All of that argued for skipping the race. Olson, however, was bedeviling him, and Warren's closest advisers—at least those whom he consulted about politics—wanted him to run. As the state's most prominent Republican, Warren represented the party's best chance to recapture the governorship. And still a third option was raised by the war: Having missed combat in World War I, Warren was eager to lend his services to this conflict, and he had kept up his work with the reserves. With the war now on, Warren inquired about rejoining the Army, and about entering the service as a colonel. Nothing came of that, but weeks ticked by, and Warren's silence only fueled speculation. In late March, he called his staff together to tell them of his plans.

"[W]e sat down," said Adrian Kragen, a member of the attorney general's staff. "And he said, 'I know all these rumors are going around, that I'm going to run for Governor of the State of California. And it's caused a lot of uncertainty around this office. And I want you to know I'm not going to run.'"[14]

For the staff, that was a relief. They could go back to work and set politics aside. California's leading Republicans were not, however, in the mood for that answer. From March 13 to April 9, Warren met five times with Jesse Steinhart and once with Steinhart and William Knowland together.[15] Through Knowland, Warren was connected to his past—to Joseph Knowland and the first campaign for district attorney, to the days of anti-Communist prosecutions in Oakland and the punishing campaign to defeat Upton Sinclair. Knowland had his father's devotion to Earl Warren. By 1942, few men knew Warren better or had better sources among the conservatives who dominated the California Republican Party. Knowland had scouted out Warren's prospects well in advance, compiling his information into a thoughtful, detailed appraisal in the fall of 1941.[16] Now, with the election approaching, Knowland redoubled his campaign to draft Warren, urging him in strong terms to take Olson out. Los Angeles mayor Fletcher Bowron was considering a run, Knowland said, but he would probably lose against the incumbent. Others were similarly positioned. Only Warren, Knowland believed, could win. And so he leaned on Warren's competitiveness and irritation with Olson and on Olson's potential vulnerability to a strong challenge.

Steinhart was gentler, his pitch less political and more intended to appeal to Warren's sense of service. Steinhart was an archetype of a certain breed of public man, as rare then as it is today. He never sought elected office but helped shape a generation of California's political leadership by pressing others to service. Humble, incisive, gifted in his judgment of people, Steinhart was a successful business lawyer in San Francisco and a longtime admirer and backer of Hiram Johnson. In the 1920s, when Warren started receiving positive coverage for his work as district attorney in Alameda, Steinhart called him up and asked him to lunch. The two enjoyed each other—two such serious, civic men—and over the years since had kept in close touch, with Steinhart providing important support during the attorney general campaign of 1938. Now, Steinhart was among Warren's most regular appointments. Rarely a week went by that they did not talk, either in person or over the phone. And he brought not just depth but breadth to Warren's circle of advisers, Steinhart being a relatively rare Jew at Warren's table. Their families were close, with the Warrens occasionally spending a day at the Steinhart home in Los Altos, south of San Francisco.

On April 3, Warren, Steinhart, and Knowland met together in Steinhart's office in San Francisco. Knowland made the political case, arguing forcefully that Warren could win and that he owed it to himself and to California to run. "I pointed out to him that he was the one man in my judgment who could defeat Olson," Knowland said. "I didn't think there was any doubt that he could be re-elected Attorney General, but he would then be faced with four more years of an Olson administration."[17] Although Steinhart's advice is unrecorded, his appeal undoubtedly was to Warren's sense of mission—that their shared commitment to service demanded that he set aside personal considerations and take the office from a governor who was failing at a time of national urgency. They went over the results of a secret poll, commissioned to give Warren a sense of how he might fare in a head-to-head against Olson; the poll had gone into the field in March, so its results were fresh. How encouraging they were is unclear, as the results have not survived, but Knowland was keen to digest the figures and clearly intent on using them to bolster his case for Warren's candidacy.[18] Still, Warren refused to commit.[19]

And still, his advisers pushed. The following day, the Saturday before Easter,

Earl and Nina Warren lunched with Steinhart yet again.[20] Nina had her own reservations about a bid. Among them, Earl said later, was the question of how he might do. "[S]he asked if I thought I could win," he said.[21] Although Warren portrayed his conversation with his wife as one-sided—him announcing to her that he had at last made up his mind to run and her acquiescing after a few questions—her presence at the lunch with Steinhart on April 4 suggests otherwise. Nina Warren was not overtly political. But this would not be like 1938, when Warren was an experienced prosecutor seeking what amounted to a step up and into an open seat. To run for governor against an incumbent in the middle of a war would require Warren to campaign in a larger context, to sell his whole person to an immense state and to persuade Democrats to abandon their governor and join him. As Nina Warren surely recognized, that meant that the Warren family could no longer stay out of the campaign. Defeat would involve all of them and might well end her husband's political career. Victory would change their lives even more deeply. In addition to the required move to Sacramento—hard on five school-age children—a win in November would transform her husband into a national political figure and would bring his family along as well. For Nina Warren, defeat would be bad enough. Victory might be worse.

But whatever concerns Nina Warren had about the move were subordinated to her faith in her husband. And he had reached his wit's end. "I would not sit on the sidelines for a term as attorney general while we were in the midst of a war that threatened our very national existence," he declared.[22] After talking with him—and presumably hearing Steinhart's pitch as well—she yielded. "All right," she told her husband, "if that is the way you feel, you should do it."[23] It fell to Nina to tell the children, which she did without fanfare. One by one, she casually let them know that their father was about to become a candidate for governor.[24]

Two weeks after having told his staff he was not running for governor, Warren was back. "Contrary to what I told you," he began, and this must have elicited a chuckle or a gasp, "I have been convinced that the only way that we can save the State of California from the tremendous disaster which the continuance of the Olson administration would bring to the state, is for me to run. I don't want to run," Warren added a bit disingenuously, since it was he who felt the frustration of fighting with Olson. "I like this job, but I'm forced, as a citizen of this state, to accept the decision of others that it's the only way we can defeat Olson, and I'm running."[25]

"That was it," Kragen recalled.

On April 9, 1942, Warren announced his candidacy for governor of California.[26] The times, he said, required "a unity of purpose that rises above every partisan consideration." While Warren acknowledged his long association with the Republican Party, he said he did not consider that relevant to the issues confronting California or to those he had addressed thus far in his career. California's issues,

Warren said, were those of "the security of the people in their homes, the administration of our schools, business methods in government to prevent overtaxation,
civil service to prevent the spoils system, conservation of our resources, both human and natural, to prevent exploitation, the social services to raise living standards, co-operation with the agencies of the Federal government to carry out
national policies, and now civilian protection to further the war effort." None of
those, Warren argued, required partisanship, merely leadership.[27] Olson issued no
immediate response, but others took quick note. Wasting no time and surprising
none of its readers, the *Los Angeles Times* endorsed Warren on April 11.[28]

Although newspaper support was assured, Warren did not enter the campaign
as a favorite. He had no conventional political machine to press his candidacy. His
fundraising apparatus was essentially nonexistent, and his relations with some Republican Party leaders were tenuous. He had sparred with Herbert Hoover, Frank
Merriam, and William Randolph Hearst—a Republican former president, a Republican former governor, and a Republican newspaper baron—and all within the
last few years. He discouraged his own staff from participating in his campaigns,
telling them that the best they could do for him was to produce a record he could
run on. Some helped anyway, which Warren allowed without much comment. But
that hardly constituted a full-fledged campaign.[29] And yet Warren was not without
other resources. The anti-Sinclair campaign in 1934 had introduced him to top political operatives, and his own 1938 race had broadened his political appeal and
spread his name identification. Warren's chief task in those early days was to find
someone to organize his effort. He turned to the consulting firm of Whitaker and
Baxter, the husband-and-wife team who had overseen Sinclair's demolition.

Clem Whitaker and Leone Baxter were the best political operation in America,
and their talents were particularly well suited to the emerging politics of California—
especially the opportunities that its Progressive-era reforms had created for political operatives such as themselves.

Clem, a journalist as a teenager and young adult, came from a left-wing family.
His uncle, a Socialist minister, had delivered one of the eulogies at Tom Mooney's
funeral. And Clem himself had once been a friend of Sinclair's. But Clem Whitaker
left journalism for business, and in 1933 founded Campaigns Inc. As a businessman, he moved sharply to the right—that was, after all, where the money was—
specializing in campaigns for conservative candidates and causes. Whitaker's
partner, Leone Baxter, had started as his employee and then became his wife. He
was intensity and blaze—tall, thin, chain-smoking, fast-talking, demanding. She
was curvy and genteel, an attractive redhead with a deceptively soft touch.

What they shared was ruthlessness. Whitaker and Baxter were dedicated to the
creation of a new form of politics and devoted to winning for their clients. Long
before it became commonplace, they brought all the elements of a campaign into a

single operation—they handled media, speechwriting, advertising, public appearances, endorsements. They conducted negative research on opponents, crafted
strategy, and recruited volunteers. Cross-filing and the initiative had weakened traditional party leadership in California; Whitaker and Baxter picked up the work
that state party organizations did elsewhere. They were a full-service political operation, maybe the first of its kind. In 1942, they put that machinery to work on behalf of Earl Warren.

Four days after Warren announced his candidacy, Clem Whitaker called to
gather materials for the campaign. That initial request suggested the dual lines that
the campaign was to take: He needed a detailed story of Warren's life and a "running and complete story of the King, Ramsay, Conner case."[30] Warren's own story
would represent the campaign's positive element; Olson's pardons and paroles
would form the principal line of attack.

The first stop of the campaign was California's mining country, the string of
mountain towns along the western edge of the Sierra Mountains. Given his birth in
Los Angeles, upbringing in Bakersfield, and education in the Bay Area, Warren had
strong roots in nearly every part of California. The mining country was an exception, but he worked hard to remedy that. It was there in the California spring that
Warren went to work on the electorate. Those towns were verdant at that time of
year, the last of the winter snows melting down their flanks in swollen rivers. The
air was fresh and cool, the heat of summer still months away. Each little town had
its dusty streets and historic markers, placed there by the Native Sons and commemorating their place at California's birth. They were fierce in their attachment
to California, many first settled in the Gold Rush less than a century earlier. They
were far away from San Francisco and Los Angeles culturally and politically as well
as geographically. In these pioneer towns, there was not much regard for Olson's
vaguely socialistic notions of attacking poverty. Their citizens did not know Warren well at the beginning of 1942, but they were Warren country. As he worked
those little hamlets, Warren enjoyed their people, their small-town papers, their
cantankerous warmth. They responded in kind.

Traveling through them in 1942, Earl Warren would demonstrate, more than in
any campaign before or later, why politics was his calling. His facility for names was
astounding. In town after town, he would walk up to a man or woman, stick out his
hand, and call the person by name, often asking further about a wife or husband or
child. So remarkable was his ability to recall names, faces, and facts that an aide
once asked him how he did it. Warren responded that it was all about focus. "I
never look at their neckties," he said.[31] But Warren supplemented his natural gift
with a typically meticulous system. In his office was a card file listing every person
he had ever met, along with a few details about the person's life—spouses, colleges,
favorite sports, and the like. Sweigert and others filled up cards with details about

notable friendships or enemies to avoid. Helen MacGregor would add information on influential women. As the campaign developed, the card file formed a stockpile of political information.

On the trail, Warren stormed through California's sparsely populated interior. Warren, said his driver, "would go into a town, shake hands with half the people, make a talk, shake hands with the other half, then we'd be on our way."[32] No one was better at it. The campaign, in fact, seemed to highlight Warren's strengths and minimize his weaknesses. His sternness, for instance, was reserved for his staff— and occasionally his children—but not constituents. To them, he conveyed earnest sincerity. Greeting crowds involved just the right amount of connection for Earl Warren. He listened to the problems of others but was under no obligation to reveal any of his own. He sympathized, offered ways to help, and then, with a slap on the back and a firm grip, moved on to the next person. If he overpromised, and he did—Warren's secretaries complained about men and women showing up at the office to speak with him because he'd casually extended an invitation to do so— well, Mrs. MacGregor was there to sort that out, and she efficiently did so. So persuasive was Warren's presence, so effective was his measured garrulousness that he invariably seemed taller in memory than in person. Warren was just a shade over six feet tall, but taller men, in their recollections of him, almost always remembered looking up at him.

He was not always an easy man to work for. Speech-writing for Warren, for instance, was a difficult and often unappreciated chore. Typically, Warren would block out a speech, outlining in broad strokes the themes he hoped to express. Then he would turn it over to an aide and ask him to "put it on the typewriter." With that, Warren would often forget about the speech until the day of its delivery drew near. When the speech finally received his attention, Warren was demanding and particular. He disliked ending a sentence with a preposition, and he insisted on plain, direct language. He could be brusque if the draft came up short. In one particularly bruising episode, Warren dressed down a staff member who had prepared remarks for him on a public works speech. "This thing is no good," he raged. "I asked you to give me a strong message on public works, and you haven't done it. A high school sophomore could write a better speech without half-trying. I just don't understand what's going on around here." The sputtering aide tried to reply, as another senior member of the staff asked what they could do to improve the draft. "I don't want you to do a damned thing," Warren snapped. "I'll write my own message. Nobody ever does anything for me around here."[33]

Outbursts such as those were not common, but they did occur, and they strained relations between Warren and some of his staff. His loyal core stayed with him through many campaigns and offices, but other turnover on his staff was high, in part because of the demands he placed on them. He was notoriously stingy with raises. He guarded compliments and rationed praise. "Flattery," Warren's press secretary reflected, "was a habit to which Earl Warren was not addicted."[34] One secretary who worked for Earl and Nina for years remembered afterward always having felt appreciated but could not recall a single time that Earl thanked her.[35] Still, he inculcated a powerful sense of loyalty among his closest aides. Warren Olney, Helen MacGregor, Bill Sweigert, Oscar Jahnsen, and others would dip in and out of Warren's life, but they were loyal to the end. Sweigert agreed that Warren was "a hard man to work with." But he stayed for nearly a decade. Warren, he said, "was always fair."[36]

Until 1942, the face that Warren had presented California was in some ways that of a forbidding figure. He ran first for district attorney, then for attorney general, serious jobs for crime fighters. He rarely attempted humor in his public addresses—once, when a secretary taking dictation suggested a joke for a speech, Warren smiled, thought for a moment, and then responded, "I think I'll leave jokes to the master of ceremonies"[37]—and his campaigns up to that point had always been built around law enforcement. The result is that many voters undoubtedly had a positive but somewhat narrow view of the man who now asked to be their governor. Whitaker and Baxter saw that Warren's image needed to be completed—the prosecutor in their client was perfect to point out Olson's failings, but they needed a candidate that voters could like, not just respect. The two consultants, with their gift for imagery, realized that they needed to show Warren as a father and husband, not just as a prosecutor. His wife was the image of devotion, his children sunny and appealing. Whitaker and Baxter's task was to overcome the Warrens' resistance and bring the family into politics.

Leone Baxter pressed hard. "Nina didn't want to do that," she remembered. "She didn't want to exploit her family. But we knew we had to get that family. . . . He wasn't very colorful, and he didn't say anything particularly directed to women. You couldn't get a feel for him. So she finally agreed that it would be alright to use the picture."[38]

"The picture." In it, Earl Warren stands at the end of a line of his family. Dressed in a dark suit, his tie neatly cinched at his throat and his wife's hand gently entwined around his right elbow, Earl Warren is straight and tall. And he smiles, a wide grin of pride and appreciation. To his right, Nina beams as well. Jim Warren, handsome and tall like his dad, grins between big ears, his skinny frame tucked into a wool suit. To his right the younger Warrens are arrayed in descending order of age. Virginia wears a cheerful summer dress, Earl Jr. and Dorothy sport Scout uniforms, bandannas knotted in front. Honey Bear, always the picture of beauty and charm, laces her fingers together at the waist of her jumper. And rounding out the family is Bobby, in uniform and tie, a delighted smile tugging at the corners of his mouth as he looks offstage, tickled by something out of view.

The picture was mailed first to Warren's clubs and the friends in his card files. After that, requests came pouring in. By the time Election Day arrived, more than 3 million copies of the cards had been printed, distributed, and clucked over in homes throughout California. It was more than just a political photograph, as its popularity proved. It captured a slice of California itself—sunny and healthy, friendly, sturdy, and captivating. Displayed together, caught happily in motion, in full stride, the Warrens were pretty without being soft. They spoke to California's sense of itself, of hopefulness and health, of promise. In political terms, the picture accomplished exactly what Whitaker and Baxter had desired: It humanized their law-and-order candidate, presented him as a father, not just a prosecutor. Running against Earl Warren was bad enough, California's politicians learned right then. Running against his family was impossible.

The photograph softened and expanded Warren's image, but he was not just altering his appearance for political purposes. Day after day, Warren was facing California's people and slipping the ideological bonds of his upbringing. These men and women out in California's mining towns were not newspaper publishers or members of the Grove. They were not wealthy or powerful. But they were Californians, and he liked them. People turned out to hear him speak and stayed to share their problems with him. Many politicians treat campaigns as a necessity, a burdensome undertaking required in order to govern, or as a contest, a battle of strategies intended to yield a winner and crush a loser. For Warren, they were all those things, but they also were a chance to listen to people, to think about issues, and to learn. As the 1938 campaign for attorney general forced Warren to contemplate the significance of civil rights, so the 1942 race required him to think beyond prosecutions and public safety.

As he did, Warren began to express a more liberal vision—protective of schools and the elderly, willing to compromise on health care, and eager to embrace a new conception of the government's role in labor-management relations, not just of suppressing violence but of actual, constructive neutrality. It was not so much that Warren was becoming more liberal; it was more that he was expanding his political vocabulary. He spoke less of law enforcement, more of society and the needs of working people. All those would come to define Warren's governorship and foreshadow his jurisprudence. Only in the area of security, where Warren already had developed opinions and where his support for the internment became an important part of his election rhetoric, was he a doctrinaire Republican in 1942.

Warren's growth during the campaign of 1942 was influenced by many people, but one in particular provided the candidate with his new template. First introduced to Warren by Jesse Steinhart, Bill Sweigert had helped out in the 1938 campaign and then dropped away. In 1939, Sweigert's wife Gertrude died. He fell into a depression, took up the habit of ducking out of the office to smoke, and drifted for a time, lost in grief. Warren would not let Sweigert fade away, however. He sought Sweigert out during those months and approached him about taking a job in the attorney general's office. Sweigert saw the prospect of a restored life, and he accepted. Coming to Warren's side, Sweigert grasped his new work with the fervor of the resurrected. He took charge of the office's litigation section and went to work reorganizing holdovers from the Webb administration into an aggressive, principled group along the lines that Warren insisted on.[39] Warren liked Sweigert, and the two would often lunch together, talking about politics. They did not generally agree, but their differences drew them together, not apart. Sweigert was as enamored of the New Deal as Warren was skeptical. Over their lunches, Sweigert would argue the merits of the president's economic recovery efforts, and Warren would counter with defenses of states' rights. Sweigert trumpeted the Democratic Party's leadership, Warren complained that the Democrats were crippled by the "unholy combination" of their liberal Northern wing and their conservative Southern base.[40]

Disagree they might, but Sweigert was a man Warren trusted. Just as Warren admired Olney's thoroughness and MacGregor's efficiency, so he saw in Sweigert a man of contrasting views against whom he could test and sharpen his own. In that vein, soon after Warren entered the governor's race, Sweigert prepared a memo for him. It was plainspoken and serious, and it helped give Warren ballast, grounded his observations in a unifying theory. "There is no place today for the so-called reactionary," it began, "the person who still thinks that government exists only to protect the power of a successful few against the demands of plain people for a greater measure of health, comfort and security in their daily lives." After that brusque dismissal of California's right wing, Sweigert painted a picture of California during and after the war, and of a democratized, civilized America:

> The aspirations of our people today are not extravagant. Few of us today still want to be millionaires or tycoons. This is going to be the century of little people, little homes and little pleasures. . . . [O]ur big country, our big projects, are, and always must be, the servants of our little people, our little families.
>
> Our people want an opportunity to work, they want decent working conditions, they want their own homes and gardens, they want available education and vocational training for their children, they want available hospitalization and medical attention for their families, they want a few of the basic machines that make for comfort in and about the home in keeping with our modern age, they want a little time for leisure and a chance to enjoy a bit of their countryside. . . .
>
> [W]e must never forget that government is the instrument set up by the people to preserve their security and their freedom and that, therefore, it must never neglect the one nor destroy the other.

> The primary obligation of government is to develop policies that will advance the welfare of the people as a whole in their efforts to live decently under modern conditions.[41]

The modesty of those aspirations resonated with Warren and was confirmed by his contact with the people Sweigert described. In Modoc and Modesto, in the Sierra foothill towns and northern redwood glens, along the Mexican border, in the irrigated mud of the Imperial Valley or the apricot and almond orchards south of San Francisco, the people Warren met wanted just what Sweigert suggested—not exorbitant riches or fortunes but health care for themselves and their children, schools and roads, police officers and iceboxes, jobs and the promise of a comfortable retirement after decades of hard work. Sweigert argued that government could help, and that because it could, it should. Warren had objected to the New Deal's intrusions on a free-market economy, but there was no denying what California's people were telling him: that the government owed its citizens a chance. Warren was never one to stand on abstraction, and the theory of capitalism he had espoused as a young man seemed painfully theoretical next to the pleas of the men and women who gathered to meet him. He listened.

And as he listened, Warren also began to speak in new and revealing language. Up to this point, labor regarded Warren with suspicion at best. His 1938 commitment to civil liberties was encouraging, but next to *Point Lobos* it struck many as hollow. When Warren would protest that he was a long-standing member in the Musicians' Union, some labor leaders dismissed that as hypocritical. Now, however, Warren reached beyond his friends in the Masons or at the Grove and met with union members. As he did, Warren explored the middle in a state that up to that point had had little experience with a neutral politician on the subject of unions.

"We need a great deal more intelligence and less force in the handling of our labor problem," Warren said on June 17, 1942. "[W]e need government officials who don't belong to either side, but who can command the confidence of both. There is no more critical problem facing us in the reconstruction period ahead—and as Governor I would do my utmost to deal with it fairly and constructively, not as a partisan of either labor or management, but as the Governor of the people of all California."[42] In some cases, that meant avoiding the organized labor tempest of the moment rather than entering such debates on behalf of business. The so-called "Hot Cargo" bill, for example, was intended to win back for labor what the legislature in 1941 had taken away, the right of unions to join together to strike back at an employer by refusing to handle goods of another company. The legislature, over Olson's veto, had barred such secondary boycotts, under which union members refused to buy products of one employer in order to put pressure on another—boycotting a department store, say, for its advertisements in a newspaper that was the target of a strike or labor action. Thwarted in the legislature, where Warren's

Republican allies dominated, labor exercised its rights under one of California's Progressive-era innovations—the referendum—and took the issue to the ballot in 1942. Olson instinctively and predictably backed labor, and Warren was just as naturally expected to side with employers. Instead, he refused to take a position, and the Republican Party's platform for 1942 similarly skirted it. "I believe it is absolutely imperative that bitterness and controversy should be avoided at this time on any issue which tends to divide our people," Warren declared.[43] That was tactical, but it disappointed some Republicans, and it telegraphed Warren's determination to keep the right wing at arm's length.

Similarly, the campaign forced Warren to think broadly about the question of state pensions for the elderly, a dominant concern in those years, as the economy at last shrugged off the Depression, but its effects continued to haunt a generation of Americans. Here again, the appeal of the issue was partly political. Well-organized groups, taking advantage of California's referendum laws and the large population of anxious elderly Californians, sponsored a series of crackpot pension schemes during the Depression years. Olson had disappointed backers of one of them by giving some help to its supporters, only to then oppose the proposal itself. That proposal, known as "$30 every Thursday" or "Ham and Eggs," was pandering economics—it attempted to alleviate the suffering of California's jobless by having the state issue $30 worth of warrants every Thursday[44] to every unemployed Californian over the age of fifty. FDR denounced the plan, as did Upton Sinclair, so Olson was hardly alone among liberals in viewing the giveaway as unsound economics (FDR even questioned its constitutionality, on the grounds that only the federal government is empowered to issue currency). Where Olson stumbled, however, was in suggesting that he was with its backers, whose enthusiasm for the idea bordered on the obsessive. Olson's abandonment of the Ham-and-Eggers thus was not bad government, but it was bad politics. "Thousands have been bitterly disappointed," Warren reminded Olson supporters, as if they needed reminding.

Warren could have stopped there—the reminder had served its purpose. It highlighted Olson's ineffectiveness as well as his untrustworthiness. But Warren was no longer campaigning as a prosecutor or merely as an opponent of the incumbent. He was asking to be a governor, and those old people who shook his hand as he passed through their towns impressed him. Warren never endorsed Ham and Eggs or the various pension schemes that resembled it, but over the course of the campaign, he came to see government-supported pensions not as a luxury or an extravagance but rather "as a right."

"I believe that we should stop thinking of an old-age pension as a dole which we grant to the needy," Warren said on June 21. "I believe that every elder citizen, when he reaches the age fixed in the statute, should have the right to retire on an annuity, or a pension."[45] As the primary campaign neared conclusion, Warren amplified that idea. By then, even his defense of states' rights was wavering. "[T]he solution of this problem lies in a uniform Federal Old Age Pension System, so that progressive, liberal States will run no risk of being penalized for their generosity. But in the meantime, I believe that here in California, where we have cradled many of the liberal reforms of the nation, that we should blaze the path and light the way for a sound, humane, progressive pension system."[46] Until Earl Warren, California Republicans did not often stand for "humane, progressive" social programs, especially expensive ones. He was changing. And because he was now his party's leader, Republicans were now along for Warren's ride.

In the area of education, Warren the candidate discovered for the first time some of the fundamental values that Warren the justice would extend to all citizens. In 1942, the emphasis was on protecting education from wartime cuts; in 1954, it would be on extending education to citizens regardless of race. The principles Warren discovered during the 1942 campaign, however, would underlie both. He vowed that even the war would not close schools. The alternative, he argued, was the erosion of American society itself. "Education," he said, "has been recognized and acclaimed as the very foundation of democracy. A people without the education that will give them a knowledge of the world in which they live and the mental training to think out their problems cannot function efficiently as citizens under a democratic system of self-government."[47] Warren himself had never been much of a student, but he understood education's place as an engine of progress and opportunity. It was, as he said, "the foundation of democracy," and thus it had to be available to all for democracy to have meaning. Never after the 1942 campaign would Warren's commitment to educational opportunity waver; few people of his time would do more to secure that opportunity.

Finally, the 1942 campaign, taking place as it did against the backdrop of war, caused Warren to think more expansively about America's role in the larger world. Although he was never an isolationist, Warren now asserted with vigor the notion not only that America was part of a larger international community but also that it was required to lead other nations and reform domestically to be worthy of that leadership. He described that mission as "one hundred percent Americanism," the slogan used by the American Legion. But Warren's use of the phrase was a mischievous appropriation. Where the Legion was quick to identify enemies of Americanism and to punish them for perceived disloyalty, Warren argued that patriotism required tolerance. The war, he said, had created a new camaraderie in America. It had "wiped out all lines of demarcation, social, political and racial." In 1942, America abroad faced enemies motivated by racism; Warren recognized that America had to be fair to be different.

The war and the campaign were working on Warren. "We must," Warren said at an Independence Day gathering, "accept as an unalterable fact that we are a moving part of the world, that this is the American Century—the century in which we attain our maturity as a nation and assume a leadership among the society of nations; the century in which we will make come true the dream of Thomas Jefferson that all men are created equal."[48] Those values blossomed in 1942, ripened through his governorship, and eventually defined his tenure as Chief Justice of the United States. In the meantime, Warren's internationalism would reach a symbolic high point in 1945, when he hosted the San Francisco meeting of delegates from fifty nations who gathered at The City's Opera House on June 25 of that year to sign the charter creating the United Nations.

Warren's embrace of social justice and international leadership, and his solidifying identification with working people, was not to be confused with softness. He kept up his attack on Olson throughout the campaign, and regularly derided the incumbent as bungling, partisan, inept, and unfit to lead a great state in a time of war. One particularly hard-edged piece of campaign literature was entitled "California Indicts Governor Olson." It listed area after area in which the Warren campaign contended that Olson had put the state's defenses at risk, and contrasted Olson's wavering sympathies toward California's Japanese with Warren's firm resolve. Olson, it said, received delegations of Japanese in Sacramento and "intimated he 'had his own plans' for dealing with the Japanese situation—a plan to the rather vague effect that evacuation was unnecessary." At the same time, the flyer noted, Warren created his maps of Japanese land holdings and supplied "federal authorities with factual data necessary for the prompt evacuation of the Japanese from California."[49]

Whitaker distributed copies of that mailer to key civic groups and campaign leaders in mid-August. More than 100,000 were printed. Whitaker, always happy to be on the attack, was pleased. "To my mind," he wrote to a friend, "this is the most effective thing we've had in the campaign."[50]

That duality—Warren as tough on foreign enemies but generous toward children, the elderly, union members—made him a formidable candidate in 1942. And yet, despite his strong appeal, Warren did not receive lavish financial support in the primary. Many of the state's conservative Southern California financiers remained uncertain about Warren's ability to win, and believed their money would be better spent on legislative races, where they hoped to build Republican representation and check any initiatives by Olson. Although that limited Warren's campaign at the outset, it was to prove a blessing, as it encouraged him to run a frugal effort, unencumbered by the interests of financial backers. Warren made no promises in return for money, and thus later there were none to be redeemed.

The primary was in August, and Warren appeared on the Republican and Democratic tickets. Olson, having eschewed bipartisanship as a value, ran only as a Democrat. With Election Day approaching, Whitaker reached out to a reliable friend in the press for advice. In a telegram to Kyle Palmer, the political editor of the *Los Angeles Times,* Whitaker asked for his "frank analysis" of the approaching vote.[51] Palmer's reply demonstrated both his acumen and the unembarrassed place that the *Times* occupied in state Republican politics:

> Unless I am more mistaken than usual, Warren can pile up a very impressive showing in the Democratic primaries if his campaign gets the gun from now on, until Election morning. Our checks here show him to be giving Olson a real run which is sufficient reason in my opinion for going all out. This plan is being followed in this area to the best of our ability and resources.[52]

On August 25, Warren smashingly defeated Olson. The attorney general swept the Republican primary, to no one's surprise, but also tallied 404,778 Democratic votes, barely coming in behind Olson's 514,144 on the governor's own ticket. Added to Warren's Republican tally of 635,230 votes, his primary victory was a two-to-one drubbing. Those returns gave Warren a decided, almost insurmountable advantage heading toward the general election.

So ringing was Warren's victory that he allowed himself a rare moment of gloating in a private letter to his friend and confidant William Knowland:

> There is no doubt but what they are panic stricken by the results. Olson is now in Washington and I was told that he is begging for support of the administration as a drowning man clutches for straws. Whether he gets it remains to be seen, but I think it is at least doubtful whether the President would enter a fight way out here in California, where the Republican candidate has made his campaign on the basis of supporting his war effort more faithfully than has the Democratic Governor during the past couple of years. I would like to believe that, of course.[53]

Warren was right. FDR, who had let Sinclair sink rather than ride to his rescue in 1934, did the same with Olson. With the Democrat clearly in trouble, the same donors who had shunned Warren during the primary now were eager to take command of his fundraising. Warren refused, leaving it in the hands of Gordon Campbell, the lone Southern California business leader who had stood up for Warren in the primary. Campbell took the position that latecomers to the campaign were somewhat suspect. "Why are you offering to contribute *now*?" Campbell would ask prospective donors. "Don't think there is anything for it because there is nothing for sale." Warren described that as "abrasive honesty" and added, "I gloried in his spunk."[54]

Warren was in command of the race, but it was not over yet. In October, Warren had his one brush with political danger. Before a packed and partisan crowd whose affections were for Olson, the two candidates met on the same stage in San Francisco for their only debate on October 11. It was a rollicking encounter—"a fire in the Currant Theater" was how the *San Francisco Chronicle* described it.[55] Olson and Warren had not spoken in private in nearly four years, and they now took the chance to flail each other in front of a raucous audience. Warren accused Olson of frittering in the face of war, of excessive partisanship, and of allowing relations with the legislature to fall apart. Olson charged Warren with subverting his efforts to defend California, of fronting for the state's reactionaries, and of lying about his commitment to nonpartisan government. Nonpartisanship, Olson said, "in the presence of these sharp and fundamental differences is sheer nonsense. Moreover, to profess nonpartisanship is to confess a lack of honest, firmly held convictions, without which no man is fit or competent to be a governor."[56] Abundantly clear from the debate was that by that point the two men had come genuinely to dislike each other. During one exchange, for instance, Warren attempted to explain his criticism of Olson's State Defense Council, only to be interrupted. "You've been as dumb as an oyster," Olson snorted. "If I've been that dumb, I couldn't have been as much of an obstructionist as you've tried to make me," Warren responded, his best retort of the afternoon.[57]

The debate did not go especially well for Warren. As the front-runner, he had more to lose than Olson, and Olson proved puckish. Nina Warren, listening to the radio broadcast while doing housework, heard the boos directed at her husband and was so distraught that she cried. She feared "all was lost."[58] Still, Warren shrugged it off. It "didn't prove anything, but it did put a little fire into the campaign," he wrote later.[59] And it came too late to affect the outcome. Olson challenged Warren to more debates, but Warren refused. Newspaper attention moved to other, closer races, a sure sign that Olson's time was running out.

Already, the campaign had broadened Warren's politics. In the final weeks, he continued to press for Democratic votes, espousing liberal positions and affiliating himself with FDR. Critics questioned his sincerity. Olson accused him of cowardice for refusing to acknowledge his partisanship, and bitterly denounced the attempt to curry Democratic support. "This non-partisan, non-political propaganda is a piece of colossal deceit," he said during the waning days of the primary campaign. "It is essentially a lie."[60] It was natural that Olson should think that, just as it was predictable that he would have seen Warren's early civil defense efforts as politically motivated; in both cases, Warren's moves were without much precedent in California's political history, and Olson's interpretation was a natural act of projection from his own partisanship.

In fact, however, Warren was steadily acquiring new politics and cutting away the old. As he drew closer to the ideas of Sweigert and Steinhart, he moved further from those favored by his own campaign managers, Whitaker and Baxter. Ten days

before the final vote, Warren tossed them over the side. They would forever disagree about what caused their final break. Reflecting on it thirty years later, Baxter
blamed Warren's temper. According to her, Warren authorized the release of a text
of a speech he was to deliver on the elderly. Whitaker sent embargoed copies to
leading reporters, giving them the chance to read it before publishing it a few days
later. In the meantime, however, Warren changed his mind about the speech and
demanded that Whitaker retract it. When Whitaker refused, "Earl got very angry,"
Baxter recalled. "He wasn't accustomed to being reversed on anything."[61]

Whitaker was just as stubborn as his boss. He said he would quit if Warren recalled the speech. Warren retracted it anyway. Although Baxter said that other
Warren supporters talked them into staying with the campaign, Warren did not call
on them during the final days, effectively ending their relationship on the eve of
victory.

As Warren remembered it, Whitaker and Baxter were under pressure from another client, Frederick Houser, running as a Republican for lieutenant governor, to
produce an endorsement by Warren for his candidacy. Houser had been dogging
Warren for weeks for an announcement of their joint campaign, but Warren refused. Such an announcement, Warren reasoned, would undermine his claims of a
commitment to nonpartisanship. As Houser became more desperate for Warren's
support, he threatened to pull out of the race and say Warren had double-crossed
him.[62] Nothing could have been more calculated to incur Warren's resistance, and
he stiffened in the face of Houser's demands. But Houser continued to press
Whitaker to secure Warren's help, and with just days remaining before the election,
Whitaker issued a press release in the name of both candidates, subtly suggesting
that they were working together. "I called [Whitaker] and told him to close the office and issue no more bulletins," Warren wrote. "That was my last personal experience with Whittaker," he added in his memoirs, adding insult to injury by
misspelling Whitaker's name.[63]

Warren coasted into the final days, a 4–1 favorite among bookies to win. He delivered. On Election Day, 1942, there were 1,275,287 ballots cast for Earl Warren; in
a state that had a solid Democratic majority, just 932,995 voted for the Democratic
incumbent, Culbert Olson. Olson would never again return to elected politics.

For Warren, the campaign had been enlightening and uplifting. He ended it a
winner, of course, but the victory was more than a political one. It was transfor-
mative, not just satisfying. Warren had felt his way to a new political center and
then had proven that it could win. He created a space between the cranky, old-
guard Republican Party and the testy, self-destructive liberal Democratic Party. He
had created Warrenism, a blend of hard politics and genuine compassion for the
poor and underprivileged. Warren sensed the importance of what he had gone
through, and he was elevated by it. "It is a great experience even to campaign for the

governorship," he reflected a few months later. "No one can really appreciate the size and complexity of our State until he has tried to cover it in a campaign and discuss the problems with the people. Whether I had been elected or not, I would have considered the campaign one of the great experiences of my life."[64]

Olson ended the campaign in a far darker mood. As he prepared to vacate his office, he ran into Earl and Nina Warren. "Warren," he said to the governor-elect, "if you want to know what hell is really like, just wait until you have been governor for four years."

"Governor," Warren replied, "I hope it won't be that bad."[65]

Two days after the election, the new governor-elect of California went fishing. Clem Whitaker called the office. Finding Warren out, Whitaker left a message instead. "Clem Whitaker," it read, "is as happy as you are over the results."[66] Warren never returned the call. Instead, the new governor and his former consultants moved into opposing corners. The state's fierce politics eventually would reunite Whitaker and Baxter with Warren. It would not be as friends.

Chapter 10

# ASSUMPTION
# OF POWER

*Warren was our first real "serendipitist" in California politics, one who has the
faculty of making happy and unexpected discoveries by accident.*

ROBERT KENNY[1]

T O THE ATTENTIVE EAR, Earl Warren's first inaugural address, delivered
beneath the state capitol dome on January 4, 1943, heralded the
changes in the man who now ascended to California's governorship.
Warren rose to the dais in California's General Assembly at three in the afternoon.
He stood beneath the Assembly's motto, emblazoned in gold letters across a pale
green background: *Legislatorum est justas leges condere,* "It is the duty of legislators
to pass just laws." The shade of green was taken from the British House of Com-
mons (and snickered over by generations of California reporters as having been
chosen because it resembles the color of money), and the columns to Warren's left
and right were meant to evoke ancient Rome. Warren took the oath of office from
California chief justice Phil Gibson, and then was introduced to the legislature and
audience by Charles Lyon, speaker of the California Assembly.[2]

Warren spoke for nineteen minutes. Before him, Warren's principal audience
was the California state legislature, composed largely of grim, wizened men, mostly
conservatives, pleased to have a Republican leader back before them after four exasperating years of Culbert Olson.

To them, Warren reiterated his commitment to nonpartisanship—"[W]e must
cut out all the dry rot of petty politics, partisan jockeying, inaction, dictatorial
stubbornness and opportunistic thinking"—and recited the requisite Republican
positions: Taxes should be lowered; the state's windfall, $60 million surplus should
be managed, not given away; and all programs should yield to the war effort, for

which no expense could be spared. Supporters highlighted those passages. The speech passed into history with little note.

But Warren's address was more than that, and its forgotten sections illuminate the man behind it at this seam in his political life, coming to power after digesting Sweigert's memo and internalizing the lessons of the 1942 campaign. In this speech, Warren's first as a statewide chief executive, he affirmed his determination to govern in a new way. He spoke of broad, humane goals and of an active government committed to intervening to achieve them. He spoke in terms undeniably more liberal than his audience. He decried the miserable health conditions faced by arriving migrants. He demanded that schools be protected from cuts. "The permanence of a democracy," he said, "will . . . depend upon the training and inspiration provided for its youth." He cited his long experience in law enforcement and noted that it had led him to the conclusion that crime prevention was more important than crime suppression. "I have come to feel with certainty that we have been making a wrong approach to our crime problem," he said, surprising words from a man whose entire professional life had been dedicated to that problem. He asked that prisoners be given work and encouraged to reenter society. On the divisive issue of care for California's elderly, Warren called for state pensions, as he had during the campaign, to be based not "upon the requirement of pauperism" but rather "as a social right."

As Warren spoke, the frost was lifting outside over the fields of the abundant Central Valley, and the afternoon sun burnt off a nearly freezing night. The war industries hummed along California's coasts. Young conscripts and volunteers came by the thousands, landing at airfields and military bases, anxious at what lay ahead. They stayed long enough to be outfitted and trained as sailors and soldiers, and while in California, to experience briefly its allure. Many would never return home; of those who survived the conflict even then raging over the horizon, many thousands would come back to the state where they trained. And all around, an ever-widening flood of farmers and shopkeepers, dockworkers, ranch hands, fruit pickers, and fishermen streamed into California from every state in America—a migration of humanity that, as Warren used to reflect, brought 10,000 new residents to his home state every week.

They were of every race and social class. Some came to manage California's industries, bringing with them wealth and sophistication. Many more crossed the state's borders in rags, owning nothing but what they carried, desperate for homes, schools, hospitals, police officers, running water, and sewers. A trickle of blacks entered the state from Texas, Arkansas, and Oklahoma, arriving mostly in Los Angeles to take up jobs vacated by its missing Japanese. In months, Los Angeles's Little Tokyo was transformed into a center of African-American life and culture. In that flood of immigrants and the change they wrought, many of Warren's Republican allies saw depravity and dissolution, a threat to their Mediterranean paradise. But Warren's own mother and father were part of an earlier California migration, and as he looked into that mass of humanity streaming across the borders from Nevada, Arizona, and Oregon, he saw the realization of the plea etched in the capitol dome beneath which he spoke that Monday afternoon. "Give me men worthy of my mountains," it enjoined. The arriving migrants were those men—and women and children.

Warren, too, determined to be such a man, to stand not against but rather with those migrants. As he prepared to govern the nation's fastest-growing state, one that had transformed in Warren's own lifetime and that was in the process of transforming yet again, the new governor imagined ribbons of highway connecting factories and fields. He envisioned the state's resources guarded, not for aesthetic appreciation but rather for future use and enjoyment. He planned for safe, humane prisons, and health care that treated the mentally ill instead of incarcerating them. He wanted clean beaches and safe cities. He imagined a fair, decent place for those men and women to raise children in security and comfort. Warren asked members of both parties to join him in constructing that future. "No clique, no faction and no party," he proclaimed, "holds priority on all the rights of helping the common man."

Earl Warren spoke most clearly in one sentence: "I visualize adherence," Warren said, "to a policy in all government activities which reflects a sincere desire to help men, women and children to develop and unfold the best that is within them." Just as Sweigert had proposed, Earl Warren's government would not merely incarcerate or educate—it would not confine itself to security. It would undertake big projects for little people. It would reach into their lives to help them. Earl Warren's government would not abstain from activism. It would embrace it. Not one member of the majority Republican legislature applauded that line or any other of his speech.[3] Warren spoke to silence.

As their sullen response indicated, California's leading Republicans were in no mood to be lectured about activist government by their new leader, triumphant over a Democrat whose support for just such activism had earned their derision. At the *Los Angeles Times,* editors did what they could to mold the public's sense of their candidate into a vision that conformed with their own. Warren's focal sentence—his call to an activist government intervening on behalf of the development of its people—was edited from the transcript of his speech as reprinted in the following morning's *Times.*[4] Gone, too, was Warren's endorsement of crime prevention and his call for protection of schools. The edited transcript removed a passage in which Warren called for sympathy for prisoners—"Procedure could be established," Warren said, "under which these men could be restored to community life and permitted, through rightful living, to earn pardon recognition from the courts

in the community in which they have demonstrated a right to such consideration"—
and also his commitment to a pension system even while the federal government
debated the matter. "We should not permit this thought to delay our own efforts to
build and maintain a pension structure within the limits of our ability to pay," Warren said. The *Times* clipped that as well.

Space undoubtedly dictated many of the cuts—newsprint, always at a pre-
mium, was especially scarce in those war years—and some of Warren's language
had been offered and reported during the campaign. But the cumulative effect of
the *Times*'s published transcript was to make Warren appear more conservative
than his own words. When some would later complain that he had changed as governor, had abandoned his early friends, they would in part be right; Warren did
learn and grow in his ten years and nine months as governor of California. But they
also would misunderstand his transformations because their sense of Warren was
based on the view of him allowed by his allies in the Republican press.

For now, however, Warren's challenge was to govern. In the months after his
election but before his inauguration, Warren began the methodical business of
building his staff. Helen MacGregor was one of the first. Warren had appreciated
her signature calm and professionalism during his district attorney years and had
kept her with him through the attorney generalship. After winning the governor's
race, Warren received a letter from a woman seeking a job; MacGregor read it first,
as she did most of his mail. The woman, a politically active Republican, asked for a
job as his staff secretary and suggested that he should consider her because it was
important to have a woman on his senior staff. As she and Warren were driving to
Sacramento one day and going over business in the car, MacGregor passed that
message along without comment. Warren took it in and said he agreed with the
writer. "But I'm not going to appoint her," he said to MacGregor. "I'm going to appoint you."[5]

As he moved to fill his other ranks, Warren shrugged off demands from Republican supporters that they be rewarded for their political loyalty. Sweigert, a Democrat, came with Warren as his executive secretary, and a few other Democrats were
selected for top positions. Warren later would insist that he never asked about a job
candidate's political makeup, an exaggeration but only a slight one. In fact, a few of
the memos composed by Sweigert and MacGregor noted a potential nominee's
politics—considering a candidate for the post of director of natural resources,
Sweigert described him as "Republican, geologist, sportsman, fine citizen"—but
politics never dominated Warren's considerations. Indeed, his refusal to give more
weight to political allegiance annoyed many of his Republican backers.

"[A]fter I was elected," Warren recalled, "many of my supporters said, 'We have
had enough of this nonpartisan foolishness. Now we will get down to business.'"[6]

They underestimated Warren's commitment to his word. One of the first to discover that was Murray Chotiner, a lawyer and political operative who had supported Warren but was soon to become chiefly associated with a new star in California's political constellation, the up-and-coming Richard Nixon. After Warren was elected, Chotiner complained on behalf of himself and other Southern California Republicans. "Chotiner," Sweigert said, "is concerned over failure to give hearing to some who were active in campaign."[7] Sweigert said Chotiner specifically cited Raymond Haight, who had steered Warren's Southern California effort, but also asked for personal consideration. "Murray Chotiner wants some prestige," Sweigert wrote to Warren, "and expected Professional and Vocational Standards." So sure was Chotiner of his pending appointment that he pushed Sweigert to act quickly "in order that he may arrange his professional affairs concerning his law practice." Warren ignored him.

At home, the new governor moved with his family to the ramshackle governor's mansion, and faced a problem his constituents could appreciate: The house was a mess. Warren's predecessors had been older men, none with young children, and had neglected to care for the house. After Olson's wife had died inside, he had abandoned it altogether. Rooms were boarded up inside the stately Victorian. Floors were ridden with termites, drapes with moths. The front steps were worn and dilapidated. The third floor had been shut off entirely, and had become a home to bats. When Nina Warren first laid eyes on the mansion, she burst into tears.[8] California's legislature, however, was not prepared to house the state's new governor and his photogenic family in a hovel, so a modest appropriation for renovation was approved, and Warren asked ever-faithful Oscar Jahnsen to supervise the project. For months, laborers crawled over the house, and Nina Warren shuttled back and forth from Oakland, consulting decorators, supervising the work.[9] The first floor was public space—greeting and dining areas. The second floor was reserved for bedrooms, while the third, formerly a ballroom, was converted into an office for the governor. It perched more than fifty steps above the ground, with views to Sacramento's intersecting rivers.

Nina worked on a budget, but she was resourceful. A California store, W. & J. Sloane, had a set of oversized Oriental rugs that it could not sell in the middle of the Depression. It offered to donate them to the mansion rather than let them sit out the years in storage. Nina and Oscar Jahnsen picked out four they liked—glowing red for the parlor, blue in the living room, garnet in the music room, and a fourth, its color now forgotten, for the dining room.[10] The rugs brought color back to the mansion. To appoint it, Nina picked out department-store imitations of Victorian furniture and inexpensive pieces. When two visitors admired antique portraits of what they assumed to be Warren ancestors in one of the downstairs living areas, Nina laughed and confessed, "I bought them at Gump's last month."[11]

Finally, as the school year neared summer break, the renovation was complete. The Warren children finished up their studies in Oakland, then joined their father in Sacramento, seventy miles to the northwest. The Sacramento telephone book listed California's new governor with conspicuous lack of pretense. "Earl Warren, 1526 H Street," the notation read, alongside the listed phone number, there for anyone to call. And inside the newly refurbished rooms, Earl and Nina Warren set out on the next phase of their family's life.

First was the business of installing the children. Room assignments followed an unmistakable theme: Girls got big ones, boys little ones. Earl Jr. was given a corner, overlooking the carriage house, quiet for the studious young boy to tend to his work; inside, Earl Jr. set his mind on his studies and his passion for taxidermy. Outside, he took over a nearby lot and converted it into a victory garden, to the delight of many Californians and his own oldest brother, Jim, who designed the family Christmas card that year around the theme of the garden. Bobby's quarters were spare as well, built over the covered driveway along the home's western edge. (Although small, Bobby's room later was distinguished by a snarling boar's head, the prize of a hunting trip in 1947 during which he, the youngest member of the party, shot and killed the wild animal and was allowed its head as a trophy.)[12] Virginia, by contrast, drew a front room with a fireplace. Dorothy secured a quiet space in the back of the house; it was decorated with busy wallpaper that she never liked and chose instead to cover with Hollywood movie stills and posters. And Honey Bear took the second floor's most opulent room, one with its own shower, quarters that later generations of first ladies would occupy. Her father, ever doting, allowed it with a private chuckle.

The move was hard on the children at first, particularly the younger ones. Bobby moped through his early days at school. Honey Bear was even more morose.[13] At the end of each school day, she would return home, pull out sad records, and play them on the family phonograph. Through the warm fall of Sacramento, she whiled away afternoons to the mournful voice of Lena Horne. One day, her father returned home early to find her that way. His heart, always tender for his youngest daughter, broke at the sight of her. In his youth, Earl Warren had been comforted by his loyal donkey, Jack. Now, seeing his daughter in distress, Warren lit upon a solution: Honey Bear got a pony, a pinto she named Peanuts. From that day onward until a tragic morning in 1950, Honey Bear spent part of almost every day on the back of a horse.[14] She and Bobby shared the pony, and Honey Bear's horseback riding became one of the emblems of the Warren family legend, one more aspect of the big, handsome, healthy family.[15]

The Warren children were neither shy nor pretentious. When they worried about what other children would think of them being chauffeured in an official state car, Bobby persuaded the driver, Pat Patterson, to pull over a block or so away. Out of view of their classmates, the children would tumble out, each one hustling to his or her own campus—elementary school for the little ones, high school for

Virginia, with the rest following. Being the governor's children made them objects of attention, naturally, but they bore the attention well. Earl Jr. drank beer with other boys on the levees outside Sacramento, and though the thought of getting caught and turning up in a newspaper story crossed his mind, it didn't keep him at home.[16] All the children experimented with smoking, climbing up to the top of the mansion to sneak cigarettes. Their parents did not do much to catch them. Sometimes the children could smell the smoke on one another, nervously tittering at dinner, convinced that they would be caught. Earl and Nina either silently tolerated the habit or preferred not to notice.[17]

Mischief notwithstanding, the Warren children mostly asserted themselves in the ways that parents would hope. "I remember how the governor used to kiss Bobby goodbye every morning," Pat Patterson recalled for Warren biographer John Weaver. "Then as he got older, Bobby began to get embarrassed. He'd duck away. The governor got the point. I'll never forget the first time he stuck out his hand to Bobby instead of kissing him."[18]

For all its obligations, the governorship in some ways actually reunited Warren with his family. Where his job as attorney general had forced him to miss many a dinner at home, now he was just blocks from work and able to join his family more often in the evenings. Dinner was the highlight of the Warren family day, as Nina and Earl Warren took their places at opposite ends of the rectangular dining room table and the five children occupied the flanks. Conversation was lively, though never rowdy. At the table, Earl Warren led the conversation as he always had, asking questions and drawing his children into gentle debates.

After dinner, Warren usually enjoyed a few quiet moments, often in the company of Honey Bear. He sipped tea while she peeled grapes for him. Sitting at her father's elbow, she entertained him with news of her day, while he listened quietly, interjecting with a question or praise.[19]

Mornings were, as they had to be in a home with five school-age children, more frenetic. The children pounded down the stairs to the kitchen at the rear of the house, where they wolfed down breakfast before heading for school. For a few minutes there would be quiet, and then the governor would dress. Nina Warren took care to pick his suits out for him, and she left them painstakingly arranged. Each shirt hung in the closet, pressed without starch, cufflinks already in the cuffs. Jackets had pens in the breast pockets. Earl Warren, almost as if a fireman, merely slipped on his uniform and was ready for work.[20] He then headed for the capitol, taking in the ten blocks in his big, assertive strides. Crossing over onto the capitol grounds at K Street, Warren jaywalked across the middle of the block. He often paused to chat with a gardener or pedestrian or to have his shoes shined at Fourteenth and J. Warren was too hearty to dislike, too open to suspect, and yet too serious and driven to be taken lightly.

His serious professionalism made him a quick hit with a tough audience, the Sacramento press corps. Those reporters were not easily impressed; having seen enough graft, greed, and cynicism in elected officials, they were wary of those who pretended otherwise. And yet Warren, from his very first days in office, struck them as different. An early, minor controversy helped set that tone. Soon after Warren took office, Oscar Jahnsen was inspecting the governor's suite and noticed some suspicious wiring. He traced it back through the walls and discovered a room upstairs in the capitol where the wires connected to recording equipment. He suspected that meant the governor's suite had been bugged, but Jahnsen could not find the microphones. After a flurry of activity, a source in Southern California tipped off the speaker of the Assembly that the microphones could be found in a janitor's closet. The speaker, Charles Lyon, called Helen MacGregor, who invited him over to investigate. Before opening up the closet, the two rounded up three newspaper reporters so they could witness the hunt. When the door to closet #7 was opened, the sleuths uncovered cleaning supplies, some vases, and in a wooden box, five telephone sets. Their cords were cut, and when one of the newspapermen unscrewed the bottom, they found the insides hollowed out and replaced with a microphone.[21] Olson explained away the embarrassing discovery. The devices, he said, were merely installed to record the debates of the legislature (why the microphones needed to be hidden in hollowed-out phones was never entirely explained). But what may have left the most lasting impression was that the press was invited along on the search.

"Warren's relationship with the press was not close," recalled one reporter, William Allen. "It was professional. We were invited once a year to the mansion for a very nice event, but most of the contact was formal."[22] Though he rarely granted exclusive interviews—Warren's press aides worried about alienating newspapers— he held press conferences regularly, alternating between mornings and afternoons so both cycles of papers would get their firsts, and spoke at such length that they sometimes ended without questions, Warren having answered everything the reporters could think to ask. He could be stiff around reporters, but they did not feel deceived, and his honesty charmed them. Morrie Landsbaum, bureau chief of the Associated Press and dean of the Sacramento press corps, admired him, as did the leading reporters and editors at the *Sacramento Bee* and the *Los Angeles Times*. Warren sought out each—trips to Los Angeles generally included a personal meeting with Kyle Palmer, not to mention social visits with the Chandlers.[23] And Warren occasionally asked Walter Jones at the *Sacramento Bee* for advice on judicial nominees or people under consideration for important state jobs.[24]

Toward the end of each year, the press corps would gather over drinks and informally designate its man of the year. Skeptical by nature and training of elected officials, the press invariably gave the honor to a man outside the elected circle. That continued under Warren—a press favorite was Warren's finance chief, James

Dean. But Warren occasionally came in second, a high mark indeed for a man in a position reporters yearned to disparage.[25] "[T]he working press in Sacramento," Warren wrote, on reflection, "treated me with what I considered to be kindness and generosity throughout my years there."[26]

After the liberal message of his inaugural, Warren tacked back to the center, at least symbolically. On January 5, one day after proclaiming his commitment to "the common man," Warren fired Carey McWilliams from his post as the head of the state's Division of Immigration and Housing. The job, Warren remarked, had "grown out of all proportion" and had encroached on areas best left to local government.[27] There was no question of McWilliams's staying. Gubernatorial cabinets leave along with governors. Still, Warren dropped McWilliams with particular gusto, and Warren's friends approved. McWilliams, in the words of the *Los Angeles Times,* was "known as a left winger," and even the increasingly big tent that Warren was erecting to house his personal philosophy had no room in those days for a liberal of McWilliams's convictions.

Warren came to office as California moved decisively to the war footing that upended the state—and did so in curiously symmetrical fashion. Having been born in the Gold Rush and shaped by that mass migration of young men who came to work the fields and streams of the Sierras, California was born again in a second cascade of young men, this time stopping over along its coast before embarking on their voyage into the War of the Pacific. The military's wartime embrace of California began in 1942 with the establishment of the Desert Training Center east of Los Angeles. There, a California native, General George Patton, began drilling in desert conditions resembling those he would soon discover in North Africa.[28] San Diego already was dominated by the Navy; now, with the Pacific fleet's Pearl Harbor in tatters, that city teemed with the arrival and departure of sailors. The federal government seized 122,000 acres north of San Diego to establish Camp Pendleton, where divisions of Marines trained before shipping out. Still farther up the coast, San Francisco's Presidio was the Army's Western headquarters, nestled among the eucalyptus trees with an inspiring view of the recently completed Golden Gate Bridge, whose span was joined in 1937, a year after the Bay Bridge linked San Francisco to Oakland. On the other side of the Golden Gate, forty miles up one of the slivering tributaries of San Francisco Bay, Camp Stoneman welcomed 30,000 men every month. There, they rushed through final paperwork, received last-minute instructions and equipment, and shipped out. By the time the war was over, more than a million men had spent an average of one to two weeks at the camp; for many, those would be their final footsteps on American soil.[29]

Among those who volunteered for service in those tumultuous days was Warren's oldest boy, Jim. He had broken his arm as a youngster, and it had been set poorly. When a military recruiting officer, thinking of doing the governor a favor,

used that as an excuse to block Jim's enlistment as a paratrooper, Warren was furious. "How dare one man interfere with another man's life like that," he thundered.
Jim kept at it, was accepted, and shipped out to the Pacific Theater.[30]

Defense industries clustered around military bases, and they too churned into
high gear. The economy, so encumbered by poverty during Lorena Hickok's tour,
now burst with activity. All California factories combined produced $2.8 billion
worth of goods in 1939. By 1944, that number had nearly quadrupled, to $10.14
billion.[31] In 1939, California employed 400,000 people in manufacturing. By 1943,
it had increased to more than 1 million, and many of the new workers were
women, often embarking on their first jobs.[32] Company after company expanded
to meet the demand for material. In 1937, Lockheed built 37 airplanes; by the time
the war ended, it had built 18,000.[33] The Kaiser shipyards north of San Francisco
pushed out new vessels with extraordinary, sometimes alarming, speed. More than
a quarter million workers built aircraft in California during the war, joining hundreds of thousands more in other defense-related industries. Wages soared, unemployment evaporated. California, in just a matter of months, had become a land of
wealth, flush with its second Gold Rush.

As that mass of young men passed through California, it created frictions. In
June 1943, just six months after Warren took office, two sailors out for the evening
in Venice, a neighborhood in West Los Angeles, approached a pair of Mexican-
American young women. Male friends of the women interceded, and pushing and
shoving soon became a melee. Local military commanders perversely encouraged
the fighting by allowing servicemen to leave their bases to join it. The so-called
Zoot Suit riots surged back and forth across Los Angeles for days. The spectacle was
dispiriting: American soldiers pausing en route to fight a racist enemy in order to
indulge in racist violence.[34] When order was restored, Warren convened a commission to examine the outburst, and its clear-eyed criticism of the violence was a
model of citizen inquiry. Unbeknownst to the governor, Carey McWilliams was behind the idea but had the sense to lobby for it through Robert Kenny, whom Warren had liked and trusted ever since his influential 1938 endorsement.[35]

Amidst wartime plenty, wealthy Californians argued that the government could
now afford to refund some of the money the state claimed in taxes. Warren naturally was sensitive to the popularity of such a move, especially among his Republican base. He could have proposed deep tax cuts and returned all of California's
surplus to those who had paid it. Instead, he consciously protected the programs
and institutions he had trumpeted in his inaugural address, and commissioned a
citizens' panel to study tax reform. That group recommended a measured set of tax
cuts, and Warren endorsed its approach. "It is true we should have some tax reduction," Warren said soon after taking office, "but it should be temperate and without
materially affecting the base of the structure."[36]

The cuts that eventually were enacted reflected Warren's evenhandedness, as well as his faith in the citizens' group that studied the issue. Sales taxes, which hit the poor hardest, were reduced by a half cent per dollar. The maximum income tax rate, which fell most heavily on the rich, was reduced, as were bank and corporation franchise taxes. The overall package reduced California taxes by $56.5 million in a single year, the first overall reduction in taxes enacted in the state's ninety-three-year history.[37] Although the tax cuts had been approved as a temporary measure, Warren and the legislature extended them year after year until the 1940s were ending, and one of California's periodic pension measures won voter approval and forced Warren to pay for it.[38]

His first budget, developed during the transition between the Olson administration and his own, set a pattern that Warren would follow for most of the decade. He found more money for universities, state colleges, and lower education; for new prisons and juvenile correction facilities and programs; for social welfare and state workers. Even after those increases, the state had money left over, and Warren cautioned against those who would either spend it on popular but ephemeral programs as well as against those who would deplete it by tax cuts. The existence of a surplus, Warren said in 1943, "constitutes a sacred trust for those who have the power to spend, for it has been collected from all the people and should be expended or preserved only for uses which will redound to the benefit of all."[39]

At his request, the legislature approved a $25 million "war catastrophe fund" to be spent in the event that California was attacked and needed to rebuild quickly. In later years, he would also convince the legislature to set aside $50 million to provide for unemployment relief when the war ended and industries were expected to shut down, and more than $140 million for a postwar construction fund, intended to pay for large capital projects at the war's conclusion, when materials marshaled for the conflict could be redirected to civilian use and when the predicted economic slowdown would create a need for job creation. Other surplus money was dedicated to retiring the debt that had been amassed under Governor Olson.

Warren's second full budget, that for 1945–47, added money for a new University of California campus at Santa Barbara, increased spending for public health and industrial relations ("to improve standards of industrial safety and accident prevention"), paid to build new mental health clinics and improve care at state hospitals, and added money for the Corrections Department in order to improve the conditions inside California's prisons. It added no new taxes. And when all that was spent, Warren and his staff estimated that California would register a two-year surplus of $144,786,145.

Sheer abundance of revenue allowed Warren to avoid choices that might have revealed his core principles. He was never forced to show whether he cared more about tax cuts or public health, because he was able to provide both. "Under such circumstances, Miss Shirley Temple, aided by the same advisers and with the same newspaper support, could make a fairly popular governor of California," Carey McWilliams wrote in 1943.[40] Although McWilliams was rarely wrong over the course of his extraordinary career, his piece for the *New Republic* that fall must be considered one of his unusual clunkers. Warren's handling of the state surplus, McWilliams wrote, was solved "quite in keeping with his past record, by reducing taxes instead of husbanding this wind-fall against the emergency demands of the post-war period."[41] In fact, Warren had done both.

Warren shrugged off such sniping and proceeded to overhaul California government. Once assembled, his team of department heads began moving to address areas within their spheres. They were, by all accounts, an impressive group. To a man—and they were all men—the Warren team was professionally well regarded and intensely loyal to the governor. Almost without exception, they agreed to take cuts in pay in order to join the administration (Warren's generosity for programs never did extend to the salaries of his top deputies).[42]

Warren established a clear pattern in recruiting them. He asked experts in a field whom they considered to be their most accomplished peer—in prison administration, say, or public finance, public health, or mental health. After talking to a number of people, Warren would set his sights on a candidate, then invite him for a personal visit. There, knowing his own ability to charm, Warren would grill the man for hours and, if satisfied, offer him a post. In some cases, the candidates had no idea they were even being interviewed for a job until the offer was extended. One, Charles Purcell, was well known as the engineer who designed the Bay Bridge, the industrial-gray span that linked Oakland to San Francisco in 1936, but he also was famous for his bluntness, not a characteristic many politicians appreciate in a manager. When Warren summoned Purcell to his office one day, Purcell assumed he was either being fired or introduced to the new head of the Public Works Department. He even brought along briefcases full of records in case Warren was planning to investigate his work. Instead, Warren offered to make him the department's director. "Me?" he replied. Purcell took the job and soon established a reputation for removing political considerations from highway planning. Purcell served in that post for nine years, up until his death in 1951.[43]

Los Angeles County Probation Officer Karl Holton was selected by Warren to draft a new philosophy for handling child criminals. Under the proposal, which Olson had signed, the idea was to train children for the future and treat their problems rather than punish them for their crimes.[44] In keeping with Warren's admission in his inaugural that the state had been wrongheaded for too long on fighting crime, the Youth Authority under Holton's leadership opened forestry camps and focused on the conditions that child offenders faced in their upbringing, rather than solely on punishing them for crimes once committed.

A third, Wilton Halverson, was a plainspoken Seventh-day Adventist who accepted Warren's offer to become the state's health director as a matter of personal mission even though it meant halving the salary he had been making as Los Angeles County's public health officer. Halverson set out to clean the state of its health hazards, the by-product of California's phenomenal growth. Warren promised to run political interference for the doctor, and he did, even when it meant closing Los Angeles beaches until voters approved a bond to pay for a new sewage treatment facility.[45] Halverson and his staff worked to care for crippled children and pregnant mothers. They paid for research into communicable diseases. They expanded testing on food and drugs, and they subsidized hospital construction by California counties. When Halverson took the job, he oversaw a budget of about $750,000 a year; before the end of the decade, Warren would see to it that he had more than $4.8 million a year to spend.[46]

Warren elected not to address the state prison system until late 1943, facing as he did an already long agenda in the early months of that year. Instead, he began the quieter work of drafting a bill—one intended to remove political oversight of the system and to turn it away from strict incarceration and toward a rehabilitative model, again, in keeping with the remarks of his inaugural. "It was our idea," he said, "to get away from patchwork on our prison system, and to create once and for all a complete, centralized system."[47] That drafting took place in private, as Warren began looking for a chance to introduce it in a way that maximized its chances. His success with the bill ultimately reflected his shrewd timing, as well as his increasingly confident use of the press to further his objectives. In late 1943, San Francisco police chief Charles Dullea called Warren to warn him of a potentially embarrassing situation: two Folsom Prison inmates, Dullea said, had been leaving the prison every weekend—presumably by bribing authorities—and coming to San Francisco, where they were spending their time in a local hotel, holed up with women and enjoying themselves. To add insult, one of the convicts was Lloyd Sampsell, one of the so-called yacht-bandits. Sampsell was a dashing young bank robber who had set up shop in the Bay Area, living off a luxury yacht and paying for his playboy life by periodically holding up banks. The case drew wide publicity, especially after Sampsell and his cohort nearly escaped from custody while awaiting trial. Given the notoriety of the case, the district attorney of Alameda County had elected to prosecute it personally. And the DA in those days was Earl Warren.

So it was with some trepidation that Dullea called to tell Warren that failures in the prison system that he now oversaw as governor were allowing a prisoner he himself had put away to make a mockery of his incarceration. Other politicians might have seen the potential for ridicule. Warren saw something else. "Charlie," Warren said, "the next time they come down, you just arrest them and give it all the publicity you can give it." [48]

"The arrest of Lloyd Sampsell during his illegal sojourn away from Folsom was the exact break I needed to do something about the prison system," Warren realized.[49] On November 29, 1943, Warren appointed the Governor's Investigating Committee on Penal Affairs. It took just two months, as the committee delivered its report on January 21, 1944.[50] Warren then ordered the legislature back to Sacramento for a special session on prisons, and by May 1944, Warren had his bill. Once signed by Warren, the new law created a director of corrections, placed the entire correctional system under that person's authority, created a new entity for considering eligibility for parole, and also gave the governor the power to appoint special commissions on crime, which Warren would end up doing five times, the most important in 1948 with the formation of the Organized Crime Commission. That gave Warren the structure he wanted, and he then set out to get a manager worthy of it. Legislators were acutely worried that Warren would use the choice to install a political appointee loyal to himself, so he departed from his general recruitment practice and allowed a committee to conduct a national, written test of applicants. That committee recommended Richard A. McGee for the position, and Warren persuaded McGee's boss, Washington governor Arthur Langlie, that McGee was more desperately needed in California.

Sealing their deal, Warren said to McGee, "Mr. McGee . . . I don't know you and you don't know me, but I just want to tell you how we're going to operate in the future. I will never do anything political to interfere with your prisons if you come here. And, if I ever find out that you have done anything political, I'll fire you. What do you think of that kind of an arrangement?"

McGee smiled and responded, "That is good enough for me."[51]

Two Warren innovations launched early in his tenure helped shape his administration in both style and substance. Tellingly, neither was partisan, and neither was explicitly political in nature. The first was Warren's "governor's council," a cabinet of his top advisers that met monthly to brief him and debate a range of policy issues. The council, reminiscent of Warren's early staff meetings in the Alameda district attorney's office, became the forum to resolve financial debates and to set the administration's spending and other priorities. Just as in the Alameda days, differences were welcomed at the council up to the point that Warren reached a decision. Then, also as in the prosecutorial years, he expected his aides to follow.

The other Warren creation was a series of "conferences" on various topics facing the state. Governor's conferences were not strictly a Warren invention; many chief executives before and since have convened commissions or committees as a way of soliciting public input or as a means of softening opposition to an idea. Rarely, however, has such an approach more clearly been an extension of a governor's personality. For Warren, the conferences were an outgrowth of his Progressivism and an expression of his love for clubs. Through the 1940s, Warren convened conferences on a wide variety of subjects, including aging, employment, highways, prisons, public health, mental health, water, juvenile justice, and educational television—sixteen overall, of which ten produced long written reports.[52] In addition, Warren turned to smaller citizen groups for advice on taxes, crime, and other subjects, notably his tax committee in 1943 and a slate of crime commissions appointed in 1947 to help the state Department of Corrections analyze the full range of issues confronting the criminal justice system.

Each Warren conference was organized along essentially the same lines—familiar ones to those who followed his practice in picking top aides. Warren asked experts for their thoughts on a subject, as well as their recommendations for others who were knowledgeable. Once he had selected those he considered the best in the field, he turned over the planning of the conference to them. Each conference was attended by 1,000 to 2,000 delegates, gatherings so large that they were held in Sacramento at the city's municipal auditorium. The sessions usually took place during the legislative session, allowing delegates to consult with legislators and ensuring that legislators were exposed to the work of the groups, either directly or through the extensive news coverage that most attracted. As the conference opened, Warren welcomed the delegates—generally a range of business, social, and civic leaders chosen because they were "people who apprehend that the only certain antidote for disaffection and radicalism is a government whose basis is an enlightened public that will put its hearts and minds to work upon the fundamental problems of life."[53] But once the sessions were under way, Warren did not attempt to direct their work. "This conference is yours," he said at the outset of one such event, a conference on aging held in 1951. "You will discuss what you choose to discuss."[54]

The gatherings could be meandering but they produced results. Warren's programs on public health and mental health both reflected the work of gubernatorial conferences, as did his proposals for a fair employment practices law, adjustments in worker benefits, an increase in monthly pension payments to the elderly, and plans to construct new facilities for treatment of alcoholism and mental illness.[55] In one instance, a 1949 conference on sex crimes, Warren endorsed the work of the conference wholesale and asked the legislature to adopt all its recommendations.[56]

Even where Warren was less enthusiastic about the substantive work of the conferences, he enjoyed the process. Bringing more than a thousand people from all walks of life under a single roof to hash out a matter of public concern appealed to his sense of a functioning democracy with enlightened leadership. He enjoyed stimulating public conversation, nonpartisan debate, on issues that affected the lives of his state. "These gatherings took much of my time and energy," Warren wrote later, "but they were also great educators for me as to both public affairs and people."[57] The conference thus became an end unto itself, a fulfillment of citizen democracy, with Warren at its head. He benefited, to be sure, as those who participated left with the strong sense of inclusion in California's affairs and connection to its governor. But for Warren, the conference was more than the achievement of political advantage; it was "public affairs and people," the reasons for governing at all.

"What better way was there to plumb group opinion and still control the outcome to a degree?" asks Richard Harvey, an astute political analyst of the Warren governorship. "What superior method to stimulate that unity so cherished by the Governor?"[58]

Although effective on his own terms, Warren's style of leadership was curiously impersonal, especially when viewed by a modern eye. Warren rarely attempted to steer the legislature—he proposed, it debated, he decided. That was partly out of respect. Warren honored the separation of powers between his office and those of California's legislators. It was also a measure of political realism: Squabbling with the Assembly and Senate had reduced Olson's stature, and Warren preferred the high ground. For the most part, he succeeded, though legislators also found it, on occasion, easy to defy him, knowing that Warren was unlikely to come down off his perch and attempt to get even. In his relations with the legislature, as in other facets of his life, Warren was deliberate rather than emotive. Warren, it was said, never roused an audience to laughter or tears—nor did he put it to sleep. Indeed, a temperamental consistency united his parenting, his governance, and his political style. Warren presented himself to aides, children, and voters in essentially the same way—as a plodding but persistent leader, intolerant of mistakes while generally optimistic and even-tempered. He was attentive to detail—a typographical error in a letter from his office was unthinkable to the secretaries in his pool. He was cautious—as the debate over the Corrections Department demonstrated, Warren liked to wait for a political issue to develop before committing himself, then strike at what he saw as a propitious moment to capitalize on public anger or interest. And once he was committed to a policy, Warren was fierce. He was, as a clerk later would describe him, a "stubborn Swede," slow to anger, hard to budge.[59] Of himself, Warren liked to say that he emulated Lincoln. He took slow steps, Warren said, but never backward.

Warren's approach did not thrust him immediately to national prominence. There was too little controversy about him to bring on instant reviews. But California, which had struggled so mightily under his predecessor, came to life with Warren in the governorship. As jobs filled and the state budget swelled, national political attention overcame its Eastern bias and the limelight found California's governor. Once it discovered him and his photogenic family, it would never again leave him for long.

On January 31, 1944, *Time* magazine published its first issue ever printed in California (a breakthrough it announced with a special banner across the cover). On its cover was Earl Warren. Beside him was an elephant—*Time*, like Warren, was

Republican. The elephant held an orange that radiated beams of energy. The story was an homage to Warren, championing him for national office despite what it called his "safe, dull political prose." His record, however, was big and growing, and *Time* imagined great things for Warren. "Big, blond, blue-eyed Governor Warren seems to radiate goodness and warmth," the magazine reported. "Impressed by his relaxed good nature, his evident simplicity, the eager 'yes-yes' and 'uh-huh, uh-huh' with which he indicates earnest interest in everything they have to say, his visitors often begin to fit him into a scheme of history. They see him not merely as a perfect political candidate, but as the forerunner in U.S. politics of a new era of friendly men to succeed the recent era of angry men."[60]

As the 1944 Republican National Convention approached, many party leaders sought to persuade Warren to join the ticket. He was, in the thinking of the day, the perfect counterpart to New York governor Tom Dewey, two moderate Republicans from opposite coasts, each compiling impressive records of management in two of the nation's largest states. Roosevelt, his health failing, was seeking a fourth term, and some Republicans hoped the country might at last have wearied of his stewardship.

Warren knew better. Although his instincts for national politics would prove erratic in the coming years, in 1944 Warren saw more clearly than many of his Republican allies the strength of Roosevelt's appeal. He determined to keep his distance from the ticket and succeeded in fending off Dewey's advances to join as vice president. At one point, Warren pushed back too hard, publicly suggesting that to leave the governorship so soon would be a dereliction of his duty to his state, an awkward pronouncement given that Dewey was preparing to do just that. "I have made certain commitments and assumed certain obligations to my state which are yet unfulfilled," Warren wrote to members of the Oregon delegation when they attempted to draft him. Warren emphatically urged the delegation not to nominate him for vice president.[61]

Warren escaped the vice presidential nomination—it went to Ohio senator John Bricker—and instead delivered a keynote address to the delegates gathered that year in Chicago. He prepared carefully for the occasion, soliciting and receiving help from, among others, Raymond Moley, by then a disenchanted New Dealer working at *Newsweek* magazine. Moley advised Warren to stay "far above the political battle. It is a time," he stressed, "for the eternal verities."[62] Warren strove for that, continuing to labor over drafts only days before the convention opened, but what he produced was less lofty than it was obvious. Where his strength at home was always in his devotion to facts and practical solutions, he found it difficult to project those virtues to the nation, where he had less command of his subject and where audiences, less familiar than Californians with his record, craved a more effusive personality. So Warren fell back on rhetoric, never his strength, and he teetered between appeals to national unity and to Republican enthusiasm. States with Republican governors, Warren argued, were producing much of the American war machine. "From the record of those states," he concluded, "it is clear that Dr. Win the War is a Republican."[63] In the next breath, however, he insisted that the war tolerated no partisan differences—generals and admirals served their nation, not their party. Warren renounced the New Deal, blaming it for centralizing power under one man, destroying the Democratic Party, and threatening basic American freedoms. But he offered little in its place other than the assertion that Republicans were better.

Returning to California and more comfortable terrain, Warren did his best for the doomed Republican ticket of 1944. Bricker brought little strength to the campaign. His ardent isolationism reassured the piece of the Republican Party that was uncomfortable with Dewey, but he alienated many moderates, including Warren. Still, Warren understood his duty. He praised the ticket and urged support for it. In October, Bricker came to California, where Warren and he made a joint appearance at the Senator Hotel, a Sacramento office building across from the capitol.[64] Warren introduced him there and at a second appearance that day in San Francisco. Bricker praised Warren as "one of the finest Governors you have ever had," and Warren returned the compliment. "No one who meets and hears him," Warren said of the Ohio senator, "but realizes he has lifted the candidacy of the Vice Presidency to a new high level."[65]

On October 17, with the election just weeks off, Warren arrived for work as usual and put in a few hours. He and Sweigert went to lunch together at the Sutter Club, a short walk from the capitol. Warren excused himself at one point and went to the men's room. Returning, he was pale. "You know," he said to Sweigert, sitting down, "I just passed some blood."[66] Warren secured an appointment with his doctor, Red Harris, who concluded that Warren was suffering from a kidney infection and required hospitalization. Warren was admitted the same day.

As Election Day approached, Warren reached out from his hospital bed to make one last effort on behalf of the Republican ticket. "The New Deal machine," Warren said of FDR's coalition, "is being held together today by the domination of one man, not by a common philosophy of government or by any common program for the future of America." By contrast, Dewey and Bricker, "men of youth and courage and determination," stood able to conclude the war and prepare America for a lasting and prosperous peace, Warren declared.[67] He was still too sick even to speak into a microphone, so his comments were transcribed and read over the radio, as well as widely published in the state's appreciative Republican press.

Roosevelt and Truman thumped Dewey and Bricker. The Democrats carried all but twelve states. And in California, Warren's pleadings had little effect: The same state that had resoundingly elected a Republican governor in 1942 went heavily for FDR in 1944, delivering him a 13-point victory over Dewey.

It would be nearly three more weeks before Warren dragged himself to the office, ending the longest illness of his life. When, just before Thanksgiving, Warren reappeared at work, he confided to Robert Kenny that the experience had been enlightening. Not only had he weathered a painful ordeal, the governor said, the long rest had given him a chance to consider the difficulties of working people forced out of a job for weeks or months at a time, with little cushion to support them financially. Recalled Kenny:

> [W]hen he got back to his desk, he told me he'd done a lot of thinking while he was flat on his back. "What does a fellow on a fixed income do when he has to go to the hospital?" he said, and then he told me what had happened to him when he was attorney general and having trouble stretching his salary from payday to payday. His check was late one month and he missed a payment on his health insurance, so it was cancelled. He called the company and got it reinstated right away, but he couldn't help wondering what an ordinary working man would have done in a case like that.[68]

Earl Warren returned to work and announced that in the coming term, just a few days away, he would propose that California become the first state in America to create and support a system of compulsory health insurance. No longer, Warren said, would middle-income residents need to worry about the financial effects of a catastrophic illness. This governor, a Republican, would see that the common men and women of California were protected by their Progressive, activist, compassionate government. Warren intended to offer them health care, fulfilling the message of his inaugural and the spirit of his campaign. It was a natural response to his personal experience and utterly in line with his compassion for others. For Warren, health care for working people was as logical as accident insurance, as indisputable as public sanitation or unemployment relief. For his enemies—and Warren was about to discover just who they were—it was something else entirely.

Chapter 11

# CALIFORNIA'S
# FAIR DEAL GOVERNOR

*He's trying to out–New Deal the New Deal.*

ASSEMBLYMAN GEORGE COLLINS[1]

W ARREN'S HEALTH CARE INITIATIVE was self-consciously aimed at
helping California's working class. The wealthy did not face sudden
ruin because of illness—and neither did the very poor, those qualified under California law to receive state government assistance. But the middle,
the same middle whose politics Warren was pioneering in California, had neither
personal resources nor public help. They were left to fend for themselves in a system that could swallow them with a single illness or accident. Having pondered
that question while sick himself, Warren returned to work and decided to fix it.

It was a prototypical Warren exercise: The problem was broad and tangible, the
victims spread across ideological lines. The path to success was satisfyingly strewn
with surmountable obstacles. By avoiding partisanship, Warren believed he could
create a program that would help common Californians through one of their most
persistent worries. The governor was no New Dealer, contrary to the grumbling of
George Collins and others. He was not prepared to put the state budget into the red
to finance the program, and he did not launch his health care initiative to stimulate
the economy or create jobs. But he was clearly no conservative, either: Warren saw
the opportunity for state action, and believed the needs of common people were
sufficient to justify an entirely new system of health insurance, backed by an assertive government paying its way as it went forward.

Warren may have been relatively new to the governor's office as 1944 closed, but
he was sufficiently seasoned in politics to know that his program would founder if

he could not win at least the acquiescence—and with luck, the support—of those most affected by it. In this case, that meant a visit to one of California's most slavishly conservative organizations, the California Medical Association. In mid-December, Warren met with Philip Gilman, president-elect of the CMA.[2] Warren had reason to believe that he might win the backing of the association, at least in principle, for an insurance system paid for by worker and employer contributions. The association had supported a version of such a program in 1935, when the Depression had cut badly into the medical profession. The desperation of those years, however, had jarred many people and organizations into aberrant positions; stability had cooled the CMA's ardor for reform. By 1944, it had settled back into its habitual complacency.

Warren may or may not have sensed that, but he knew enough not to rely solely on the organization's good will. Beneath his pitch, then, was a subtle threat. California's working middle class, Warren reminded the doctors, lived with the danger of a catastrophic health event. And that situation—millions of people living in fear—was not suited to stability. Stimulated by the promises of the New Deal, those residents would demand more from their government. If they did not get something soon, Warren warned, they might well demand a program more far-reaching than Warren was prepared to give or than the medical establishment could endure. Many of those who wanted better health care, Warren reminded Gilman, did not share their appreciation for private enterprise. They could not be expected to remain silent forever. Having posed the threat, Warren then, in broad strokes, proposed a publicly financed insurance program, guaranteed by the state but designed to be self-supporting.[3] Employees would pay 1.5 percent of their salaries, up to $4,000 a year, into the system, an amount that employers would match. The money would be collected by the state and administered by an eleven-person board overseeing the new California Health Service Authority. Those members would be appointed by the governor. The act specified that three would represent employers, two would be drawn from organized labor, and one from a state employee association; three would be doctors, one would be a dentist, and one member would be the state director of Public Health. Any California worker earning more than $300 a year would be eligible for coverage—the very poor already received health care through the publicly funded system of county hospitals. Benefits would pay for doctors' services, specialty care as ordered by a doctor, hospitalization for up to three weeks, drugs, X-rays, nursing care, and treatment of severe dental problems. Dependents also would receive coverage. Crucially, patients would be free to choose any doctor who was enrolled in the system. The authority would set "rates, fees or charges" for doctors in the system, but no doctor would be required to register, and those charges would not necessarily be uniform throughout the state.

Warren emphasized that the program did not compel patients to use the insurance, nor did it compel doctors to enroll in the system. Only one aspect of the proposal was compulsory: workers and employers would be bound to contribute to it, and their mandatory contributions would provide the pool of capital that would pay for insurance for all those who qualified.[4]

Warren saw himself not as an advocate for a radical notion but rather as a proponent of a sensible, modest social program. He compared it to California's Workmen's Compensation System (now known as Workers' Compensation). That program, adopted during Hiram Johnson's years, provided for worker and employer payroll deductions, which were pooled and used to underwrite insurance that paid medical bills for employees who were hurt at work. "Before adoption of Workmen's Compensation in California in 1915, an employee injured on the job was in very much the same situation as an employee and his family today when confronted with serious illness or non-industrial injury," Warren's staff emphasized in an internal memo.[5]

Discussing this with Gilman, Warren thought he sensed the doctor's support, and he moved to capitalize on it. At his request, Gilman arranged for Warren to make a presentation to the CMA's executive committee, which Warren did on December 13, appearing on a stage at the Family Club in San Francisco with Gilman and John M. Cline, another leader of the association.[6] Cline remembered the discussion as "very vague," with Warren parrying the doctors' queries but offering few specifics. In hindsight, it seems obvious that the doctors interpreted Warren's vagueness as tactical, but their suspicion reflected their basic misunderstanding of the governor. Warren was principally interested in a program that would insure middle-income Californians; he was, as he often was in complex and important matters, flexible on the details. Concerned that Warren was playing them, the doctors hedged. "This is a matter far too important to the health and welfare of the people of California and to the medical profession for any group of twenty men to decide," Cline concluded. "This will require a special meeting of our House of Delegates to discuss."[7]

While the doctors misjudged Warren, he did the same with them. In his case, wishful thinking clouded his analysis of the CMA. He left their initial gathering believing that the reaction was at worst noncommittal and at best promising—Sweigert, for instance, described Warren as having gotten "a nice reception"[8]—when in fact the doctors harbored grave doubts that they withheld from him. Compounding the misjudgments on both sides was a misunderstanding about the process: Cline said he concluded the meeting believing he had a promise from Warren that no public statement would be forthcoming until the legislature convened in January and that the CMA had until then to formulate its response. Warren had no intention of waiting that long.

On December 29, the governor unveiled his plan to the public. "I am not for State medicine," he declared. But he had given up on voluntary programs, Warren added, "because everybody will not join."[9] In support of his argument that health care was lacking, Warren noted that more than a third of Californians called to military service in the war—"38 out of every hundred of our boys," as he put it[10]—were rejected as "medically substandard." He thereby linked his program to the national defense effort, seemingly a strong argument in those still-tense days of war.

Early reaction was temperate, as the state's Republican press contemplated this latest move by the governor. The proposal, the *Los Angeles Times* offered cautiously, "raises questions that need mature consideration." Tactically, the governor also bolstered his case by embedding the proposal in his larger package of legislative proposals for the coming year. That package also included Warren's support for an extension of the tax cuts enacted in 1943, the single aspect of his record that had the strongest support among conservatives.[11]

For the Medical Association, however, the public announcement was not only a surprise but one with the strong suggestion of a betrayal. They countered with an insistence that they would not accept any plan that in any way hampered the medical profession's control over medical services.[12] And when they began to raise the alarm, Warren too felt deceived, believing he already had secured the association's support or at least neutrality. "The doctors thought he'd double-crossed them, and he thought they'd double-crossed him," one member of Warren's staff confided to biographer John Weaver. "I believe he thought at first he could win them over, but we couldn't even get a doctor to come help us draw up a bill."[13]

On January 8, 1945, Warren welcomed the legislature back to Sacramento. His address to the legislators, carefully tuned by his staff and pored over by him in the early days of the year, reflected his optimism about California and his commitment to its betterment.[14] In terms reminiscent of his Inaugural Address two years earlier, Warren again sounded the call to Progressive state action, embarked upon by a state flush with tax revenue. And he again trumpeted the virtues of cooperation between his office and the legislative leadership, alluding to the darker period during Olson's administration when no such cooperation existed. "I report to you that your government is sound," Warren said, "sound in finances, in integrity and in conformation to the spirit and the policies established by your honorable body."[15]

As Warren spoke, World War II was entering its final months. Paris had been liberated the previous August, followed by Brussels and Antwerp. Rommel, implicated in an attempt to kill Hitler, was dead by his own hand. Soviet troops pressed Hitler from the east, the Battle of the Bulge was under way, and the American fleet had regained control of the Pacific, moving toward the recapture of the Philippines on its way toward Japan. With the end of the war in sight, Warren framed his speech through the eyes of California's soon-to-be-returning servicemen:

As I visualize their return to the homeland, these service men and women of ours will want to have the opposite of what they have experienced in foreign lands. First, they will want peace—peace that comes from the elimination of racial prejudices, religious bigotry, and political intolerance. They will want an opportunity to work and to help develop the vast natural resources of our State. They will want industrial peace. They will want to be protected against the ravages of mass unemployment. They will want to see new evidence that we realize the importance of strong and vigorous health programs, for they will have seen sights which give urge to a search for perfection in this field.

They will want wholesome recreation for their families, as well as for themselves, and a high standard of educational opportunity offered in every part of the State. They will want safety at their work and in their homes and justice in all their relations with government.[16]

Health insurance—sensitive to the implications of the word "compulsory," Warren chose to label his program "prepaid" medical insurance—was squarely a part of the society that Warren argued those veterans were entitled to come home to. "Public health has always been considered the responsibility of community and State," Warren said. "I want to see it remain such a responsibility. . . . We have had enough investigation and enough talk to be ready for action. We have ample evidence that our people desire the protection. This is the time for action."[17]

The fundamental liberalism of Warren's inaugural had escaped notice. Not this time. The California Medical Association turned its full legislative energy to the defeat of Warren's proposal, and to do that it enlisted a natural ally, Clem Whitaker. They instructed him to kill any compulsory health insurance bill advanced by Warren or anyone else. Angered by their treatment by Warren in 1942 and philosophically opposed to a proposal they saw as socialistic, Whitaker and Baxter set out to destroy the principal policy objective of the Warren administration. For Whitaker and Baxter, this was business but also something more—a chance to get even.

Clem Whitaker believed in attack. "You can't wage a defensive campaign and win," he liked to tell clients.[18] When he had worked for Warren in 1942, Whitaker had been most pleased by the campaign's challenge to Governor Olson's war record; now he and Warren were on different sides, and Whitaker recognized that Warren's plan was vulnerable to criticism from the same quarter that had criticized Olson's—the conservative California press. In one sense, such criticism was unlikely: Warren was a Republican, after all, and one elected with overwhelming press support in 1942. But this plan was different, and Whitaker knew his audience. He had been working reporters and editors for years, through initiative campaigns, the anti-Sinclair effort in 1934, the campaign to defeat Ham and Eggs. And he knew publishers, too. In California, they were generally Republicans and conservatives, and though many supported Warren, Whitaker suspected he could sour them on the health care proposal if it was presented to them as a challenge to the free market. So Whitaker and Baxter labeled Warren's plan "socialized medicine," and they tapped the CMA's vast political budget—every member of the organization was levied a mandatory fee to help support the campaign[19]—and began to work on the press. They took out ads, they wrote feature stories and analyses, and they and their employees personally visited hundreds of newspaper offices up and down the state. Initially, about 50 of California's papers expressed at least mild support for Warren's proposal; after Whitaker and Baxter had gotten to them, the number dropped to about 20. Those opposing the plan started at about 100; by the end, 432 California papers had expressed opposition to its passage.[20]

Whitaker occasionally put pen to paper himself, and one of his columns captures the inflated sense of alarm marshaled against Warren's proposal. "National Health Insurance," Whitaker wrote, "with the cost being deducted from workers' paychecks, as proposed in California, has existed in England since 1911—and has been in operation long enough, therefore, to permit of realistic appraisal. Except for Nazi Germany, where the system may be considered in suspension, the British system furnishes the outstanding example of a government-controlled medical program."[21] "Government-controlled," "National Health Insurance," the wry evocation of "Nazi Germany"—these were all earmarks of a Whitaker and Baxter effort. In his column and in the campaign he managed, Whitaker went on to sneer at British inefficiencies and to complain of oppressive state oversight. As the campaign built, the Warren program thus became synonymous simultaneously with soft socialism and dangerous fascism, a neat trick of political invective.

Opponents took the threat personally. Warren aides complained that once the doctor learned who their boss was, they would be refused treatment; political allies reported that they suddenly found themselves accused of being Communists.[22] "It was amazing," Virginia Daly, Warren's eldest daughter, recalled more than sixty years later. "Suddenly, my father was hated."[23]

Warren was understandably taken aback, but he professed to have expected this reaction. "I was not surprised, of course, to witness opposition to the program develop," he said in a radio address on February 21, 1945. "Such proposals invariably develop passionate friends and violent foes. Such is the case here. But the comforting thing from my viewpoint is that the opposition has not argued, and I believe will not attempt to argue, that the people of our state are receiving or have ever received adequate medical care. On the contrary, it is generally admitted that such care is not now available."[24] Warren tried to return the issue to "facts," citing the health problems of draft-age young men uncovered by the Selective Service system, and stressing that he was open to suggestion for amendments to his proposal as written, so long as any alternative provided for universal coverage of the state's middle class. Trying to cool the debate off, Warren urged listeners to ask that "further light instead of heat be turned upon the subject."

The California Medical Association responded with a denunciation that called Warren's proposal "outrageously impractical." Its adoption, the CMA contended, would drive business from California and force huge tax hikes to pay for a program that would quickly spiral out of control.[25] Warren counterpunched again. California's climate, economy, and infrastructure would always make it attractive to business, he argued, and industry would only be further enticed by the prospect of a "healthy, happy working population." Warren reiterated that no patient would be forced to see a certain doctor, and that no doctor would be forced to participate. Those decisions would continue as before. The difference, Warren said, would become evident only in the moments that a working family most dreaded. Speaking of a hypothetical father, who had had 1.5 percent of his paycheck deducted for payment to the state insurance program, Warren then described that moment:

> Let's look ahead to a night when he is suddenly awakened to learn that his young daughter is seriously ill. What does he do? He calls the family physician. I hope you are following me closely now for I am talking about the procedure under the prepaid health plan. He calls the family physician just as he has always done and when the doctor arrives, he entrusts the child to the doctor's care just as he has always done.
>
> Should the family physician determine the child must be moved to a hospital, he consults with the doctor in regard to which hospital, just as he has always done.
>
> For this father and for most of us, it will be at this point that the real distinction between present-day procedure and procedure under the plan begins to become definitely apparent. It will come in the form of a sense of relief from financial worry, for the father will know when his child goes to the hospital that the bill is already paid.[26]

This time, Warren's foe was not Culbert Olson or Japanese-Americans. He was up against a determined and wealthy adversary acting in defense of what it believed were its core interests. What's more, though the CMA pushed its argument with hyperbole, it had genuine points to make. The threat of a health care bureaucracy was real, and though Warren and his allies argued that it paled beside the reality of an underinsured state, it alarmed some legislators, particularly Republicans. Whitaker and Baxter capitalized on that, as did the medical profession's lobbyists. Warren had tangled with banking lobbyists in considering his tax plan in 1943 and 1944; now the assembled medical lobby turned on him as well, deepening his conviction, which he never abandoned, that lobbying was a pernicious business that served to undermine democracy. Complicating matters still further, organized labor drafted legislation of its own, even more aggressive health insurance legislation. This was the prospect Warren had warned about—that more extreme voices would demand to be heard. The introduction of the labor bill probably increased public awareness and support for mandatory insurance, but it also had the effect of dividing support between labor's legislation and Warren's.

The Warren and labor bills were referred to the Assembly's Public Health Committee, where the Republican strategy soon became obvious: stall the matter in committee and avoid a roll-call vote that would expose members to retaliation. Warren worked furiously to dislodge his program—by March, Sweigert had convened a daily five P.M. meeting of cabinet secretaries to plot strategy.[27] In speeches and press conferences, Warren hammered at his opposition. When they refused to yield, Warren's comments reflected his deepening irritation. "They reminded me of the people whom Abraham Lincoln said 'could not distinguish between a horse chestnut and a chestnut horse,'" he wrote later.[28] The tension surrounding the bills grew as the Public Health Committee staged hearings in March. At one, Warren's point person on his bill, Nathan Sinai, fended off sharp questions about the program. Then one Republican opponent of the legislation, who had promised reporters a show at the hearing, grilled Sinai about his credentials. Sinai explained that he had multiple degrees, but the assemblyman wanted specifically to know about his medical education. When Sinai reluctantly admitted that he was credentialed as a veterinarian, the room burst into laughter. Merrell "Pop" Small, then a small-town newspaperman but soon to join the Warren administration, was watching from the press section. He realized at that moment that Warren was done. "Warren's health insurance bill," he wrote later, "was laughed to death."[29] It was, Sweigert admitted, "very embarrassing."[30]

Still, Warren fought on. Working through his chief legislative ally, Assemblyman Albert Wollenberg, Warren pushed for a vote to dislodge his bill from committee and force full consideration by the Assembly. On April 10, 1945, Wollenberg requested that the full Assembly consider the bill; his motion failed by a single vote, 39–38. Warren's bill was finished.

Less than a month later, on May 7, Admiral Karl Dönitz, having ascended to command of the German Reich upon Hitler's suicide a week earlier, announced his nation's unconditional surrender to Allied forces. At 11:01 P.M. the following day, fighting in Europe ended.[31] In the Pacific Theater, the war continued and appeared destined to culminate in a protracted and devastating island-to-island campaign. Military leaders predicted that hundreds of thousands would die on each side. Parents anxiously awaited word of the war's next turn. And then, on August 6, the atomic bomb destroyed Hiroshima, and on August 9, Nagasaki fell in a single blast. With those cities reduced to rubble by the only atomic weapons ever used in combat, Japan's emperor surrendered. He spoke to his nation over the radio on August 15 to announce that its war was lost. It was the first time the Japanese people had ever heard his voice.

World War II restructured the world. It left a scarred and devastated Europe, its fields trod upon by millions of boots, its cities gutted by gunshot and bombs. Germany lay in ruins, as did Poland, Italy, the Low Countries, and the western Soviet Union. Britain was resurrected from the Blitz, and staggered back to its feet. Europe's Jews were not so fortunate. Across the globe, two of Japan's industrial cities had evaporated in a single blast each, and the world contemplated the implications of those blinding explosions on the future now before it.

Beyond the physical ruin of Europe and Japan lay the political reassembly that the end of the war wrought. A curtain, as Churchill put it, came down across the center of Europe. Behind it, the grim Soviet empire consolidated its territorial gains and girded for the next war, the global struggle between communism and capitalism foreseen by Marx and encouraged by the Soviet heirs to his ideology.

The world's peace was America's victory, but it came at a staggering price. World War II cost America 405,399 lives in battle. Another 78,000 men, more than the number of Americans killed in Vietnam, were simply lost, forever declared missing in action. Thousands of children would grow up without fathers, thousands of widows would raise those children alone. And yet the war also had freed the nation from the Depression and unleashed its industry. The era defined by streams of Okies heading west, straggling across the California border in search of promise—the ravaged faces captured by Dorothea Lange, the dusty, dissipated lives memorialized in fiction by John Steinbeck—ended with the vitality of war. Now there was work and industry, and with them wealth. "At the end of the Depression decade, nearly half of all white families and almost 90 percent of black families had still lived in poverty. One in seven workers remained unemployed," writes David Kennedy in his unsurpassed account of that era. "By war's end unemployment was negligible. In the ensuing quarter century the American economy would create some twenty million new jobs, more than half of them filled by women."[32]

California lost its share of young men in combat during World War II. All told, 23,628 Californians perished in that conflict, dying in the myriad ways that the battlefield claims victims—of shots and explosions, of wounds, injuries, and illness, on ships at sea, in trenches, on cobbled streets and stifling jungles, and in the slow death of prison camps. Another 176 Californians vanished, their families deprived even of the solace of their remains.[33] And yet nowhere was the resurgence of American might more evident than in California. In place of those nearly 24,000 men lost to battle would come 850,000 more, streaming into the state from which many had shoved off during the war.[34] Most settled into the suburbs of Los Angeles, San Diego, and San Francisco. And just as their forebears had sent for family after the Gold Rush had peaked, so now did these men gather wives and children around them. They desperately needed housing, and a sizzling home-building industry hastened to supply it. They bought cars and set out on the new highways California was hurrying to pave. They brought energy and optimism—they had survived a war and were ready to live again.

"Along the highways into California," *Life* magazine reported in 1946, "are lines of automobiles bearing license plates from every state. New Californians are flooding auto courts, drive-ins, super-markets and schools."[35] *Life*'s pictures illustrated that cavalcade of newcomers: a farm family from Oklahoma in California for picking season but hoping to stay; an Ohio veteran dishing out ice cream at the local soda fountain; a Navy lieutenant who passed through California on his way to the war and came back to sell Buicks (cars were in such demand that the lieutenant started off by repairing cars, waiting for more Buicks to arrive); a doctor unable to find office space and instead working out of a lean-to; a sign painter from Memphis who shipped out to Manila from California during the war and who settled there afterward for the climate and because, as *Life* put it, "he noticed there were more signs there than anywhere else in the country."[36] Those men and women needed schools and electricity and water and jobs and every other amenity that modern life had to offer. Warren flogged the state government to supply them.

The war's end brought that new era to California, and as the conflict drew its final breaths, the state and its governor experienced a moment that brought past, present, and future together. On August 6, 1945, the same day that the United States exploded the atomic bomb over Hiroshima, Hiram Johnson, Earl Warren's idol and California's principal contribution to Progressive politics in America, died at the Naval Hospital in Bethesda, Maryland.[37]

Johnson's final bequest to his political heir, the sitting governor of California, was an opportunity: Warren had the chance to fill the vacancy created by Johnson's death, the power to appoint a United States senator. Warren used the opportunity to repay an old family friend, his first patron and trusted adviser, J. R. Knowland of the *Oakland Tribune,* whose support had helped Warren win his first seat as Alameda County district attorney and whose son had guided Warren into the 1942 contest for governor. William Knowland, then an Army officer stationed in England, was plucked from his military service and installed in the United States Senate. It was, self-evidently, the repayment of a personal and political debt, made easier by the competence of the man whose appointment fulfilled it. Still, for Warren, who loathed the notion of alliances based on anything but merit, it was hard to repay the family that had launched him. One reporter at his news conference announcing the appointment recalled years later that it was the only time he ever saw Warren uncomfortable.[38]

Knowland and Warren, friends in California and later in Washington, would govern side by side for decades, allies for most of that time, estranged nearer the end, when mental instability caught up with Knowland. Both died in 1974, Warren of age, Knowland of a self-inflicted gunshot wound.

Through the end of the war and the peace that followed, Warren continued to push his health care proposal, dogged effort in a losing cause. He amended his legislation to cover merely hospital costs, then tinkered with it in other ways intended to mollify the medical community. Each time, the CMA successfully opposed him, and their campaign against Warren turned from disagreement to bitter animus. Warren reciprocated. He forever believed that Whitaker and the association had, out of misguided self-interest and misfocused politics, undermined California's best hope to lead the nation in protecting its residents from illness. "[O]ur state," he wrote in his memoirs, "would have reaped great benefits from it."[39]

If Warren's critics outmaneuvered him in the health insurance debate, however, their victory was largely Pyrrhic, at least in political terms. Warren's fight on behalf of the legislation put him at odds with conservative Republicans for most of 1945 and 1946. The result was that when it came time to run for reelection in 1946, Democrats were hard-pressed to make an argument for unseating him. Even worse, they had no obvious candidate, so thoroughly did Warren now dominate the political landscape. Divided among themselves and unable to stomach the unopposed reelection of a Republican governor in a state that had not elected the same man twice in a row since Hiram Johnson, they turned to their only statewide elected official, Attorney General Robert Kenny.

That the burden of running against Warren should fall to Kenny was ironic and unfortunate. It was Kenny who had given Warren an important boost in Warren's first statewide campaign, the 1938 election that made Warren attorney general. Kenny had weathered Democratic criticism then for crossing party lines, but had survived it to become attorney general himself in 1942. Since then, he and Warren had resumed their collegial relations, finding common, practical solutions to the issues that confronted both as elected leaders of California.

Kenny had helped Warren respond to the Zoot Suit riots in 1943, and the two had worked together to provide for the compassionate reabsorption of the state's Japanese when the federal government at last ordered the internment camps closed near the end of 1944. "I am sure all Americans," Warren said, "will join in protecting constitutional rights of the individuals involved, and will maintain an attitude that will discourage friction and prevent civil disorder. It is the most important function of citizenship, as well as government, to protect constitutional rights and to maintain order."[40]

Warren warned law-enforcement agencies that he expected their forces to protect the returning internees and to intervene assertively in order to thwart violence and the threat of violence. Kenny, as the state's top law-enforcement officer, joined Warren in insisting on that as well. "Two county sheriffs," Kenny recalled years later, "openly defied our efforts to obtain peace officer cooperation for the peaceful relocation of the Japanese. Gov. Warren backed me up, and said that if the local constabulary did not protect the returning Nisei, he would see that state forces did so."[41] The sheriffs backed down. Although there were isolated acts of violence against the returning Japanese, amazingly, in light of the powerful emotions that had led to the internment and the continuing bloody war with Japan, the internees returned largely in peace and quietly resumed jobs and places in the life and economy of California, though often finding their homes and possessions scattered in their absence.

By 1946, then, Warren and Kenny had long admired each other across party lines. What's more, the two men genuinely liked each other. Kenny appreciated Warren's direct honesty, and Warren delighted in Kenny's raconteur wit. Still, politics is politics, and California's Democrats in 1946 were desperate. They prevailed on Kenny to run. Reluctantly, he agreed, then proceeded to run one of the worst campaigns for governor in California's history.

Just after announcing, Kenny informed reporters that he would be traveling to Nuremberg as a guest of U.S. Supreme Court Justice Robert Jackson, then acting as prosecutor for the war-crimes trials. Kenny laughed off those who questioned the strategic wisdom of missing the first two weeks of his own gubernatorial campaign. As long as he was out of the country, he argued, at least he couldn't make any mistakes.[42] Charm was not enough for Kenny. It was no easy job for a Democrat to take on Warren in 1946. Warren had championed health care, had built hospitals, and had asked the legislature for a full-employment bill. He supported a Fair Employment Practices Act, intended to "guarantee economic opportunity" to all.[43] Conservatives grumbled about their Republican governor, but Democrats could find no real way to get to Warren's left. Through most of the campaign, Kenny avoided even criticizing Warren, and when he did, it was so gentle as to often escape notice. The uneventful contest warranted just a single sentence in Warren's memoirs.

Its outcome, however, established Warren's preeminence in California politics beyond any other measure. On June 4, Republican voters unsurprisingly named Warren their candidate, preferring him to Kenny by 774,502 votes to 70,331. That was no great surprise. What was breathtaking was the action of California's Democrats. By a margin of 593,180 votes to 530,968,[44] the state's Democrats selected as their candidate a lifelong Republican who twelve years earlier had chaired his party during its campaign against Upton Sinclair and who just two years earlier had delivered the keynote address at the Republican National Convention. With the 1946 primary election, the Republican Party of the *Los Angeles Times* and the Associated Farmers and the Democratic Party of Sinclair and Carey McWilliams agreed on one thing: Both picked Earl Warren to lead them. Warren thus effectively sealed the election in the primary (he still faced token opposition in November from a Prohibition candidate and a write-in, but neither gave him trouble). Kenny took the loss with typically good humor: "I saved him from oblivion in 1938 and end in oblivion myself. You've got to be careful whom you help in politics."[45]

Among those heartened by Warren's victory were his friends in the FBI, who worried about the left-wing support they perceived for Kenny. The election, according to the Bureau's San Francisco special agent in charge, "provided a stunning blow to the Communist Party . . . and those laboring unions active in supporting political candidates." Kenny, the agent reported to headquarters, had been "supported, although not publicly endorsed, by the Communist Party," so his defeat "caused considerable doubt and speculation in the minds of Communist functionaries responsible for political activity."[46] Warren's victory thus pleased his proud benefactor in Washington, J. Edgar Hoover.

Sweigert, in his running, poetic ode to Warren, put it more brightly:

> . . . Earl had a trusted weapon
> Just suited to his style,
> And brandished it with gusto,
> 'Tis called the great Cross File.

> And with it mighty Warren
> Made all the yokels swoon;
> Not waiting for November,
> He slew young Bob in June.[47]

No other gubernatorial candidate had ever won such a victory, and none ever replicated the feat. It remains a singular achievement in the history of California politics. Warren thus emerged from 1946 as a virtually unassailable figure in his home state. His straitlaced liberal politics had become California's. His fusion of prudent spending, care with taxes, and lavish support for social and educational programs, his belief in free enterprise and public help—these values had become his state's. California's political center had at last arrived, in the program of its Republican governor and in the person of Earl Warren.

Chapter 12

# IN COMMAND

*You know Earl.*

Los Angeles Times POLITICAL EDITOR KYLE PALMER TO HERMAN PERRY,
FRIEND AND BENEFACTOR OF RICHARD NIXON[1]

W ARREN'S HISTORIC VICTORY in 1946 cemented his hold on the leadership of both California political parties. It also meant that he effectively won his seat in June, as the November general election now was turned into a mere formality. That gave Warren not only influence but also the latitude to use it, since his own political fortunes were, at least for the moment, secure.

Given that, others naturally looked to Warren for help. One of those in 1946 was a young Navy veteran, attempting his first foray into politics with a campaign for a Southern California congressional seat. Richard Nixon had plenty to recommend him to the voters of his district: He was young, smart, and ambitious. He was, moreover, an archetype of Southern California, emblematic of its emphatic bond with the Midwest and of the strong pulls of religious piety and social conservatism. "Lt. Nixon comes from good Quaker stock and is about thirty-five years of age," his first patron, bank manager Herman Perry, wrote in introducing Nixon to a Republican fact-finding committee searching for a candidate. "He is a graduate of Whittier College and a member of the Board. By hard work he obtained a scholarship to Duke University law school. He is a very aggressive individual. He was an orator and debater in high school and college."[2]

Nixon was no Earl Warren, however. In fact, they seemed almost to mirror each other, their opposing images portending the life of conflict upon which the two were embarking in the early months of 1946. As they each campaigned that spring and summer, Warren was fifty-five years old, tall, strapping, and handsome; Nixon, at thirty-three, was charismatic, to be sure, but his appearance was more glowering than garrulous. Warren was a graduate of U.C. Berkeley, the state's archetypal institution of higher education; Nixon came from the smaller, more parochial Whittier College. In their political demeanor, Warren was sunny and approachable, the model of a friendly leader floating above the tumult of politics. Nixon seethed; his signature political posture was the attack. And where Warren prided himself on his professional nonpartisanship, Nixon believed strongly in the contest of the two-party system. He was firmly and unequivocally a Republican. When his daughter Patricia was born in 1946—just in time for her birth to figure in his campaign—Nixon announced, "Patricia is a lucky girl. She will grow up in the finest state in the union, in the greatest country on earth. She will grow up, go to schools and when the time comes she will register and vote Republican."[3] It is impossible to imagine Earl Warren ever uttering such a sentence.

Whatever schools she would attend and however she would register, Tricia Nixon would also grow up in the era of Earl Warren. For as Richard Nixon set out to launch a career in California politics, he did so in Warren's shadow, which had important ramifications for their relationship and for Nixon's early political development. Warren, by defining and personifying the political center of California, exerted a gravitational force on the state's ideological universe. Others bent toward him. Those who attempted to defy that force risked appearing marginal or strange. That tug was never stronger than in 1946, and one of those thus pulled into Warren's orbit was the young Richard Nixon. Temperamentally, Nixon was his own man. He railed hard against Communists, but the young candidate nevertheless presented himself as an advocate of "practical liberalism," a self-conscious attempt to appeal to the middle that Warren had carved for Republican candidates in a Democratic electorate. In his first run for political office, Nixon cross-filed as a Democrat and a Republican, this fiercely competitive Republican thus emulating the tactic that Warren had pioneered as a self-described nonpartisan.

If all of that reflected Warren's tug on Nixon's politics, however, the more penetrating impact of Warren's influence was in the tone it established between them: From the very beginning, the relationship between Nixon and Warren was characterized by Nixon's resentment of Warren and Warren's contempt for Nixon. Nixon was in a tough race in 1946. He was challenging Democrat Jerry Voorhis, an able and intelligent iconoclast with a base among Southern California's Left and an incumbent who already had spent a decade in the House. So Nixon's associates reached out to Warren, hoping the popular governor would consider an endorsement—valuable in any race but especially in one where Nixon hoped to cast Voorhis as extreme while Nixon argued that he was the genuine moderate in tune with the district. Warren refused. Adding to the slight, Voorhis made the most of

Warren's silence, releasing a complimentary letter Warren had written to him ear-lier and even endorsing Warren as "the better man" in the governor's race. Eager for any word to rebut those comments, Nixon's camp urged Warren at least to recant the letter to Voorhis. Warren again refused.[4]

Nixon's supporters were livid. "[H]e was a man who wanted everyone to sup-port him when he was running for office, but never wanted to give anyone else any help when the other fellow was running for office," Earl C. Adams, a Los Angeles lawyer who helped encourage Nixon to run in 1946, remembered in a 1975 inter-view. "It was all for Warren."[5]

In the June primary, when Warren won both party nominations in his historic rout, Voorhis appeared to finish comfortably. He won the Democratic victory and tallied half as many votes as Nixon on the Republican side. It was then, however, that Voorhis made his critical mistake. He viewed those numbers through over-confidence, failing to appreciate how far Nixon had come in a few short months. Thinking he was safe, Voorhis challenged Nixon to a series of debates. That ele-vated Nixon to Voorhis's stage (a tactical error) and overlooked Nixon's talent for the cut and thrust of personal politics (a substantive mistake). Voorhis gave Nixon his chance. Nixon made the most of it.

Their first debate was on Friday, September 13, at a junior high school in the tiny, conservative town of South Pasadena. Introduced by Murray Chotiner, Nixon arrived late but ready. When Nixon accused Voorhis of being supported by a left-wing labor organization known as the CIO-PAC, Voorhis demanded that Nixon prove it. Nixon then reached into his pocket and took from it a copy of *Action of Today*, a publication of the National Citizens Political Action Committee, which worked with the CIO and which Nixon accused of supporting Voorhis.[6] In fact, the PAC elected not to endorse Voorhis, but the congressman was unaccountably caught by surprise and mumbled an unconvincing reply, managing to damage himself further by conceding that there was a "grave question" of Communist in-fluence at the CIO.[7] Nixon partisans at the debate booed Voorhis lustily, and the congressman's career drained out of the hourglass. After the debate, Voorhis asked a longtime friend and admirer how he had done. "Jerry," his friend answered, "he murdered you."[8]

The pattern was set for the balance of the debates. Nixon was plucky and ag-gressive, Voorhis wavering and unsure. Still, Voorhis was an incumbent and popu-lar among Democrats. With the election approaching, some Nixon confidants continued to hold out hope that Warren would give them a boost. In September, Warren proved that he was not averse to all endorsements, as he announced his support for William Knowland's senatorial campaign. That was hardly a surprise—Warren, after all, had named Knowland to the Senate—but it suggested that Warren might be open to helping another fellow Republican. At Nixon headquarters, however, the phone never rang.

Despite Warren's refusal to help, Nixon defeated Voorhis in 1946 by nearly 15,000 votes. This marked the beginning of his extraordinary career, one filled with accomplishment and setback, destined to unfold alongside that of Earl Warren. For now, the two men shadowed each other, Nixon heading off to Washington, miffed that the governor had not helped him, and Warren settling in for his second term as governor, astonished that Nixon's people would even have asked.

In Sacramento, Warren returned to office with barely an interruption. His command of California was confirmed by his reelection, and he now enjoyed surveying his domain from a favorite perk of office. Warren converted a National Guard C-47 plane into one at the service of the governor. He nicknamed it "Grizzly Bear" and loved riding in it up and down his far-flung state, typically logging seven or eight trips a month and eventually amassing more than 250,000 miles in it.[9]

Warren's second inaugural address, delivered on January 6, 1947, continued along the lines Warren had established in his first term. With the war now over, Warren redoubled his denunciation of partisanship—"There has been little blind partisanship or personal controversy to hinder our attention to the job to be done," he said—insisted that the state pay for programs as it went, argued for extension of the 1943 tax cuts, and called for expansion of programs and institutions that served the state's growing population. Warren never raised his voice, never harangued or pleaded, but his enthusiasm for the task of leading permeated his address.

"Our task will not be easy," he said. But he added, "It can be thrilling."[10]

Addressing the state's principal problems, Warren identified two, both associated with its rapid growth. Housing was needed to accommodate returning veterans and new immigrants, and Warren was unwilling to wait for the private sector to adjust to the need. Housing materials were available as a result of the federal government's closing of bases and the like, and Warren proposed that the state take over that material and put it to use. "It is the obligation of State Government to assist in every way to make this material easily and promptly available to veterans who desire to purchase it," he said. Similarly, Warren urged legislators to take advantage of a building boom in order to "make it possible to eliminate the blighted areas of our cities." Here again, the pattern of previous political advocacy held: Warren used veterans to justify a program, then found ways to extend it to others, largely the poor and middle class. Turning then to another area of concern, Warren added, "Comparable only to the distress resulting from the housing shortage is the tragic situation in which we find ourselves as the result of an outgrown highway system. Our streets and roads have become places of frightful danger, and our economic development is being retarded."[11]

The governor did not tell legislators that afternoon what he intended to do about the state's "frightful" highway problem but did announce that he was calling the legislature into special session to address the issue. In California, the special session was—and still is—a device used by governors to focus the legislature on a particular topic and to allow bills enacted at such sessions to take effect more quickly than under normal circumstances. By calling the session on highways, as he had on health insurance in 1944, Warren elevated the issue to the top of the state's political agenda and created a path for quick action.

The following Monday, he made clear what it was precisely that he had in mind: an increase in the gas tax to pay for road and highway construction. Californians in those days paid 3 cents a gallon of state taxes on gasoline, and Warren proposed to double it to 6 cents. That was a significant tax, but one with the potential for real return. Russell H. Conwell, in his "Acres of Diamonds" speech that made such an impression on young Earl Warren, had advised that "he who can give to this city better streets . . . he will be great anywhere."[12] Warren believed that all his life, and his gasoline tax was meant to fulfill it. Under Warren's proposal, the money from the tax would fund highway construction across the state, construction he argued was needed to make roads safer but also to uncork California's economy, which depended in large measure on swift transport of goods across large distances only barely touched by railroads. The state's leading oil executives were flabbergasted. Many had contributed to Warren's campaigns in 1946. And now he proposed to tax them.

As did the medical association, the oil companies fought back. And like the medical association, they did not always fight cleanly. Led by the Western Oil and Gas Association, which represented nearly all of California's oil producers, the oil interests mailed postcards to California car owners, asking such leading questions as "Do you want your taxes raised?" When owners replied that they did not, the cards flooded the legislature.[13] While the legislature debated Warren's tax increase, the oil companies raised gas prices, first in August 1946 and again in January 1947. Furious at the increases and still angry at his treatment by the medical association, Warren wheeled on these new right-wing adversaries with the full legal and political force of his office. He denounced the companies and their executives, publicly asked the United States Department of Justice to investigate the antitrust implications of the gas price hikes, and consented to a rare deal in order to win passage of his measure.

The Justice Department's announcement that it would open an antitrust case rattled the oil companies; in Warren's dry retelling, "the cohesion of the opposition disintegrated."[14] In the state Assembly, however, the oil companies pressed on, and seemed to have victory in hand, though by the barest of margins. Warren, unwilling to lose two battles in two terms, stumped hard for the tax and lashed back at the oil companies: "While the slick lobbyists of the oil companies are overwhelming the capital with false propaganda and presumably are sobbing for the motorist, who is being asked to pay only his fair share for decent highways which will protect the lives of our people, the oil companies have connived to siphon off the loose change of the people before the Legislature arrives at a conclusion."[15]

This was unusually prickly coming from Warren, but the governor had been checkmated in the health insurance debate by one group of conservative opponents and their lobbyists; he was in no mood to lose again. That is also evidenced by his rare departure from his self-imposed ban against horse trading for votes. The Assembly was closely divided over the measure, and Warren's aides told him it might come down to a single vote. One Los Angeles assemblyman, they added, might be willing to deal his vote in exchange for Warren's willingness to sign a piece of legislation close to his heart, a bill requiring that any pet food containing horse meat be labeled as to whether its contents had been inspected. Warren looked at the bill, saw no reason to object, and agreed. With that, the assemblyman joined the gas-tax ranks, and dog food sold in California thereafter was labeled "inspected" or "un-inspected."[16]

"This was the only time I ever made a trade with a legislator for his vote," Warren wrote later, "but it was for an important one."[17] Warren had his victory, and with it, California had its highways.

Warren and the oil companies parted as enemies in that debate, and one in particular would come back to haunt the governor. William Keck, head of the Superior Oil Company, had angrily fought the bill, and the oil industry had threatened to pull the companies out of California if the tax passed. Warren called the bluff, and won.[18] Keck, whose wealth and family foundation would make him a significant force in California social history, went away mad, but his pique must rank among the most shortsighted in the history of special interest complaints. The tax that Warren succeeded in passing over Keck's objections helped to pay for paving thousands of miles of California highways. Cars multiplied and took to those roads. By the mid-1950s, California's image was inextricable from that of the automobile. Those cars ran on the gasoline that Keck and his company sold, and they piled up miles on highways that Keck had fought against.

Beyond the gas tax, Warren pressed the balance of a social agenda whose liberal tilt was becoming undeniable. In 1947, he submitted the first single-year budget in California history, the state having outgrown its practice of budgeting in two-year cycles. "We are dealing with a bigger and more diversified postwar California, with expansion in almost every field," he announced. Given that, Warren found almost every one of the state's problems worthy of more government spending. He proposed the construction of two new mental health clinics; improvements in medical, surgical, and hospital care; a new school for juvenile delinquents and a medium-security prison for adults; more money for crime prevention, for education, and for a vast expansion of the state's social welfare system, whose spending Warren boosted from $6.7 million a year to $61 million a year, mostly in grants to counties for taking care of the problems of California's poor and indigent. As before, he proposed those expansions not only without new sales or income taxes (he was supporting the gas tax hike, but only for the specific purpose of road and highway construction), but actually with the continuation and extension of his 1943 cuts. Warren's budget, like those before, survived the legislative process largely intact. As much as conservatives might find to dislike in him, they also found him persistently difficult to beat.[19]

Over time, Warren's spending bore witness to his ideology—not once as governor would he substantially curtail any program that benefited poor or working people; not once but twice did he seek tax increases in the face of determined special interest opposition. Moreover, his commitment to social justice found purchase in a much smaller but telling act, only barely noticed at the time or remembered later. It was executed with Warren's signature professionalism and calm. The results, not the rhetoric, testified to its importance.

In 1945, five Mexican-American fathers, fed up with the segregation of their children into so-called Mexican schools in Southern California, filed a lawsuit, led by Gonzalo Mendez, challenging the existence of that separate school system. The Orange County school district defendants argued that the separation was based on language, not race, but the reality of their schools belied that. Language testing was rudimentary, and assignment to the schools was based not on one's command of English but rather on one's appearance and last name. Students assigned to a Mexican school were not permitted to leave it once they mastered English; they remained there until graduation. The result was unambiguous racial discrimination. In the small town of Westminster, for instance, two elementary schools educated local children. One, Westminster School, enrolled 628 Anglo children and 14 Latino children. The other, Hoover School, had 152 students, all of them of Mexican descent.[20] In another district, two schools shared the same property, their entrances just 120 yards apart. One had 83 "English-speaking" students and 25 "Spanish-speaking" students; the other had 249 "Spanish-speaking" children and not a single white.[21]

The United States Supreme Court still sanctioned "separate but equal" education in those years, so the federal judge who heard the Mendez lawsuit, Paul J. McCormick, could easily have dismissed it. Instead, he ruled on behalf of the Mexican-American families that the districts were deliberately discriminating on racial grounds and denying those families the equal protection of the law. His ruling amazed and angered the school districts, whose lawyer then appealed to the Ninth U.S. Circuit Court of Appeals. That appeal was taken up in 1946, and then Attorney General Robert Kenny, serving out the end of his term after having lost to

Warren in the governor's race, entered an amicus brief for the State of California on behalf of the families. There is no evidence that Warren himself participated in the filing of that brief, but he soon made his views clear on the subject of segregated education. While the appeals court upheld McCormick's ruling, it did not embrace some of his reasoning, finding on narrower grounds. The Ninth Circuit ruling could have ended the matter; had it, the Orange County schools would have been desegregated but California's education code would have remained burdened by two racist artifacts of the Progressive era. Those code sections, while not authorizing discrimination against Mexican-Americans, did allow for the segregation of Indian children and those of "Chinese, Japanese or Mongolian parentage."[22]

In June 1947, those sections were struck from the code upon the signature of California's governor, Earl Warren. For those who would later express surprise at Warren's position in *Brown v. Board of Education,* the *Mendez* case should have offered a clue. But, like much of Warren's building legacy in those years, it was accomplished with little fanfare. By the end of 1947, racial segregation in California schools was illegal; by the end of 1954, it would be for the nation as well. The same man was responsible for both.


As GOVERNOR, Warren was surrounded by aides and acquaintances, many of them eager to presume friendship. In fact, he befriended few. He was guarded and cautious, and not many men, and even fewer women, crossed the threshold from cheerful acquaintance to trusted friend. His top staff, including MacGregor and Sweigert, were devoted but subordinate, trusted aides but not exactly friends. Bill Knowland was a political friend and a good one, but he was in Washington, placed there by Warren.

And yet a few did penetrate Warren's reserve. Warren Olney never was far away for long. And during the years that Warren served in Sacramento, he met three men who would find their way through into the closest circle of his friendship. Bart Cavanaugh, the city manager for Sacramento, shared a love of sports and children with Warren. The two started by taking in local games together—their boys attended high school together, and Warren and Cavanaugh liked to sneak over to the stadium to catch their football games. In time, they settled into the robust life of fans, traveling to San Francisco or Los Angeles and taking in a weekend full of sports. Warren usually would root for the local team—he enjoyed his partisanship on the field if not in the office—and during baseball games, he would keep a meticulous scorecard.[23] One exception to Warren's local centrism was the Yankees, for whom he rooted faithfully. Even there, the reason was based in California: The Yankees' great star Joe DiMaggio came from San Francisco. Warren, later to become a habitué of Toots Shor's in New York, came to know DiMaggio on and off the field, even attending the funeral of DiMaggio's mother with Cavanaugh. For their trips to games, Cavanaugh made arrangements, taking care to line up with the rest of the fans and to buy their tickets so as not to be accused of accepting freebies. Their devotion to sports established their bond, which deepened over their children. Each suffered the illnesses of their youngsters, and confided his pain in the other. Their friendship stretched across decades and led, in later years, to an annual pilgrimage; the World Series has known few more devoted fans than Earl Warren and Bart Cavanaugh.

Another lifelong friendship was struck by happenstance in the clattering comfort of a train. It was the summer of 1944, and Earl and Nina were returning to California from Chicago on the City of San Francisco, which ran the route in those days. Jesse Steinhart was on board as well, and he introduced the Warrens to another passenger, Benjamin H. Swig. Swig was one of the most ambitious and successful real estate investors in America, having mastered a system of purchasing expensive properties with little cash outlay of his own. None of that would have impressed Warren much, but Swig also nurtured an abiding appreciation for public service, and as the two men talked, they found much to like about each other. Swig was on his way to take over his newest acquisition, the Fairmont Hotel, an iconic San Francisco monument that had survived the 1906 earthquake, only to fall into shabbiness during the Depression. Swig appreciated luxury, and he would soon refashion the Fairmont into one of San Francisco's great hotels—it would become The City's traditional Election Night home for Democratic candidates, and in later years the Warrens' home away from home, when they would return to California from Washington for holidays. With his canny eye for a deal, Swig also assumed another role for the Warrens. A lifetime of public service gave Warren power and importance, but it did not make him rich. As a result, he worried about money, and Swig helped ease those concerns by guiding Warren's investments. He kept an eye out for promising real estate opportunities in the West, and eventually got Earl and Nina Warren a share of the Fairmont itself.[24]

The third of Warren's new friendships in those years was, in at least one way, the least likely. Reporters liked Warren. His professionalism was so thorough that it overcame their doubts, and they allowed that he was straight and honest. But that admiration was not often reciprocated. With rare exceptions, Warren did not confide in reporters. He presented to them and answered their questions, but they were kept apart from him. One exception was Drew Pearson. A sharp-tongued liberal, educated in elite private schools, Pearson was an enthusiastic champion of the New Deal and a fierce advocate of American involvement in World War II (as with Warren, Pearson's support for the war had triumphed over his commitment to civil liberties; he too supported the internment of the Japanese). Pearson launched his career as a correspondent for the *Baltimore Sun* but moved in the early 1930s to the

*Washington Post,* where he wrote a widely syndicated and much-feared column, "The Washington Merry-Go-Round." Pearson was flashier than most Warren friends—no one would ever accuse Warren Olney or Bart Cavanaugh of coveting the limelight. But Pearson was passionate about his work and his country. He was connected to power but not in awe of powerful men or women. All that appealed to Warren, who appreciated Pearson's work more and more as they came to know each other—Pearson would, in fact, help Warren decode some of Washington's mores when Warren's career took him there in 1953.

They first met on November 7, 1947, "on a floodlit platform on Sunset Boulevard in Hollywood," as Pearson remembered it.[25] Pearson then was stumping for a project he had conceived and promoted in his column, a Friendship Train intended to solicit food contributions for Europe and to embarrass President Truman for not doing more to help the continent then paralyzed by strikes, suffering under a poor harvest, and still trying to shrug off the ravages of war. Pearson hoped the train would stir American sympathies and invited governors to join him in order to drum up support for the idea; their endorsement, he hoped, would bring the campaign credibility and seriousness, would elevate it beyond a mere columnist gimmick. "I confess therefore to a feeling of considerable gratitude when I met the Governor of California on the platform," Pearson wrote, adding that Warren arrived with Nina and "one statuesque blond daughter." They rode together on the train that day, and Warren spoke at each stop, "nothing very pretentious," but sincere and political—Warren made a point of telling each audience that no federal official was aboard the train. At each little city, local volunteers brought another bundle of food. By the time the Friendship Train arrived in Sacramento, the project was a success, and Earl Warren and Drew Pearson were friends.[26]

At home, the Warrens were settled into their public life. Their children were growing, and, as Pearson was hardly the only one to notice, attracting attention. Virginia was an eye-catching young woman, and men and boys regularly would write to her unbidden. During the war, she took to corresponding with servicemen. She did it as a wartime duty, and most appreciated the notes in the spirit they were sent, but at least one of her correspondents took it too far. He showed up one day at the mansion to ask Virginia on a date and explained to the guard that they had been writing each other. Virginia was suddenly confronted with her own growing effect on men: "I got kind of scared," she confided to her mother's assistant. "I sort of stopped writing letters after that."[27] Earl Jr. was more studious, while Dorothy was quiet and levelheaded, and she sometimes seemed forgotten between her magnetic older and younger sisters.[28] Bobby and Honey Bear were the family spitfires, athletic and spirited. There was little they would not attempt. Honey Bear took up skiing as a youngster, and headed off on adventures by herself. Before dawn on Saturday mornings, sometimes as early as three-thirty A.M., she trudged to the local bus stop with her skis and equipment and caught the bus for Lake Tahoe. She spent the day on the slopes, then came back the same night (the bus trip took four to five hours). It was nine P.M. by the time she got home, but Nina would run her a bath and bring her dinner in bed. The next morning, she was off again. Honey Bear was a fixture on the slopes as she was in the California imagination; when Squaw Valley opened in 1949, Honey Bear was the first person after the ski patrol to ski the mountain. A friend on the patrol got her the first ride.[29] One person who watched her grow up remembered that Honey Bear "had no physical fear of anything."[30]

Bobby was just as daring. So driven was he on the football field—as a high school junior, he started as a defensive guard, and in his senior year moved to starting at offensive center—that his mother refused to go to games, afraid to see him hurt. Bobby played anyway, making the all-city team that year and going on to an impressive college career as well. He also followed his sister's footsteps into skiing, with one difference: As a boy, Bobby was allowed to spend the night at Lake Tahoe, rather than having to return and head for the slopes again the next morning.[31]

Initially apprehensive about being California's First Lady, Nina came to enjoy it and balanced its obligations with her responsibilities for the Warren children. Her small staff adored her. She was blessed, her aides liked to say, with an "educated heart."[32] When she traveled with Earl, she would spy trinkets or modest presents to give to staff members, picking them with care and explaining the gift in such a way that made it more personal. When she gave her secretary, Betty Foot Henderson, a cashmere sweater, Nina explained, "Once you have a cashmere sweater, nothing else is quite as comfortable. My girls just love these, and so do I, and so I just thought you should have one, too."[33]

Nina's attention to others extended beyond her staff. There was a woman who lived nearby in Sacramento. She was alone and on welfare, and survived on modest meals cooked on her hot plate in a one-room apartment. Somehow her path crossed with Nina's, and Nina was touched by her situation and her pride—the woman refused offers of help. Every so often, when Earl was scheduled to be out of town, Nina would cook a large meal—a turkey, say. She would then call one of the governor's security officers and instruct him to take it to the woman and to explain to her that Nina had made it expecting the governor to return and then had learned that he was busy for dinner. Nina would then phone the woman and urge her to take the food. "Please do me a favor and take this food off my hands," she asked. Happy to do so, the woman would then invite other struggling neighbors to join her in a meal provided by California's First Lady. "So you see," Betty Foot Henderson recalled, "Mrs. Warren's gifts were more than giving."[34]

Nina Warren enjoyed her husband's success, and ran the governor's mansion with the same cheerful efficiency that she had shown at 88 Vernon. Earl Warren's rising stature did, however, expose him to a wider range of celebrities, and Nina oc-

casionally displayed a protective streak. There was, for instance, the time that Warren was invited to lead a parade in the coastal city of Monterey. His staff accepted
the invitation, but Nina Warren asked to skip the event and stay home. When that
was communicated to the sponsors, they suggested that Ginger Rogers accompany
the governor. Warren's aide agreed. "The governor will be very happy," he said.
"Miss Rogers is a friend of theirs." Earl might have been agreeable to spending
an afternoon in an open car with a beautiful actress, but Nina was not about to let
that happen. When her assistants heard of the arrangements, one turned to another
and remarked, "I'll bet Mrs. Warren decides to go." The parade went off as scheduled, led by two cars. One carried Ginger Rogers, the other bore Nina and Earl
Warren.[35]

WARREN'S EXTRAORDINARY record and centrist appeal—the tax-cutter who still
managed to attack segregation and build roads and water projects, hospitals, prisons, and mental health facilities—drew him back to national politics through the
1940s. As in 1944, the run-up to the 1948 Republican convention centered first on
Dewey, the party's presumptive nominee, but Warren remained a contender in his
own right. Coming to Philadelphia as the head of California's delegation and with
its votes pledged to him, Warren stood an outside chance at securing the nomination if it deadlocked between Dewey and his principal rivals, Harold Stassen, Arthur Vandenberg, and Robert Taft.

On June 23, 1948, Warren's old friend, University of California president Robert
Gordon Sproul, placed Earl Warren's name in nomination for the presidency of the
United States. His speech was given in Warren's name and in keeping with his
gentle style of persuasion. No rivals were derided, no nastiness expressed. "Our
pleasant difficulty," Sproul told the delegates, "is the selection from among these
well-qualified aspirants, of that one [who] will most surely appeal to the majority
of the voters of the country, in all its parts and from all walks of life."[36] Sproul's
nomination of his friend was relatively brief—just fifteen minutes—but it wittily
and thoughtfully summed up Warren's appeal. Warren, Sproul said, was a man
raised modestly, a university graduate—"and of no mean university," the university
president added for laughs—a lawyer, a veteran, and a dynamic, vigorous leader:

> He is a modest man, with a high sense of duty, who surrounds himself with men of sim-
> ilar character, with records of achievement elsewhere than in a corrupt city or county ma-
> chine. . . . As Governor of California, a commonwealth larger, wealthier and more complex
> than many of the nations of the world, Earl Warren has demonstrated unusual capacity to
> replace public dissatisfaction with government by good will, confidence and cooperation.
> He is calm, logical and judicial in his approach to the problems of government.[37]

Explaining Warren's political philosophy to the delegates, Sproul was emphatic: "Earl Warren is a liberal," he said, "but only in the true sense of that much-abused word, i.e. he understands the basic forces at work in our society, and recognizes the weaknesses and defects of our system, as well as the unmatched merit of its performance and promise." Finally, after recounting Warren's tremendous string of political successes in California, Sproul insisted that Warren could win nationally as well. "Make no mistake about it," Sproul said, "this man Warren has the mark of victory upon him."[38]

Not in 1948. Warren hoped protracted disagreement would turn the convention to him, but he did little to help his own cause. He arrived with California's 53 delegates in his pocket and hoped for a long enough deadlock that other candidates would fold and release their votes. Instead, Dewey came on strong. Needing 548 votes to secure the nomination, he got 434 on the first ballot. He picked up 81 more in the second round and was clearly rolling toward a victory when Warren, seeing there was no more use in fighting, called to concede and to pledge California's delegates to Dewey's cause. That sealed the nomination, and then Dewey turned to the same idea he had tried but failed to execute in 1944. He leaned on Warren to accept the vice presidency. At four-thirty A.M. on June 25, with the sky still dark over Philadelphia, Dewey summoned Warren to his hotel suite and began to work on him.[39] For hours, the New York governor tried to persuade Warren to take a spot on the ticket—the same spot Warren had turned down in 1944 and vowed not to accept this year. Warren attempted various defenses. He objected to taking a cut in pay to become vice president; Dewey vowed to seek an increase. Warren complained that he would have little to do beyond presiding over the Senate; Dewey promised to make him a member of the cabinet. And this time, Dewey impressed another fact on Warren: Party leaders would not come calling forever. Warren might prefer the top of the ticket, but it was not his, and should he continue to rebuff the party, it might well lose interest in him.

Sometime during those talks, Eugene Meyer, patriarch of the *Washington Post,* found a moment to twist Warren's arm further, implying that Warren's resistance was egotism. "No man," Meyer told the governor, "is too big to run for Vice President."[40] It was this year or nothing, Warren became convinced. Sometime after dawn Warren gave in.[41] He trudged back to his hotel suite and broke the news to Nina, who reluctantly endorsed the idea but worried her husband would not take well to running in Dewey's shadow.

"For the first time in my life, I know what it feels like to get hit by a street-car," Warren told the convention. He proceeded to stammer out an acceptance speech and pledged to wage a "great crusade" for the Republican ticket and to give Dewey his full support as president. That night, Warren called home to tell his sons the news. Bobby answered the phone, and his father told him he had been nominated by the Republican Party to run for the vice presidency of the United States. "Is that good?" Bobby asked.[42]

The crusade was a curious one, reflecting both Warren's discomfort in the fast waters of partisan politics and Dewey's firm conviction that the presidency was his to lose. He had reason to think this was a Republican year. The Democrats spent much of the summer tearing themselves to pieces. Young Strom Thurmond led the States' Rights Party, known as the "Dixiecrats," in their abandonment of Truman; they instead held their own convention and named Thurmond as the South's candidate for president. Henry Wallace, meanwhile, attempted to stake out the left, launching his own presidential bid under the Progressive banner. Amid that confusion, Warren and Dewey conducted a mild, issue-free effort. In fact, Warren took the first weeks of the campaign off, heading to Santa Monica to join his family for time at the beach.

When Warren did begin the campaign in earnest, he followed orders issued by the top-heavy Dewey organization. They made a few perfunctory joint appearances, including a memorable one with both their families. At that gathering, Tom Dewey, Jr., found himself transfixed by Dorothy Warren—"Look at the camera, please, Tom," his father implored.[43] After that, however, the two candidates largely campaigned independently of each other. Warren's principal contribution was a thirty-one-day train trip that took him to most of the United States—outside the South, that is, where Republican inroads were deemed impossible.

When there were just six weeks to go before Election Day, Warren boarded his special campaign train in Sacramento and headed east, accompanied by his wife Nina and daughter Virginia, as well as stalwart Bill Sweigert, who joined the campaign in order to lend Warren help writing speeches. As the train prepared to pull away, the Warrens came to the rail and smiled broadly for the crowd. Warren leaned forward toward the camera, his flashy tie jutting from his double-breasted suit. At his left elbow was Nina, striking in a flowered hat, gloved hands gently resting on the rail. Behind and between her parents Virginia beamed.[44] The fourteen-car train, the Aleutian, then pulled out of the station. On board, Warren settled in with the newsmen. He drank three bourbon highballs and in between them sucked on lemon drops for his voice. He carried a copy of Churchill's *The Gathering Storm*. Warren worked, read, and socialized. By midnight, as the train raced through the night and across the Nevada plain, he was asleep.[45]

Although the atmosphere of the train in those weeks was exciting—devoted crowds met the governor and his party at every stop—it also was wearing. It was, Warren recalled later, "a grind."[46] Warren woke early, rising sometimes on the train, sometimes in a local hotel. He spoke to a crowd almost every morning, then the train pulled out and stopped once or twice during the day. Between stops, while newsmen and staff relaxed, Sweigert would organize his thoughts and then put the next speech on paper. He then would share it with Warren, who would pull it back apart, and both men then would try to put it back together yet again. It was agonizing and repetitive. "My life," Sweigert said, "was a life of misery on that train."[47] What's more, the speeches were singularly uninspired, as Warren was under strict orders from the Dewey team not to rock the boat. This was to be a safe campaign, and so the speeches were written to be bland. Nothing was to be said or done that would disrupt the Republicans' ordained return to power that year.

So convinced were the pundits of the ticket's victory that solidly Republican *Time* magazine treated Warren's tour more as a victory lap than as a barnstorm. On the second night of the trip, Warren addressed a Republican gathering in Salt Lake City and asked what *Time* and others called the central question of the campaign: "Is the present national administration displaying the unity, the competence and the leadership to warrant extending its tenure to 20 years? Or has the time come for better housekeeping methods that can only be supplied by new leadership and a new broom?"

Warren asked the question. *Time* answered it: "By every available piece of evidence, the voters had already made up their minds to answer: yes, it's time for a change. That was why Earl Warren could afford to campaign like a big, friendly Saint Bernard, tail-wagging his way east across the nation. The Republicans had only to raise no ruckus, make no thumping blunders, keep their fingers crossed against a world upheaval—and their election seemed assured."[48]

That plan guaranteed a dull campaign, and Warren helped provide it. Traveling through the West, Warren held forth about the region and its growth, its emerging position as the American center of gravity, an empire unto itself. He knew the West and showed it. He remarked on dams that had helped conserve its water, he discussed the issues of farmers and developers, the importance of migration and resources, the common Spanish heritage of the Southwestern states. His familiarity was charming, and even his gaffes were appreciated, as when he began one speech by praising Governor Dewey for his "great record in the State of California." The crowd laughed, and Warren corrected himself: "I mean in the State of New York. You know I can't get away from California. I never wanted to, anyway."[49]

That last aside was revealing. Throughout the record of his thirty-one-day voyage, one senses his longing for California. Warren dutifully performed the role of vice presidential candidate. He lamented the disjointed state of American foreign policy, he demonstrated his own Republican internationalism by embracing the United Nations, he even launched a brief attack on the Truman administration's vulnerability to domestic Communists. "If Tom Dewey becomes President of the United States," Warren said in Cincinnati, ". . . you will have no further trouble about getting Communists out of the national government because he will just never let them in." Communists had infiltrated the Truman government, Warren added, "because at times the national administration has become soft on Communists. They have catered to their votes, and when they got their votes they owed them something, and because they owed them something, some of them infiltrated our government."[50]

But Warren's appearances felt forced, and the attack on Truman's handling of Communists demonstrated it. To suggest that Truman's trouble with Communists was the result of electoral politics—that he needed their votes and rewarded them with jobs—fell somewhere between nonsensical and laughable. In either case, it was far below Warren's normal standards for political debate and suggests the extent to which he was operating out of his element. Virginia Warren, while enjoying the summer—with its professional, high-speed hubbub of reporters and staff—also describes her father as a harried figure in those weeks, always forced to write another speech and welcome another dignitary.[51]

While Warren and Dewey cautiously circled the country and tried to run out the clock, Harry Truman campaigned his way. He summoned the Republican-majority 80th Congress back to Washington and dared it to follow the lead of its party platform in enacting humane legislation. When Congress adjourned with little to show for itself, Truman had an issue. And on the stump, he was as feisty as Dewey and Warren were staid. Two days after Warren left California for his tour, Truman set out on his own, taking one of several train trips from which the phrase "whistle-stop campaign" was born. (Robert Taft, deriding Truman's rambunctious campaign, accused the president of "blackguarding Congress at every whistle stop station in the West." Truman turned the remark to his own populist advantage; at each stop, the president would ask the crowds whether they considered themselves residents of a "whistle stop" or a town.[52]) The beginning of the trip also gave the campaign its most memorable sound bite. As the train pulled away from Washington, Truman's running mate, Alben Barkley, yelled to the president, "Mow 'em down, Harry!" Truman responded, "I'm going to give 'em hell!" From then on, at almost every speech, someone would yell from the crowd, "Give 'em hell, Harry," to which Truman would often reply, "I'll just tell the truth, and they'll think it's hell."[53]

Truman's vigor merely underscored the torpor of Dewey and Warren. Constrained by their analysis of the race, they made little news. And Dewey compounded voters' suspicions with his arrogance. For Warren, one moment crystallized the frustrations of their failing effort: Campaigning away from Warren, Dewey too was on a train, and one day as he addressed a crowd, the car jerked (the engineer, Warren speculated in his memoirs, may have been testing the air brakes, an observation less interesting for its accuracy than for the fact that Warren, writing in his seventies, still remembered a thing or two about trains). "They should take that engineer out and shoot him at sunrise," Dewey exclaimed to the crowd. Warren groaned. It was, he wrote, "a most unfortunate utterance."[54]

Only in the final leg of the trip, as the Warren train rolled back across the northern plains and again hit the West Coast, did the vice presidential candidate seem to relax. Rounded up by Helen MacGregor, the younger children joined the Warrens in Wenatchee, Washington, a few days before the trip concluded. They boarded the train to help celebrate their parents' anniversary, and then to ride the last miles home to California. The governor showed off his youngsters and joked as he introduced them to the crowd early that morning. "And here's the man of the family," Warren said, picking on Bobby. "You know, we had Bobby believing a few moments ago that he was going to have to make a speech here." The crowd laughed along with the Warrens, comfortable in their company again.[55]

Four days after the Warren children joined the train in Washington, the Warrens were home. "I can't begin to tell you how good it feels to get back to California," Warren said as the Aleutian arrived in Sacramento. "I say that without any disparagement of the 31 other states we have visited since we left Sacramento on this tour Sept. 15. You who live in California know that no apologies are necessary when a Californian declares he is glad to be back in this wonderful state of ours."[56] Over the course of thirty-one days and nights, those were the truest words that Earl Warren uttered.

Those final weeks brought every indication of a Republican victory. On October 11, *Newsweek* asked fifty political columnists for their prediction; all fifty picked Dewey. The final Gallup poll of the campaign, released on October 30, said Dewey by 5 points. Elmo Roper, another respected pollster of the day, discontinued polling on September 9. He had Dewey up by 13 points, and decided it was a waste of his time to continue sounding out the public given the landslide taking shape.[57]

Consequently, much of the nation went to sleep on Election Night believing it had elected Tom Dewey and Earl Warren. Editors of the *Chicago Tribune* reached their most embarrassing low with their early-edition headline: "Dewey Defeats Truman." Truman, the actual winner, brandished the paper triumphantly as he relished his needle-threading, 2,136,525-vote victory (out of more than 47 million votes cast), in which he navigated between Thurmond and Wallace while holding off the Republicans. Combined, the Republican votes and those for the minor candidates would have been enough to topple Truman, but individually, each of the other candidates fell to the incumbent. Truman went home to the White House, Dewey back to New York, and Earl Warren to the state capitol in Sacramento, where he was at his desk the morning after Election Day.

Just after Election Day, the FBI finished up work on a curious analysis of Earl Warren, whose record and overtures to Hoover had stitched up their friendship through the 1930s and 1940s. Labeled an "Espionage" file, it was a multipage profile of Warren. Long passages were deleted from the document before it was released under the Freedom of Information Act, but it presents a thoroughly admiring portrait of the California governor. Warren, it states, "is considered above reproach," a "strong family man [and] not a drinker or carouser." The memo notes Warren's nomination for president, though it garbles Sproul's name, identifying him as "Norman Sproul," and does contain a few hints of skepticism about the governor. It notes, for instance, that Warren is "peculiar to Republican policies in that he has gone very far for socialized medicine" and "has backed many Democrats." While personally admirable, it adds, Warren "is egotistical regarding his own abilities."[58]

Those subdued criticisms did nothing to undermine the Bureau's relationship with Warren. Through the 1940s, the FBI maintained regular and helpful communication with him. So frequent were the contacts that the Bureau grouped them together under the category "Cooperation with Governor Warren," a heading that described the FBI's errands for Warren and his endorsement of its work. Time and again through those years, Warren sought out the FBI's quiet assistance in vetting nominees to state positions. Before naming a person to a government post, Warren would ask the FBI to search its files for any "derogatory information." The Bureau complied and relayed its findings back to Warren. Usually it came up empty, but in some instances, it did surface concerns.[59] Warren relied on the FBI not only to check out potential appointees but even, on occasion, to brief him for meetings in order to avoid possible embarrassment. When one group asked to meet with him regarding an upcoming execution, Warren inquired whether the group was considered "Communist-infiltrated." The FBI replied that it was, or at least that its West Coast national director had been an officer of the Communist Party for some time.[60] By the end of the 1940s, Warren's relationship with the FBI was so trusting that he could even call upon its agents for personal favors. Hoover arranged for cars and drivers to assist Warren while traveling, and on the eve of a scheduled trip to Scandinavia, the Warrens discovered that citizenship records of Nina's were missing and were complicating their travel arrangement. An agitated Warren asked the FBI for help, and Hoover himself scrawled on the bottom of Warren's request: "Do everything possible."[61] For his part, Warren often mentioned the FBI in speeches, invariably to praise it; agents passed along Warren's compliments to Hoover, who would, on occasion, thank Warren for the praise. Hoover's notes in those years were addressed to "Dear Earl."[62]

The 1948 presidential campaign marked the first time that voters anywhere had said no to Earl Warren. And yet, even in defeat, this campaign—like the one for attorney general in 1938, when Warren focused on civil rights, and like the gubernatorial election in 1942, when Warren expanded into issues beyond public safety—marked an important stage in his personal political development. As with 1938, the occasion was a request for him to define himself, then in terms of civil rights, this time in the form of a query from the *New York Times,* which asked him to define "liberalism" and to describe what it meant to him as a philosophy. On his own, Warren was not inclined to philosophize, but when asked in 1938 to do so on civil liberties, he formed his ideas around his response. Now he did so again. Warren's reply to the *New York Times* linked his politics and those of Hiram Johnson but did so in a way that made clear that Warren was not bound by the old-style definition of a Progressive. He had grown beyond Progressivism's proscriptive notions—the elimination of vice and corruption—and turned it into a more affirmative and constructive philosophy. With his response, Warren also served notice that those inclined to see him as simple and hardworking but unimaginative had not looked hard enough. His approach to governing, developed in five years as governor, had in fact hardened into a philosophy, reflective and practical, deliberately moderate but ambitious, too. For the rest of his life, whether as governor or as chief justice, Warren would never substantially depart from its basic principles. Warren's answer, quoted here at length:

I particularly like the term "Progressive," not necessarily as a party label, but as a conception. To me it represents true liberalism and the best attitude that we could possibly have in American life. It is distinguishable from both reaction and radicalism, because neither of these philosophies make for real progress.

The reactionary, concerned only with his own position, and indifferent to the welfare of others, would resist progress regardless of changed conditions or human need.

The radical does not want to see any progress at all because he hopes that our democratic institutions will fail and that in the collapse he will be able to take over with some form of alien tyranny.

The progressive, however, realizes that democracy is a growing institution and that, if it is to succeed, we must make steady advances from day to day to constantly improve it and adapt it to human requirements on an ever-widening base.

The progressive has faith in democracy, and he is determined to work for its improvement and greater effectiveness; he realizes that, as with everything else in human affairs, we must work at it patiently, with forbearance and good will. He has the courage to develop it through trial and error, seeking to assure real freedom, not merely for a few, but for all, and to this end he is willing to subordinate his private interest to the common good.[63]

Chapter 13

# LOYALTY

*I would cut off my right arm before I would willingly submit my youngsters to the wiles or infamy of a Communist faculty. I don't believe that the faculty of the University of California is Communist; I don't believe that it is soft on Communism, and neither am I.*

GOVERNOR EARL WARREN[1]

N INETEEN FORTY-NINE opened with the menace of international Communism gathering around the world. Much of the Western world felt threatened and afraid, and their preoccupations turned to the question of loyalty. In California, much of the state's conservative press and leadership decided that Communists were a danger not just in Peking and Moscow and their orbits of satellites, but at home, in state offices, and in schools. And in order to identify those who posed a danger to the government, the defenders of the Republic settled on an approach: they determined to ferret out Communists by administering an oath. The oath would demand rejection of Communism. Those who refused to take it presumably would be Communists, who could then be fired or prosecuted or otherwise harassed.

At first, there was little to suggest that loyalty—and the oaths meant to validate it—would upend institutions. The anti-Communist leadership in California was personified by state senator Jack Tenney, whose oafish obsession with the subject made him an object of something close to ridicule in Sacramento. He boasted of having gotten his start playing piano in a Mexican whorehouse—perfect training, the joke went, for a life in politics. Tenney's fame and fortune derived from a song: He was the author of the maudlin little border waltz "Mexicali Rose" ("Dry those big brown eyes and smile, dear . . ."), and with its royalties Tenney sought a place for himself in the ferment of 1930s Los Angeles politics. In 1936, he won his first campaign for the Assembly, debuting as a leftist admirer of Upton Sinclair's and a protégé of California's premier lobbyist, liquor industry representative Artie Samish. Tenney served for a time as the leader of the local musicians' union, but after he lost that post, he pivoted to his right. As Samish recalled in his colorful memoir, "He saw reds under every bed. As a chaser of Communists, he made Martin Dies and Joe Mc-Carthy seem like pinkos."[2] And yet while Tenney might have been humorous, even absurd, he also was an elected official. He could reach into California's budget, and he had a grasp of its legislative machinery. Tenney could be laughed at, but he could not be ignored. When, in early 1949, he began his familiar rumble with a host of bills intended to cleanse California of its menace, others took note.

Tenney thought he spied subversion in the university ranks, and he meant to take care of it. One of his bills proposed stripping the University of California regents—a panel of appointees named by the governor and confirmed by the legislature—of the power to determine the loyalty of university employees. Under that bill, vouching for the loyalty of university staff—faculty as well as nonfaculty employees—would move instead to the legislature itself, where Tenney and his allies were poised to wreak mischief. The bill was intended as a deliberate affront to the university's ability to manage its own affairs.

Sproul, president of the University of California system, eyed the clouds forming with concern but not panic. Clever as well as smart, Sproul had begun his time at Berkeley as a student and then, after a brief period away, had commenced his rise through its administrative ranks. He understood its finances, and he knew politics. He was strongly supported by its faculty—notwithstanding that he himself did not have a doctorate—and he was devoted to the university's health and prosperity.

What's more, Sproul had in Warren an extremely well-connected friend. The two men had been students together at Berkeley, Warren a year ahead of Sproul. Like Sproul, Warren loved his alma mater, and he respected few men so much as the university's president, a campmate in the redwood glens of the Bohemian Grove. Sproul and Warren were frequent, cordial correspondents, and often guests in each other's homes. Earl Warren could be counted on to stand up for Bob Sproul just as Sproul had done with his nominating speech for Warren at the Republican National Convention in 1948.[3]

If Sproul had experience and relationships on his side, however, Tenney seemed to have timing on his. In those early months of 1949, Communism as a global force was terribly real and genuinely threatening to American interests. From behind the Iron Curtain across Eastern Europe, Stalin consolidated his dominion through the late 1940s. Communist parties waged disruptive uprisings in Greece and Turkey in 1947, rattling the Truman administration. By 1948, Stalin was sufficiently confident to cut off Berlin, and to blockade that stranded city behind his forces. Truman countered in June 1948 with Operation Vittles, an airlift of supplies to the residents of West Berlin otherwise trapped inside East Germany. Peace in that theater hung on the discipline of young troops, eyeing one another as they patrolled a narrow boundary, always a single mistake away from war.

As the superpowers waged that knife-edge conflict, the hunt for domestic Communists gathered intensity as well. On December 15, 1948, Alger Hiss, a once promising diplomat and statesman, was indicted for perjury, accused of lying about his relationship with Whitaker Chambers. Hiss was the quarry; his pursuer was a young congressman whom Warren knew well: Richard Nixon.

A month later, Communists came to power in China, and Mao would soon travel to Moscow to meet Stalin for the first time. By the end of 1949, the Soviets had exploded an atomic bomb. Aided by the espionage that helped secure the bomb and now bolstered by its power, Communist rule extended from the Elbe River to the Formosa Straits.[4] And the maw was not satisfied. Stalin pined for Western Europe. Mao eyed Korea and Southeast Asia. Communism was formidable and growing, well armed and disciplined; its agents had insinuated themselves into positions of influence in America. Next to it, democracy seemed frail, and not just to alarmists.

In that context, the hunt for Communists at home and the use of loyalty oaths to find them seemed alternately vital and absurd. With armies in the field, spies at work, scientists pioneering new weapons, and diplomats struggling for strategic advantage, American security hardly seemed to turn on the question of whether a university admissions officer or PE teacher was willing to pledge loyalty to the United States. On the other hand, with such stakes rising monthly, almost no measure seemed too much if it might protect a nation that understandably saw itself in danger.

Sproul took heed of those sentiments and struck what he believed would be a defensible middle course. Urged on by university vice president James Corley, who was concerned about Tenney's potential for punishing the university by pinching its budget, Sproul proposed what he believed would be a harmless addition to the oath already required of state workers, including university employees.[5] Rather than simply swear to uphold and defend the Constitution, as all government officers were required to pledge, Sproul suggested adding an explicit rejection of Communism. In order to remain employees of the university, all workers—professors, administrators, and others—would have to pledge the following: "I do solemnly swear or affirm that I do not believe in, and I am not a member of, nor do I support any party or organization that believes in, advocates, or teaches the overthrow of the United States Government, by force or by any illegal or unconstitutional methods."[6]

Earl Warren was not present when the regents considered that proposal. Although California's governor sits as an ex officio member of the board of regents, neither Warren nor his predecessors or successors made a regular practice of attending. So Warren was not there when, after a brief discussion about the precise language, the regents adopted the oath, amending the state oath that had already existed since 1942, by a unanimous vote. Sproul promised the regents that the new oath would be included in the annual contract given to university employees.[7]

Sproul believed university employees would readily accept the additional language containing the specific rejection of Communism. Instead, as faculty members learned of the oath with the school year drawing to a close—the first official notice of it came in the May 9 issue of the *Faculty Bulletin*—they were suspicious.[8] To many faculty members, the requirement that they take an oath or lose their right to teach represented an attack on intellectual freedom and a challenge to the principle of tenure—the idea that professors, once tenured, could be removed only under extraordinary circumstances. Moreover, the decision to impose a special oath on university employees implied suspicion of them—no other state workers were being asked to swear their abhorrence of Communism—and while many professors were willing to disavow Communism, they resented being singled out to do so.

Through 1949, the controversy surrounding the oath grew and shifted. Although Sproul had been the first to propose the oath, he represented the faculty, and his position became increasingly tenuous in the face of faculty resistance. He began to search for a way out. As he shifted his position, however, regent John Francis Neylan moved to counter him. Born in 1885, Neylan was a Progressive of the old school, a Hiram Johnson backer who had drifted into isolationism along with Johnson and Neylan's boss, William Randolph Hearst, whom Neylan had served as lawyer and San Francisco representative for years. Warren and Neylan had first met in Warren's young days as Alameda DA, when the newly appointed county prosecutor sought relief from punishing press coverage of his handling of the murder of Bessie Ferguson. Neylan's intervention at that delicate, early stage of Warren's career had helped the naïve young prosecutor sidestep a mine.[9]

In the years since, Warren and Neylan had been polite but restrained correspondents, with Neylan presuming a more confidential and personal tone than was reciprocated by Warren. Typical was one exchange in 1943: Neylan sent along a book by a Harvard philosophy professor, suggesting that "when you find yourself driven half-crazy by the job seekers and those with crackpot schemes to relieve the treasury of the surplus on hand, you take ten minutes to read it aloud to Mrs. Warren." Warren did not respond. Instead, press secretary Verne Scoggins delivered Warren's "acknowledgment and thanks."[10]

Neylan was first appointed a regent in 1928 (regents served for sixteen-year terms) and was reappointed to the board by Warren in 1944. Boastful and intimidating, Neylan was a force eager to unleash his powerful intellect on an adversary. When Sproul first proposed the oath, Neylan opposed what he considered a pointless requirement. Now, however, as Sproul moved to withdraw in the face of an angry faculty, Neylan switched his position, too, and decided to defend not so much the oath as the regents' right to impose it. He would not back down, because Jack Neylan did not back down. The regents ran the university and had the power to require an oath, and even if Neylan was never much impressed with the oath itself, he was devoted to making the faculty bow to the regents.

With a small but important minority of the faculty unalterably opposed to the oath and Neylan and his allies insistent that they take it or leave, the two sides dug in for a destructive debate. Across the nation, the loyalty oath debate in California became a kind of ideological touchstone, reminiscent of *Point Lobos,* Tom Mooney, or the IWW trials: Supporters of the faculty saw their opponents as dim ideologues hunting for reds among professors who had given no hint of disloyalty; supporters of the oath viewed at first with suspicion and then alarm the intransigence of elitist academics unwilling to state simply that they were faithful to the government that paid their salaries. Thus what started over a few sentences in an annual university contract expanded into a larger debate over freedom, Communism, and security, with a notable class subtext—tweedy academics and their allies against frightened working people.

Warren entered that debate tentatively. Twice before he had been squeezed by imperatives of security and freedom—once in the early prosecutions of IWW members and once in the debate over removal and internment of the Japanese. Both times he had opted for security and sacrificed liberty. But he was governor now, a veteran of the 1942 and 1946 campaigns, of the health care and highway tax debates. More and more, his friends and allies were liberals, his opponents to his right. And yet he deplored Communism and recognized a duty to defend his state against what he believed to be a genuine enemy. Moreover, Lieutenant Governor Goodwin Knight, also a member of the regents and, in late 1949, openly a candidate for governor, supported the oath and threatened to make an issue of it in a Republican primary if Warren opposed it.

The tension between those competing impulses was evident in Warren's actions. Although he would recall his participation in the loyalty oath debate as unequivocal, in fact it rarely was, at least viewed in the ideological and philosophical terms under which it played out—terms Warren himself accepted in retrospect. Writing in his memoirs, Warren portrayed opponents of the oath as devoted believers in academic freedom and constitutionally protected speech. Having done that, and writing then from the perspective of an internationally acclaimed standard-bearer for civil liberties, he reflected that he had consistently supported the faculty views against the shrill anti-Communism of Neylan and his allies. Warren also portrayed his own actions as swift and unambiguous. Noting, for instance, that he had not been present at the meeting where the oath first was presented to the regents, Warren added, "[A]t the next meeting I pointed out that it could do nothing but create dissension in the university and was unenforceable."[11]

Warren's analysis of the debate was correct—it did pit civil liberties against anti-Communism—but his statement regarding his own actions is false, as are other details of his memory. Warren did not attend the next meeting of the regents after their March 1949 adoption of the oath, nor did he speak out publicly at that time. Indeed, Warren remained physically absent and conspicuously silent on the issue for month after month that year. Not until early 1950 was he drawn to the debate. When he was, it was by his friends.

The fall of 1949 represented a particularly tense period in the oath debate. The regents had required obedience to the oath for employees to return that year and had expected easy compliance. As the fall term began, however, a significant number—around fifteen percent—of the university professors still had not signed. Their holdout enraged Neylan. He wanted compliance, and he determined to secure it, even at the cost of firing dozens of faculty members. On the other side, some of the university's finest professors resisted the encroachment of the regents on university tenure, and questioned their legal right to impose an oath that made political fidelity a precondition of university employment. The fall of 1949, Gardner writes, "had been a period of retreat from the stability of common resolve, harmony of purpose, and respectful goodwill which had for so long characterized relations within the University."[12]

It was out of the fear of what that meant for the university's future that three key players in the debate sat down on November 22 in San Francisco. Over lunch in the elegant dining room of the Palace Hotel—the same hotel where Earl Warren had launched his statewide political career as the Republican Party chief during the campaign to defeat and destroy Upton Sinclair—regents Edward Heller and Farnham Griffiths warned Sproul that they felt the debate was getting out of hand. Agreeing, Sproul said he would call Warren and urge him to join the matter. Less than two months later, Warren also received a visit from another friend, Berkeley economics professor Frank L. Kinder, who had served as an economic adviser to Warren and who became an important part of the faculty opposition to the oath.[13]

Those overtures turned Warren's head. Kinder was an admired economist who had lent his thoughts to Warren's presidential effort. Sproul was a longtime friend. And in Griffiths, Warren had yet another trusted ally, one who had backed Warren politically and helped him as a young politician gain entrance into California's most elite social circle. Eight years before the oath controversy erupted, it was Griffiths who had proposed Warren for membership at the Bohemian Club and who had helped steer his application toward acceptance. Warren's campmates at the Isle of Aves now included Griffiths and Sproul.[14] Still, Warren hesitated. Not until Knight gave up his thoughts of running for governor did Warren move.

Only then, with his right flank secure, did Warren join the debate. He attended his first regents meeting on the matter in January 1950, and the following month made his first public comments regarding it. The oath, said Warren, was unfairly intended to single out university employees on the suspicion of disloyalty and was suspect under California law, which permitted only one oath for all public employees—the same oath Warren had sworn upon becoming attorney general and later governor. Finally, Warren was paraphrased as saying that the oath was one "any Communist would take with a laugh."[15]

From that point forward, Warren was the most important opponent of the oath among the regents. He was, in that sense, a principled defender of the faculty and its president, as he remembered in his memoirs. But Warren's public comments on the issue do not suggest that he was stirred by the call of academic freedom or the civil liberties concerns raised by the administration of a political oath. At the time, he focused on the aspects of the oath that seemed most to offend him: that it singled out the university and that it contravened state law that required a single oath of all public employees.

International events, meanwhile, conspired to escalate the debate. On March 2, the same day the Los Angeles Times published an interview with Neylan explaining his position, the news from London was that Klaus Fuchs, a British atomic scientist, had pleaded guilty to spying for the Soviet Union. Or as the Times colorfully put it, "Fuchs, 38, Jekyll-Hyde wizard of science, pleaded guilty today and was given the maximum sentence of 14 years in prison for betraying American and British atomic secrets to Soviet Russia."[16] Some in Britain called for a purge of the nation's intelligence services. In such an atmosphere, it was hard to communicate a defense of professors unwilling to pledge their allegiance. One result is that press coverage within California was notably unsympathetic to the oath opponents, even contemptuous. The position of the Los Angeles Times on March 3 was typical: "To anybody who says that to require such a statement in the given circumstances would infringe academic freedom or reflect on the probity of honest teachers, we say bosh."[17]

Warren already had antagonized doctors and oil industry executives. Another jab at conservatives was risky, especially on an issue with national security overtones, however overwrought. So Warren consolidated his position before leaping. Through the early spring, three vacancies opened on the regents' board. L. Mario Giannini, president of the Bank of America and heir to his family stewardship of that California bank, came to the end of his term. Giannini was no Warren favorite and was Neylan's chief ally in the oath battle, but to dump him amid the controversy would have caused turmoil and damaged Warren politically. He stayed. In his other appointments, however, Warren strengthened his side. He named Cornelius Haggerty, a leader of the California State Federation of Labor with long connections to Warren, to fill one vacancy. For the second, he tapped one of his closest friends, lawyer Jesse Steinhart of San Francisco. The governor was lining up his votes. Or as Neylan saw it, "making appointments to pack the board."[18]

Neylan was not yielding, however, and the two sides pushed for a showdown on March 31, when the regents were to take up the "sign or quit" measure designed to force out faculty members who continued to resist the oath.[19] At the fateful March meeting, the Warren forces and the Neylan forces bitterly denounced each other. In his comments, Neylan revealed how deeply committed he was to facing down the faculty:

> Finally it kept coming back and coming back that evidently all these months this minority was powerful enough to reject the President's original oath. . . . I was convinced last Saturday night that the minority is still there and is still powerful enough to keep on doing what it has been doing during the last year. Now is the time to find out if that minority is going by threat and menace to run the University of California.[20]

If Neylan was typically combative, Warren was disarmingly personal. "I have an added interest in this university," Warren stated. "I am an alumnus myself and have three youngsters in the university today. God willing, I will have two more in two or three years on one of the campuses of the university." He continued,

> I would cut off my right arm before I would willingly submit my youngsters to the wiles or infamy of a Communist faculty. I don't believe that the faculty of the University of California is Communist; I don't believe that it is soft on Communism, and neither am I. I believe that in their hearts the members of the faculty of our university are just as sincere on the things they represent against Communism as any member of this Board, and I want to say here that I have absolute confidence in the faculty of the University of California.[21]

After five hours of debate, the roll was called. Warren's allies stuck with him and he with them. The final tally was 10 to 10 to rescind the oath and to allow the non-signing professors to stay. Since a majority was required to overturn the oath, Warren had fallen one vote short. The professors—sixty-two were holding out as of that day—were given until April 30 to sign or be fired.[22]

That might have ended the matter, but the faculty nonsigners were stubborn in defense of their view, and Warren was a tenacious friend. Through the spring and early summer, he, with Sproul, continued to seek a way out of firing the nonsigners. That fight took place against a darkening political sky, as the spy cases of early spring gave way to far graver and more immediate evidence of the Communist threat to America. In the hours just before dawn on a rainy Sunday morning, June 25, 1950, North Korean forces stormed across the 38th parallel, the political divide separating them from the South. Confused South Korean troops were quickly overrun, trapped by the North Koreans' circling maneuvers and lines of tanks. With those antagonists in armed conflict, their patrons—the United States, China, and the Soviet Union—faced one another in their first shooting battle of the Cold War. Secretary of State Dean Acheson reached President Truman at home in Independence, Missouri, with news of the attack; Truman returned to Washington the following day, as the United Nations stirred in anger at the news of an attack on a member state. On July 7, the United Nations, with the Soviet Union absent (the Soviets boycotted the sessions because the UN had refused to seat Communist China), authorized the creation of an international fighting force and directed the United States to name its commander.[23] Truman picked General Douglas MacArthur, whose American troops already were in combat with the North Koreans.

Fighting on unfamiliar terrain against a well-supplied enemy, American forces did not fare well. Seoul, the South Korean capital located just a short drive from the 38th parallel, fell four days after the initial invasion.[24] Under heavy artillery fire along the Kum River, American troops held North Korean forces at bay for a time, but by July 16, Communist divisions had pushed the Americans back. Dispirited American forces grumbled over their participation in a conflict not even worthy of being called a war as a ferocious enemy, pressing for a quick victory, stormed down the peninsula in heavy tanks. President Truman three days later spoke to the nation. "We are united in detesting Communist slavery," he said in his radio broadcast on the evening of July 19. "We know that the cost of freedom is high. But we are determined to preserve our freedom, no matter what the cost."[25] Truman asked Congress for $10 billion. Military units were mobilized and readied for action. And on July 20, Warren activated the California Guard.

In such a climate, some of the professors who had held out for more than a year on the oath now capitulated. Still, as the July regents meeting approached, thirty-nine remained unwilling to sign and determined to be fired rather than capitulate.

Warren prepared carefully. An attempt at yet another compromise in April had led to Giannini's sudden decision to submit his resignation. That gave Warren a one-vote margin, and he also was working stealthily to blunt newspaper demands for the ouster of the professors. Warren's most significant effort in that regard played out far from public view and was revealed only decades later.

Warren had come to depend upon the editorial support of the *Los Angeles Times*. Harry Chandler, son-in-law and heir of General Otis, backed Warren in his early races, and Norman Chandler, now the *Times*'s publisher, had his father's admiration for the stolid, hardworking governor. Though Warren tended to stand to the paper's left, the Chandlers understood the value of his Republicanism in a state where Democrats outnumbered Republicans. Still, the *Times* believed in the loyalty oath and showed no sympathy for the quibbling of academics and their ivory tower objections. That concerned Warren, who faced reelection in 1950. Warren well knew that the *Times* would never back a Democrat to replace him, but he also was painfully aware that he needed the paper's enthusiastic support to shore up his southern base, always the most tenuous part of his coalition.

Tipped off by *Times* political editor Kyle Palmer that Chandler wanted an editorial criticizing the governor for opposing the loyalty oath, Warren asked Chandler to first talk the matter over with him. They agreed to meet in the shadow of the redwoods at the Bohemian Grove, where both were members, Warren a part of the Isle of Aves, Chandler a member of the Lost Angels camp. There, Warren recalled later, the redwoods "added a cathedral-like solemnity"[26] to a discussion between California's two most important Republicans about the merits of the oath and the degree of Communist infiltration into the faculty of their state's great university. Although Warren recalled the discussion as turning on questions such as the Bill of Rights and its vitality to a free press and a free academy, those recollections were summoned by the retired chief justice, then immersed in the life of the Constitution. It seems more likely that his arguments in 1950 would have been practical ones—the unfairness of singling out the university, the questionable legality of the oath, the unlikelihood that it would ferret out real Communists but rather would only target stubborn, principled faculty members. What is clear is that whatever Warren said that day to his fellow Bohemian Club member, whatever passed between those two veterans of California's brutal politics, Warren left with the assurance that the *Times* would not abandon him. He was free to attack the oath without fear that it would cost him his alliance with the paper.[27]

So he did. On July 21, the regents met on the ninth floor of San Francisco's Crocker Building. Giannini was absent while Warren dawdled over whether to accept his resignation.[28] Neylan continued to demand the firing of the nonsigners, Warren rehashed his arguments for backing down and stressed that not one of the thirty-nine professors at issue had ever been accused of being a Communist; they objected to the oath as an oath, not because of what it would reveal about them. Then Warren called the roll. This time, by a single vote—his own—he won. The regents, voting 10–9, agreed to let the thirty-nine professors keep their jobs.

The victory was short-lived, as Neylan regrouped his forces for the following meeting, and the regents then fired thirty-one professors (the number kept dwindling as professors signed or resigned) over Warren's objections. But Warren again prevailed, predicting that the courts would reinstate those fired. He was right, and eventually the oath controversy settled into a standoff. It revealed no Communist infiltration of the faculty, and it established no grand precedent for control of the university. But it left Warren whole politically, and it preserved his central mission: the protection of the university and its faculty. That was no small feat under the circumstances and in the climate of 1950.

Evidence that Warren's mission was about protecting the university—not about a civil libertarian objection to the oath itself—is what he did next. On September 20, Warren welcomed the California legislature to a special session with a call to emergency action against Communists at home. Warren appealed now to the public's fear, warning that an atomic attack on the United States was "a possibility."[29] He further warned of the presence of Soviet agents in the United States and called for the creation of a civil defense office to protect Californians from harm. Given such urgency, Warren asked, in his message transmitted to the legislature the following day, that all state employees in effect be deputized as part of the civil defense effort, and that they be required to swear an oath denying affiliation with Communism. In the legislature, Senator Tenney, undoubtedly surprised to find Warren in his camp, took up the call. Within days, Warren had signed and California had adopted the so-called Levering Oath, named for its assembly sponsor. It was passed as an emergency measure, and thus took effect immediately; it was binding on all public employees in California, from the governor to janitors and jail guards— including, notably, university employees.

In substance, the Levering Oath was in many respects worse than the oath Warren had fought for so many months at the university. It required those who signed not only to swear to support and defend the Constitution but also to pledge not to advocate or be a member of any organization that advocated the overthrow of the government. In addition, workers were required to state specifically that they had not been members of any such organization within the past five years and to promise not to join any such organization in the future. Substantively, then, Warren appeared to have capitulated to advocates of the oath and to have extended its reach beyond the university to all public employees.

Then and since, some have speculated that Warren was motivated by politics. His November reelection was just a month away when he signed the Levering Oath Act, and he was facing James Roosevelt, son of the revered former president. That, however, ignores the realities of the campaign by that point. By the time the Levering Oath came to him for his signature, Warren already had dispensed with the threat of conservative opposition (indeed, Warren seems far more likely to have been motivated by politics in 1949, when Knight was challenging him from the right and he stayed out of the debate). By 1950, when he was effectively unopposed in the Republican primary, Warren carried all fifty-eight California counties. If he felt any pressure going into the November election, he felt it from his left, as Roosevelt had virtually no crossover appeal for Republicans or conservatives. As a result, Warren had little reason to worry about his restive conservative allies in September and October of 1951 and thus no reason to appease them with an oath.

Only those who viewed the oath controversy in philosophical or ideological terms, however, would find Warren's support for the Levering Oath hard to explain. If Warren's actions in the university debate are viewed, rather, as a defense of the university and its president, they become entirely consistent with his later support of the Levering Oath. The university oath was odious not because it was an oath per se but rather because it implied disloyalty by the university. Warren had attended that university and had sent his children to be educated there. He would tolerate no suggestion that it was undermined by Communism. Tellingly, those issues—the singling out of the university and the legally suspect quality of the oath requirement—were what Warren identified as the basis for his opposition when he reflected on the matter in 1954, just a few years after it had subsided. In an unsigned memorandum, but one typed on his typewriter and kept with his papers, Warren listed those issues as the reasons that he opposed the oath. The words "academic freedom" and "rights of expression and association" never appear in that document.[30]

Warren's stand was, in fact, about loyalty, but not about loyalty to an idea or even to government in the abstract. It was about loyalty to his friends, to his family, and to his university—the tangible, real-life loyalties that always for Warren prevailed over theory and abstraction. He had attended the University of California with Bob Sproul; he trusted Sproul and determined to see him through. That meant squashing Neylan, not on the principle of loyalty as articulated by the oath but on the principle of loyalty to one's friends. Sproul stayed as president, and professors were not asked to sign anything other than that given to all state workers. On his terms—the terms he set in 1949 and 1950—Warren won.

LIFE WOULD be simpler for governors if it served them up one issue at a time—if tax cuts gave way to health insurance and health insurance was resolved before prison reform was required and if a new prison system was in place before the legislature considered a gas tax. Such is rarely the case, however, and certainly not in the fast-moving epoch of Earl Warren's governorship. For even as Warren tiptoed through the loyalty-oath debate, his old frustrations with corruption and Sacramento lobbyists crested in one imbroglio, which in turn segued into another.

Those interlocking issues had their genesis in the 1946 election, when Warren defeated Kenny in the primary. Kenny vacated his seat as attorney general to challenge Warren, and the Los Angeles district attorney, Frederick Howser, ran for Kenny's slot. Warren was wary of Howser even before he arrived—while serving as district attorney in Los Angeles, Howser had arranged for Tony Cornero, captain of the *Rex*, to return his gambling business to Southern California, undermining Warren's celebrated victory over Cornero in 1939. Despite that, Howser had the audacity to ask for Warren's support in the 1946 elections; Warren refused. Howser instead relied on the less savory support of Sacramento liquor lobbyist Artie Samish. Thanks to Samish's backing—and to the similarity of his name to that of Lieutenant Governor Fred Houser—Howser won. The next act was predictable: Within months of Howser's taking office, Warren heard rumors that organized crime was extending feelers into the state. "The word was out," he said, "that the state was to be opened up to gambling and other illegal activities."[31] Warren warned Howser he knew what was developing. Howser professed innocence, and though promising to act, did not. Warren then did what Warren did in situations where the public interest was at stake and he was hamstrung: He called Olney.

Olney was then in the midst of one of his periodic returns to private life, but Warren prevailed upon him, as he had before, to leave it for public service, this time to serve as counsel to Warren's California Crime Study Commission on Organized Crime. Howser objected to the formation of the commission, arguing through the summer and fall that reports of organized crime in California were exaggerated, that, in effect, he had matters under control. Warren did not believe him from the start; after June 20, 1947, few others did, either. It was that day that Benjamin "Bugsy" Siegel, founder of Las Vegas's Flamingo Hotel and a flamboyant mobster, was shot to death in his mistress's Beverly Hills home. Confronted with the hard-to-deny facts that the bullet-riddled body of a known mobster had now turned up in an elegant Southern California neighborhood, Howser continued to insist that there was no real problem. On September 12 of that year, Howser called together California police and sheriffs—he did not invite the FBI—and downplayed the talk of troubles. Organized-crime conditions in California were, he insisted, not "as bad as they have been indicated." Howser also remarked that he was "tired of the talk of 'some people' on this subject."[32]

Warren was not persuaded, and chose retired Admiral William Standley, a Navy man of great distinction and a former American ambassador to Russia, to head the commission. Olney agreed to serve as its chief counsel. As expected, the commission soon clashed with Howser, who professed a desire to cooperate with the commission even as he worked to undermine it. By 1948, Howser was trying to push Olney off the commission staff, alleging that the commission somehow had signed him on improperly. Indignant, Warren cabled his support: "Mr. Olney has performed his duties fearlessly and in the public interest. His job is not yet completed. It must be completed." If there were problems with Olney's hiring, Warren promised to pay his $625-a-month salary out of his own pocket.[33]

Olney stayed on the job through 1952, as Warren's first commission and then a second probed organized crime activity throughout California and submitted extensive reports on bookmaking, rackets, and other manifestations of the mob. The commission did not adopt Howser's sanguine view of the situation. "The menace of organized crime is one of the major problems of contemporary political life," the commission concluded. "Organized rackets are not managed by ignorant men or desperate nitwits. They are controlled by greedy men who are as alert and sagacious as they are ruthless and persistent."[34] The commission was as thorough as it was biting. Included in its report were biographies of leading California mobsters and even pictures of their luxurious homes and the resorts they frequented. Even before the commission had submitted its final work, it had effectively devastated Howser.

The undoing of California's attorney general also had the effect of drawing attention to Samish, who compounded his difficulties by encouraging that scrutiny. The presence of lobbyists in Sacramento was a nettlesome one for Warren from the beginning. Banking representatives agitated him during the debate over taxes in 1943, and lobbyists for doctors and oil companies bedeviled him thereafter. But the issue jumped to public attention with the publication of a two-part series in *Collier's* magazine in August 1949. Entitled "The Secret Boss of California," the series profiled Samish, whose fame and influence had grown through the 1940s. By 1949, Samish was a controlling force in the state legislature, and power had made him brazen. When Lester Velie of *Collier's* came to write about Samish, the lobbyist forgot the cardinal rule of backroom influence, which is that to maintain it, one must keep it in the back room. Instead, Samish boasted and mugged and posed for a fatal picture, in which he held a ventriloquist's dummy in his left hand and pretended to address it: "How are you today, Mr. Legislature?" the caption read.

Samish represented beer, liquor, bus companies, railroads, cigarette manufacturers, banks, racetracks, and chemical companies—among others. To Velie and *Collier's,* he boasted of putting Howser in office; of controlling votes on the state Board of Equalization, which regulated liquor laws and tax assessments; and of a conspicuous willingness to reward friends and punish enemies with his acute sense of a legislator's needs. "I can tell if a man wants a baked potato, a girl, or money," Samish offered.[35] When Warren was asked by Velie who was the most influential person in the legislature, Warren replied, "On matters that affect his clients, Artie unquestionably has more power than the governor."[36]

Warren's comment raised the question of why a governor so offended by lobbyists and so intolerant of corruption had in fact tolerated Samish for so long. Sensitive to that charge, Warren asked the legislature for a bill to curb lobbying, and though he got less than he wanted, he signed such a bill in 1949. With that, he was through with Samish, but Olney was not quite. Samish would eventually be prosecuted for income tax evasion, and the prosecutor in that case was none other than Olney, then working for the Justice Department but then, as always, a premier expert on crime in California. Samish was convinced that he would have beaten the case against him, that the government simply would have tired of poking through his records, had it not been "for my old friend Warren Olney III."[37]

Samish eventually served twenty-six months in a federal penitentiary. As for Howser, his association with Samish and his transparent efforts to whitewash the threat of organized crime persuaded voters that Warren and the Crime Commission were right—that Howser was not to be trusted. He served out his term and then was gone from public office, replaced by Democrat Pat Brown.

WITH THE Crime Commission under way and the university's loyalty oath controversy largely superseded by the enactment of the Levering Oath, Warren turned to his reelection in early 1950. He announced his candidacy in February and prosecuted it with practiced efficiency. As had become his routine, Warren began his campaign with a trip through the Mother Lode counties, speaking once, twice, sometimes even three times a day in those old Sierra mining camps through May.[38] The electorate knew Warren and trusted him. Now when he said he intended to govern in nonpartisan fashion, he was taken at his word, particularly since he could point to a record of accomplishment that would be the envy of almost any official.

In plain, calm language, Warren reminded voters of the change he had managed for California in his eight years as governor: 20,000 classrooms and at least that many new teachers to serve a student population that had grown by 500,000 children in ten years; improved mental health centers serving 10,556 more patients; an increase of 1.45 million jobs; a tripling in the annual value of state crops; construction of 4,025 miles of new highways; and despite acute housing shortages in some parts of the state, a galloping boom that saw the construction of 625,000 new homes, a fourth of all new homes built in America, in the five years beginning with the end of the war. All that with a balanced budget and a reduction in state taxes over the same period (though also with the imposition of California's gas tax).[39] Moreover, though social issues did not form the mainstay of Warren's reelection effort, there was substantial evidence supporting Warren's claims of nonpartisanship as he turned to Democratic legislators for support for his social agenda—health care, for instance—and Democrats readily complied.[40]

While he was governor, Warren's social record had mounted. He had signed the bill that ended discrimination against Mexicans in schools. He backed the creation of a Fair Employment Practices Commission and supported fair employment legislation as well as nondiscriminatory housing requirements, substantial increases in public pensions, and expansion of eligibility for receiving government support.[41] Some critics, Warren conceded late in the campaign, "believe we have been too liberal. I don't. I believe that most Californians want our State to be as liberal as our finances will permit."[42]

Under Warren's leadership, California had transcended the historical extremes that so long had marked its history. Supported by an enthusiastic and diligent Warren, the great water projects planned for the Central Valley would soon bring rivers from the cool north to the arid south, where they would irrigate rich, loamy fields. The grand distances that once made Los Angeles and San Francisco remote and opposite provinces now were shortened by highways and rail lines. Government-supplied electricity cooled California's desert homes and warmed those in its northern forests. Under Warren's watch, it had become a nation-state, its economy robust, its natural resources abundant and in use.

Jimmy Roosevelt would go on to an honorable career as a member of Congress, but in 1950, he ran a mean and occasionally stupid campaign for governor of California. In August, he attempted to capitalize on war fears by proposing that California construct a series of "open cities" inside the state. Those were intended to be fully functional metropolitan areas that would sit vacant unless and until California was attacked, at which time 4 million residents could evacuate to them. More perplexed than threatened, Warren described the plan as "hysterical, nonsensical and wholly demagogic."[43] Beyond that proposal, Roosevelt was elitist in every sense that Warren was not, and Roosevelt even came with the hint of scandal, as newspapers probed his business dealings and political connections. All that hampered Roosevelt's effort and threatened to make him a laughingstock. When Roosevelt made his first speaking trip as a candidate to Sacramento in February, the *Los Angeles Times* played the story on the same page as a piece headlined "Other Planets Send Saucers, Navy Man Says."[44] So what did Earl Warren have to fear from little Jimmy Roosevelt? The name, of course.

As usual, Sweigert understood and captured Warren's mood:

The Earl of Warren rallied
'Til one night in the dark,
He saw a figure moving—
The ghost of old Hyde Park.

"I know that voice," said Warren,
"But not that baldish head."
And then cried out in horror—
"Is Franklin really dead?"[45]

In 1942, Warren beat a failed Democrat in part by drawing Democratic support away from the incumbent. In 1946, he so thoroughly dominated the state's politics that Democrats abandoned Robert Kenny and claimed Warren as their own candidate. Now, however, there was the risk that voters were tiring of Warren, and Roosevelt offered the glamour of his father's presidency. Why, Roosevelt's candidacy implicitly asked voters, settle for Warren's milder New Deal when here was the real thing? Roosevelt's mother appeared on her son's behalf in September in order to draw that connection more explicitly. Her appearance drew a rare witticism from Warren as he brushed off her significance to the election. "I don't like to argue with a mother about her boy," Warren told reporters.[46] And yet Warren may have seen Roosevelt as more threatening than he really was. Warren had just come off the experience of running nationally in 1948, when all signs pointed to an easy Republican victory, only to have Truman outcampaign the cocky Dewey-Warren ticket. It was one thing to lose the vice presidency, an office Warren never much coveted anyway. To suffer a loss at home, in defense of his own seat, would be quite another.

Those were months of tough politics in California. For as Warren and Roosevelt waged their campaign in the flickering light of the Loyalty Oath controversy, two vigorous contestants vied for a California seat in the United States Senate. Congressman Richard Nixon was running against Helen Gahagan Douglas, an attractive, liberal congresswoman from Southern California, for an open United States Senate seat. With Murray Chotiner helping to direct the campaign, Nixon unleashed a scaled-up version of his Voorhis strategy, suggesting in this campaign that Douglas was sympathetic to Communism and comparing her voting record to that of leftist New York Congressman Vito Marcantonio—"a notorious Communist party-liner," as the flyer pointed out;[47] a "red-ass red," as one Nixon associate colorfully recalled.[48] The Douglas-Marcantonio comparison was exaggeration, its visual impact enhanced by Chotiner's decision to print the flyer on pink paper. It became known as "The Pink Sheet." "We put it on pink paper," Nixon aide Frank Jorgensen said later. "People drew their own conclusion."[49]

For Nixon in 1950 as in 1946, a kind word from Warren would have had huge ramifications, as it would have helped persuade moderates that they could trust the young congressman. But as in 1946, Warren was unwilling, and Nixon's camp this time decided to try to bait him. For weeks, Nixon aides hectored Douglas at public events, demanding to know whom she would support for governor. Finally, their pursuit paid off when she cracked and acknowledged that she favored Roosevelt. Warren still would not endorse Nixon—which was telling, given that both were Republicans and Nixon now was running against an avowed Warren opponent—but the governor did allow this: "In view of her statement . . . I might ask her how she expects I will vote when I mark my ballot for United States senator on Tuesday."[50] Chotiner had what he wanted, and trumpeted Warren's hedged remark as an endorsement. Warren filed it away, part of his growing accumulation of grievances against Nixon and his friends.

In his own race, Warren pounded Roosevelt with a ferocity he had never unleashed on Kenny. When Roosevelt argued that Warren had not done enough for schools, the indignant incumbent responded, "James Roosevelt has never been in a public school in his life, except to make a political speech."[51] Roosevelt countered that Warren was an illusory friend of labor, a Republican feigning appreciation for unions solely to curry their votes. Warren knew enough to see he could be vulnerable to that charge. There were still those who remembered *Point Lobos* and Upton Sinclair, and there was no shortage of voters who were squeamish about members of the Bohemian Club or friends of the Chandlers. Still, Warren felt entitled to labor's appreciation. He was raised in a union home and found early work helping union men to their trains on time. He still carried his musicians' union card.

On November 3, 1950, with the election just days away, Warren vented his full fury at Roosevelt and staked his claim for the votes of California's working people. Appearing at the Sailors Union Building in San Francisco, Warren asserted his support for the "procedure of collective bargaining," and described his accomplishments as having been judged "through the years for their fairness by the working men and women of our State."[52]

And then Warren cut to the point:

> It is great for me, in such surroundings, to look working people in the eye and refute as absolute falsehood the distortions, the insinuations, and detractions that have been used by my opponent to insinuate himself into the Governor's office.
>
> I use the term "insinuate himself into the Governor's office" because it is the only way he could hope to arrive there in this campaign. He has absolutely no record of accomplishment of any kind in the public service, or in the civic life of our State. And outside of foraging for political insurance, the only private employment of any kind he has ever had was his employment at $25,000 a year by a group of left-wingers in Southern California which his own party eventually forced him to repudiate as a dangerous group.
>
> I want to say to you, ladies and gentlemen, that I have not heretofore made reference to this sordid page in the history of Mr. James Roosevelt, nor have I said anything about his business activities which have received such notoriety in recent years throughout the country.
>
> But when he repeatedly and intentionally tells the working people of California that I am a labor-hater, and that my administration has ground working people down, I not only am entitled as a matter of fair play to show the falsity of his statements, but also to make an observation based upon the facts that will throw some light on the situation.
>
> I came from a humble workingman's home. My father worked with his hands as a mechanic. Both he and I have worked twelve hours a day, six days a week, at 25 cents an hour. I know what better wages mean to a home. I know what better hours mean to a family. I know what better working conditions mean to the safety, the health, and the well being of all working people.[53]

Left unsaid, barely, was that Roosevelt—raised at St. Albans, Groton, and Harvard—knew none of that, that his upbringing of wealth and privilege undermined his claim to the hearts of labor, just as Warren's dusty youth in Bakersfield and rearing in California's public schools entitled him to their attention. Rarely had Warren spoken of an opponent in such personal and strident tones. He was, as the election of 1950 drew near, tired and angry, defeated once nationally and worried that a loss could finish him. He would not lose to a liar.

Warren delivered a last radio plea on Monday evening from Los Angeles, then, accompanied by Nina and Virginia, returned that night to San Francisco, where the three stayed at the St. Francis Hotel. They rose early the following morning and shuttled across the bay to their old home precinct, back to the Alameda Court- house that had given Earl Warren his public start. There, they voted as the polls opened at seven A.M. They then joined old friends for breakfast at their home, hop- ing to spend a relaxing morning before settling in to hear the results of Warren's seventh election in California.[54] The prospects of a seventh victory, a third term, and an amiable evening seemed strong indeed.

In Sacramento, the day began differently. Seventeen-year-old Honey Bear had been feeling poorly that week, nursing a fever, fidgeting and uncomfortable. As her mother, father, and sister barnstormed the state for one last time, Honey Bear and Earl Jr. stayed home. Earl tended to his ailing sister—the flu, doctors said. He rubbed her legs and soothed her to sleep. On Tuesday morning, at about the same time Earl and Nina Warren cast their ballots for his reelection, Earl came into his sister's room to check on her. Stripping back her blankets, he glanced at her legs and knew there was trouble. The heating pads he had given his sister the night be- fore to ease her legs had burned them. Honey Bear had not felt a thing.[55]

In a panic, Earl Jr. summoned doctors and sent word for his parents. Reached by an aide at the Oakland home where they were having breakfast, the Warrens im- mediately hurried home to Sacramento, driving through a thick fog.[56] They arrived to find Honey Bear at Sutter Hospital in Sacramento. She had a fever of 102 de- grees. Her body ached. Most terrifyingly, she could not move her legs. The lovely girl, daughter of the governor, image of horseback riding and swimming and Cali- fornia sun, was diagnosed with polio.[57]

"It's not so bad," Honey Bear told her worried father. "Oh Daddy," she added, "I've spoiled your big day."[58]

Turning to her mother, Honey Bear suggested they go home and rest. And with that, the months of strain and the wear and tear of an election all piled up. Earl Warren never could stand to see Honey Bear in distress; the mere thought of her unhappy at moving to Sacramento had pushed him to buy her a pony. Now she was in pain. She might never walk again. She might, in fact, die. Earl Warren had to be exhausted. He had just completed a year in which he fought for his friends at the university and himself at the polls. His long campaign—every campaign is a long one for those at their centers—was ending that day, almost certainly in triumph.

And yet here was his little girl, here in a hospital bed urging him not to worry about her. Honey Bear was, simply, "his heart."[59] The man famous for his earnest stoicism, the governor who had shown his grief in public just once—in the hours after his father's murder—walked out of his daughter's hospital room, his broad shoulders slumped and tired. Outside, in a quiet hallway, he wept.[60]

Earl Warren was overwhelmingly reelected that night to the governorship of California. He was the first person ever to win a third term in that office. His political record, achieved on November 7, 1950, was never equaled, and the later imposition of term limits on the governorship makes it unlikely ever to be again. Warren's political legacy now reached beyond that of any other governor ever to preside over California. His state was sound, his electorate satisfied, his opponent vanquished. Warren had created California's center and now he commanded from it. But on that night of victory, Warren attended no parties, made no public appearances. He paced and fretted with his family. The next few days were crucial, doctors warned. The polio could creep up her body, paralyzing more and more of Honey Bear. Or it could subside.

Special serum was administered on November 8, and doctors reported some hope that the crisis had passed.[61] Still, Warren worried. He canceled all appointments during what should have been that celebratory week. On his calendar, he drew a light pencil X across one page after another.[62] Instead, he conferred worriedly with Bart Cavanaugh, whose own children were battling polio. They fretted together and with their wives. Not until November 13 did Warren allow himself so much as a lunch, finally breaking from his worries to dine with Attorney General Pat Brown. Nina spent hour after hour by Honey Bear's side. Her secretary handled the phones for her—the mansion was deluged with calls—while Nina tended to her namesake daughter. She struggled for composure. "I don't know what I would have done if you hadn't been here this week," she told her aide after days of straining. With that, Nina's strong voice cracked.[63]

Honey Bear improved. With her trademark vigor, she willed herself back to health, recuperating dutifully in a closed-off wing of Sutter Hospital. She moved from bed to wheelchair to walker, straining for motion and strength in her legs. Earl and Nina struggled with her, consulting daily with her doctors and praying. The combined anxiety of his daughter's illness and the workload of the new term finally got to Warren. On February 6, he felt a sharp pain in his arm and went to the hospital to have it checked out. He was diagnosed with neuralgia, and the painful disorder gripped him for weeks. Hospitalized through February 24, he canceled that month's meeting of the Governor's Council and then, in early March, accepted a ride on a National Guard plane that took him to Southern California, where the recuperating governor and his recuperating daughter settled in with Nina for a rest. By the shores of Lake Arrowhead, east of Los Angeles, Earl Warren read papers while Honey Bear swam, at first tentatively, then with growing strength.[64] Both governor and daughter soon were on the mend. Honey Bear was able to spend half a day in a wheelchair on February 26.[65]

Her illness and pluck deeply touched the state. Honey Bear got polio, one long-time California political journalist said years later, and all of California got sick.[66] Press reports suggested Honey Bear probably had contracted polio at school, where three other students had gotten the disease. Across California, parents pulled their children out of public pools and only warily allowed them into crowded class-rooms. In letter after letter, they poured their fears and wishes out to Honey Bear. Servicemen stationed across the world wrote her pained notes, beseeching ones, telling their own stories of injury and fear. The bellboys at the Biltmore Hotel in Los Angeles put together an elaborately drawn card, addressed simply to "Miss Nina Warren—That's Honey Bear—Executive Mansion, Sacramento, California." Beneath it, they added a note: "Hurry Postman. She's Needing Mail These Days!" Admirers sent her pins, songs, candy, perfume, flowers, food, art books, collages, notepaper, and dozens and dozens and dozens of flowers.[67]

Honey Bear's recovery was remarkable and complete. By May 1951, Warren was able to report that she was "walking more and more."[68] The following month, she walked across the stage to receive her high school diploma. By the summer after that, no traces of the illness remained, at least to those who saw her. That year, War-ren's longtime aide and friend Warren Olney arrived at the Warren's summer cot-tage in Santa Monica to deliver papers to his boss. Thinking he would only be a moment, Olney asked his teenage son Warren IV to wait in the car. Young Olney did, but as he whiled away the minutes, he suddenly looked up to find the Warren daughters at his window, asking if he would join them for a walk to the beach. Dressed in their bathing suits, beaming with California summer, the girls took his breath away. More than forty years later, telling the story on a sunny morning in Venice, just ten miles from where it occurred, Warren Olney IV, now an accom-plished journalist accustomed to a world of fame and beauty, stammered at the memory of teenaged Honey Bear, recovered from polio, bounding away to the beach, leaving him flustered in his father's car. He was struck numb by his en-counter with the Warren girls' radiance, and as he later remembered, only a visit from Mrs. Warren snapped him out of it. She had spied him in the car and invited him inside for cookies.[69]

Nineteen fifty had been a year that tested Warren's loyalties and found them solid. Asked to choose between loyalty to an oath and to his alma mater, he chose the latter. Asked to weigh the abstraction of a Communist threat against the fact of personal friendship, he picked friendship. And forced, in one of his darkest hours, to choose between celebration of a political victory and devotion to his ailing daughter, he stayed with his daughter, crying in the hall. Having fought the loyalty oath debate through that difficult time, Warren soured even on the word "loyalty," at least as many used it. In later years, when he searched for a way to describe the bond between a person and his nation or government, Warren chose "love of country." "I prefer 'love of country,'" he wrote, "because the other terms [*loyalty* and *patriotism*] have occasionally been adopted by extremists as labels for their own exclusive brand of 'Americanism.'"[70]

In the end, Warren's loyalties were vindicated. Honey Bear recovered, and the loyalty oath controversy petered out in Warren's third term. In 1952, the California Supreme Court sided with the fired professors and ordered them reinstated. The regents, firmly under Warren's control by then, acquiesced quietly. When finally Neylan completed his term as a regent, Sproul wrote to Warren to gloat. Warren, who generally shied away from personal remarks in writing, this time could not resist. Lamenting that he'd missed a chance to see Sproul in person, Warren added, "I had looked forward to it for a long time and was prepared to rejoice with you over the great thing that happened at the University when Neylan resigned. The sun must have shown much brighter in California for some time."[71]

Much as Warren would have preferred to be finished with the loyalty issue, California in his governorship was not through debating the meaning of loyalty and the methods of testing it. In 1952, with the Korean War still grinding on, voters were given the chance to consider a pair of ballot measures to bar "subversive persons" from holding public office and to mandate still another oath for public employees. Warren by then had had enough of oaths, and he opposed the measures. His implacable Republican colleagues were furious again. They protested, but he held firm, even as it became clear that he would lose this round. On November 4, 1952, voters did, despite Warren's objections, approve the new oath and the accompanying bar on public employment by subversives. The following day, an old colleague sat down to write Warren. The two men had supported each other and worked together. They had even run against each other for office, but their bond survived that. They shared respect and loyalty to each other as persons, not as causes. On that day in 1952, those ties were stronger than their differences.

"You and I have been corresponding on the subject of civil liberties since 1938," Robert Kenny wrote. "I think your stand on the two propositions in the midst of the current hysteria is one of the finest things that you have ever done."[72]

Chapter 14

# "TRAITOR IN OUR DELEGATION"

*Honorable men don't stab their friends—or enemies—in the back!*

KYLE PALMER[1]

E ARL WARREN SET OUT on a familiar journey on a hot afternoon in 1952.
The day was typical for July in California's Central Valley: it had peaked at
98 degrees, and the light breeze off Sacramento's intersecting rivers did little to take the edge off a sizzling afternoon. As the sun began to drop toward the
horizon, Warren boarded yet another train, headed for Chicago, as he had so many
times before. He was accompanied again by fellow Californians, carrying again the
mantle of that state's favorite-son status to the quadrennial convention of the nation's Republican Party. As he had in 1948, William Knowland, son of Warren's patron and Warren's own selection for the United States Senate, headed the California
delegation. And as they had before, the California delegates—seventy in 1952—
anticipated casting presidential ballots for their governor, Earl Warren.

There was, however, a difference in 1952. In 1952, Warren intended to win.

"I go to Chicago," Warren announced as the train prepared to leave, "without
the intention of making any deals of any kind."[2]

With that, Warren and the delegates boarded the eighteen-car Warren Special
and headed east. The air-conditioning units had been off all afternoon. Delegates
asked porters to deliver buckets of ice to their cars, then sat around them, dipping
into them for drinks and straining for a breath of cool air. It was, one delegate recalled, "hotter than the hinges of hell."[3] The train strained upward through the
Sierra Nevada. Delegates and families elbowed with reporters and jostled in the drink
and dining cars. Some played cards or read. Mostly they gossiped about the days

ahead, when history seemed to offer the Republican Party yet another prime opportunity to regain the White House after a full generation of Democratic control.
The train was professionally festive, relaxed but taut, comfortable but tinged with
excitement.[4]

Warren had begun his exploration of a presidential bid in January at a meeting
of the Republican National Committee in San Francisco. There, he had methodically checked in with old friends and political bosses, with journalists and influential officials; by the time the committee meetings were complete, Warren had a list
of seventy-two people he'd met with over the three days.[5] His strategy was not to
ride a national wave of delegate support for first-ballot victory—he had no national
organization to support such a time-consuming and expensive campaign—but he
had learned in 1948 that coming with California's delegation alone was not enough.
In 1952, then, he decided to mount a strategic challenge in one or two states outside
of California, enough to show a national presence and to hope that, combined with
his likely California win, he would come to the convention well positioned to
emerge as a compromise candidate able to carry the party to victory in November.
He built a campaign plan and organization suited to that strategy. Through mid-
February, Warren constructed his political and fundraising apparatus. He opened
offices in San Francisco, Los Angeles, and Sacramento and set out to raise the
$100,000 or so that his finance chairs believed was necessary to run in three states
and enter the convention with a respectable showing of delegates.[6]

Warren entered the Wisconsin primary on February 19 and campaigned there
even as the California legislative session kept him pinned in Sacramento for much of
the time. An old friend wasted no time in declaring his allegiance: Two days after
Warren announced, Drew Pearson proclaimed him the "surest shot to win for the
GOP next November."[7] Buoyed by the support of friends, Warren worked in the California capitol every Monday through Wednesday, then flew to Wisconsin for long
weekends of campaigning. The trips, made in the thick of the Wisconsin winter, were
grueling, typically taking Warren to more than a dozen events a day—greetings, talks,
speeches from sound trucks—all in the home state of Senator Joseph McCarthy.
Warren gave the phlegmatic senator a clear rebuke—he made clear that "blanket indictments against groups of people without naming them or substantiating them by
substantial evidence" did not, in his view, "serve the best interests of our country"[8]—
but he did not engage the home-state senator in direct debate. Warren hoped instead
to animate the surviving members of LaFollette's Progressive base without driving
away the remainder of the Republican electorate.

Fighting the demands of his schedule and the angry anti-Communism of Mc-
Carthy and his admirers, Warren persisted. He spoke on behalf of the United
Nations and international cooperation, and he met with crowds in the easy, gentle
fashion with which he campaigned in California. Despite a thin organization and

limited time, Warren polled more than 260,000 votes on Wisconsin primary day, finishing second to Senator Robert Taft. Warren carried Madison and a few other districts, enough to have delegates from outside his home state.[9] He had proven he could get votes outside of California.

His second effort, in Oregon, was less successful. The American Medical Association, still angry about Warren's health care proposal, opposed him. And though Warren campaigned with vigor, condemning Truman's seizure of the nation's steel mills and warning of the administration's "great complacency," Eisenhower was gaining strength rapidly by that point in the contest. Ike polled more than 150,000 votes, while Warren, though he finished in second place, finished short of Eisenhower by more than 100,000 votes.[10]

That left Warren far short of the front-runners but still viable. In the weeks leading up to the convention, most political insiders picked Taft, whose father had been president and who, by 1952, was the unchallenged standard-bearer for the Republicans' conservative wing. Nicknamed "Mr. Republican," he was noted for an isolationism so deep-set that he opposed aid to Britain during World War II and the creation of NATO after the war's conclusion. He deplored the expansion of presidential power under FDR and Truman, and his commitment to personal freedom included opposition to the military draft. Taft commanded the GOP's political machinery, and his reach in 1952 was at its peak: He controlled the most basic party decisions, down to such a level of detail that even the seating of delegates and their guests in the Chicago hall was cleared by him.[11]

With the convention approaching, Taft and his allies worked to fasten up votes and give the senator a first-ballot victory. But they confronted a fast-rising force in the Republican Party, one whose late entry into the race was scrambling the conventions of American politics. Dwight Eisenhower was the general who had saved Europe, the man most responsible for D-Day, the liberation of France, and the destruction of Hitler. He was an American hero with an infectious grin, a bounce in his step, and a keen, clever mind. Although a committed Republican, Eisenhower kept his politics so quiet after the war that Truman had personally lobbied him to accept the Democratic nomination and had contrived ways to bring Ike into the administration's response to the outbreak of the Korean War. For a time, Eisenhower agreed to advise Truman and his generals, but eventually he backed out, preferring to criticize the administration publicly rather than to counsel it privately.[12]

As Ike moved about the country in 1950, he did so firmly denying any intent to run for president. Besieged by requests, he demurred, not even conceding to his diary that he would consider such a draft. And yet Eisenhower acted like a candidate. He spoke forcefully about the war and the president. He met political leaders to hear their analysis of the campaign—the campaign he insisted he would not join. He conferred with business and civic leaders. Indeed, the same week that Earl Warren buttonholed *Los Angeles Times* publisher Norman Chandler in the redwood glens of the Bohemian Grove, Dwight Eisenhower arrived at the Grove as a guest. There, Eisenhower introduced himself to the other members of the Republican leadership and sidled up to a young congressman from Southern California then engaged in a tough campaign for the Senate, Richard Nixon.[13] Warren was not terribly impressed, especially when Eisenhower used the occasion to extol loyalty oaths.[14]

And still, Eisenhower resisted entreaties through all of 1950 and 1951. The general returned to his post in Europe, where he was building NATO. From there, he fumed at Taft's isolationism and Truman's stingy defense spending. A choice between those two candidates, Eisenhower ultimately concluded, was so grim that it required him to intervene. His supporters placed his name on the New Hampshire primary ballot in January 1952 (apparently against his wishes). The following month, after viewing a film of an Eisenhower rally in New York, the general was moved to tears by the emotion of the crowd. He agreed to run.[15]

Four months later, the Republicans prepared their arrival in Chicago. On the eve of the convention, reporters estimated that Eisenhower could count on 414 delegate votes, and Taft had the support of 516, though Eisenhower was gaining fast and some believed delegates were swinging his way. It was important that both were short of the votes needed to win on the first ballot—leaving a small window of hope for Earl Warren, who arrived with 76 delegates pledged to him.[16] Although numerically far behind, Warren was stronger than his delegate count. He, like many Republican observers, believed going into the convention that Taft's strong hold on the party would deny Eisenhower the delegates needed to win. And since Warren represented the socially moderate, internationalist element of the party—Eisenhower's wing—the general's delegates were much more likely to see Warren as acceptable than Taft should their champion fail. What's more, Harold Stassen of Minnesota commanded a handful of delegates himself, and he too was inclined to favor Warren over Taft, if that's what it came to.

Said Warren, "Either somebody has a majority of the votes when he goes to Chicago, or he hasn't. And if he hasn't, it's a wide-open convention."[17] With less than a week before the delegate count began, no candidate had a majority. It was, then, at least in Warren's view, "wide-open."

The trip through the Rockies took longer than expected. The Warren Special arrived in Denver about two hours late. There it stopped and took on the only delegate who had not left California with the rest of the group. Senator Nixon had been in Chicago, working on platform matters, but flew to Denver to join the delegation for the final leg of its trip. As Nixon boarded the train that night, the mood turned detectably sour. After climbing into the train, Nixon immediately slighted Warren by heading straight for his own car, not bothering to pay the governor the courtesy of greeting him first. That might have offended Warren in any event. Formality was important to the governor. But it was especially vexing in Nixon's case, as their antagonism toward each other was already a barely concealed fact of California politics, the residue of their strained relations in the 1946 and 1950 campaigns. By 1952, Warren and Nixon had plenty of reason to distrust each other.

And the early months of that year had been trying. Nineteen fifty-two was the time when Warren's enemies found one another and put aside their many differences to oppose Warren's presidential bid. From the loyalty oath debate came John Francis Neylan, still mad, now on the attack, charging that Warren's campaign was egotistic and that his politics were dangerously liberal.[18] From the gas tax debate came Bill Keck, still smarting over Warren's successful push for that tax hike. Loyd Wright, the pompous president of the State Bar Association—a "domineering little Napoleon," one Warren supporter called him[19]—felt Warren had betrayed his party and was looking for a candidate who spoke to its traditional conservatism. The American Medical Association, never to forgive Warren's compulsory health insurance efforts, asked members to give $10 each to the Taft campaign. The Associated Farmers, once so fond of the governor they helped elect, now found themselves increasingly distressed by his unwillingness to defy organized labor. "[Y]ou have abandoned Republicanism," the farmers concluded.[20] In 1952, Keck, Neylan, Wright, and the others gave up on Warren for good and instead sought out Congressman Tom Werdel of Bakersfield, Warren's hometown, to challenge Warren's presidential primary candidacy in California.

Although Werdel was hardly Earl Warren, his challenge was distracting, and posed some real threat. Warren was difficult to assail from the right during a general election—Democrats could be counted on to cross over to vote for him, and Republicans could hardly abandon him for an even more liberal opponent—but a Republican primary brought out more conservative voters, those who might be more unhappy with Warren and more willing to consider an alternative. In addition, the Werdel group had money—doctors, oilmen, wealthy conservatives—linked by their common exasperation with the governor. Given all that, Warren needed protection from conservative friends. Nixon agreed to help.

On November 8, 1951, Nixon signed—along with Knowland and other leading California Republicans—a public letter asking Warren to seek the nomination. When the Werdel faction emerged to challenge Warren, Nixon stood by the governor, at least publicly, bragging that he did so despite the risk of offending some conservative supporters. "You can rest assured," one constituent wrote him, that we "will remember when another election comes around."[21] But even as Nixon publicly allied himself with Warren, he played both sides. In order to appease Werdel supporters, Nixon assured them that he eventually would work for Taft at the convention anyway—that he would protect the party's conservative plank under the cover of the Warren delegation.[22] Nixon, in fact, was courting the favor not of Taft but of Eisenhower, but the Werdel supporters did not know that.

Werdel went ahead anyway, and his critique of Warren brimmed with years of repressed anger by California's conservatives. "His Trumanistic idolatry is well known," the group's "Declaration of Policy" proclaimed of Warren. "His record supports the conclusion that he endorses socialistic governmental policies, including limitless taxation and planned inflation; that he is vacillating in his opposition to Communism and government, and that for all these reasons he has forfeited any claim to the voting support of this delegation at the convention."[23] Warren fought back through the spring and summer of 1951. His calmer logic eventually prevailed, and Warren defeated Werdel by a 2–1 margin. The race had been difficult, however—Werdel actually carried Orange County—and served as a reminder that the right wing and Warren had now permanently parted ways. In addition, Warren had cut some deals to protect himself. He agreed, for instance, to allow Nixon to name some of the delegates who would compose the Warren slate at the Republican convention. It was a fateful compromise.

Just a week after the campaign ended but before the convention began, Nixon once again sought to distance himself from Warren's candidacy despite his public pledge of support. Using the free mailing privileges given to members of Congress for nonpolitical constituent communications, Nixon sent 23,000 cards to California Republicans asking them to name their favorite candidate for president in 1952 in the event that Warren failed to win the nomination.[24] Nixon's poll was accompanied by a misleading letter—"I am writing to a selected group of those who were active in my campaign . . . for the purpose of obtaining their views on this problem"—and the poll made it clear that Nixon was looking for a backup when, not if, Warren fell short.

Nixon demanded secrecy in handling the returns; indeed, he promised confidentiality to those who responded. But he also made sure select politicians and journalists knew the results favored Eisenhower. Nixon, whose support from the *Los Angeles Times* was a bulwark of his political base, shared the results with Kyle Palmer. Nixon undoubtedly expected a positive response from Palmer, who had championed Nixon at every turn and who occasionally blanched at Warren's overtures to the left. This time, however, Palmer reacted strongly in the opposite direction. Rather than protect Nixon's secret, Palmer promptly told Warren, who was understandably angry. "I told Palmer that was not consistent with the oath that all the delegates had taken to support my candidacy," Warren said.[25]

What Palmer said in private to Nixon is not known. But there is no secret about how he felt, for on June 20, the *Times* published Palmer's regular column and it came as close as the *Los Angeles Times* would ever come to flaying the senator. Without naming Nixon, Palmer wrote in the *Times* of Knowland's honor, noting that

Knowland could be counted on to support Warren unless and until Warren freed him to do otherwise. "Why am I so sure?" Palmer asked. "He is an honorable man. He didn't make any pledge to support Earl Warren for President with any shabby reservations. Honorable men don't stab their friends—or enemies—in the back!"[26]

A chastened Nixon pulled back and did not release the poll generally. His backers later would cite that as evidence of his intention not to harm Warren. In fact, however, Nixon already had achieved what he wanted. Publicly, he remained a Warren loyalist. But insiders, those whose attention Nixon sought, now understood that he was not there for the governor. For the stated purpose of helping to form his views on the nomination, the poll had always been a useless exercise; for telegraphing his ambivalence about Warren and his attachment to Eisenhower, it was superbly effective.

Nixon's efforts were encouraged by his closest friends, who, almost to a person, resented the governor and his politics. Murray Chotiner was still mad that Warren refused to give him and other Republicans special consideration after the 1942 victory, and others picked up their grievances as well. Herman Perry, the man who had launched Nixon into politics and was still a loyal friend, angrily wrote in April to Bernard Brennan, one of relatively few California Republicans allied with both Warren and Nixon, to express his mounting anger toward Warren. Unable to contain his irritation, Perry deprecated Warren as "the great white father," and demanded that he release the convention delegates to Nixon and Knowland's leadership.[27] Three weeks later, that still had not happened, and Perry wrote again to Brennan, again insisting that Warren withdraw his public insistence that his delegates back him. Perry called that stand "selfish" and "unrealistic" and added, "[W]ith Earl Warren out of the picture, I am further convinced that the candidate for Vice President on the Republican ticket could be Bill Knowland or Richard M. Nixon."[28]

In June, a month before the convention and with his poll in the field, Nixon himself wrote to Brennan. Labeling the letter "personal and confidential," he urged Brennan to confer with him in person before the convention began. Nixon warned that he felt Taft was close to securing the necessary delegates, and he dismissed the prospects for Warren. "I don't believe that any of us should have any illusions on the possibilities of Warren being selected for the top spot," Nixon wrote. "As a matter of fact as a result of Knowland winning the primary, he has completely supplanted Warren as the Vice Presidential prospect and several people have been talking about Knowland as the best bet of a dark horse in the event of a deadlock. I am laying these facts right on the line because I do not feel we should go into the Convention without knowing what we are going to be up against."[29]

Not only was Nixon convinced Warren was headed to defeat, he also was determined not to be aligned with that defeat, his pledge of support notwithstanding.

Perry urged Nixon not, under any circumstances, to agree to place Warren's name in nomination for the presidency. "The feeling is that if anyone is to stick his neck out in this instance, it should be Bill Knowland," Perry wrote, adding, "I believe by proper manipulation you yet can come through the critical period of the Convention without being harmed."[30] Nixon needed no convincing: "I have neither the desire nor the intention of accepting such an assignment."[31]

Nixon and his admirers would long deny that Nixon secretly worked through those weeks to deny Warren the nomination. It was Warren, they insisted, whose selfishness threatened the unity of the delegation in the service of his own far-fetched ambition. And they were right insofar as they stressed that Warren's chances were remote. But at least two aspects of the episode are undeniable. First, despite professing loyalty to Warren, Nixon undermined him at several important moments: He signed on to Warren's ticket but privately sought to advance another candidate's prospects; he conducted a poll, illegally using taxpayer money to do it, and saw that results damaging to his own candidate made their way to key decision makers; and he privately pressured Warren through intermediaries to back down. The other clear message from those months of 1952 is that Warren came to see Nixon not just as generally devious—an impression he already had from the campaigns of 1946 and 1950—but now as a personal adversary. And so when Nixon boarded the train in Denver on that summer night in 1952, the seeds of suspicion were well tended.

As the train pulled away in the dark, the engineer pressed it for speed, trying to make up for time lost in the Rockies. As it whisked through the plains east of Denver, Nixon mingled among the delegates; he reported from Chicago on the platform work he had been conducting in recent days, and passed along the latest gossip from the back rooms. Chester Hanson, the *Los Angeles Times* reporter accompanying the Warren delegation, wrote that Nixon supplied a "shot in the political arm" for the Warren supporters by publicly reporting that a deadlock could still deliver the convention to the California governor. But Hanson also noted that Brennan, then serving as one of Warren's convention managers, "was like a nervous mother coaching the bride just before the wedding."[32]

What Hanson picked up was more than nerves. Brennan knew of the tension between Nixon and Warren and was doing his best to navigate it.[33] Nixon moved from car to car that night, conferring mainly with the delegates loyal to him. In each case, his message was substantively the same: Warren was finished, and for the California delegation to be relevant, it needed to swing to Eisenhower. "Nixon felt that, in view of the fact that in his opinion Warren's chances were not good, that the California delegation could effectively insure Eisenhower's victory by voting for Eisenhower forthwith," recalled John Walton Dinkelspiel, one of the California delegates loyal to Nixon aboard the train. As Nixon spoke to one group or another, ru-

Earl Warren held elected offices in California from 1926 to 1953, winning seven straight elections. He enjoyed campaigning, and engaged in it with diligence and attention to detail. Asked how he could recall people with precision, Warren replied that he avoided distractions: "I never look at their neckties." *(University of California, Berkeley)*

Born in Los Angeles and raised in Bakersfield, Earl was part of a small family and was especially close to his father. Here with him are his mother, Chrystal; his father, Methias; and his older sister, Ethel. Earl was small for his age as a boy and, because he started school early and skipped a grade, young for his class as well. Perhaps partly as a result, he was shy and did not blossom, physically or emotionally, until college.
*(University of California, Berkeley)*

As a boy in Bakersfield, Warren was surrounded by pets. He had dogs, sheep, even an eagle. His favorite was a donkey named Jack, who accompanied him on romps through the San Joaquin Valley countryside.
*(University of California, Berkeley)*

Warren (front row, third from left) graduated from Bakersfield High School in 1908; his own children would attend California public schools, too. Despite his later successes, he showed little promise of greatness in high school. Reflecting on this at the time of his graduation, he remarked: "I know many things, but nothing distinctly." *(University of California, Berkeley)*

Warren came to adulthood in an age of clubs, and he joined with enthusiasm. Among his most lasting and important memberships was that with the Masons, which he joined in 1919 and through whose ranks he rose during the 1920s and 1930s. In 1935, he was elected grand master of the California Masons; he is at the center in this photograph. *(University of California, Berkeley)*

Earl Warren and Nina Palmquist met at a pool party in 1921 and were married four years later. Theirs was an enduring, happy, traditional marriage of two practical people who loved and appreciated each other deeply. *(University of California, Berkeley)*

Although Warren held important public positions without interruption from 1919 to 1969, he tried to reserve time for his family, usually in the evenings. This picture, taken around 1937 in the breakfast room at 88 Vernon Street in Oakland, shows all the Warren children except for the eldest, Jim, who was away at school. *(University of California, Berkeley)*

On Saturday, May 14, 1938, Earl Warren's father was beaten to death at his home in Bakersfield. Warren, then the district attorney of Alameda County and a candidate for state attorney general, received the news the next morning, when his father's body was found. Here he prepares to leave for Bakersfield with George Helms (left), a member of his staff, and Nina. *(University of California, Berkeley)*

As Warren embarked on his campaign for governor in 1942, his consultants Clem Whitaker and Leone Baxter convinced him that he needed a softer, more approachable image. The Warren family previously had not been part of his campaigns, but this time Nina agreed for herself and her children to be featured in a photograph. It was a hit—more than three million copies of the picture were distributed in California. Other politicians complained that it was hard enough to beat Warren alone; to beat his whole family was too much. *(University of California, Berkeley)*

The Warren family spent part of most summers in Santa Monica. Here, Bobby and Honey Bear join Earl and Nina for a night of grunion fishing. With them (at center) is Leo Carrillo, one of the first successful Mexican-American actors in Hollywood, best known for his portrayal of Pancho, sidekick to the Cisco Kid. Carrillo supported Warren politically and campaigned with and for him among Latinos. *(Private collection of Bill Beebe)*

Warren was a devoted baseball fan, who, after 1952, rarely missed a World Series. Here, in 1940 or 1941, he throws out the first pitch of the season in Sacramento. He was naturally left-handed, but his elementary school teachers forced him to favor his right; for the rest of his life, he wrote right-handed but played sports left-handed. *(University of California, Berkeley)*

Jim, Nina's son by a previous marriage, whom Earl adopted and raised after they were married, was significantly older than the rest of the Warren children; he supplied the elder Warrens with grandchildren when their other children were still young. Here, Jim and his wife and their three young sons—Jim, Jeffrey, and John Albert— join the rest of the family during Warren's gubernatorial years. As these grandchildren grew older and the other Warren children had children of their own, the grandchildren would visit Earl and Nina during the summer in Washington.
*(University of California, Berkeley)*

The national Republican Party yearned for Warren to be on the ticket in 1944; he demurred, and delivered an unremarkable keynote address at the GOP convention. New York governor Tom Dewey selected Ohio senator John Bricker as his running mate, and the ticket lost overwhelmingly to Franklin Roosevelt. *(Associated Press)*

By 1948, Warren recognized that he could not say no again to the Republican establishment if he hoped to remain a viable national candidate. This time, when Dewey asked, Warren reluctantly agreed to accept the vice presidential nomination. He campaigned mostly by train—a grueling enterprise made more difficult by the strictures of Dewey headquarters. Only near the end of the campaign did Warren seem to brighten; he was joined by his family as he and Nina celebrated their wedding anniversary and the campaign train returned them to California. (*Associated Press*)

Dwight Eisenhower appointed Warren to the court in 1953 and supported him through a deceitful attempt to derail his confirmation. By the late 1950s, however, relations between the two had become strained and cursory; Warren was deeply disappointed that the president did not lend support to the Supreme Court's desegregation efforts, and Eisenhower was enraged at the Warren Court's defense of communists. This photograph shows the two in the fall of 1953, in more convivial times. *(Associated Press)*

## WANTED!

### EARL WARREN
### FOR *IMPEACHMENT*

For giving aid and comfort to the **COMMUNIST CONSPIRACY,** the mortal Enemy of the United States and the American People!

Opposition to the Warren Court coalesced in the early 1960s, with the John Birch Society waging its long and highly public campaign to impeach the chief justice. Although impeachment proceedings were never initiated, billboards and pamphlets such as this one bitterly attacked Warren and the Court.

As chief justice, Warren could not openly engage in politics, yet he found ways to telegraph his favorites. In 1961, with Governor Pat Brown preparing to face a challenge from Richard Nixon, Warren went out of his way to signal to voters that he favored Brown. On December 20, the two went on a hunting trip in Colusa, California, and posed together for photographers. When Brown (at left) won the election, Warren was delighted. *(Bettmann/Corbis)*

On November 20, 1963, Warren led the Court to its annual White House dinner, hosted by President John Kennedy and his wife. At cocktails before dinner, Warren joked that Kennedy should take care on his upcoming political mission to Texas. "Watch out for those wild Texans, Mr. President," Warren said. "They're a rough bunch." The Kennedys left the next day. (Bettmann/Corbis)

Warren accepted Lyndon Johnson's invitation to head the President's Commission on the Assassination of President Kennedy with great reluctance, and only after Johnson exerted pressure on him to take the post. Ten months later, on September 24, 1964, Warren and his fellow commissioners delivered their 888-page report to Johnson. Behind Warren in this picture is Representative Gerald Ford, another member of the Commission. *(Associated Press)*

In 1973, the retired chief justice returned to his birthplace, Los Angeles, to swear in that city's first black mayor, Tom Bradley. Bradley's wife, Ethel, stands between them in this photograph. (Los Angeles Times)

Warren died on July 9, 1974. His final days were spent at Georgetown Hospital, near the Water-gate complex, locus of the unraveling Nixon presidency. Despite their long animus, Nixon honored Warren's passing and escorted Nina to the funeral at the National Cathedral on July 12. Less than a month later, Nixon resigned the presidency. *(Associated Press)*

Earl Warren 1891–1974.
*(AP Photo/U.S. Supreme Court handout)*

mors raced through the cars. "If you're on the front end of the train you have to run pretty fast before the statement gets to the back end of the train," Nixon aide Frank Jorgensen remembered of that night.[34]

The delegates ate, drank, gossiped, and lobbied hour after hour. As sunrise and Chicago approached, the train clattered across the Great Plains, the light spirit of the first night replaced by the darker throb of intrigue. Just before the train reached Chicago, Nixon ducked out again, his late-night meetings complete. When the Warren Special arrived in Chicago, it pulled up as it had departed from Sacramento, missing the junior senator from California. Awaiting the delegates were buses to take them to the hotel. Chotiner had arranged for the transportation, and as the train neared the station, Warren aides got wind of yet another act of mischief: The buses set aside for the Warren delegation were draped in "Eisenhower for President" banners. Warren loyalists hastily rewrapped the buses before Warren arrived, but when Warren later learned of the stunt, he was "blistering mad."[35]

Once in Chicago, the machinations between Warren, Eisenhower, Taft, and Nixon continued, with Eisenhower and Taft elbowing for advantage and Warren holding out hope for sufficient deadlock to permit his emergence. The Eisenhower and Taft campaigns all were headquartered in the same Chicago hotel—though the California delegation was staying elsewhere—and Warren quickly made his way to Eisenhower's suite to meet the general; although their paths had crossed before, this was to be their first serious conversation. Arriving, Warren knocked on the door and was admitted by none other than Chotiner. "Imagine my surprise," Warren noted archly, indulging himself in a rare note of sarcasm.[36]

Eisenhower and Warren liked each other. Natural leaders with similar politics and easy smiles, they were rivals but not enemies. For Warren to succeed, Ike had to fail, but Warren would far sooner have seen Eisenhower get the nomination than have it fall to Taft, and Eisenhower similarly favored Warren over Taft, if it came to that. Indeed, Warren's meeting with Taft, later that same week, only reinforced Warren's preference for Eisenhower. Taft used the occasion to try to cut a deal, offering Warren the vice presidency or any other spot in a Taft administration (Taft had already offered the vice presidency to MacArthur but assured Warren that he could make that awkward problem go away) if Warren would deliver him the California delegation on the first ballot. As with Nixon's attempts to steer the delegation to Eisenhower, this backroom offer offended Warren's integrity at the same time that it undermined his personal political position. Moreover, Warren did not like or trust Taft—just days earlier, Taft and his deputies had used their control over the convention seating to put Warren's family up near the rafters. As Warren later put it mildly, "I was not particularly enamored of Taft as a candidate."[37]

By 1952, Warren had led California's Republicans to their national convention four times. He knew a thing or two about the mechanics and complexities of those affairs, and he knew that this year, when he came to win, he might at some point require the services of a trusted emissary, someone who could communicate directly with Eisenhower without reporters sniffing out the contact. So Warren set out to make sure he had such a person lined up. Well before the convention began, Warren invited a close associate of Eisenhower's, who had served with the general during his tenure at Columbia University, to join him for lunch in Santa Monica. They discussed Warren's presidential efforts, and Warren expressed some irritation at Eisenhower's comments on the loyalty oath controversy (Warren and Eisenhower never would see eye to eye on oaths or Communism, among other things). A month later, Eisenhower's associate wrote back to Warren asking if he needed any help at the upcoming convention. Helen MacGregor returned the message and asked him to go ahead to Chicago, to check into a hotel, and to await a call from Warren. He did as instructed.

On July 8, the day that General MacArthur—once Eisenhower's boss, then his rival, and often the object of his scorn—spoke to the convention, pledging the party, "so help us God," to victory in the fall, Earl Warren called for his emissary and entrusted him with a message to deliver to the general. The California delegation, Warren told him to tell Eisenhower, was becoming difficult to hold together. "The problem is this," Warren said:

> We have a traitor in our delegation. It's Nixon. He, like all the rest, took the oath that he would vote for me, until such time as the delegation was released, but he has not paid attention to his oath and immediately upon being elected, started working for Eisenhower and has been doing so ever since. I have word that he is actively in touch with the Eisenhower people. I wish you would tell General Eisenhower that we resent his people infiltrating, through Nixon, into our delegation, and ask him to have it stopped.[38]

A "traitor." Could any description have been more calculated to reach the general? Warren was not prone to hyperbole—or to threats, though he leveled one here as well. "I tell you," he confided in his intermediary, "but you needn't tell Eisenhower, at this time, that if he doesn't do that we're going to take measures that will be harmful to his candidacy." Eisenhower replied that he had no designs on California and was not intending to undermine Warren, that indeed he wished Warren well in the event that he himself should fall short of the nomination. Though Warren may have accepted Eisenhower's assurances—it is plausible that Eisenhower did not know of Nixon's attempts to sow discord among the California delegates— the general's reply did nothing to convince Warren that Nixon was trustworthy.

Again and again, Warren resisted any attempt to wrest his delegates from him on the first ballot, and found time to lobby on his own behalf with several other state delegations. But on the convention's key procedural matter, he chose a different course, one that revealed his character as surely as Nixon's maneuvering revealed his. At issue was the seating of a number of Southern delegates, those from Texas and Georgia, loyal to Taft. Given Taft's control of the party machinery, he was in a strong position to place his delegates in voting roles, a move contested by the Eisenhower forces who sought to seat their own, rival groups of delegates. Before either group could take its place at the convention, however, the question for the remaining delegates was whether the contested, pro-Taft delegations should be allowed to vote on their own seating. Eisenhower naturally opposed that, as it would allow Taft delegates to vote to seat themselves. He moved to block it, and his political adviser, Herbert Brownell, shrewdly labeled his counterproposal the "Fair Play Amendment." So many delegates were at stake and the voting was so close that the nomination hung in the balance—by most tallies, allowing the Eisenhower slates to be seated would all but ensure his nomination. By contrast, if the Taft delegates were allowed to vote to seat themselves, it might deny Eisenhower a quick victory and thus force a protracted convention. That route, a long and contested convention, also was Warren's one chance, as he still held out hope that if Eisenhower folded, those votes would come his way. On this issue, then, Warren and Taft had common interests.[39]

Thomas Mellon, a member of the California delegation, knew well—they all did—what a vote for Eisenhower on the seating matter would cause: It would show Eisenhower's strength, add to his vote total, almost definitely ensure the general's victory and Warren's defeat. Knowing that, Mellon asked Warren, whom he greatly admired, what he should do. "Well," Warren replied, "of course I'd enjoy seeing the Taft delegation supported and seated. [But] you people have to go back to California. You have an obligation, and it seems to me that you have to discharge that obligation in a way that satisfies your conscience."[40]

On Wednesday, July 10, 1952, the California delegation voted 62 to 7 to seat the Eisenhower delegations from Georgia and Texas, delivering the general the votes he had sought for "Fair Play." The following day, Warren was nominated for president amid fanfare and appreciation; William Knowland submitted the name of his old friend, saying Warren would provide "honor and purpose in both domestic and foreign affairs."[41] Twenty minutes of applause and excitement followed, yet for Warren that was the end. He fought a principled campaign for president, but did so hamstrung by an unprincipled adversary in his own delegation. When the California delegation swung over to Eisenhower on the rules vote, Ike's contingent was impressed, as it had been for months, by the young senator. As soon as Eisenhower was nominated, he asked Brownell to lead a group of political insiders in a discussion over who should be the vice presidential nominee. Warren was invited but declined, convinced that Nixon already had the inside track. It was, he wrote later, "a fait accompli."[42]

Nixon received the nomination, and Warren congratulated him through gritted teeth. With the train trip behind him and his chances of ever becoming president now effectively gone, Warren turned to a friend and confessed his bewilderment at what had occurred. "How do you account for him doing a thing like this?" Warren asked, speaking to himself as well as his listener. "I just can't understand anybody doing such a thing as that."[43]

Warren never publicly vented his full anger at Nixon over the events of that night and the days to come. But it rankled him as few other events in his life did. The full measure of his unhappiness would come to light only in glancing admissions and occasionally unguarded remarks. In later years, Warren would grumble to his clerks and children, would complain to an occasional close friend. And he would, in time, find ways to get even. But while their feud was a long one, and did not begin in 1952, it was that night on the train that would sear Warren's impression of Nixon as untrustworthy. As with the internment, his memoirs offer a clipped version, one in which he ratcheted down his anger while still displaying a telltale sliver:

> [D]uring the night [that Nixon arrived on the train], the Nixon delegates—but not the senator as far as I know—held caucuses and urged other delegates to vote for General Eisenhower on the first ballot. Some of those who were importuned came to me and asked what the situation was. I told them what I had told the voters: that the delegation was not a front for anyone, and that no matter what happened it was obligated to vote for me on the first ballot at least.[44]

Those terse sentences contain hints of Warren's feelings—the indignant insistence that he would not "front for anyone," the pointed notation that the delegate caucuses did not include Nixon "as far as I know," even the reference to "Nixon delegates" when in fact all those aboard were at least nominally pledged to Warren. Those all suggest a still-angry Warren recalling that night nearly twenty years later. An even clearer sign comes from the reaction of one person close to him reading those same words. When Warren sent his manuscript draft to Merrell Small, an old friend and colleague from the gubernatorial years, Small read those sentences and suggested that Warren was pulling his punches:

> Have you not treated Richard Nixon with too kindly a touch? This book you are writing becomes part of the written history of America, and although he is President now and that office must have our respect, your account deals with conditions precedent. . . . I have had the understanding that you believed Richard Nixon was at least prepared in 1952, at the Republican convention in Chicago, to cut your political throat.[45]

Nixon came to Sacramento in August, and now it was the forty-year-old senator who held the spotlight, the governor twenty years his senior accompanying him, dutifully posing for photographs and calling on Republicans to unite.[46] A few days later, Eisenhower himself, taking a break from his postconvention vacation in Colorado, arrived in Los Angeles to address a convention of the Veterans of Foreign Wars, a group naturally well disposed toward the general. Warren, still smarting, again accompanied Nixon—and this time Eisenhower, too—but the event went poorly. Eisenhower asked Warren, Warren remembered later, "to take no part in the affair," by which he apparently meant not to take part in planning the visit. Warren held back, then watched in amusement as it flopped.

A parade was scheduled for late afternoon, when Los Angeles traffic made it impractical. The motorcade shoved off early, taking the few people lining the route by surprise. And at the Los Angeles Coliseum, a sparse crowd greeted the nominees. The *Los Angeles Times* did its best for its fellow Republicans, seeking out just the angle to make the stadium appear as full as possible. Even those efforts were not enough. The corners of its photographs on the full page devoted to pictures of Eisenhower's day showed empty bleachers, undermining the paper's insistence of an electrifying address before "thousands of cheering listeners."[47] Warren's testy recollection was closer to the truth. "The affair," he wrote, "was a complete washout. . . . It was a humiliating and almost ludicrous experience." Riding with Eisenhower to the airport, Warren assured him that the sparse crowd along the route and the embarrassing spectacle of speaking to a nearly empty stadium would not be repeated. "We would fill the stadium for him," Warren said, and one can imagine him leaning on the "we" in that sentence. He then added with evident satisfaction, "We did exactly that sometime later, giving him a rousing welcome."[48]

After that bumpy start, the Republican campaign settled into a more favorable rhythm in September. Running against Adlai Stevenson, Eisenhower led in most polls. But Warren's friends, despite their surface support for their party's ticket, continued to nurse their convention wounds. In mid-September, they retaliated, and just as surely as June and July had launched Nixon's national political standing at the expense of Earl Warren, so did September nearly finish it, this time at the hands of Warren loyalists.

In mid-September, Nixon departed on a train trip through California, starting in the south and traveling north, heading eventually for Oregon. Warren was invited to join, but declined, citing a previous engagement.[49] As Nixon's train passed through Southern California on September 18, Keith McCormac boarded and showed Nixon a copy of a newspaper. For a moment, Nixon was dumbfounded. "He was just sitting there, looking at it," McCormac said. Nixon aides shuffled the candidate into a car by himself and canceled the next whistle-stop on the tour. It was not until Tulare that Nixon had regained enough composure to appear again in public.[50]

The story being carried in the nation's newspapers that day had been slow to break, and its bounce startled the Nixon team. For months, sources in California had trafficked in the rumor that Nixon kept a "secret fund," a stash of money raised from supporters to help him make ends meet. In one sense, the fund was not secret at all. Wealthy donors, many from the well-to-do Los Angeles suburbs of Pasadena and San Marino, had been asked for contributions, and had complied, sending checks to Dana Smith, a friend of Nixon's who had the job of managing the fund. Nixon had discussed the fund with at least one reporter, Peter Edson, who had given the story a light treatment, referring to the money as "an extra expense allowance" and stressing not only that donors were not entitled to ask for favors in return for contributions but even that the names of donors were concealed from Nixon to prevent any such overtures.[51]

The version of the story by *New York Post* reporter Leo Katcher was notably different—in tone as well as in effect. "Secret Rich Men's Trust Fund Keeps Nixon in Style Far Beyond His Salary," the tabloid headline blared. The fund, Katcher reported, accurately if luridly, was "devoted exclusively to the financial comfort of Sen. Nixon."[52] It was that account that struck Nixon dumb that September morning. The next several days were the most agonizing of Nixon's life, up to that point at least. His handlers first tried to ignore the story, then argued that it was the sensationalized work of leftist opponents of Nixon, Communist foes afraid of what it would mean for them should he be elected. The former approach was futile—the story, with its charges that Nixon had amassed $18,000 for his personal and political benefit, now had legs, and ignoring it was doing nothing to make it go away. The latter response was disingenuous—those behind this charge were not Communists. Suddenly, the heavily favored Republican ticket was in jeopardy, and Eisenhower came under pressure to dump Nixon.[53]

Tom Dewey warned Nixon that his days could well be numbered. "Did Ike tell you that he went to lunch with a lot of his old friends today, and that everyone of them except one thought you ought to get off the ticket?" Dewey asked Nixon on September 20. Ike had told Nixon no such thing. In fact, he told Nixon nothing. Instead, he deliberately, cruelly, left him hanging. Days passed, and Eisenhower declined to speak with Nixon or to come to his aid. He waited, refusing to be rushed. Finally, on the twentieth, the two men spoke by phone, and Nixon snapped.

After remarking on how difficult the past couple of days had been for young Nixon, Eisenhower cautiously made clear that he remained undecided about Nixon's future. "This is an awful hard thing for me to decide," he ventured.

For Nixon, that was too much. "Well, General," he responded, "I know how it is, but there comes a time in matters like this when you've either got to shit or get off the pot."[54]

Men did not speak that way to General Eisenhower. They did not bully him, and they did not curse at him. Faced with Nixon's impertinence as well as his advisers' conviction that the senator was fast becoming a liability, Eisenhower forced the matter back into Nixon's hands:

> I have come to the conclusion that you are the one who has to decide what to do. After all, you've got a big following in this country, and if the impression got around that you got off the ticket because I forced you to get off, it's going to be very bad. On the other hand, if I issue a statement in effect backing you up, people will accuse me of wrongdoing.[55]

The next day brought more bad news, and a further increase in the pressure. Harold Stassen, long-standing leader of the Republican Party's liberals, wired Nixon to tell him to pull the plug. "After a thoughtful review of the entire situation, Dick, I have regretfully reached a conclusion which [I] feel that I should frankly tell you," he wrote, forwarding along a statement for Nixon to read. Its conclusion: Nixon, Stassen felt, should offer to quit. "If [Eisenhower] decides to accept your offer," Stassen said, "Earl Warren should be named to step in."[56]

Warren was silent. Just as Warren's fall in Chicago had paved the way for Nixon's ascent, so now did Nixon's potential fall offer opportunity for Warren. He watched and waited. As late as September 22, four days after the stories had first broken, Warren remained aloof, "withholding comment . . . until all the evidence has been presented."[57] Finally, on September 23, Nixon spoke. He addressed the nation on television, speaking from Los Angeles at six-thirty that night. Forever remembered as the "Checkers" speech, Nixon's address emphasized that he had received none of the money from the fund, that it had underwritten expenses but paid him no salary, that in contrast to his well-to-do Democratic opponents, Nixon and his wife Pat were a couple of modest income. "I should say this," he implored, "that Pat doesn't have a mink coat, but she does have a respectable Republican cloth coat; and I always tell her that she'd look good in anything."[58]

The speech's signature passage, however, was one of mawkish defiance:

> One other thing I probably should tell you, because if I don't they'll probably be saying this about me, too. We did get something, a gift, after the election. A man down in Texas heard Pat on the radio mention the fact that our two youngsters would like to have a dog; and, believe it or not, the day before we left on this campaign trip we got a message from the Union Station in Baltimore saying they had a package for us.
>
> We went down to get it. You know what it was? It was a little Cocker Spaniel dog, in a crate, that he'd sent all the way from Texas; black and white spotted, and our little girl, Tricia, the six-year-old girl, named it "Checkers." And you know, the kids, like all kids, love the dog; and I just want to say this right now, that regardless of what they say about it, we are going to keep him.[59]

That was Nixon's touch: He was a decent, average man, and his opponents were the type of people who would take a puppy from a six-year-old. His tactical success, meanwhile, was in asking viewers to register their response to his speech by wiring the Republican National Committee. Nixon promised he would accept the committee's judgment. With that, he left the stage, angry with himself for overrunning his time, sure that he had failed.[60] He had not. Thousands of letters and telegrams poured in, overwhelmingly in support of Nixon. Not everyone liked the speech; Eisenhower, for one, was furious at Nixon's demand that the Democratic candidates disclose their personal finances; the general well knew that if they complied, he would have to as well. As Nixon reached that point in his address, Eisenhower, holding a pencil and a legal pad, pressed so hard that the pencil point snapped.[61] But once the public had spoken, Eisenhower had no choice. He summoned Nixon to Wheeling, West Virginia, and, when Nixon arrived, greeted him at the plane. Nixon was flustered and responded that Eisenhower had not needed to meet him.

"Why not?" Eisenhower asked. "You're my boy."[62]

Nixon's future was saved, and the Checkers speech passed into history as a signature act of self-recovery. Less remembered, however, is how close Nixon's career came to ending that September. And still less recalled is the role that Warren played in it. While Warren did not himself leak the secret-fund story, people loyal to him apparently did. Leo Katcher, the *New York Post* reporter who was among the first to break the story, would later go on to write an admiring biography of the then chief justice in 1967, and Warren, alarmed that Katcher would embark on such a project, took unusual pains to make sure others knew he was not cooperating with it.[63] In that book, Katcher would claim that he first heard of the fund from "an intimate of Nixon," and would discount rumors that Warren friends were behind it,[64] but years earlier, when the story was still fresh, he attributed it to a "Warren Republican"[65] unhappy with Nixon's selection as vice president. Warren himself, though tactically distant from the leak, nevertheless was happy to let Nixon dangle and to let others lean on Eisenhower. When Nixon saved himself, Warren had no choice but to come back to the ticket. He had, however, enjoyed the spectacle.

Once the fund controversy had subsided—aided substantially by the fact that Adlai Stevenson also kept such a fund—the Eisenhower-Nixon ticket got back on track. Aided by a confused Democratic ticket—in a vain effort to achieve balance, the Democrats paired liberal intellectual Stevenson with Alabama senator John Sparkman, added to attract Southern voters uncomfortable with Stevenson. The gambit partially succeeded—the Deep South stayed with the Democrats in November. But the price for the continued loyalty of those votes was the failure of the ticket in virtually every other part of the country. In the West, Warren did his duty, appearing for Eisenhower and Nixon and helping to put out a late-breaking controversy. When Eisenhower had bumblingly implied that he would not support federal government involvement in the further development of Western water and power, Warren was hustled in to deliver a speech to California, Oregon, and Washington, which depended on those resources. "Out here," Warren reported calmingly, "Eisenhower stands for the development of our great river basins, the development of hydroelectric power, irrigation and all the other multiple purposes that water can be used for."[66] That crisis averted, Eisenhower succeeded in carrying all three of those states, along with the rest of the Western United States. His war-hero popularity and the Democrats' uncertainty on issues such as civil rights—exemplified by their cobbled-together ticket of North and South, urban and rural—carried Ike to sweeping victory. On Election Day, he won over 33 million votes, almost 55 percent of those cast. His victory included the first Republican inroads on the periphery of the Old South since the Civil War, as Virginia, Tennessee, and Florida all went to Eisenhower and Nixon.

Eisenhower then moved to construct his cabinet, finding no place there for Warren that Warren wanted. Warren instead returned to Sacramento, where his first post-election act was the naming of a new senator to fill the vacancy left by Nixon's departure for the vice presidency. Warren picked Tom Kuchel, then serving as California's state controller. Kuchel, a liberal Republican in Warren's tradition, accepted the post but asked Warren if he could take Merrell Small, Warren's top press aide, with him to Washington. Kuchel needed Small, he explained, because he was going to Washington without any experience or contacts there and needed an assistant he could trust. "Tom, I have stolen so many men from friends of mine to set up my organization that I can hardly object to your committing a little larceny on me," Warren replied.[67] With Kuchel's appointment, Warren's influence on the California congressional delegation went from substantial to profound: Kuchel joined Knowland in Washington, so both California senators now had been placed there by Warren.

Small's departure stirred speculation that Warren was closing up his governorship and preparing to move to Washington (later in the summer, the rumors would redouble, as Warren named Helen MacGregor to serve as a member of the board overseeing the California Youth Authority). He continued to serve, however, and on July 1, 1953, signed the Ralph M. Brown Act, providing for public and press access to the meetings of state and local governments. It was a fitting act for an heir to Hiram Johnson, whose tenure would always be remembered for its forceful ejection of the Southern Pacific from the back rooms of California government. Now Warren moved to complete that crusade by opening the rooms themselves. Although the Brown Act has been subjected to much criticism over the years—some government officials complain that it forces them to do too much in the open, slowing deliberations and confining their ability to cut deals—it survives and sets the parameters of an open government in California.

Warren realized, however, that it was time to move on. He was sixty-two years old and had served longer than any man before him as governor of California. He had accomplished more than he had once imagined possible, but was increasingly at odds with powerful elements of his own party. So when Eisenhower proposed that Warren become solicitor general, Warren accepted, taking the post with the understanding that he was there to warm up for a Supreme Court vacancy. And then, on September 8, 1953, Chief Justice Fred Vinson died of his heart attack, and Warren held Ike to his word, extracting from him the chief justiceship of the United States.

On October 2, Warren said farewell to his home state, the state whose politics he had revolutionized, whose rivers he had dammed, whose highways he had built, whose children he had educated, whose extremes he had tempered, softened, and mollified. He left behind an angry right wing, an appreciative Democratic Party, and a jubilant Republican lieutenant governor, Goodwin Knight, at last cleared for the office he had impatiently sought in Warren's shadow. On that final Friday night of his tenure, Warren's calm voice—the familiar flat accent, the stylized formal diction—beamed out to California one final time. Some of those who listened had never voted for another governor; some had a hard time imagining California without him. To his colleagues, his voters, and his home, he said good-bye.

"My fellow Californians," Warren began that Friday night,

For many years I have made a report to you each month over this ABC network concerning the affairs of our State government. Tonight as I leave the service of my State to assume national office, I conclude those reports by endeavoring to say goodbye to my associates who have served both you and me so well throughout the years and to you who have made it possible by your suffrage for us to serve you. . . .

I have been in the service of my city, my county or my State since January, 1919—almost 35 years. It is a long time, and the road we have traveled was not always smooth. But it has been a satisfying experience—every year of it. It is always satisfying when those whom we serve are understanding of our efforts, tolerant of our mistakes and fair in their appraisal of the results obtained. That is exactly the kind of treatment I have received from the people of California during my many years of public service. For it I am very grateful, and in the turmoil and confusion of politics it would have been so easy at times for them not to understand.[68]

Warren then listed, his pride rich and evident, the accomplishments of his eleven years as governor of the state he had tamed. He spoke of the schools and colleges, highways and canals, hospitals and prisons. He marveled at all that he and California had done, of all those who had come to share in its experience and had arrived to find jobs and welcome. Four million people—four million—migrated to

California while Earl Warren was governor. Its Japanese had been expelled, to his great shame, and reabsorbed, to his great credit. When he was a boy, California had shaped him; as an adult, he had refashioned it. Now Warren prepared to leave a state nearly twice the size of the one he inherited, one immeasurably larger, more modern, more sophisticated than the one he grew up in, when Western shoot-outs had captivated him in his Bakersfield boyhood. When Earl Warren became governor of California, the state had 2.9 million cars and 24,000 state workers; when he left it, its bustling freeways carried 5.9 million cars, and the state employed 56,545 workers. The state was in debt when he arrived; he left a balanced budget.[69] A hotel maid working in California in 1940 made about $19 a week; by 1953, she made nearly $45 a week. Salaries for auto workers, aircraft builders, and other manufacturing workers similarly tripled or quadrupled. In the state's motion picture business, a man or woman working in production took home about $55 a week the year before Warren became governor. When he left, that same person made twice that.[70]

"Where on earth have so many new people been integrated into a Commonwealth in so short a period of time?" he asked. "It is my belief that this accomplishment, which is your accomplishment, will be recorded in history as one of the most outstanding of our generation."

And then he concluded:

> I do not intend to cut my moorings from my State. Here I was born. Here Mrs. Warren and I have reared our family. Here our children have attended the public schools. . . . Here our fondest memories and our greatest hopes are. Here my home will always be. . . .
>
> I thank all of you—the people of California—from the bottom of my heart. You have been so gracious to me and to my family. I thank you all for your kindness through the years, and I pledge you my continued interest in the welfare of your California and my California—the greatest place on earth in which to live.[71]

Warren would never again appear before California's people as their governor. His speech concluded the second great act of his three-act life, bringing to a close the years in which he fashioned a new California out of his own solidifying politics. He had begun 1942 as a politician seeking firm principles. That year's campaign had helped broaden and toughen him; the gubernatorial years had only furthered that development. His centrism in 1953 was no longer merely a middle course between left and right but an activist, humane philosophy of leadership. Warren had invented affirmative nonpartisanship for California; now he prepared to carry that with him to Washington, where the nation was about to learn what it meant to be governed by Earl Warren's humanism.

But before he finished and left for Washington, Warren had one last piece of business to conclude, one remaining loose end whose string connected back to his youthful rise. Warren's political ascent could well be said to have begun with his *Point Lobos* prosecution. That case had established his credentials on the business side of California's then wide labor-business chasm. That case had helped Warren befriend the Chandlers, helped seal his attachment to the Knowlands. It had angered Carey McWilliams, Max Radin, and California's vigorous, engaged left. By 1953, few people remembered it. The emotions it aroused, once so intense, were now quieter, more reflective. But a shadow of that case remained.

Ernest Ramsay, freed by Culbert Olson over Warren's denunciations, in fact remained just part free in 1953. His criminal conviction still haunted his record, and that year he faced deportation to Canada because he was a felon. His appeals were exhausted, and Ramsay was on the verge of removal from the United States. For nearly thirty years, the lives of Ernest Ramsay and Earl Warren had been intertwined by the events in a darkened cabin on the *Point Lobos*—by Warren's prosecution of that crime, by Ramsay's prison sentence for it, by Olson's release of Ramsay, by Warren's anger over that release.

Earl Warren would never admit he was wrong about *Point Lobos*, never admit that his office overstepped, much less concede that Ramsay or the other defendants were anything but guilty as charged.[72] But now, in those final hours of his governorship, he and Ramsay crossed paths one more time. Just before leaving for Washington, Earl Warren reviewed Ramsay's case, asked whether Ramsey would be willing to testify if the lone fugitive from the case ever turned up, and was assured that Ramsay would.[73] With that, Warren signed the pardon for Ernest Ramsay, wiping his record clean.[74]

The governorship was over. Earl Warren had cut the last mooring that tied him to his youthful life as a prosecutor. The following Monday morning, Warren was sworn in as Chief Justice of the United States.

# PART THREE

# AMERICAN JUSTICE

Chapter 15

# THE CHIEF AND HIS COURT[1]

*Where there is injustice, we should correct it; where there is poverty, we should eliminate it; where there is corruption, we should stamp it out; where there is violence, we should punish it; where there is neglect, we should provide care; where there is war, we should restore peace; and wherever corrections are achieved we should add them to our storehouse of treasures.*

EARL WARREN[2]

W HEN EARL WARREN departed California, he left behind a personal staff of advisers, more than a dozen department heads, and a team of secretaries. He had commanded a $1 billion budget with functions spread across America's second-most-populous state. Arriving in Washington, he put all of that behind him. Now Warren had a secretary and three law clerks, along with a handful of Court workers, messengers, security guards, and custodial workers. He brought just one assistant with him, a personal secretary named Maggie Bryan, to handle California mail.

Though he was chief in name, Warren in fact was colleague to eight men, heirs to an institution unlike the other branches of federal government—one whose members served for life and answered to no voter, one whose character blended the cool reasoning of legal analysis with the hot urgency of national politics, and one distinctly male. Not until Sandra Day O'Connor's appointment in 1981 did a woman sit on the Court. Until then, the men who occupied America's high bench at times resembled nine elbowing brothers, each with his own place at a boisterous table. With no terms of office, the justices fought, then returned to fight again, year after year. Isolated from conventional politics, bound by the secrecy of their deliberations, their colleagues became their families; wives of deceased justices remained part of the Court even after their husbands had died, returning for annual dinners, joining in retirement celebrations and funerals. When children married, the justices would chip in and buy a silver platter for the new couple. They were "the brethren."

Proximity and time fused them in a common endeavor, but also ripened differences. By the time Warren joined the Court in October 1953, the surface commonality of the bench—the other eight members had been placed there by Democrats during the party's long reign from FDR through Truman—belied deep doctrinal and personal disagreements. Those had been nursed over time, and flared occasionally in public, more often in the weekly conferences of the justices.

One of the Court's most embarrassingly divisive and public conflicts came a few months before Warren's arrival. As the Court prepared to recess for the summer, lawyers for Julius and Ethel Rosenberg, both convicted of espionage and sentenced to die, brought their final appeal to the Supreme Court. Justice William O. Douglas vacillated with the Rosenbergs' case—for months, he had cast votes against them in conference. But then, as the execution date approached, he heard their arguments and abruptly decided he should stay their death sentences. On Wednesday, June 17, 1953, Douglas ordered the stay and then, without informing his colleagues, got into his car and headed West, dropping out of touch as the nation rose in outraged fury at the possibility that two convicted Communist spies would not meet their expected end. One telegram to Douglas summed up the nation's feelings: "If you grant the Rosenbergs a stay, there will be a lynching party waiting for you here," it read.[3] The Court was deluged, as bands of angry protesters, some screaming anti-Semitic epithets, gathered outside the Court and the White House. Chief Justice Fred Vinson, urged by the Eisenhower administration, exercised a power he did not have and called his colleagues into special session. After a series of motions and votes, the Court agreed to hear oral argument on the issue that had persuaded Douglas to issue the stay. (The Rosenbergs had been convicted of conspiracy to commit espionage, and during the course of that conspiracy, federal sentencing laws spelling out the punishment for it changed; the question, then, was under which set of rules they deserved to be sentenced. It was an important matter, since at the outset of the Rosenbergs' activities, the sentence would have called for death, but by the conclusion, that penalty had been reduced.) The Court then vacated the stay over the objections of three justices, including Douglas, who had hurried back to Washington after hearing on the radio that Vinson had called the Court into session.

Desperate, and with the nation arrayed against them, the Rosenbergs' allies and family pleaded with Eisenhower to grant clemency. At Sing Sing prison, Julius and Ethel were allowed to spend the afternoon together, separated by wire mesh. They wrote a final letter to their children. "We wish we might have had the tremendous joy and gratification of living our lives with you," Ethel wrote. "Your Daddy who is with me in the last momentous hours, sends his heart and all the love that is in it for his dearest boys." Ike read the clemency appeal that night and refused it. The Rosenbergs were separated at 7:20 P.M. and put to death within the hour.[4]

That quenched the thirst of a manic American public eager to see the young couple killed for their acts of espionage. It also advertised the deep divisions within the Court, as the two sides had wrestled publicly with their differences on a matter of great passion. Summer for the Court in 1953 thus began in the shadow of the deaths it had authorized; vacation had not healed any of those wounds. Vinson's death in September opened them yet again.

In broad terms, the Court that Warren joined in 1953 can be considered as two groups: four extraordinary jurists who would leave their imprint on American history for generations and four lesser justices. Yet even the dimmer lights were men of consequence. Sherman Minton was a commonsense man who was elected to the Senate from Indiana in 1934. While there, he served with such luminaries as Harry Truman and Hugo Black, both of whose lives would overlap considerably with Minton's. The Indiana senator was intensely devoted to the New Deal and FDR, and those loyalties hurt him among Indiana's conservative voters in 1940, when they cast him out. Without office but still helped by friends in high places, "Shay" Minton, as he was known, was given a place on the 7th Circuit Court of Appeals. Then, in 1949, with Truman in the White House, Minton was nominated for the Supreme Court. His former Senate colleagues approved him amidst much hope for Minton. As a justice, however, Minton followed an undistinguished course, his time on the bench almost as well remembered for his tobacco-chewing—during oral arguments, Minton would avail himself of the Supreme Court spittoon, in the process occasionally spraying an irritated Harold Burton when he missed[5]—as he was for his jurisprudence. Minton shrank from the challenge of wielding ultimate judicial authority. When Truman seized the nation's steel mills in 1952 to prevent their shutdown by strike during wartime, six justices used the occasion to curb the president's power.[6] Minton dissented. His timidity in that and other national security and criminal cases disappointed some of his early supporters.

Harold Burton was the only Republican on the Court when Warren arrived in 1953. Nominated by Truman, the former mayor of Cleveland was extraordinarily charming, attentive to his friends, and beloved by his colleagues on the Court. His nomination to the Supreme Court was unanimously confirmed by the Senate— and on the same day that it was received. Yet, as a justice, Burton proved a mixed bag. He was cautiously, unpredictably liberal in his view of government power and the Constitution, and in retrospect is considered to be Truman's most progressive appointee. Unlike Minton, for instance, Burton voted with the majority to thwart Truman's seizure of the steel mills. Some Court observers thought him lazy, the result of his seeming absence from a leading role on important cases, but that was not true. Burton worked hard and was appreciated by his colleagues.[7] He was not, however, armed with a clear sense of mission, and he exerted no effort to break new constitutional ground. Burton, one of the Court's preeminent scholars noted, "was far happier in the role of follower than leader."[8] His legacy to the Court is most felt in connection with a personal habit, not an act of judging. Burton kept a diary of his Court years; it provides a running and relatively neutral—if sometimes spare—narrative of the Court during Burton's years on the bench.

Joining Minton and Burton on the follower end of the 1953 Court were two justices from the periphery of the South, Tom C. Clark of Texas and Stanley F. Reed of Kentucky. Reed—whom William O. Douglas considered "the kindest, friendliest and most polite and courteous Justice"[9] other than Burton. Reed had studied law at the Sorbonne, Columbia, and the University of Virginia, but had degrees from none. He learned practical law in the office of a Kentucky lawyer. Public service eventually drew him to Washington, where Roosevelt chose him as solicitor general—so overwhelmed was Reed by the position that he was said to have fainted at the opening of his first argument before the Court. Recovering from that setback, Reed amassed a run of well-regarded defeats as the government's attorney in the early days of the administration, when the Court was in a surly mood toward reform. Reed moved to the Court in 1938, where he was a genteel though colorless figure, voting with the government in most cases and during the late 1940s tentatively wading into the tangle of desegregation. Indeed, segregation was a matter that Reed took personally: In 1947, when the Court clerks proposed to invite black Court messengers to their annual Christmas party, Reed refused to consider attending. Felix Frankfurter pressed him to reconsider, but integration was more than Reed could stomach. "He said this is a purely private matter and he can do what he pleases in regard to private parties," Frankfurter noted in his diary.[10] Reed's courtliness endeared him to his colleagues, but in the bright light of more assertive justices, he cast little shadow of his own.

Tom Clark was more dynamic, and was, upon Warren's debut, one of few justices with whom the new chief was acquainted. "The spindly Texan," as Justice William J. Brennan, Jr., was later to call him,[11] was hardworking and assertive, jaunty in his bow tie but generally cautious in his judicial writing and in his manner—"delightful, placid and slow-talking," in the words of Drew Pearson.[12] As a lawyer for the Justice Department during World War II, Clark had worked with Warren in the tragic effort to remove and then intern the nation's Japanese-American population. Their paths also had crossed in matters relating to gambling and state-federal relations during the time that Warren was governor and Clark was the United States attorney general under Truman. Since his coming to the Court in 1949, however, Clark's presence had faded, obscured by the dominating figures of that Court. His irritating habit of switching votes, sometimes in important cases close to decision day, tested the patience of his colleagues, and his loyalty to law enforcement, particularly the FBI, placed him at odds with the Court's civil libertarians. Truman came to regret placing Clark on the bench. "It isn't so much that he's a bad man," the splenetic Truman remarked. "It's just that he is such a dumb son of a bitch. He's about the dumbest man I think I've ever run across."[13] That was unfair. Clark was bright and accomplished, and his stature grew over time. But Truman was right to suggest that on the Court where Clark served, he would never lead.

Clark, Minton, Burton, and Reed labored in the shade of four others, each committed to a constitutional and judicial philosophy, each seeing in the new chief a chance to add a vote to his column. To a man, each had been disappointed by Vinson, whose attempts to corral them had fallen short and irritated them in the process. Now they circled one another.

Rarely has the Court featured four such forceful and intelligent members as William O. Douglas, Hugo L. Black, Robert H. Jackson, and Felix Frankfurter, so different in temperament and philosophy, so bound by their position and era. The four were, when Warren arrived, engaged in disputes large and small, but none was as consequential as the debate over judicial activism, a dispute framed by the New Deal circumstances that placed each of them on the bench. Roughly speaking, Justices Jackson and Frankfurter had become advocates of a restrained judiciary, while Black and Douglas argued a view that gave the Court a more robust place in American life. Those were broad definitions, and all four were too complex and thoughtful to subscribe to them without caveat, but they set the basic terms of the pre-Warren Court.

Frankfurter was the Court's professor. A tiny man of enormous energy and roving intellect, he had emigrated to the United States from Austria as a boy, then grew up on the Lower East Side of Manhattan and eventually taught a generation of Harvard Law students the intricacies of Supreme Court decision-making before coming to the Court himself in 1939. Frankfurter was a brilliant writer and a dedicated teacher—widely considered the nation's preeminent constitutional scholar— but his restless intelligence pushed him beyond the academy. He helped found the *New Republic* magazine, championed the cause of Sacco and Vanzetti, and lobbied for a new trial for Tom Mooney. After graduating from Harvard Law School in 1906—when Warren was still in high school—Frankfurter worked briefly on Wall Street, but opportunities there were limited for a Jew, and he was lured by Henry Stimson to the United States Attorney's Office for the Southern District of New York.

Like Warren, Frankfurter came of age as a Progressive, though his experience of Progressivism had a decidedly Eastern, intellectual cast. Still, there were parallels. Both approved of government action, of intervention intended to neutralize big business and to level the relationship between industry and labor. Both abhorred vice and what it did to working people. Among Frankfurter's cases during his brief prosecutorial career were prosecutions of smugglers, gamblers, counterfeiters, and gunrunners, cases that placed him in defense of social order. That same band of defendants could easily have passed through Warren's offices on the other coast.[14]

But while Warren and Frankfurter each began their political lives in the thrall of Progressivism, they extrapolated different lessons from it. To Warren, the Progressives were inspiring because they took on fights and won them for common people; they taught Warren the values of nonpartisanship and stressed, for him, the value of bringing apolitical experts to the job of governing. Frankfurter would not have disagreed, but where Warren experienced politics as an actor and an extrovert, Frankfurter's more incisive legal mind reached in a different direction, analyzing Progressivism in terms of its effect not only on government generally but also on the relationship between the institutions of government. Specifically, Frankfurter concluded that effective Progressive government required a restrained, deferential judiciary, one that allowed experts to lead and innovate in the legislative and executive branches. As he honed his thoughts on judging during his years as a leading constitutional scholar and Harvard law professor, Frankfurter increasingly came to see the judiciary as "cumbersome and ineffective" in the face of pressure for political change.[15]

His views were reinforced by the great debates early in FDR's term, when the Court stood in the way of the president's efforts to stimulate the economy. With the Depression casting millions of Americans out of work, Roosevelt understandably viewed his 1932 election—and overwhelming reelection in 1936—as a mandate for federal government intervention in the economy. Congress complied, passing attempt after attempt to stimulate the collapsed consumer demand that throttled attempts at recovery. The Court, however, was in no mood to defer. Led by the so-called Four Horsemen, the Court held the line against economic experimentation through the early 1930s, overturning any legislation that interfered in private rights of contract in order to secure socially desirable ends. The Court threw out laws providing pensions for railroad workers, setting prices and wages, setting minimum wages for women, and paying unemployment benefits, among others.[16] Time and again, Roosevelt proposed, Congress approved, the Court cast aside.

By 1937, Roosevelt had been returned to office, and on the strength of that mandate, he set out to overcome the Court's resistance. Without acknowledging the underlying purpose of his proposal—namely, to bring to the Court justices more amenable to his economic plans—FDR called on Congress to allow the president to name a new justice for every sitting member of the Court who was over age seventy. This, the president said, would help alleviate the strain on the Court, whose aging justices were struggling to keep up with their docket. The insult to the justices cost Roosevelt support there—Louis Brandeis, generally a New Deal supporter, was particularly incensed. More important, the obvious falseness of that position undermined Roosevelt's credibility, and the proposal quickly was exposed for the "Court-packing" plan that it was. And yet, though it failed, the justices got the message: Owen Roberts, who had joined the Four Horsemen in overturning many of the earlier New Deal programs, in early 1937 reversed field and decided to uphold a minimum-wage law from Washington state. Although Roberts changed his vote in conference before FDR announced his Court-packing proposal, the decision was announced afterward. Many have speculated that it was at least influenced by the growing public antagonism toward the Court and at most directly affected by early knowledge of FDR's proposal. In either case, the "switch in time that saved nine" achieved what the president was seeking without adding new members to the bench. It brought the Court into line with the new economic demands of the Depression and the perceived need for aggressive executive action without judicial interference.

To Frankfurter, then at Harvard and both a friend and an adviser to Roosevelt, the Court's resistance to change through those early Depression years validated his belief that judges should defer to executives in order to make way for social and economic progress. In that view, Frankfurter was heir not only to Progressivism but also to the considered jurisprudence of some of the Court's great visionaries, notably Brandeis and Frankfurter's idol, Oliver Wendell Holmes.

By the time Warren arrived, in 1953, Frankfurter had been on the bench for more than fourteen years and had sharpened his views on judging into a hard philosophy of judicial self-denial. He had, moreover, become something of a scold. Fond of lecturing his colleagues, Frankfurter steadily had worn away his welcome with several; Douglas in particular had given up suffering Frankfurter and turned instead to nettling him. Eventually, Douglas would grow so exasperated that he would walk out of the conference room while Frankfurter was speaking, tossing back over his shoulder instructions to be summoned when Frankfurter had finished. The rest of the justices accepted his cloying condescension with varying degrees of equanimity, but Frankfurter's manner, by the early 1950s, had left him increasingly in a fight for support. In Warren, then, he hoped for a colleague and a vote, a fellow Progressive who had served as an innovative chief executive, just the sort of leader who, Frankfurter hoped, would allow great latitude by reining in the judiciary. Frankfurter thus greeted Warren's arrival with great hope.

Frankfurter's most eloquent ally on the Court in 1953 was Robert H. Jackson, arguably the greatest courtroom advocate ever elevated to the Supreme Court of the United States. Precise and direct, a master of the simple metaphor and the gentle witticism, Jackson was so gifted at argument that during his years as solicitor general, Justice Brandeis once remarked to Frankfurter, "Jackson should be Solicitor General for life."[17]

In contrast to Earl Warren's lackadaisical youth, Jackson showed his promise early, excelling under the tutelage of a high school teacher in the rural New York where he grew up. He was, from his earliest days, determined and independent. Taken young by the law, Jackson defied his father, who saw no future for a lawyer and refused to help his son pay for law school. Robert Jackson borrowed the money instead, and attended a year of law school before striking out on his own. After passing the bar, Jackson built a successful small-town practice and caught the eye of New York's governor, one Franklin Roosevelt. As president, FDR shuffled Jackson through a series of important posts. Jackson served as general counsel to the Internal Revenue Service, where he earned national attention for his tax-evasion prosecution of Andrew Mellon (Mellon was forced to pay $750,000). Jackson then moved rapidly through a series of Justice Department positions before becoming solicitor general in 1938, a role at which he was so effective that some maintained he elevated the Court itself by the logic of his arguments.[18] In 1940, Jackson became FDR's attorney general, succeeding Frank Murphy in that job at the age of forty-seven. The following year, when Chief Justice Charles Evans Hughes retired, Jackson followed Murphy again, this time to the Supreme Court.

From his earliest time with the brethren, it was clear that Jackson belonged among them. A case in point was his decisive impact on the Court's view of religious freedom. Shortly before Jackson joined the Court, Frankfurter had written for the majority in a case brought by Jehovah's Witnesses who objected to their children being forced to pledge allegiance at the opening of the school day. Frankfurter, who always resisted granting special protection to First Amendment rights, was unmoved by the Witnesses, concluding, "The ultimate foundation of a free society is the binding tie of cohesive sentiment."[19] He added his familiar note that the legislature, no less than the Court, is committed to "the guardianship of deeply cherished liberties" and with that, upheld the compulsory pledge against the objections of the Witnesses.

Three years later, Jackson had joined the bench, and World War II was at its height. Again, the Court considered the pleas of the Witnesses, this time along with the PTA, Boys and Girls Clubs, and other civic organizations in West Virginia. Drawing its support from the Court's earlier ruling by Frankfurter, the state had ordered a compulsory flag salute, and had directed that any student who refused to take it would be found insubordinate and expelled.[20] Nothing of consequence had changed since Frankfurter's opinion in 1940; if anything, the years of war had only hardened the patriotic impulses behind Frankfurter's earlier decision, which won a majority of the Court. But a new voice had arrived in the form of Jackson, and it was a persuasive one. Jackson's opinion witheringly dissected Frankfurter's reasoning, overturning it with a new and magnificent conception of the relationship between patriotism and government power:

To believe that patriotism will not flourish if patriotic ceremonies are voluntary and spontaneous instead of a compulsory routine is to make an unflattering estimate of the appeal of our institutions to free minds. We can have intellectual individualism and the rich cultural diversities that we owe to exceptional minds only at the price of occasional eccentricity and abnormal attitudes. When they are so harmless to others or to the State as those we deal with here, the price is not too great. But freedom to differ is not limited to things that do not matter much. That would be a mere shadow of freedom. The test of its substance is the right to differ as to things that touch the heart of the existing order.[21]

It was, however, Jackson's most memorable paragraph that established his reputation as the Court's prose poet:

If there is any fixed star in our constitutional constellation, it is that no official, high or petty, can prescribe what shall be orthodox in politics, nationalism, religion, or other matters of opinion or force citizens to confess by word or act their faith therein. If there are any circumstances which permit an exception, they do not now occur to us.[22]

Justices Douglas and Black, who had joined with Frankfurter in 1940, now abandoned him for Jackson and the poetry of his logic. Frankfurter was not used to being outthought, and he responded with a personal dissent that crystallized his discomfort with the self-restraint he adopted to fulfill what he believed was his judicial duty. "One who belongs to the most vilified and persecuted minority in history is not likely to be insensible to the freedoms guaranteed by our Constitution," he wrote. "Were my purely personal attitude relevant I should whole-heartedly associate myself with the general libertarian view in the Court's opinion, representing as they do the thought and action of a lifetime. But as judges we are neither Jew, nor Gentile, neither Catholic, nor agnostic. . . . As a member of this Court I am not justified in writing my private notions of policy into the Constitution."[23] This time, Frankfurter's exhortation of restraint was unpersuasive; freedom, as articulated by Jackson, carried the day over deference.

Jackson's stirring opinion in *West Virginia Board of Education v. Barnette* demonstrated his independence from Frankfurter, but the two men in fact were doctrinally not so different. Both were New Deal liberals, determined to allow Roosevelt the opportunity to lead the nation with a minimum of judicial interference. Thus, through their early years together, Jackson and Frankfurter generally upheld the government, and despite Frankfurter's dismay over the flag cases, Jackson's real rival was not the Harvard law professor but rather the Southern individualist anchor of the Court wing that Frankfurter sneeringly dubbed "the Axis." That justice was Hugo Black.

Hugo Lafayette Black was the youngest of eight children, born on a rainy night in 1886 in the backcountry of Alabama, "a Clay County hillbilly," as he described himself.[24] He grew up poor but in an atmosphere of learning, of farming and small-town stores and a home full of books—a Southern version of Earl Warren's Western childhood. But where both Warren and Black were taught to love reading, Hugo Black's personal library was a particularly distinguished one. Young Earl Warren read *Peck's Bad Boy;* young Hugo Black was given Shakespeare, Milton, and the Bible.

Black's ascent through the country politics of post–Civil War Alabama began, as Jackson's did in New York, with a small-town law practice. Unlike Jackson, who was lured to government service by appointment, Black sought it through politics. He was elected to the Senate as a Democrat from Alabama in 1926, and there joined Roosevelt as an aggressive proponent of the New Deal. Black was armed with an abiding sense of personal loyalty, an extraordinary memory and an intensely probing intellect, a man whose searching mind was in "constant intellectual rebellion," biographer Roger Newman notes in his extraordinary study of the justice.[25] Black joined the Senate in 1927, starting slowly but building into a forceful legislator who used his position to bully opponents and champion friends, including labor and especially President Roosevelt. He was gracious and generous, in love with his wife and an enveloping, devoted father to two sons and a daughter. But Black could be vicious in a fight, "a cruel strategist with a biting tongue. . . . Men who had crossed swords with him rarely forgot or forgave the experience."[26] Within a short time, the Senate was full of men who had their grudges with the senator from Alabama.

Court-packing did not give Roosevelt the spots he had hoped for on the Court, but time yielded what politics did not, as Roosevelt's reelection in 1936 extended his time in office. Black had demonstrated his loyalty to the New Deal and had supported Roosevelt in the Court-packing debacle as well. When it came time at last to name a justice of his own, Roosevelt predicted that the Senate would be forced to take Black because of its long tradition of senatorial courtesy, notwithstanding Black's unpopularity in that body and the persistent rumor that he had been, or even might still be, a member of the Ku Klux Klan. With a flourish, FDR signed the nominating letter in front of Black and sent along the name to the Senate.

During the confirmation process, some senators and others rumbled quietly about the rumors of Black's Klan membership. He did not address them publicly but allowed colleagues to deny them for him. With that matter on the periphery of the debate, the Senate, as FDR had predicted, fell into line behind a colleague and confirmed him just five days after the president sent the nomination to the Hill. Black then sailed for Europe. While he was away, Ray Sprigle, an enterprising reporter from the *Pittsburgh Post-Gazette*, traveled to Alabama, where he struck up a relationship with a former Grand Dragon. The Klansman gave Sprigle Black's Klan membership card, a list of committee assignments, and his resignation from the organization, among other things. The story broke as a series in September 1937, and Sprigle not only presented the evidence that Black had been a Klansman but also suggested that he still was (Black had, in fact, resigned from the Klan at the outset of his 1926 Senate campaign). That placed the Senate in an awkward position, as it had just confirmed Black and now was faced with the jurisdictional debate over whether it still could take action against a justice who had been confirmed but not yet seated. Black retreated into silence, fending off, among others, a young James Reston who tried and failed to elicit comment from him for the *New York Times*.[27] Eventually, however, the uproar became too much for Black to ignore. He returned home and delivered a radio address to the nation; so anticipated was it that it attracted the second-largest radio audience of all time up to that point in history, surpassed only by Edward VIII's abdication of the British throne. With millions tuned in across America, Black admitted that he had been a member of the Invisible Empire, denied any current ties to the order, and emphasized that his liberal record in the Senate made clear that his membership had been practical, not heartfelt. With that, he refused to speak of it again, and took his place on the Court.

Soon enough, the nation would be convinced that Black was no Klansman. He went, the old joke had it, from dressing up in white robes to scare black people to dressing in black ones to scare white people. Hugo Black soon developed a vigorous constitutionalism that was at once strict and personal, empowering and limiting. Black believed that the Constitution and its Bill of Rights meant precisely what they said. Thus, when the First Amendment stated that Congress shall make "no law" respecting establishment of religion or abridging speech or press, Black assumed it meant exactly that—no allowances for minor abridgements or insignificant aid to religion. No law, to Black, meant no law. That was true across the rest of the Constitution and the Bill of Rights as well. So devoted was Black to its literal language that he carried, until the day he died, a copy of the Constitution in his jacket pocket.

Black was a gracious gentleman, but a tough one, and the cloister of the Court did nothing to diminish that streak in him. Inevitably, his ambition drove him up against colleagues on the Court, especially Jackson. The object of their fight was the chief justiceship, as that seat suddenly became open in 1946 with the death of Harlan Fiske Stone. Black and Jackson each had reason to believe he might ascend to the Court's center chair—Black was the senior Democratic appointee and Jackson had been promised consideration for the job before. Their rivalry was intensified by mutual disdain. They also had just concluded a bitter debate over a mine workers' case from which Jackson believed Black should have recused himself because of his previous Senate action on the matter and because the lawyer for the mine workers' union was a former law partner from Black's Alabama days.[28] Black refused, casting a fifth vote in favor of the United Mine Workers. Jackson wrote the dissent, joined by Frankfurter, Chief Justice Stone, and Owen Roberts. In addition to substantive differences over the case, which involved overtime pay for mine workers, Jackson believed the majority had rushed its decision in order to help John Lewis and the mine workers prevail in a strike. Jackson left "seething," and considered resigning from the Court.[29] When the losing side in the mine workers' case appealed to the Court for rehearing, the appeal was rejected, but Jackson and Frankfurter released a statement noting that they could find no authority to "exclude one of its duly commissioned Justices from sitting or voting in any case."[30] Their clear suggestion, though one not widely noticed at the time, was that had they been able to find such an authority, they would have used it against Black. The denial for rehearing was released on June 18, 1945. That same day, Jackson, exhausted by the Court's infighting and eager to return to advocacy, left for Nuremberg, where he was to serve as the lead prosecutor in the trial of Nazi war crimes.

With Jackson away, reports circulated in Washington that Black and Douglas were threatening to resign if Jackson were promoted above them. Then, on May 16, the *Washington Star*'s Doris Fleeson reported on what she described as the "Supreme Court feud" between Black and Jackson. The story was cast sympathetically toward Black, and its insights into the Court, particularly into the coal and mine worker cases, suggested that Black could have been a source for the reporter—a suggestion strengthened by the fact that Fleeson was a friend of Black's and a frequent guest in his home. Jackson, then immersed in the war crimes trials, waited until Truman had picked Vinson for chief justice, then succumbed to his disappointment.

Jackson cabled Truman from Nuremberg to complain that he believed he had been passed over because of Black. Jackson used the cable to tell his side of the mineworker controversy and hinted that he now was considering leaving the Court. Truman replied quickly that Jackson was "grossly misinformed," that he had not discussed the chief justice position with Black or any other justice, and that he had not even read Fleeson's article.[31] Truman urged Jackson to let the matter go, and pointedly advised him not to release his cable. Jackson chose not to listen. Without telling Truman, Jackson consulted his son and another associate, redacted some of the personal insults about Black from his cable to Truman, and then sent it to congressional leaders at the same time that he made it public to reporters. The reaction was swift. Some of Jackson's colleagues were appalled at his discussion of the confidential Supreme Court conference and believed he would be forced to leave. Black, amazed at Jackson's self-immolation, withdrew into silence and let the matter pass. In time, Jackson returned from Nuremberg and rejoined Black on the bench. Relations were understandably frosty, but it is the unusual and endearing character of the United States Supreme Court that nine justices must find ways to disagree and yet return, day after day, to new cases and new contests for their values.

With Jackson back among the brethren, Black plunged into the central quandary of his jurisprudence and one of the defining debates of twentieth-century American law. Because the Bill of Rights was adopted as a mechanism for restraining the federal government only, it had limited effect in American life. States were not constrained by its language, no matter how rigorously or literally one applied it. But in the years after the end of the war, Black studied deeply—if selectively—the history of the Fourteenth Amendment. He emerged with an insight that reshaped first his philosophy of judging and ultimately the nation itself. Taken as a whole, the Fourteenth Amendment extended the protections and requirements of the Bill of Rights to all the states, Black concluded. That view, known as incorporation, represented a break from the Court's precedents, as it had held during the 1830s that the Bill of Rights restrained only the federal government, in effect allowing the states to infringe the rights protected under those amendments.

Rather than extend the entire Bill of Rights to the states, the Court in those years began the piecemeal process of deciding which rights were so important that the states were prohibited from violating them under the Fourteenth Amendment. That approach was known as selective incorporation. Frankfurter, one of its advocates, argued, for instance, that police could not engage in conduct that "shocks the conscience,"[32] but still refused to accept that the entire Bill of Rights was binding on state governments. Black rejected that doling-out of rights and, with it, launched his historic debate with Frankfurter.

Black first expressed his incorporation view in a 1947 opinion that he later called his most important. In *Adamson v. State of California*, Black dissented from the majority when it concluded that the prosecutors in the murder trial of Admiral Adamson, a black California man (Admiral was his name, not his rank—Adamson had no connection to the Navy), were entitled to comment on Adamson's decision not to take the stand at his trial. Under federal rules, that would have been barred by the Fifth Amendment, which prevents defendants from being forced to testify against themselves and, by implication, bars punishment for those who invoke that right. But the majority in *Adamson* concluded that the Fifth Amendment's protection against self-incrimination did not apply in state prosecutions. It was, the majority concluded, a matter of "settled law" that the Fifth Amendment right did not extend to state trials, because the Bill of Rights limited only the federal government, not the states. Black disagreed:

My study of the historical events that culminated in the Fourteenth Amendment, and the expressions of those who sponsored and favored, as well as those who opposed its submission and passage, persuades me that one of the chief objects that the provisions of the Amendment's first section, separately, and as a whole, were intended to accomplish was to make the Bill of Rights applicable to the states.[33]

Black's "study of historical events" was limited to the Congressional debate over the Fourteenth Amendment and did not address the larger discussion that accompanied ratification. That alone made it suspect. When his clerk showed a draft of Black's *Adamson* dissent to Frankfurter, the justice read it while the clerk waited. Reaching the end, Frankfurter tossed it aside. "At Yale, they call this scholarship?"[34] he demanded. Black was not one to take Frankfurter's condescension, however. From that moment on, he would shrug off Frankfurter's disapproval and apply the letter of the first ten Amendments to the states. Moreover, Black would insist that his literal reading was not just an opportunity to extend civil liberties but was in fact his judicial obligation. Black thus fused original intent—at least his interpretation of the Fourteenth Amendment framers' intent—with judicial restraint and civil liberties into a single, uniquely personal philosophy. Through the late 1940s, much of Black's effort would be made in dissent, thwarted by Frankfurter, Jackson, and the other justices arrayed against his Axis. And as the 1950s opened, Black fell further into gloom. The death of his wife at the end of 1951 left him bereft. His children helped him rally, as he slowly did. Black's day was coming.

The Black-Jackson feud was the Court's most public airing of its factionalism, but its most combative member was William O. Douglas. It is difficult to imagine a man more intellectually capable or temperamentally ill-suited to sit on the Supreme Court than William Douglas. Douglas was a man of mountains, self-consciously contemptuous of convention. Born in Minnesota and raised in Yakima, Washington, Douglas was the Court's only Westerner until joined by Warren. But where Warren came from politics and loved company, fellowship, and family, Douglas relished his isolation. He was the first Supreme Court justice to divorce while in office and would go on to marry three more times. As he wrote, traveled, and worked, Douglas paid little attention to the niceties of life among the brethren. Indeed, if the brethren can be thought of as nine brothers working under the same roof, William Douglas played the role of unruly son. He was rude to his clerks, he twitted Frankfurter's pomposity with delight, and he would often leave for his summer vacation before the Court's work was concluded, as he did with tragic consequences in the *Rosenberg* deliberations. Rarely did Douglas seem to care if he wrote for the majority or in dissent; his vision was so singular and his self-esteem so enormous that he preferred speaking his mind to negotiating the compromises sometimes needed in the Court.

Douglas was a nationally renowned law professor and the flamboyant head of the Securities and Exchange Commission before turning forty, the age at which he joined the Court.[35] When he arrived in April 1939, Douglas was more than ten years younger than his next oldest colleague. Many thought he would not stay long, that the Court was a way station on his route to the White House. He would end up serving longer than any justice in history. His restlessness was evident, however. Long after moving to the bench, Douglas continued to dabble in politics. He considered leaving the Court during the war when Roosevelt talked with him about taking over some defense operations. And in 1944, when Roosevelt was ailing and the vice presidency thus an important prize, Douglas came close to making the ticket, only to see the nomination go to Truman. Meanwhile, Douglas's scattershot intellect nurtured his love of travel and his fondness for writing. While his opinions were often brief to the point of brusqueness, Douglas was a talented and prolific writer who published more than thirty books, their royalties helping him to cover his mounting alimony obligations. His travel works are models of curiosity; his treatises are exhortations of individualism (titles like *Points of Rebellion* and *International Dissent* tell much of the story); his two-volume autobiography is both tantalizing and riddled with factual errors, typical of Douglas in both its pugnacity and its inattention to detail.

Douglas's closest friend among the brethren was Black. They wrote together often, feeling their way in the early years toward the libertarian liberalism that would become their hallmark. Off the bench, at least in the early years, they were friends and confidants. Douglas turned to his senior colleague for guidance during his periodic bouts of restlessness with judging. Doctrinally, they also were close, though they arrived at their philosophies differently. Where Black constructed a literalist reading of the Constitution and the Bill of Rights and melded it to his individualism, Douglas evolved into a more pure libertarian. He developed that orientation on the bench, characteristically, as an expression of defiance. The arrogation of power offended Douglas and drove him toward the defense of individual liberty. Particularly searing for Douglas was the Court's consideration of the Smith Act in 1951. Written by Representative Howard Smith of Virginia and formally if misleadingly titled the Alien Registration Act of 1940, the legislation made it illegal not just to attempt to overthrow the government but to advocate, abet, advise, or teach the "desirability, or propriety of overthrowing or destroying the government of the United States or the government of any State, Territory, District or Possession." The act thus punished not just those who actively sought to overthrow the government but also those who merely talked about it or believed it to be desirable even without doing anything to bring it about. Using that broad definition of subversion, the government charged eleven members of the American Communist Party in 1948, indicting Eugene Dennis and his codefendants for conspiracy as defined by the Smith Act. All eleven were convicted on October 14, 1949.[36] The Vinson Court accepted the government's contention that the Communist Party leaders, through their words, were planning and encouraging the overthrow of the government and rejected the argument that the First Amendment allowed them to do so. "We reject," the majority concluded, "any principle of governmental helplessness in the face of preparation for revolution, which principle, carried to its logical conclusion, must lead to anarchy."[37] Instead, the Court adopted the approach of Judge Learned Hand: "In each case [courts] must ask whether the gravity of the 'evil,' discounted by its improbability, justifies such invasion of free speech as is necessary to avoid the danger." That calculus was used to uphold the convictions of Dennis and the other Communists.

Douglas was incensed, and his anger elicited his eloquence, as he rose in defense of the principle of free speech:

> Full and free discussion has indeed been the first article of our faith. We have founded our political system on it. It has been the safeguard of every religious, political, philosophical, economic, and racial group amongst us. We have counted on it to keep us from embracing what is cheap and false; we have trusted the common sense of our people to choose the doctrine true to our genius and to reject the rest. This has been the one single outstanding tenet that has made our institutions the symbol of freedom and equality. We have deemed it more costly to liberty to suppress a despised minority than to let them vent their spleen. We have above all else feared the political censor. We have wanted a land where our people can be exposed to all the diverse creeds and cultures of the world.[38]

Black dissented as well, and in the years to come "Black and Douglas, dissenting," would become a staple of the Vinson Court. By the time Warren arrived, Douglas's views were steadfast and hardening. He believed simply that government intruded too deeply in the lives of its citizens, and as a judge he enjoyed clipping the wings of government officials at all levels who stymied civil liberties. Douglas eventually would draft the Court's signature work on the privacy of the individual, and thus of the limit of legitimate government interference in the lives of its citizens. The Court, in Douglas's view, existed to protect those citizens—to demand the fulfillment of their rights in the face of a government sometimes all too willing to subordinate them. In his core, Douglas was an individualist, and though he would become the whipping boy for generations of conservatives, he was, in many ways, one of them: rugged, independent, suspicious of the state, and committed to the individual.

Black appreciated Douglas's idiosyncrasies. They were singular men, willing to live apart from those around them. Black in his years as a justice would disappoint many of his Alabama friends. Douglas would disappoint almost everyone who cared about him personally. And so they found each other, and they liked and appreciated each other. When Stone died on the bench, Douglas hoped Black would ascend to the chief justiceship. When Vinson died in his apartment, Douglas again pulled for his Southern colleague. This time, it was Warren who received the nod.

In 1953, Warren and Douglas were two of America's most prominent Western politicians, and though they were of different parties, their paths had crossed. Warren recalled meeting Douglas at legal gatherings, but said they were only "slightly acquainted."[39] Douglas thought their bond deeper, and was one of thousands who took the time to write to Warren to express his sympathies and well-wishes for Honey Bear when she was struck with polio. The letter, Warren said in reply, "touched us deeply," adding that Honey Bear was looking forward to reading Douglas's memoir, *Of Men and Mountains*.[40] Given his regard for Warren, Douglas remembered being "more delighted than surprised" when Eisenhower named Warren to the Court.[41]

And so, on the first weekend of October in 1953, Warren signed the papers resigning the governorship of California and flew to Washington to join his new colleagues, whose work had now become his and whose family he would now preside over. So quick was Warren's transition from governor to chief justice that he arrived without a robe and had to borrow one. At precisely noon on October 5, 1953, the Court clerk read Warren's appointment, and Warren took the judicial oath. He then was escorted to the Court's center chair, reserved for the chief justice, and as he stepped up to occupy it, Warren tripped on the hem of the borrowed robe, almost falling into the chair. "I suppose it could be said that I literally stumbled onto the bench," he remembered.[42]

President Eisenhower and his wife attended the ceremony, as did Richard and Pat Nixon. Warren's old friend and trusted aide Warren Olney III was on hand as well, waiting for admission to the Supreme Court bar, as he had come to work for the Justice Department as an assistant attorney general. Nixon moved for Olney's admission (and muffed his line, presenting Olney for "nomination" rather than "admission," a slip that Warren noted and could not resist including in his memoirs).[43] From his post, Warren administered the oath to his old friend.

Black was the senior justice, and Warren knew formalities well enough to seek him out first, presenting himself at Black's chambers just moments after first arriving at the Court and introducing himself to his clerks and personal staff. Flattered, Black welcomed the new chief with grace, and introduced him to the rest of the brethren. Their first stop was Burton, and Warren mischievously assumed an intimacy with his new colleague, urging him not to let any of his more senior colleagues, notably Reed, know that Warren had come to see Burton first.[44] Already, Warren was making friends under the approving eye of Black. To Black directly, Warren acknowledged his unfamiliarity with the Court's procedures and again flattered his senior colleague by asking him to take over the conference while Warren settled in. Even more deferentially, Warren asked Black what he should read to learn about opinion-writing. "Aristotle on Rhetoric," the classically self-educated Black replied. That night, as midnight approached, Warren was reading Aristotle in his chambers.[45]

Warren moved slowly to assume the full scope of his duties, but his friendly presence immediately lightened the mood of the Court, as his fellow justices warmed to his personality and came to his assistance. Burton, an amateur historian, forwarded to Warren a copy of his history of the site on which the Court stood, a monograph that traced the land from 1550 through eight periods, culminating in the construction of the Court as it was completed in 1935.[46] Douglas sent over a copy of "Washington and Manifest Destiny," an address he had delivered a few months earlier.[47] Clark offered help finding an apartment, recommending a place on Connecticut Avenue.[48] Frankfurter delighted in taking Warren under his wing, commencing a series of lectures for the new chief on desegregation.[49]

Warren was grateful for the courtesies of his new colleagues. From the first days, his notes to them—and theirs to him—conveyed fondness and respect. They were, as Warren's notes almost always were, formal, but they went beyond stiff collegiality; they were genuinely appreciative. A few days after Warren's arrival, Black wrote to his sons. In his note, Black demonstrated his keen eye for character. He had only known Warren for ten days, but already Black had intuited his essence. "The new Chief Justice is a very attractive, fine man," Black wrote:

> Just a short acquaintance with him explains why it was possible for him to get votes in both parties in California. He is a novice here, of course, but a man with his intelligence should be able to give good service. I am by no means sure that an intelligent man with practical, hard common sense and integrity like he has is not as good a type to select as could be found in the country.[50]

Chapter 16

# SMEAR

*The biggest lot of tommyrot ever brought before a Senate committee.*

SENATOR ARTHUR V. WATKINS[1]

W ARREN'S EARLY MONTHS with the Supreme Court were tentative; as the recipient of a recess appointment, he was guaranteed his position only until Congress returned and took up the matter of his nomination to the position permanently. It was not until early 1954 that Congress set about the awkward business of deciding not whether Warren deserved to be seated on the Court—he was already there—but rather whether he should be allowed to stay.

Warren himself said little about his confirmation, but that was not because he enjoyed it or took it lightly. Like other experiences that deeply upset Warren, he responded by minimizing it, in this case pushing it out of his official history altogether. His memoirs dismissed his confirmation as Chief Justice of the United States in a footnote supplied by his editor: "The Chief Justice, in writing this book, did not feel that the accusations brought against him had enough validity to deserve attention at the expense of other matters."[2] Because Congress by statute seals its own judicial confirmation records for fifty years, Warren's decision to skip over the story of his own confirmation has meant that no serious examination of it has ever been undertaken or published. Warren's biographers have been unable to access the relevant files, so the only descriptions have come from contemporary accounts, based solely on the public workings of the Senate Judiciary Committee and on some enterprising reporting at the time, most notably by James Reston of the *New York Times*. Only in March 2004 did the Judiciary Committee records at last become available. Their contents reveal a smear of the first order, a deliberately deceitful attack on Warren's character by the committee's chair, aided by a self-aggrandizing political disciple and a delusional California private investigator.

As the cast assembled for that episode in late 1953, Warren was suffering in silence. He was, in those early months on the Court, alone and unhappy. Nina accompanied him to Washington and attended his swearing in, but the next day she returned to California. There, Nina packed up their things, while Goodwin Knight impatiently waited for her to vacate the mansion. The Warren children were in school or on their own, and so the new chief justice was by himself. And Earl Warren without Nina Warren was a diminished, sulky man. "I was," he remembered later, "perfectly miserable."[3] It was Nina who organized the details of Warren's unofficial life, she who cooked and kept their home, who laid out his clothes, who made sure his shirts were cleaned without starch—even the slightest bit of starch would give Earl Warren a rash.[4] Nina oversaw their modest social schedule and charmed friends and neighbors with her devil's food cakes. Earl Warren liked order—depended on it, in fact—and it was Nina who brought order to his life. Without her, even briefly, he foundered.

Friends were also hard to see. Most were far away, in California, and those in Washington were difficult to socialize with under the new strictures of his work. Chief among those was Olney, whose new position as associate attorney general of the United States meant that he and Warren were both in Washington. At first, they resumed their friendship, as the two men enjoyed walks together along the Potomac, reminiscing about California and warming in their old, deep camaraderie. Some nights, Warren would eat at the Olney home, reconnecting with the family as well.[5] Soon, however, it became clear to both that it was potentially compromising for the chief justice to maintain a friendship with a senior official from the Justice Department. The walks ceased, as did most unofficial contact between two men who had grown up professionally together and who both were now far from home. Olney took special care never to argue a case before the Supreme Court during the years that he was with Justice; he and Warren reduced their social contacts, and though they saw each other occasionally, those events were few and far between. The separation was difficult—and, as it turned out, temporary—but while it lasted, both accepted it with the stern self-discipline that was the mark of their common professionalism.[6]

While some aspects of the sanctum of the Court were comfortable for Warren in those early days—he welcomed the new and complex work—Warren also found it confining. In California, Warren's schedule was full of public events—speeches, receptions, radio addresses. He was used to speaking his mind, and enjoyed the response it generated. Now he rarely appeared in public outside the Court, and he was especially cautious during the months that his confirmation was held in abeyance. Not until January did he deliver a significant public address. And then it was one so bromidic that it was sure not to give his Senate critics material to use against him. Speaking at Columbia University on January 14, 1954, Warren proclaimed that freedom of thought was the tool by which free nations would prevail over Communist and fascist ones. "Liberty, not communism," Warren said, "is the most contagious force in the world." Only in one passage did Warren hint at a controversial notion, his willingness to tolerate excess in the name of freedom:

> When men are free to explore all avenues of thought, no matter what prejudices are aroused, there is a healthy climate in the nation. Dissenters can let off steam. That is important, too. The greatest figures in American history have always recognized this as inherent in our system. The founding fathers themselves were not orthodox either in thought or expression. They recognized both the right and the value of dissent in their generation.[7]

Two days later, the United States Senate received President Eisenhower's nomination of the acting chief justice. It was promptly referred, as judicial nominations typically are, to the Judiciary Committee, which appointed a subcommittee to examine Warren's qualifications. And there the trouble began. The chairman of the Judiciary Committee at that time was North Dakota's senior senator, the strange and irresponsible William Langer. Hawk-nosed and jowly, with piercing eyes that peered from beneath heavy lids, Langer was a strange blend of abstinent and indulgent: He refused to touch alcohol but chomped a cellophane-wrapped cigar. As a prosecutor, he pursued felons with zeal but amassed a long rap sheet of his own, including arrests for inciting a riot, defrauding law clients, and engaging in numerous suspicious financial deals.

Nevertheless, Langer clawed out a political career, eventually rising to governor of North Dakota. While in that job, he was convicted of conspiracy and then declared martial law rather than vacate his office. Ousted despite his efforts to hold on, Langer then saw his conviction overturned on appeal and in 1940 ran a successful Senate campaign. That victory brought him to Washington in 1941, but Langer held his office provisionally for over a year as the Senate debated denying him a place in the chamber; only in March 1942 was Langer seated, and then over the objections of thirty senators, including Harry Truman. The nation's newest senator was among its oddest. His behavior was too erratic to be ignored.[8]

Once allowed to take his official place among his new colleagues, Langer, whose nickname "Wild Bill" was in his case an understatement, built an agenda shaped largely by three factors: his radical isolationism, his genuine desire to advance the interests of North Dakotans, and his near physical unwillingness to accept no for an answer.

Langer opposed the formation of the United Nations, the military draft, the

Marshall Plan, and every foreign aid bill that was presented to him. He opposed foreign entanglements of all types, but reserved a special hatred for Britain. On the final day of 1951, as Winston Churchill was approaching the United States by ocean liner, Langer cabled the vicar of the Old North Church in Boston. Langer asked him to hang two lanterns in the belfry.[9] Such antics made Langer easy to ridicule—he bore some resemblance to California's Jack Tenney—but he was nothing if not determined, and through his nearly two decades in the United States Senate, Langer solidified his North Dakota base with his intense commitment to delivering services and appointments to his constituents. With the seating of the 83rd Congress, Langer's seniority landed him atop the Judiciary Committee, and he happily set out to use that position, as he had his place on the Postal Committee, to force the administration to give North Dakotans positions of influence.

In 1950, Langer had announced his intention to block any nominee to "head any office" unless that person came from North Dakota.[10] The following year, Langer proved he was not kidding when he refused to back Eisenhower's pick for ambassador to Switzerland—no North Dakotan, Langer announced, had ever been named an ambassador. By 1954, most of Washington appeared to have forgotten Langer's pledge or underestimated his grit. But he was steadfast, and thus it was with predictable dismay that Langer received word that a Californian, not a North Dakotan, would occupy the next important judicial opening. Moreover, Warren was not Langer's type. Warren had demonstrated considerable fondness for international engagements—he was a long-standing supporter of the United Nations and comfortable within Eisenhower's internationalist wing of the Republican Party. Gallingly, from Langer's perspective, Warren had even recently returned from Britain, where he had acted as one of Eisenhower's emissaries to the coronation of Queen Elizabeth. And in general, Warren was philosophically and temperamentally something of Langer's opposite: Warren the stable political moderate, in contrast to Langer the ping-pongy individualist.

Through the fall of 1953, while Warren had been settling in at the Court, some of his detractors had written to the Judiciary Committee to express their disapproval of his appointment.[11] Langer husbanded them carefully, and by early 1954, he had in hand a stack of material regarding the nominee. On February 2, the senator convened a public hearing of the committee, which heard from witnesses for and against Warren's nomination, but that session was overshadowed by a closed-door meeting of the panel. It was there, Langer announced later, that he presented his colleagues with ninety-seven "protests" against Warren's confirmation. The protests, Langer said, included numerous charges against the nominee and required investigation by the committee and by the FBI. But Langer used those protests tactically, not forthrightly. He initially promised them to the FBI so that agents could investigate, then withdrew that offer; similarly, he showed the stack of letters to his colleagues but would not let them read them.[12] Leaving the meeting, Langer explained to reporters that a vote on Warren's nomination had to be delayed because "too many charges" had been leveled against him to be evaluated in a single session.[13]

That was where the matter stood, as far as the public knew, in early February 1954. In fact, as the long-delayed opening of the Judiciary Committee files revealed fifty years later, the letters were a jumble of unsupported allegations and expressions of ideological disagreement. The vast majority included no charges at all. Any FBI agent or committee member would have recognized the irrelevance of those communications instantly—had Langer allowed them to see the correspondence. Typical was the note from Claudia Babcoke of Los Angeles: "As one lone voter, I protest the appointment of Earl Warren, former Governor of California, as Chief Justice. Why can't Senator Joseph McCarthy get something as important as that?"[14] Or Mr. and Mrs. Fulton of Glendale, California, who warned the committee in a single-page, handwritten note that Warren "leaned too far to the left."[15] Or Michael Gorke of Little Neck, New York, who sent a postcard stating simply, "Warren's appointment is a disgrace."[16]

Those letters—and dozens more in the committee files—contained no allegations to investigate, no charges of any kind. Of the 122 letters received by the committee during the weeks leading up to the nomination and preserved in its files, just fourteen included any allegation regarding Warren.[17] And most of those "charges" were ludicrous on their face. One former inmate charged that Warren, as governor, had used his "despotic power" to lock him away for an unfair sentence;[18] another promised "unquestioned evidence" that Warren had been an officer of the Ku Klux Klan while serving as district attorney in Alameda.[19]

One letter was different. It did in fact contain allegations of wrongdoing by Warren. Specifically, it detailed ten charges arising from Warren's time as attorney general and governor. It alleged: (1) As attorney general, Warren practiced and encouraged discriminatory prosecution against migrants during the Dust Bowl years; (2) Warren was under the domination of liquor lobbyist Artie Samish; (3) Warren, as "chief magistrate" of California, failed to rein Samish in, encouraging his illegal lobbying; (4) Warren had allowed organized crime to flourish in California; (5) unemployment trust fund money was missing, lost during his administration; (6) California administrative procedures were misused for the purpose of "taking over of a corporate state," a development the writer compared to Mussolini's tactics in Italy; (7) Warren permitted gambling at California racetracks; (8) Warren encroached on the legislature's authority; (9) Warren ignored allegations of corruption by California officeholders; and finally, (10) Warren prosecuted or investigated allegations of corruption only when they involved people in disfavor with his administration.[20]

Those at least assumed the form of charges, as Langer had told the press. But even a cursory examination would have exposed their falsity without delay. Warren was not even attorney general during the Dust Bowl. Far from encouraging race-track gambling, he actually had shut it down. His efforts against organized crime had been among the most aggressive in the nation, and had been publicly recognized as such. The two charges relating to Artie Samish were undermined by the fact that Warren had criticized Samish and supported stronger legislation to curb lobbying—legislation specifically inspired by Samish's record. Although Samish had been prosecuted federally, not by the state, it was Warren's old friend and ally, Warren Olney, who had led that prosecution, further evidence of Warren's distaste for the flamboyant liquor lobbyist. Indeed, Samish himself blamed Warren for much of his trouble.

Two more allegations in the letter, those relating to public corruption, were so vague that investigating them would in all likelihood have been impossible, and they were contradicted by the known fact that Warren had built much of his reputation in California on his anticorruption work as a prosecutor. That left the two administrative charges—that unemployment money had been misspent and that administrative procedures had been misapplied. Neither was directed at Warren personally, and thus they were allegations more of neglect than of misconduct. Still, the first, if true, might have merited committee attention; the second, with its allusion to Mussolini, seemed to say more about the alleger than it did about the accused.

So ridiculous were some of the charges—and so shaky many of the accusers—that Olney believed those making the allegations were fronts for Warren's California enemies, notably the still-angry Bill Keck, left over from the gasoline sales tax debate. Keck, Olney knew, "hated Earl Warren like poison."[21] Warren accepted that theory as well.[22]

Keck may well have been behind the effort—he had motive, and it was not beneath him. Nominally at least, however, Warren's accuser was a man named Burr McCloskey, who put his charges in a letter to the committee on the letterhead of a Chicago-based group called the American Rally. McCloskey was an odd figure, perennially on the fringes of Midwestern politics. A series of alliances and memberships had led him to found the American Rally, a self-described nonpartisan organization dedicated to "promoting the principles of peace, abundance and the Constitution."[23] A young man drawn to grandiosity rather than principle, thirty-four years old in 1954, McCloskey had flirted with left- and right-wing fringe politics, first attracting attention as a high school student in Akron, where he organized the United Students Alliance to challenge his school administration.[24] He attended the University of Akron from 1937 to 1938, then dabbled in various shades of left-wing politics before joining the Army on November 12, 1943;[25] he was discharged in 1945. On Christmas Eve of 1948, a month after divorcing his first wife, he married again, this time to a woman named Brunhilde. McCloskey continued to work as an organizer, affiliating with a group known as the United Labor Party, which advocated the formation of a national union. That party in turn gave birth to the American Rally. But while much of McCloskey's political résumé suggests a somewhat aimless leftist, he also considered himself a "farmer's rights fighter,"[26] he countenanced Senator Joseph McCarthy, and he was critical of the Senate for failing to rally behind McCarthy's anti-Communist purge.[27] McCloskey, taken with his own importance, urged the FBI to investigate him in order to discover his true political beliefs. The FBI declined, though agents did conduct an interview with him.[28] Other members of American Rally, meanwhile, were alarmed by McCloskey's embrace of right-wing causes and candidates; some feared he was stalking for fascist elements.[29] For a man thus more drawn to the spectacle of politics than to its content, the nomination of a Supreme Court justice was a tempting opportunity to ascend the national platform that had eluded McCloskey his entire restless life. Recognizing his moment, he grabbed it. It was, one observer at the time noted, the "crowning achievement of his career."[30]

And yet even as he grabbed a sliver of the national spotlight, McCloskey took care to insulate himself against reprisal. In his letter, for instance, he noted that he was serving merely as a conduit, relaying reports he had received from the American Rally's California representative, a similarly shady character named Roderick Wilson. Invited to appear before the committee, McCloskey showed up late and instead forwarded his allegations in writing. He was gone from Washington by the time they were received.

All of that smelled suspicious, but the true deceit belonged to Senator Langer. Without evaluating the substance of the charges against Warren—and while still clinging to exclusive control over the other letters received by the committee— Langer had the committee's lawyer produce a charge sheet summarizing the allegations. The lawyer struck a few but included most of the McCloskey/Wilson allegations, along with others plucked from the mail. The additions included charges that Warren, while the Alameda DA, was "many times . . . so drunk . . . that his assistants had to help him stand up in court," that as governor he uniformly supported the "Marxist . . . revolutionary line," and that he knowingly appointed and promoted dishonest judges.[31] The drunkenness charge was culled from a single note. It read, in its entirety:

> Dear Sir,
>
> Yes, it was well known around Oakland when Warren was the DA, he was often so damned drunk his assistants had to hold him up in the courtroom! Chief Justice? Wow.[32]

It was signed: "News Reader" and included no return address. From that, counsel and chairman of the Senate Judiciary Committee listed Warren's courtroom drunkenness as a charge worthy of investigation by the United States Senate. While still refusing to share the letters, Langer asked the Justice Department to direct the FBI to investigate Warren's background. Deputy Attorney General William Rogers pointed out that no chief justice had ever undergone such an inquiry—the Constitution's doctrine of separation of powers cast some doubt as to whether it was appropriate for the legislative branch to direct the executive branch to investigate a sitting member of the judicial branch.[33] When it became clear, however, that Langer would not proceed with the nomination unless he got his investigation, Rogers backed down. On February 9, Rogers told the FBI that "we have no other choice but to make a quick investigation," but he suggested that the Bureau keep it short—the issue, Rogers insisted, was in fulfilling the principle of requiring an FBI report rather than submit a genuinely thorough review.[34] After ensuring that Rogers understood that the Bureau would submit only a "limited" report, Hoover dispatched agents to check Warren's background. The same week, one visited an old colleague of Warren's in Sacramento, who told Warren of his visit and assured him that nothing seemed amiss. The agent, Warren's friend wrote, "indicated it was pretty much of a formality."[35]

Hoover had been doing favors for Warren for more than a decade, and the FBI background check reflected Hoover's protectiveness of his charge. It amounted to little more than a collection of testimonials to Warren's abilities and character. It cited two picayune associations between Warren and Communism—a written greeting that Warren had sent to a pageant commemorating the third anniversary of Russia's war against Nazi Germany (America's war, too, after all), and his attendance at a 1945 banquet in San Francisco hosted by the American-Russian Institute, later identified as a Communist front organization by the attorney general.[36] There were a few Warren critics quoted, though even some of those said they supported the nomination. The bulk of the report was devoted to synopses of interviews with Warren backers, who praised him lavishly, describing him as of "good moral character," as the "best-informed man in the three branches of government," "superb," "completely devoid of bias," and "one hundred percent in every respect."[37]

The report was transmitted to the Justice Department and shared with Langer on February 16. That same day, an FBI agent assigned to the Judiciary Committee proceedings made one last attempt to convince Langer to share with him the accusations that had been filed with the committee. Langer had been dodging the Bureau for days, publicly insisting that the accusations merited review but refusing to let them be reviewed, at least by the FBI. Now, on February 16, Langer admitted he had nothing. "Langer stated he had gone over the complaints and that he had concluded that they were of no value and, therefore, he would not turn them over for investigation."[38]

That, then, seemed likely to end the matter. Langer admitted he had nothing incriminating on Warren, and the FBI turned up nothing, either. But three days later—three days *after* acknowledging that his files contained nothing damaging against Warren—Langer called his colleagues into session. As the hearing opened, Langer directed the counsel to read the charges against Warren (they had been edited yet again, and as presented no longer included the allegations regarding drunkenness; the balance of the allegations were included). Warren was accused of permitting organized crime in California, of collaborating with Artie Samish (that was news to Samish), of favoring the "Marxist line," of running an escrow racket, and of mishandling government funds, among other things. Langer knew those charges were baseless—he had admitted it to the FBI three days earlier. But the public did not know that, would not know it for more than fifty years. William Knowland, Warren's old friend and then the majority leader of the Senate, was in the audience when Langer had the charges read in an open hearing room, with press and public present. "I would not submit a town marshal to this type of anonymous charge," Knowland complained.[39]

After the session, he added, "The procedure followed today in the case of Chief Justice Warren is the most shocking event I have observed in my eight years in the Senate."[40] Another Californian, Vice President Richard Nixon, echoed Knowland's anger and pivoted in Nixonian fashion. "Rather than wasting its time investigating the charges [against Warren]," Nixon suggested that it "could well spend some time investigating those who made them."[41] Eisenhower, vacationing in Palm Springs, released a statement standing by Warren, whom he described as "one of the finest public servants this country has produced."[42]

Across the country, editorial boards rose up with unusual unanimity. Outrage poured from the *Memphis Press-Scimitar* and the *Oregon Journal*, the *Long Beach Press-Telegram* and the *Tampa Sunday Tribune*, the *New York Times* and the *Santa Monica Evening Outlook*. The *Outlook*'s editorial nicely captured the national revulsion: "The North Dakota Senator, who had some reputation as a screwball before, has now climbed far out on the special limb hitherto occupied by the nastiest little viper in the Senate and has told Senator Wayne Morse to move over."[43]

Curiously, Langer's attention to the seedy charges against Warren distracted from three areas where Warren's record might have provided legitimate grist for senators considering his worthiness for the Court. One letter writer had argued that Warren's support for the internment of the Japanese should count against his ascending to a tribunal charged with the protection of civil liberties, a worthwhile point but one that Langer chose to ignore altogether.[44] Several others questioned Warren's actions during the loyalty oath debate in California. There, the risk to Warren was less substantive but more political: Eisenhower and Warren had different views on the value of oaths, so Warren's contrary position in the California debate could have surfaced a policy difference between the president and his nominee. Again, Langer's attention was focused elsewhere.[45] Finally, a third and potentially fruitful avenue for inquiry was Warren's continued membership in the Native Sons of the Golden West. Nearly seventeen years earlier, Hugo Black's ascension to the Court had been disturbed by the revelations of his past Ku Klux Klan membership. The Native Sons were not the Klan, but they too had espoused an openly racist agenda, in their case with respect to California land ownership. And whereas Black had resigned his membership in the Klan, Warren remained a dues-paying Native Son. But Langer was more offended by internationalism than racism. There is no evidence that he ever considered probing Warren's relationship to the Native Sons.

Langer's actions could have been explained by eccentricity or bad judgment were it not for two facts that he deliberately concealed from the committee and the public. Langer knew when he aired the charges against Warren that they were without merit. That was proof of bad faith. Even more telling was a subtler act of deceit. Through both the public and closed sessions of the committee, Langer presented himself as a disinterested fact finder. He professed to be surprised, even offended, by the allegations but duty-bound to investigate them. But Langer was hiding the truth. After the blowup on February 20, Langer's subcommittee met in secret to evaluate the allegations against Warren that Langer had made public the day before. There Olney, now in his role as associate attorney general, presented the committee with the Justice Department's research on the chief accusers, Wilson and McCloskey. As Olney laid out the facts of McCloskey's history, Langer sat quietly, interjecting a question or two but volunteering nothing.

What Langer did not say was that he had known McCloskey at least since 1938—perhaps earlier—that he had given him advice throughout his career, that McCloskey considered the senator his political idol, and that the two had been working together on a variety of fronts in the months leading up to the Warren hearings. Nearly a year earlier, McCloskey, addressing the senator as "Dear Bill," urged Langer to weigh in on a raging farm battle outside Detroit. The letter was friendly and familiar, closing with "I thank you from the bottom of my heart for all past favors, and remain, Very sincerely yours."[46] Responding, Langer addressed "Dear Burr" and promised that he would make a staff member from the Judiciary Committee available to meet with McCloskey and review the dispute.[47] Their correspondence continued through 1953 and early 1954, as the Warren nomination came before Langer's committee. In November, writing on the letterhead of the American Rally, McCloskey updated Langer on the farm situation, invited him to address two of the organization's state conventions, and for the first time raised the idea of contesting Warren's appointment (Warren had taken his seat the previous month). In that note, McCloskey detailed for Langer the American Rally's efforts to place a candidate on the California ballot in the 1952 elections. "In this struggle, I became well acquainted with the corruption of both machines and the culpable relationship of then-Governor Earl Warren," McCloskey wrote. "I understand that your Senate Committee will shortly conduct hearings on the fitness of this Earl Warren to be approved as Chief Justice of the U.S. Supreme Court. I am here petitioning you for time as a witness before your Committee in order to protest the Warren appointment."[48]

And yet when McCloskey and American Rally were attacked by the Justice Department representatives in the closed session of the Judiciary Committee, Langer feigned ignorance. "What is the American Rally?" he asked.[49]

Langer denied knowledge for a reason. The transcripts do not supply it because no one in the room during those hearings knew enough to challenge Langer. But context provides what the text cannot. Ignorance of McCloskey suited Langer's purposes. He did not want to appear vindictive toward the chief justice, whose confirmation he knew to be likely. All Langer wanted was to smear Warren, to discredit him and the Eisenhower administration. To denigrate Warren without openly opposing him, it benefited Langer to strike a pose of neutrality and to have McCloskey bear the burden of leveling the specific charges. Langer even went further than that, unctuously proclaiming during a closed session of the committee that he, in fact, supported Warren—"He is one of the best friends I have," the senator said, undoubtedly to the disbelief of his colleagues.[50] It was a smear, not the first and certainly not the last leveled against a judicial nominee, but distinct in its mendacity and deviousness.[51]

Warren himself gave the hearings a wide berth, no doubt concluding that his presence would only lend dignity to a proceeding that was collapsing of its own weight. He declined, for instance, an invitation to appear before the committee and defend himself. That is not to say, however, that he was not aware of or troubled by the attacks on him. Olney remembered Warren being "irked" by the proceedings, by the parade of false charges and dubious witnesses and by the committee's retreat into closed sessions, where Warren was left to imagine what they were hearing.[52]

Even after the tumultuous public meeting of February 19 and the contentious private session on February 20, Langer was not quite willing to let Warren go. The following week, he convened the committee, again in secret, to hear from Roderick J. Wilson, the California representative of the American Rally whose allegations McCloskey had forwarded with Langer's encouragement. Wilson was a private investigator of dubious credentials, wanted for perjury and apparently lying low to avoid a warrant for his arrest. More alarming to the committee, he was a rambling, incoherent witness. His allegations against Warren turned out to be drawn mostly from his reading. His charge that Warren had abetted organized crime, for instance, was based on the findings of the California Crime Commission. That commission was created by Warren and chaired by Olney, who not only could refute the charges but also happened to be in the room as Wilson testified and interjected to correct the witness. Wilson then turned to question Olney, infuriating the dignified Olney and his colleague, Deputy Attorney General Rogers. "I do not think we should submit to cross-examination by this witness," Rogers finally said, interrupting, his patience at an end. "I resent it very much."[53]

Bad enough for senators to have been dragged through Langer's hoax; now they were party to a circus, and they were done. Senator Arthur Watkins of Utah dismissed Wilson's testimony as "fourth-rate hearsay," and another member then called the question, moving that the committee favorably report Warren's nomination to the Senate. The vote was 12–3, with Senators James Eastland and Olin Johnston voting against the nomination on substance—both Southern Senators were concerned about Warren's views on civil rights—and Senator Harley Kilgore bizarrely joining them to send a message to the newspaper editors and columnists who had expressed dismay over the committee's handling of the appointment. If Walter Lippmann would agree to apologize, Kilgore said, he would vote for Warren.[54] Exasperated, his colleagues recorded the final vote. The event's laughable coda: Langer voted in Warren's favor.

Even with the recently released materials and the light they shed on the story of Warren's nomination, they leave one question pregnantly unresolved. Why? Why would Langer go to such lengths to denigrate a sitting chief justice named by a popular president of his own party, especially when he had to know there was almost no chance that he would succeed? Part of the answer to that question rests with Langer himself, whose perverse sense of political theater was gratified by the Warren fight. Reston was the first to uncover Langer's old pledges to block any non–North Dakotans from office, and that observation, widely repeated in subsequent coverage, provided the most complete rationale in its day. And as discussed, Langer had plenty of reason not to like Warren: The Californian was too moderate, too internationalist, and too accommodating on civil rights, among other things, for Wild Bill's taste.

By themselves, however, none of those facts seems enough to warrant the scathing and unfounded public attack that Langer encouraged. A more specific possibility is suggested by a single document in the confirmation files and by later events that reunited Langer and McCloskey. As Langer listened to Wilson's pained testimony, with its loopy conspiracy theories and unconnected dots, the senator doodled on a pad. He made line drawings of masks and swirly figures, some resembling the letter S or an infinity sign. Several times, he sketched the number 5. And then, near the bottom of the page, he wrote "1955" and underlined it elaborately. Just above it, in bold writing, obviously traced again and again, was another number: "'56."[55]

Was Langer looking ahead to the next elections as he contemplated Warren's fate? If so, he was either scheming or prophesying. In 1956, Langer, nationally renowned in part for his stand against the controversial Earl Warren, would be urged to run for president of the United States. The American Rally, in its newspaper ("The Newspaper That Believes in the American People"), championed "Fighting Bill Langer" and titled its series on the senator "The Making of a President."[56] Later that year, the newly formed Pioneer Party, affiliated with the American Rally, convened delegates from sixteen states and drafted Langer as its nominee. Although Langer declined the third-party nomination—accepting it would have cost him his seniority in the Senate—the party picked him anyway. For his running mate, its nominee for vice president of the United States, the Pioneer Party chose Burr McCloskey.

Langer emerged from the hearings better known, if not better liked. Warren came through them having felt the sting of a legislative power not to legislate but to defame. And having felt that lash against himself, he did not need to consider the effect of legislative inquiry in the abstract. Two days after the public airing of the laundry list of allegations against Warren, a Philadelphia man named Burton Crane wrote to the chief justice to express his sympathy and outrage. Warren, he suggested, might well learn something from the experience he was undergoing:

> Too many timid men have kept silent in the face of roving prosecutions sanctioned by the Senate. . . . With both your reputation and the high office you hold, I submit that it is your duty as a citizen of this country to add your voice in protest against the marauding bands ambushing our freedoms. Now that you have been shot at, you know what it is like.[57]

The message was received.

Chapter 17

# ALL MEN ARE
# CREATED EQUAL[1]

*The humanitarian idealism of the Declaration has always echoed as a battle-cry in*
*the hearts of those who dream of an America dedicated to democratic ends. It can-*
*not be long ignored or repudiated, for sooner or later it returns to plague the council*
*of practical politics. It is constantly breaking out in fresh revolt.*

VERNON L. PARRINGTON[2]

AMERICA'S DECLARATION OF INDEPENDENCE proclaims that all men are
created equal—endowed by the same Creator, they are equally entitled
to unalienable rights, among them life, liberty, and the pursuit of happiness. Government, the drafters of that profound and poetic document concluded,
exists not to bestow but merely to secure the God-given rights of men. So elemental
was that charge that the Declaration reserved for the people the right to destroy a
government that failed to protect its people's rights. America's Constitution, struck
just eleven years later, makes no such promises or threats. The Constitution was a
triumph of ingenuity and a model of compromise, but its rights were more stingily
proffered, and it brought into being a nation that embraced slavery, not to mention
the disenfranchisement of women and most landless workers. The nation was the
Constitution's victory; slavery was its curse. The trade dehumanized its victims and
debased its practitioners while warping both the economy and the morality of the
American South. Slavery recalculated values, aroused furies, and undermined
America's place at the head of human liberty. And most perniciously, because the
Constitution accepted slavery in order to make a union, it stood between America
and its own Declaration. As late as the mid–twentieth century, the Declaration was
best understood as a grand but unfulfilled pledge.

It was that chasm—between the ideals that gave birth to the nation and the rules that it chose to govern itself—that was responsible for America's defining trauma, its soul-wrenching debate over the place of blacks in American society. As presented to the United States Supreme Court in the early 1950s, the broad question for the justices, one burdened with nearly two centuries of neglect, was this: Were black men and women—whose ancestors were brought to this country in bondage, then freed into a world of legal oppression—to be allowed the full blessings of liberty promised by the Declaration, or were they to remain subjugated by law as well as custom?

While that was the question the justices knew they faced, the cases upon which they were to write the answer were, as cases always are, more narrowly cast. In this instance, the specific issue—presented to the Court prior to Warren's arrival but there still for him to decide—was whether Negro boys and girls were constitutionally entitled to attend the same public schools as white boys and girls. Much of the nation's history and of the Court's jurisprudence suggested they were not.

To understand why not, one must briefly step back to the end of the Civil War and the reunification of the nation under the postwar constitutional amendments, the Thirteenth, Fourteenth, and Fifteenth Amendments to the original Constitution. Those amendments, respectively, freed the slaves, promised the full rights of citizenship and equal protection of the laws to those who had been freed, and prohibited withholding of the right to vote on account of "race, color or previous condition of servitude." Of the three, the Fourteenth was the amendment with the most far-reaching implications, as it extended to all American citizens the "privileges and immunities" of their citizenship, regardless of the state in which they lived. Moreover, it promised those citizens due process of law against any attempt to deny them life, liberty, or property and guaranteed, for the first time, the "equal protection of the laws."

The language of the Fourteenth Amendment would seem to speak for itself, but it was written in an era of casual discrimination. Indeed, the same Congress that passed the amendment also continued to fund segregated schools in Washington, D.C. As applied by the Supreme Court in the late nineteenth century, the Fourteenth Amendment thus came to stand for protections far different from those suggested by its plain language. Through a series of rulings after the amendment's adoption in 1868, the Court used it to protect contracts and corporations but withheld its guarantees from those whom the amendment was pointedly intended to help, Negro Americans. As the century drew to a close, the Court read into the amendment segregation itself, a finding it explicated in one of the most intellectually dishonest rulings in its history, *Plessy v. Ferguson*.[3]

Homer Plessy was a man seven-eighths and by all appearances white. Even that thin rivulet of Negro blood in him was too much for Louisiana, which required him and all other Negroes to ride in black-only railroad cars. Louisiana's law was plain discrimination, but state authorities contended it did not violate the Fourteenth Amendment's guarantee of equal protection, because those cars were "equal" to the cars set aside for whites. Plessy challenged that rule, sat in the car reserved for whites, and was arrested. He was convicted of violating Louisiana's law and appealed his conviction all the way to the United States Supreme Court, which took the case in 1896. The purpose of the Fourteenth Amendment, the justices conceded, "was undoubtedly to enforce the absolute equality of the two races before the law." But, they added, "in the nature of things, it could not have been intended to abolish distinctions based upon color, or to enforce social, as distinguished from political, equality, or a commingling of the two races upon terms unsatisfactory to either."[4]

As Richard Kluger, in his defining account of the Court and desegregation, aptly points out, one might well ask of the *Plessy* authors: Why not? Why couldn't the Fourteenth Amendment have been intended to abolish distinctions based upon color when that is precisely what its language purports to do? And what, by the way, was meant by "in the nature of things"? Most appallingly, the Court had the audacity to blame Negroes for assuming that the establishment of separate facilities was intended to demean them. "The underlying fallacy of the plaintiff's argument," the Court ruled, lay in "the assumption that the enforced separation of the two races stamps the colored race with a badge of inferiority. If this be so, it is not by reason of anything found in the act, but solely because the colored race chooses to put that construction upon it."[5] There are few instances in American history where men of such esteem have joined in a decision that was more hardhearted or more plainly false.

The one justice who disagreed, Justice John Marshall Harlan, denounced the opinion's deprivation of liberty and equality. Harlan did not deny his own pride of race—his opinion specifically trumpets his belief that whites dominate society and predicts they will continue to—but for him and him alone on his Court, the Constitution was not the place to write one's prejudices:

> The white race deems itself to be the dominant race in this country. And so it is, in prestige, in achievements, in education, in wealth, and in power. So, I doubt not, it will continue to be for all time, if it remains true to its great heritage, and holds fast to the principles of constitutional liberty. But in view of the constitution, in the eye of the law, there is in this country no superior, dominant, ruling class of citizens. There is no caste here. Our constitution is color-blind, and neither knows nor tolerates classes among citizens. In respect of civil rights, all citizens are equal before the law.[6]

Notwithstanding that, the Court's ruling in *Plessy* became the law. An ebullient South embraced it and used it to construct Jim Crow, the separate society for

American blacks. Blessed and encouraged by the Court, that separation had become all but complete by mid-century. Theaters, parks, beaches, courtrooms, drinking fountains, public bathrooms, trains and buses, restaurants, and schools all were separated by race.

Against that tide rowed a few lonely but determined advocates, chief among them Charles Houston and Thurgood Marshall. Houston was an austere man driven by an abiding purpose, the construction of a civil rights strike force under the banner of Howard University, whose law school he transformed and whose students he inspired. Marshall was cut from different cloth, but stood out among those whom Houston had tutored. Witty and earthy, energetic and stubborn, Marshall grew up in a middle-class black Baltimore neighborhood, raised by tough parents and stern teachers who attempted to squeeze scholarship out of the mischievous boy. Luckily for Marshall—and the nation—his elementary school principal would punish his misbehavior by making him read and memorize sections of the Constitution. He was in trouble so frequently, Marshall would recall later, "before I left that school . . . I knew the whole thing by heart."[7] He studied first to be a dentist, but switched to the law when he clashed with a biology professor. Marshall's law school options were limited, however: the University of Maryland law school in the early 1930s did not admit blacks. Accepted instead at Howard, Marshall studied under Houston and then joined him in one of the defining crusades of American political history: the painstaking, brave quest to roll away the nation's segregation laws.

At first, the education cases were aimed not at the "separate" or segregationist prong of *Plessy* but rather at its command that such separate facilities be "equal." Marshall, Houston, and their colleagues accepted, for a time, the existence of segregated schools but demanded equal pay for Negro teachers, and later fought for equal educational facilities. In 1935, Marshall made the University of Maryland pay for its unwillingness to admit him when he successfully sued to force its integration. Three years later, Houston brought a similar case to the United States Supreme Court, where he argued on behalf of Lloyd Gaines, a promising student who was president of his class at Missouri's black college, Lincoln University. Gaines wanted to go to law school, but Missouri offered no legal education for blacks. Instead, it proposed to give him a scholarship to study elsewhere or to open a new law school at Lincoln just for Gaines.[8] Neither option appealed: Gaines wanted the advantages of studying law in his home state, and he well knew that a one-man law school was no law school at all.

Charles Evans Hughes wrote for the majority that rejected Missouri's solution. "The admissibility of laws separating the races in the enjoyment of privileges afforded by the State rests wholly on the equality of the privileges which the laws give to the separated groups within the State," Hughes wrote. "The white resident is

afforded legal education within the State; the negro resident having the same qualifications is refused it there and must go outside the State to obtain it. That is a denial of the equality of legal right to the enjoyment of the privilege."[9] Hughes's
opinion for the Court breathed new commitment into equalizing educational opportunities, but it notably did not attack segregation itself. If schools were equal,
they could still be separate (the bitter, aging Justice McReynolds would not have
given even that much; in dissent, he noted that Missouri could opt now to close its
law school for whites or could break down segregation and, in the process "damnify
both races."[10]).

*Gaines* gave Marshall and Houston a significant new tool for attacking separate-
but-equal, and through the 1940s they wielded it again and again at states that
were offering a façade of equal education to blacks. Those cases, which were collectively referred to as the "graduate-school cases," were among the proudest of Chief
Justice Vinson's tenure, though they did not accomplish as much as he and some
observers have suggested. In 1946, the University of Oklahoma refused to admit
Ada Lois Sipuel, and she sued. Oklahoma courts upheld the university's right to
discriminate against her, but she pressed her cause. The Supreme Court heard argument on January 7 and 8 of 1948 and ruled less than a week later, brusquely reminding the Oklahoma courts of the *Gaines* decision and stating unequivocally
that Sipuel was "entitled to secure legal education afforded by a state institution."
Oklahoma, the justices declared in their brief per curiam opinion, was obligated to
provide it to her "in conformity with the equal protection clause of the Fourteenth
Amendment."[11]

Two years later, the Court took up the more complicated case of Heman Sweatt,
a Houston mailman who was barred from becoming a clerk because of his race and
so decided to become a lawyer. At the time, Texas did not provide a law school for
blacks, but it rushed to build one in the face of Sweatt's lawsuit. By the end of 1946,
it had a law school ready to accept a Negro student, but Sweatt wanted none of it,
and no wonder. The University of Texas law school, open only to whites, had sixteen professors, 850 students, a library stocked with 65,000 books, "many distinguished alumni, and much tradition and prestige."[12] The hastily constructed law
school for Negroes was ready to take Sweatt in early 1947, but it was to be staffed by
four professors on loan from the University of Texas; it had ordered 10,000 books,
but few had arrived. It had no librarian and was unaccredited. By 1950, when the
case had reached the U.S. Supreme Court, the school had just five professors,
twenty-three students, 16,500 books, and one alumnus who practiced law. Sweatt
wanted a real legal education and the real benefits that might flow from it; he refused to accept the knockoff version offered to him by Texas. In Texas, the trial
court rejected Sweatt's lawsuit, finding that the school for blacks was "substantially

equivalent" to that provided to whites, a finding upheld on appeal and allowed to stand by the Texas Supreme Court.[13]

Vinson wrote for his Court. Despite their quarrels, here the justices spoke as one and borrowed from their own experience as law students to say what the Texas courts would not admit. "Few students and no one who has practiced law would choose to study in an academic vacuum, removed from the interplay of ideas and the exchange of views with which the law is concerned," the Court ruled. "The law school to which Texas is willing to admit [Sweatt] excludes from its student body members of the racial groups which number 85% of the population of the State and include most of the lawyers, witnesses, jurors, judges and other officials. . . . With such a substantial and significant segment of society excluded, we cannot conclude that the education offered [Sweatt] is substantially equal to that which he would receive if admitted to the University of Texas Law School."[14]

The decision in *Sweatt* was announced the same day as a second challenge to a segregated graduate school. In Oklahoma, George McLaurin, who already had a master's degree, hoped to continue with his studies and secure a doctorate in education. He applied to the University of Oklahoma and was rejected because of his race. An Oklahoma judge, citing the *Gaines* and *Sipuel* rulings, ordered McLaurin admitted. Before Oklahoma would make a place for him, however, its legislature attached humiliating conditions to his schooling. McLaurin was given a desk in an anteroom off the main classroom, behind a sign reading, "Reserved for Colored." He had a designated library area and was prohibited from the regular reading room. He was segregated as well in the cafeteria, where he ate at a different time from the white students. While he sued to correct those demeaning impositions on his schooling, the school altered some of them, but when he came to the Court in 1950, McLaurin still was the subject of practices intended to emphasize his remove from his fellow students: He sat alone in a row of classroom desks, he had his own place in the library, and though he now was permitted to eat at the same time as the white students, he sat alone there as well.[15] The Court recognized that even if it removed the barriers to his integration, McLaurin's fellow students might shun him; still, the Court could not help but find that isolating McLaurin by law was depriving him of a fully meaningful education. "There is a vast difference—a Constitutional difference," Vinson wrote for the Court, "between restrictions imposed by the state which prohibit the intellectual commingling of students, and the refusal of individuals to commingle where the state presents no such bar."[16]

*McLaurin* represented a particularly important advance for the Court, though it took that step reluctantly and almost invisibly. George McLaurin had access to the same classrooms and library as his white counterparts; only the obnoxious conditions of that access differentiated him. It was his separation from his fellow students that caused the inequality of his education, the Court realized. The restrictions that set McLaurin apart from his fellow, white students "impair and inhibit his ability to study, to engage in discussions and exchange views with other students, and, in general, to learn his profession," Vinson said for the unanimous Court.[17] With that recognition, the Court was tantalizingly close to saying that segregation was inequality. It had admitted, after all, that separation within a school denied a black student equal protection. How, then, could it help but conclude that the exclusion from a school itself would also constitute a constitutional offense? And yet the Vinson Court could not quite bring itself to say that.

Thus, while the decisions in *McLaurin* and *Sweatt* opened educational opportunities for the plaintiffs, they did not, as some have written, represent a "chipping away" at *Plessy*. In fact, the Court specifically refused to accept Marshall's attempt to coax it into using the cases to strike down separate-but-equal. "Broader issues have been urged for our consideration," Vinson wrote. But, he added, "we adhere to the principle of deciding constitutional questions only in the context of the particular case before the Court."[18] The justices were prepared to enforce *Plessy* and demand equal facilities for black students; they were not ready, under Vinson, to accept the notion that separate facilities were by definition unequal.

As the Court waded cautiously through the school segregation debate, blacks were challenging a range of other Jim Crow laws and traditions. The white primary—Southern Democratic primaries in which only whites were permitted to vote—was under assault, as was segregation in public accommodations and transportation. Enlightened public opinion was moving, however haltingly, against those who separated black and white. The fight against Hitler inevitably cast questions back upon the United States: If racism was so invidious in Nazi Germany, how could it be easily tolerated at home? The rise of Communist Russia also gave poignancy to Jim Crow. Again, the question for segregationists was a hard one when posed against the nation's international objectives: How could America denounce sham elections in Communist countries when it denied the vote and education to its own black citizens?

Those doubts were reinforced by the 1944 publication of *An American Dilemma*, Gunnar Myrdal's epic work of sociology, a two-volume study of American race relations as pathology. Myrdal's candid exploration of sexuality and the fear of miscegenation recast racism not just in moral but also in psychological terms, and humiliating ones at that. Moreover, his accumulation of anecdotal and statistical information made his findings difficult to ignore. Myrdal instantly became a villain to much of America's white South, which pounced on his socialist leanings and cast him as an outside interloper interfering in long-established customs and mores. But America's liberal intelligentsia now had its antisegregation text, seemingly refutable only by *ad hominem* attacks on the author.

Blacks and whites were integrating in other aspects of American life as well, though not without difficulty. The most notable of those breakthroughs came in 1947, when Jackie Robinson joined the Brooklyn Dodgers. Robinson endured cat-calls, death threats, and the sustained attack on his health and humanity, but he played with breathtaking skill and spirit, and even the tumult around him could not keep him from winning the Rookie of the Year Award. With time, Robinson's grace and talent won over many of those initially hostile to the integration of the national pastime and cleared the way for many other blacks to follow. Earl Warren—while governor of California and, as always, an inveterate baseball fan—was among those who cheered Robinson's arrival. For Warren, Robinson appealed to two sources of pride, his love of baseball and of California. Robinson was raised in Southern California—the "Pride of Pasadena," as his hometown liked to call him—and educated in the same university system as Warren.

If white and black baseball players could coexist, then why not white and black soldiers? On July 26, 1948, President Truman signed Executive Order 9981. In it, he declared that there "shall be equality of treatment and opportunity" throughout the military. Truman did not order desegregation overnight, and his language re-flected the strong sense that integration was best handled slowly. The new policy, according to the order, "shall be put into effect as rapidly as possible, having due re-gard to the time required to effectuate any necessary changes without impairing ef-ficiency or morale."[19]

At the end of the decade, the cause of black equality received yet another ad-vance. In 1950, the same year that the Court decided *Sweatt* and *McLaurin*, Ralph Bunche became the first black American to win the Nobel Peace Prize, awarded for his diplomatic work in pursuit of peace in the Middle East; in that light, it was dif-ficult for any but hardened racists to claim intellectual inferiority for blacks.

And yet those signs of progress were sometimes hard to spot on the landscape of American racism in the early 1950s. Lynchings were rare but still occurred. In eight states, most public facilities were segregated; eleven required Negroes to ride in the backs of buses; fourteen states segregated mental patients; six prohibited black and white prisoners from being chained together. And in the area of educa-tion, seventeen states required school segregation, while another four allowed it. The District of Columbia, home of the federal government, practiced segrega-tion.[20] And though much of intellectual America had moved away from it, the practice was not yet consigned to ignominy. As late as 1956, William Faulkner, him-self a winner of the Nobel Prize and the great sage of the South, counseled Ameri-can blacks not to claim their freedom too quickly. Faulkner's rejoinder to the NAACP: "Go slow now."[21]

It was against that backdrop that Marshall and the NAACP took a brave step as the 1950s opened. One week after the Court decided *Sweatt* and *McLaurin*, Marshall convened a meeting of lawyers and professors to plot a strategy for ending segregation "once and for all."[22] Later that month, an NAACP conference approved a resolution adopting the policy that all pleadings in all education cases going forward would be "aimed at obtaining education on a non-segregated basis and that no relief other than that will be acceptable."[23] That was a daring departure, highly controversial within the NAACP itself. Despite the victories that the organization had won for individual plaintiffs, no one could be sure whether the Supreme Court was willing to reconsider separate-but-equal schools. The Court had, after all, upheld the notion time and again, even in rulings favoring Negro plaintiffs. Just as troubling was the possible reaction of the NAACP's own base. The school equalization cases had scored substantial victories, and even some of the most stubbornly segregated states in America were moving to improve Negro schools in order to head off litigation. To drop such a successful strategy just as its results were beginning to show was, for Marshall and his colleagues, to risk the support of their clients. Still, staying the course was perilous as well. It meant a nearly endless series of lawsuits aimed at equalizing schools one state or community at a time. That road was long and expensive. And its pursuit would always be halfhearted, as it forced Marshall to swallow the principle of segregation in order to help those victimized by it. However cautious he was as a litigator—and Marshall was a decidedly careful lawyer—he also was a black man tired of the indignities that his nation permitted to be served upon him.

And so as the 1950s began, Marshall and the NAACP traversed the American South, identifying school districts and plaintiffs that might give them their landmark case. Eventually, five lawsuits—one each from Kansas, South Carolina, Virginia, Delaware, and the District of Columbia—would be consolidated into a single action. Collectively, they would become known as *Brown v. Board of Education* (actually, the D.C. case would be decided separately, but in the popular imagination, all five cases were lumped together). Individually, they began in the modest and personal struggles of families resolved to secure the best life possible for their young children.

The man for whom it was named was Oliver Brown. Brown was a welder and a pastor, a union member but not, interestingly, a member of the NAACP. He was a quiet man, a veteran, married to a beauty queen. One of his main complaints about his daughter's school was not that it was inferior to the local white school but that his little girl, Cheryl, was forced to cross a rail yard to get there when the closer, whites-only school would not have subjected her to that danger. Brown was not the first to file his lawsuit—that honor went to the South Carolina parents—but he was chosen as the lead plaintiff in part because he was a man (NAACP lawyers saw that as potentially an advantage), in part because his union membership protected him to some degree from reprisals, and in part because his solid personal résumé rebutted the stereotype of NAACP members as radicals. In addition, placing the challenge to Topeka's school board at the top of the litigation highlighted the fundamental issue—that of segregation, not of unequal facilities. Of the school district defendants, Topeka stood out in that it offered a remarkably sound education to its black children. It was, however, a segregated education, and on February 28, 1951, the NAACP filed suit on behalf of Oliver Brown to end it.[24]

After a trial in June 1951, the three-judge panel overseeing the case unanimously upheld Topeka's segregation law and concluded that the facilities for white and black students were sufficiently equal to be constitutional under the separate-but-equal doctrine. Within the ruling against the plaintiffs, however, was a finding by the Court that would come to play an important role in the ultimate outcome. School segregation, the Court concluded,

> has a detrimental effect upon the colored children. The impact is greater when it has the sanction of the law; for the policy of separating the races is usually interpreted as denoting the inferiority of the negro group. A sense of inferiority affects the motivation of a child to learn. Segregation with the sanction of the law, therefore, has a tendency to [retard] the educational and mental development of negro children and to deprive them of some of the benefits they would receive in a racial[ly] integrated school system.[25]

The Kansas court could not bring itself to read away *Plessy;* the case was, after all, the work of the United States Supreme Court and still stood as the law. But it had come a long way from accepting that segregation bore no indignity other than what blacks read into it. In Kansas, the Court had announced it was objectively bad for blacks. A pillar of the sociological reasoning in *Plessy* fell quietly.

Delaware, although also a border state, practiced a less benign, more nakedly venal racism. There, a white woman named Sarah Bulah fumed that the bus for white boys and girls would pass her house every day without stopping, while Sarah had to drive her adopted little girl, Shirley, two miles to the Negro school. Sarah Bulah complained, was rebuffed, and sued. All of that was grindingly predictable, but the Delaware litigation was assigned to a decidedly atypical judge named Collins Seitz. He visited the white and Negro schools and examined for himself the facilities. The white school, No. 29, had lush grounds, with pines and roses, a nurse's office, and an auditorium. At Shirley Bulah's school, the urinals were broken; there was no auditorium or nurse's office, just a first-aid kit for emergencies.[26] Like the Kansas court, Seitz could not rule that segregation itself was unconstitutional. He could and did find, however, that the state had failed to provide equal educational facilities to its Negroes, and he too found that segregation was itself harmful: "I conclude from the testimony that in our Delaware society, State-imposed segregation in education itself results in the Negro children, as a class, receiving educational opportunities which are substantially inferior to those available to white children otherwise similarly situated."[27] Having registered those findings,

Seitz then shockingly ordered the white schools integrated. Of the cases that came to the Supreme Court under the banner of *Brown*, only the one from Delaware was appealed by the government.

Kansas and Delaware lay on the periphery of the Old South. South Carolina and Virginia were its political and cultural center. Rural Clarendon County in South Carolina was the testing ground for the NAACP's attack on segregation in a decidedly inhospitable forum, a little sharecropper community well below what Marshall playfully but ominously called the "Smith-and-Wesson line." Clarendon County was overwhelmingly black—approximately 70 percent of its residents—so any desegregation of that district necessarily would place white children in the minority of an integrated district, a prospect that many Southerners found all but unimaginable. Even equalizing facilities was anathema in Clarendon. Black children attended schools in shacks, often without electricity or plumbing. In a district with three times as many black children as white children, the district spent $282,000 to educate its blacks and $395,000 to educate its whites.[28] Preserving that inequity was high on the list of Clarendon County's white priorities, and blacks signed the lawsuit at their peril, but did so anyway. When it was filed, Harry Briggs, a local mechanic, war veteran, and father of five children, topped the alphabetical listing of plaintiffs. Briggs promptly lost his job—the service station where he worked was owned by the mayor—and his wife lost hers at a local motel.[29]

Despite threats and punishments, the case moved forward under Marshall's personal direction and with the prodding of a rebellious local judge, J. Waties Waring, once a member of South Carolina's political and social establishment but by the early 1950s a renegade whose divorce had ostracized him from his former peers. So itching for a fight was Waring that when Marshall initially left the door open for Waring to rule against Clarendon's schools by finding the black and white schools unequal rather than by attacking segregation itself, Waring rejected the pleading and urged Marshall to redraft it as a direct challenge. Chastened, Marshall did, and then the case was put before a three-judge panel. Waring could deliver only his own vote, however, so when the Briggs case made its way to the Supreme Court, it did so on appeal of a lower-court rejection of the NAACP lawsuit.

Virginia's case was different from South Carolina's in at least one important respect: it was started not by parents fearful for their children but by children themselves. On the morning of April 23, 1951, black students at Robert R. Moton High School in Prince Edward County went on strike to protest overcrowding and leaky, badly heated buildings that had been erected as temporary facilities but then had been allowed to stay. The students were led by a sixteen-year-old girl, Barbara Johns, whose charismatic uncle, Vernon Johns, was an early and inspirational advocate of desegregation on moral and religious grounds. Barbara learned her uncle's lessons, and added to it a resourceful mischief of her own. Eager to rouse students but not to implicate their sympathetic principal, she or one of her friends placed a call to the principal that morning to say that two students were in trouble with the police downtown. He rushed to their aid, not realizing he'd been tricked. Then Barbara Johns had notes delivered to each classroom informing teachers and students that they were wanted at an assembly. Puzzled teachers arrived with their classes, and the adults were told to leave. When they resisted, young Barbara Johns rapped her shoe and shouted, "I want you all out of here!" They left the room.[30]

This was not the NAACP's way to launch a lawsuit, and the students' demands—mainly for better buildings—did not conform to the organization's newly adopted pledge to attack segregation directly rather than pressing merely for improved conditions at segregated schools. But when the students wrote to the NAACP to ask for help, the organization sent along Oliver Hill and Spottswood Robinson, two Howard graduates and veterans of the school equalization lawsuits. The lawyers told the students that they would file suit if the students would agree to press for ending segregation, if the students would end their strike, and if their parents would join in the litigation. The matter was put before the community on May 3, when students and parents gathered in church. There, Barbara Johns addressed her friends, her parents, her neighbors. After she finished, Reverend Francis Griffin spoke for all: "Anybody who would not back these children after they stepped out on a limb is not a man," he said. The community approved the lawsuit, and it was filed on May 23, 1951.[31]

It took the Virginia court just one week to rule against the plaintiffs from Prince Edward County, in the heart of old Virginia, and though "frankness required admission" that at least the buildings at Moton High School required improvement, the court declined even to issue an injunction to assure that. Instead, the court accepted the school district's promise that improvements were on the way. In seventeen other counties and eight cities, it concluded, black schools were "better" than white ones. The court refused to order desegregation of any type at any school.[32]

The last of the cases that found their way under the popular banner of *Brown* arose in the District of Columbia. *Bolling v. Sharpe* was the only one to work its way through the trial courts without significant input from the NAACP, and it was distinguished from the others by the applicable law. Congress itself had sanctioned segregated schooling in the same period that it adopted the Fourteenth Amendment, so any analysis of its intentions for the District was complicated for the plaintiffs by the clear evidence of Congress's actions. Moreover, because the Fourteenth Amendment established "equal protection" only for residents of the states, it did not reach the District, which lay under federal jurisdiction. Different constitutional principles thus applied to the issues in the District case.

And yet while bound by different law, the black students of the nation's capital experienced conditions that were woefully familiar to those of their counterparts across the Deep and peripheral South. Overcrowding was common, and facilities were in disrepair. Like Barbara Johns and the Moton High School students, some children in the District struck to protest. In this case, it was a junior high school whose halls suddenly went quiet in the face of youthful unrest. Their parents sued the school board, which refused to budge even as the strike dragged on. That lawsuit, filed by Marshall's old mentor, Charles Houston, initially sought improved conditions. It was rejected. After the Supreme Court handed down its decisions in *Sweatt* and *McLaurin,* eleven black students attempted in the fall of 1950 to enroll in the white school. They were denied again, and this time their lawsuit sought not to equalize conditions but to gain them admittance into an integrated school. They were represented now by a new lawyer, James Nesbrit, who replaced Houston. Charles Houston spent decades in the urgent struggle to achieve equality for his people. He yearned to hear the United States Supreme Court command that equality, and he trained a generation of lawyers to pursue it. But Houston would not live to see the day he imagined his whole adult life. He died in 1949.

As those five cases worked their way through their appeals, the justices of the United States Supreme Court knew that history was bearing down on them. They dithered as long as they could, uncomfortable with the notion of being backed into the corner of a direct challenge to separate-but-equal. By 1952, the time for stalling had run out. On June 9, 1952, the justices voted to hear *Brown* and *Briggs,* and then later consolidated those cases with the remaining three. Argument was set for December 1952, conveniently after the November elections.[33]

The arguments that day—and the briefs that set the stage for them—were divided by the individual cases, with *Brown* going first, followed by *Briggs* and then the rest. Each of the individual presentations had their moments, but the marquee lawyering matchup came in *Briggs,* the South Carolina litigation. There, for the plaintiffs, appeared Thurgood Marshall, fluent in his case and his area, disarmingly folksy, penetratingly smart. For the state of South Carolina appeared an even more familiar face to the justices. John W. Davis was arguably the most esteemed lawyer in America. No man had argued more cases before the United States Supreme Court. So wide was his fame and great his renown that the Democratic Party nominated him for president in 1924. Davis was staid and careful, a brilliant orator, a dignified relic of the antebellum South. In 1952, Davis was nearing the end of his extraordinary career, and his life and work were formed in the era of Jim Crow. Raised in that world and steeped in its customs, Davis could not fathom life apart from it. He accepted South Carolina's invitation to defend segregation in schools and ultimately worked without a fee. In one respect, Davis and his adversary had a heritage in common: Segregation was Thurgood Marshall's world, too. But far from romanticizing it, he felt its insult, the presumption that assumed his inferiority to men such as Davis. Marshall was younger and less tested than Davis. But Marshall came to Court with the strong sense that history was to be his. And he, like Davis, arrived as both advocate and symbol—of an idea, of a time, and of a place.

On December 9, 1952, Marshall and Davis waited their turns as the session began and the lawyers from the Topeka litigation started off. Then, just after 3:15 P.M., Marshall took the lectern. Exquisitely prepared by long nights of brainstorming with his colleagues in little hotel rooms with plenty of Jack Daniel's, Marshall seemed at ease as he made his case and fended off the questions of the justices, particularly the inquiring Frankfurter, famous for shredding the incomplete arguments of lawyers just as he had once done to those of his students. Nor did Marshall shrink from wit. When Justice Jackson inquired as to whether Native Americans might find comfort in Marshall's desegregation claims for blacks and suggested that Marshall might want to bring some lawsuits on their behalf as well, the lawyer drolly replied, "I have a full load now, Mr. Justice."[34]

Davis was not easily outdone. The justices knew him well and respected him. They listened intently as he laid out his argument, barely interrupting him. When reminded by Justice Burton that the Constitution is "a living document" and asked whether changed circumstances did not compel new readings of its mandates, Davis responded as best he could: "[C]ircumstances may bring new facts within the purview of the constitutional provision," he said, "but they do not alter, expand or change the language that the framers of the Constitution have employed."[35] The framers of the Fourteenth Amendment never contemplated that it would force integrated schools, Davis argued. No change in sociology could undermine that fact, no new customs or ideas altered the written text or the intentions of those who wrote. No act by the Supreme Court could justify rewriting the text that bound their decisions. After he and the other lawyers had finished their arguments, Davis was overhead to say to a colleague that he believed, based on the presentations and the questions of the justices, that his side was likely to win, "five to four, or maybe six to three."[36]

Much has been written about the Vinson Court's initial attempt to grapple with the desegregation cases, but any honest assessment must begin with the admission that it is impossible to know precisely how each of the justices analyzed the cases. That is in part because the justices decided at the outset not to record a tentative vote. Instead, they discussed the matter informally, with several justices keeping notes. The notes are incomplete and at times suspect, as they are refracted through the particular points of view of the justices taking them. That said, they do portray a deeply divided Court, one strained by doctrinal and philosophical differences and burdened with a leader unworthy of the case before him.

The chief justice traditionally speaks first when the brethren gather in their conference, so on that Saturday morning, Chief Justice Vinson led off. Vinson began by observing that *Plessy* remained binding and that the "body of law" arising from it upheld segregation. It was, he said, hard to "get away" from the continued acceptance of the practice under the sanction of the Court.[37] Reed, who genuinely believed in segregation (it was Reed, remember, who had refused to attend a Supreme Court Christmas party if black workers were to be invited), and Clark, who tended to follow Vinson's lead and who emphasized the Court's role in leading the South to believe segregation was appropriate, agreed. That meant that three of the Court's four Southern members were prepared to extend the practice of segregation into the second half of the twentieth century.[38] On the other side, Black was the lone Southerner to find segregation unconstitutional by the terms of his cherished Fourteenth Amendment. Burton and Minton joined him without hesitation, and Douglas, in his inimitable way, declared that the matter was "very simple for me."[39] Though he recognized the complexity of fashioning an order to abolish it and was willing to consider asking for more argument on that point, Douglas was prepared to say simply that all racial discrimination was illegal. With that, four justices stood solidly to overturn segregation and three seemed almost as determined to uphold it.

The views of the remaining two—Jackson and Frankfurter—are harder to pin down with certainty. No doubt that is because they, more than any of their brethren, were genuinely conflicted about the cases, which pitted their personal politics against their judicial philosophy. None of the justices in 1952 had a more developed record of support for black Americans than Frankfurter. He had lent his legal skills to civil rights organizations and had picked the first black clerk ever to serve a Supreme Court justice, William Coleman, who clerked for Frankfurter in 1949. There could be no doubt that Frankfurter supported school desegregation and would have cheered any president or Congress that moved for it. But it is equally true that few justices have given more thought to the duties and constraints of the judiciary—or have ever taken those matters more seriously—than Frankfurter. As the Jehovah's Witnesses cases had amply demonstrated, Frankfurter was capable of deciding cases against what he saw as society's substantive best interest in order preserve the proper place of judges.

On that December morning, Frankfurter delivered an equivocal view to the brethren. He was agitated, as he often was, by Black's certainty regarding the meaning of the Fourteenth Amendment. "How does Black know the purpose of the 14th Amendment?" Frankfurter demanded, adding that he had read all of the history of the amendments and could not conclude, as Black did, that they commanded desegregation.[40] Douglas, in his reflections on the case, put Frankfurter down as a vote to reargue the cases, but also noted that Frankfurter remarked that he "can't say it's unconstitutional to treat a negro differently than a white." Jackson, who would have listened to Frankfurter with a more sympathetic ear, noted that his colleague was prepared to strike down segregation in the District of Columbia as a violation of the due process rights of black citizens under the federal government's protection, but he, like Douglas, noted that Frankfurter wanted more argument.[41] Douglas concluded that Frankfurter would abolish segregation in the District of Columbia but sustain it in the states.[42] What seems clear, at a minimum, is that Frankfurter had yet to figure out a way to overturn segregation in the states.

Jackson joined with Frankfurter in seeing the cases "with great alarm."[43] He was, like Frankfurter, a New Deal Democrat, though one with fewer attachments to the cause of black equality. And he tended to frame cases in Frankfurter's style, pulling back from what he saw as judicial excess. Moreover, he was more comfortable in the philosophical company of Frankfurter than of Black and Douglas, whom he disliked personally. Beyond all that, Jackson was a scrupulous reader of the Constitution, an elegant and brilliant man with words. And the Constitution, as he read it, did not supply the same easy solutions that it did for Black and Douglas. There was, he told the others, "nothing in the text that says this is unconstitutional." Moreover, there was nothing in the opinions of the Court that struck the practice of school segregation and, notwithstanding Black, nothing in the history of the Fourteenth Amendment that did it, either. "On the basis of precedent," Jackson said, he would have to conclude the segregation was constitutional.[44] That had to have been wrenching for Jackson, but he believed in the law and, at least in late 1952, saw no escape from its commands.

In the months after that argument and conference, Jackson attempted to think his way through the dilemma of the segregation cases, of the law and his responsibility to it, as well as of society itself and the duties it required. His was a singular mind, searching and dedicated. Its task in those months was as great as any he had ever put it to.[45]

The tally, then, stood not far from what Davis had predicted at the end of the oral arguments. Although it is puzzling to imagine how Davis believed there could be six votes in his column, there were certainly four votes to strike school segregation, and there were almost certainly three—and possibly even a majority of five—to uphold it in the states. Indeed, Douglas would later say with certainty that had the case been decided that year, "we would have had five saying that separate but equal schools were constitutional."[46] As with the rest of Douglas's memoir, that should be regarded with skepticism. Still, he was almost certainly correct when he noted, in a memo for the files, that "it is apparent that if the cases had been decided in the 1952 Term there would have been a wide divergence of views."[47]

What happened next is Frankfurter's great contribution to the cause of American equality. Recognizing the price that the nation would pay for a divided Court on a matter of such historic magnitude, Frankfurter devised a stall. As he indicated during the conference in late 1952, he proposed holding over the cases for reargument the following term. When the brethren showed interest in that idea, Frankfurter, working with his clerk Alexander Bickel, devised a set of questions for the lawyers to research and answer. They came up with five questions probing the roots of the Fourteenth Amendment, the power of the judiciary in the absence of clear guidance from the Constitution, and the form a desegregation decree might take if the Court ordered one.[48] The attorney general was invited to share his thoughts as well, and the matter was put over until the following fall.

And then, with Frankfurter's work done, fate intervened to vindicate his stall. In the early morning hours of September 8, 1953, Vinson's smoking habit caught up with him. The decent Vinson, who tried and failed to rally his Court, succumbed to his heart attack.

The cases returned for oral argument on December 7, 1953, twelve years to the day from the Japanese attack on Pearl Harbor. This day would prove almost as historic. At 1:05 P.M., the school segregation cases were gaveled to order for their second oral argument in two years. The same cast of lawyers presented themselves to the Court. Many of the same arguments were contained in the briefs and memos of the justices. Only one thing had changed, really. The man whose hand wielded the gavel on that Monday afternoon was not Fred Vinson. He was not afraid to wrestle with the intellects of the Court or one to shrink in the face of its duty. It was a big, comfortable hand that gripped the Court's gavel that day; a man at ease with power, confident and capable, a centrist by temperament but an activist, too—a man who liked responsibility, a master of forging agreement, and a leader who refused to let doctrine blind him to real life. He was eager to translate his views of fairness and justice into a working program for America. Earl Warren held the gavel that day. The country was about to learn what that meant.

Chapter 18

# JUSTICE

*Nothing is more certainly written in the book of fate*
*than that these people are to be free.*

THOMAS JEFFERSON[1]

W HEN WARREN arrived at the Court in 1953, he came with a record
that suggested he might sympathize with the Negro plaintiffs in the
desegregation cases, but that record was incomplete and in some
ways contradictory. As a governor and as a candidate for national office, Warren had
signed the legislation ending California's Mexican schools, backed the Fair Employment Practices Commission, and spoken out favorably on civil rights. He was a Progressive Republican, which in those days represented an enlightened sliver of the
American political spectrum on race—the Democratic Party had its liberals, but the
party as a whole was freighted by its long-tenured Southern leadership. All that
seemed to suggest that Warren would fit naturally into the Court's desegregation
bloc. On the other hand, there was his shabby record in the Japanese internment debate. And though some of the country's great civil libertarians, including his new
colleagues Hugo Black and William Douglas, had fallen down in that episode as
well, Warren's testimony before the Tolan Committee during that dark period was
enough to cast doubt about how protective he would be when it came to American
blacks. Summing up Warren's civil liberties résumé as he arrived at the Court,
*Newsweek* was among those reluctant to draw firm conclusions. "The only guide to
Warren's stand," it wrote, "is his generally liberal position."[2]

In December, when the desegregation cases were reargued before the Court
with Warren now in its center seat, Warren spoke occasionally, but still said nothing to reveal himself. Beneath his opaque gaze, the advocates for the states and the

NAACP rehashed their differences, each now familiar with the arguments of the other. Marshall and his associates pleaded that the Fourteenth Amendment meant what it said, that divining the original intent of its framers was impossible given the politics surrounding it, and that even if those framers had countenanced school segregation in 1868, it did not mean that the Court could not strike it in 1953. (Historians do not rate Marshall's argument that day as particularly effective, but he did impress at least one justice. Burton, as was his habit, jotted notes and assessments of each of the lawyers who appeared before the Court; next to Marshall's name for that day, he wrote "very good." In parentheses, however, he also noted: "colored.")[3] The United States government brief and argument largely echoed those positions, concluding, too, that the history of the Fourteenth Amendment left the Court free to decide the case in favor of the NAACP.

For his side, Davis countered that intent did matter, and the existence and acceptance of segregation during the nineteenth century gave it credence. Southern states had determined that segregation was best for both races. Congress and the Court had allowed, even encouraged, the practice. As a matter of law, Davis asked, what had changed? The same Fourteenth Amendment was in place in 1953 as in 1896; how could today's Court conclude that its words or intentions were different from what they had been for decades? And how could John Davis's cherished South be blamed for adopting a practice that had, for so long, enjoyed the sanction and blessing of the same Court before which he now stood? "[S]omewhere, sometime," the old orator proclaimed, "to every principle comes a moment of repose when it has been so often announced, so confidently relied upon, so long continued, that it passes the limits of judicial discretion and disturbance."[4]

Had that moment arrived in segregation? Had the Court's tolerance of the practice, even if initially misguided, now extended across so many decades that the South had reason to believe it was constitutional and thus believe in the right to continue it? After three days of that argument, the Court took the matter under submission again and turned to that question in the privacy of its conference. It did so without obvious rancor, the differences of the justices on many matters notwithstanding. Civility, even among adversaries, was—indeed, still is—highly valued in the Supreme Court. As was the long-standing custom of the Court, the conference that December Saturday began with each justice shaking the hand of every other. The justices then took their seats in the Court's grand old conference room, seating themselves at its long table, over which so much history had been made.

Warren had neither judicial experience nor scholarly depth with which to impress his brethren. But he understood what power he did have, and he used it. He had, most plainly, the right to speak first. On that morning, December 12, 1953, he did. There was, Warren told his brethren, no way to duck the question any longer. After more than a year of argument and contemplation, after the death of one chief justice and the arrival of another, the Court was "now down to [the] point of deciding the issues."[5] And for Warren, the matter that had so vexed the Court was in fact simple. There was, he said, only one way that he could imagine for upholding segregation. *Plessy* could only stand upon the "basic premise that the Negro race is inferior."[6] The Southern states had repeatedly denied that racial superiority was the essence of racial segregation, but that was a barely concealed fiction. Plainspoken as ever, Warren simply stated what others knew but would not say: Segregation was not equally good for blacks and whites. It was created by whites and imposed on blacks, intended to protect whites from blacks and thus to extend their power over blacks. Given that, Warren said, he had come to believe that for the Court to endorse school segregation, it would have to embrace the notion of racial superiority. That, Warren added, he would not do.

Warren rumbled along in his commanding voice that Saturday morning. A slow drizzle fell outside the Court, while inside it, the chief justice's meaning washed over his colleagues. The others had yet to speak, but they knew well where one another stood, and Warren's declaration of his views now joined him with the four justices—Black, Douglas, Minton, and Burton—who had previously announced their intention to strike the practice. Five justices are a majority, so it was clear a majority had formed since Vinson's death. Almost as important, Warren's conclusion that segregation rested upon a premise of racial inferiority reframed the implications of the case for the wavering justices. It was one thing for Frankfurter, say, to resist the judicial activism required to overturn segregation; it was quite another for a man whose life and reputation were bound up in liberal causes to join a dissent that would be accused of resting on racism. Finally, Warren's presentation to the conference was important for what he did not say or do. Warren did not blame the South for its predicament; it had relied on the Court's interpretation of the Fourteenth Amendment in good faith. He did not blame the justices for their more cautious approach to *Plessy* in the years before he arrived; they had attempted to apply precedent in a thoughtful and conscientious way. Warren was not there to blame or to look back. As a governor, Warren had assumed the good will of his adversaries until it was proven otherwise. As a justice, he saw no need to change that practice.

The Court's senior justice, Hugo Black, normally would have spoken next, but he was tending to a sick family member.[7] Instead, he sent word that his views had not changed, that he continued to believe the time had come to abandon school segregation. With Black absent, the conversation moved to Stanley Reed. Later, Warren would maintain that there had "not been a division of opinion expressed on the Court at any time,"[8] but that was written after his retirement and after *Brown* was the established and accepted law of the land.[9] In fact, Reed, undoubtedly taken aback by Warren's insistence that Reed's belief in segregation implied one of white supremacy, choked out a defense of race separation. Reed insisted that segregation was based "not on inferiority but on racial differences. It protects people against mixing races." If Congress wanted to change the law, it could, Reed argued. But he stood firm on the notion that segregation was constitutional so long as the two races received substantially equal treatment, in this case in school facilities.[10]

With Warren and Reed thus staking out the poles, the rest of the justices filled in, speaking in order of their commissioning to the Court (although Warren was the junior justice, the protocol does not apply to the chief). Frankfurter was next, and Douglas recorded him as continuing to worry about the application of the Fourteenth Amendment. Always bothered by what he saw as Black's glib reading of the Amendment and its application to the states, Frankfurter stiffened in the face of the professed assurances of Warren and Black as to its application here. The "history in Congress and in this Court indicates that *Plessy* is right," Frankfurter insisted, according to Douglas.[11] But while Douglas took that as a sign that Frankfurter was considering a dissent, it seems more likely that Frankfurter was still struggling with his conscience.

Next came Douglas, about whom there was never any doubt. Douglas would strike down segregation happily and without pangs of judicial propriety. He said so crisply, wasting no time with any pretense of indecision.

Then came Jackson, who took the strange view that striking segregation was the right thing to do but that the Court should simply acknowledge its work as an act of politics, not the law. The Court, he said, "can't justify elimination of segregation as a judicial act."[12] But rather than join Reed in supporting segregation, Jackson instead proposed to have the Court adopt an admittedly political approach. His comments must have puzzled the other justices; they were sufficiently confusing for Douglas to record Jackson as a likely vote to uphold the Southern states. Jackson and Frankfurter, Douglas wrote later, "expressed the hope that the Court would not have to decide these cases but somehow avoid these decisions."[13] Warren would have none of that. As he had said in his opening remarks, the chief justice was determined to resolve the cases this term. Frankfurter and Jackson soon would be forced to choose.

The remaining three justices spoke in turn, though their comments were anticlimactic. Burton already had made clear in the prior term that he intended to abolish school segregation, and he repeated his position that day. Clark, who had for so long labored under Vinson's shadow and only now was emerging from it, spoke more ambiguously. He stressed the importance of carefully considered relief that would not antagonize Southern states or his native Texas. If such an order could be drafted, Clark said, he would reluctantly join the apparent majority forming beneath the new chief.[14] Then Minton, who despite four years on the Court remained its junior justice, added his emphatic support to the antisegregation bloc.

Before adjourning that day, Warren dealt one more significant political stroke. Normally, the justices record their tentative votes at conference, and if he is in the majority, the chief justice assigns that opinion for drafting. Here, the informal conversation made it clear that Warren was in the majority, but he asked his brethren to refrain from a vote. Once votes are cast, they are harder to change, and Warren wanted more than a majority. He wanted a solid Court, ideally a unanimous one, to speak with a single, clear voice on a matter of moral urgency. So instead of voting, the justices agreed to continue talking.[15]

Beyond preserving the Court's flexibility, Warren had at least two reasons to favor a short delay. First, he still was not the confirmed Chief Justice of the United States. Were the Court to vote on the segregation cases before he was confirmed, Southern senators surely would have voted against keeping Warren on the bench. More important, Warren knew that time played to his great strength. For although he was modest about his abilities, he never was blind to them, and Earl Warren knew that few people were better than he at persuasion. When the conference ended on December 12, 1953, Warren set out to do what he did best—work the room.

Burton's diaries and Warren's calendars for late 1953 and early 1954 illustrate the breadth and thoroughness of Warren's campaign.[16] That Saturday afternoon, during the break in the justices' conference, Warren lunched with Burton, Reed, Douglas, Clark, and Minton, effectively surrounding the two most doubtful justices with four of the most decided. Over the next five days, Warren lunched with Reed no fewer than five times, and each time took care to invite Burton and Minton, who were solidly in favor of striking segregation. In addition, Warren made sure that the justices who might antagonize Reed—Frankfurter, in particular—were not at the table; after his first lunch with the rest, the prickly Douglas did not join the group again for some time.[17]

As 1953 turned to 1954, Warren continued his small lunches, private meetings in chambers, conversations at the justices' homes, and walks around the block. Patiently but insistently, Warren urged each to consider the possibilities for the Court and country should a united group of justices lead the nation away from segregation. Alternatively, he warned of the consequences of division. An opinion of the Court upholding segregation now was impossible, he reminded those who were in doubt; the only remaining question was whether the Court would project a united voice or a conflicted one. Through those weeks, Warren suffered Frankfurter's misgivings on the role of the judiciary, and he weathered Reed's deep ambivalence about race relations. Warren was persuasive not so much because he offered new arguments or dazzling insights but rather because he listened to his colleagues' reservations and coaxed them into becoming comfortable with the ruling's inevitability. And through it all, Warren was gracious. On January 15, he hosted a lunch for all his brethren. Friends had sent Warren a hearty supply of fresh duck and pheasant; rather than store it, Warren invited the justices to join him in a feast. All attended. Eight, including Warren, had duck. Frankfurter preferred pheasant.[18]

Warren was equally tactical in the Court's weekly conferences. There, he shifted discussion from the underlying question of segregation's constitutionality to the more complex matter of how the Court should draft a decree to carry out that decision.[19] Warren's sensitivity to the pressures on the South helped soften Clark's concerns about the proposed integration of schools and also addressed Reed's fear of that result. Even Black, whose vote was never in doubt, was gravely worried about the manner in which the Court might proceed. And as the Court discussed how to frame such a decree, gradually the justices found themselves no longer talking about whether segregation was legal but rather assuming that it was not and debating how best to dispose of it. Over those weeks, they became more and more accustomed to talking about segregation in the past tense.

While Warren worked his colleagues, he too was the subject of pressure, administered in his case cloddishly by Eisenhower himself. Eisenhower was a brilliant strategist, a brave military commander, and a shrewd administrator. He understood military power as few men of any generation have, and he projected calm, capable leadership to the nation and world. But for all his many strengths, Eisenhower was a dunce on matters of race. He had allowed Herbert Brownell and the Justice Department to support desegregation in the legal filings and arguments in the *Brown* case, but the president himself never fully warmed to the idea of the government intervening to place blacks and whites together. He was sophisticated enough not to advertise his discomfort with integration, but one evening during the months that the Court was deliberating over *Brown*, Eisenhower tipped his hand to Warren.

The occasion was a White House dinner, one of the stag affairs the president hosted regularly. Warren accepted the invitation reluctantly, as the events were an occasion to talk politics, and though Warren loved few topics more, he was reluctant to discuss political matters in public, even the guarded public of a White House dinner. Still, he was not a man to say no to a president, much less the president who had appointed him, so he accepted.[20] Arriving that cold February night, Warren was seated to Eisenhower's right, and within speaking distance of them both was John W. Davis, South Carolina's lawyer in the *Brown* case. That alone was more than enough to offend Warren's sense of propriety, but as the night wore on, his tension increased as Eisenhower again and again made a point to tell Warren what a fine and impressive man Davis was. Thurgood Marshall, of course, was nowhere in sight, so Davis's presence alone demonstrated that the president's admiration for the lawyers in the desegregation cases was limited to the premier lawyer for the South, not his NAACP counterpart. Then, as the dinner ended,

Eisenhower led his guests into an adjoining room for drinks and cigars. As the two men passed from one room to the next, Eisenhower took Warren by the arm and confided in him. The Southern states, Eisenhower said to Warren, were full of good will and good intentions. "These are not bad people," the president said. "All they are concerned about is to see that their sweet little girls are not required to sit in school alongside some big overgrown Negroes."[21] Warren never forgave Eisenhower that crude and stupid remark.

As the justices discussed the segregation cases together in conference and in smaller groups of two and three, Warren found time for a short retreat. He arranged with his chauffeur, a black man, to go on an overnight tour of Southern Civil War monuments outside Washington, D.C. They headed south through Virginia, touring various sites. As afternoon slipped into evening, Warren asked his driver to stop at a local hotel for the night. The two made arrangements for the man to pick Warren up in the morning, and then Warren went inside to register, not really paying attention as his driver shrank back. Perhaps, Warren thought distractedly, he was heading for a cheaper place to stay for the night. The following morning, when the chauffeur came to pick Warren up, it was clear to the chief justice that the driver had spent the night in the car. "What happened?" Warren asked. "Didn't you go to a hotel? Have you slept here all night?"

"Well, Mr. Chief Justice," the driver replied hesitatingly, "I just couldn't find a place—couldn't find a place to . . ."

Listening to his chauffeur's halting reply, it suddenly dawned on Warren that he had brought a man to a town that would not allow him a room, that the personal assistant of the Chief Justice of the United States was not worthy of a bed in a segregated hamlet within a day's drive of the nation's capital. "I was embarrassed," Warren remembered toward the end of his life. "I was ashamed. We turned back immediately."[22]

Warren was a man who felt most strongly what he experienced directly, and on that day, he was slapped by this direct confrontation with such an odious practice. One can well imagine him in the car, the miles rolling by as he seethed at the indignity to his aide, angry with himself for creating the opportunity for that shame. Warren retained the bitter memory of that day for twenty years, telling it to his children and grandchildren and recounting it to a reporter just a few months before he died.[23]

The indignity of segregation hit Warren hard, but it was not enough, by itself, to shock the Court into action. Even as the end of the term approached, some of the justices remained doubtful about their authority to bar a practice so long sanctioned by the Court. Of the uncertain justices, none was more conflicted than Jackson. A few days before the second round of oral arguments in *Brown*, Jackson had begun to draft a long rumination on the case, one that appears to have been styled as a concurrence.[24] The justice continued to work on it in the early months of 1954, and in his memo, Jackson fretted about the implications of "judicial fiat," even when directed at so worthy a cause as Negro integration. Jackson wished that Congress would abolish segregation, but worried that if the Court did what Congress would not that it would undermine the Court's prestige and call its legitimacy into question. "Precedent, a usual source of law, is wholly against the idea that the Constitution requires not only equal facilities but mixed and unseparated use of them."[25] And yet for all his reservations, Jackson could not bring himself to uphold school segregation. Instead, nearing the end of his long memo, he concluded that Negroes had advanced so far in their years of segregation that they had "overcome the presumptions on which it was based." It was a tortuous analysis, revealing the intense strain upon Jackson as he wrestled with one of the most difficult decisions of his life.

Fortunately for Jackson, one of his clerks that term was E. Barrett Prettyman, Jr., an intellectually gifted and personally brave young man. Prettyman urged Jackson to reconsider his approach and not to make a decision undermined by its own argument. Prettyman put his thoughts down in writing, typing them up himself and hand-delivering the copy to his justice. Prettyman implored Jackson to think again, in legal as well as political terms. Whatever the Court decided, Prettyman wrote, the American people "should be made to feel that the decision is honestly arrived at, confidently espoused and basically sound. They should feel that it expresses certain truths, even if they aren't quite prepared to accept fully those truths themselves or to practice them." Jackson's clerk proposed that the justice turn his opinion upside down, beginning with the assertion that "there is no longer a basis for separate but equal facilities," and only once having stated that as a matter of law going on to express caveats or concerns. "I say this in all frankness," Prettyman wrote, "if you are going to reach the decision you do, you should not write as if you were ashamed to reach it."[26]

Reflecting on Jackson's work years later, Prettyman explained, "I thought it said some things which would give grounds particularly to those in the South who were combating any decision striking down segregation."[27] Prettyman knew Jackson intended no such thing. Prettyman's heroism was his willingness to tell his justice of the trap he was creating; the young man's grace was in his ability to say that convincingly.

By the end of February, Warren was confident that most of the wavering justices were preparing to join him. It was then that he brought the matter to a head. In his memoirs, Warren recorded that the justices first voted in late February, but others at the Court believe it more probably occurred in early March, and that seems more likely, since Warren received his belated Senate confirmation on March 1.[28] Whatever the date, it sealed the outcome. A clear majority now was on board to rule for the NAACP plaintiffs; the exact number would depend on the opinion itself. The justices urged Warren to write, believing that the Court would speak most authoritatively in the voice of its chief. And so Warren took pencil to yellow legal paper in the privacy of his chambers and began to work. Revising as he went, the new chief justice sketched the opinion in broad, simple strokes.

Warren opened with a straightforward if uninspired recitation of the cases and their histories, recounting briefly their route to the United States Supreme Court. That section ended with the Court's assumption of jurisdiction, then left a space in which Warren intended to recount the basic question underlying the litigation. By page 3, Warren had turned to the reargument and the questions relating to the Fourteenth Amendment and the intentions of its authors. Here, Warren reached the conclusion that the justices had finally come to, and relied most heavily on the presentation of the government to bolster his conclusion. "It [the government] concluded that the Legislative history and the contemporary statements . . . of the Amendment as it applied to these cases were"—and here Warren struggled for the right word, crossing out several attempts before writing, "inconclusive." "This is not surprising," he added, "because neither the Constitution itself nor any of its amendments have been adopted under circumstances comparable to those in 1868 surrounding the adoption of the Fourteenth Amendment."[29]

Specifically, Warren wrote, the "fratricidal warfare around the status of the negro in American life" created such turmoil and division in the nation that its shadow over the debates on the Fourteenth Amendment clouded its true intentions. This was not Warren at his finest. The Constitution itself, after all, was written in the aftermath of a bitter war and agreed to amid deep divisions over the status of Negroes. How, then, could one rely on the intentions of its framers if not on those of the Fourteenth Amendment? But he was new and still drafting.

By page 5, Warren was writing more quickly and more forcefully. The pages were clearer, with fewer evident reconsiderations. Here Warren turned to *Plessy v. Ferguson,* and he took his sharpest aim at the Court itself. Warren accused the 1896 Court of attempting to "serve two masters, 1, the master of equality under the laws and 2, the master of racial concept as it existed at the time in the Southern states of the Union." After that sentence, he added an elaboration in the margin: "It endeavored to retain both the philosophy of the Dred Scott case and the principle of the Fourteenth Amendment." He then turned to the judicial history that had arisen from that tension, leaving a space to later insert the details of the Court's line of education cases that attempted to implement the doctrine of separate-but-equal.

Concluding that passage, Warren turned to his sociological argument: Whatever the framers had believed in 1868 and whatever the Court had meant by its attempt to balance equality and social customs, the changing nature of education had rendered both moot. Here Governor Warren was comfortable expounding. Whereas public education was "not an accepted fact" at the time of the Fourteenth

Amendment's adoption, contemporary public education, Warren noted, represented the "major function and expense of local and, in many states, state government." The relationship between students, parents, and government was, in contemporary life, a highly intertwined one, he went on. Students were required to attend school, and parents allowed school officials certain rights of supervision and discipline. In return, schools were responsible for equipping their students for "a place in local and national life." It may not have been true in the nineteenth century, but in the twentieth century, Warren wrote, "No child can reasonably be expected to succeed in life today if he is deprived of the opportunity of an education."

Those sentences represented an important and fateful choice. With them, Warren was deliberately confining his decision to education, thus limiting its attack on *Plessy v. Ferguson.* For while *Plessy* sanctioned all manner of segregation, Warren built an argument only for striking it down in schools. Children might, after all, be expected to succeed in life despite the inconvenience or indignity of separate-but-equal railroad cars, just not classrooms. By limiting the scope of his ruling, Warren shrank the opportunity for resistance, a tactic deliberately intended to soften *Brown*'s immediate impact. In addition, its emphasis on the growing vitality of schools allowed him to avoid a direct confrontation with those who believed they had built their schools in compliance with both custom and law. They had done nothing wrong, Warren was saying in effect. It was just that times had changed. In retrospect, limiting the scope of *Brown* would prove a weakness in the decision, as the Court relied on its holdings to justify desegregation of other institutions. It was difficult to see later how *Brown* supplied the rationale for desegregating beaches or water fountains, say, when it so explicitly identified the harm caused to children in schools. But in 1954, Warren was principally concerned with overcoming the expected resistance to school desegregation. He was not ready to fight a wider war.

Having done what he could to limit the ruling, Warren then built to the decision's high point, framed as a question and then answered. He was at page 8 now, and it is clear from his draft that he labored over it. Sentences were crossed out, words and other sentences inserted. By the time he was finished, the page was covered in tiny script, thoughts presented, abandoned, and revised. But the stirring, simple words that would mark *Brown*'s ultimate passage were there, in Warren's hand: "Does segregation [and here Warren inserted the following three words; emphasis added] *of school children* solely on the basis of color, even though the physical facilities may be equal, deprive the minority group of equal opportunities in the educational system? We believe that it does."

Warren there added a memorable margin note that revealed much about its author: "To separate [Negro children] from others of their age solely because of their color puts the mark of inferiority not only on their status in the community but upon their little hearts and minds in a fashion that is unlikely ever to be undone."

If Warren's section on education was the governor writing, this was the father, the man so hurt by Honey Bear's loneliness that he bought her a pony; the man so shattered by her illness that he wept in the hospital hallway; the father so attentive to his adopted son that he took him as his own and never gave him reason to feel distant from his siblings; the son who looked up to his own limited father, only to see him murdered; the man so guarded with so many of his feelings and yet so singularly vulnerable to the pain of children. How could such a man not be moved by wounded "little hearts and minds"? Warren felt for those black children. And where Earl Warren's heart went, his sense of fairness followed.

Warren finished his work sometime in late April. On April 29, 1953, he turned it over to a young man he had met barely seven months earlier.[30] Earl Pollock was one of the bright young clerks whose time with the United States Supreme Court has enlarged its thinking even as it prepared them for their futures in the law. Pollock was a graduate of Northwestern Law School and had won a coveted clerkship with Chief Justice Vinson. He arrived in the heat of a Washington summer in 1953 and settled into the imposing surroundings of his new workplace. Vinson was a congenial boss, and Pollock liked him. One night in September, Pollock and his wife gave the chief justice a ride home to his residential hotel. Vinson seemed in good health and cheer. Two days later, word arrived over the radio that Vinson was dead. As the nation grieved, so did Pollock. And for him, the death of the chief justice also meant a potentially abrupt conclusion to Pollock's own service to the Court. "I was very unclear in my mind about whether my clerkship had ended," he remembered.[31] He was temporarily assigned to Black and began sifting through offers to join one of several Washington law firms. But one of Warren's first stops upon arriving at the Court was in his new chambers, where Pollock and two other clerks, as well as secretary Margaret McHugh, anxiously awaited his first words. After hearty handshakes, Warren assured Vinson's team that he wanted them all to stay on. Relieved, Pollock went to work for his new boss, struck, as virtually all new Warren acquaintances were, by the radiant vitality of the man.

Pollock never saw the yellow sheets of legal paper upon which Warren recorded his initial thoughts. Warren's secretary typed those for him. But what he received were Warren's words, along with specific instructions that illustrated Warren's hopes for the final product. The opinion was to be kept short so that newspapers would reprint it. It was to be written simply, because its audience was not meant to be just lawyers and judges but the millions of laypeople whose lives would turn on its reasoning. It had to be, Warren stressed, "accepted and understood by the American public."[32]

Pollock took the draft home and went to work. He kept intact much of Warren's recitation of the case history, though he amplified it considerably. With what he called the "hubris of youth,"[33] Pollock tossed out Warren's inartful rendering of the intent of the Fourteenth Amendment's authors, substituting instead a more thoughtful examination of the gaps in the congressional record. Pollock retained Warren's passages on the evolving nature of public education and found ways to elaborate while still holding on to the essence of Warren's analysis. He worked around the clock, energized by the thrill of writing legal history, writing in longhand, barely pausing. In the end, his work adopted the best of Warren's cool reasonableness and of his calm, signature phrasing while dropping some of his least careful legal reasoning. Finally, Pollock realized in the drafting that Warren could not resolve all five cases in one opinion, since the Fourteenth Amendment was directed at the states and thus could not be construed to apply to the District of Columbia.

Pollock straggled back to work on Monday morning, his rewritten *Brown* opinion in hand, along with his recommendation for the separate opinion in *Bolling* and for some of the language that it might contain. Under no circumstances would Warren sanction opinions that struck segregation in the states but preserved it in the nation's capital, and Pollock proposed a way to avoid that. The Fifth Amendment bars the federal government from depriving any person of "life, liberty, or property, without due process of law." "Liberty," as interpreted by the courts, includes the "full range of conduct which the individual is free to pursue," and thus denying black children of their right to an equal education represented an unwarranted intrusion on their liberty. Happy to see a way out of the conundrum, Warren readily agreed to Pollock's argument and sent his clerks to work on a separate opinion in *Bolling*.

Warren's other clerks set about that work, and the draft that they completed and that Warren approved was, in its own way, a clearer expression of Warren's heart. Writing there, Warren authoritatively proclaimed that the due process clause, like the Fourteenth Amendment, stemmed "from our American ideal of fairness."[34] One might well ask, Whose idea of fairness? But Warren was profoundly confident of his own footing. If he knew one thing when he saw it, it was fairness. He was not to be disabused of his abiding intuition when it came to simple matters of right and wrong. In an ironic capstone, given his own shameful conduct in the Japanese internment cases, Warren now cited the reasoning from that period in support of desegregation. The majority in *Korematsu v. United States* had upheld the internment but warned that racial classifications were to be permitted only when they served an important government objective—in that case, national security. Segregation served no such legitimate purpose, Warren now wrote, so the same rules that upheld his views of the internment now upheld his views on desegregating schools. Warren's most revealing line in *Bolling*, one suggested by Pollock but accepted by his boss, was this: "In view of our decision that the Constitution prohibits the states from maintaining racially segregated public schools, it would be unthinkable that the same Constitution would impose a lesser duty on the Federal Government."[35] For Warren, it was "unthinkable" because the Constitution was a good and fair document written for a good and fair country. In such a country, it was "unthinkable" that acts of manifest unfairness could be constitutional.

The opinions written, Warren circulated them for suggestions and votes— "joins," as they are called at the Court. It was May 8, a Saturday, when Warren and his clerks hand-delivered copies of their work to the justices, some at work, others at home. Hugo Black, indomitable on his home tennis court, got his copy there. He put it aside and read it when he finished his game.[36] Others jumped to it more quickly, and liked what they saw. Burton, who had supported desegregation from the beginning, read Warren's work and recorded his reaction in his diary. It was, he wrote, "a magnificent job that may win a unanimous Court."[37]

Unanimity was still not guaranteed, however. One of the justices who received his copy from the chief himself was Robert Jackson, and he took it lying down. Jackson had suffered a heart attack on March 30, and by the time the Court was at last coming to grips with *Brown,* he was seriously ill. Warren, ever solicitous, wrote comfortingly to Jackson after the heart attack and visited him in the hospital.[38] With an opinion to share, Warren took it to the justice on Thursday, May 13.[39] Prettyman was with Jackson when Warren arrived, and the younger man excused himself while the two justices spoke. Then, informed by a nurse that Warren had departed, Prettyman reentered the room, and Jackson handed him the opinion. "Go read it," he said. For more than a year, Jackson had agonized about this moment, had turned himself into knots trying to rationalize a decision that squared his politics with his belief in his role as a justice. Prettyman had tried his best to help Jackson in that struggle, and now the justice lay ill, the climax at hand. Prettyman took the opinion, left the room, read it, and then returned, searching Jackson's face for a sign of his response. What Prettyman saw was relief, relief that the opinion was one he could join. It was, Jackson believed, "a master work."[40] Jackson's hard-won vote was now secure.

Frankfurter, too, now set aside his reservations and joined the gathering confidence of his brethren. "He saw this movement toward unanimity and clearly felt that was the most important thing," one of his clerks recalled later. "So he was ready to jump on the bandwagon."[41] Being Frankfurter, he continued to tinker, suggesting small changes, some of which Warren adopted. Clark also agreed to join, and his only request was a trivial one: One footnote citing the social science evidence on the harmful effects of discrimination cited an author, identifying him only as "Clark." Justice Clark asked that the author's initial be added so that no one would think he was the researcher in question. Later, Warren would have cause to regret having not looked more carefully at that footnote. For now, he agreed to Clark's request without hesitation and left the rest of the footnote as written.

The most stalwart defender of segregation among the brethren had been Stanley Reed. He had practiced it, argued for it, and defended it. But Warren was a hard man to resist, and in this case Reed's dignity and patriotism both made him susceptible to the chief's main line of argument. The Court was going to strike segregation with or without Reed; the only question was whether his dissent, should he offer one, would accomplish anything for the country he had so long served or whether it would merely divide and prolong conflict over the institution of segregation. At some point, Warren brought the matter to the point. "Stan," the chief said to his colleague, "you're all by yourself now. You've got to decide whether it's really the best thing for the country."[42] Reed held out for the promise that the South would be given time to implement the Court's order. Once so assured, he joined. And with that, the prospect of a dissent in *Brown* disappeared.

Earl Warren had done in less than a year what had perplexed and befuddled Fred Vinson for his entire tenure. He had united his brilliant Court into a single voice on an issue of moral urgency. On May 15, the justices met at the regular Saturday conference and voiced their approval for the final drafts of *Brown* and *Bolling*. Both were unanimous. It was, Burton noted to his diary, "a major accomplishment for [Warren's] leadership."[43] Had the matter been decided a year earlier, Burton speculated, it would have come out 6–3 for striking segregation, precisely the sort of divided Court that would have encouraged segregationists in the belief that theirs was a defensible idea.[44]

That Sunday was the first sunny weekend day of the month along the Eastern Seaboard, and families celebrated with days outdoors. In Brooklyn that afternoon, the Dodgers split a double-header in front of a sellout crowd; fans cheered as Jackie Robinson was intentionally walked in the sixth, and then Gil Hodges made the Reds pay for it when he hit a grand slam to score Robinson, Pee Wee Reese, and Duke Snider. Across town, Willie Mays made a sensational catch in the deep reaches of the Polo Grounds to end the Braves' fourth inning, then homered in the fifth, leading the Giants to a win in their nightcap.

In Washington, Warren spent the day in the company of his colleague William O. Douglas doing what Douglas loved most. They hiked along the C&O Canal, an old route from Washington out to Maryland that ran along the banks of the Potomac River.[45] As in New York, it was a beautiful day, cool in the morning, and warming as the two met at eleven-thirty for their walk. It grew warmer still as the sun beat down on the backs of those two colleagues joined together at a pivotal moment in the history of the country they both served.

Douglas and Warren had much in common. Both were born in the closing years of the nineteenth century. Both were raised in the West before coming East to find their places at the head of a nation, dreaming first of the presidency but finding their ways blocked there, settling in instead at the Court. Both were outdoorsmen, though of different types: Warren hunted and fished, enjoyed nature in the style of men of his generation; Douglas was a more modern environmentalist, one touched by the poetry of wilderness. The canal along which he and Warren walked that day was a particular love. When the *Washington Post* had dared to suggest a highway for Douglas's prized 185 miles of canal, the justice challenged the paper's editorial writers to join him on a hike and did so with the poetry of which he was capable. Douglas predicted that anyone who came to these woods would "hear the roar of wind in thickets; he would see strange islands and promontories through the fantasy of fog; he would discover the glory there is in the first flower of spring, the glory there is even in a blade of grass; the whistling wings of ducks would make silence have new values for him."[46] The writers accepted the challenge and then, bowing to the intrepid Douglas, backed down, as he had predicted. The paper soon withdrew its endorsement of the highway.

Warren and Douglas may have come to their positions by different routes, but on this glorious spring morning, they set off together along the river. Douglas probably moved quickly. He usually did. Warren, a languid bear to Douglas's gazelle, would have struck a more temperate pace. If their common ideals reflected that which Warren and Douglas shared, their gaits hinted at their profound differences as well. Douglas could be a bitter man, estranged from colleagues and family, accustomed by then, his fifteenth year on the Court, to dissenting, often just with Black. For Douglas, judging had become easy. He was secure to a fault, insufferable at times, unwavering and uncompromising in his judgments of the law and of others. With him that day was, by comparison, a neophyte of judging, a justice on the eve of his first major decision. Warren was a more compassionate and open man than Douglas, immersed in a stable and happy family from which he drew great comfort. Warren did not have Douglas's crackling genius, nor did he share Douglas's bleak isolation from those around him. But William Douglas did not begrudge Earl Warren his intelligence, and Warren did not object to Douglas's iconoclasm. That afternoon, these two men—the Court's established, cranky genius and its still new, genial leader—walked the canal with the knowledge that within hours, they would make history together.

The justices had gone to lengths to protect against leaks in the desegregation cases, but by Monday morning, word had begun to spread within the small circle that surrounds the Court. Warren, who had had dinner with Attorney General Herbert Brownell on Saturday, tipped him off that Monday would be a smart day to show up at the Court; Brownell was in the audience, as was Secretary of State Dean Acheson. So was Nina Warren, making a rare appearance at her husband's workplace, this time arriving with a surprise for Warren. Nina was accompanied by their old friend Helen MacGregor, there to seek admission to the Court bar. Despite the magnitude of the occasion, Warren did a double-take when he saw his old friend.[47]

Most telling was the arrival of Jackson, who dragged himself from his hospital bed over Warren's protests, determined that his unexpected return to the Court should emphasize the brethren's unity.[48] Among the clerks, anticipation had been building for weeks as the end of the term drew near. That morning, one of Clark's clerks came back from the Court printshop and noticed a batch of opinions without a docket number, which suggested that a secretive move was a afoot. "Something's going to happen," he told his colleagues.[49]

The justices took the bench at precisely noon. There were other cases to be announced, and at first the session seemed routine. Some of the reporters covering the Court were downstairs in the pressroom, lulled into complacency by the assurance of a court official that it looked like "a quiet day."[50] Then Banning H. Whittington, the Court's information officer, slipped his coat on and moved toward the stairs. "Reading of the segregation decisions is about to begin," he announced. Reporters leapt from their chairs and rushed for the door. As they entered the courtroom, it was 12:52 P.M. Warren had just begun.

"I have for announcement," he said, "the judgment and the opinion of the Court in Number 1: *Oliver Brown et al. v. Board of Education of Topeka*." For several minutes, Warren read from the opinion, with its union of his original language, Pollock's deft edits, and the minor revisions adopted at the request of the brethren. He recapped the history of the Fourteenth Amendment and the uncertainty about its framers' intentions; *Plessy*'s introduction of separate-but-equal; the Court's rulings that admitted black students to graduate schools but never took direct aim at *Plessy* itself; and the modern primacy of public education in American life. Not until the tenth paragraph of the fifteen-paragraph opinion did Warren indicate which way the Court was headed. It was then he read the question that he had posed as to whether segregation itself deprived black children of equal opportunity. He answered the question as he had in his initial draft. "We believe that it does," Warren said from the bench.

Two more paragraphs summed up the cases *Sweatt v. Painter* and *McLaurin v. Oklahoma State Regents*, which established the principle that equal educational opportunity extended beyond mere classrooms and facilities and reached to intangible factors. Warren then cited the Kansas court that had found, even in upholding segregation, that separating white and black children was bad for black children. Segregation was not equality. Warren acknowledged that such a finding might not have been reachable at the time of *Plessy*. It was reachable now, however, and Warren and his brethren endorsed it.

The document before Warren then read, "We conclude that in the field of public education the doctrine of 'separate but equal' has no place. Separate educational facilities are inherently unequal." Those words were stirring enough. With them, the segregated school systems of seventeen states were struck down as unconstitutional.

But Warren amended them as he delivered the opinion from the bench, adding a word that gave moral clarity to the legal result. "We *unanimously* conclude . . ." he read. With that, the nation took a deep and satisfying breath. Sitting before the Court, Thurgood Marshall turned his amazed look at Stanley Reed. Reed stared down from the bench and nodded almost imperceptibly. As Marshall watched, Reed wiped a tear from his cheek.

From his seat at the center of the Court's great bench, Warren too felt the rumble of his words. "When the word 'unanimously' was spoken, a wave of emotion swept the room," he wrote in his memoirs, "no words or intentional movement, yet a distinct emotional manifestation that defies description."[51]

Cheryl Brown's mother was working at home in Topeka when the news came over the radio in a bulletin. She went on with her ironing. Their historic case, which bore her husband's name, was finished.[52] In Alabama, a young man named Martin Luther King, Jr., had just become pastor-designate of Dexter Avenue Baptist Church.[53] His parishioners also received the news quietly, but it soon burrowed its way into King's consciousness. With the unanimous Court behind it, *Brown*, the young pastor wrote, "came as a joyous daybreak to end the long night of human captivity. . . . It was a reaffirmation of the good old American doctrine of freedom and equality for all men."[54]

King was right to cite "good old American" doctrine, with its echo of the first document that established America's independence and singularity. The Court's opinion, in Warren's hands, had effectively written the Declaration of Independence—and its long-neglected promise of equality—into the Constitution. With one opinion, one *unanimous* opinion, the Warren Court was born. Over the next sixteen years, the nation embarked on what would prove an uneven, controversial, halting, and noble drive to imbue the Constitution with the values of the Declaration. The urgent pursuit of American equality, so long promised, so long avoided, was under way. Earl Warren was at its head.

Chapter 19

# RESISTANCE

*It is not defiance for defiance sake, but for the purpose of raising basic and funda-
mental constitutional questions. My action is raising a call for strict adherence to the
Constitution of the United States as it was written—for a cessation of usurpation
and abuses. My action seeks to avoid having state sovereignty sacrificed on the altar
of political expediency.*

GOVERNOR GEORGE WALLACE, BLOCKING ENTRANCE
TO THE UNIVERSITY OF ALABAMA[1]

BROWN V. BOARD OF EDUCATION had many contributors, but in the end
it was Warren's feat. Its unanimity was his singular accomplishment. Beyond that, the opinion itself expressed much of what constituted his
most impressive self. It was restrained, committed to principle, self-conscious of
political ramifications. It was, above all, fair. He had aimed to expand the reach of
liberty and to codify the Declaration of Independence's great promises. In that, he
largely succeeded. But Warren's concern for the politics of *Brown* also had convinced him it was important to offer gentle encouragement to moderates, particularly in the South, so that they would lead the way to the liberty that the Court
commanded. In that, he did not succeed, at least in the short run. And he had himself to blame, in part. For just as *Brown*'s strengths were Warren's, so too were its
weaknesses.

Among the first to spot the vulnerability of *Brown* was the *New York Times*'s
James Reston. Reston was a sparkling little Scotsman, irrepressible in pursuit of a
story and bitingly intelligent. In 1954, he was coming into his own as the greatest
reporter of his generation, emerging from Lippmann's shadow, awing Washington
with his diverse, well-connected sources, and seducing readers with his easy command of language. Reston was versatile—he had started as a sportswriter and had
worked as a correspondent in London, where in 1937 he had confronted a surly

Justice Hugo Black with questions about Black's prior membership in the Ku Klux
Klan. Since returning to the United States, Reston had mastered many things but
understood few more thoroughly than politics. He watched Warren settle into the
Court and greeted the early indicators with approval, reporting just days after Warren's confirmation that the other justices appreciated their new chief's hard work
and friendly manner as well as his "self command and natural dignity."[2] As that column made clear, Reston could penetrate even the most cloistered institution. And
as Reston read *Brown* the day the decision was announced, he grasped that its
significance—as well as its underpinnings—went beyond the law. The decision,
Reston wrote in the next morning's *New York Times*, "read more like a paper on
sociology than a Supreme Court opinion."[3] Reston made that observation appre-
ciatively; indeed, he closed his column by favorably quoting the revered justice
Benjamin Cardozo: "The final cause of law is the welfare of society."[4]

Reston welcomed the Court's sociology, for Reston, like Warren, was a man of
basic values. He appreciated fairness and saw its evidence in *Brown*. Others, once
clued in to *Brown*'s sociological premises, were not so understanding. For those
critics, the sociology of *Brown* was that of an amateur outsider, no more valid than
the South's own social structure. They had a point. The Court's legitimacy is based
on its legal reasoning, not its sociological expertise. And sociological convictions
can change, raising difficult questions for the law. Sociologists had concluded that
segregation was bad for black children, and the Court had at least in part relied on
that finding to hold it unconstitutional. What, then, if sociologists were someday to
decide that segregation was good. Would it then become constitutional again?

As Southern leaders mounted their campaign to discredit *Brown* and the Court
that wrote it, they were aided by a tool that Warren inadvertently provided, what
was to become the notorious footnote 11. *Brown*'s eleventh footnote cited neither
precedent nor legal text; instead, the Court reached to a collection of psychological
and sociological works, most controversially Myrdal's *An American Dilemma*. The
footnote appeared near the end of the short decision and was offered merely to
support the District Court finding of fact in the Kansas case: "Segregation of white
and colored children in public schools has a detrimental effect upon the colored
children." After listing six psychological and sociological studies, the note then
glibly tacked on Myrdal's work under the heading of "See generally."[5] That was not
only provocative. It also was gratuitous. What footnote 11 suggested was what
many Southerners suspected: the Court was striking down school desegregation
not because the law commanded it but because modern experts no longer approved of it.

Warren would long grouse about the attention to footnote 11. He was not inclined to labor over the footnotes of his opinions, and there is no evidence that he
gave great thought to this one. Had he done so, he undoubtedly would have deleted

it, for footnote 11 to a great extent undermined the purpose of unanimity in *Brown.* One goal of a unanimous Court was to convey to the nation that there was no honest legal support for segregation. Warren's unanimous Court had in fact conveyed just that sentiment. But footnote 11 seemed to suggest that the Court, as Reston reported, found its support not just in law but also in the more ephemeral discipline of sociology. Reston was right to call Warren on it, and Warren and his colleagues were caught on a mistake of their own making. Warren sulked.

Now, despite Warren's great care to present his Court as a united front, the forces opposed to him and his colleagues began their work.

One man had the credibility and stature to demand compliance with *Brown.* As a candidate in 1952, Eisenhower had broken the Democrats' hold on the segregated South, proving that his esteem trumped even long-established party loyalties. In 1954, Eisenhower's strong support for the Court could have shown the nation the resolve that Warren had hoped to demonstrate by delivering a unanimous Court. But Eisenhower, as his comment to Warren at their February dinner that same year made clear, was unconvinced of integration's wisdom. Having done his best to dissuade Warren from that course, the president now was irritated to have the burden of enforcing the order that his Court had thrust upon the administration. And so Eisenhower equivocated.

Speaking at a news conference on May 19, two days after the ruling, Eisenhower struck what was to become his standard reply to questions about *Brown:* "The Supreme Court has spoken, and I am sworn to uphold the constitutional processes in this country. And I will obey."[6] That was hardly the ringing endorsement that would encourage compliance; indeed, Eisenhower's reticence was reinforced in his private communications to friends and allies, where he expressed the hope and expectation that the Supreme Court justices would not press too hard for the rights they had unanimously proclaimed. "My own guess," the president told his old friend Swede Hazlett that fall, "is that they will be very moderate and accord a maximum of initiative to local courts."[7]

Eisenhower's deliberate refusal to stand with the Court infuriated Warren, and relations between the president and the chief justice effectively collapsed. After *Brown,* Warren wrote, "I can recall few conversations that went beyond a polite 'Good evening, Mr. President' and 'Good evening, Mr. Chief Justice.'"[8]

While *Brown* broke new ground for equality, Warren deferred difficult choices in order to achieve unanimity. In effect, the Court had told the Southern states that they were engaged in an unconstitutional act, the racial segregation of schoolchildren. But it had not ordered it ended immediately, nor had it suggested what should be done. Instead, they deferred a decree and asked the parties to return the following term with proposals on how to proceed. That was remarkable by itself: When the Court finds a violation of the Constitution, it orders it halted. So the reargument signaled the difficulties in this area, and the justices played for time. As a result, they still had before them in 1954 and 1955 the problem of how to draft a decree that would enforce their desegregation opinion. The questions there were not mere details. Would schools be ordered to integrate at once? If not, how long would school districts have to begin the process and by what time would they be required to complete it? And by what theory would the Court pronounce that Negro children had a constitutional right to a desegregated education but not be allowed to enjoy that right immediately? A right, after all, is a right, not a privilege to be dispensed by the Court or others at their convenience.

Once again, the answers were found in a balancing move between the now clear constitutional rights of the plaintiffs and the fear of moving so quickly or broadly as to invite disobeying the Court. As with the original *Brown* case, the justices sought advice and time by scheduling reargument and inviting the Justice Department to participate as well. Again to the Court came the now familiar group of lawyers, though this time without John Davis, who withdrew from the case following South Carolina's defeat in 1954 and who died a few weeks before the reargument. (Reed, the justice most sympathetic to Davis's position on segregation, suggested to Warren that the chief justice read a statement from the bench honoring Davis and noting that "his appearances in this Court were in the best tradition of the American Bar." Warren declined.[9])

With Davis absent, his place was filled at the April 11 argument by S. Emory Rogers, whose combative presentation brought Southern resistance directly to Warren's angry attention. Rogers was there to argue for a position similar to that predicted by Eisenhower in his letter to Hazlett the previous fall—the idea that lower courts should be given maximum latitude in overseeing desegregation of Southern schools. Rogers wanted time and wanted local courts to be able to judge the particulars of the circumstances in their areas. Warren was not averse to either of those positions, but Rogers made the mistake of attacking Warren's authority rather than appealing to it.

As Warren attempted to pose a question to Rogers regarding how quickly his district would conform to the Court's order, Rogers interrupted: "To say we will conform depends on the decree handed down."

Warren was jolted. "It is not a question of attitude," he reminded the lawyer. "It is a question of conforming to the decree." Surely, Warren was saying in the bluntest possible terms, Rogers was not standing in the United States Supreme Court and arguing that the states would only adhere to a decree that they liked. American law—indeed, American society itself—is predicated on the primacy of the Supreme Court in matters of the Constitution. States have no right to refuse it. Could Rogers be daring to suggest otherwise in the presence of the Court itself?

Rogers tried to turn the discussion back to his request, that the lower courts have the discretion to fashion decrees in tune with local needs. But Warren wanted a straight admission of the Court's authority. He tried again. "But you are not willing to say here that there would be an honest attempt to conform to this decree . . . ?" he demanded.

"No, I am not," Rogers replied. Gesturing directly at Warren now, the lawyer then pushed to the edge of contempt. "Let's get the word 'honest' out of there."

"No," the smoldering chief justice responded. "Leave it in."

And still Rogers would not yield. "No," he said again, "because I would have to tell you that right now we would not conform. We would not send our white children to the Negro schools."

Warren hesitated, visibly straining to rein in his temper. As the lawyers for the Southern states winced and anticipated his response, the chief justice pulled himself together, ending the exchange with a brusque "thank you." Rogers barely escaped without a contempt citation, and Warren had nearly lost his self-control at a moment that required maximum deftness. Never again would he underestimate the ferocity of the Southern antipathy toward *Brown*.[10]

That Saturday, the justices met again in conference, but it was a changed group that traded handshakes. Justice Jackson, who had abandoned his reservations and cast off his illness to join his brethren in *Brown*, had soon thereafter given up the struggle. In the autumn of 1953, the great and eloquent justice, his long feuds with Black behind him, his graceful wit diminished by time and stress, had at last succumbed to his weakened heart. Earl Warren, who had known Jackson for only one historic year, led the members of his Court to the National Cathedral to pay homage to the justice, then to Jackson's native Jamestown, New York, for his burial near his boyhood home. Every member of the Court attended.

Jackson's death deprived the Court of one of its greatest advocates and writers, but it gave Eisenhower his second vacancy in just over a year. This time, the president named John Marshall Harlan, an elegant Wall Street lawyer and grandson of the first John Harlan, who had so memorably dissented in *Plessy v. Ferguson*. Ideologically conservative, as well as a dignified, patrician man, Harlan would prove much more to Eisenhower's liking than Warren. But Harlan was also his grandfather's progeny. He would not be the one to break the Court's hard-won unanimity in *Brown*. As the justices took their seats that Saturday, Harlan now occupied the junior chair. He would speak last at conference. Warren went first.

Warren began in much the same vein as he had in the first *Brown* conference more than a year earlier—by recommending patience and conversation, not quick judgments. He had not, Warren told the conference, "reached [any] fixed opinion."[11] But just as quickly as Warren set a tone of collegiality, he also reminded his brethren of something else that they had discovered in these discussions a year earlier—that while he valued their views and insisted on an atmosphere of respect, he was not in awe of his colleagues. Warren had opinions of his own. Warren now listed them. He summarily rejected a suggestion by Frankfurter—also contained in the Eisenhower administration's brief—that the Court appoint special masters to oversee desegregation, though he added that he would not deny lower courts the chance to do so if they chose to. He did not want a final date set for the completion of the process—here, the conflict with Rogers must have rung in his ears—and he wanted lower courts to have flexibility in the orders they struck to move the process along. Having listed what he did not want, Warren then turned to "what appeals to me."[12] He proposed that the Court shift the burden for enforcing *Brown* back down to district court judges, but that it also write an opinion to help guide those judges in applying the law. It would be cruel, Warren insisted, to deny those judges such guidance and instead "let them flounder." Finally, Warren rejected the suggestion that the Court only grant its relief to the individual plaintiffs who had sued in the four states and the District of Columbia. The cases were, he said, class actions, and thus the Court's ruling on *Brown*'s applicability ought to apply to all segregated children in the districts that were sued, not just those whose families had shown the courage to file and pursue lawsuits.[13]

Black surprisingly disagreed with Warren's recommendation on the reach of the cases. Despite his intense devotion to civil liberties—at least those enumerated in the Bill of Rights—Black was a Southerner and he saw trouble ahead. "I was brought up in an atmosphere against federal officials," Black reminded his colleagues. Time had softened some of that feeling, he added, but federal intervention on behalf of Negro children would stir it again, fueling the South's historic antipathy for Washington. For Black, the best decree would be the one that did the least—one that stuck by the proposition that school segregation was unconstitutional but that limited its effect just to the litigants who had brought the cases and that gave districts time to adapt. The Court, he said forebodingly, should expect "glacial movement," but though that might be frustrating, it was preferable to the alternative. "Nothing," Black warned, was "more important than that this Court should not issue what it cannot enforce."[14] And in that vein, he foresaw resistance. "Some counties," Warren said, "won't have Negroes and whites in the same school this generation."[15]

Those were sobering words from a justice whose commitment to civil rights was without peer, and it set the tone for the rest of the conversation. Frankfurter hardly needed to be pushed toward judicial caution, so his support was inevitable, and he took the opportunity to assume the credit for successfully delaying the cases. "He now says he filibustered this problem under Vinson for fear that the case would be decided the other way . . . !" Douglas scrawled in obvious exasperation.[16] Despite his irritation with Frankfurter, Douglas agreed that the Court should proceed with caution and should limit its own reach in order to achieve compliance.

Others weighed in similarly, urging unanimity and also counseling restraint. By the time the conversation reached Harlan, the junior justice, he had little left to add beyond noting that he too looked forward to the Court's moving unanimously. Black's remarks, Harlan said, had "made a deep impression."[17]

Warren again assigned the opinion to himself, and as he wrote and circulated drafts through late April, he struggled for the right balance—not shrinking from *Brown* but not provoking too much, either. Warren did not, of course, yield from the position that *Brown* and *Bolling* had declared discrimination in public education unconstitutional and thus that all local, state, and federal laws to the contrary were required to yield to that ruling. Less satisfying were his attempts to mute the outcry at that finding. The Court agreed, first of all, to limit the immediate impact of its ruling to the parties who had brought the lawsuits. Though the principle of segregation's unconstitutionality thus stood, the effect of it initially would be felt only by those families who had had the gumption to sue (in Kansas, Oliver Brown's daughter was not even affected that much; Topeka's segregated schools ended after elementary school, so she already was attending an integrated classroom).

As to timing, Warren's early drafts of the opinion—the justices had settled on an opinion as preferable to a mere decree—ordered desegregation to begin "at the earliest practicable date." That language was softened through the exchanges with other justices, and what emerged was a ruling that in effect said discrimination could continue for a very long time indeed. The most famous of the Court's equivocations was added by Frankfurter, who suggested the language of "all deliberate speed." Frankfurter was enamored of that phrase, with its intentionally equivocal implications. To him, it smacked of judicial statesmanship, and he had used it, seriously and whimsically, for years. As early as 1947, for instance, he had urged a former clerk to edit a document and return it "as the grand old chancery phrase expresses it, 'with all deliberate speed.'"[18] Now Frankfurter recommended it to give guidance to those judges asked to carry desegregation forward.

Except in Delaware, where the Supreme Court was upholding a lower court, the segregation cases were returned to the district courts, where judges were directed "to take such proceedings and enter such orders and decrees consistent with this opinion as are necessary and proper to admit to public schools on a racially nondiscriminatory basis with all deliberate speed the parties to these cases."[19] As Lucas Powe notes with typical concision and insight, the message of *Brown II* "was that the Court was willing to accept token desegregation—later."[20] In the Florida legislature, when *Brown II* was read aloud, the audience burst into applause.

With *Brown II,* Warren and his colleagues moved the front line of the school desegregation battle out of their courtroom and into the district courts. There, many brave judges would face hostile local communities and demand compliance without state or federal support. That the matter moved ahead is a testament to their work, for while Warren had established a grand new principle of American life—the idea that equality was not just an abstract value but in fact the law—he was quickly discovering the limitations of his assignment. He could pronounce law and change standards, but he was not a governor anymore. The police no longer were at his command, and the president was not required to move the Court's agenda. It would take time for Warren to understand both the reach and limits of the Court, but the balance of the 1950s would prove an essential fact of his new life: Only with political support could the Court be as effective as Warren wanted. And for the time being, the Court had precious little.

A few weeks after announcing *Brown II,* the Court recessed for the summer, and Earl and Nina Warren set off on an exploration of their family roots. It was their second trip to Scandinavia but their first since Warren's appointment to the Court. They were hosted at embassies and Warren was greeted across northern Europe as more than a dignitary—rather, as something approaching the status of a liberator, a champion of freedom whose controversies and conflicts stayed behind in America. He and Nina stayed for more than a month, touring Sweden, Belgium, Luxembourg, Germany, and Austria before making their way home to California in August. It was the beginning of a regular summer travel tradition, one in which Warren would typically meet ambassadors and judges from the nations they visited; Nina would accompany him, and would keep in touch with the children and grandchildren by her regular postcards, which they would save and share upon the Warrens' return.

Back home, the Warrens traveled to Santa Barbara for its annual "fiesta," and then returned to Washington as the summer ebbed. As would also become his habit, Earl Warren made one last trip—this one on his own—before Court began its business in early October. He ducked out of the office with old friends to take in the World Series. This year, that meant a trip to New York, where Warren and pals from his California days took in games 3 and 4. The Dodgers fought off the Yankees in both games, winning the contests at their home park, Ebbets Field, despite lackluster playing by Jackie Robinson, whose historic career then was winding to a close. Warren returned after the Saturday game and gaveled the Court into its new session on Monday morning, refreshed and ready for a new term.[21]

WARREN WAS a national figure before *Brown,* an international figure afterward. And as such, politics continued to tug him back to his still-unfulfilled quest for the presidency. With 1955 beginning, the nation's chief political question was whether Eisenhower would seek a second term; the president had made it clear that he felt his duty had been performed and that retirement was an attractive option for him. With his plans thus uncertain, two old rivals were thrown back into conflict.

Richard Nixon had every reason to believe that he should be Eisenhower's heir—he was the sitting vice president, a proven vote-getter, and an ambitious, skillful politician. But Nixon would always be Nixon, an irritant to moderates because of his red-baiting past, a source of anxiety and fear to liberals. Warren, on the other hand, was the architect of desegregation, the friendly California bear whose stature had only grown since he left the governorship and came to the Court. In early 1955, Gallup conducted a survey that found Warren the most popular Republican to succeed Eisenhower should the president not seek reelection. For Nixon, this was just one more in a line of indignities served him by Warren.

On April 15, with speculation rife about Warren's decision, Warren wrote out in longhand a stiff rejection:

> My name has been used as a possible candidate for the Presidency. This has been a matter of embarrassment to me because it reflects upon the performance of my duties as Chief Justice of the United States. When I accepted that position, it was with the fixed purpose of leaving politics permanently for service on the Court. That is still my purpose. It is irrevocable. I will not change it under any circumstances or conditions.

Concluding, Warren added, "Be they few or many, the remaining useful years of my life are dedicated to the service of the Supreme Court of the United States, in which work I am increasingly happy."[22] Before releasing the statement, Warren made only one change. He reversed the introductory clause of his final sentence, so that the final draft read: "Be they many or few . . ."

Warren's withdrawal won widespread praise. Editorial writers hailed the decision, as did law school professors and deans and many others who wrote personally to Warren. They understood that with his unambiguous statement, Warren had raised the stature of the Court by removing it and himself from electoral politics and by making it clear that the presidency was not an office worth leaving the Court to pursue. It also had the effect—no doubt intended—of diminishing Nixon by reminding voters that where Nixon would presumably engage in the messy business of seeking votes, Warren was above that and thus above Nixon. That resolved the issue for the moment, but it returned in the fall, when Eisenhower suffered a heart attack, and eyes turned again to Warren. The chief justice received dozens of letters urging him to reconsider his withdrawal, given that Eisenhower now seemed unable to continue in office for a second term. This time, Warren remained silent.

Warren even turned the dagger a notch by use of a device that would serve him well in the coming years. He sought out a friendly journalist and told his side of the story. In this case, as in many others, Warren reached out to Drew Pearson. Since their first meeting in 1947, Warren and Pearson had maintained a respectful, professional friendship, and it grew closer once Warren arrived in Washington. Warren admired Pearson's courage and talent, and Pearson wrote occasionally and favorably about Warren, whom he believed should have received the Republican nomination in 1948.[23] By the time Warren came to the Court in 1953, Pearson felt sufficiently comfortable to drop by and chat about politics.[24] With Pearson's deep affection for Nina and with the bond between Nina and Pearson's second wife, Luvie, the two families grew close through the early 1950s and formed a klatch of friends that included Adlai Stevenson and Agnes Meyer, heir to the *Washington Post.* Warren and Pearson liked each other, and helped each other. In later years, Pearson would deliver messages to the White House on Warren's behalf, and now and again Warren saw to it that Pearson got a good story.

With Eisenhower's health and future in doubt, Warren suggested to Pearson that he might consider running if it would block Nixon.[25] That gave Pearson a scoop, and allowed both Warren and Pearson to enjoy the twitting it gave Nixon, of whom they shared a loathing. Eisenhower, himself sometimes suspicious of Nixon's ambition, allowed the issue to sit, driving Nixon to distraction through early 1956. It was then that the president finally closed the speculation by announcing that he did indeed intend to seek a second term. With that, the matter rested, having only succeeded in alarming Nixon, amusing Eisenhower, and elevating Warren.

For Warren, however, the coming period in the life of the Court was to prove exasperating. Eisenhower flatly refused to push desegregation forward, while Warren flatly refused to back down. The result was a national standoff, which the resisting states exploited to delay and rebuff most serious attempts at integration. Through 1955 and 1956, the Supreme Court extended *Brown* to new spheres of American life, usually without even cursory explanation. In November, the Supreme Court upheld a Fourth Circuit opinion outlawing Baltimore's segregated public beaches; the Supreme Court did not even bother with an opinion. At the same time, it reversed another lower court that had upheld Atlanta's segregated golf courses. This time, the Supreme Court cited only its unexplained decision in the Baltimore case.[26] Those decisions were perplexing if one relied on the literal text of *Brown. Brown,* after all, was narrowly tailored to address the particulars of harm created to children by segregated public schools. Its rationale was partly based on the explicit finding that segregation was bad for children. But was it bad for golfers? Bathers? Apparently so, for the Court applied its earlier reasoning and felt no need to elaborate. But if Warren's approach was frustrating to judges and legal theorists, it was more defensible in the political terms that drove him. Warren understood that to announce the overturning of all state-sanctioned segregation was to invite rejection of the Court itself. Such a move would mean, among other things, that laws against interracial marriage would fall. Warren was too familiar with the ways of local government to delude himself about how that would be received. So he self-consciously decided to approach the problem piecemeal, never saying much, simply plowing ahead.

In that effort, Warren generally led a congenial Court, willing, even eager to follow his approach. Their comity knew its limits, however, as Warren was more aggressive than many of the other justices to push the nation along its journey toward desegregation. Late in 1955, the brethren came to an impasse in that debate, divided over whether to extend *Brown* in a precarious direction. As Myrdal had observed in *An American Dilemma,* the subtext for much of segregation was a lurking sexual distress, an unwillingness to tolerate so much as a hint of interracial sex, much less marriage. But *Brown*'s progeny seemed to suggest that the Supreme Court no longer regarded race as a suitable basis for separate treatment. What, then, of interracial marriage? Inevitably, the Court would be asked to consider that question, and in 1955 it was.

Han Say Naim and Ruby Elaine Naim were married in North Carolina, which did not bar the union of a Chinese man and a white woman. But Virginia was their home, and they had traveled to North Carolina to avoid prosecution under the Virginia antimiscegenation law. When they moved home and were caught, they argued that the equal protection clause forbade Virginia from barring their marriage. The Virginia Supreme Court disagreed. It ordered the Naims to dissolve their marriage, and, in doing so, pointedly cited *Brown* while noting that its holding with respect to public schools did not extend to interracial marriage. "Intermarriage," as the Virginia court termed it, was not, like public education, the foundation of citizenship: "In the opinion of more than half the States it is harmful to good citizenship."[27]

Mrs. Naim appealed. Her case, *Naim v. Naim,* posed an agonizing dilemma for the justices. To overrule the Virginia Court and restore the Naims' marriage would invite an uprising throughout the South and would certainly undermine the Court's attempts to impose *Brown* as slowly and dispassionately as possible. But to allow the Naims to suffer was to tolerate the very indignity that the Court was determined to wipe out. "So far as I recall, this is the first time since I've been here that I am confronted with the task of resolving a conflict between moral and technical legal considerations," Harlan told the conference on November 4, 1955, when the issue formally came before the brethren. Harlan encouraged the Court to avoid the issue, as did Frankfurter. Over Warren's objections, the Court returned the case to the Virginia Supreme Court under the pretext of asking it to complete the record. That was nonsense, as all concerned knew the record was complete. The Virginia Court called the Supreme Court on its bluff and sent *Naim v. Naim* back to Washington, standing by its original decision in an act of near-defiance. Warren was incensed—not by the Virginia Supreme Court but by the cowardice of his colleagues. The Supreme Court then, embarrassingly, folded and refused to take the case.[28]

Warren was furious at the spectacle of his Court yielding to Virginia's insolence. He contemplated a dissent from the Court's refusal to set the case for argument, then reconsidered; a dissent, he reasoned, would only advertise divisions within his own Court. But he went away mad. "That," he grumbled to his clerk, Sam Stern, "is what happens when you turn your ass to the grandstand."[29]

The intriguing irony of Warren's approach to desegregation was that the Court made least headway in the area it tackled most directly. Schools remained stubbornly segregated for years—in some cases, decades—as "all deliberate speed" came to mean much more deliberation than speed. But as Southern leaders concentrated their firepower on preserving white schools, their moral authority steadily diminished, and new converts joined the civil rights side of the struggle. Indeed, the most immediate impact of the Court's invocation of American idealism against segregation was the infusion of energy that it supplied to the nascent civil rights movement.

In December 1955, less than a year after *Brown* and five months after *Brown II*, Rosa Parks refused to relinquish her seat to a white passenger on a segregated Montgomery, Alabama, bus. Martin Luther King, Jr., came to her aid, and the bus boycott was on. Direct action did not depend on a friendly United States Supreme Court, but it benefited by it. The Court's ruling in *Brown* helped persuade advocates, black and white, that their struggle could reach the hearts of reasonable white people. On a basic, human level, it meant that Rosa Parks enjoyed the tacit blessing of the Supreme Court. Warren thus might not be able to move Eisenhower beyond terse statements of obedience to the law. But he was energizing the forces of change. He was, as he often would be over the coming fifteen years, a moral leader first and a judicial officer second.

Warren's embrace of racial justice was not part of a broader rejection of America's social order. He deplored the Communist Party and detested vice. He believed in police and prosecutors. He was no less a moderate and institutional man in 1955 than he was when he rose to the head of the Masons in California. As a result, Warren in his early months with the Court easily accepted the canons of judicial restraint in cases involving criminal justice. The clearest evidence of Warren's early deference to the government came in a case that he would later describe as his worst mistake on the bench. It involved a bookmaker from Long Beach, California, and both the defendant and the jurisdiction weighed on Warren, whose protectiveness of California law and abhorrence of vice were two powerful influences. The bookmaker, Frederick Irvine, had applied for and received a tax stamp identifying the source of his income as gambling. Long Beach police then, without any warrant, broke into Irvine's home on at least four occasions. They drilled a hole in the roof and installed hidden microphones, at first in a hall, later in Irvine's bedroom and elsewhere. They then repaired to a neighbor's garage, where they eavesdropped on Irvine and his wife for a month, accumulating evidence that he was a book-maker.[30] When the case reached the Court, the justices were dumbfounded that po-lice officers could behave so badly: "That officers of the law would break and enter a home, secrete such a device, even in a bedroom, and listen to the conversation of the occupants for over a month would be almost incredible if it were not admitted."[31]

A bare majority of the Court upheld Irvine's conviction anyway. Warren joined Jackson, Reed, Minton, and Clark in allowing Irvine to go to prison, a ruling that squared Warren's belief in the goodness of California law with his distaste for bookmakers. What that left was the misconduct of the police, which would go un-punished by the affirming of the conviction. Warren eased his conscience there by joining Jackson in an extraordinary final paragraph of the opinion. In it, he and Jackson noted that federal law permitted prosecution of officers who, acting under color of authority, willfully deprived a person of a federal right, in this case the right to be secure in one's home. Given that, Jackson and Warren concluded, "We believe the Clerk of this Court should be directed to forward a copy of the record in this case, together with a copy of this opinion, for attention of the Attorney Gen-eral of the United States."[32]

That same day, Warren Olney called Hoover directly to tell him of the Court's ruling. Hoover at first misunderstood, believing that the Court had outlawed the use of illegally obtained evidence in state trials. Olney assured him it had not, but also warned that in light of the ruling, the Department of Justice wanted to see the officers investigated, and he suggested that the FBI "go ahead with its investigation and complete it without waiting for any one."[33] Hoover was skeptical. If the FBI were to take on this case, it would invite others, he said. He did not refuse to open the case—to do so would have invited a showdown—but he hardly leapt at the prospect of the FBI's accusing police of violating the civil rights of suspects who were the subject of illegal searches. No case ever was brought against the Long Beach officers responsible for *Irvine*.

It is interesting to wonder what might have happened if those officers had been investigated and prosecuted. Warren's sense of justice might have been vindicated, and though the price would have been some erosion in the separation of powers (the Court, after all, has no business recommending prosecutions; for that reason, Minton and Reed, while signing Jackson's opinion, refused to join the personal note he and Warren attached to it), the result could well have been that Warren's impulse to govern from the bench would have been sated. None of that occurred, however. The officers went back to their lives, and Irvine went to jail. Warren, al-ready rebuffed by the Eisenhower administration on civil rights, was given new rea-son to brood about the Department of Justice and the FBI. *Brown* had taught him he could not rely on the president to enforce equality. *Irvine* came to convince Warren that he could not trust Eisenhower—or presidents generally—to enforce the Court's rules in criminal justice, either.[34]

For Hoover's part, *Irvine* offered the first hint that Warren as chief justice might not prove as accommodating as he had during his years as California's attorney general and governor. And yet if the glimmers of their subsequent relationship were visible in that 1954 exchange, it was only barely. For now, Hoover continued to look out for Warren, and Warren availed himself of the Bureau's many special services. When Congress approved a car for Warren—upon arriving at the Court, he was surprised to discover that none was provided, and Congress was shamed into providing him one after the press saw Warren step out of an airport limousine that brought him to a White House function—Warren asked the Bureau's help in finding a suitable driver. Agents did their best, but could not find one for the Court.[35]

The FBI was more helpful elsewhere. Warren was far away from home and children in 1954, and, as noted, those early months were trying ones. Back in California, Honey Bear was in college, and Warren's little girl, whom he would not allow to spend the night during her ski trips to Lake Tahoe, now was on her own. So when an acquaintance visited the special agent in charge of the Los Angeles office to raise concerns about Honey Bear's well-being, the Bureau took notice. Although the name of the busybody is deleted from the FBI's files as released, he or she warned the agent that Honey Bear was dating an actor and that the two, according to the tabloids, planned a trip together to Aspen that winter. The agent took down the information and forwarded it to Washington. On February 1, with Hoover's authorization, senior officials of the Bureau concluded that it was their duty to let Warren know that Honey Bear was rumored to have fallen in with, as their inform-ant put it, "a bad crowd."[36] The following year Honey Bear became engaged, and Warren, perhaps still concerned about those earlier reports, asked the FBI to check out her fiancé, Stuart Brien. The FBI did, forwarding its conclusions to Warren on November 1, 1955. Although its findings have never been made public, Brien passed Warren's muster. Honey Bear and Dr. Brien eloped and then settled into a long and happy marriage that pleased Earl and Nina greatly.[37]

Despite siding with prosecutors over criminals and, in his early years, giving lat-itude to the legislative efforts to uncover Communists, Warren could not shield himself and his Court from the backlash against *Brown*. It arrived in full force in late 1955, as the political leadership of the South vented its fury at the spectacle of the Montgomery bus boycott and the Supreme Court, which it perceived as responsible for this outbreak of activism. In Virginia, columnist James J. Kirkpatrick revived a discredited constitutional notion, the theory of "interposition," whereby states re-served the right to interpose themselves between the federal government and their citizens on matters relating to the states. The theory rested upon the notion that the Constitution was a contract between the states and thus that they had the right to limit the federal government's interference in their own affairs. As law, that was rubbish. The Constitution's "Supremacy clause" leaves no legitimate room for misinterpretation: "The Constitution, and the laws of the United States which shall be made in pursuance thereof . . . shall be the supreme law of the land; and the judges in every state shall be bound thereby." And if that weren't enough, there was the matter of the Civil War; one would think that would have been enough to demonstrate that the states were limited, to say the least, in their ability to defy federal authority. Ignoring all that, however, Kirkpatrick sputtered on, and did so with enough apparent authority to lend cover to those who wanted to reach his conclusions.

In early 1956, the nearly united political leadership of the South, particularly in Congress, joined to add its condemnation of the Court. "We regard the decision of the Supreme Court in the school cases as a clear abuse of judicial power," the Southern Manifesto began. After a cursory review of public education and the Fourteenth Amendment, the signers blamed the Court for disrupting "amicable relations between the white and Negro races" and for creating an "explosive and dangerous condition." The Manifesto's signers praised those states engaged in resistance and pledged themselves to "use all lawful means to bring about a reversal of this decision."[38] The Manifesto pointedly did not say what those "lawful means" would be, unsurprisingly, given that no such means existed to repudiate a decision of the United States Supreme Court. As Robert Jackson had long ago noted, the justices are not final because they are infallible, but they are infallible because they are final. The Constitution provides no avenue for rejection of its work other than constitutional amendment, and that clearly was not what the Manifesto contemplated. Nineteen senators and eighty-one members of the House—nearly the entire representation of the American South in the United States Congress—signed the Manifesto.

Still, as long as resistance to the Court was confined to the South, Warren was safe. Southern prejudices had embedded themselves deeply in the life and social structure of that region, but they were not widely shared in the North and West. The Manifesto thus was provocative—annoying, even—but unthreatening, as long as its complaints were regional. That all changed one month later when the Court announced its decision in the case of Steve Nelson, an admitted member of the Communist Party, who had been tried and convicted for subversion by the state of Pennsylvania. That state's Supreme Court, however, had concluded that because Nelson had been convicted of sedition against the United States and not against Pennsylvania, its state law was preempted by the Smith Act.

The case had come to the Court the previous fall, but now, on April 26, 1956, the ruling was ready. Warren wrote *Nelson,* and he did everything possible to contain the reaction to it. Speaking for himself and all but Reed, Burton, and Minton, Warren merely upheld in his opinion the Pennsylvania Supreme Court and did so on the same technical grounds as the court below. Moreover, he took pains to explain the limits of the ruling and even favorably to note the efforts to combat international Communism. "Congress," Warren wrote, "has devised an all-embracing program for resistance to the various forms of totalitarian aggression. Our external defenses have been strengthened, and a plan to . . . protect against internal subversion has been made by it. It has appropriated vast sums, not only for our own protection, but also to strengthen freedom throughout the world."[39]

But none of Warren's efforts could obscure the bottom line. What *Nelson* came down to was an assessment of Congress's intent in passing the Smith Act, its principal vehicle for attacking Communist subversion. And what Warren and the majority concluded was that Congress had produced such a pervasive scheme that it left no room for states to add their own anti-Communist efforts. Pennsylvania's court was right to let Nelson go, Warren ruled. The grounds were technical and the rhetoric spare to the point of dull, but the fact was that Steve Nelson, an avowed and admitted Communist, won the support of the United States Supreme Court. And the Southern legislators who had once been isolated in their attacks on the Court now had anti-Communist allies across the nation.[40]

The resolutions came in many shapes and sizes, but typically amalgamated *Brown* and *Nelson* under the general charge that the justices, so many lacking judicial experience, were incapable of understanding the law. Sensitive to charges of racism for attacking *Brown*, Southern leaders instead alleged that the Court had relied on sociologists such as Myrdal ("and their ilk" one resolution added for good measure), rather than on legal precedent. That was the price for footnote 11. The price for *Nelson* was a charge of treason. That ruling, the Georgia legislature found, constituted "aid and comfort to the enemy."[41] At least the Georgia legislature merely called for impeachment. A California group calling itself the Cinema Educational Guild recommended that Warren be found guilty of treason and condemned to the same fate as Julius and Ethel Rosenberg: death.[42]

Warren soldiered on. Even as critics derided his intelligence, experience, and loyalty, Warren joined a bare majority of the Court in laying down one of the early markers of its criminal justice jurisprudence. Decided on April 23, 1956, *Griffin v. Illinois* forced the state of Illinois to give prisoners who could not otherwise afford one a free transcript of their trials in order to appeal. Illinois required that transcript to consider allegations of error during the trial, and as long as it made the transcript mandatory, the Court ruled that the state could not deny it to the poor. *Griffin* was less momentous than the criminal justice cases of the Warren Court's heyday in the 1960s, but it foreshadowed the Court's egalitarianism, which Warren would make its hallmark. "Providing equal justice for poor and rich, weak and powerful alike is an age-old problem," Black wrote for himself, Warren, Douglas, and Clark (Frankfurter concurred in the result, supplying a majority, but he wrote a separate opinion). "People have never ceased to hope and strive to move closer to that goal. . . . In criminal trials a State can no more discriminate on account of poverty than on account of religion, race, or color."[43]

Racism and anti-Communism found each other in the spring of 1956, just as Eisenhower had recovered from his heart attack of the previous fall and decided to seek reelection. The president was in no mood to defend his wayward Court in its coddling of Communists. As clamor for action against the Court spread, Eisenhower let it spread, and even encouraged it. The president never spoke out against the Southern Manifesto, and as Congress debated legislation to overturn *Nelson*, the Eisenhower administration announced its support. Only the rapid close of Congress for the summer saved Warren the indignity of having the man who appointed him sign a law to strip him of some of his new power.[44] It did not come too soon, however, for Warren to escape a piece of political theater staged by Senators Eastland and McCarthy. Fulminating about the Court and its view of the Communist threat, McCarthy announced that there was "something radically wrong" with the chief justice. Taking up his half of the colloquy, Eastland naturally agreed, and though he made clear that he was not accusing Warren of being a Communist himself, he seemed nevertheless to be taking "the same position the Communists take when they attempt to protect themselves." Of the Court, Eastland added, "It's just one pro-Communist decision after another."[45]

While members of Congress piled on Warren, they gave shelter to those who yearned to express themselves more viscerally. Late at night on July 13, 1956, a twenty-four-year-old man named Ronald Rowley, affiliated with his local White Citizens' Council and fed up by "Earle Warren Nigger Lover," soaked some lumber in kerosene and planted two crosses outside the Warrens' Sheraton-Park residential hotel, then set the crosses on fire in the midnight quiet. He and a cohort were spotted by an alert doorman as they put matches to their work. They fled in separate cars, but not before the doorman was able to memorize the license plate number of one. Before the night was out, crosses were aflame at the homes of Felix Frankfurter, Senator Herbert Lehman (another Sheraton-Park resident, whose cross identified him as "Jew"), Solicitor General Steven Sobeloff (also labeled "Jew"), and the local head of the NAACP.[46] Rowley at first denied his involvement, then admitted it, and said he was provoked by Warren's Court. "I was just trying to make people aware of something they already know anyway . . . that the Supreme Court really was out of order." The *Washington Post* ran Rowley's comments under the headline "Rowley Issues 'Apology.' "[47]

The close of Congress cleared the way for the summer Democratic and Republican conventions, and they too provided more opportunities for mischief against the Court. At Eisenhower's request, the Republican platform that year withheld "support" for the *Brown* ruling and instead merely "accepted" that judgment while concurring with *Brown II*.[48] Democrats were no better. Still, Warren continued to walk through raindrops, in part by staying far away from presidential politics. As the two parties settled on their candidates that summer, Earl and Nina Warren returned to their travels, stopping first in New York City, where they took in a Broadway production of *My Fair Lady*.[49] The following day they left for Europe, intending to spend a long vacation in Switzerland. While there, however, they were beseeched by the Indian government to pay a visit to that country's judiciary, and after ordering up warm-weather clothing, Earl and Nina ventured to the subcontinent, their first visit to the area and the beginning of a lifelong fascination with it. Their long stay in India then was capped by a return through Hong Kong, Manila, and Hawaii. By the time the Warrens returned to California, both parties had their platforms and nominees. All that was left of the campaign was for Eisenhower and Nixon to march through the earnest but overmatched Adlai Stevenson. For Warren, that election marked a quiet transition: He cast his ballot for Stevenson, the first Democrat, though not the last, to receive Warren's vote for president.[50]

As Election Day approached, Sherman Minton announced his retirement, and Eisenhower was handed his third opportunity to leave his mark on the Supreme Court. After his disappointment with Warren, Eisenhower never again picked a nominee without a record on the bench, but judicial selection remained strangely casual to Eisenhower. This time he approached the matter with more thought to the November elections than to the character of the Court he was building. Apparently concerned about Stevenson's strength in some Northeastern states, Eisenhower asked Brownell to find him a conservative Catholic Democrat with judicial experience— preferably a state court judge, since no other member of the Warren Court came from a state judiciary.[51] Brownell recommended William J. Brennan, Jr., an impishly delightful judge then sitting on the New Jersey Supreme Court. Brownell had met Brennan by chance not long before Minton announced his retirement. Arthur Vanderbilt, still serving as chief justice of the New Jersey Supreme Court (having been passed over for Warren in 1953), had been the scheduled speaker at the National Conference on Delays and Congestion in the Courts, of which Brownell was the organizer. Vanderbilt had been forced to cancel at the last minute and had sent Brennan in his place. Grateful that Brennan delivered and impressed by his speech, Brownell not only befriended the justice but also placed his name on Brownell's running list of potential Supreme Court nominees. When Minton retired, Brownell read Brennan's opinions and found them "well-reasoned."[52] Brennan fit Eisenhower's other criteria— he was a state judge, a Catholic, and a Democrat—and so Eisenhower accepted

Brownell's recommendation and named Brennan to the Court. Once confirmed—a simple matter, with only Joe McCarthy voting against Brennan—Brennan took his place among the brethren.

As with Warren, that would prove a nomination that Eisenhower regretted, for Brennan was a committed and effective liberal. Once there—or at least once he had settled fully into the job—Brennan would become Warren's most faithful friend, deputy, and ally. Together, the two would join Douglas and Black as a solid block of four liberal votes. For Frankfurter, it was yet another promise turned sour. Brennan had studied under Frankfurter at Harvard, and now took his place beside and in opposition to him. Frankfurter once remarked that he had always encouraged his students to think for themselves, but "Brennan goes too far."[53]

Brownell brought Brennan to meet Warren on September 29, and Warren took Brennan under his wing. After they talked that afternoon, Warren suggested that he introduce Brennan to the rest of the justices over lunch that Friday. Brennan arrived as scheduled, and went first to Warren's chambers. Warren then led the younger man upstairs to the Court's third-floor lounge. The lights were dim as the two entered, but Warren turned them up, and Brennan could see that the justices were eating sandwiches and watching the 1956 World Series. Warren introduced Brennan to the brethren, who shifted impatiently during the pleasantries. Finally one called out to Brennan, "Sit down so we can see the game!"[54] After making his introductions, Warren left that afternoon for the Series himself, taking in games 3 and 4 in New York before returning to Washington to open the Court's fall session. (Warren missed, by one day, seeing Don Larsen's perfect game, which he pitched in game 5; he and his old friend Bart Cavanaugh had planned to stay for that game, but Warren insisted they leave. He was convinced the Yankees had no pitching talent that year. Cavanaugh never let him forget it.)[55]

Warren returned to Washington to a Court that now included Brennan as well. The nucleus of the Warren Court was formed.

Chapter 20

# "DUMB SWEDE"

*I stood up at a time when many people kept quiet, or became informers, or left the country. I am still an American.*

LLOYD BARENBLATT, VASSAR COLLEGE TEACHER WHO,
HAVING REFUSED TO TELL HUAC WHETHER HE WAS A COMMUNIST,
LOST HIS JOB AND WAS HELD IN CONTEMPT AND SENT TO PRISON[1]

I N 1986, long after Earl Warren was gone, Justice Brennan reflected on his then nearly three decades with the Court and identified one of its enduring truths: "In an institution this small, personalities play an important role. It's inevitable when you have just nine people. How those people get along, how they relate, what ideas they have, how flexible or intractable they are, are all of enormous importance."[2] By virtue of background and inclination, Warren grasped that essential fact of Supreme Court leadership. Indeed, with the possible exception of John Marshall himself, no chief justice ever sensed it better. From the first moments of his arrival, Warren worked to create a harmony that would ease the work of the Court and erase the Vinson legacy of discord. His first ally was Black. His most reliable would prove to be Brennan. But his main obstacle, almost from the beginning, was Frankfurter. By the mid-1950s, their deepening mutual distrust defined much of Warren's working life; by the end of that decade, it had nearly cost Warren the effective leadership of his own Court.

There probably was no avoiding a break between two such strong-willed and diametrically different men as Warren and Frankfurter. Warren was the son of Methias, raised in a restrained, Protestant, Swedish home, one with little open affection or acrimony. He spent his youth among those who respected deeds over words and he came to prominence in the compromises and calculations of elected politics. Frankfurter was a Jewish immigrant raised in New York City, steeped in the cultural milieu of verbal jousting and close textual debate. Frankfurter was a brilliant professor used to lecturing students and expecting their attention. Warren was a master at getting others to do his bidding by persuasion, not dominance. Frankfurter's judicial self-abnegation was a considered response to years of contemplating the appropriate role for the judiciary in the separation of powers. To Warren, it looked suspiciously like an excuse for avoiding hard decisions. Warren's skill and enjoyment at making those decisions was just as much a product of his professional upbringing as Frankfurter's belief in restraint was of his. And yet to Frankfurter, Warren looked suspiciously like a thickheaded pol.

With so much to separate them, it was unsurprising that after the initial euphoria of *Brown*, Frankfurter's appreciation for Warren entered a steep downward spiral. At first their disagreements flared in technical fields. In 1957, for instance, the Court tackled the second antitrust lawsuit involving the DuPont corporation that had come before it in two years. The year before, Warren had joined the dissenters when the Court found that DuPont had not violated antitrust laws in its cellophane business.[3] Now the issue before the Court was one of ownership; DuPont had acquired 23 percent of General Motors stock, and the government argued that such a large stake created an illegal monopoly, since DuPont was a General Motors supplier, not merely an investor. Always suspicious of big business—Warren still nursed one grudge from his battles with big oil in California and an even older one against the Southern Pacific—the chief justice announced at the first conference on the case that he believed DuPont had acquired its share in General Motors "for the purpose of controlling a channel for the outlet of its products."[4] That, Warren said, was enough to make it illegal under Section 7 of the Sherman Antitrust Act. Frankfurter objected to Warren's novel and expansive reading of the act, and wrote a dissent that accused the majority of disregarding the "language and purpose of the statute."[5]

That case was part of a developing pattern in the conflicting jurisprudences of Frankfurter and Warren as applied to business. Remembering his own railroad labors as well as the toll such labor took on his father and others, Warren searched for ways to relieve employees of burdens and to shift those burdens to companies, particularly big ones. Ignoring Frankfurter, Warren beginning in 1956 inserted the Court into a series of cases involving individual workers and their claims against their bosses under the Federal Employers Liability Act. Each time, Warren urged the Court to give benefits to the workers at the expense of their employers. At first, the justices, even Douglas, were puzzled, but they soon saw the cases as an expression of Warren's life and humanity. "He knew enough from first-hand experience to see the human values at stake in these FELA verdicts," Douglas noted.[6] Frankfurter viewed Warren's commitment less charitably. By 1957, he was so fed up he dashed off an intemperate note to Harlan:

The real truth of the matter is that some of our brethren play ducks and drakes with the jurisdictional requirements when they want to reach a result because they are self-righteous do-gooders, unlike Holmes who spoke of himself "as a judge whose first business is to see that the game is played according to the rules whether I like them or not."[7]

With Frankfurter, disagreement almost always slid into contempt. And in this case that natural inclination was egged on by one of those he most admired, Judge Learned Hand. Hand was a great judge, inclined like Frankfurter to see his duties in terms of self-restraint. That put him squarely at odds with Warren's sense of purpose, and as Hand took the measure of Warren he did not like what he saw. On January 1, 1956, he wrote to Frankfurter as part of their long, mutually admiring, and candid correspondence. Hand praised Warren's statesmanship and acknowledged that his leadership was helpful in the office of the chief justice. "But somehow," he added, "deep in my belly, I do long for more distinction."[8] By October, the month that Brennan arrived, Hand could not restrain himself even that much:

> The more I get of your present Chief, the less do I admire him. It is all very well to have a man at the top who is really aware of the dominant trends, but isn't it desirable to add a pinch or two to the dish of what we used to call "law"?[9]

A mutual friend of Hand's and Frankfurter's, Hand added, had taken to referring to Warren by a new nickname: "That Dumb Swede."[10] Frankfurter did not adopt the nickname in that exchange of letters, but by the end of the decade he was using it with his clerks, encouraging them to distrust and disparage the chief justice.[11] In unguarded moments with friends, Frankfurter made clear that he regarded Warren as a fool. Writing to Harlan, for instance, Frankfurter described one of Warren's opinions as "crude, heavy-handed, repetitive moralizing," and described the experience of reading it as akin to "eating rancid butter."[12]

Warren was a big and successful man. He came to the Court with a public career far broader than Frankfurter had accumulated. He was in no mood to be patronized. But Frankfurter lectured and lobbied, convinced that he could lead Warren by imposing his superior intellect on the mere politician who now served as his colleague and chief. Early on, the chief justice grew suspicious of Frankfurter's attempts to woo Warren's clerks; Warren gently but clearly directed them to cut off contact with Frankfurter.[13] In conference, Warren suffered Frankfurter's lectures with lessening patience. "All Frankfurter does is talk, talk, talk," Warren blurted at one point. "He drives you crazy."[14] For the most part, Warren suffered Frankfurter, but occasionally he lost his temper. In conference one day, Frankfurter was snickering and passing notes as Warren spoke. Warren blew: "I am goddamn tired of having you snicker while I'm talking. You do it even in the courtroom and people notice it." Frankfurter denied it, but Warren dressed him down anyway, much to Douglas's delight.[15]

Frankfurter was a distraction, but not enough of one to keep Warren from pursuing an amicable Court. Warren built his alliances upon common purpose and mutual regard. Until illness and philosophical drift helped undermine their relationship in the 1960s, Black was Warren's most important mentor, the guide who offered him a route toward judicial leadership and a genial host who provided both Earl and Nina Warren warm evenings in his Arlington home. In 1954, the two families shared Thanksgiving, the first of many holidays that would bring the Blacks and the Warrens together. Earl and Nina brought Virginia and Honey Bear; Hugo was accompanied by his daughter, Josephine, who lived with the justice for a time after his wife died.[16] "Hugo was a great friend to my father, and we loved Jo Jo," Virginia recalled decades later.[17]

At the Court, Warren relied on Black, often meeting with the senior justice just before and after Court conferences to plot strategy for those vitally important meetings. Theirs was a trusting friendship. Black felt free to make suggestions about which justices might best handle certain cases, and Warren usually concurred.[18] That gave Black enormous influence over the Court. And as Warren came to appreciate Black, it drove him still further from Frankfurter, personally and philosophically. For not only did Black offer gentility and friendship, he also presented Warren with a theory of judging that allowed Warren to be the chief justice he imagined being. Eventually, Warren would move even beyond Black, but in those early years, with Frankfurter sniping and condescending, with Black cajoling and entertaining, Warren slid easily under Black's wing.

Among the other justices, Warren tended carefully to Clark and genuinely enjoyed his bright spirit. Warren and Clark would duck out of Washington for quick hunting and fishing trips, and the two enjoyed swapping stories from their old days. For altogether different reasons, Warren developed a fondness and appreciation for Harlan, whose dignity impressed him, even if Harlan's politics were of a different sort. When Harlan suffered from health problems, Warren tended to him—late in life, Harlan's eyesight began to fade and he contemplated retirement. Warren persuaded him to stay and arranged for him to have an extra clerk to help with reading.[19] And yet even within those binds of collegiality and admiration, Brennan would always be special. He was different from Black, less a mentor and more a friend. And he was closer to Warren philosophically than any other member of the Court. Their bond began slowly but developed in the full richness of a lasting friendship, one that combined political solidarity with mutual reliance. From Warren, Brennan received key opinions and important counsel; in Brennan, Warren found a master of legal writing who could translate Warren's leadership into solid legal doctrine. It is one of American history's amusements that these two pillars of judicial activism, who hunted down injustice in order to toss it from the Constitution, were both appointed by a president who had no sympathy whatsoever for that style of judging.

For the balance of the Court, Warren attempted to forge unity by good cheer, hard work, and fair management—he distributed opinions evenly, spreading the workload among them. His own chambers were calmly professional, reminiscent of the governor's office, though on a much smaller scale. Two women—Margaret McHugh and Maggie Bryan—handled secretarial duties and scheduling, while his clerks, all of them men, did legal research and drafting. Unlike most of the justices, whose clerks worked out of adjoining offices, Warren's worked on a separate floor (space did not allow them to work next to Warren's chambers). They met frequently with Warren, however, sometimes as a group, other times individually, to discuss opinions or memoranda. Although the workweek was focused, Warren treated his clerks to lunches most Saturdays. They would generally work in the morning and then head for lunch at one of Warren's clubs or a local restaurant. There, Warren relaxed, as his clerks would politely draw him out on his favorite subjects—California and politics. Warren liked to talk on those easy afternoons. One clerk, Doug Kranwinkle, introduced him to vodka gimlets, and Warren would sometimes enjoy a drink or two as the afternoon wore on.[20] He was garrulous and comfortable, secure in the sanctity of his conversations with these close and devoted aides. And yet Warren maintained a reserve. He was welcoming but not casual, and he was deeply protective of the Court.

Once, when the Court clerks voyaged to the Justice Department for a lunch with Attorney General Robert Kennedy and ended up insulting their host, Kennedy retaliated by writing an article in which he ridiculed them. Warren, appalled, upbraided the clerks by reminding them that they did not exist as a group—that their allegiances were to their individual justices. All future lunches, he decreed, were to take place at the Court, not elsewhere. Chastened, the clerks agreed.[21]

Nina rarely joined Warren at the office or with his clerks; few of those who served Warren over the years felt they got to know Nina well. At home, however, she continued to arrange the Warrens' lives. The children were, of course, gone by the late 1950s, but they visited often, and Nina and Earl annually returned to California. In Washington, Nina performed the social graces expected of a chief justice's spouse—she presided over events involving the Court wives, and she maintained social contacts with other Washington figures. Her cakes became her signature, the recipes captured in Washington cookbooks, and her delivery honed to an art. Every January, Nina bought scores of boxes, which she stacked near the kitchen. As she baked, she packaged and delivered. Neighbors at the Sheraton-Park were frequent recipients, but Nina doled out cakes to friends and luminaries alike. When Richard and Pat Nixon traveled overseas in 1958, Nina sent their girls a pair of cakes, one with pink icing, the other with chocolate.[22]

In Washington's social circuit, Warren represented the Court and was well received. He appeared at functions almost weekly, often appearing at embassy receptions and particularly agreeing to attend those of smaller countries. Warren even managed to coax the other justices along with him in an annual public ritual. Starting in 1954, he arranged for the Court to travel as a group to the Army–Navy game, the perfect outing for a justice looking to project patriotism and still eager to take in a football game. Warren tended to the smallest details. He booked a special train car that the justices and their wives would take from Washington's Union Station in the morning. A light breakfast was served on the train, along with morning drinks. The Court and Court family then attended the game and returned to Washington by train that evening, dining together as the cars rumbled home in the dark. It was a festive, family gathering of the type that Warren loved. Most of the justices came to appreciate it as well, though Frankfurter and Black, who disagreed on so much but shared a distaste for sports, rarely attended. For those who did attend, it was both a chance to put aside their differences and a rare opportunity to present themselves in public, unrobed and as a family, not a bench.

Soon after arriving to the Court, Brennan joined the brethren on the trip to the game, bringing with him his oldest son, William Brennan III. The younger Brennan, recently mustered out of the Army, came in uniform, eager to show off his service to the members of the Court. Warren greeted him with the booming welcome of a friendly uncle. He asked about his service, his college life, his friends and family. After the game, young Brennan sat near Warren as the justices and their families dined. And upon returning to Washington, William Brennan took Virginia Warren to a movie. "It was one of the nicest days of my life," he said fifty years later.[23]

The Court's growing esteem—except, of course, in much of the South and in such places as the White House—lifted all the justices with it. Stories about division on the Court, rife in Vinson's day, gradually disappeared. Controversy surrounding the Court did not, however. On the day before Eisenhower's reelection, Steve Nelson, the Pennsylvania Communist whose earlier case had riled conservatives, returned one more time to the Court after the Justice Department was informed that a witness against him had lied in other cases. Conceding that, the government wanted the trial court to investigate whether the witness's testimony against Nelson—who was charged under his real name of Mesarosh—was truthful. Over the objections of Frankfurter, Harlan, and Burton, Warren refused and instead granted Mesarosh a new trial. "The government of a strong and free nation does not need convictions based upon such testimony," he wrote.[24] That briefly revived the uproar over the *Nelson* case, but the tribulations of that fall would seem small indeed compared with those that Warren and the brethren unleashed the following spring.

The first tremor of the Court's end-of-term rush came in an opinion by Brennan. Since just after Brennan's arrival in the fall, the justices had debated the case of Clinton Jencks, a union president who in April 1950 had filed the required affidavit swearing he had never been a Communist, only to have the government then contend that he had lied.[25] At issue was Jencks's right to confront witnesses who testified against him—specifically, the right to review reports made by the informants to the FBI so that they might be cross-examined about them. At trial, Jencks's lawyer had asked the witnesses about their reports, but both said they could not recall what they had said at the time. That cut off that line of questioning, so the lawyer asked that the reports be turned over to the judge so that the judge might review them and then decide which, if any, the defense was entitled to use in cross-examining the government informants. The judge denied the motion without explanation, and that decision was upheld on appeal.[26]

When the Supreme Court first discussed the *Jencks* case, Warren again set the tone, announcing that he could not see how Jencks could receive a fair trial without access to the reports needed to question witnesses against him. At first, the brethren were divided on the question of who, if anyone, could read the reports. Some favored giving the records to the defendant, while others would agree only to let the judge review them. "It is O.K. to let the judge see them, but not the lawyers," Clark said at the Court's first conference on the case.[27] Jencks's lawyers asked only that the material be shared with the judge, but Warren and Brennan were unwilling to stop there. Instead, they took the unusual position of arguing that Jencks deserved more than he asked for, that he himself deserved the reports if the witnesses who wrote or conveyed them were going to testify against him.

They carried the day, with Brennan writing for himself, Warren, and two others. Frankfurter joined them in all but a side discussion about the jury instructions to be given at Jencks's retrial, and Burton and Harlan joined in the outcome but urged that the trial judge be allowed to screen material before handing it over to a defendant. Only Clark dissented from the conclusion that Jencks deserved a new trial, but he did so in such angry language, the most memorable of his career on the bench, that he virtually ensured the reaction outside the Court. Allowing a defendant to peruse the reports, Clark warned, "afforded him a Roman holiday for rummaging through confidential information as well as vital national secrets."[28] The Court's critics could not have agreed more, and even as they loaded up for another round of Court-bashing, Warren and the brethren tossed them a sack of ammunition.

Four decisions were handed down on June 17, 1957, and with them the Warren Court demolished much of the nation's anti-Communist domestic-security program. Warren took charge of two cases himself, and his decision to write those opinions is revealing. Both—*Watkins v. United States* and *Sweezy v. New Hampshire*—turned on the question of how far legislative bodies can go in conducting investigations. Both Warren rulings served to curtail the power of legislatures, state and federal, to force witnesses to cooperate with legislators seeking to expose or embarrass their witnesses. In *Sweezy,* the New Hampshire attorney general, at the direction of its legislature, had corralled a Marxist economics professor from the University of New Hampshire and ordered him to discuss his lectures and involvement with the Progressive Party. The professor, Paul Sweezy, refused to answer. The attorney general then haled Sweezy into state court, where Sweezy again refused, and was held in contempt.[29]

In *Watkins,* the questions were put by the House Un-American Activities Committee and were addressed to a labor organizer named John Watkins.[30] Watkins denied that he had been a Communist but freely acknowledged that he had supported Communist causes. Watkins would not, however, tell the committee about people with whom he had associated:

> I do not believe that such questions are relevant to the work of this committee nor do I believe that this committee has the right to undertake the public exposure of persons because of their past activities. I may be wrong, and the committee may have this power, but until and unless a court of law so holds and directs me to answer, I most firmly refuse to discuss the political activities of my past associates.[31]

For asserting that principle, Watkins was convicted of contempt of Congress, a misdemeanor.

Warren well knew the gravity of challenging the right of legislatures to hunt down and expose Communists. Although McCarthy was dead by 1957, McCarthyism was kicking, and the spectacle of congressional committees dragging witnesses before the bar and badgering them into giving up their friends and associates was a grim leitmotif of the entire Cold War. The Court had long stood by and allowed demagogues to have their way with those witnesses, never mind the swath that those persecutions had cut through labor, the movie industry, and many other institutions of American life. Indeed, Warren specifically acknowledged the turf upon which he and the Court now warily trod. "We approach the questions presented," Warren wrote for his majority in *Watkins,* "with conscious awareness of the far-reaching ramifications that can follow from a decision of this nature."[32] That said, Warren did everything he could to limit those ramifications. Both cases cried out for a finding that the men cited for contempt had merely exercised their protected First Amendment rights of association and speech. In Sweezy's case, his only alleged association was with the Progressive Party and his only other contested act was delivering a lecture, surely a protected act of free speech. Likewise, Watkins

had admitted his Communist affiliations, shallow though they were; all that remained was whether Congress could bludgeon him into giving up names of old
associates. But Frankfurter and Harlan lobbied Warren to avoid a sweeping
constitutional conclusion based on the First Amendment. Frankfurter in particular leaned hard on the issue. He heavily edited Warren's draft opinion, and once he
had succeeded in scrubbing its references to free association, dashed off a handwritten note of self-congratulation to Harlan. "I have," he wrote, "deleted all references to the First Amendment."[33]

Under pressure from his right, Warren instead wrote a narrowly drawn opinion,
concluding that Watkins had not known enough about the congressional inquiry
to assess its proper scope and thus to determine whether its questions to him lay
within or outside that scope. Moreover, Warren further attempted to shield the
Court by assembling a strong majority behind the opinion. Only Clark dissented,
complaining of what he called, with some justification, the Court's "mischievous
curbing of the informing function of the Congress."[34]

But neither Warren's efforts to contain the opinion's reach nor his work to communicate the breadth of the Court's support for it could obscure the Court's revulsion at witch hunts. "No inquiry is an end in itself; it must be related to, and in
furtherance of, a legitimate task of the Congress," Warren wrote. "Investigations
conducted solely for the personal aggrandizement of the investigators or to 'punish' those investigated are indefensible."[35] Whereas Warren couched much of the
opinion in restrained language, those sentences spoke from his heart and personal
experience. As governor, he knew legislatures, and as a nominee, he had been pilloried and belittled by William Langer in 1954, had been called a drunk, and had his
loyalty questioned—all by an "investigator" interested in "personal aggrandizement" whose inquiry, at least as he conducted it, served no legitimate task of Congress. "Now that you have been shot at, you know what it's like," Burton Crane had
written to Warren at the end of Warren's travesty of a confirmation hearing. Crane
had urged Warren to add his voice "in protest against the marauding bands am-
bushing our freedoms."[36] It had taken four years, but on June 17, 1957, Warren did
just what Crane had asked him to do. "There is," Warren concluded, "no congressional power to expose for the sake of exposure."[37]

And that was not all. In addition to the two legislative cases announced that day,
the Court handed down two more. The first, *Service v. Dulles et al.,*[38] reinstated
John S. Service, a State Department China expert who had been cleared of disloyalty time and again but who was eventually fired by Secretary of State Dean Acheson in 1951 after a loyalty review board mysteriously concluded that there were
doubts about him. The second, *Yates v. United States,*[39] voided the convictions of
fourteen California Communists under the Smith Act, freeing five immediately
and ordering a new trial for the other nine. As with the other two cases decided that

day, *Service* and *Yates* were written with care not to overreach. What's more, both were the work of Harlan and thus bore his trademark craftsmanship and conservatism. In *Yates,* for instance, Harlan painstakingly dissected the meaning of the word "organize," as the defendants were convicted for their work in "organizing" the Communist Party. Having concluded that the organization of the party occurred in the 1940s and the defendants were not indicted until 1951, he announced that the statute of limitations barred their convictions, hardly a sweeping constitutional conclusion. Similarly, in *Service,* the Court did not overrule the regulations allowing the secretary of state to fire employees for disloyalty; it only concluded that those regulations had been misapplied in Service's case.

All those efforts might have dulled the reaction to the decisions, as might have the impressive majorities behind them. But no amount of care in drafting or in assembling votes could blunt the fury that the Court now unleashed. At the FBI, Hoover, so long a Warren admirer, could not believe what Warren's Court had wrought. Testifying before the House Subcommittee on Appropriations, Hoover mentioned *Yates,* the decision involving the California defendants charged under the Smith Act, and noted that the Communist Party heartily approved. One "top Communist functionary," said Hoover, called the decision "the greatest victory the Communist Party in America has ever received. The decision will mark a rejuvenation of the party in America." In contrast, some judges considered the ruling foolish, he added. One in particular, one Warren Burger, was favorably quoted by Hoover as deploring the "unfortunate trend of judicial decisions . . . which strain and stretch to give the guilty, not the same, but vastly more protection than the law-abiding citizen." Hoover understandably was accused of using his testimony to criticize the Court—saying that Communists approved of it hardly qualified as an endorsement. Aides replied by insisting that Hoover only had relayed the reactions of others.[40] Hoover and Warren remained civil after what quickly became known as "Red Monday," but their relations were on a decidedly cooling trend.

This time, the Court's critics also included not just a sulking, reticent Eisenhower but an actively angry one. The president was hosting one of his stag dinner parties on June 18, a day on which headlines across the country trumpeted the news of Red Monday. First the Court had backed the administration into an unpleasant predicament regarding segregation. Now its members had risen to the defense of Communists even as the president was engaged in a global contest for domination over Communism. And fully four members of the Red Monday Court were Eisenhower's own appointees: Warren, Brennan, and Harlan each played important parts in the cases; Charles Whittaker, whom Eisenhower had appointed just a few months earlier to replace the retiring Stanley Reed, joined the majorities in most but did not participate in *Jencks,* which was argued before he joined the Court. The president was livid. In front of his guests, he fumed that he had "never been as mad" as he was upon reading the *Jencks* decision and presumably the balance of the Court's work in the Communist cases.[41] The president's intemperate remarks quickly made it into print, and an embarrassed Eisenhower then wrote to Warren to defuse the problem. "I have no doubt that in private conversation someone did hear me express amazement about one decision," Eisenhower conceded, "but I have never even hinted at a feeling such as anger."[42]

Undoubtedly amused by the president's embarrassment—and over his attempt to mince a difference between being angry and amazed by the Court's work—Warren chose to let Eisenhower dangle a bit. Warren received the letter just before leaving for California with Nina, and waited for three weeks, until returning, to respond. His reply was a masterpiece of telling a president off without quite telling him off. First, Warren acknowledged that he'd had Eisenhower's letter for three weeks and had delayed responding only because he assumed stories would continue to be written, as if that mattered (in fact, Warren had received Eisenhower's letter on June 21 and had not left until June 25).[43] Then Warren demurred, noting that "it was considerate of you to write, but it was in no sense necessary." After noting that articles are often wrong for reasons of either ignorance or deceit on the part of the journalist, Warren added, "Whatever the reason, if unfounded, they should be ignored." "If unfounded" was plainly loaded, as Warren no doubt thought it quite likely that this story was, in fact, "founded." Turning then to the coverage of the Court's Communist cases, Warren said it too was often inaccurate, but stressed that he felt he could not respond: "While in other positions, I could and did speak out to counteract such statements. Here we do not respond regardless of what is said." Again, left unsaid was that Eisenhower's position, unlike Warren's, did allow him to speak out. Eisenhower had refused to do so after *Brown,* and now refused to do so to clarify the Court's actions in the Communist cases. Warren was chiding him. This time, Eisenhower did not reply.[44]

It was thus, isolated and angry, that Earl and Nina left for the summer. They were headed to England on the *Queen Mary,* looking forward to a break from American politics and to Earl's scheduled appearance before a meeting of the American Bar Association in London. There, it would be Warren's turn to lose his temper.

The trip across the Atlantic was a pleasant one. The Warrens departed from New York City on July 17. The skies were clear as the ship moved out of New York harbor, and Warren took in the view at the rail.[45] On board with the Warrens were legal luminaries heading for the meeting, including Attorney General Herbert Brownell and his wife. The Warrens and Brownells dined together and shared the trip, and Warren found time to mingle pleasantly with others aboard, including *New York Times* Washington bureau chief Luther Huston. After their easy passage, the group disembarked on Monday, July 22, arriving in Southampton. The Warrens then settled in at the Savoy Hotel and relaxed for the evening before the meetings began the following day. It was then that the trouble started. Warren was always a stickler for ceremony—"a bit of prickly pear," as one of his clerks said later[46]—and there was a snafu in the arrangements. Warren's calendar indicated that the dress for the evening was "informal," and so Warren arrived in a business suit. Entering the room, he discovered that the rest of the guests were in black tie. Warren suffered through the event, but felt misled and embarrassed by his hosts. Then, as the convention itself began, Warren was blindsided again, this time substantively.

Before leaving New York, the ABA had conducted a number of meetings, and Warren had come to London expecting the events there to be more ceremonial. He was thus taken aback when the convention received a committee report on "Communist Tactics, Strategy and Objectives."[47] The report's title was misleading. In fact, the report summarized much of the Supreme Court's recent case law on Communism, criticized those rulings, and recommended that Congress pass legislation to limit the Court's jurisdiction in such cases. As Warren recalled it, the report concluded with a warning: "If the courts lean too far backward in the maintenance of theoretical individual rights it may be that we have tied the hands of our country and have rendered it incapable of carrying out the first law of mankind—the right of self-preservation."[48]

Bad enough that the ABA should issue a statement that treated free expression and association as "theoretical individual rights." That it should do so without alerting Warren to its plans—and after soliciting his attendance—sent him over the edge. Warren lumbered through the week, then fled London for an extended vacation through Ireland and Scotland, where he brooded with Nina. Returning to the United States later that summer, Warren met on September 4 with the ABA's president, who came to Warren's chambers for the discussion.[49] Shortly thereafter, the Chief Justice of the United States, head of the nation's judiciary and one of its most recognizable public figures at home or abroad, quit the ABA.

Warren's feud with the ABA stretched over years, as he bitterly resented its unwillingness to lend support to the Court in the face of mounting attacks on it. But his anger went beyond pique. Warren felt personally betrayed—set up, even—by the Bar Association. Adding to that sense was an episode that occurred shortly after Warren submitted his resignation in September 1957. The bar's president asked Warren to reconsider his resignation, but Warren dropped the matter, assuming that his resignation was now final. A few months later, the secretary of the association announced that the chief justice had been dropped from the ABA for "non-payment of dues." Warren was incensed, worried what his children and grandchildren would think of him, and furious that he should be subjected to what he viewed as "absolute libel."[50] He demanded a personal letter from the bar's president clearing him of the nonpayment allegation. After several years of wrangling,

Warren received it. Satisfied but grumpy, he then recounted the episode in his memoirs at great length.

EVEN IN a presidency of unfortunate utterances, Eisenhower's comments at a July 17, 1957, news briefing were notable. This time it was not the president's evasiveness or his garbled syntax that were the problem. Instead, he spoke clearly—and dangerously. "I can't imagine," he said, "any set of circumstances that would ever induce me to send federal troops into any area to enforce the orders of a federal court."[51] From that moment forward, it was only a matter of time before some Southern governor would test the truth of the president's words. It did not take long.

In Little Rock, Arkansas, the local school board had made a better-than-average attempt to respond to the edicts of *Brown* and *Brown II*. A week after the first *Brown* ruling, the board publicly acknowledged its "responsibility to comply with Federal Constitutional requirements" and added, "[W]e intend to do so when the Supreme Court of the United States outlines the method to be followed."[52] The following year, even before *Brown II* was handed down, the board adopted a plan for integrating high schools first, followed by junior high and elementary schools. The entire district, under that plan, was to be integrated by 1963. Little Rock residents did not like it much, but they acquiesced. Those modest efforts of Little Rock were too much for opportunistic Arkansas state politicians. The legislature passed a slew of new laws aimed at blocking integration and directing the state attorney general to fight "in every Constitutional manner the unconstitutional decisions [*Brown* and *Brown II*]."[53]

Nine Negro students were scheduled to enter Little Rock's Central High School on September 3, 1957. Before they could, Governor Orval E. Faubus, under fire for not being segregationist enough, concluded that their admittance threatened the safety and well-being of the state of Arkansas. He mobilized the Arkansas National Guard and directed its armed soldiers to Little Rock. When the students arrived to begin classes, they were met by an angry mob and turned away from school by their state's National Guard.

Eisenhower might not have cared much for judicial activism or racial integration, but he understood power, and he knew that to allow Faubus to prevail was to announce the effective end of his own authority. The president was on vacation in Rhode Island, and he invited the governor to Newport to discuss the matter. Faubus cautiously agreed, coming to meet with Eisenhower even as his lawyers in Arkansas tried to persuade a visiting United States District Court judge, Ronald Davies, to delay the integration of Central High. Neither the summit in Newport nor the hearings in Little Rock resolved the crisis. At the September 14 Newport meeting, Eisenhower wrested from Faubus a public concession that the *Brown* decision, regardless of what he thought of it, "is the law of the land and must be obeyed." But Faubus also continued to insist that "changes necessitated by the Court orders cannot be accomplished overnight."[54]

Back in Little Rock, Faubus fought on until September 20, when Judge Davies ordered the desegregation of Central High to go forward and directed Faubus to get out of the way. Faubus's lawyer stormed out of the courtroom in protest, to the amazement of Thurgood Marshall, there to argue for the NAACP. Then the governor, his constituency now fully stirred, withdrew the Guard and turned Little Rock over to the mob (indeed, Faubus's actions were even worse than that, as an associate of the governor stayed with the mob and continued to agitate, according to Little Rock's mayor).[55] As Faubus knew it would and encouraged it to do, that mob then descended on the boys and girls who arrived on Monday, September 23, 1957, to begin school. The images of that morning remain, fifty years later, some of the most searing and venomous of the entire civil rights struggle. At least hundreds, perhaps thousands, of angry white men and women rebuffed the boys and girl, their neat clothing evidence of their dignity in the face of spitting and howling hatred. Little Rock's mayor and police department attempted to protect the students and usher them to school but could not withstand the mob, and eventually the Negro students were taken home for their safety.

The following day, September 24, was worse, and the mayor's morning telegram to Eisenhower verged on desperate:

SITUATION IS OUT OF CONTROL AND POLICE CANNOT DISPERSE THE MOB. I AM PLEADING TO YOU AS PRESIDENT OF THE UNITED STATES IN THE INTEREST OF HUMANITY LAW AND ORDER AND BECAUSE OF DEMOCRACY WORLDWIDE TO PROVIDE THE NECESSARY FEDERAL TROOPS WITHIN SEVERAL HOURS.[56]

Faubus stood back and watched. Eisenhower returned from Newport to the White House, where he solemnly addressed the nation, beginning by pointing out that he did so from "the house of Lincoln, of Jackson and of Wilson," about the action he was taking in Little Rock.[57]

In that city, under the leadership of demagogic extremists, disorderly mobs have deliberately prevented the carrying out of proper orders from a Federal Court. Local authorities have not eliminated that violent opposition and, under the law, I yesterday issued a Proclamation calling upon the mob to disperse. . . .

Whenever normal agencies prove inadequate to the task and it becomes necessary for the Executive Branch of the Federal Government to use its powers and authority to uphold Federal Courts, the President's responsibility is inescapable.

Even then, Eisenhower declined to lend his authority and popularity to the cause of integration. "Our personal opinions about the decision [*Brown*] have no bearing on the matter of enforcement," he insisted, reiterating his oft-repeated sentiment on that topic. As he neared the end of his address, Eisenhower emphasized that he had many friends in the South, even in Little Rock, and that he was confident that they joined him, whatever their views on school segregation, in recognizing the rule of law. In closing, Eisenhower urged the citizens of Arkansas to end their resistance to the federal courts and allow "peace and order" to return to Little Rock.[58]

The following morning, no such compliance was forthcoming. And now Eisenhower was out of options. Jotting notes to himself, he began by observing the obvious. "Troops," he wrote, "not to enforce integration but to prevent opposition by violence to orders of a court."[59] Still, troops were troops, as no one knew better than Eisenhower. And dispatching them to control a Southern city summoned a history he dearly wished to avoid resurrecting. He had tried every way to avoid it, but at 12:08 P.M. on September 25, Eisenhower issued the order authorizing the United States military to quell the violence in Little Rock and force obedience to the federal court.[60] Seven minutes later, he called the general overseeing the Army's 101st Airborne Division, and a thousand paratroopers were in Little Rock by nightfall, occupying an American city.

Hatred is the force of a mob. Cowardice is just as surely the essence of its character. The arriving soldiers were greeted with derision. One popular sign among the demonstrators read, "Join the Army and See the High Schools!"[61] But the protesters who were happy to stand up to unarmed high school students backed down in the face of rifles and bayonets. The Little Rock nine were escorted to school and guarded in classrooms. Integration, albeit nominal and at the point of a gun, had come to Little Rock.

Warren never commented on the Little Rock crisis of 1957 in public, but there is every reason to believe that he followed it intently. It was, after all, the culmination of the events that he had launched with *Brown* in 1954 as well as the consequence of Eisenhower's infuriating tolerance for Southern resistance. Moreover, Warren remained personally invested in the implementation of *Brown,* and even though his relations with Eisenhower were frayed, he remained in close contact with the administration through Brownell. On September 20, the same day that the district court in Little Rock ordered Faubus to back off, Warren had dinner with Brownell at Brownell's Washington home.[62]

Little Rock threatened to reerupt the next year, and local officials once again sought a delay from the district court, where they asked that integration be discontinued for two years and the Negro students already admitted to Central High be resegregated and sent to black schools. (Of the original nine, one had graduated and one, Minnie Jean Brown, had let down her guard for one moment. After months of silence, she snapped back when a white student called her a "nigger bitch." Minnie responded, "White trash," and was expelled.)[63] This time, the judge granted Little Rock's request, approving a two-year postponement in the desegregation effort in order to give the community time to cool off. The NAACP appealed, and the judge's delay order was overturned by the Eighth Circuit Court of Appeals. The Supreme Court then rushed into special session to consider the case and decide it in time for the new school year to begin.

Oral argument was set for August 28, and Warren hurried back to Washington from his vacation in California. He arrived on August 27, and met privately first with Black and then with Frankfurter. The following morning, he called the Court together into conference for an hour before he led the justices through the red velvet curtain. Thurgood Marshall was back again for the NAACP, and Richard Butler represented the Little Rock school board. Marshall was his comfortable self, graciously received and interrupted only occasionally as he rehashed arguments he had made before: The rights of the Negro boys and girls of Little Rock could not be placed on hold merely because the citizens of that city objected or because school or state officials believed more time would allow a smoother transition. The school district had used its time; now was the moment for implementation. "The rights we seek," Marshall reminded the justices, who needed no reminding, "are rights that have been recognized by the federal courts."

Butler knew he was arguing his case to an unsympathetic audience, but he managed through most of his time to make it without obviously agitating Warren or the brethren.[64] That surface amicability broke down near the end, however, as Butler returned after lunch to conclude and quickly locked horns with Warren. Earlier, Warren had attempted to express the Court's understanding of Little Rock's difficulties, trapped as it was between a Supreme Court edict and a recalcitrant governor, but when Butler tried to turn that sympathy into a defense, Warren bristled.

"Regardless of whether or not the people of Arkansas *should* recognize the United States Supreme Court decisions as the law of the land," Butler began, "the plain fact is that they *have not,* and it is most difficult for them to do so if not impossible when the governor of the state says that that is not the law of the land, that only Congress can really say what the law of the land is." That would have been pushing his luck, but Butler then attempted to reach Warren by reminding him that he, too, had "been the governor of a great state."

To equate Warren of California with Faubus of Arkansas was more than Warren would allow: "I never tried to resolve any legal problem of this kind as governor of my state. I thought that was a matter for the courts, and I abided by the decision of the courts, whether they were the courts of my state or, in their proper jurisdiction, the federal courts."

Butler should have stopped there, but in the heat of his argument, he pressed on. "We all realize that, sir," the lawyer insisted. "The point I'm making is this: that if the governor of any state says that a United States Supreme Court decision is not the law of the land, the people of that state, until it is really resolved, have a doubt in their mind and a right to have a doubt." That was lunacy—the suggestion that a governor's publicly expressed doubts about the law meant that it was not "really resolved"—and it cut to the flaw in Little Rock's argument. If true, it meant that the Court's word on *Brown* was not in fact final until and unless Faubus said it was. Warren had heard enough of interposition and defiance. He could contain himself no longer.

"But I have never heard such an argument made in a court of justice before," he said, his voice tight and his words coming unusually fast. "And I've tried many a case over many a year, and I have never heard a lawyer say that the statement of a governor as to what was legal or illegal should control the action of any court."

Butler tried to dig himself back out, saying that he only was trying to point out that the people of Arkansas were understandably confused when their governor preyed on their hope that there was something not final about the word of the Supreme Court. They were particularly susceptible to Faubus's claims, Butler said, because he was a respected state leader. "The short answer to that," Warren growled, "is that if they want to believe it, they'll believe it no matter who says it."[65] That was, for all practical purposes, the end of Butler's presentation and of his case.

So brusque was Warren with Butler that a legend has grown up around that day's argument. Often repeated is a reported exchange at the outset of the argument, when Butler was said to have begun by introducing himself as appearing "on behalf of the people of Little Rock." At that, the legend has it, Warren interrupted to demand, "What people?" From which Butler is said never to have fully recovered.[66] That exchange, though recalled by Ira Michael Heyman, a brilliant young man who clerked for Warren that term (and whose career soared afterward, eventually taking him to the head of Warren's alma mater, the University of California, Berkeley), is not borne out by the transcript or the tape recording of that day's argument. Yet its persistence says much about what those close to Warren saw of his mood in those weeks. Warren was a patient man, but Southern resistance had toppled his reserve.

After concluding the argument, the Court set a second session for September 11, determined to resolve the standoff in Little Rock before the beginning of the school year. That morning, before the lawyers came to Court, Warren met privately with Brennan. As he had demonstrated during the August oral argument, Warren was fed up—frustrated by a president who could only be goaded into action by a direct threat to his authority; furious at the presumption of Southern officials, even among the lawyers who appeared before him, that they could openly question the Court's authority; dumbfounded by the silly and dangerous spread of "interposition." This case offered Warren and his brethren the chance to assert the Court's power and clarify the duty of others to accede. Frankfurter remained convinced that there was a viable political center in the South, and he hoped the opinion and the argument would reach those moderates; he went so far as to urge Warren to open the argument by complimenting Butler on the district's attempts to integrate.[67] Warren disagreed. He was done urging.

Butler barely had a chance to present his argument, so often was he interrupted by the justices. He tried time and again to elicit sympathy for the school board he represented by pointing out that it was caught in the middle of a conflict between the state and federal governments, that it had tried to implement a desegregation plan but found itself thwarted by a governor who refused any integration and a federal government that insisted its courts be obeyed. For the Court to accept Butler's position it would in essence have had to agree that its own orders could be ignored. And Warren's unwillingness to do so was underscored by his barely suppressed fury that four years after it commanded desegregation, so many parties continued to avoid their duties under *Brown.* "If we stop that program [Little Rock school desegregation], we are denying this same right to approximately 40 percent of the children of your community, aren't we?" Warren asked Butler, referring to the Negro children of Little Rock.

"We take the position that you are not denying the right. You are delaying the fulfillment of a constitutional right which you have said they have," Butler replied.

"Well, this decision, the *Brown* decision, was in 1954," Warren said with a sigh. "This is 1958. Two and a half years will bring it up almost to 1961. Now if all those children are denied the right to go to the elementary schools, aren't they being denied permanently and finally a right to get equal protection under the laws during their primary grade years?"

"They would be deprived of the personal fulfillment of what we consider an intangible right expressed by this Court," Butler said.

It took a moment for that to sink in, but Warren then pounced on Butler's revealing reply. "Why do you call it an intangible right?" he asked.

Butler was caught. "Well, I was distinguishing that as against monetary rights," he responded lamely.

"If somebody was to deprive you of life, liberty or property, would that be an intangible right?" Warren asked. Butler's answer—"I did not have in mind that sense"—spoke volumes about the vacuity of his argument.

All that was left was for Thurgood Marshall to dispense with the notion that the Little Rock School Board deserved the Court's sympathy rather than its order. Marshall did so in fine fashion. Yes, he acknowledged, the past months had been difficult. There was the gauntlet of the previous year, the mobs, the troops, the threatening letters and phone calls. But there also were Negro children who had been promised an integrated classroom by the unanimous Supreme Court of the United States. They had entered those classrooms through mobs. And now Little Rock proposed to take them out again, to yield to the mob rather than to the pleas of those whose rights were being violated. They were not abstractions, those children. They were young boys and girls with constitutional rights. If that made life difficult for the school board, so be it. Marshall's best line summed up the case in three words: "Democracy is tough."[68]

The second oral argument in *Cooper v. Aaron* was intriguing for what it said about Warren's mood, but the Court had already made up its mind, and announced its decision the following day. Little Rock officials were directed to proceed with integration; the district court's granting of the delay was overturned. It took a few more weeks for Brennan, working closely with Warren throughout, to polish his opinion—Harlan tried his hand at a draft as well, but the final work relied much more heavily on Brennan's approach.[69] When it was released, it bore the earmarks of Warren's exhausted patience. *Cooper* asserted, once and for all, that the Court was the last word on the Constitution and that all officials, state and federal, must accept it. Enough of interposition, it effectively said: We are the law; you will obey. The opinion spoke that command most forcefully and eloquently in a passage written by Black and used at the outset:

> As this case reaches us it raises questions of the highest importance to the maintenance of our federal system of government. It necessarily involves a claim by the Governor and Legislature of a State that there is no duty on state officials to obey federal court orders resting on this Court's considered interpretation of the United States Constitution.... We are urged to uphold a suspension of the Little Rock School Board's plan to do away with segregated public schools in Little Rock until state laws and efforts to upset and nullify our holding in Brown v. Board of Education have been further challenged and tested in the courts. We reject these contentions.[70]

After an exhaustive review of the facts and legal history of the case before it, the Court then upbraided Arkansas officials with a condescendingly rudimentary lesson in constitutional law—citing John Marshall for the elementary proposition that the Court interprets the Constitution and no intervening state authority may contravene that. Then, at the suggestion of Harlan, the opinion drew to a close by calling explicit attention to the unanimity of *Brown* and the continued unanimity of the Court despite the departure and replacement of three members of the original *Brown* Court. "Since the first Brown opinion three new Justices have come to the Court," the opinion noted. "They are at one with the Justices still on the Court who participated in that basic decision as to its correctness, and that decision is now unanimously reaffirmed."[71] Rather than merely bearing the name of its principal author, Brennan, and listing the other justices as having joined, *Cooper v. Aaron* was signed by all nine members of the Court, a legally meaningless flourish but a memorable one meant to highlight the Court's resolve even in the face of its changing membership. *Cooper* was about demonstrating that the Court meant business.

As Brennan was putting the final touches on *Cooper*—incorporating Black's stirring opening passage and adopting suggestions by Harlan for the conclusion—Frankfurter once again annoyed Warren. Despite Frankfurter's long belief in the power of unanimity in the segregation cases, he chose this moment to write for himself, apparently believing that his tutelage of so many lawyers as a professor gave him a special ability to persuade the ever-elusive Southern moderate to listen to the Court. When Warren learned that Frankfurter intended to write a concurrence to *Cooper,* he was furious. He, Brennan, and Black tried mightily to persuade Frankfurter not to do it, but Frankfurter was adamant. "This caused quite a sensation on the Court," Warren recalled.[72] In fact, Frankfurter's concurrence—which substantively added little if anything to the ruling of the Court, which he joined—ended what was left of the relationship between Warren and Frankfurter. They now openly disliked each other; the rift from *Cooper* never healed.

Warren's insistence on obedience to his Court was both constitutionally correct and emotionally inevitable. He had struggled from 1954 through 1958 to protect minorities and dissidents from an often indifferent American political leadership. And yet even as *Cooper* made clear that the Court meant to be taken seriously, Warren and his colleagues effectively withdrew.

Conventional wisdom records the history of the Warren Court as a straight line—an unbroken series of activist rulings on behalf of individual rights. In fact, as Powe astutely notes, 1958 was a signature year in the Court's history, for it combined two nearly opposite events: the assertion of power in *Cooper* and the near loss of that power in Congress, what Powe terms the Court's "near-death experience."[73] The latter event shook the Court's libertarianism and effectively displaced Warren as its leader for a time.

The first signs that the Court's political support was bottoming out came early in 1958, when Learned Hand, prodded by his friend Frankfurter, completed and delivered the Oliver Wendell Holmes Lectures at Harvard.[74] By 1958, Learned Hand was an old man, eighty-seven, and his lifetime of thought about the proper role of judges in a democratic society poured out in the lectures. There was a tinge of bitterness in Hand's work, but there was eloquence, too, and deep consideration, the melding of judicial notions that he had honed in his long service on the bench and his extensive, unguarded correspondence with friends such as Frankfurter. While Hand in his lectures never mentioned Warren or his court by name, Hand's discomfort with Warren specifically and of activist judging generally was laced through the three discussions, particularly in the final day. "For myself," Hand told his standing-room-only audience near the conclusion of his talk, "it would be most irksome to be ruled by a bevy of Platonic Guardians, even if I knew how to choose them, which I assuredly do not. If they were in charge, I should miss the stimulus of living in a society where I have, at least theoretically, some part in the direction of public affairs."[75]

Hand's critique was far too scholarly to be generally appreciated—indeed, many of those who did understand it disagreed—but it encouraged the Court's two main legions of critics, the anti-Communists and the Southern racists. Buoyed to be in such learned company and still stinging over Red Monday and the never-ending in-dignities of the desegregation cases, those two camps pooled their efforts and intro-duced a host of bills intended to limit the Court's authority or otherwise curb and embarrass it. By spring, the Congress was teeming with ideas for how to restrict the power of the Court. The chief vehicle for doing so became known as the Jenner-Butler bill, which sought to strip the Court of its jurisdiction over domestic-security cases, an idea which, if adopted, would have vastly reduced the Court's power to control its own docket and to police lower court decisions in that field. In addition, passage would have emboldened the Court's critics and opened the door for further congressional tampering.

Warren refused to give quarter. Through late 1957 and early 1958, he and Frankfurter fenced over the case of Albert L. Trop, who, while serving as a private in the Army stationed in Morocco, escaped from the stockade in Casablanca and was arrested the following day on the road to Rabat. He was sentenced to three years of hard labor for desertion and was dishonorably discharged. That might have ended Trop's ill-conceived desertion, but years later, when he applied for a passport, it was denied because the government concluded that he had forfeited his citizenship by deserting from the Army. Hard labor was one thing, citizenship an-other. Trop sued to regain it, arguing that Congress did not have the power to pass a bill to strip him of his most basic American right—the right to be an American.[76] Frankfurter sided with the government, and initially the Court did as well. His drafts from late 1957 are listed as an "opinion of the Court." But Warren worked his justices as he circulated his thoughts. As late as March 14, 1958, Warren still thought he would file a dissent, but that draft included a new statement about the vitality of the Constitution, and it picked up enough votes to transform it into a majority opinion, one whose language would prove among the most resilient of his work.[77] Analyzing the Eighth Amendment's protection against cruel and unusual punishment, Warren wrote, "The Amendment must draw its meaning from the evolving standards of decency that mark the progress of a maturing society."[78] Rarely has the idea of an evolving Constitution found better expression.[79]

A more timid chief justice might have let *Trop* go the other way. For as Warren won over his Court in that case, the pressure in Congress against it was rapidly building. By the summer of 1958, the situation was bleak indeed. In highlighting this nearly forgotten episode in the Court's history, Powe compares it to the brinks-manship of the Court-packing debate early in FDR's tenure. That fracas drew much more public attention because it centered so personally on the justices. But the 1958 clash over Jenner-Butler was in some ways even more dire, as it threatened not just the personnel of the Court but its structural and political integrity. And where Court-packing was handily defeated, Court-stripping came within a razor-thin margin of victory at a time when President Eisenhower was in no mood to save it. Indeed, Eisenhower had grown so exasperated with Warren—and by now, Brennan, too—that when Burton went to talk to him that summer about retiring, the president "evidenced disappointment" with those two appointments, remarkably indiscreet of the president given that Burton was a colleague of Brennan's and Warren's.[80]

The first round of that year's attack on the Court went to the justices when Learned Hand, having encouraged the Court's foes, then refused their invitation to testify on behalf of the bill. Hand deplored much of what the Warren Court had wrought, but he was too intellectually honest to join its most frothing critics. Moreover, although Hand declined to comment on the bill's constitutionality, he did allow that he did not think its provisions removing jurisdiction from the Court were good for the nation.[81] The Court's attackers had stumbled into intellectual credibility; now it was taken away. Still, they shouldered on in both houses, amending the bill through the spring and summer and eventually bringing it to the floor of the Senate on August 20. It was there that Majority Leader Lyndon Johnson, who was even then building his national résumé to run for president and thus eager to distance himself from Southern attacks on the bench, worked mightily to keep the bill's supporters from gaining the upper hand. Johnson's efforts barely succeeded, as 41 senators voted against the motion to table; 49 supported the motion, however, and the bill died.

That was not quite the end, as a second bill, this one from the House, proposed to rewrite existing law on Communist investigations and prosecutions so as to make them invulnerable to the Court's opposition. That bill came even closer. The Court's supporters lost their motion to table, then Johnson managed to adjourn the Senate for the day. After berating Hubert Humphrey for miscounting the votes and allowing the motion to table to fail, Johnson alighted upon another tactic to kill the bill. He found Utah Republican Wallace Bennett and persuaded him that if the motion resulted in a tie, Vice President Nixon would have to vote to break it. That vote would haunt Nixon politically, Johnson warned, hurting him no matter which side he came down on. When the roll was called, Bennett, a supporter of Nixon, voted to send the bill back to committee, where it died.[82]

Across the street, Warren and his colleagues exhaled in relief. One vote had saved them, and it had been cast not in defense of Warren and his Court but in defense of Nixon. The legislation, Warren wrote in repose years later, "evoking as it did the atmosphere of Cold War hysteria, came dangerously close to passing."[83]

Some of the justices recoiled at their close shave. Warren himself showed no signs of retrenching, but Frankfurter, already inclined toward restraint, now moved aggressively to back the Court away from controversy. In domestic security especially, but also in segregation and criminal justice cases, the Court withdrew into a period of stunned quietude, a period that lasted until roughly 1960, ending decisively only with Frankfurter's retirement in 1962.

One early test involved the double-jeopardy case of Alphonse Bartkus, who was accused of robbing a savings-and-loan in Cicero, Illinois, on December 18, 1953. Tried in federal court, Bartkus was acquitted, but officials were unwilling to let the matter drop. Federal authorities gathered up their investigative file and shipped it over to state prosecutors, who presented it to a state grand jury and secured an indictment and ultimately a conviction of Bartkus in state court. Because of his prior record, Bartkus was sentenced to life in prison.[84] His conviction having been upheld by Illinois courts, Bartkus brought his complaint to the United States Supreme Court in 1957, and the following January, the Court split 4–4, thus allowing Bartkus's conviction to stand.[85] He then asked for a rehearing, and the Court granted it, restoring the case to its docket in May 1958 and taking it up again in the fall, when the summer's brush with Congress was fresh in the justices' minds.

Warren, Douglas, and Black never had any doubts about how the case should be resolved. The Constitution bars "double jeopardy," trying an individual twice for the same crime. In this case, Bartkus had been tried twice for robbing the same bank, and both juries heard evidence gathered by the same investigators. The only substantive difference was the courtroom—in one case, it belonged to the federal government; in the other, to the state of Illinois. That was a meaningless distinction to Warren—and, no doubt, to Bartkus. The chief justice announced from the start that he would overturn the conviction.

Frankfurter had different ideas and several overlapping agendas. First, *Bartkus* offered him an opportunity to tweak Black yet again over their different interpretations of the Fourteenth Amendment and whether it had imposed the Bill of Rights on the states. For years, Frankfurter had been losing that battle incrementally, and here, in *Bartkus*, he wanted the chance to state emphatically that Black was wrong and he was right. Second, keeping Bartkus in jail would send up a white flag to those who believed the Court hell-bent on putting criminals back on the streets. As an act of judicial diplomacy, Frankfurter saw in *Bartkus* the opportunity for tactical retreat.

Initially, Brennan indicated some sympathy with the *Bartkus* prosecutors. Brennan, his clerks recalled, "agreed that two separate prosecutions by a state and the federal government for the same act were not prohibited by the Constitution."[86] But as Brennan reviewed the record, he became troubled by the cooperation between the state and federal governments, by the sharing of information that had rendered the state trial in effect a rerun of the failed federal prosecution. The second prosecution, he concluded, "while in form a state prosecution, was in essence a second federal prosecution and thus was barred by the Constitution."[87] That brought Brennan to his natural place—the company of Warren, Black, and Douglas. And it left both sides—the unrepentant individualists and the world-wary judicial statesmen—looking for a fifth vote. Their feud grew "hot," in Brennan's word, fueled by the groaning pressure on the Court; it settled on the decision of Justice Potter Stewart.[88]

Stewart was one of two new Eisenhower justices. The first to arrive, Charles Whittaker, took his seat from the retiring Stanley Reed in March 1957. Whittaker was a skilled Missouri lawyer first named to the federal bench by Eisenhower in 1954. Just two years later, at the urging of the editor of the Kansas City Star but over Whittaker's objections, Eisenhower elevated him to the Eighth Circuit Court of Appeals. And then, again with Whittaker objecting, Eisenhower placed him on the Supreme Court in 1957. The judge's rapid rise gnawed at his insecurity, which then mushroomed on the high bench. Whittaker developed the belief that at least one justice should read the entire record of a case, a record that can include thousands of pages. Overwhelmed by the responsibility of serving as a justice and ill-prepared for it, Whittaker struggled terribly. Reflecting back on his tenure in later years, he ruefully characterized his service in baseball terms. "I went to first on a walk, second on a fielder's choice, and I was sacrificed around third to home," one of his clerks recalls him saying.[89]

The fifth and last of Eisenhower's appointees, Stewart came less than a year later, taking his place after Burton retired in 1958. Stewart came from a conservative Ohio family and arrived at the United States Supreme Court from the Sixth Circuit Court of Appeals. He was a pragmatic man who would, in his twenty-two years on the Supreme Court bench, often find himself between the magnetic poles of his colleagues, joining the liberals in some instances, though more often siding with the conservatives. But while Whittaker agonized at the stress of centrism, Stewart seemed to like it. He was fond of Warren personally, admiring the chief justice's patriotism while not always accepting Warren's views of the Constitution. Because he replaced the fundamentally conservative Burton, Stewart did not significantly alter the Court's ideological balance, but his arrival, combined with Frankfurter's more aggressive retreat, initially helped push Warren into dissent on major opinions of the Court.

Bartkus was argued in the shadow of the congressional debate over the Court's jurisdiction, and it thus marked an early test of strength between the two opposing camps on the Court. Both sides lobbied Stewart. Brennan and Frankfurter made their cases in competing memos, and once their cases were on the table, Stewart tipped the balance by joining Frankfurter. The Court upheld Bartkus's conviction by a 5–4 vote. Black, Douglas, and Warren were irritated and let it show in Black's dissent. "The Court," Black wrote, "apparently takes the position that a second trial for the same act is somehow less offensive if one of the trials is conducted by the Federal Government and the other by a State. Looked at from the standpoint of the individual who is being prosecuted, this notion is too subtle for me to grasp."[90] Bartkus went to prison.[91]

For the moment, that was where the Court rested—torn between Warren, Douglas, Black, and Brennan on one side and Frankfurter, Harlan, Stewart, and Clark on the other. Sometimes Stewart would join the Warren bloc, and the ninth justice, Whittaker, would move from one camp to the other depending on the case. That perpetuated the standoff that in turn led to the slowing of the Court's activism. It also placed an enormous strain on Whittaker.

As the 1950s drew to a close, the Court wallowed and feuded. So bitter were the relations between Warren and Frankfurter, the heads of their respective blocs, that at times they leaked out in public. On June 30, 1958, Frankfurter delivered a long, charged dissent from a case involving California's procedures for evaluating the sanity of defendants. As Frankfurter spoke, Warren became visibly agitated and finally could not contain himself. "Neither the judgment of this Court nor that of California is quite as savage as this dissent would indicate," he said when Frankfurter concluded.[92] Their running spat would continue to flare after that, making its way to the front pages in 1961, when they again tussled over a Frankfurter dissent. The headline on the jump page of that day's New York Times said it well: "Warren Is Irked by Frankfurter."[93]

Two of the cases that shouted the Court's new posture came together, announced on a sort of Blue Monday as counterpart to 1957's Red version. On 1959's end-of-term Monday, the Court handed down two rulings—with Warren dissenting in both—that substantially gave back to Congress and state legislatures the very powers to "expose for the sake of exposure" that it had denied just two years earlier. In the first, a thirty-one-year-old Vassar College teacher named Lloyd Barenblatt had been brought before the House Un-American Activities Committee and ordered, as so many others had been before him, to divulge whether he or his friends had ever been Communists. He refused to answer and was held in contempt. As he fought his conviction, Barenblatt understandably was heartened by the Court's ruling in Watkins, when it found that HUAC's authorization was so vague that Watkins could not be convicted for refusing to participate. Two years later, HUAC was still sputtering away, and Barenblatt had every right and reason to assume that the Court's decision in Watkins would apply to him as well.[94]

But Barenblatt underestimated the effect of fear. In *Watkins,* Warren had acceded to Frankfurter's urging and ducked the First Amendment ruling that would have decided that case on constitutional terms. Yet Warren still had delivered a strong majority that set Watkins free. Those were bolder days. Now Barenblatt confronted a Court with barely a congressional vote to spare. Harlan, writing for the five-member majority that included Frankfurter, ruled that *Watkins* did not impose a "broad and inflexible" protection for those confronted with uncertainty about the legitimate reach of HUAC. On the central question of whether the First Amendment protected the confidences entered into in political discourse, the Court said, simply, No. "The protections of the First Amendment," Harlan wrote, ". . . do not afford a witness the right to resist inquiry in all circumstances." Instead, the government's interests (those of self-preservation) had to be balanced against those of the person being questioned (those of free speech, privacy, and the right to associate with others of like mind). And the balance in this case, the majority concluded, tipped against Barenblatt, as one might expect it would when "self-preservation" sat on one side of the scale. He was ordered to answer or be held in contempt.[95]

Warren never was and never would be an absolutist. He did not accept Black's belief that because the First Amendment specifies that Congress shall enact "no law" abridging speech, literally any law curbing speech was unconstitutional. But here, as his majority slipped away from him and he was forced to watch a young man bullied, the chief justice agreed to sign on to Black's dissent. And though Black never did persuade his colleagues that "no law" meant literally "no law," he was rarely more stirring than in his defenses of a robust debating America, one where people were free to test their ideas against one another without fear of government repercussions. Here, set against the sterile arguments of a cowardly majority, he let loose. "The First Amendment says in no equivocal language that Congress shall pass no law abridging freedom of speech, press, assembly or petition," Black wrote as he warmed to the meat of his opinion. "The activities of this Committee, authorized by Congress, do precisely that, through exposure, obloquy and public scorn."[96] Black acknowledged that in some instances government could balance its interests against those of protestors but stressed, as he would with increasing conviction in later years, that only conduct might be regulated—a man seeking to broadcast his political views over a loud phonograph, say, could be ordered to turn it down. It was important, however, that here it was only the public peace that was allowed protection—the public did not need protection from ideas. Beyond that, balancing was a fiction and the majority had misconstrued the government's side of the ledger, Black wrote:

> At most it balances the right of the Government to preserve itself, against Barenblatt's right to refrain from revealing Communist affiliations. Such a balance, however, mistakes

the factors to be weighed. In the first place, it completely leaves out the real interest in Barenblatt's silence, the interest of the people as a whole in being able to join organizations, advocate causes and make political "mistakes" without later being subjected to governmental penalties for having dared to think for themselves. . . . It is these interests of society, rather than Barenblatt's own right to silence, which I think the Court should put on the balance against the demands of the Government, if any balancing process is to be tolerated.[97]

This was more strident language than Warren would write himself, but he was at his wit's end, and it was difficult to resist such clear logic and strong prose. He signed on with Black, as did Douglas and Brennan, the latter of whom wrote a brief separate opinion but endorsed the work of Black as well. None of that helped Barenblatt. Rebuffed by the Supreme Court, he reported to authorities to serve his six-month sentence for contempt of Congress. After time in District of Columbia jail and federal prisons at Lewisburg and Danbury, he regained his freedom, which he reclaimed without the compromise of repentance.

Barenblatt was just one of two men to suffer on June 8, 1959, from the Supreme Court majority's failure of courage. The second was Willard Uphaus. Uphaus was nearly seventy years old when his case came to the United States Supreme Court, and he had spent years fencing with New Hampshire's attorney general, Louis Wyman, the same attorney general who had unsuccessfully sought to question Sweezy a few years earlier. Uphaus was a Methodist minister and a tough, flinty old character. A pacifist and leftist who had made trips to Moscow and Warsaw, he was the director of the World Fellowship Center, a quiet spot on a New Hampshire pond where, every summer, several hundred politically engaged men and women gathered to talk and listen to speakers. Uphaus's unapologetic embrace of leftist causes drew Wyman's attention and then ire, as Uphaus refused to give the attorney general a list of employees and guests of the camp. As he had with Sweezy, Wyman dragged Uphaus to court and asked him again, this time in front of a judge. Uphaus arrived ready. He came to court that day with a copy of the Bill of Rights in his hand and said his piece: "In the final analysis, after one has prayed, after one has thought of all aspects, one must, before God, make up his own mind or his own heart and conscience as to what he shall do. . . . I don't want to involve innocent people in the attorney general's network."[98] Unimpressed, the judge held him in contempt and ordered him held until he divulged the names; when he continued to refuse, Uphaus faced the real possibility that he could spend the rest of his life in jail.

Uphaus came to the Supreme Court with all the same reason to believe he would find relief there that Barenblatt had expected. Like Barenblatt, he would leave disappointed. The majority, again a majority of one, upheld Uphaus's contempt citation and cried crocodile tears over the effect that turning over the names of guests would inevitably have. Exposure, Clark acknowledged for his brethren, "is an inescapable incident of an investigation into the presence of subversive persons within a State."[99] Never mind that "exposure for exposure's sake" was all that Wyman had in mind; there was no allegation that any person attending the camp had broken any law by being there. And never mind, too, that the Court had prohibited forced disclosure of NAACP records by Alabama under strikingly similar circumstances. The Supreme Court had paid a price for standing in defense of Communists and leftist dissent for long enough. With Barenblatt and Uphaus, it was washing its hands of these burdensome allies.

Warren, however, was not. He joined again with Brennan, Black, and Douglas in puncturing the majority's reasoning. Brennan's opinion in *Uphaus* lacked the fire or eloquence of Black's in *Barenblatt,* but it ultimately sided with Uphaus in defense of his right to protect the names, not just for Uphaus's sake but for the sake of a society that depends on the uninhibited exchange of sometimes unpopular ideas. "In an era of mass communications and mass opinion, and of international tensions and domestic anxiety," Brennan wrote, "exposure and group identification by the state of those holding unpopular and dissident views are fraught with such serious consequences for the individual as inevitably to inhibit seriously the expression of views which the Constitution intended to make free."[100] Although the United States Supreme Court would not stand with him, Uphaus still refused to turn over the names, and spent a year in jail rather than submit to Wyman. Exhausted by the conflict, he finally was released just before Christmas in 1960. "I was able at the end of the year to emerge victorious, and to say I had peace in my heart, first because I had stood firm, and second because I held no hate in my heart for any human being," Uphaus later reflected.[101] He had kept his courage where the Court had not.

The term ended that summer with Warren in a foul mood. Some of the pressure on the Court had subsided, but only because it had gone soft. An editorial in the *Washington Post* commended the cooler temper in Congress regarding the Court, crediting leaders there but also noting that "the total output of decisions of the Court's last term seemed to be more moderate than in the previous term."[102] That might have helped ease pressure on the Court, but for Warren, it was nothing to be proud of.

At the *New York Times,* Arthur Krock was even more pointed, writing on June 14, 1959, that the Court appeared to have slipped away from Warren and surmising that the new majority was beating its retreat in response to congressional and public pressure. "Two Supreme Court 5 to 4 decisions last Monday [*Barenblatt* and *Uphaus*] have produced a deluge of speculation and firm assertions that 'conservatives have recaptured the majority from liberals,'" Krock wrote. Those conclusions, he added, seemed somewhat off, but not entirely. Speculating as to why, Krock argued that the "Supreme Court is trimming its sails to ride out a gale." The columnist even compared the 1959 decisions to the Court when it pulled back in the face of Roosevelt's Court-packing proposal, and he concluded by noting that Harlan now was leading the Court's "rechecking process," while Warren was consigned to dissenting.[103] To his credit, Warren did not waver. It is never comfortable for a chief justice to write in dissent—it advertises his lack of control—but since Warren was both too principled and too stubborn to soften his views, that was all that was left for him to do.

As summer approached, Earl and Nina looked forward to their annual trip overseas—this time to Europe and the Soviet Union—but first had a few stops to make on the Washington social circuit. At one of those, on the night of June 28, Warren's accumulated frustrations blew. The subject, as it so often was in his life when frustrations came to a head, was Richard Nixon.

By 1959, Nixon was well on his way toward announcing his candidacy for president of the United States, the position he had patiently pursued ever since his vice presidential election in 1952. The speculation near the end of Eisenhower's first term about who might succeed him if he did not or could not run again disappeared when Eisenhower chose to seek reelection. Warren had so firmly taken himself out of that race that few raised it again in 1959, as the administration wound down. But Nixon was openly a candidate. One element of that many-headed effort was the need to soften Nixon's public persona. Seen by many as little more than Eisenhower's youthful attack dog, Nixon craved a more complete personality, one that would attract the wider spectrum of supporters needed in order to capture the presidency.

An author named Earl Mazo offered Nixon the chance to achieve just that. Mazo was at work on a biography of Nixon, and his take was decidedly sympathetic. Nixon cooperated extensively with Mazo, and the resulting book was published in 1959. Warren read reviews of the book with irritation (he insisted he did not read the book itself), and on that June evening in 1959, he ran into Mazo at a dinner party celebrating the twenty-fifth wedding anniversary of two West Coast journalists, Naomi and Barney Nover.[104] In his memoirs, Warren recalled the argument that then broke out between himself and Mazo as centering on Warren's complaint that Mazo had resuscitated "an old political canard"—namely, that Warren had sought to block Nixon's career in retaliation for Nixon's treatment of Helen Gahagan Douglas. That, of course, was not true. Warren had withheld his support for Nixon even before Nixon wheeled on Douglas, and Warren's real resentment of Nixon dated from the 1952 convention, not the 1946 congressional campaign. But if the facts were off, the underlying point was uncomfortably close—that Warren had stifled Nixon and Nixon had lived uncomfortably under Warren's shadow for years. Sensing that Mazo was close to the truth and still indignant that his facts were wrong, Warren gruffly insulted the author. The exact words remained in dispute even decades later—a journalist overhearing the exchange reported that Warren had called Mazo a "damned liar," which Warren denied—but the essence of the exchange was clear. Warren insulted Mazo, in a room full of journalists there to honor the anniversary of two colleagues, and one of the reporters in attendance could not resist publishing the outburst, despite Washington's general presumption in those days that parties were off the record.

Whether Warren called Mazo a liar or just incompetent, whether he raised his voice or spoke through gritted teeth, the argument demonstrated more about Warren's state of mind than it did about the book. Warren prided himself on self-control, and on that June evening, after so many indignities, after the irritations of Frankfurter, the slights of Eisenhower, the defiance of racists, the campaigns of anti-Communists, the rumblings of old and new congressional foes, and now, God forbid, the resurrection of Richard Nixon, Warren blew. And, of course, the controversy only served to sell Mazo's book and promote the candidacy of Richard Nixon. Warren was lost.

He left that summer in a funk, brooding over the aimlessness of his Court, unsure of what the coming year would bring. Earl Warren was sixty-eight years old. He had governed California in triumph and had righted the nation's moral purpose in his early years on the Court. But what was next for him? He fell back on routines—travel that summer, the World Series in October, social graces with the Court in the fall. Every member of the Court was invited to dinner at the Warrens' in late October. Everyone but Frankfurter came.[105]

And then, as suddenly as the Court had been frozen and Warren trapped into inaction, so did those constrictions begin to thaw. In February 1958, Learned Hand had shocked the Court with his erudite denunciation of its work and his snide allusion to Warren and his colleagues as "Platonic Guardians." Two Februaries later, a new wind blew through American life, this time not the hard gale of one of its most esteemed legal minds but rather the freshening breeze of a group of North Carolina college students who had been pushed too far.

AT FOUR P.M. on February 1, 1960, four young black men, all students at North Carolina A&T College, wandered into the Main Street Woolworth's in Greensboro, North Carolina. They shopped for a few minutes, mingling with black and white customers, and then made their way to the all-white lunch counter. They sat down and tried to order. They were ignored. The minutes ticked by as puzzled, anxious customers and employees eyed their silent act of disobedience. At five P.M. the counter closed. The students left, having never been served.

The following morning, they were back. Accompanied by sixteen classmates, they arrived at ten-thirty, sat down, and waited for service. Whites came and went, eating or drinking as they chose. The black men sat quietly, still ignored even in the middle of the mounting disturbance their presence was creating. One of them, Ezell Blair, Jr., promised a long winter for the Woolworth's if it did not reconsider its position on serving blacks. "It is time for someone to change the situation," Blair told the local newspaper. "We decided to start here."[106]

Within weeks, sit-ins were being staged across the South, as the tactic democratized the campaign and replaced litigation with mass action as the movement's most compelling strategy. Uncoordinated by any central group, sit-ins allowed energetic and brave black men and women to take their fortunes into their own hands. Hundreds eventually would. And the results were gratifyingly immediate: On July 25, just six months after the four "first-dayers" sat down at the counter and were ignored, the Greensboro Woolworth's served the first black customer in its official history. The tremors of the movement shuddered outward from the South and into that year's national political campaigns. In Boston, young Senator John Kennedy took note. So, in Washington, did Richard Nixon.

And so, too, did Earl Warren. A Nixon presidency represented the most dangerous of all possibilities for the Warren Court. It would replace Eisenhower with a president at least as conservative as the current one, and where Eisenhower nominally appreciated Warren in personal terms—he had, after all, nominated him—Nixon resented him personally as well as politically. Moreover, Nixon was crafting a new Republican Southern strategy that held ominous implications for relations with Warren and his Court. Aimed at breaking the Democratic hold on those states, it depended on linking Southern white Democrats with Northern white Republicans—a bond built in part out of their common anti-Communism and support for a robust patriotism at home and abroad. Kennedy's coalition was far less threatening to the main pillars of the Warren Court's jurisprudence. Its key constituencies included union members, racial minorities, big-city bosses and their followers, and enough die-hard, yellow-dog Southern Democrats to hold off Nixon's appeal to them on ideological terms. Warren preferred Stevenson. He could live with Kennedy. He could not stand the idea of Nixon.[107]

The Kennedy–Nixon contest of 1960 was one of history's great campaigns, a clash that Kennedy wisely framed as generational and that featured a historic realignment in the place of blacks in American politics. The Warren Court loomed large in its backdrop, as the nation continued to debate the principle of desegregation, a matter brought again to the forefront by the sit-in movement. For the most part, both candidates gave civil liberties a fairly wide berth. Pushed by New York governor Nelson Rockefeller—and over the objections of Barry Goldwater and other conservatives—Nixon persuaded the party to adopt a more expansive civil rights platform but otherwise said little about the issue, hopeful as he was of luring conservative Southerners to his ticket.[108] Kennedy straddled, too, in order to avoid antagonizing either wing of his inchoate coalition.

Once Kennedy and Nixon had their nominations, the race introduced new wrinkles. Campaigns always do. Henry Cabot Lodge, Nixon's vice presidential running mate, surprised his own team by promising that Nixon would put a black in the cabinet. Kennedy's selection of Johnson as his running mate disappointed liberals and raised questions about the candidate's commitment to civil rights. Johnson's record there was mixed: He did not approve of *Brown v. Board* when it was first announced ("Like you, the Supreme Court decision left me shocked and dismayed," he wrote one constituent[109]). But his ambitions had driven him to the Court's defense against conservative assault in 1958. He had not signed the Southern Manifesto, but that, too, was evidence more of ambition than of principle. Still, Johnson's addition to the Kennedy ticket, if confusing as a matter of principle, was clear as one of politics. With Johnson on the ticket, Kennedy believed he could carry the key state of Texas and perhaps some other Southern states as well. To pull that off, roiling the waters on behalf of Negroes was not part of the Kennedy campaign plan.

Just weeks before Election Day, the efforts of both campaigns to steer clear of civil rights were challenged by what at first seemed a noteworthy but not critical matter. On October 19, with Election Day less than a month away, Martin Luther King, Jr., set aside weeks of agonizing and joined a sit-in at the Rich's department store in his hometown, Atlanta. He had not particularly wanted to be part of the demonstration but had finally been persuaded by the student organizers that his participation was vital, since the event was taking place in his hometown and since Rich's, an icon of middle-class Atlanta, was such a prominent target. After being denied service at Rich's lunch counter and in its upstairs, fancier restaurant, King and the other protesters were arrested and taken to Fulton County jail. Negotiations then ensued to spring the culprits, but in King's case, they were complicated by an old traffic case in which he had received a suspended sentence, terms of which the judge, Oscar Mitchell, now said were violated by King's participation in the sit-in. After a hearing at which King arrived shackled and manacled, Mitchell revoked the suspended sentence and ordered King to spend four months at hard labor. Mitchell also denied King the chance to post bond. King, that same night, was rousted from his bed by jailers and shipped, again in handcuffs and shackles, to the maximum-security prison at Reidsville.[110]

For Nixon and Kennedy, King's arrest offered opportunity and risk. Here was an icon of the movement, imprisoned in one of the Confederacy's most terrifying prisons, denied bail in what was in effect a traffic case, for which he would labor on a chain gang in obvious peril to his safety. Whatever one's beliefs on civil rights, this was a human story of national and international scope. And yet neither candidate wanted this: Nixon still held out hope of carrying a handful of Southern states; Kennedy needed those same states and could not afford to antagonize his allies among the Southern Democratic leadership. So the candidates tried to stay quiet. Jackie Robinson, campaigning for Nixon, deplored King's incarceration, but Nixon himself rejected appeals from aides to say something publicly in defense of King.[111] At the Eisenhower Justice Department, Lawrence Walsh, later to gain fame as the special prosecutor in the Iran-Contra case, drafted a statement urging King's release, but did not complete it until the episode had passed; in any case, neither Nixon nor Eisenhower would approve the release of the statement with the election so close.[112] Kennedy's aides similarly rejected a public statement on King's behalf and stirred uncomfortably when Atlanta's mayor announced that he was working for King's release at Kennedy's behest. What Kennedy did agree to do, however, was accede to the urging of Harris Wofford, his civil rights representative, that he place a comforting call to Coretta King, then pregnant and panicked at the thought of her husband in a Southern prison.

"I know this must be very hard for you," Kennedy said after being connected with Coretta by Sargant Shriver. "I understand you are expecting a baby, and I just wanted you to know that I was thinking about you and Dr. King. If there is anything I can do to help, please feel free to call on me."

Coretta replied, "I certainly appreciate your concern. I would appreciate anything you could do to help."[113]

The call infuriated Bobby Kennedy, who accused Wofford and Shriver of going behind his back and endangering his brother's chances in the delicately balanced South. But it largely escaped white attention even as it powerfully spoke to blacks. King's father, Daddy King, was a lifelong Republican. When Judge Mitchell relented and let King out of prison a few days later, Daddy King was there to take his son home. Greeted by fellow protesters, Daddy King publicly expressed the family's gratitude for Kennedy's call. "I had expected to vote against Senator Kennedy because of his religion," King said. "But now he can be my President, Catholic or whatever he is."

Kennedy was amused at Daddy King's bigotry. "We all have fathers, don't we?" he joked to Wofford later.[114] Unlike his father, Martin Luther King, Jr., would never endorse Kennedy, but the Democratic nominee's call to Coretta rippled through the black electorate, aided by Wofford's daring decision to publicize it, without Kennedy's knowledge, through a hastily assembled blue pamphlet, known thereafter as the "blue bomb." On Election Day, an estimated 250,000 blacks voted for Kennedy in Illinois; he carried the state by 9,000 votes. In Michigan, 250,000 blacks cast their votes for Kennedy, and he won by 67,000. And in South Carolina, where Nixon had been headed at the time of King's forced trip to Reidsville, 40,000 blacks voted for Kennedy; he took the state by 10,000. The call to Coretta can plausibly be said to have placed John F. Kennedy in the White House.

No person was happier at the outcome than Earl Warren. Nixon and Eisenhower were gone, off to contemplate the nation's rejection of their legacy and campaign. Sweetening the victory was the nature of Kennedy's election. Not only was a new president in office, but the efforts of black voters, those whose interests Warren and the Court has so assiduously protected, were in no small measure responsible for the outcome.

As the year drew to a close, Warren's personal fortunes improved as well. Virginia Warren, the beautiful young woman who was Warren's eldest daughter, set aside her long and boisterous dating life—one that had included political luminaries and business tycoons—and married John Daly, a confident journalist and television talk-show host. Earl and Nina were thrilled. They both liked Daly, who was more conservative than Warren but not in the least intimidated by him. His union with Virginia would usher in a new tone to Warren family gatherings, as Daly and Earl Warren cheerfully argued issues of the day—though never the business of the Court—generally concluding with a clap on the arm or a playful roll of the eyes.[115] Virginia's choice of him as a husband would warm and complete the Warren family, and they celebrated the occasion by hosting a lavish wedding in their West Coast headquarters, the Fairmont Hotel in San Francisco. Ben Swig, the Warrens' friend and the owner of the Fairmont, was delighted to have the affair at his flagship hotel, and afterward complimented Warren on the event—even after giving Warren a friendly discount, Swig acknowledged that the "bill was high enough as it was!"[116]

At the Court, the year closed on a happy note as well. Jesse Choper, one of Warren's clerks that year and on his way to becoming one of the nation's most esteemed legal scholars, struggled that fall with the case of a young black law student who had been headed home to Alabama on a bus from Washington, D.C. The bus left in the evening and the student, Bruce Carver Boynton, got off in Richmond, Virginia, to get a bite to eat. Inside the bus terminal, he found a restaurant, but it was divided into "white" and "colored" sections. The black section had not been recently cleaned, while the white section had. Boynton, the son of civil rights activists and soon to be a lawyer, knew his conscience and so he sat down in the white section, and ordered a cheeseburger and tea. He had not planned to make a protest out of that act, but the waitress ignored him and then the manager appeared at his table. "Nigger," he told Boynton, "move." "That," Boynton recalled more than fifty years later, "resolved it."[117] He refused to budge, an officer was called, and Boynton was arrested, tried, convicted, and fined $10 for staying on the premises after being ordered to leave.[118]

As Choper analyzed the case, he was troubled: He sympathized with Boynton, but Choper could find no legal basis for the Court to rule on Boynton's behalf. The restaurant was not owned by the bus company and thus was a private entity, beyond the reach of the ban on racial discrimination in public transportation. Reluctantly, Choper recommended to Warren that the Court dismiss the case—in legal terms, as "improvidently granted." Another case will come along, he told Warren in a memo, in which the record will be better.[119] After reading Choper's memo, Warren called him down and confessed that he had two problems with it. The first was that Boynton was a law student and the conviction, even for such a trivial offense, might keep him from becoming a lawyer. That offended Warren's sense of fairness. Moreover, Warren acknowledged that another case might come along, but added, "I may not be here." Given that, Warren preferred to keep searching for a way to overturn Boynton's conviction. Eventually, Black found it in an argument not raised by Boynton's lawyers—no less than Thurgood Marshall and others—at the Supreme Court. While conceding that the restaurant was privately owned, Black noted that the owner had acknowledged that it primarily relied on bus passengers for its business. The restaurant held a lease with the bus company and was located inside the bus company's terminal in order to service the bus company's passengers. All that added up to such a strong relationship to the travel of interstate passengers that the restaurant was treated as part of commerce and Boynton "had a federal right to remain in the white portion of the restaurant."[120] Boynton's conviction was overturned, and his law career was uninterrupted. Warren joined the decision with satisfaction and relief, his underlying belief in fairness upheld.[121]

Nineteen sixty-one thus opened for Warren fresh. His enemies were vanquished—Nixon and Eisenhower were gone, the Court was back in his hand. America preened with excitement over the dashing young couple preparing to move into the White House. On Inauguration Day, Warren led the justices across the street to take their place at the swearing in. Beneath them lay a blanket of newly fallen snow, but the day was clear and sunny. Robert Frost, the great poet of New England and America, rose to read a poem he had written for the occasion, but the glare of the snow and sun was too much for his aging eyes. After stumbling with it briefly, he abandoned it and instead recited from memory a much older work, "The Gift Outright":

> The land was ours before we were the land's.
> She was our land more than a hundred years
> Before we were her people. She was ours
> In Massachusetts, in Virginia.
> But we were England's, still colonials,
> Possessing what we still were unpossessed by,
> Possessed by what we now no more possessed.
> Something we were withholding made us weak.

Until we found out that it was ourselves
We were withholding from our land of living,
And forthwith found salvation in surrender.
Such as we were we gave ourselves outright
(The deed of gift was many deeds of war)
To the land vaguely realizing westward,
But still unstoried, artless, unenhanced,
Such as she was, such as she would become.[122]

After reciting that final line, Frost amended it by one word: "Here, for this occasion," he said, "let me change that to 'what she *will* become."[123] Warren sat in his chair, just an arm's length away while America's great poet, eyes watering in the sun, recited those American lines, infused with the special optimism of that January day. Warren, whose college years gave him poetry but whose lyricism would never match that of those he admired, drank in the poet's lines from the dais, the crowd gazing upward in silent apprehension, pulling for Frost, swimming in his words. Then Frost sat and Warren stood. Behind the chief justice, Eisenhower glowered in a dark coat and a long white scarf wrapped around his neck against the cold. Facing Warren directly was the new president. Behind Kennedy, Nixon gamely smiled. The chief justice guided Kennedy's hand to the Bible between them. Speaking in his gravelly voice, bareheaded in the cold, somber in his unadorned robes, Earl Warren administered the oath of office to the new president of the United States. Kennedy took it in strong and confident voice and addressed the nation as its president for the first time.

Kennedy spoke of the simple patriotism and service that always animated Warren. He heralded renewal and change, rejected his election as a victory of party— just as Warren had refused to claim his governorship as a prize of partisanship—but rather trumpeted it as a "celebration of freedom." Invoking the Declaration of Independence—the Declaration whose values Warren had imported into the Constitution—Kennedy reminded the nation of the "revolutionary belief" that "the rights of man come not from the generosity of the state but from the hand of God." In his most memorable passage, Kennedy raised his voice to a near-shout and proclaimed, "And so, my fellow Americans, ask not what your country can do for you. Ask what you can do for your country. My fellow citizens of the world, ask not what America will do for you, but what together we can do for the freedom of man."

Kennedy concluded on a stirring note. "With a good conscience our only sure reward, with history the final judge of our deeds, let us go forth to lead the land we love, asking His blessing and His help but knowing that here on Earth, God's work must truly be our own."

With that, Kennedy smiled and sat down. For Warren, the moment was splendid indeed. The day was clear, the air crisp, the snow fresh. Warren's family was healthy and growing. For two long years, his command of his Court had been tested, and he had lost his share of fights. But as 1961 opened, it was Warren on the dais with Kennedy and Johnson, with Frost. He stood face to face with America's young president and just a few feet away from his stylish wife, swearing in a new era to an eager nation. The prose of Eisenhower had given way to the poetry of Kennedy. What promise, what destiny, lay atop that snow-covered land on that January morning in 1961.

Chapter 21

# KENNEDY, KING, AND A NEW ERA

*Although [it is] not possible for all of us to be your clerks,*
*in a very real sense we are all your students.*

JOHN F. KENNEDY TO EARL WARREN[1]

ARL WARREN was twenty-six years older than John Kennedy, old enough to be his father. And though Kennedy was older than Warren's own children, there was an element of paternalism in Warren's attraction to the young president and his wife. Similarly, Kennedy approached Warren with palpable deference, partly in acknowledgment of Warren's position but also partly with the refined instincts of a younger man in the presence of a distinguished elder. John Kennedy was the first American president born in the twentieth century; Earl Warren was the last chief justice born in the nineteenth. Earl Warren served peripherally in the first of the twentieth century's great wars; Kennedy fought with heroism in the second. Both were tough on foes, and they happened to share a common adversary: John Kennedy shook his head in amazement when the Republican Party missed its chance at Warren. "How can you hope for anything from them?" Jack muttered to Jackie one night in frustration. "They nominated Dewey and Nixon when they could have had Earl Warren." Warren watched with glee as Kennedy dismantled Nixon in 1960.[2] Together, Warren and Kennedy would lead America from the residue of its eighteenth-century moral backwardness and into the fullness of its maturity. Kennedy would not live to see the journey completed, but he would provide Warren with the grace, the courage, and the friendship to see that it would, in time, be fulfilled.

On January 25, four days after he assumed the presidency, Kennedy initiated their correspondence, writing to thank Warren for administering the oath earlier that week. "I need hardly tell you that I am delighted that you are presiding over the

Court during my administration," Kennedy wrote. "I wish you all continued success in the days that lie ahead."[3] Warren responded in kind, his note simple and sincere, stripped of all the edge that occasionally crept into his correspondence with Eisenhower. After acknowledging Kennedy's note to him, Warren wished the new president and his administration "happy sailing on the course which you so thrillingly outlined to the American people at the Inauguration."[4]

That cordial exchange was followed by an even more personal overture. Warren turned seventy on March 19, 1961. To mark the occasion, a group of current and former clerks arranged a surprise party that week, and Kennedy arrived unannounced to pay his respects. Warren, sensitive as always to the nuances of protocol, was touched by the gesture, which confirmed for him his initial enthusiasm for the president. "He had great affection and admiration for Kennedy," recalled Dennis Flannery, who served as a Warren clerk in the mid-1960s.[5] "Kennedy," agreed another clerk, Kenneth Ziffren, "he just loved Kennedy."[6] The sentiment ran both ways. Pierre Salinger, one of Kennedy's trusted intimates, said both men confided in him their regard for the other. "The Chief Justice expressed his pleasure at the way President Kennedy had taken hold of his duties. He liked Kennedy's vitality and imagination." And as for Kennedy, he "had a deep respect for the Chief Justice, both as Chief Justice and as a man. He was always meticulous in his dealings with him."[7]

The first of its Kennedy-era landmark cases came to the Court less than two weeks after Warren's birthday. Dollree Mapp and her daughter were living upstairs in a two-story Cleveland home in 1957 when police officers received a tip that a bombing fugitive was holed up in the house. On May 23, officers arrived at the home, knocked, and asked to be allowed to look around. Mapp made them wait while she called her lawyer, then told the officers she would not permit them to enter without a warrant. A few hours later, they came again to the door and this time forced their way inside, breaking down a door in the process. Mapp demanded to see a warrant. When an officer handed her a piece of paper, she shoved it in her bra. The police forcibly "recovered" the paper and roughly placed a yelling Mapp in handcuffs. Her lawyer, who had arrived amid the commotion, was denied the right to speak with her. The officers never did find their suspect or anything connecting Mapp to him; they did find a trunk in the house, however, and it contained some lurid photographs and pamphlets. Mapp said the trunk belonged to a former boarder, but Ohio law proscribed possession of "an obscene, lewd or lascivious book," and since material roughly fitting that description was found in her house, Mapp was arrested, charged, tried, and convicted. She was sentenced to seven years in prison.[8]

Had Mapp been tried in federal court, the evidence seized—without a warrant, while her lawyer was held at bay—would have been excluded from her trial, and

Mapp would have gone free. But the Supreme Court had never held that a defendant in state court was entitled to the same protection against search and seizure as applied in federal proceedings. Warren himself had refused to extend the Fourth Amendment's protection against "unreasonable searches and seizures" to the states, ruling in the 1954 *Irvine* case that the police there had behaved atrociously but that that was not a reason to let the bookmaker go free. Dollree Mapp was to receive the benefit of Warren's hard lesson in *Irvine*. Tired of inaction by others, Warren acted himself.

Soon after the initial argument, Warren led the conference on *Mapp*, and assigned the opinion to Clark, who had grudgingly concurred in *Irvine* but had warned of precisely the result that had now come to pass. In the absence of a rule limiting the introduction of evidence seized by overzealous police, misconduct by police would surely continue, Clark noted in 1954: "Unpredictable reversals on dissimilar fact situations are not likely to curb the zeal of those police and prosecutors who may be intent on racking up a high percentage of successful prosecutions."[9] Proven right by time, Clark now drafted for a majority that included Warren and Brennan, with Douglas and Black joining in the result, though for varying reasons— Black found his recourse in the idea that the search violated a combination of search-and-seizure rules as well as a defendant's Fifth Amendment right, technically the right not to be forced to testify against oneself but here construed by Black as a broader right not to be forced to supply incriminating evidence against oneself. Stewart provided a sixth vote to free Mapp, but he explicitly refused to join the majority's constitutional conclusions. Harlan did his best to talk Clark out of a broad ruling, suggesting that the Court free Mapp by finding that Ohio's law against mere possession of obscene material went too far toward state imposition of "thought control."[10] But Clark wanted more and got it.

The result was hardly elegant—a divided Court articulating a grab bag of principles. But *Mapp* made bold new law almost despite itself, and it lightened the stain that the early, judicially immature Warren had allowed his Court to create in *Irvine*. Over the objections of Frankfurter, Harlan, and Whittaker, *Mapp* told police that they would comply with the Constitution or their suspects would go free. "There is no war," Clark wrote, "between the Constitution and common sense."[11] Certainly Clark would get no argument there from Warren.

*Mapp* represented the first of the major Warren Court forays into criminal justice, and it overturned the practices of half the states, which until *Mapp* had permitted the introduction of evidence regardless of the police conduct in obtaining it. Moreover, as Lucas Powe points out, *Mapp* was a pure criminal justice case, not an effort to extend or solidify the Court's desegregation opinions. As such, it represented new ground for the Court as it entered the 1960s.[12] And yet *Mapp* was mere portent. Its bevy of concurrences, dissents, and memoranda for a time cloaked one aspect of its significance. Beneath the changes it wrought in the law itself was a lurking message: Warren had control of his Court again; restraint had run its course.

FOR THOSE who feared and detested Warren's work, the resumption of his control posed a threat to their values, and they moved in response. In 1961, the John Birch Society launched its campaign to drive Warren from the Court.[13] Within months, the billboards calling for Warren's impeachment began to sprout up along American roads and highways, many to remain there until his retirement in 1969. The Birch Society's billboards became a ubiquitous and literal part of the American landscape, and remain a landmark of the imagination in history's depiction of Warren and his Court.

The Birch Society was led by the single-minded Robert Welch, a onetime candy-maker who concluded that America was rife with Communists bent on selling out the nation to the Soviets—even Eisenhower was suspect in the eyes of the Birch Society.[14] Welch founded the Society at a December 1958 meeting in Indianapolis, and within two years, its "cells" had formed across the United States. Those cells cobbled together a motley coalition of serious conservatives, many of them wealthy, and right-wing misfits—"a collection of wealthy businessmen, retired military officers and little, old ladies in tennis shoes," as California attorney general and Warren friend Stanley Mosk once described them.[15] After two years of aimless anti-Communism, the Society settled on Warren as its enemy, and with him as its target, found its voice and place in American life. The campaign was unique in the annals of Court criticism, and it served both to heighten attention on the Court as well as to amplify the significance and coffers of the Society.

"We are aware that the whole Supreme Court is a nest of socialists and worse," the Society argued in its bulletin launching the effort. "We have nothing but contempt, which we believe to be completely justified by the records, for a number of its justices." Of Warren specifically, the Society noted, "We are demanding that Warren be impeached by the House, because we are convinced that the evidence of his abuse of his high office is amply sufficient to warrant his arraignment."[16]

In listing its grounds for impeachment, the Society started with *Brown v. Board of Education*, which it labeled "the most brazen and flagrant usurpation of power" in the history of American jurisprudence. It also cited the *Nelson* case overturning state anti-Communist laws, and the *Sweezy* opinion curbing the New Hampshire attorney general's investigation into alleged subversives there. There were, the Society added, too many offenses to list them all. Members were urged to write their congressman, to write letters to the editor, to talk with friends and neighbors, pass resolutions, put up stickers ("This is a Republic," the stickers stated), form organizations, and be inventive in crafting ways to challenge the chief justice. "The future of your country—and of your children—is at stake," the bulletin asserted. It bore Welch's signature.[17]

The campaign was good for the Society. In 1961, when the "Impeach Earl Warren" campaign began, the Society reported $534,241 in income; two years later, it had nearly doubled, to $1,043,656.[18] That money paid for a visible, sustained attack on the Supreme Court and its chief. By 1963, there were thirty-five coordinators of the impeachment movement, being paid $8,000 a week, while forty-one home office employees of the Society were earning $3,000 a week. The Society reported that its campaign was doubling every five to six months.[19]

The manifestations of that effort suddenly flooded the American landscape. At the Indy 500, a huge sign greeted visitors to the speedway in the mid-1960s: "Save Our Republic. Impeach Earl Warren!" The same message or variants of it greeted civil rights marchers in Selma and motorists on Highway 27 outside New Orleans; on federal Route 22 near Allentown, Pennsylvania; and on state highways throughout Florida, Alabama, and Georgia.[20] Warren impeachment packets were available in Massachusetts, while a bedsheet hung near Montecito, California, proclaimed that America had fallen under the cruel dictatorship of "Communist Warren." "If we do not kill him, he will enslave all of us," it read.[21] In the predawn of September 17, 1962, one protester brought the campaign to Capitol Hill, tacking up twenty-eight posters on trees around the House and Senate office buildings and the Lincoln Memorial. "Be a super patriot," they urged. "Impeach Earl Warren."[22]

The Birch Society campaign was both irrelevant and historic. At no point did it reach anything close to the support required to bring articles of impeachment against Warren, so its threat was abstract. Nevertheless, its breadth and duration revealed the intense animus that the Court inspired in those years, and even if that animus was confined to a segment of American society, that segment was large enough to sustain itself and angry enough to go on year after year.

Warren always professed to be unaffected by the Birch Society, but those close to him dispute that, and even he conceded that it took a toll on Nina. Some clerks from those years remember the grim tightening of his jaw, the cold stare, the abrupt end of pleasantries when the subject of "Impeach Earl Warren" was raised. Still, when one clerk, Doug Kranwinkle, called Warren's attention to a sign that read "A Man's House Is His Castle: Impeach Earl Warren," the chief justice tossed it off.[23] Warren suppressed his irritation, to be sure. He knew better than most that to respond to a political adversary was to elevate that adversary. Had Warren engaged the Society, its leaders would have enjoyed a platform with the Chief Justice of the United States, rather than on the kooky margins of American politics. Instead, he rationed his fire, betting that the threat would fade. "I recognized it for what it was," Warren wrote, "an expression of dislike on the part of vested interest groups who were offended by the Court's interpretation in various cases that came before us."[24] Years later, with the campaign over, hints of Warren's irritation and amazement crept through. "In all my years in politics in California, I had never been subjected to any such treatment," he noted.[25] Of the campaign against the Court, Warren conceded, "The organization, using the device of making people hate some group by blaming that group for the ills of the nation, as Hitler blamed the Jews in Germany, chose the Supreme Court as the object of its attack."[26]

While Warren did his best to ignore the Society, he cheered those who took it on, especially in the press. In 1960, management of the *Los Angeles Times* passed to Otis Chandler, and he signaled the arrival of responsible journalism at that paper by its publication in 1961 of a five-part series on the Society. The series began on March 5, and it profiled the Society in careful, balanced articles all week. Conservatives used to seeing the *Times* as their defender were puzzled, and then, with the publication of a Sunday editorial authorized by Chandler himself, furious: "The Times," the editorial ran, "does not believe the argument for conservatism can be won—and we do believe it can be won—by smearing as enemies and traitors those with whom we sometimes disagree. Subversion, whether of the left or the right, is still subversion."[27] Under Otis Chandler's oversight of the *Times*, it shed its disreputable past and ushered in a remarkable journalistic era for the paper. It did not, however, sit well with all his family. Philip Chandler, his uncle, waged a behind-the-scenes attempt to discredit Otis in the wake of the Birch Society stories. Writing to Norman Chandler—Philip's brother, Otis's father, and a longtime friend and supporter of Warren—Philip warned of the paper's lack of appreciation for the threat of Communism. Closing his letter, Philip noted, "No one can deny the fact that the danger of Communism (not to mention the trend toward Socialism in the U.S.) is the No. 1 problem of the free world."[28] Responding, Norman Chandler thoroughly scolded his brother for his attack on the paper and invited him to present his criticisms "face to face."[29] There is no record of whether such a meeting occurred.

Up the coast in Santa Barbara, the publisher of that city's paper launched a campaign of his own against the Society and in defense of Warren, an old friend. Tom Storke's editorials infuriated the Society, whose followers hanged him and Warren in effigy in that city's stately downtown. Storke's work secured the only Pulitzer Prize in the history of the *Santa Barbara News-Press*. Warren delighted in his friend's courage.[30]

Support from newspapers and old friends helped soften the Birch Society's campaign. In time, the Society's campaign against the Warren Court became more curiosity than threat. Yet the fringe right wing, as exemplified by the Birch Society, never let go of Warren. Typical is his entry in the *Biographical Dictionary of the Left*, which portrayed Warren as a "compulsive publicity seeker" with a "strange" code of ethics and "contempt for the division of powers."[31]

———

WHEN FORCES gathered against the Warren Court in Eisenhower's years, he let them have their way and occasionally even encouraged them—an obfuscation here, an outburst there. With Kennedy in the White House, however, Warren acquired an ally. Kennedy's open support for the landmark rulings of the Court during his brief presidency—and his careful, dignified handling of Warren himself—deprived the Court's critics of even implicit support from the White House. Nowhere was that more evident than in the response to the Warren Court's second great blockbuster opinion, exceeded in historic significance only by *Brown* itself and, in the estimation of Warren, even more important than that.

By the 1950s, voters in Tennessee had exhausted their options for trying to reform that state's voting rules. They pleaded with the legislature and argued with the governor, to no avail. The state had no mechanism for popular initiative, and the officials who had been elected under its voting rules understandably defended those rules against those who were hurt by them. Finally, having lost patience with their political representatives, the marginalized voters filed a lawsuit in federal court. Their argument was simple: The state's practice of allocating representatives by county meant that sparsely populated areas were overrepresented at the expense of growing urban areas. That, they said, denied equal protection of the laws to those Tennessee voters whose votes in effect counted for less than those of others. The Fourteenth Amendment, they contended, guaranteed them that equal protection— and not coincidentally, the effect of its denial in their state was to ensure that white rural voters continued to have more power than black urban voters, even as urban areas grew.

This was not a problem that had troubled Warren as governor of California. When labor groups had sponsored an initiative in 1948 to redistribute California's voting power along population lines, Warren opposed it. The racial implications of the state's voting system were not the issue in that campaign, so there is no benchmark of Warren's consideration of that question. What is clear is that in 1948, California's voting rules worked to elect Warren, and since Warren saw himself as a good and progressive governor, he saw no reason to amend those rules. Reflecting on it later, Warren realized he was wrong, and made no attempt to justify himself. "It was," he recorded in his memoirs, "frankly a matter of political expediency."[32]

As chief justice—and, moreover, as a chief justice who by 1960 was all too familiar with the use of legislative power to thwart minority interests—he understood the question of voting power differently. The Tennessee case, *Baker v. Carr*, first came to the Court in 1960, and at their initial conference to discuss it, the justices moved to their now familiar positions. "Justice Frankfurter unleashed a brilliant tour de force," Brennan's clerks recorded, "speaking at considerable length, pulling down Reports and reading from them, and powerfully arguing" that the Court should steer clear of what he framed as essentially a political conflict.[33] In Frankfurter's view, the Court already had foreclosed the area of legislative districting with its decision in *Colegrove,* a 1946 opinion that turned down a challenge by Illinois voters who complained that congressional districts in that state were unfairly distributed. In his opinion for a shorthanded Court (Black, Douglas, and Murphy dissented; Jackson, who was off in Nuremberg during the consideration of the case, did not participate; and Rutledge concurred, though on grounds that suggested he might have ruled otherwise if faced with somewhat different facts), Frankfurter acknowledged that the disparities between districts were real and objectionable but concluded that the Court should not resolve them. "To sustain this action would cut very deep into the very being of Congress," he wrote, and then he invoked the metaphor that appeared so often in his writing: "Courts ought not to enter this political thicket."[34] That was hardly a departure at the time of its writing. Through the late nineteenth and early twentieth centuries, the Court declined time and again to assert authority over certain aspects of American life, even when the rules governing those areas were a part of the Constitution. As a result, *Colegrove* was amply justified by the precedents that Frankfurter cited in it. "It is," Frankfurter wrote, "hostile to a democratic system to involve the judiciary in the politics of the people. And it is not less pernicious if such judicial intervention in an essentially political contest be dressed up in the abstract phrases of the law."[35]

But while that held a Court in 1946, much had changed since then. In the interim, for instance, the Court had considered and decided *Gomillion,* a lawsuit brought by black voters of Tuskegee, Alabama, who sued after the state legislature there redrew the boundaries of their city, including white neighborhoods but dropping black ones. When they were done, all but four or five of its four hundred Negro voters lived outside Tuskegee and thus were not allowed to vote in its elections. The Court in that case concluded that the Fifteenth Amendment, granting blacks the right to vote, was offended by a scheme deliberately intended to dilute the power of that vote. Frankfurter also was the author of that ruling, which, unlike *Colegrove,* spoke for a united Court, save a strange concurrence by Whittaker, who joined in the result while inexplicably concluding that the Fourteenth Amendment, not the Fifteenth, protected the right of Negroes to vote.[36]

So now the question before the Court was whether the complaint of Tennessee's voters more closely approximated the facts of *Colegrove* or those of *Gomillion*— and whether the Court was willing to wade into the "thicket." The aging Frankfurter unleashed his "tour de force" in defense of restraint. Harlan was with him. So was Clark. Warren, Black, Douglas, and Brennan were not persuaded and unlikely to be. Indeed, by 1960 Warren had become convinced not only that restraint had allowed political inequities to fester but that it had in fact encouraged them. "Because of timidity," he wrote, "it made change hopeless."[37] In Warren's view, restraint as a defect had gone beyond reticence; it had become cowardice. And since Frankfurter was its chief proponent, there can be no question about how far that relationship had sunk.

That left Stewart and Whittaker in the crucible, and with their votes wavering, the case was put over from 1960 into the following term. When it came back, Douglas summarized the view of the liberal justices in one characteristically pithy sentence: "Governed by *Gomillion*."[38] When Stewart spoke, his ambivalence showed through, as he at length expressed sympathy with the problem presented by Harlan and Frankfurter—the danger of the Court immersing itself in the intricacies of legislative boundary-drawing. In the end, however, he could not stomach the inequities of districts that so blatantly reduced the power of one voter over another. He tentatively sided with the Warren camp, giving it a fifth vote, but his ambivalence made it clear that his vote was not assured. Moreover, Stewart's desire for a narrow opinion so conflicted with Douglas's interest in a ringing one that the burden now shifted to Warren: To whom would he assign the opinion, and how would he keep both his most aggressive colleague and his most cautious on the same opinion?

Warren's work over the ensuing several weeks represented his most important and effective coalition management of the Court since *Brown* in 1954. He initially contemplated writing himself or assigning the decision to Stewart—one common tactic to assure a wavering justice's vote is to have him write, thus sealing his position. But Warren worried that Stewart might write in such a way that either Douglas or Black would break from the majority, and he also saw that Frankfurter was burrowing in for an extended opinion intended to break up the majority. After consulting with Black, Warren chose Brennan, Warren's doctrinalist.[39] Brennan's mission was to write an opinion that could hold its own against that of his former professor; Warren's was to hold their fragile coalition intact.

Harlan saw an opportunity to peel off votes from the majority, and made a direct appeal to Whittaker and Stewart, urging them to consider not just the merits of the case but the place of the Court in society and history:

> I need hardly argue to you that the independence of the Court, and its aloofness from political vicissitudes, have always been the mainspring of its stability and vitality. Those attributes have been assured not alone by the constitutional and statutory safeguards which surround the Court, but also to a large extent, I believe, by the wise restraint which, by and large, has characterized the Court's handling of emotionally-charged popular causes. I believe that what we are being asked to do in this case threatens the preservation of these attributes.
>
> Let me be as concrete and frank as possible. Today, state reapportionment is being es-

poused by a Democratic administration; the next time it may be supported (or opposed) by a Republican administration. Can it be that it will be only the cynics who may say that the outcome of a particular case was influenced by the political backgrounds or ideologies of the then members of the Court?[40]

Harlan sent a copy of his note to Frankfurter, who commended him for having "rendered a service to the Court, whatever the outcome."[41]

While they attempted to add to the conservative ranks, Brennan went to work for the liberals, digging deep into the historical and judicial record. Through the winter of 1961 and early 1962, he selectively circulated drafts, mollifying first Stewart, then Douglas. On January 31, 1962, the full Court received his opinion, and Frankfurter was incensed, complaining to Clark that the majority had done just as he had expected all along. Frankfurter then promptly circulated his dissent, and the Court nearly fell apart. Clark and Harlan appeared to join with Frankfurter, Douglas threatened to bolt from the majority, and then Stewart indicated that he too was abandoning the coalition. Into the turmoil stepped the calming Warren. The chief justice, a Brennan memo would recall later, "was Gilbraltorlike [*sic*] in his support for Justice Brennan. . . . With our 'two wings' flying off and no saying where matters might come to rest," Warren helped restore order.[42] Over the next twenty days, Warren sounded out his colleagues, seeking to solidify Stewart, calm Douglas, and talk with Clark. Brennan continued to hope that Stewart would return and that he and Douglas, once his irritation had passed, would provide the fourth and fifth votes needed to assure a majority. Then, in late March, Clark emerged from his study of the matter to declare that he had decided to leave the Frankfurter camp and join the majority. He informed Warren, who called Brennan at home with the news. The phone call, "never to be forgotten," began with Warren spending the first minutes laughing happily in Brennan's ear.[43]

On March 26, Brennan announced the opinion of the Court for a majority that, in the end, included all but Harlan and Frankfurter. There were an array of concurrences and dissents, and the majority opinion by Brennan was encumbered by its exhaustive recitation of the legal history. But it had secured the votes needed to assert that federal courts did in fact have the authority to review and overturn state legislative districts. The Supreme Court did not overturn Tennessee's lines in *Baker,* but it sent the matter back to the district court to do so, explicitly authorizing that court to undertake what many had assumed to be a matter purely for legislatures. Warren was delighted, and passed a note to Brennan as the two sat together on the bench that day. "It's a great day for the Irish," Warren wrote. Thinking again, he crossed out "Irish," and wrote, "It's a great day for the country."[44]

It was, however, a trauma for the Court. Both sides had ridden their positions hard, and while Warren prevailed, Frankfurter scorched the earth in defeat. In particular, he thrashed the wavering Whittaker, and Whittaker broke under the strain. With the two sides mounting their final offensives that March, Whittaker considered joining the majority, but Frankfurter relentlessly lobbied him to stay. On March 6, Whittaker, who suffered from depression exacerbated by extreme stress, visited Walter Reed Medical Center for a physical examination, and his doctors warned him that his health was perilous.[45] Whittaker confided his condition to Warren, who, partly out of compassion and no doubt partly knowing that Whittaker's removal might clear the way to strengthen his own hold over the Court, assured him that he could leave anytime, that his clerks and staff would be cared for.[46] When *Baker* came down on March 26, Whittaker did not participate. His retirement from the Court was effective April 1.

For Frankfurter, *Baker* was a clear and final defeat. He would never again write a major decision of the Court.

Whittaker's departure gave Kennedy his first opportunity to alter the composition and tone of the Court. Kennedy initially had his eye on William Hastie, an appeals court judge who would have become the first black man to sit on the Supreme Court. But Kennedy asked his brother Bobby to sound out Warren on Hastie, and Warren "was violently opposed." According to Robert Kennedy, Warren warned that Hastie was "not a liberal, and he'd be opposed to all the measures that we're interested in, and he would just be completely unsatisfactory."[47] Douglas also advised against it on the grounds that Hastie was too conservative.[48] Kennedy heeded that warning and turned instead to an able deputy from his campaign. Byron White was an extraordinarily diverse and accomplished man, the only member of the National Football League Hall of Fame ever to sit on the Supreme Court and the first Court clerk ever to make it to the bench. Ideologically, the switch of Whittaker to White did not change the Court's balance, but it brought smoother workings and faster dispatch of cases, as White was far more at ease with the workload and responsibility than Whittaker had been. White joined the Court in April, less than a month after *Baker* had been handed down.[49]

The real change came later that year, when Frankfurter, badly weakened by a stroke he suffered just weeks after concluding his work on the *Baker* case, informed the president that he could not return to his work. He resigned with trademark formality, the old dignity shining through the more recent defeats. "To retain my seat on the basis of a diminished work schedule would not comport with my own philosophy or with the demands of the business of the Court," he wrote. "I am thus left with no choice but to regard my period of active service on the Court as having run its course. I need hardly tell you, Mr. President, of the reluctance with which I leave the institution whose concerns have been the absorbing interest of my life."[50]

And with that one-page note, the defining twentieth-century feud within the United States Supreme Court was over. For more than a decade, Black and Douglas had squabbled and debated with their resolute rival. After his settling in, Warren had joined them in their activism, and then Brennan, Frankfurter's onetime student, had come aboard and defied his former teacher. As the ranks of that wing of the Court thus grew, the other side dwindled away, its demise postponed mainly by the force of Frankfurter's personality and intellect. Jackson long ago had gone, as had Reed and Minton and the other holdovers of the New Deal period when restraint was a liberal judicial value. Clark retained a residue of it, and Harlan embodied a different, more patrician conservatism, but neither was a dominating figure in the mold of Frankfurter. Stewart had come to the Court during those years, but he now moved from camp to camp, never destined to be a standard-bearer in that long battle. When Frankfurter gave up the work in 1962, his speech slurred, his hands shaky, and his body weakened, "the Axis" was the only remaining solid bloc of justices left standing at the Court. And yet even then, Warren, Black, Douglas, and Brennan were one vote short of a consistent majority. Kennedy's next appointment would determine whether that group would emerge as a majority or whether it would, as in *Baker,* find itself in regular search of a fifth and deciding vote.

Kennedy moved quickly, advised again by Douglas and Warren and guided by certain political imperatives. He wanted a Jew, as Frankfurter's departure left the Court without Jewish representation. He wanted a loyal Democrat and an intellect. He found all those in the person of Arthur Goldberg, the blazingly intelligent secretary of labor. Goldberg charmed the Judiciary Committee so thoroughly at his confirmation hearings—he had been well briefed by, among others, former Whittaker and Warren clerk Jim Adler—that he sailed through the Senate with just a single no vote, that of South Carolina Senator Strom Thurmond, no friend of Kennedy liberals, nor, for that matter, of Jews.[51]

In the summer and fall of 1962, Kennedy did more than give the Warren Court two justices. He also gave it essential political support through the crucible of two potentially divisive cases. Senator Richard Russell of Georgia, whose distaste for Warren already was intense, led the negative response just one day after *Baker* was announced. It was, he said with an obvious nod to *Brown,* "another major assault on our Constitutional system."[52] But Russell's complaints this time would have a different effect from the one they had after *Brown.* When Southern politicians had attacked *Brown,* Eisenhower let them. This time, they found a far less tolerant president. Even as Russell was challenging the Court, Attorney General Robert Kennedy praised its work as a "landmark in the development of representative government."[53] And at his press conference two days later—the same press conference at which he would announce the retirement of Whittaker—President Kennedy himself, in response to a question, declared that the principle of votes counting equally was "basic to the successful operation of a democracy." While the president acknowledged that political change is most tidily handled through the political process, he rejected the Frankfurter argument that the Court must avoid such entanglements. "If no relief is forthcoming" through elections and lobbying, Kennedy said, "the judicial branch must meet a responsibility."[54] No president had ever spoken so supportively of a controversial Warren Court decision, and Kennedy's praise was both heartening and timely, as the Court had one more blockbuster to deliver before calling it a session.

Just two months after *Baker*, on the final day of the term, the Supreme Court invalidated the short prayer that the New York State Board of Regents had authorized and encouraged its teachers to recite each morning to the children in their classrooms. Drafted specifically to be nondenominational and kept deliberately short, the prayer read, in its entirety: "Almighty God, we acknowledge our dependence upon Thee, and we beg Thy blessings upon us, our parents, our teachers and our Country."[55]

Simple and voluntary though it was, that prayer meant that young children were forced to choose between reciting their devotion to God or risking ostracism from friends and teachers. Such a choice inherently involved the government in the endorsement of God, a function that the Court now ruled was a violation of America's history and law. "When the power, prestige and financial support of government is placed behind a particular religious belief, the indirect coercive pressure upon religious minorities to conform to the prevailing officially approved religion is plain," Black wrote for the six-member majority, including Warren. Black's opinion stressed that it was not hostile to religion but only to state sponsorship of religion. In that, it was a hallmark of his long-argued constitutional libertarianism. "It is neither sacrilegious nor antireligious," Black wrote, "to say that each separate government in this country should stay out of the business of writing or sanctioning official prayers and leave that purely religious function to the people themselves and to those the people choose to look to for religious guidance."[56]

Coming so soon after the shock of *Baker*, the *Engel* case was a bell clap. Anthony Lewis, in his perceptive analysis of the decision in the *New York Times*, noted that it not only would reach public school practices across the country but also "might indicate a stricter attitude in the Supreme Court toward breaches of what it has called the 'wall of separation' between church and state."[57] Just a few years earlier, the combination of two such explosive topics—in that case, segregation and Communism—had given Warren's enemies the chance to band together against him. As anger from *Engel* swept through Catholic churches and divided Protestant faiths—only Jewish leaders voiced general agreement—the Court risked a new coalition of opponents, this time of the religious right and rural politicians. Warren anticipated such a reaction, and he got it. Former Presidents Truman, Eisenhower, and Hoover all denounced the decision, as did members of Congress, from liberal Republican Prescott Bush in Connecticut to conservative Democrat Herman Talmadge in Georgia. Congress boiled for a time with constitutional amendments to overrule the Court in *Engel*. This time, however, the criticism was limited to railing. Whereas Eisenhower had allowed those opponents of the Court to dominate the conversation, Kennedy cut them off. Addressing the decision two days after it was handed down, Kennedy unequivocally stood behind it. Americans, he said, should go to church and pray there and at home, not in school. Reporting on Kennedy's comments, the *New York Times* ran its story the next day beneath the headline "President Urges Court Be Backed on Prayer Issue."[58]

The summer of 1962 was one of transition for the Court, but it also, for Warren, was a return home to familiar contests. In California, Richard Nixon rose from the depths of his 1960 defeat by John Kennedy to reclaim his place in politics, this time as the governor of California, a step in what he was charting as his march back toward national political leadership. Nixon was, of course, a national figure in 1962 and had carried California over Kennedy two years earlier. He was the nominal leader of the Republican Party and was assessing his options for a return to power. In that calculation, the California governorship offered considerable advantages, giving him a platform to demonstrate executive ability and returning him to his base, where he had never lost an election. All that appeared to stand in Nixon's way was the incumbent governor, Pat Brown, whose record was viewed by Republicans as sufficiently uninspired to provide an opportunity for Nixon.

Warren's position on the Court precluded his playing any overt role in the 1962 campaign. But no one close to him could doubt where his sympathies lay. Their different parties notwithstanding, Pat Brown was an heir to Warren's legacy of California centrism. Initially a Republican who switched to the Democratic Party during the FDR years, Brown was a builder, a moderate, a governor who openly modeled his administration on Warren's example. He credited himself, immodestly but probably truthfully, with helping to temper some of Warren's early conservative instincts. "It may be a conceit on my part, but I do think I influenced him to some extent," Brown confided to Carey McWilliams after Warren's death.[59] Warren and Brown also had grown close personally, overcoming early turf disputes—Warren's Crime Commission claimed some of the field in California law enforcement that Brown understandably saw as his domain—and settling into what Brown described as "leisurely talks" during the Warren gubernatorial years when Brown was attorney general.[60] Warren liked Brown and appreciated him— most men did, as Brown was an avuncular and warm personality. So in 1962, Warren set out to do all he could, within the bounds of his office, to secure Brown's election in California.

First was the matter of the Warren family. So long a mainstay of Warren's political image in California, the sunny boys and girls, now grown, remained a public
window into his beliefs, and they, unlike him, could support anyone they chose. So
it was with considerable fanfare that Earl Warren, Jr., announced that he had
switched his registration from Republican to Democrat and was supporting the
candidacy of Pat Brown. Brown, Earl Jr. recalled years later, "was carrying on my
father's traditions. . . . And then, of course, [there was] Nixon. He was no family
friend."[61]

Earl Jr. did more than just endorse. He campaigned aggressively for the governor, appearing across California and taking the Brown campaign into Republican
areas where Brown himself would have been coolly received.[62] And everywhere Earl
Warren, Jr., appeared, he was assumed to carry his father's blessing. Reinforcing
that, Warren himself pushed the boundaries of judicial propriety by going on a
widely noticed hunting trip with Brown in late 1961 and, later, by praising California's development under Brown's leadership. In Oakland for the dedication of a
new federal courthouse, Warren complimented California's progress. "I believe
that the standard of law enforcement in this State is greater than any other State in
the union."[63] Brown himself was scheduled to be at the dedication, and one story
noted that he was there. He was not pictured in the photograph, however, so he
may have missed that opportunity to make a joint appearance with the chief justice
and California icon.[64] Nevertheless, Warren's message was received—and only was
reinforced by a late-campaign resurgence of the debate over Nixon's role in the
1952 Republican Convention. Warren encouraged the assumption that he was supporting Brown by confirming it to reporters off the record. Privately, Warren was
even more outspoken. "Nixon," he told one reporter after securing a promise that
the two were off the record, "has to be stopped."[65]

Nixon formally filed his papers the same day the Warren Court announced its
decision in *Baker v. Carr*. He entered the race a heavy favorite. But he squandered
his lead through the spring and a divisive Republican primary, during which, ironically, he paid a political price for denouncing the Birch Society. By Election Day,
Nixon knew he had lost, and he took it sourly. With his career in tatters, Nixon
blamed the press corps:

I leave you gentlemen now. And you will now write it. You will interpret it. That's your
right. But as I leave you, I want you to know, just think how much you're going to be
missing. You don't have Nixon to kick around anymore. Because, gentlemen, this is my
last press conference, and it will be one in which I have welcomed the opportunity to test
wits with you. I have always respected you. I have sometimes disagreed with you. But unlike some people, I have never cancelled a subscription to a paper, and also, I never will. I
believe in reading what my opponents say. And I hope that what I have said today will at

least make television, radio, the press first recognize the great responsibility they have to report all the news and second, recognize that they have a right and a responsibility if they are against a candidate to give him the shaft but also recognize if they give him the shaft, put one lonely reporter on the campaign who will report what the candidate says now and then. Thank you, gentlemen and good day.[66]

That crude, self-pitying display captured what so many, especially Earl Warren, had learned to loathe about Richard Nixon. Warren thoroughly enjoyed it. Later that same week, Warren and President Kennedy were aboard *Air Force One*, traveling together to the funeral of Eleanor Roosevelt. Near the front of the aircraft, Warren saw Kennedy and beckoned him over. When the president sat down, Warren pulled from his pocket a handful of clips detailing Nixon's self-immolation. Mary McGrory, a *Washington Star* correspondent on board that day, watched as the president of the United States and the nation's chief justice sat together, reading clips to each other and "laughing like schoolboys."[67]

ONE OF THE DUTIES of the chief justice's clerks is to sift through the thousands of petitions filed each year by prisoners seeking review of their cases. Warren's clerks read those petitions and summarized them in short memos to the conference. The memos were typed with carbon copies, and the copies thus were known as "flimsies." The clerks recommended dismissal of the vast majority of those petitions, but there were those that demanded attention. One arrived at the Court in 1962—the handwritten petition of Clarence Earl Gideon, a Florida man convicted of breaking and entering a pool hall in Panama City. Too poor to afford a lawyer, Gideon had asked the state to give him one, but it had refused. Florida only supplied indigent defendants with lawyers when the defendant faced the death penalty or when "special circumstances" required it (an illiterate defendant, for instance). Acting as his own lawyer, Gideon was convicted and sentenced to five years in prison for stealing wine, cigarettes, and less than $100 in cash.[68] The justices took the case, recognizing that it offered them an opportunity to consider whether the right to counsel, already provided in federal trials, extended to the states as well.

Since Gideon had no lawyer to make that argument for him, Warren got him one. Abe Fortas—graduate of Yale, protégé of William Douglas, friend of Lyndon Johnson, founder of a distinguished Washington law firm—was considered in 1962 nothing less than the best lawyer in America. He accepted Gideon's case, and Fortas's argument to the Court on January 15, 1963, ranks with the best ever presented in its chamber, standing with the graceful logic of Robert Jackson, the orations of John Davis, and the earnest, earthy conviction of Thurgood Marshall. Fortas's deep, calm voice curled around carefully chosen words. Throughout, he addressed the question posed to him by the Court when Warren asked him to take the case: Should the Court overrule its own precedent, established in 1942 with a case known as *Betts v. Brady,* and force states to appoint lawyers to indigent defendants in all cases, not just those where special circumstances required it? Fortas might have argued that Gideon deserved to go free because the special circumstances of his case commanded that he be given a lawyer, but Fortas had found no such circumstances, and so he forced the Constitutional question:

> If you will look at this transcript of the record, perhaps you will share my feeling, which is a feeling of despondency. This record is not, does not indicate that Clarence Earl Gideon is a man of inferior natural talents. This record does not indicate the Clarence Earl Gideon is a moron or a person of low intelligence. This record does not indicate that the judge of the trial court in the state of Florida or the prosecuting attorney in the state of Florida was derelict in his duty. On the contrary, it indicates that they tried to help Clarence Earl Gideon. But to me, if the Court please, this record indicates the basic difficulty with Betts against Brady. And the basic difficulty with Betts against Brady is that no man, certainly no layman, can conduct a trial in his own defense, so that the trial is a fair trial.[69]

The absence of a defense lawyer made any trial an unfair trial, Fortas argued; the Sixth Amendment required a fair trial in federal courts; the Fourteenth Amendment required that states do the same. Against that truism stood the proposition that federalism required the Court to accede to the rights of states to structure their criminal justice systems, to hold its tongue in the face of what were admittedly unfair trials. There was "no possible escape hatch," he insisted. For the Court, then, the only options were to allow unfair trials or to curb federalism. That was the direct conflict that Warren had hoped to create when he tapped Fortas to argue Gideon's case.

Close Court watchers suspected that *Betts*'s days were numbered even before Fortas came to take it head-on. A year earlier, Warren had signaled his willingness to overrule *Betts v. Brady,* joining with Douglas and Black in finding: "Twenty years' experience in the state and federal courts with the *Betts v. Brady* rule has demonstrated its basic failure as a constitutional guide. Indeed, it has served not to guide but to confuse the courts as to when a person prosecuted by a State for crime is entitled to a lawyer."[70] The majority in that case, *Carnley v. Cochran,* overturned the conviction of a man who had molested his thirteen-year-old daughter, but the justices, fearful of setting a major precedent on the back of such a depraved defendant, instead concluded that the special circumstances of that trial—the defendant was illiterate—required that he be given a lawyer under that provision of *Betts.* That allowed the justices to dispose of *Carnley* without the reaction that setting a major constitutional principle in order to free a child rapist would surely have provoked.[71]

Clarence Gideon offered no such drawbacks. His relatively innocuous crime gave the Court the chance to make important law with a minimum of controversy. What's more, the votes were there: Brennan and Warren had shown their willingness to overturn *Betts*. Black and Douglas had dissented from *Betts* when it was first decided; their views were clear. With the addition of Goldberg, there was little doubt of a fifth liberal vote. Inside the Court, the shift was even more apparent, as the justices already had voted, in *Douglas v. California*, to require California to provide indigent defendants with a lawyer for their appeal.[72] There was no way to require a lawyer for appeal but not for trial, so *Gideon* was a foregone conclusion, though that was invisible outside the Court, as *Douglas* had been held over and not been announced when the justices took up *Gideon*.[73] Thus, the outcome of his case was preordained before Gideon wrote to the Court from his cell and before Fortas made his historic argument on Gideon's behalf.

If that undermines *Gideon*'s romance—of the poor defendant scratching out his appeal with pencil and paper, reaching out to the nation's highest tribunal, and finding a fair and receptive audience willing to do justice—it does nothing to detract from *Gideon*'s importance. In 1963, five states—Florida, Alabama, Mississippi, and North and South Carolina—routinely forced indigent defendants to represent themselves in criminal trials. It fell to Hugo Black to wipe out that blot. Black argued not that circumstances had changed since *Betts* was decided or that new principles had been developed or revealed. Instead, he insisted, as he had in 1942, that *Betts* was wrong then and wrong still. It was, as twenty-two states had argued in their brief on Gideon's behalf, "an anachronism when handed down."[74] The right to a lawyer was so basic to fairness, Black wrote, that states could not deny it any more than the federal government could.

With *Gideon*, Black finally prevailed in *Betts*. And he did so for a unanimous Court. Only Harlan was left to grumble at the abrupt overturning of *Betts*. He agreed that it should go, but complained that it was "entitled to a more respectful burial than has been accorded."[75] Harlan used his concurrence also to stress that the Court was not, with *Gideon*, adopting Black's long-standing view that the Fourteenth Amendment incorporated wholesale the Bill of Rights and made those requirements binding on the states. Still, *Gideon* was now the law, so held by a unanimous Warren Court. With its announcement, on March 18, 1963, another obstacle to the equality of Americans and the fairness of their nation fell.

Clarence Gideon, represented this time by a lawyer, was tried again and acquitted. His story became the basis for Anthony Lewis's gripping *Gideon's Trumpet*, and *Gideon* helped launch the Warren Court of lore. Like *Baker* and *Engel*—the redistricting and religion cases—it attracted the support of the Kennedy administration, where Bobby Kennedy enthusiastically endorsed it. More important, its appeal to such a fundamental American understanding of fairness blunted the crit-

icism that resulted from the Court's other landmark rulings of the early 1960s—
and of those still to come. That conclusion was perfectly Warren, and though it was
Black who put the Court's rule into words, it was Warren who steered the case to
that outcome—from his appointment of Abe Fortas to argue it to the assignment
of the opinion to Black. For Warren, *Gideon* was right because it was fair. Clarence
Gideon's victory was Warren's as well.

That was the spring of 1963. Kennedy had been in office for two years, and
much of the nation was charmed by its glamorous President and First Lady, awash
in a happy and productive period. Kennedy was laying early plans for his reelection, a campaign made easier by the self-destruction of Richard Nixon. But the stir-
rings of liberty and patriotism that so moved so many supporters of the president
had not reached all Americans. Indeed, some of the progress toward a more equal
America—the progress initiated by the Warren Court, pleaded for by sit-in protesters, and cautiously nurtured by the Kennedy administration—had created a thirst
for more and a frustration at the slow pace of change. And thus, as 1963 unfolded,
the demands for faster progress toward the elimination of state-supported racism
quickened.

This time, the battle would occur at the time and place of Martin Luther King's
choosing. He and his closest aides picked Birmingham, Alabama, and they spent
months honing their program for a confrontation with that city's notorious Bull
Connor. The White House was not consulted, though FBI agents had picked up
rumblings in their wiretaps.[76] Two days before the scheduled kickoff of the campaign, which a King adviser had code-named "Project C" (C standing for "Confrontation"), an Alabama judge issued an injunction barring 133 people, starting
with King, from waging any sort of public protest. King elected to defy the order,
and took to the streets as promised, on Good Friday. He was tossed inside a paddy
wagon and taken to jail, where he was placed in solitary confinement. While locked
away, King wrote his "Letter from the Birmingham Jail."[77]

While King's removal from the streets temporarily quieted Birmingham, on
May 2, the two sides confronted each other again; this time, King was accompanied
by 958 children, waves of them marching toward City Hall. By nightfall, 600 Birmingham boys and girls were in jail. "I have been inspired and moved today," King
announced that night to a nervous crowd of parents. The following morning, the
march went on again, so many children flooding the streets of segregated Birmingham that Connor directed Fire Captain G. V. Evans to spray the youngsters down.
Much of the crowd fell back, but a few held their ground. Firemen then ratcheted
up the pressure in the hoses, turning to special nozzles so strong that they could
knock bricks from buildings. When they opened those hoses up on the children, it
scattered them like leaves tumbling across pavement. Screaming and in disarray,
some tried to throw bricks or rocks, others fell back and formed their peaceful

protest lines once more. Connor then unleashed the dogs. Turning on bystanders as well as protesters, officers allowed the dogs to maul Negro children. One image told the story of Birmingham: In it, a white police officer in dark sunglasses held the leash of his German shepherd as the dog sank its teeth into the abdomen of a fifteen-year-old black boy. The photograph, Taylor Branch memorably records, "struck like lightning in the American mind."[78]

Americans winced at the images of shattered, bitten children. Volunteers flooded Birmingham. Where hundreds had at first risked liberty and safety, now thousands rose to take their place. Birmingham leaders, in the midst of a contested election that divided their leadership, struggled to shed their new image as the center of American racism while still resisting direct talks with the Negro leadership that they held responsible for the violence. The White House desperately attempted to broker a truce. King and the Kennedys warily circled each other, talking and threatening through intermediaries. Finally, after weeks of protesting and often dispiriting negotiations, city and civil rights leaders struck a tentative deal on May 10. The protests would stop, and in return, Birmingham would desegregate lunch counters, restrooms, dressing rooms and drinking fountains; Negroes would be hired to fill city jobs, and the city's white leaders would help secure the release of those then in jail.[79] News of the deal enraged the local Ku Klux Klan, which expressed itself by bombing the home of King's brother and the hotel that King had only shortly before departed. Furious, Birmingham's Negroes wandered into the streets, and some fought with police, who then went on a rampage of retaliation. Andrew Young, King's reliable lieutenant, rushed back to Birmingham from Atlanta to calm the black community even as King's destroyed hotel room, Room 30, smoldered.[80]

In Washington, Kennedy edged toward the dispatch of federal troops, and announced that he would not permit the deal in Birmingham to be unraveled by violence. Slowly, gingerly, calm returned to Birmingham at the point of a gun. Jackie Robinson came to visit and was overcome by emotion, telling a church audience that his own children had asked to come with him and be arrested, too. King closed the campaign with exhortations to optimism and pleas for forgiveness. Project C, launched on Good Friday of 1963 and carried to victory on the backs of more than two thousand children, celebrated its triumph on Mother's Day.

Warren was an observer to the escalating civil rights struggles of 1963, standing in the wings as Kennedy and King played the central parts. But he continued to contribute from his position, as the Court found ways to reinforce the efforts of the civil rights advocates in the field. From even before the *Brown* decision in 1954, many of the South's efforts to contain civil rights activity focused on trying to demonize and criminalize the NAACP. Resistance varied state-by-state, as Southern leaders experimented with ways of eliminating the organization or at least tying it down in litigation. Virginia was among the states that pioneered attacks on the NAACP, and in 1956, it enacted a statute to redefine and expand the definitions of legal malpractice as they related to soliciting clients. When the NAACP's case challenging that statute reached the Supreme Court, it posed special complications: Virginia had a right, as all conceded, to regulate the legal profession in order to ensure high standards for it, and the law at issue was neutrally written—that is, it did not name the NAACP specifically, though there was no real doubt about who its intended target was. But allowing the statute to stand would have real consequences, about which none were deluded. To allow Virginia to outlaw the NAACP practices was, in effect, to concede defeat on desegregation litigation arising from that state, as no other organization was positioned to take over the effort should the NAACP be driven out.

The case wound its way through the Virginia courts, where the statute was upheld by that state's Supreme Court. The United States Supreme Court agreed to hear it, and lawyers for the two sides made their first appearances in November 1961, with Robert Carter making yet another trip to the Court to argue on behalf of the NAACP. When the justices first weighed in on the matter, they sided with Virginia, over the objections of Warren, Douglas, Black, and Brennan. Frankfurter wrote for the narrow majority, while Black drafted a dissent.[81] Had the case been handed down in the summer of 1962, as the Court was scheduled to do, it would have represented a sobering setback for the NAACP, whose efforts had consistently been defended and appreciated by the Warren Court. Fate intervened, however, with the breakdown of Whittaker and then with Frankfurter's stroke. That took two votes away from the majority, and the justices agreed to hold the matter over to the following year.

When the Court reconvened the following fall, Brennan immediately went to work on the new justices. He sent each a memo urging them to consider the NAACP's long and difficult work on behalf of school desegregation in Virginia and he suggested that the Court could find for the NAACP with an opinion that defended its rights of speech and association without having to find that the Virginia legislature was intentionally discriminating against it.[82] At the conference, both new justices agreed—Goldberg enthusiastically, White with less vigor—tipping the balance now solidly in favor of the NAACP where just six months earlier it had been on the verge of going the other way. Warren, probably with an eye on the effectiveness of Brennan's memo, asked him to write for the new majority. Brennan did so with some difficulty, but he managed to hold a fragile coalition together and keep the NAACP in business. "The NAACP is not a conventional political party; but the litigation it assists, while serving to vindicate the legal rights of members of the American Negro community, at the same time and perhaps more importantly, makes possible the distinctive contribution of a minority group to the ideas and beliefs of our society," the Court ruled. "For such a group, association for litigation may be the most effective form of political association."[83] That ruling was handed down one day before the fabled Fortas argument in *Gideon*.

Thus, by the time King marched in Birmingham, Warren and the Court had been doing what they could to protect King's movement from extinction for nearly a decade. In the White House, meanwhile, Kennedy resisted King's early entreaties to take leadership on the issue, worried about its consequences for his political standing among Southern Democrats. After Birmingham, Kennedy chose to go a different way. On June 11, he spoke to the nation about civil rights in terms that King had long urged. For the first time, Kennedy framed the quest for civil rights as a "moral issue" and placed himself and his office squarely behind a civil rights bill that would force integration of public accommodations. With the exception of Bobby Kennedy, the president's advisers were opposed to the speech, which they worried would commit the administration to a doomed bill.[84] Kennedy spoke anyway, and the speech marked a historic moment for his administration and for the cause of racial equality, the same cause that had occupied so much of Earl Warren's life for the past ten years. The issue, said Kennedy, "is as old as the Scriptures and is as clear as the American Constitution." Continuing, he added,

> The heart of the question is whether all Americans are to be afforded equal rights and equal opportunities, whether we are going to treat our fellow Americans as we want to be treated. If an American, because his skin is dark, cannot eat lunch in a restaurant open to the public, if he cannot send his children to the best public school available, if he cannot vote for the public officials who represent him, if, in short, he cannot enjoy the full and free life which all of us want, then who among us would be content to have the color of his skin changed and stand in his place? Who among us would then be content with the counsels of patience and delay?
>
> One hundred years of delay have passed since President Lincoln freed the slaves, yet their heirs, their grandsons, are not fully free. They are not yet freed from the bonds of injustice. They are not yet freed from social and economic oppression. And this Nation, for all its hopes and all its boasts, will not be fully free until all its citizens are free.[85]

Hours after Kennedy finished speaking, an NAACP worker in Mississippi, Medgar Evers, was shot in the back. Evers's murder, so soon after the elation of Kennedy's speech, was a terrorizing reminder of the space between a promise and its fulfillment. And yet with Kennedy's moral and political pledge, the civil rights leadership now could count as allies both the president and the Chief Justice of the United States.

Kennedy's address to the nation on June 11 was close to his best, but in that summer of great American rhetoric, Kennedy finished second. For despite the pleadings of Kennedy's administration, King and other civil rights leaders pressed forward with their plans for a March on Washington, and it was there, in the heat and humidity of Washington in August, that Martin Luther King stood on the steps of the Lincoln Memorial, at the feet of the man who had freed America's slaves, and there riveted the nation. King had written most of his speech, poring over it the night before at the Willard Hotel, where he and Young and others were staying. It evoked, in the language of the pulpit and Scripture, the same message that Earl Warren had delivered in constitutional terms: the demand that America fulfill the promise of its Declaration. To Warren, that promise was one of fairness, and the Constitution was the vessel for its ultimate fulfillment. To King, that promise seemed sadly like "a bad check."

"It is obvious today that America has defaulted on the promissory note insofar as her citizens of color are concerned," he said to the hundreds of thousands, black and white, who lined the Washington Mall. "Instead of honoring this sacred obligation, America has given the Negro people a bad check, a check that has come back marked 'insufficient funds.'" Waves of applause and shouts of endorsement wafted up the Mall to where King stood, then approving laughter as he added, "But we refuse to believe that the bank of justice is bankrupt." Now, King insisted, was the time for democracy to make good on its promises. "Now is the time," he repeated. As King reached the end of his prepared text, he departed from it to ask those who heard him that day to take their "creative suffering" back home, "knowing that somehow this situation can and will be changed." Then, the great gospel singer Mahalia Jackson, who stood behind him on the stage, shouted out, "Tell 'em about the dream, Martin."[86]

King took flight, and his soaring imagery that afternoon established him as America's poet of freedom. With Scripture and spirituals, with majesty, King described the America of his dream. Its words and cadences were all his own, but in its evocation of the Declaration of Independence, it spoke to Warren's dream as well. "I have a dream," King rumbled, "that one day this nation will rise up and live out the true meaning of its creed: 'We hold these truths to be self-evident, that all men are created equal.'"

Warren was vacationing in Greece when King summoned the Declaration with such power. Even from that distance, he was impressed, and he passed along news of the peaceful demonstration to his fellow travelers "with a note of thrill in his voice. . . . He felt it was a great triumph for them [the demonstrators] and for civil rights."[87] At the White House, Kennedy watched on television. He knew something about speechmaking. As King spoke, the president turned to an aide and remarked, "He's damn good."[88]

That summer of rising American passions coincided with the tenth anniversary of Warren's nomination to the Court. No honest observer could deny that the nation was a changed one because of Warren's tenure. In 1953, segregation was legal and the accepted practice of much of the nation. Exposing Communists for the sake of degradation was a popular pastime in Washington and elsewhere, its wreck-age strewn across ruined careers and lives. Police routinely violated the Constitu-tion's order that they respect the security of home and papers. Five states sent poor defendants to jail without ever giving them the chance to speak with a lawyer. Schools opened their days with prayers and dared children who did not believe to separate themselves from classmates. By 1963, all of that had ended—and without an act of Congress or a presidential decree. It had changed because Warren and his colleagues had determined that a just country required more. The Supreme Court had been pilloried, and Warren had come under particularly personal attack. He had been ignored by the president who put him on the Court. Fanatics wanted him impeached or worse. But by 1963, the crises and isolation of the Eisenhower years had passed and the embrace of the Kennedy administration provided cover and support.

That fall, Warren presided over the groundbreaking of a new legal center at his alma mater, the University of California, Berkeley. There were the requisite protests, the "Impeach Earl Warren" placards that now accompanied his every pub-lic appearance. But the school where Warren had paid more attention to drinking songs and manly poems than to academic achievement now named the centerpiece of its law school the "Earl Warren Legal Center." Warren had succeeded beyond any boyhood dream, any imagination of Methias and Chrystal Warren in their little home in their dusty little Western town. He was at the peak of his profession and atop a nation.[89]

On Warren's birthday in March, Kennedy had gracefully added his voice to those wishing Warren well, sending along a telegram to the annual clerk dinner that he closed with a touching remark: "Although [it is] not possible for all of us to be your clerks," Kennedy wrote, "in a very real sense we are all your students."[90] Now, with the anniversary of Warren's service at hand, Kennedy outdid himself. He marked the occasion with a note that left no doubt about the depth of his admira-tion and respect. Addressing it to "Dear Mr. Chief Justice," Kennedy captured War-ren's dignity and significance, alluded to the personal bond between them, and flattered Warren justly:

> You have presided over the work of the Supreme Court during ten years of extraordinary
> difficulty and accomplishment. There have been few decades in our history when the
> Court calendar has been crowded with so many issues of historic significance. As Chief
> Justice, you have borne your duties and responsibilities with unusual integrity, fairness,
> good humor, and courage. At all times your sense of judicial obligation has been unim-
> paired by criticism or personal attack. During my time as President, I have found our as-

sociation to be particularly satisfying, and I am personally delighted that during this week you will receive not only the acclaim of Californians, but also the respect and affection of all Americans whose common destiny you have so faithfully helped to shape throughout your public career.[91]

Warren tucked the president's good wishes away and returned the next week to Washington to open the new term of the Court, overseeing a docket that brimmed with historic conflicts involving the freedom of the press, the state of civil rights, and the meaning of voting in a modern democracy. Warren and the justices settled in, this time without any changes in personnel, that October. They heard arguments through the month, and Warren settled into his now-established routines— arguments during the week, conferences on Fridays, lunches with his clerks on Saturdays, football on Sundays.

Warren's life in the early 1960s was as tranquil as his work. He and Nina initially had hoped to buy a home in Washington, but a frustrating search in 1953 and 1954 came up empty. They settled instead at the Sheraton-Park, a residential hotel where they rented a spacious suite.[92] The Warrens, who had not owned a home since selling 88 Vernon Street in Oakland, took to the Sheraton-Park and accumulated overlapping circles of friends. The brethren and their wives were, of course, the innermost of those bonds, but there were others as well. Drew and Luvie Pearson, Adlai Stevenson, and Eugene and Agnes Meyer all were part of a close group that included the Warrens. They dined at one another's homes, took summer trips together, joined for weekends in the country. When Eugene Meyer died in 1959, Earl Warren delivered a eulogy.[93] When Phil Graham, Meyer's son-in-law and heir to the *Washington Post*, killed himself in 1963, it was Warren, then vacationing with Agnes Meyer and the Pearsons, who helped break the news to her.[94] Nina, of course, supplied charm and gifts, and her warm appreciation of her friends helped cut through her husband's reserve.

Almost entirely separate were Warren's male friends, with whom he hunted, fished, and took in ball games. Wally Lynn, in California, was a regular duck-hunting companion—he owned land in the state where Warren would often spend a few days during the family's winter sojourns out West. Bart Cavanaugh made it to most of Warren's annual trips to the World Series, and he and Warren and generally another companion or two would spend the day at the ballpark and then retire to Toots Shor's in Manhattan. There they would rub elbows with Joe DiMaggio and Casey Stengel, both of whom became Warren friends. In Washington, Warren followed the Senators but, like so many in that otherwise divided city, was drawn especially to the Redskins. Edward Bennett Williams, the great trial lawyer who worshipped Warren and who was part owner of the football team, made sure that Warren was a regular guest in the owners' box, and a fair number of Warren clerks made their way from his service into Williams's firm over the years.[95] Although Williams could be a complicated friend—he made regular appearances before the Court—he cherished his relationship with Warren, and Warren admired few lawyers as deeply.[96]

Williams and Warren bonded around sports, though they appreciated sporting events with notably different styles. Where Warren liked to keep careful score no matter who was up or down, Williams paced and fretted if his team was losing, nearly frantic if his Redskins were underperforming. Still, Williams revered his friend and fellow fan, and he grandly recalled an exchange between Warren and a sportswriter during a slow Saturday game between the Washington Senators and the Chicago White Sox. "Is it true, sir," the reporter asked Warren, "that you read the sports pages every morning before you read the front page?"

"It is," Warren replied, explaining: "The sports pages report men's triumphs and the front page seems always to be reporting their failures. I prefer to read about men's triumphs rather than their failures."

After telling that story at a memorial for Warren in 1975, Williams concluded: "Earl Warren was the greatest man I ever knew."[97]

Beyond the chummy company of men and the assembling of intimates out of Washington's social milieu, there was family—and near-family. In 1958, Warren Olney was on the verge of leaving Washington. Olney was just as frustrated as Warren over the Eisenhower administration's reluctance to enforce civil rights, and Olney finally quit his job at the Justice Department in a huff. His house was sold and his car was packed to leave when the phone rang and Warren offered him an alternative. Rather than return to California, Warren proposed that Olney serve as director of the administrative office of the United States courts. Olney agreed, and their reunion ended the awkwardness of their arm's-length days when the two could not sustain a friendship while one ruled on the cases developed by the other. Through the early 1960s, the Warrens and Olneys resumed their enduring tie, picking up where they had left off in California.[98]

In 1960, the Warrens began a tradition that would further knit their family together across distance and generations. Every summer, Earl and Nina would invite a teenaged grandchild to visit, usually for several weeks. Jim Warren, the eldest son of Jim, was the first, arriving that summer on a humid afternoon at Friendship Airport in Baltimore. Nina—Mama Warren, as she was known to the grandchildren— met sixteen-year-old Jim there. She wore gloves and a hat despite the heat, always mindful that there could be a photographer and she would want to look her best. Arriving at the apartment, Jim discovered his grandfather had already prepared a list of activities for them. For the next several weeks, the Chief Justice of the United States visited the monuments, drove out to Gettysburg (where he told Jim the story of his driver spending the night in the car and of his shame at discovering it the next day), and carted his grandson to the Court. Jim did his best to play the role of dignified grandson, but sometimes it was hard. As he squirmed during the oaths administered to newly admitted members of the Supreme Court bar one Monday, a page appeared before him with a note. Jim sat up straight and opened it. "Don't worry," it read. "It'll be over soon." Jim looked up at the bench, and Justice Tom Clark waved.[99]

With Thanksgiving approaching, Warren led his Court on an annual trip that November. Together with their wives—Douglas had recently remarried and brought his third wife, twenty-four-year-old Joan Martin—the justices traveled down the hill to the White House, where they had drinks and dinner with the Kennedys. Earl Warren sat next to Jackie that night, charmed by her as so many older men were, awash in her coy sophistication, impressed, as usual, by the cool intelligence of her husband. She was just tentatively emerging back in public from a miscarriage, and her effect on Warren undoubtedly was amplified by his sympathy for her. Nina was stately in a royal blue dress, Earl big and broad-shouldered in a dark blue suit. Jackie wore red, her skirt just below the knee, her jacket open and modern. John enjoyed a drink before dinner and carried himself with grace. He looked ahead to later that week, when he was planning an early political foray to Dallas, a city that had voted against him last time.[100] Warren knew a thing or two about politics, and offered his friendly advice: "Watch out for those wild Texans, Mr. President," he called out from the sofa where he was enjoying his drink. "They're a rough bunch."[101]

Chapter 22

# THE LONGEST YEAR

*It was like losing one of my own sons.*

EARL WARREN, ON THE DEATH OF JOHN F. KENNEDY[1]

T HE UNITED STATES Supreme Court is an orderly place, one where customs are honored across generations of justices. It was only after long deliberation that Warren persuaded the brethren to move the conference from Saturday to Friday. Once he had succeeded, that new routine was steadfastly observed. So it was that on November 22, 1963, a Friday, the justices began their conference at ten A.M. They exchanged their traditional handshake and settled into their deliberations. Having recently heard arguments in a series of legislative apportionment cases, the justices now faced the question they had raised but not completely answered in *Baker v. Carr*. Where that case had established that voting districts could be challenged as a violation of equal protection, now before the Court were the natural conflicts about how much redistricting was required, how often, and by what criteria—in short, of how much equality of the vote actually was commanded by the equal protection clause of the Fourteenth Amendment.

Without Frankfurter there to lead the voices of restraint, Warren pushed against an open door. Goldberg had given Warren his fifth vote, and as the justices announced their positions that Friday to one another, it was clear that a new era in voting rights was taking shape at the long table in the wood-paneled conference room of the nation's high court.

So sacred is the privacy of the Court's weekly conference that only the most monumental events are permitted to intrude. When news must be passed to the justices, it comes in the form of a knock on the door. All conversation ceases while the door is opened, a note is handed in, and the door is closed. So rare are those intrusions, so high the threshold for their acceptability, that on that Friday afternoon, Margaret McHugh fretted about whether to interrupt when she heard the news from Dallas. She asked one of Warren's clerks, Frank Beytagh, whether he believed the justices should be bothered. Beytagh assured her that it was important enough, so she sent in a note with a rap on the door.[2] Justice Goldberg, the newest of the brethren, rose from his seat to answer it and took the note without reading it. Goldberg passed it to Warren, who then read it to the justices. Tears welled in Warren's eyes and the blood drained from his face as he relayed the reports that the president had been shot.[3] He then quickly adjourned the conference, and the justices streamed out of the room. Most gravitated to Brennan's chambers, where they watched the news on his television set. Warren returned to his office alone, turned on the radio, and listened, hoping in vain "until all hope was gone."[4]

A stricken Warren wrote a statement for the press, expressing his anguish but also revealing himself in an unintended way. "A great and good President has suffered martyrdom," Warren wrote, "as a result of the hatred and bitterness that has been injected into the life of our Nation by bigots."[5] To Warren, who had been pilloried by racists for nearly a decade, Kennedy's death appeared naturally to result from its location—Dallas. It had been just two nights since Warren, sitting across a coffee table from the president, had warned him of Dallas's snarling reputation for hatred. Warren's warning had been offered in political jest, but now it seemed to have been proven all too true.

Those first hours after the shots in Dallas were terrifying as well as tragic. In Washington, the city's phone system buckled under the panic. Many callers found busy signals or no dial tones, confirming for some the fear that America was under attack, that the assassination was the first prong of a coordinated strike. Leading members of the Kennedy cabinet were en route to Japan when the shots were fired in Dallas; they had to be recalled, and their distance from shore fueled fears that the assassination was deliberately timed to take advantage of the scattered national leadership. At the Justice Department, headed by the now dead president's younger brother, aides leapt into motion to respond to Vice President Johnson's urgent inquiry about how best to formally occupy the presidency. One aide called the Supreme Court asking whether anyone there had a copy of the presidential oath. Told that it was in the Constitution, the tightly wound aide blurted out, "Do you have one there?" Yes, he was told, the Court had a few copies lying around.[6]

As the hours passed and no attack came, the mood of the nation and its leadership sank from terror to a crushing sadness. The death of the young and vibrant president, the widowing of his elegant bride, and the calamity to his young children moved millions of Americans—though few more profoundly than the nation's chief justice. The same president who socialized with Warren on Wednesday night now was hurtling home in a casket, his brains splattered across the presidential limousine, his blood staining Jackie's pink suit and matching pillbox hat, so carefully chosen for that trip, so indelibly marked by its tragedy.[7] A new president, Lyndon Johnson, led the entourage that had fled Dallas that afternoon and now droned its way above a nearly hysterical country. *Air Force One,* carrying the nation's new president and the body of its fallen one, plowed through the afternoon toward Andrews Air Force Base, outside of Washington.

Warren was determined to be on hand to greet it, to demonstrate the continuity of government and to greet the nation's widowed First Lady. He called for his driver, Jean Clemencia, but discovered he was stuck in panicked traffic as he tried to drive Nina Warren home from a lunch in suburban Maryland.[8] So Warren asked his clerk, Beytagh, to drive him to the base. As Beytagh navigated the busy streets, Warren reminisced about the young man whose presidency he had so appreciated. There were times when Warren enjoyed banter with his clerks—in their Saturday lunches, over an occasional football or baseball game, in the early mornings, or as the day's work wrapped up. But Beytagh recognized that this was no such time. Warren needed not to discuss but merely to unburden himself, to relieve his sadness and fear, to give voice to his broken heart. They drove together through the fading sunlight, the seventy-two-year-old justice speaking softly of what he and the nation had lost. His young clerk piloted the car in silence.

Arriving at the gate of the air force base, the two were stopped by a pair of tense Marine guards. Beytagh informed them that he was transporting the Chief Justice of the United States. The guard looked across Beytagh at Warren and saw only a white-haired passenger whom he did not recognize. The guard refused to let them pass. Beytagh, a veteran and member of the Navy reserve, was momentarily thrown. Then he reached into his wallet and produced his Navy identification card. The Marine saluted and waved him in. Warren allowed himself a brief grin. Under the peculiar circumstances of that night, Earl Warren's clerk was more trusted than he.[9]

Once through the gate, Beytagh shepherded his chief as close as he could to the waiting area, where dignitaries huddled in the lights, awaiting the plane. The clerk asked whether he should wait for Warren, but the chief waved him off, insisting he could find a ride home. Beytagh then departed, and Warren nudged his way into place at the chain-link fence, elbow-to-elbow with Hubert Humphrey and Averell Harriman, when the lights suddenly went out and *Air Force One* abruptly appeared before them in the darkness.[10] The sight of Jackie Kennedy, with her husband's blood still caked on her dress and jewelry, staggered those who stood beneath the jet. Warren expressed his condolences to Johnson, then reeled away into the night; Beytagh never knew how the chief justice made it home.[11]

The next day, as the nation absorbed the body blow of Kennedy's assassination, Earl and Nina Warren watched with the rest of the country, following the developments from Dallas as police accumulated evidence and pandered to the press corps. Lee Harvey Oswald had been arrested soon after the assassination of Kennedy, the wounding of Governor John Connally, and the murder of Dallas police officer J. D. Tippit—shot to death at 1:16 P.M. less than one mile from Oswald's rooming house in Dallas.[12] Shamed that the assassination had taken place in their city and staggering under the scrutiny of the world, police and prosecutors now rushed to demonstrate their investigative competence, trotting out evidence as they gathered it and arranging for displays of their suspect during breaks in his interrogation. Warren was horrified.[13] A prosecutor at heart, though one whose insistence on fairness had deepened appreciably from the vantage point of the Supreme Court, Warren was appalled at the unseemly release of information that would not have been allowed before a jury. (Authorities disclosed, for instance, that Marina Oswald had told them her husband owned a rifle, a statement that she could have refused to offer at trial by invoking the spousal privilege; similarly, reporters were informed that Oswald had refused to take a lie detector test, which would not have been admissible in a trial.) Led by District Attorney Henry M. Wade, authorities helped generate a climate of conviction around Oswald, and made a number of mistakes that would give rise both to legitimate questions and to outlandish theories concerning the assassination.

That Friday night and Saturday while the rest of the nation grieved, Oswald was questioned. He admitted nothing, but he acted like a guilty man: He lied about his purchase of a rifle, suggested he was a victim of police brutality, and even denied to newsmen that he had been questioned about killing the president. In its own way, this may have been satisfying to Oswald. During his small, violent life, he had yearned to be a grand historical figure. Now, at least briefly, he was. Oswald laid his head down in his cell while the nation drifted into a restless sleep.

In Washington, the jangle of the telephone interrupted Earl and Nina's crushing night. Warren put the receiver to his ear and was stunned to find Jackie Kennedy on the line. The president's widow was on the minds of most Americans. Few could shake the image of her devastated face and bloodstained dress as she made her way off *Air Force One*, supported by her brother-in-law Bobby Kennedy. Now Warren heard her voice for the first time since Friday's events. She was calling to ask a favor, to wonder whether the chief justice would deliver a eulogy for her husband the following afternoon, when Kennedy's body would lie in state under the dome of the Capitol. "I was almost speechless," Warren recalled. He stammered out a reply, naturally agreeing.[14] For Warren, that was the beginning of another long night, during which he struggled for words under the weight of the emotions piling upon him. For hours, he sat blankly pondering his remarks. Finally, at midnight, Warren gave up. He set his alarm and decided to try again when his mind was clearer.

Warren rose early and returned to work; he was nearly finished when his daughter Dorothy burst into the room to tell him that Oswald had been shot. Warren reprimanded her for accepting the latest rumors swirling around the case. "But Daddy," she cried back, "I saw them do it."[15] Warren dashed into the other room, saw the replay of Jack Ruby's attack on Oswald, and then, in a rush to make it to the Capitol on time, asked his wife to type up his eulogy.

Under the circumstances, Warren had no time to ask others to review the comments he was to deliver. What poured from him was rawer than Warren's typical addresses, less carefully modulated, less thoughtfully crafted for its impact or audience. He delivered it on a day of profound mourning and despair, a day when the heavy rain that fell across Washington felt darkly appropriate to the national mood. Warren spoke in the rotunda of the Capitol, his thick voice barely under control. He stumbled only once, near the end of his short eulogy. Thousands of mourners listened in silence; there was barely a stir. Before Warren were Jackie and Caroline. Young John, about to celebrate his third birthday, had been taken aside. After greeting those present and acknowledging the nation outside, Warren moved to the heart of his eulogy, expressing his personal loss along with that of the country:

John Fitzgerald Kennedy—a great and good President, the friend of all people of good will; a believer in the dignity and equality of all human beings; a fighter for justice; an apostle of peace—has been snatched from our midst by the bullet of an assassin.

What moved some misguided wretch to do this horrible deed may never be known to us, but we do know that such acts are commonly stimulated by forces of hatred and malevolence such as today are eating their way into the blood stream of American life. What a price we pay for this fanaticism!

It has been said that the only thing we learn from history is that we do not learn. But surely we can learn if we have the will to do so. Surely there is a lesson to be learned from this tragic event.

If we really love this country; if we truly love justice and mercy; if we fervently want to make this Nation better for those who are to follow us, we can at least abjure the hatred that consumes people, the false accusations that divide us and the bitterness that begets violence. Is it too much to hope that the martyrdom of our beloved President might even soften the hearts of those who would themselves recoil from assassination, but who do not shrink from spreading the venom which kindles thoughts of it in others?

Our Nation is bereaved. The whole world is poorer because of his loss. But we can all be better Americans because John Fitzgerald Kennedy has passed our way; because he has been our chosen leader at a time in history when his character, his vision and his quiet courage have enabled him to chart . . . a safe course for us through the shoals of treacherous seas that encompass the world.

And now that he is relieved of the almost superhuman burdens we imposed on him, may he rest in peace.[16]

Reaction to Warren's speech was decidedly mixed. Jackie appreciated it, but Warren's continued insistence that "hatred," code in those days for racism, was in some way responsible for the president's death rang a hard note in the ears of many Southerners, already by then accustomed to finding fault with the chief justice. Warren's clerk, Beytagh, worried at how others would respond to those remarks, correctly predicting that some would wince at the suggestion that their passionately held views on race were somehow responsible for the horror that had befallen the Kennedy family and the nation.[17] Warren himself evidenced no second thoughts about the eulogy. He sent copies to his colleagues on the Court and reprinted it in full in his memoirs, acknowledging none of its controversial insinuations.

With the eulogy delivered, Warren assumed his formal responsibilities in connection with the assassination were complete. He and Nina attended the funeral the following day and trudged up the hill at Arlington Cemetery for the lighting of the torch, but he was not called upon to speak again. The country tottered back to its feet the following week, and Johnson delivered his first formal address as president on Wednesday, November 27. Speaking to Congress, the new president placed the power of his office and the already gathering aura of Kennedy's legacy in support of the Civil Rights Bill, whose progress had come to a halt that fall. "[N]o memorial oration or eulogy could more eloquently honor President Kennedy's memory than the earliest possible passage of the civil rights bill for which he fought so long," Johnson announced to the Congress where he so long served and to the nation that he now suddenly led. "We have talked long enough in this country about equal rights. We have talked for one hundred years or more. It is time now to write the next chapter, and to write it in the books of law."[18] Having labored for so many years in that field alone, Warren could only have welcomed Johnson's pledge with relief.

That Thanksgiving, the day after Johnson's speech, was a somber one, as Americans struggled to imagine what they could be grateful for after that terrible week. The Warrens marked the day as did many, in quiet reflection. They attended a Thanksgiving mass and then Warren, late in the day, paid a visit to an old California acquaintance, Senator Clair Engle, who, like Warren, grew up in the little dusty town of Bakersfield, when times seemed simpler and America less troubled.[19] Elected to the Senate in 1958, Engle had replaced Bill Knowland there and had soon befriended Warren. Engle was, on that sad, rainy day in 1963, near the end. A brain tumor was eating away at him. First it robbed him of his voice—when he cast a vote for a civil rights bill the next year, Engle could not speak; he was forced to point to his eye in order to register his "Aye"—then it took his life. Engle would be dead by the end of 1964.

On that Friday afternoon, Warren was shaken with grief. Kennedy had died and Engle was dying. Much of Washington remained closed. Warren made it to the

Court, where he met with Beytagh that afternoon. Warren said there were two main issues he wished to discuss. The first was to inform Beytagh that the brethren had agreed to address the issue of legislative reapportionment, and that Warren himself intended to write for the Court, as he viewed that topic as the most important matter before the justices that term. The cases challenging various legislative districting schemes would be consolidated in a single decision, Warren said, and it was up to the chief justice and his clerks—in this case, Beytagh—to compose the opinion that would rewrite the rules of American voting and representation. The second matter, Warren said, was that he felt Beytagh should know that he had been approached that afternoon by two senior Justice Department officials, Nick Katzenbach and Archibald Cox, who had urged him to accept an assignment of national importance, the chairmanship of a commission that Johnson was forming to study the Kennedy assassination. Warren held a dim view of previous extrajudicial undertakings by sitting justices—Owen Roberts's report on the aftermath of Pearl Harbor had stirred the passions that led to Warren's worst mistake, his advocacy of the Japanese internment in 1942; Robert Jackson's service in Nuremberg had annoyed his colleagues and strained relations at the Court. He told his clerk he had listened but firmly declined.[20]

The two then turned back to the business of the Court, only to be interrupted by the phone. It was the White House calling, Lyndon Johnson himself asking if Warren would not come down the hill to discuss a matter of urgency. Beytagh excused himself while the two men talked, and then Warren quickly exited for the White House. Before leaving, he asked Beytagh to stick around so that they could resume their conversation when he returned.

Warren arrived and was shown into the Oval Office at 4:30 P.M. on Friday afternoon.[21] Johnson immediately went to work, skipping over any attempt to soft-sell his Commission proposal and jumping instead to Warren's most vulnerable places—his concern for the nation's safety and his patriotism. Johnson told Warren that the rumors of foreign involvement in the assassination were contributing to a dangerous international situation, one that, if left unchecked, could propel the nation toward war, even a nuclear war. If that weren't enough, Johnson pointedly warned Warren, the administration's top security and defense officials estimated that such a war could claim 60 million American lives.[22] Johnson's reasoning was tenuous—it was a significant leap from rumors of foreign involvement to 60 million American dead—but it was a hard pitch for Warren to resist. Still, he tried to say no, erecting his stiff formality in response to Johnson's increasingly feverish demands. And then Johnson capped it, as only Johnson could, with the dagger to Warren's heart—the appeal to his love of country. "You've worn a uniform," Johnson reminded Warren. "You were in the service in World War I. This job is more important than anything you ever did in the uniform."[23] There was nothing left for

Warren to do but to give in. The entire conversation had lasted less than half an hour. By Johnson's account, Warren left the office in tears.[24]

When Warren returned to the waiting Beytagh that evening, he was as downcast as the clerk had ever seen him.[25] Deflated to the point of exhaustion, Warren knew he had yielded on a point that he should have held, but, he complained, the appeal to his patriotism was more than he could withstand.[26] Warren did not wallow. With the decision made, he plunged ahead into the work that he had agreed to shoulder. At the age of seventy-two, he would spend most of the coming year simultaneously presiding over the United States Supreme Court and the President's Commission on the Assassination of President Kennedy. The world would come to know it as the "Warren Commission"; Warren himself never called it that.

Warren was placed at the chairmanship of an esteemed and intentionally disparate group. From the House of Representatives came Hale Boggs, House majority whip and a congressman from Louisiana for nearly two decades. Boggs, one of just two Democrats on the Commission, was, by 1964, one of the House's most respected members. First elected in 1940 at age twenty-six, Boggs was then the youngest member of Congress; he lost his seat, left to fight in World War II, and then returned to New Orleans, where he resurrected his political career by winning a New Orleans congressional seat. Like Lyndon Johnson, Boggs studied under the tutelage of House Speaker Sam Rayburn, who nurtured their early careers and ambitions. In 1956, Boggs was among those Southern representatives who signed the Southern Manifesto denouncing the Court's decision in *Brown*.

Joining him from the House was an up-and-coming Michigan congressman, Gerald Ford. Though in the House nearly as long as Boggs, Ford had labored in its Republican minority, rising in 1963 to the chairmanship of the House Republican Conference, where he led a group of younger Republicans asserting leadership in order to counteract the youthful vitality of the Kennedy administration. Solid and reliable, he seemed a safe bet for Johnson as he sought to demonstrate his bipartisanship by tapping a House Republican. Moreover, Ford was known to be friendly with J. Edgar Hoover and supportive of the FBI. Since Johnson required the FBI's active participation in the investigation and analysis of the case, Ford offered advantages there as well.

From outside the government, Johnson selected two veterans of public service and pillars of American power. Allen Dulles had served as director of Central Intelligence under President Eisenhower and in the early months of the Kennedy administration. Few men in the American intelligence community were more widely recognized—or reviled. None had overseen more covert actions of the American government; few, if any, knew more of its mid-twentieth-century secrets, and few had failed more spectacularly. Dulles had helped oversee the disastrous Bay of Pigs episode early in the Kennedy administration, and after it, John Kennedy's distrust of the CIA grew so intense that he asked his brother Bobby, from his post as attorney general, to in effect ride herd over the intelligence agency. Dulles shortly thereafter retired, ending his career as the longest-serving director of America's relatively young intelligence service.

For the other public slot, Johnson turned to John J. McCloy, like Dulles a member of long standing in the nation's international apparatus. McCloy's public duties had included stints as assistant secretary of war, president of the World Bank, and U.S. military governor and high commissioner for Germany after World War II. So varied and deep was McCloy's background that the Warren Commission's premier scholar, Max Holland, described him as a "Wall Street lawyer, banker, and diplomat who personifies the versatile statesmen who serve Democratic and Republican presidents alike."[27]

Completing the Commission were two members selected from the United States Senate. John Sherman Cooper was a veteran of the House and a Kentucky judge, first elected to the Senate in 1946 to fill out a term of a resigning member. He lost his reelection bid in 1948, then filled out another term, this one caused by the death of Senator Virgil M. Chapman, starting in 1952, only to lose again at the polls in 1954. His on-again, off-again Senate career, however, said more about the difficulties of being a Republican in Kentucky than it did about Cooper's reputation. Cooper was highly regarded by leaders in both parties, a genuine Southern moderate at a time when few such animals existed. He also had been close not only to John but also to Jackie Kennedy, who felt in him a "great kindness."[28]

The final slot on the Commission went to the man Johnson trusted most, but he only agreed to accept it under the sternest pressure and even some duplicity on the president's part. Richard Russell was one of Washington's most intriguing figures, a lonely bachelor who had long since abandoned hopes of a wife and marriage and devoted himself instead to the business of the United States Senate. Heir to one of Georgia's great political families, Russell was sworn in to the governorship by his father, the state's chief justice and himself a failed candidate for that office. Once he moved to the Senate, Russell amassed influence with his quiet intelligence, his abiding modesty, and his reputation for telling the truth. By 1963, he was the Senate's most powerful man. Leaders of both parties recognized that he controlled the pace and outcome of legislation, that he could and would win passage of what he favored and would filibuster what he did not. He was devoted to America and to the American South.

Kennedy's death had only heightened Russell's power, for the White House now was occupied by one of his most grateful protégés, Lyndon Johnson. Johnson represented more for Russell than a friend in power. Russell had dreamed his whole adult life of a Southerner's ascending to the White House, rising above the animus of the War Between the States and taking his place at the head of the united nation. Johnson was the fulfillment of that dream. Johnson owed his rise in part to Russell, and Russell relished what Johnson had achieved. Russell admired presidents; he *loved* this president. It was thus entirely natural that Johnson would choose Russell for such a delicate and important task. There was only one serious problem: As much as Russell loved Lyndon Johnson, he also detested Earl Warren. In Russell's eyes, no cause was greater than the preservation of the Southern Way of Life, and no man had done more to debase that cause than Warren.

When Johnson called Russell on the evening of November 29 to update him on plans for the Commission, the president knew he was going to be pushing Russell into an assignment. So Johnson deliberately waited until he had announced the formation of the Commission before bothering to tell Russell that he was a member.[29] Calling Russell just before nine P.M. that evening, Johnson read him the announcement, featuring Warren's appointment as chairman and Russell's as the next name on the list. Russell was dumbfounded. When Johnson finished reading the statement, Russell sputtered, "I don't have to tell you of my devotion to *you,* but I just can't serve on that commission. I'm highly honored you'd think about me in connection with it. But I couldn't serve there with Chief Justice Warren. I don't like that man." Johnson had proved all day that he would not take no for an answer, though, and he proved it again that night. He first fell back on the arguments he'd used with Warren—that a nuclear war loomed if rumors persisted, that millions of Americans could die, that Russell would put on a uniform if asked by his president. Russell continued to protest, and Johnson mixed threats with appeals to their long friendship. "You're *my man on that commission, and you gonna do it!*" Johnson exclaimed. "And don't tell me what you can do and what you *can't* because . . . I can't arrest you. And I'm not going to put the FBI on you, but you're *goddamned sure gonna serve,* I'll tell you *that.*"[30] By the time their conversation was over, Johnson had flattered, threatened, and cajoled—"Nobody ever been more to me than you have, Dick . . . except my mother," Johnson noted at one point. The weary senator, complaining still at the thought of serving with Warren, nevertheless succumbed and agreed to take his place on the president's commission.

The other members fell much more quickly into line (Ford would later tell Arlen Specter that he, like his then more famous colleagues, resisted; in fact, the congressman and future president accepted his place without protest).[31] They were in some senses a homogeneous group: All seven members were men; all were white; all were lawyers. And they were all, indisputably, among the most admired members of America's political leadership. But they also represented a diversity of backgrounds and views. They came from different parties (five Republicans and two Democrats) and different parts of the country—none, by design, from Texas, but Cooper, Russell, and Boggs all came from the South or border states. Most important, they arrived with different conceptions of what had happened in Dallas. War-

ren believed the assassination was motivated by hatred and bigotry; Russell was inclined to see Castro and Cuba as the agents of the deed. McCloy, too, believed others were at work. They were not, individually or as a group, predisposed to believe
that Oswald acted alone. Nor were they inclined to agree out of friendship or common worldview. When others wondered much later about whether the Commission collaborated on a cover-up, Warren snorted in reply, "As if Gerry Ford and I
could conspire on anything!"[32]

At ten A.M. on December 5, Warren opened their first session. "Gentlemen,"
he began:

> This is a very sad and solemn duty that we are undertaking, and I am sure that there is
> not one of us but what would rather be doing almost anything else that he can think of
> than to be on a commission of this kind. But it is a tremendously important one. The
> President, I'm sure, is right in trying to make sure that the public will be given all of the
> facts of this sordid situation, so far as it is humanly possible to do it, and I feel honored
> that he would think that I, along with the rest of you, are capable of doing such a job, and
> I enter upon it with great feeling of both inadequacy and humility because the very
> thought of reviewing these details day by day is really sickening to me.[33]

With that, the Warren Commission was at work. Johnson had encouraged the
Commission to take a small view of itself, and Warren accepted that. He initially
conceived the Commission's work as limited to reviewing the work of the FBI, analyzing that work, and reporting its findings. Given that narrow task, the Commission would not, in Warren's view, need to conduct an independent investigation of
its own. Warren came to that first meeting believing that the Commission did not
need subpoena power and would not hold public hearings. Although he would be
forced to reconsider each of those positions, they were natural ones for a chairman
who wanted to make quick work of this panel and who, as a governor, had entrusted much to the work of his commissions in California, where he placed confidence in small gatherings of experts to lead government to dispassionate,
nonpartisan conclusions.

It was McCloy who first suggested that the Commission needed a top-notch
general counsel—a "rattling good counsel," in his words—and Warren clearly had
been thinking along the same lines. In fact, he arrived at the meeting that day with
one in mind.[34] It was, unsurprisingly, one of the men he had trusted most for the
longest time, a friend and colleague of estimable reputation and one arguably
closer to Warren than any man alive: Warren Olney III. Since returning to work
with Warren in 1958, Olney had brought his lifelong devotion to detail and professionalism to the post, which gave him administrative authority over all federal
courts and courthouses except the Supreme Court itself. Olney monitored budgets,

congressional hearings, the status of legislation, and delicate matters such as complaints against judges. He met regularly with Warren, and Warren relied on his judgment.[35]

To the Commission, Warren presented Olney's credentials, his education at the University of California, Berkeley; his lineage as part of one of California's most esteemed legal families; his service to Warren in a series of positions; his well-regarded tenure at the Department of Justice; his studied aversion to partisan politics. Before coming to the Commission that day, Warren had discussed with Olney the general counsel position, and Olney had agreed to take it.[36] But Warren had barely laid Olney's merits before the Commission when Gerald Ford spoke up to object. "There can be some," Ford interjected gingerly, "unfairly perhaps, who would then say that the Chief Justice is dominating the Commission and it will be his report rather than the report of all of us."[37] When McCloy added that he was reluctant to approve Olney right away for a different reason—he sensibly noted that there was no reason to jump at the first name put before the Commission—Olney's appointment was shelved for the day in order that the commissioners could make inquiries.

They returned the next day, and Olney was knocked out of contention. The commissioners, conscious that a stenographer was recording their comments, albeit in executive session, talked around the reasons why Olney was unacceptable. Warren withdrew his name rather than debate the matter in a forum that might someday become public. All that was said in that early discussion was that commissioners had checked up on Olney and decided he was not the right man for the job. Late in the session, however, McCloy let the reason slip. The issue that had tanked Olney and deprived Warren of his trusted aide was, McCloy said, "that he was at swordspoint with J. Edgar Hoover."[38] What McCloy did not say, but what was later to become evident, was that Hoover and the FBI were determined to exercise influence over the Commission. They monitored its work, withheld information from it, and meddled in its business. And at its outset, they had help from an especially well-placed and eager informant, Congressman Gerald Ford.

THE INITIAL MEETINGS of the Commission had not gone well for Warren. The other members challenged his conception of the panel's work and rejected his choice of a top assistant. And yet Warren seemed to regain his footing after those setbacks. In that, Warren was aided by the hiring of a general counsel who, though not his first choice, brought a rational and more expansive view of the Commission's work. Warren knew J. Lee Rankin from the latter's service as solicitor general in the Eisenhower years, and the two men liked and respected each other. Rankin, in the view of the chief justice before whom he had so often argued, was "a splendid man in every respect."[39] Russell may have harbored some doubts about Rankin, who was prominently associated with desegregation, but the Commission already had scotched Warren's first choice, and it now moved to accept Rankin with Warren's blessing.

Ten days later, at the commission's December 16 executive session, a new tone crept into the proceedings—one of confidence, manifested both in the Commission's own steps to organize and in its new willingness to exercise skepticism about the reliability of the agencies whose work would supply it with much of its material. Warren opened the December 16 meeting by having his old colleague, now retired Justice Stanley Reed, swear in the Commission, then ticked off the Commission's organizational accomplishments: Rankin had accepted the position, 10,000 feet of office space in the newly built Veterans of Foreign Wars Building had been arranged—the fourth-floor offices were "clean as a thistle," Warren proudly reported. Commissioners also had received the FBI's initial report, as well as one from the State Department; others from the Secret Service and the CIA were expected soon.[40]

But if those were the signs that the Commission's work was coming into focus, the enormous scope of that work also now was becoming clear. Having read the FBI report, Warren and several of the others found little to praise. "To be very frank about it," said Warren, "I have read that report two or three times and I have not seen anything in there yet that has not been in the press."[41] Russell agreed, as did Boggs, who noted that "reading the FBI report leaves a million questions."[42] Dulles voiced his dissatisfaction with the reports of Oswald's activities in the Soviet Union during the period of his defection. McCloy wanted more information on the attempted shooting of General Walker, a right-wing military man living in Dallas, whom Oswald was accused of trying to kill in the months leading up to the Kennedy assassination. As the expressions of dissatisfaction mounted, Warren presented his colleagues with a motion to require the various agencies to turn over their raw materials to the Commission so that it could conduct its own analysis. With that, the Warren Commission moved subtly from reviewing the analysis of government agencies to conducting its own, more thorough and probing investigation. Neither Warren nor the other members were under any illusions about the implications of the expansion of their work. Commenting on the documents they were now requesting, Russell bemoaned, "[I]t will take a truck." Warren replied, "Yes, I have no doubt."[43]

The Commission's unhappiness with the report was reinforced by skeptical press coverage of the document, which was leaked to reporters at about the same time it was transmitted to the Commission. Hoover professed fury at the leak and blamed Warren for handing it to Pearson. "I informed the Attorney General [Bobby Kennedy] that Pearson got a good portion of the story from the Chief Justice with whom he is very close," Hoover told his top aides.[44] Although Hoover was right about the friendship between Warren and Pearson, he almost certainly was wrong about the leak. Press accounts of the report's contents began appearing even before the Commission received the document, suggesting that the sources for it were within the FBI itself.[45] While it thus seems more likely that FBI officials, perhaps without Hoover's knowledge, were the source of the leaks, Hoover's willingness to blame Warren—and to do so with the brother of the dead president—says much about how far gone were the days of the Bureau's "Cooperation with Governor Warren." With Hoover now angry over the leak, and Warren thwarted by Hoover in his desire to select Warren Olney, the old ties that once bound them were unraveling fast.

The new, self-imposed mandate of the Warren Commission—to review the raw reports included in every government document relevant to the assassination—necessitated a new staff plan as well. Rankin, with the support of the Commission, divided the assassination into topic areas and began to recruit a full staff of lawyers. Former NYPD Commissioner Francis Adams and Chicago trial lawyer Albert Jenner were the first two picked for the Commission, and Rankin was given permission to go out and recruit more. Through late December, he did just that, drawing on personal and professional contacts to assemble two tiers of legal talent: senior lawyers drawn from top law firms and public service, and a second group of young attorneys who would end up carrying the bulk of the Commission's work. Warren interceded only occasionally in that process, helping to bring on three lawyers he knew and admired: Joe Ball of Long Beach, a leading member of the California bar and longtime friend of Warren's; Sam Stern, who had clerked for Warren at the Supreme Court and then was practicing in Washington; and Richard Mosk, a recent law school graduate and veteran whose father had once been Culbert Olson's chief of staff—and in those years, a Warren foe, but his family had grown close to Warren during Warren's governorship. Mosk wrote to Warren to ask for a place on the staff before beginning a clerkship on the California Supreme Court. Warren brought him on.[46]

One other aspect of the Commission's December 16 meeting is worthy of note, if only because of the controversy that would come to shadow its findings. At that session, Warren clearly believed others might have assisted Oswald. The man who frequently gave Oswald a ride to and from the home where Marina Oswald then was living, for instance, "certainly had to be checked out," Warren said, as others added their suspicions regarding Oswald's time in Russia and other movements. Whatever one may say later about the Commission's conclusions, it is clear that as it began its work, its members were open to the possibility that Oswald was not a lone gunman but rather someone working with the help of others.

The FBI monitored those developments closely and despite the secrecy of the proceedings heard about them almost immediately. Less than twenty-four hours after the Commission had met in closed session—with just its seven members, general counsel, and a stenographer present—the FBI knew of its work plan, its reaction to the FBI's report, and even the names of those it was interested in hiring. It knew all that because it had a source inside the room: congressman and future president of the United States Gerald Ford. On December 17, Ford met with Cartha D. DeLoach, a senior official of the FBI, and briefed him in detail. He reported to the FBI the Commission's initial reaction to the Bureau's work on the case, though Ford presented that reaction far more favorably than the Commission had actually responded. He told DeLoach that two commissioners had doubts that Kennedy had been shot from the window of the Book Depository, he briefed DeLoach regarding the initial appointments to the legal staff, and he passed along the displeasure of some commissioners at public statements by a former Secret Service chief. All of this was dutifully recorded in the files of the FBI, and Ford's contact passed information back to him as well. Ford, the FBI suggested, should tread carefully with his new colleague, Chief Justice Warren. The Bureau also warned that Warren was known to be close to Drew Pearson and thus might leak material to him.[47]

Ford and the FBI closed their December 17 session with Ford making a request: He wanted to take the FBI report with him skiing over the Christmas holiday and wondered if the Bureau could get him a briefcase with a lock; the bureau delivered Ford an "agent briefcase" the following day.[48]


THE AGENDA of the United States Supreme Court is partly its own. The justices choose the cases they hear, and any combination of four justices is enough to take up a case and either set it for argument or decide it on the briefs. But the Court cannot dictate what lawsuits will be filed, what cases prosecuted, what appeals pursued. It cannot avoid decisions because its members, even its chief, are preoccupied. And so, as the Warren Commission ground through its early labors, the Warren Court took stock of a momentous agenda. Warren had agreed at the first Court conference to write in the reapportionment cases, and even though he had since accepted the chairmanship of the president's Commission, he refused to hand off the work. So now, as Rankin began hiring lawyers, Warren returned to *Reynolds v. Sims*. *Reynolds* was the first case of its kind to come to the Court in the post-Frankfurter era, and Warren now operated with the latitude that only Frankfurter's absence could have provided.

Alabama's constitution was adopted in 1901, and it provided for a two-house legislature, which, as the 1960s opened, consisted of 35 senators and 106 members of the state House of Representatives.[49] The state's political balance had been struck with the adoption of its constitution, and in the sixty years since, it had grown unevenly, with cities such as Jefferson, Mobile, and Montgomery growing faster than rural areas. Although the state constitution also required a decennial reapportionment, Alabama's leaders had ignored that provision, and its courts, while finding that a violation, took the Frankfurter view that politics was beyond the reach of judges.[50] The result was a pattern of voting that denied urban—and thus, black—voters anywhere near the power afforded to rural whites. Bullock County, for instance, had a population of 13,462 and was given two representatives in the state legislature; Mobile, with a population of 314,301, had three. It was, in the language of the law, an "invidiously discriminatory plan completely lacking in rationality."[51] And yet it stood.

Warren set out with *Reynolds* to complete the work of *Baker v. Carr,* but he did so while also chairing the Warren Commission. As a result, he relied heavily on his clerk, often talking with him by phone or meeting at the beginning or end of long days. Beytagh and Warren settled on some early drafts and began to circulate them among the justices. It was immediately clear that they would prevail. "The opinions issuing from the chambers of the Chief Justice in those cases were joined without the slightest apparent hesitation or reservation by Justices Black, Douglas, Brennan, and Goldberg," Brennan's clerks recorded that year.[52] That gave Warren a majority, but a slim one, and he asked Beytagh to continue to hone the writing, specifically with an eye toward attracting White's vote. Beytagh drafted and corrected drafts, and Warren worked on White personally, dropping by his chambers, urging him to consider the fairness implications of rules that gave so much more power to some voters than others. By spring, White was wavering, and Beytagh and Warren were discussing the finer points of the ruling, among them the question of how often legislatures should be required to redraw district lines. In his draft, Beytagh had proposed a decennial reapportionment to coincide with the census. Warren was not convinced.

In that case, Beytagh said, "I have an alternative. We can go back to the *Brown* case and use 'all deliberate speed.'"

"No," Warren replied, shocked at the idea of reviving the phrase that had caused him and his Court such grief. "I'm not going to do that."

"I'm just pulling your leg," Beytagh said, and the two relaxed in a moment of laughter. Laughter came all too rarely in 1963 and 1964.[53]

By the end of the term, White had come around on *Reynolds,* and he eventually joined in its reasoning and its memorable language, much originally the work of Beytagh, though all of it supervised by the chief justice. "Legislators represent people, not trees or acres," the opinion for the Court noted. "Legislators are elected by voters, not farms or cities or economic interests."[54] More than four decades afterward, those remain the most quoted words of the *Reynolds* opinion, but *Reynolds* also contains a parting shot by Warren at Frankfurter and the votes he once commanded:

We are told that the matter of apportioning representation in a state legislature is a complex and many-faceted one. We are advised that States can rationally consider factors other than population in apportioning legislative representation. We are admonished not to restrict the power of the States to impose differing views as to political philosophy on their citizens. We are cautioned about the dangers of entering into political thickets and mathematical quagmires. Our answer is this: a denial of constitutionally protected rights demands judicial protection; our oath and our office require no less of us.[55]

Harlan dissented with a thorough and complex work, accompanied by two appendixes. Warren contemplated a reply, but then abandoned the idea at the last minute. *Reynolds* stood on its own, and it, along with *Baker v. Carr*, came to be the opinions that Warren valued above all others.[56] It was natural that they should. Warren, who believed so deeply in the fundamental principles of American democracy, in its Declaration and in the conviction that its Constitution required fairness, saw the right to vote and the right to have every vote count equally as predicates for the fair society he was helping to build. If the rights and responsibilities of society were to be administered through its government, Warren believed, "it must be done by representatives who are responsible to all the people, not just those with special interests to serve."[57]

That conviction first was expressed in *Baker*, though that was Brennan's writing. It was reinforced and expanded by *Reynolds*, this time in Warren's words. But it was pushed to a limit that demonstrated just how serious Warren was in one of *Reynolds*'s companion cases, *Lucas v. Colorado General Assembly*. There, Warren wrote for a Court that not only insisted that voting districts be drawn according to population but also specifically rejected an attempt by the voters of Colorado to draw them otherwise. "An individual's constitutionally protected right to cast an equally weighted vote cannot be denied even by a vote of a majority of a State's electorate, if the apportionment scheme adopted by the voters fails to measure up to the requirements of the Equal Protection Clause," Warren wrote. "A citizen's constitutional rights can hardly be infringed simply because a majority of the people choose that it be."[58] In effect, Warren—the old Progressive, still convinced that enlightened leadership acted as ballast against the swings of populist bandwagons—said in *Lucas* that democracy was so important it could not be curtailed even through the democratic process. Democracy was essential to achieve fairness; fairness could not be subverted, even by democracy.

Warren's determination in the legislative redistricting cases thrust the Court into its third great battle of his tenure, following the attacks on its decisions regarding segregation and domestic security. This time, the reaction came in the form of a sneak attack. The Council of State Governments met in December 1962 in

Chicago and there adopted three resolutions. The first would require the Congress to certify any constitutional amendment passed by two-thirds of the state legislatures; the second proposed creation of a Court of the Union, composed of the chief justice of each state Supreme Court, with the power to override the United States Supreme Court on any matter that asserted rights reserved to the states or people under the Ninth or Tenth Amendment to the Constitution; the third would overrule *Baker v. Carr*.[59] Where other challenges to the Court's jurisdiction or authority had attracted wide attention, this one passed with little note—except in state legislatures, where elected officials exercised about *Baker v. Carr* took up the call and quietly passed the proposed amendments. By the spring of 1963, twenty-four states had passed some version of the amendments with barely a whisper of opposition. Warren learned of those developments with alarm, and used a scheduled set of speaking engagements that April and May to draw attention to a threat against his Court and the framework of federal-state relations. Speaking at Duke University on April 27, Warren demanded that the nation's lawyers take note of the movement: "If lawyers are not to be the watchmen of our Constitution, on whom are we to rely?"[60] That drew press attention, as did his reiteration of that call three weeks later at a meeting of the American Law Institute. Warren marshaled his prestige against the proposals, and once exposed to scrutiny, they withered.

The reapportionment decisions were the most momentous of the term, and they placed the Court in its most precarious political debate, but the most contentious disagreement among the brethren occurred elsewhere. In earlier times, Warren would have turned to Black for support in the term's divisive deliberation, but this time they would part ways, their first significant break over civil rights. The sit-in cases that confronted the United States Supreme Court that term had been working their way to the Court for some time. In the fall of 1963, the Court accepted three new cases: *Bell v. Maryland; Barr, Bouie v. City of Columbia, South Carolina;* and *Robinson v. Florida*. Another case, *Griffin v. Maryland*, had been argued the previous term and held over, so it too was before the justices as they contemplated the balance between the rights of private property and those of equal protection. Each case brought slightly different facts, but all centered on the same basic question: How far could state and local governments go to enforce racial segregation by owners of private facilities? In other words, if a privately owned restaurant refused to seat black customers and the police then assisted in ejecting those customers, had the state lent government support for segregation or merely assisted in the protection of private property from trespass?

On October 18, 1963, in its first conference on the subject, the Court voted in favor of the protesters in two of the cases—*Griffin* and *Bouie*, though both were by 5–4 majorities and the Court in neither reached the basic constitutional question of whether private owners could discriminate and rely on the state to enforce their discrimination. In *Bell* and *Robinson,* however, the Court was inclined to address that basic question, and in both instances, an equally thin majority rallied behind Black to uphold the rights of private property over those of assembly and protest. In one sense, Black's position was predictable. He had always drawn a distinction between speech and action, and in his view the actions of the demonstrators exceeded the protections of the First Amendment, at least when they were placed in conflict with the rights of private property holders. Making that point to the brethren, Black drew upon his usual constitutional literalism but this time added a distinctly personal touch: Black's "Pappy," he told the justices, had run a little store in Alabama, and Black refused to believe that his Pappy was obligated to serve just anyone; it was his store, his property, and his right to choose who came inside.[61] The Court's more conservative justices, unaccustomed to having Black in their corner, endorsed his view. That gave Black the company of Clark, Harlan, Stewart, and White and placed him at odds with his traditional allies—Warren, Brennan, and Douglas—along with the newly arrived liberal, Goldberg.

It had been months since Birmingham and the March on Washington had convinced Kennedy to introduce his Civil Rights Bill, but that legislation was still before Congress when the Court first took up its five sit-in cases that fall. With Black's exhortation on property rights and his departed Pappy, he thus placed himself in opposition to the leading civil rights imperative of that year. Brennan and perhaps Warren, apparently swept up in the heat of the discussion, threatened to do all they could to stall the Court's decisions—a ruling against the protesters, particularly one bearing Black's prestige, would, they feared, badly hurt chances for passage of the bill.[62] Such overt reference to politics is highly unusual inside the Court, and the conservative justices understandably took offense at the threat to gum up pending cases merely to advance a political interest. "The suggestion of delay," Brennan's clerks admitted, "caused a certain amount of hard feeling among the Justices."[63] The battle lines thus hardened and remained set through the fall, through the death of Kennedy, and into the New Year. With Warren preoccupied by the reapportionment cases and the assassination commission, it fell to Brennan to lead what was, in effect, a prolonged stall.

The first move was a page taken directly from Frankfurter's slowdown of the *Brown* deliberations. It was to ask for more briefing, in this case in the form of an amicus brief from the federal government. Proof of how testy the discussion had become can be found in the fact that the vote on that relatively benign proposal broke 5–4. Harlan at first joined with those seeking more argument, then reconsidered overnight, undoubtedly having realized that he was being used as part of the delaying tactic.[64] The request for reargument passed only because Stewart, who was allied with the conservatives on the basic question, went along with the liberals seeking more information. Then Warren took his time informing the solicitor general, who, soon after receiving it, asked for another extension.[65] It did not arrive at the Court until early 1964. When it did, it contained one small but important revelation: Attorneys in that office, in the course of researching Florida's segregation laws, found one that regulated toilets by race. Because that was clear state action, it provided a basis for reversing the convictions in the *Robinson* case, and it bought the liberals even more time, since Black had structured his main opinion in the sit-in cases on *Robinson* and now was forced to retool it around the facts in the *Bell* case.[66]

Still, time appeared to be running out for the liberals, as Southern Democrats waged a historic filibuster to block the Civil Rights Bill even in the face of President Johnson's active support. My mid-March, Brennan had concluded that he could not outlast Black's forces, but he continued to try to pick off one vote from the other side, since one defection would be enough to change the outcome. As Black circulated drafts through March and April, he was fighting hard to hold on to his five votes—"a scant and scared majority," as his wife put it to her diary.[67] Brennan responded, circulating dissents, trolling for another ally. The debate grew complicated and fierce, until, on May 15, Clark suddenly announced that he was inclined to side with Brennan. Black was shocked and angry. The conference discussion that day was, in the words of the Brennan clerks, "brief and exceedingly tense, with Justices Black and Clark saying virtually nothing."[68] The matter continued even after that, however, as Clark agreed only to join a narrow ruling that passed on the larger constitutional questions; Douglas, typically, wanted broader strokes, so now Douglas threatened to bolt the liberals even as they edged toward victory. That technical debate, made more emotional by the wrangling among the brethren, finally subsided after a final gasp of acrimony.

On Friday, June 19, Congress passed the Civil Rights Act and sent it to Johnson for his signature. It prohibited discrimination in any place of public accommodation, defined in the act as any restaurant, cafeteria, lunchroom, lunch counter, or soda fountain; any hotel or motel; any movie theater or gas station. Three days later, the Court announced its rulings in the sit-in cases; Douglas had already left for the summer; Black now spoke only for himself, Harlan, and White, having lost Clark and even Stewart in the term's endgame; Brennan delivered the majority opinion in *Bell*. Johnson signed the act, the most important piece of civil rights legislation in American history, on July 2. "Five votes," Brennan remarked near the end of the session, "can do anything around here."[69]

The sit-in cases were explicitly about civil rights and the Court's role in protecting that movement against its opponents. The term's other historic decision also was, at its core, a civil rights case, though its larger impact was on the development of a modern free press. *New York Times v. Sullivan* began with a fundraising advertisement in the *Times* that appeared on March 29, 1960, beneath the headline

"Heed Their Rising Voices."[70] The ad charged that Negro protesters who engaged in nonviolent resistance to segregation were being met "by an unprecedented wave of terror," and it asked readers to contribute money to support the student protesters, to assist in securing the right of Negroes to vote, and to help pay the legal defense bills of Martin Luther King, Jr., in a perjury case.[71] In the ad, student protesters were said to have sung "My Country, 'Tis of Thee" on the steps of the Alabama state capitol, for which they were allegedly expelled from school. "Truckloads of police" were accused of ringing the Alabama State College campus, and when the students refused to reregister for classes, "their dining hall was padlocked in an attempt to starve them into submission." "Southern violators" were accused of directing intimidation and violence at King, who, along with his wife and child, had been bombed, assaulted, and arrested seven times, the ad reported.

Many of those statements turned out to be false, though many were trivially so. The students sang the national anthem, not "My Country, 'Tis of Thee." They were expelled from school, but not for demonstrating at the capitol; their expulsions were for a lunch-counter sit-in. The dining hall was never padlocked, and though large numbers of the police were deployed during the protests, they never "ringed" the campus. King had been arrested only four times, not seven.[72]

L. B. Sullivan was one of three commissioners of the city of Montgomery, and though his name never appeared in the ad, he filed the libel suit against those whose names appeared on it and against the *Times* for running it. Sullivan said the ad defamed him because it was widely known that the city commissioners oversaw its police and therefore the ad's misstatements about police actions could logically be inferred to be about him. As to the accusations against "Southern violators," he argued that because those charges also included references to police action—King's arrests—the ad again implied that he was responsible. Sullivan did not show that he had suffered any damage as a result of the ad—one could argue that it only helped his standing in Montgomery in 1960—but Alabama's juries and courts happily lent their assistance to his campaign against a Northern newspaper in a climate of anger toward "outside agitators." After a trial in Alabama, the *Times* was ordered to pay Sullivan $500,000 in damages, an award upheld by the Alabama Supreme Court.

That alone threatened the ability of the *Times* to cover news in Alabama, and in the weeks following it, others piled on. By the time the case had reached the United States Supreme Court, in 1964, there were eleven pending libel cases against the paper in Alabama alone, seeking a combined $5.6 million.[73] Few doubted who would win those cases in Alabama courtrooms. The effect on the *Times* was potentially devastating; while *New York Times v. Sullivan* was pending, the paper pulled its reporters out of Alabama, achieving precisely what the state had hoped—an end to national attention to its racial policies, at least in the pages of the *Times*, and a portent of diminished coverage by other national news organizations.[74] What's more, the *Times* was not the only defendant in the case. Ralph Abernathy, who helped pay for the ad, was sued as well, along with three other civil rights leaders. Their personal financial security was at stake, and the movement depended on drawing attention to its suffering in order to change minds. If innocent mistakes, as interpreted by hostile Southern juries, would be enough to shut down coverage, then the movement itself was in peril.

It was that threat, more than sympathy for the newspaper, that captured Warren's interest and attention. By 1964, he had spent a full decade confronting Southern authorities as they attempted to shut down dissent. He had led the Court through years of keeping the NAACP in the fray, and certainly he would not fold his cards now. The *New York Times* case was argued on January 6, 1964, and Warren, then less than a month away from beginning to take testimony for the President's Assassination Commission, looked to hand it off. Warren turned, as he so often did, to Brennan. For three months, Brennan circulated drafts, trying to articulate a rationale that would dismiss the lawsuit against the *Times* and the other defendants while holding open the possibility that a future public official, confronted with more egregiously bad reporting, might be able to bring and win a libel suit. Through his seven drafts, Brennan settled on the idea of "actual malice" as the relevant standard, meaning that public officials could recover libel damages from news organizations only if the reports about them were not just false but also willfully or recklessly malicious.[75] Stories or advertisements about public officials conducting public business could be false and they could be defamatory, and the defendants could still be protected from lawsuits if those false and defamatory statements were innocently made.

"The constitutional guarantees require, we think, a federal rule that prohibits a public official from recovering damages for a defamatory falsehood relating to his official conduct unless he proves that the statement was made with 'actual malice,'" Brennan wrote, "that is, with knowledge that it was false or with reckless disregard of whether it was false or not."[76] That language set the new standard simply by declaring it, and what the Court did next helped make clear its main objective: to shut down this litigation and others of its type. Rather than send the case back for a new trial in order to determine whether Sullivan could show that the *Times* and the civil rights leaders had in fact acted with "actual malice," Brennan established the new standard and then simply declared that Sullivan could not meet it. "Since respondent may seek a new trial," he wrote, "we deem that considerations of effective judicial administration require us to review the evidence in the present record to determine whether it could constitutionally support a judgment for respondent."[77] The Court was not naïve; it well knew what the outcome of a new trial would be. There would be another judgment for Sullivan, upheld again in Alabama's courts, and more years of delay and squelched dissent. So the Court ended the case while it could, freeing the *Times* to return to reporting and the civil rights leaders to resume their work, the work blessed and encouraged by the United States Supreme Court.

*New York Times v. Sullivan* freed the press to pursue its momentous coverage of the civil rights movement and greatly strengthened national debate in other areas as well. It was, one scholar noted, "an occasion for dancing in the streets."[78] Over time, some cracks in its edifice undermined that early euphoria. By relying on malice as a standard, the ruling allowed plaintiffs latitude to explore the motives of reporters and editors, an intrusion into newsgathering that press organizations would come to lament. It also sanctioned substandard reporting, as it allowed news organizations to make mistakes without legal consequence, a zone of protection that would be expanded in later rulings, that the press would too often exploit, and that even its defenders would have difficulty defending. Edward Bennett Williams represented the *Washington Post*. He worshipped Earl Warren and cherished their friendship. But even Williams worried about *New York Times v. Sullivan*. When a judge complained to him that the opinion gave the press a "license to lie," Williams responded, "That's right."[79]

Those were long-term consequences, none of them salutary. But in the context of early 1964, the ruling achieved all that Warren and Brennan had hoped: it removed the threat to the civil rights movement, and it kept public attention focused on Southern racism. *Sullivan* was greeted with relief and exultation by the press. The point of *New York Times v. Sullivan* was the same as the point of the stall in the sit-in cases—it was to keep civil rights alive, and it succeeded.

Legislative reapportionment would stand as one of Warren's most significant contributions to the Court and the nation. The deft handling of the sit-in cases would help Congress along its bumpy path toward enactment of civil rights legislation that Warren saw as vital to the nation's development. The protection of speech extended in *New York Times v. Sullivan* would expand the role of an assertive American press, for better and for worse. And yet those monuments of 1964 were, for Warren, backdrops to the excruciating work of determining who killed President Kennedy and how.

ON JANUARY 20, Warren and Rankin addressed the staff of the assassination commission for the first time. Summoning the majesty of his office and the weight of his own reputation, Warren explained to the lawyers gathered that day at the office that he had reservations about the job, that he had resisted Johnson's entreaties until he felt he had to agree. Warren warned that the nation needed certainty about Kennedy's death, that rumors were dangerous, and that the truth, only the truth, would satisfy the public's need for closure. Truth, he said, "is our only client."[80]

Warren meant that gravely, and no one worked harder than he did to direct the Commission's work. Over the coming nine months, Warren often would begin his day reading at home before dawn. He arrived at eight A.M. at the offices of the Commission, where he would work until just before ten A.M. He would then walk down the block to the Court, gavel it to order at ten, and preside over its business for the day. At its conclusion, he would then return to the Commission, often working into the evening or even the early hours of the following morning. He was, one staff member recalled later, a "constant presence," his devotion to the work nothing less than "heroic."[81] For nearly a year, Warren supervised a nationally scrutinized investigation into the murder of a president without ever missing a scheduled session of the United States Supreme Court. His health paid the price of his diligence. Early that winter, Warren contracted a bronchial infection. It depleted the chief justice for much of the year, leaving him rheumy, congested, and tired.[82]

Rarely during that entire time was there a break from the pace of the Commission's work. Just two days after Warren met with the staff, Texas officials warned the Commission that they had stumbled upon an explosive rumor—that Oswald had been an undercover FBI agent. In support of that report were tantalizing "facts," including the monthly payments that Oswald was said to have received and the FBI's identifying number, 179, allegedly attached to him. Warren urgently summoned the Commissioners into a special session of the panel that evening to brief them about, as he told them, "something you shouldn't hear from the public before you had an opportunity to think about it."[83] Commissioners then listened as Rankin laid before them the frightening possibility that the assassin of the president might have been an agent of the government.

The commissioners took the matter seriously. As a group, they conceived a plan to investigate it, both by approaching the FBI directly and by checking it through sources independent of the Bureau. They soon discovered that it amounted to less than it seemed. The source, it turned out, was not one with any special access to classified information but rather a reporter for the *Houston Post,* who had passed it along to a Secret Service agent. By February 24, the Commission had interviewed the reporter and checked the rumor against records and sources and had concluded that it was false.[84] To those who believe to this day that the Commission participated in a cover-up, its response to that early rumor is telling. It is true that the Commission had two motives in chasing that report: Commissioners wanted to discover any hidden allegiance between Oswald and the FBI, but they also recognized the implications of such a rumor and they were eager to dispel it. That tension— between the Commission's role in finding the truth and its responsibility for mollifying a frightened public—is what causes some to question whether the Commission would sacrifice truth for peace. In fact, however, that tension proved more hypothetical than real, and in its quest to discover whether Oswald worked for the FBI, the Commission at no time gave any hint that any member was willing to cover up the truth if the rumor proved correct.

That is not to say that Warren or the Commission pursued every lead or disclosed every piece of evidence. Warren made pivotal decisions to circumscribe the inquiry, and he had no qualms about doing so, then or later. Some commissioners and members of the staff wanted to take Jacqueline Kennedy's testimony early and to subject her to questions about the president's wounds and the shots fired. She was, after all, the person sitting closest to Kennedy when he died. Warren resisted. His affection for the First Lady—and his paternalism toward those most closely affected by the assassination—inclined him to a gentler approach. When Jackie Kennedy eventually was questioned, it was only briefly, and it took place at her Georgetown home, with only Warren, Rankin, and Bobby Kennedy present. Similarly, Bobby Kennedy, though the nation's attorney general, would be questioned only in writing, and his evasive responses about his lack of knowledge, particularly with respect to potential motive by Castro, would be accepted without challenge. Each of those concessions had consequences, but far more serious was Warren's decision not to admit autopsy photographs taken of the dead president. Unwilling to allow ghoulish exploitation of those photographs, Warren instead viewed them himself. "[T]hey were horrible," he recalled.[85] Concerned that the pictures might be exploited "for sordid commercial purposes, and perhaps for spite purposes," Warren arranged to keep them out of the official record.[86] Warren's solicitousness was in one sense predictable. He was moved by the suffering of Jackie and Bobby Kennedy, protective of them and the president's children; he thought of Kennedy as nearly a son, after all, and thus as family. That was understandable but naïve. His solicitousness of the Kennedy family deprived the public of a complete record, and offered doubters a vacuum into which to pour their worst suspicions.

The Warren Commission called its first witness, Marina Oswald, on February 3, 1964. Marina Oswald was the third woman widowed by the events of that November weekend, and she too received the benefit of Warren's sympathy. The chief justice welcomed her and her lawyer to the hearing, informed her of her rights, and let her know the Commission was mindful that she had recently had a baby and would want a break to be with her. "If at any time you should feel tired or feel that you need a rest, you may feel free to say so, and we will take care of it," he said.[87] During her testimony, when Marina Oswald testified that she had seen a gun owned by her husband, she said she could not tell whether it was a rifle or a shotgun. "You men. That is your business," she testified. Warren was understanding. "My wife wouldn't know the difference, so it's all right," he assured her.[88]

For four days, Marina Oswald, accompanied by a lawyer, painted a damning portrait of her deceased husband. She identified his rifle, which he had denied owning. (Shown Exhibit 139 and asked to describe it, she replied, "That is the fateful rifle of Lee Oswald."[89]) She described in detail his seething anger, his tendency to violence, his admission to her that he tried to kill General Walker, his alienation from all those around him, and his final, telling act on the morning of the Kennedy assassination, when, for the first time in their marriage, he slipped off his wedding ring and left it behind as he departed for work.[90] Lee Harvey Oswald's widow had little doubt about who had killed President Kennedy or why: "From everything that I know about my husband, and of the events that transpired, I can conclude that he wanted in any way, whether good or bad, to do something that would make him outstanding, that he would be known in history."[91] Warren had sized up witnesses before, and he believed Marina Oswald. "I was convinced," he told Drew Pearson four years later, "she was telling [the] truth."[92]

Marina Oswald's testimony, like that of all but one Commission witness, took place in a closed room. Though the transcripts of all testimony would later be released, Warren and the rest of the Commission believed public hearings would encourage some witnesses to grandstand and would intimidate others. Warren urged that approach from the outset, and it reflected his lifelong belief in a sort of limited open government—in a government whose actions were subject to scrutiny but not at the mercy of the mob. Like so many of his important decisions over the years, this one was informed by his old Progressive instincts, in the idea that enlightened leadership was preferable to unfettered majority rule. In this case, as with Warren's decision to withhold the autopsy photographs, that instinct would expose the Commission to later criticism, but he showed no hesitation in pushing the panel toward the limited openness that it practiced.

Although the hearings themselves were closed, the Commission was subjected to intense daily coverage. In the jostling press area outside the hearing room, Warren made a mistake early on that would cast a pall over the Commission. Marina Oswald was appearing for her first day on the stand when the press corps caught Warren and asked him if or when the Commission would release all the testimony it gathered. "Yes, there will come a time," he answered. "But it might not be in your lifetime. I am not referring to anything especially, but there may be some things that would involve security. This would be preserved but not made public."

Warren had barely uttered the words before realizing he had made a mistake. He tried the next day to clear up what the *New York Times* charitably said had "appeared to be a misunderstanding."[93] Addressing the same reporters, Warren emphasized that the Commission so far had heard nothing that would be withheld—it was, after all, hearing from only its first witness—and that he expected the public would receive a full report. Even Warren realized that was too late. The idea of the Warren Commission as an agent of cover-up had found purchase.

Over the next eight months, the Commission heard from 552 witnesses, 94 of whom testified before the Commission itself, and 395 of whom were questioned by staff members. Sixty-one people supplied affidavits.[94] Two gave statements. Because the Commission determined early on to avoid extensive pretestimonial interviews, the accounts that appeared in its official record—the report itself and twenty-six accompanying volumes of transcripts and exhibits—were subject to all the vagaries of lapsed memory and differing vantage points that are common to any criminal investigation of a violent crime, exacerbated in this case by the enormity of that crime. Throughout the Commission's long testimonial sessions, Warren was a patient and gentle chairman.

On some occasions he was even more than that, displaying a depth of human compassion that astounded his staff and colleagues. One such moment occurred during the testimony of a young man, Arthur Rowland, who had been standing outside the Texas Book Depository Building waiting for the president's motorcade to pass by that day in Dallas. As Rowland waited with his wife—they were just eighteen, and had recently married—he glanced upward and saw a man in a window holding a rifle. A police officer was just a few feet away, but it did not occur to Rowland to point out the man to the officer. By the time Rowland appeared before the Warren Commission, he had replayed that scene time and again in his mind, asking himself if he might have changed history had he merely called out to the officer. Rowland brought that self-inflicted agony with him to the Commission, and when Senator Cooper asked him about it, he could contain himself no more. "This is a recurring dream of mine, sir, all the time, what if I had told someone about it," Rowland said. "I knew about it enough in advance and perhaps it could have been prevented. I mean this is something which shakes me up at times."[95]

With that, Rowland collapsed into tears. Warren then called for a brief recess, and took the boy under his arm, speaking quietly as Rowland sobbed, the chief's voice low and comforting. The Chief Justice of the United States was a father and a grandfather, and he understood something about young people and anguish. He told Rowland that he needed to stop blaming himself, that no bystander was responsible for President Kennedy's death, that no person deserved to carry such guilt. Gradually, Rowland calmed down. It was, Commission lawyer David Belin recalled, "an unforgettable experience" to see Warren comfort the troubled young man.[96] When Rowland was quiet enough to speak again, Warren asked whether he had been able to see the sights in Washington during his visit. "I've tried," Rowland answered, "but walked my feet off." When Rowland completed his testimony a few minutes later, Warren's car was waiting for him.[97]

Through the spring, other members of the President's Commission began to waver in their attention to its proceedings. Ford was a fairly regular participant, and McCloy attended most of the significant hearings, but Russell became less and

less engaged, and Boggs was often called away by congressional duties. Only Warren remained fully dedicated, attending almost every one of its scores of sessions,
though often ducking in and out. Tough on himself, he was equally demanding of
his staff. His temper could flare, and he was unyielding in his insistence that the
staff work as hard as necessary in order to finish by his proposed deadline of June 1.
Few excuses were tolerated. When Richard Mosk slipped off to Massachusetts one
Saturday to get married, he postponed his honeymoon and was back at work on
Monday morning. His mother, an old friend of Warren's, made sure Warren knew
of her son's dedication. Warren's response, "Why wasn't he here Sunday?" had a bit
of edge.[98]

But Warren was respected, even revered, by Mosk and the rest of his staff. He
gave the lawyers wide latitude to develop their areas as they saw fit, and he trusted
their judgments. There were times when they disagreed with his decisions—Belin
and Specter, among others, were furious at Warren's decision not to include autopsy photos of President Kennedy; they and others also objected to Warren's
decisions to question Jackie Kennedy privately and to accept a statement from
President Johnson rather than present questions to him.[99] Those disagreements,
however, were overshadowed by a wider admiration for the chief justice, and that
admiration was sealed for many by the way Warren single-handedly fended off an
attack on one of the staff's most admired members, Norman Redlich.

Redlich was a young law professor at NYU when Rankin recruited him for the
Commission. In the months since, Redlich had established himself as the Commission's leading intellectual and one of its hardest workers. He reported directly to
Rankin and assisted lawyers in each of the Commission's working groups. By May,
no lawyer on the staff, with the possible exception of Rankin, understood the work
of the Commission or its investigative findings more clearly than Redlich.[100]

Because the Commission had set to work so quickly, its staff members had proceeded without full background checks by the FBI. Notwithstanding that, most were
reading highly sensitive, sometimes classified material even as the FBI probed them
for loyalty. In May, the FBI's field reports were completed and forwarded to the
Commission. Included in those reports were entries on the leftist affiliations of two
staff members, Joe Ball and Redlich. Ball's affiliation was glancing—he joined with
other members of the California Bar Association in approving a resolution denouncing the House Un-American Activities Committee. The Commission decided
with little discussion that it did not merit concern. Redlich was another matter. A
passionate activist for many liberal causes, Redlich drew particular notice for his
work with a group known as the Emergency Civil Liberties Council. It too had actively opposed HUAC, and HUAC had treated it as an enemy, listing it as a Communist front organization.

The disclosure of Redlich's affiliations, which he had made no attempt to hide, came at a particularly embarrassing juncture for the Commission. It already had placed him in a position of influence and allowed him to read classified government material. To find now that he was a security risk would thus raise questions about the Commission's judgment. Moreover, the FBI material about Redlich found fertile minds among some members of Congress, including Ford. The congressman knew that to challenge Redlich on the basis of the FBI's assessment of his liberal associations was to invite a confrontation with Warren, so Ford prepared meticulously for their showdown.[101] It came on May 19, 1964.

As was his usual practice, Warren opened the session by asking Rankin to summarize the issue. He then heard from commissioners. Russell, though apologizing for having missed so much Commission business, nevertheless said he worried about taint to the panel if Redlich stayed. Boggs was less strident, but he too voiced reservations. Then Ford spoke at greater length. After praising Redlich's ability and intellect—"I think he is a brilliant man," Ford said—and after stressing that he did not question Redlich's loyalty, Ford nonetheless concluded that Redlich's activities were such that Ford would have objected to his hiring had he known of them. "That being the case," he added, ". . . it is hard for me to say now that we should continue the employment of any [such] person."[102] Cooper was noncommittal but clearly concerned about the Commission's reputation if it kept Redlich; Dulles argued for letting him go.

Warren heard all of that in silence, but when it came time for him to speak, he reversed the clear momentum of the Commission. "As far as I can see, the only real criticism against him is that he has been against the Un-American Activities Committee of the Congress," Warren said, simplifying the case somewhat for effect. "And there are some very, very fine Americans who are so recognized in all circles who have exactly the same views." That was arch. Warren's fellow commissioners did not need to be reminded that among those "very, very fine Americans" was Warren himself. Warren then added a sly endorsement of Ford's view of Redlich, concurring with the congressman that Redlich was indeed able and dedicated.[103]

To those points, Warren added a dramatic human observation and a deft parliamentary maneuver. Lest his fellow Commissioners fool themselves about the consequences of letting Redlich go, Warren reminded them that they would be casting off a member of their staff in the face of allegations that he was disloyal to his country. They would subject him and his family to harassment. His wife would suffer, as would his children. And that suffering would go on and on. To be branded disloyal, Warren reminded all of them, "is a hurt that can never be remedied as long as a man lives." That sobering observation then led Warren to his conclusion: If the Commission was inclined to question Redlich's loyalty, Warren insisted that the professor be granted a hearing where he could present his own evidence and challenge those who questioned him. Such a hearing in the midst of the Commission's work would be a time-consuming spectacle, as Warren well knew. None of the commissioners was prepared for such a course, but none dared challenge Warren's authority to demand it. Suddenly, the issue was turned—the human costs of casual dismissal were now before the Commission and the practical matter of how to carry it out was now vastly more daunting.

McCloy was the first to speak when Warren concluded, and he joined Warren in arguing that Redlich should be allowed to stay. Ford continued to insist on an up-or-down vote on Redlich's continued employment, but Warren again maneuvered. The chief justice insisted that the Commission first vote on whether to grant all its staff members, including Redlich, their security clearances. Since Ford already had acknowledged that he had no question about Redlich's loyalty, he could only vote in favor. The motion passed unanimously. And then, once Redlich's loyalty was off the table, the idea of firing him became more complicated. Fire him for what, precisely? And for those who wanted him gone as a way of appeasing the Commission's critics, what of Warren's threat to expand the matter with a full hearing? Still hoping for a vote that would allow him to go on the record against Redlich, Ford moved to force the issue. "It seems to me that from the position I take, that there ought to be some action by the Commission affirming his continued employment—if that is what the majority of the Commission wants to do," Ford insisted. But his allies were dropping off. Dulles now saw the futility of that approach and began to craft an alternative. Warren had the momentum, and he allowed himself the luxury of losing his temper with Ford. "Jerry, there are no charges against this man," Warren said, dropping his customary formality and addressing Ford by his first name. "There are no charges against him."

Other members of the Commission then jumped in, urging Ford to withdraw his motion, which no member would agree to second. All members of the Commission staff, including Redlich, were granted their clearances and allowed to continue working. Chastened, Ford retreated, but he did not soon forget Warren's handling of the matter. "He was given that job to run the show," Ford remarked forty years later. "And he did."[104]

As with so much of the Commission's work that spring, the Redlich debate sapped Warren's strength. When the Commission adjourned that evening, Warren headed home, where his old friend Bart Cavanaugh waited for him.[105] Nina Warren had asked Cavanaugh to spend some time with Warren, to help revive him from the wearing months of early 1964. Arriving in Washington, Cavanaugh was distressed to find Warren in shaky health. His weight, which normally hovered around two hundred pounds, was way down. He was watching his diet carefully, and he was accompanied everywhere by Secret Service. "It was getting to him," Cavanaugh realized.[106]

So that Friday, at Nina's urging and without tipping off the Secret Service, Cavanaugh hijacked his friend, piled him into a car, and headed for New York. They arrived in time to catch the late innings of a baseball game, then went for dinner and checked into a hotel. They stayed through the weekend, watching games during the day, relaxing at night. Warren liked Toots Shor's and New York's other grandly male habitations; he liked a scotch at the bar, a booth with friends, and a steak. He and Cavanaugh enjoyed the city for two days and nights, then headed home, Cavanaugh at the wheel. Warren was back at work on Monday morning.

On June 7, Warren and Ford led a small Commission delegation to Dallas. Warren was in good spirits that morning. He picked up Arlen Specter in his limousine on the way to Andrews Air Force Base, and he chatted brightly with Ford during the flight.[107] In Dallas, it fell to Specter to explain to Warren the theory that he had developed regarding the shots to Kennedy and Connally—namely, that a single bullet had struck Kennedy from behind, had passed straight through his neck without striking any bones, and had exited his throat, nicking his tie as it tore through his body and clothing. That bullet, continuing in a direct line but wobbling slightly, then struck Connally in the back, just to the left of his right armpit and, after hitting a rib, exited below his right nipple. It then passed through the back side of Connally's left wrist and, at last spent, hit him in the thigh. That shot—later to be derided as the "magic bullet"—was followed by another, which struck the back of Kennedy's head and exploded out of the right front of his skull, the force of that aerial explosion snapping his head backward. Warren initially was skeptical of the single-bullet theory, as were many upon first hearing it.

And yet that theory was consistent with all the medical evidence in the case—consistent with the wounds to Kennedy's neck and throat and Connally's injuries. It was consistent with the positions of Connally and Kennedy and with the so-called Zapruder film, which the Commission reviewed and which captured the moments of the assassination. It was supported by the majority of witnesses who heard the shots and recalled that there were three, one of which apparently had missed. It explained Kennedy's motions—his hands pulled toward his throat after first being shot in an involuntary muscle reflex; his head slumped forward, but his back was propped up by the brace he was wearing that afternoon; after the next shot, the right side of his skull blew up and jerked backward. And it answered another vital question: If Connally and Kennedy were struck by separate bullets, then where was the additional bullet, the bullet that struck Kennedy in the back but that was subsequently unaccounted for?[108] It should have lodged in the car, and yet none was there. Specter's theory, meanwhile, was supported by the bullet found on Connally's stretcher, only slightly damaged. When fired, that bullet had weighed approximately 160 to 161 grains; when recovered, it weighed 158.6 grains, with the balance being explained by the fragments recovered from Connally's wrist and thigh. Specter laid out the evidence for Warren in about eight minutes, talking with the chief justice as the two stood in the window of the Book Depository where Lee Harvey Oswald had been spotted by witnesses moments before the shooting. Warren stared down at Dealey Plaza. He said nothing. He quietly turned and walked away.[109]

The second act of that trip—the only trip that Warren would make to Dallas in connection with the assassination probe—was to interview Jack Ruby. Warren had avoided Dallas during the time that Jack Ruby was on trial, but by June, Ruby had been tried for the murder of Oswald and had been sentenced to death. Late that morning, after taking in the scene of Kennedy's murder and visiting that of Officer Tippit's death, Warren and his entourage arranged to meet Ruby in the kitchen of the local sheriff.[110] Specter retired downstairs to watch the Giants-Phillies game on television, but after about an hour, he was summoned back into the interrogation. Ruby, who was Jewish and who, in his consuming paranoia, was convinced that Jewish children were being murdered in the jail, had asked for a Jew to be present during his questioning. Specter filled that role.[111]

With Texas officials, Ford, and Specter all on hand, Warren began the session, but even before Ruby was sworn in, he asked that he be allowed to take a lie detector test. Warren was not a believer in lie detectors and tried gently to dissuade Ruby, but added, "[I]f you want such a test, I will arrange for it."[112] From there, the interrogation spun away, with Ruby holding forth about subjects at best tangentially related to the assassination. He went on at great length, for instance, to describe his decision to close his burlesque club after the Kennedy assassination, and he frequently interrupted himself to make sure Warren was tracking him. To the extent it was possible, Warren seemed to. He urged Ruby along, hearing him out, eliciting from him a wobbly tale of the anguish that Ruby felt over the assassination and of his two-day descent into violence. That Sunday morning, after Ruby read a public letter to Caroline Kennedy in the *Dallas Times Herald,* his emotional state fractured: "Suddenly I felt, which was so stupid, that I wanted to show my love for our faith, being of the Jewish faith, and I never used the term and I don't want to get into that—suddenly the feeling, the emotional feeling came within me that someone owed this debt to our beloved President to save her [Jackie Kennedy] the ordeal of coming back [to Dallas, presumably to testify at Oswald's trial]."[113]

Ruby's testimony was hard to follow, but one fact alone seemed to eliminate the idea that his Sunday morning murder of Oswald was part of a larger plot. That morning, Ruby came to downtown Dallas to wire $25 to one of the dancers who worked at his club. A copy of the receipt for that wire provided solid evidence that Ruby was in the Western Union office at 11:16 A.M. Oswald had been scheduled to be moved by that time, so Ruby's movements that morning would have precluded him from being at the police station at the right moment had Dallas police carried out the transfer as scheduled.[114] Instead, Oswald's departure was delayed, and when Ruby emerged from the Western Union office, his gun in his pocket as usual and his business with his dancer complete, he walked down the jail driveway and into the loading area just as Oswald emerged from the building. There, with a breathless nation watching, he pulled his gun, shoved it toward Oswald's stomach, and fired—at 11:21 A.M. on Sunday, November 24.[115] Coincidences may not be satisfying to the conspiratorially minded, but there was no evidence that Ruby's arrival at the driveway at just that moment was anything but a coincidence.

A weary Warren returned that night to Washington. He had hoped that the Commission would be done by now—June 1 was his target date, apparently picked to have it out of the way in time for that year's political conventions—and he hoped still that it might conclude its business within the month. He was to be bitterly disappointed. As the deadline approached, Warren met with Redlich and another commission lawyer, and Warren exploded when told that the staff was not ready to finalize its report. So furious was Warren that one staff member worried he might have a heart attack.[116] Then resignation set in. "Well, gentlemen, we are here for the duration," Warren remarked quietly.[117]

Warren did squeeze in a vacation that summer, but he cut it uncharacteristically short. He had lunch with Rankin on July 6 and departed that night for Oslo. He was gone for three weeks of fishing. His first meeting after his return was with Rankin again.[118] Normally, Warren would have been in Europe or California for the notorious Washington August, when few government officials who could leave town chose to stay. This time, he supervised the Commission staff as it prepared its findings and submitted them to the full panel. Warren also enlisted his Court clerks for their help, and they proofread copies of the report as sections were completed. Warren had learned the value of a unanimous opinion in *Brown*, and as the Commission neared the end of its work, he lobbied hard for a report that would speak for all its members.

It had not been easy in *Brown*, and it was not easy now. Russell in particular remained unconvinced that Oswald had acted without help, and dickered regarding the language by which the Commission dismissed all conspiracy theories. And Ford hesitated as well. "Both refused to sign," Warren told Drew Pearson afterward. Ford "wanted to go off on [a] tangent showing [a] communist plot," Pearson's notes of their 1967 conversation say.[119] Convinced that unanimity was more important than the precise language used to describe the Commission's conclusions, Warren agreed to accommodate them, especially Russell.[120] Rather than state that conclusion without equivocation, the Commission reported only that it had "found no evidence that either Lee Harvey Oswald or Jack Ruby was part of any conspiracy, domestic or foreign, to assassinate President Kennedy."[121] That left open, at least a bit, the possibility that new evidence could change the report's central conclusion. The Commission similarly debated the single-bullet theory, but eventually agreed that it was the only satisfactory explanation for the injuries to Kennedy and Connally.

Russell professed not to be entirely satisfied. "I tried my best to get in a dissent," he told Johnson a few days before the report was delivered, "but they'd come 'round and trade me out of it."[122] Even then, with the Commission's work complete, Russell demonstrated how badly he had misunderstood the significance of the single-bullet theory, insisting that it "don't make much difference" whether a single bullet struck Connally and Kennedy.

The commissioners delivered their report to Lyndon Johnson on September 24, 1964. Early reactions were widely positive—at the *New York Times,* James Reston wrote that the Warren Commission had "fulfilled its primary assignment," while also predicting that the assassination would long continue to occupy American imaginations.[123] Polls later that year showed that the American people overwhelmingly accepted the Commission's conclusions.[124]

At the FBI, reaction was far less restrained. Hoover fumed at the Commission's refusal to adopt the Bureau's reconstruction of the shooting—Hoover never would accept the single-bullet theory—and at its mild rebuke of the FBI's work. With the release of the Commission report, the long and complicated relationship between Warren and Hoover at last came to an end. The two men would never again regard each other with anything more than coldness. Three months after the Warren Commission report was published, Hoover dropped Warren from the Bureau's Special Correspondents' List, a group of trusted Bureau allies entitled to receive regular updates from the FBI. The two then settled into a long standoff, broken only by Warren's announced retirement in 1968. Then Hoover sent along a note and addressed it in their old style, to "Dear Earl." A staff notation on Hoover's letter made clear, however, that the address was an act of nostalgia, not warmth. Until the time Warren was "deleted" from the correspondents' list in 1964, the notation read, "He was . . . known to the Director on a first-name basis."[125]

Public regard for the Commission was short-lived. Some of the early works critiquing the Warren Commission were genuine inquiries intended to raise serious questions about whether the report had solved the murder. Others were unscrupulous, and none more so than the work of Mark Lane, who was at odds with the Warren Commission even before it finished. On Tuesday, February 11, 1963, Marguerite Oswald, the eccentric mother of the assassin, returned for her second day on the witness stand, accompanied by Lane as well as another lawyer, John Doyle. Doyle offered to withdraw if Lane was to represent Mrs. Oswald, and in the confusion over who was her counsel, Warren asked her directly whether Lane represented her. "No sir, he does not," Mrs. Oswald replied. When Lane protested,

Warren gave him little quarter. "Mr. Lane, now really," the exasperated Warren noted, "either you are here as the attorney for Mrs. Oswald or you are not entitled to be in this room—one of the two."[126] Lane was shown the door.

After Lane wrote articles and held a number of press conferences challenging the Commission and suggesting that he had evidence that would rebut its findings, the panel invited him to testify on his own. Lane appeared twice as a witness, both times engaging the Commission in an infuriating game of cat and mouse. At his first appearance, on March 4, Lane testified that one witness who picked Oswald out of a police lineup as the man she saw shoot Officer Tippit gave Lane a description of the assailant that was inconsistent with Oswald; according to Lane, she had told him the murderer was "short, a little on the heavy side, and his hair was somewhat bushy."[127] The witness was confronted with Lane's statements when she appeared before the Warren Commission, and she denied having met with him or having described Oswald as Lane testified that she had. To back up his version, Lane insisted he had a tape recording of the conversation. In July, the Commission asked him to appear again, paying his way to return from a speaking tour in Europe so that he might supply the tape and clear up the confusion regarding that testimony. Lane appeared but refused to supply the tape.[128]

Lane similarly alleged that an informant had told him of a potentially important sighting—of Oswald and Ruby together before the assassination. If true, that would contradict Ruby's insistence that they had never met and would bolster the contention that Ruby and Oswald were involved in a conspiracy. Lane was asked to supply the name of that informant during his first appearance before the Commission. He promised to check with the source and see if he could reveal the name; when he returned in July, he was asked again, and this time refused.[129]

The work by Lane, first in *Rush to Judgment* and later in increasingly attenuated attacks on the Commission, was highly selective in its use and analysis of evidence. Commenting on the witness who saw Oswald fire the shots, Howard Brennan, Lane chose to emphasize Brennan's inconsistency regarding whether Oswald was sitting or standing at the time, rather than to acknowledge that Brennan had testified that he had no doubt about whom he had seen.[130] Lane also clipped and excerpted testimony in order to bring out details favorable to his argument while ignoring those that hurt it. Writing of the three men at the Depository window, for instance, Lane questioned why they had not gone upstairs when they heard the shots. "Representative Gerald R. Ford asked [one of the men, Bonnie Ray] Williams, 'Why didn't you go to the sixth floor?'" Lane wrote. "Williams replied, 'We just never did think about it.'"[131]

The quote is accurate, up to a point. But Williams's next sentence was "Maybe it was because we were frightened."[132] Lane omitted that sentence. The shortened version seemed to suggest that the men had no good explanation for why they did not apprehend the assassin themselves; the full quote made clear that they had a perfectly understandable reason for avoiding a killer. Lane chose the short version because it supported his account.

There are countless such examples of distortion and selectivity in Lane's work. Warren would never forgive Lane for his dodging during the hearings or his exploitation of the assassination. The chief justice complained about Lane to friends and colleagues,[133] and in his memoirs, treated him with disgust. Refusing even to name him, Warren said he believed most Commission critics were unconvinced by the Commission's conclusions because Oswald had not received a public trial. Warren sympathized with those critics, but he had no patience for "those who wrote or lectured for money while deliberately using false hypotheses."[134]

Lane's writing preyed on the public thirst for a larger explanation of Kennedy's death, on those whose great and admired leader was above being murdered by such an insignificant assassin. Others joined him, offering a mélange of theories stubbornly at odds with one another—Communists and anti-Communists, CIA critics and defenders, supporters and opponents of American foreign policy all claiming Oswald was in league with their enemies to kill the president. Addressing as they did that psychological need, the conspiracy buffs had claimed the field from the Warren Commission by the end of the 1960s and they held it for more than thirty years.

That sustained attack on the Commission was greeted with silence from Warren, who insisted that the report stand on its own and who urged that the Commission members not dignify the critics with a reply. Warren held his tongue even when Jim Garrison, a showboating New Orleans district attorney, launched a highly public investigation of what he claimed was a conspiracy to kill Kennedy. Garrison charged a New Orleans businessman, Clay Shaw, in connection with the assassination. There was, Garrison claimed, "an infinitely larger number [of people involved in the conspiracy] than you would dream,"[135] among them Texas oilmen, Cubans, the FBI, and the CIA. Before he was through, Garrison would suborn perjury, override the warnings of his top deputies, and intimidate witnesses; he would accuse Bobby Kennedy of impeding his investigation, attempt to bribe at least one witness, and file patently false criminal charges against his critics.

Once, when questioned about the investigation during a trip to Tokyo, Warren ventured cautious skepticism about Garrison's probe. Garrison leapt to the chance to tangle with Warren and responded in Garrison fashion: "The heavy artillery whistling in from Tokyo means that everything is in place, all the infantry lined up and the lull is over." Garrison said his staff had reviewed the Warren report and concluded that it was a "gigantic fraud, quite possibly the largest in terms of effort and scope and effect ever perpetuated on the planet." As if that weren't enough, Garrison added that the "fairy tale" concealed the true nature of Kennedy's assassination "for political reasons."[136] The FBI monitored Garrison's comments and passed them along to Warren, but Warren refused to engage in a running debate with a self-promoting prosecutor. The chief justice, according to the FBI, "wanted to skirt this issue very carefully due to the possibility the case might some day come before the Supreme Court."[137] Garrison never again received the satisfaction of a comment from Warren. It took two years for Garrison to build his public case against Shaw, and the jury took less than an hour to acquit him. Shaw was bankrupted by the prosecution. He never recovered his fortune or health.[138]

Garrison's prosecution was a shameless affront to the truth, and it had profound consequences, not just in the shortened and maligned life of Clay Shaw but also in the development of conspiracy theory. Before it, those inclined to find that Oswald had been helped generally regarded the government inquiry, including the Warren Commission, as incompetent or duped. After it, conspiracy believers would tend to cast the Warren Commission as a participant in the assassination or its cover-up. That was due to Garrison, whose case amounted to nothing and whose pursuit of it damaged not just humans but history as well.

Warren encouraged the other members of the Commission not to engage their critics, and though Ford published a book about the investigation—to Warren's irritation—the Commission and its staff largely followed Warren's lead.[139] Without the Commission there to defend itself, the conspiracy theories continued to prosper. By the mid-1970s, Congress was drawn back into the inquiry, convening a House Select Committee on Assassinations. Established in 1976 and reconstituted the following year, the Select Committee was charged with investigating whether government agencies had provided full disclosure to the Warren Commission; in its final report, the Committee supported the Warren Commission in virtually all its essential findings, but the Select Committee highlighted areas where the FBI and CIA had failed the Commission, and the Committee introduced one new, important allegation that ultimately proved untrue.

Warren Commission members had been aware of one act of FBI cover-up. A page from Oswald's address book contained the name and number of James Hosty, an FBI agent, but it was not included when the book was forwarded to the Commission in December 1963. Commission staff members discovered the omission and pressed the FBI on it. They were told the FBI had removed the page because the bureau did not consider that page evidence; reprimanded by the Commission staff, the FBI then provided the page.[140] Although Redlich and others were annoyed by the clumsy attempt to shield Hosty from embarrassment, it was a blunder without larger implications. It was, the Select Committee concluded, "regrettable," but "trivial in the context of the entire investigation."[141] The Warren Commission knew all that, but what it did not know was that Hosty had also received a note from Oswald about two weeks prior to the assassination. After Oswald's murder by

Ruby, Hosty destroyed the note at the direction of his supervisor.[142] The note reportedly warned Hosty to stay away from interviewing Marina Oswald, but when Oswald was murdered, Hosty's supervisor suggested tossing the note out, since there could be no trial. Its destruction was a bracing reminder of how far the FBI would go to protect itself, even at the expense of the whole truth.

The CIA's withholding was of a different sort. After the calamitous failure at the Bay of Pigs, John Kennedy resolved to dispose of Castro's regime. Jack put his most trusted adviser, Bobby Kennedy, in charge of supervising the secret effort from his post as attorney general. In that capacity, Bobby Kennedy applied his singular talents to developing plans to overthrow Castro, plans that were to be carried out by the CIA and that included assassination as an option. Years later, Lyndon Johnson, then retired, would refer to the CIA's willingness to entertain assassination as a tool as "Murder Inc.," and it provided Castro with a motive to do the same to his American counterpart. Those plans were never revealed to the Warren Commission—Kennedy declined Warren's invitation to appear before the Commission and ducked Warren's question to him about whether there was additional material that might shed light on the investigation (Kennedy's reply indicated only that no such material was within the Department of Justice, which Warren had not asked, while not volunteering that such information might be elsewhere). Allen Dulles had been director of Central Intelligence; he never informed the Commission. Ford and Russell had knowledge of CIA covert activities, though perhaps not assassination plans; they, too, remained silent.[143] When information regarding the CIA's role in plotting to kill Castro first came to Rankin's attention in 1975, he was outraged. "We were assured that they would cooperate fully and give us everything that would have any bearing on the investigation," Rankin told Committee investigators. "Now apparently they didn't."[144]

That said, the hostility between the Kennedys and Castro was no secret—the Bay of Pigs was an internationally public act. As a result, while the CIA was not as forthcoming as the Commission staff would have liked, its withholding did not deprive the Commission of any meaningful insight into possible motive by Castro. Anyone inclined to believe that Castro might have been behind the assassination knew from the newspapers that he might want Kennedy dead. The CIA's reticence thus must be considered in the context of its Cold War mandate. It divulged what it believed to be germane, and it protected its secrets beyond that. Secrecy may not be attractive. In the mindset of the Cold War, however, it was expected.

The deceptions by the FBI, by contrast, were of real consequence. And since the Warren Commission had relied in large measure on the work of that agency, much of the remaining faith in the Warren Commission came tumbling down with those revelations. That process was accelerated by another finding of the Select Committee, albeit a hotly contested one even within the panel itself—namely, that acoustical evidence suggested that there was a fourth shot fired in Dealey Plaza that afternoon. Since Oswald only fired three times (a finding the Select Committee endorsed), that meant a second gunman and thus a de facto conspiracy. At the same time, the Select Committee abandoned the long-held notion in conspiracy circles that Kennedy had been hit by a bullet fired from the grassy knoll. The committee agreed with the Warren Commission that three shots had come from the Book Depository, fired by Oswald, that one missed, one struck Kennedy through the throat and then hit Connally, and one hit Kennedy in the head, killing him. The fourth shot, according to the committee, missed altogether. In the years since, the acoustical evidence for that shot has been repudiated, in part by enhancements to the Zapruder film that strengthen the single-bullet theory and also by subsequent scientific studies of the acoustical evidence itself.[145] The Warren Commission findings in that area have only grown stronger.

Lost in much of the response to the Select Committee was the fact that it supported the Warren Commission in nearly every major conclusion. It agreed that Oswald was the gunman, that he fired three shots from the Book Depository, missing once, striking Kennedy and Connally with one bullet, and killing Kennedy with his final shot. It concluded that Oswald also was the murderer of Officer Tippit. The only evidence of conspiracy was that of a fourth shot, a miss, and that evidence would eventually be discredited. Nevertheless, the die was cast for a new generation of conspiracy theorists, as the committee provided government support for the notion of government deception.

The determination to find conspiracy behind Kennedy's assassination reached its cultural zenith in 1991 with the release of Oliver Stone's *JFK*. The movie was a technologically adventurous web of distortions and dramatizations woven together in visually arresting fashion. Stone spliced actual footage of Kennedy and the assassination with dramatic renderings, moving back and forth between them in such a way as to dramatize and deliberately deceive. Along the way, Stone managed to ridicule the scientific evidence supporting the single-bullet theory and insist that Kennedy was shot from the front, notwithstanding proof to the contrary. His principal premise was that the CIA, with the help of Lyndon Johnson, killed Kennedy in order to prevent Kennedy from withdrawing American forces from Vietnam. For Stone, the troubles with that theory might have included the facts that Kennedy was an ardent Cold Warrior, with a proven disinclination to shrink from conflict with Communism, and more important, that not one scintilla of evidence has ever pointed to Johnson as a conspirator. Neither fact was enough to deter the moviemaker. Meanwhile, Jim Garrison, whose shameless prosecution of Clay Shaw had been brought in disregard of Garrison's duties as a prosecutor, was elevated into a hero. Garrison lived to see this resurrection of his reputation, by then in tatters even within the community of conspiracy theorists. Conscienceless to the end, he appeared in a cameo in the film—in the role of Earl Warren. *JFK* was the venal work of a self-aggrandizing charlatan, but for those too young or too busy to compare it with the actual record, it substituted for history.

The Stone movie was, in fact, useless as history but helpful in one regard. It provoked Congress to order a further release of theretofore sealed Warren Commission records. With their release came further bolstering for the Commission. Ardent conspiracy theorists refused to be disabused, but their work took on an increasingly frantic or incoherent tone, exemplified by the 1993 publication of *Deep Politics and the Death of JFK*. In it, author Peter Dale Scott offered the novel notion that the Kennedy assassination was best understood by focusing not on the murder itself but rather on the "structural defects in governance and society that allowed this huge crime to be so badly investigated. . . . In simpler words, how could American institutions harbor and protect such evil?"[146] In clearer words, Scott assumed the existence of a conspiracy, then asked why no one found it, then assumed, from the failure to find it, a broader conspiracy.

The new century brought a new entry into the conspiracy field, with the 2005 publication of *Breach of Trust*, by Gerald D. McKnight. McKnight's work avoids many of the hyperbolic pitfalls of Lane, Stone, and Scott, none of whom is cited in McKnight's work or even appears in his bibliography. McKnight's book builds a case for investigative failings. It is less convincing when it attempts to pin blame on the Commission, however, and it is burdened by small factual errors and more serious lapses of logic. Among the former, House Speaker John McCormack is presented as "McCormick," and the delegation that visited Warren to ask him to chair the Commission is said to have been headed by Robert Kennedy, when it actually consisted of Nicholas Katzenbach and Archibald Cox. On page 120 of McKnight's book, the weight of a bullet grain is said to equal the weight of a postage stamp; on page 182 he writes that a postage stamp weighs two grains; by page 222, the same stamp weighs 2.5 grains. Those are trivial errors, but when others err, McKnight sees conspiracy. His own book is a reminder that mistakes often are just mistakes.[147]

In McKnight's work, as in so much of that produced by conspiracy theorists, the Commission and those involved in the investigation can do no right: McKnight sees the Commission as beholden to the FBI, but gives it no credit for the single-bullet theory, which defied the FBI analysis and angered Hoover, nor does he acknowledge that one result of the Commission's work was that it severed a thirty-year relationship between Warren and Hoover—hardly consistent with the idea that the Commission deferred to the FBI. Beyond that, McKnight portrays the Commission as a single-headed representative of the American political elite but brushes away its many internal disagreements and antagonisms; he makes much of Russell's skepticism of the single-bullet theory but pays little note that Russell's woeful attendance record meant that he missed much of the evidence that supported it. Throughout, Mc-Knight attributes to individuals the knowledge and motives of their organizations—CIA agents in Mexico are assumed to know all that Washington knows; the FBI's agents, with the exception of Hosty, are portrayed as in lockstep compliance with Hoover. In real life, the FBI, like any bureaucracy, has its miscreants along with its organizational loyalists, but because acknowledging such complexity would threaten the conclusions of conspiracy theorists, many, McKnight included, simply overlook those complexities. McKnight's work is a far cry from that of its disreputable predecessors, and he deserves credit for acknowledging that he has produced no "smoking gun," but in the end he proves only that many people may have wanted Kennedy dead and that the investigation of that crime was not perfect.

To those inclined to think more clearly, the Commission's initial findings grew more solid over time. Today those findings are beyond reasonable doubt. Lee Harvey Oswald, a lifelong misfit desperate to secure a place for himself in history and preoccupied by the Kennedy administration's challenges to Cuba, fired three shots from the Texas Book Depository. One missed, one hit Kennedy and Connally, one exploded the president's skull. The weapon he used was a mail-order Italian military rifle with a four-power scope, purchased using a money order in the amount of $21.45 and delivered to a post office box held under the name A. Hidell, an alias that Oswald used. Oswald's palm print was found on the rifle; his fingerprints were on the boxes in the Depository window from which the shots were fired. After shooting Kennedy and Connally, Oswald left the Book Depository, boarded a bus, then got off when it became stuck in traffic, taking a cab from there to the area near his boardinghouse. He changed clothes and picked up a handgun—ordered to the same post office box—then took off on foot, only to be stopped by Officer Tippit. Eyewitnesses watched Oswald shoot Tippit to death. Oswald took off at a fast walk, breaking into a jog. Police responded to the scene, and Oswald ducked inside a store to avoid them. The manager spotted his suspicious behavior and then watched him enter the Texas Theatre without paying. He informed the ticket taker and they called the police. When the police arrived to search the theater, Oswald pulled the gun on them. They wrestled it from him and arrested him for carrying a concealed weapon. At the station, they discovered that their suspect in the Tippit killing bore the same name as that of a Book Depository employee unaccounted for after the shooting. When he was questioned by police and others on the night of November 22 and the day and night of November 23, Oswald lied repeatedly as the evidence against him mounted.

The rifle recovered in the Book Depository was owned by Lee Harvey Oswald, and it fired the bullets that killed President Kennedy. The gun in Oswald's hand when he was arrested was his, and it fired the bullets that killed Officer Tippit; handgun shells were still in Oswald's pocket when he was arrested. Five witnesses picked Oswald out of a police lineup on the evening of November 22 as the man they saw shoot Tippit; a sixth identified him the following day.

None of those facts is seriously disputed today. Together, they amount to proof beyond any reasonable doubt on the question of who killed President Kennedy and Officer Tippit.

They are only strengthened by the questions that those who seek to refute them cannot convincingly answer. If Oswald did not kill Kennedy, why did he kill Tippit? If Oswald was innocent, why did he lie to police about owning a rifle? Why did he tell them he had brought curtain rods with him to the Depository that morning? Why did he deny that a picture of him holding a rifle in one hand and the *Daily Worker* in the other was real, when his wife clearly remembered taking it, others remembered seeing it, and scientific evidence confirmed it was taken by his camera? If a conspiracy killed President Kennedy, why has no evidence of such a conspiracy ever surfaced, and why have those who believe in that conspiracy been forced to resort to deceit and obfuscation in order to argue for it?

There was no reasonable evidence in 1964 that anyone helped Oswald carry out those murders or covered up for them afterward. There is no such evidence today.

For many, Earl Warren's chairmanship of the Warren Commission would stand as the most momentous act of his large life. And for those inclined to see conspiracy in the Kennedy assassination, the Commission's report has marked Warren as a dupe or even a fraud. Even some of his admiring biographers have tended to view the Warren Commission as an aberration from a grand career, a blemish standing alongside Warren's advocacy of the Japanese internment. The criticism of Warren for abrogating the rights of those Japanese and Japanese-Americans is more than upheld by history. But the attack on his Warren Commission service is manifestly unfair, as time and sober reflection have made clear.

The Warren Commission was not perfect, nor was its chairman. But they were right.

Chapter 23

# AN ENFORCED CODE
# OF DECENCY

*Once loosed, the idea of Equality is not easily cabined.*

ARCHIBALD COX, WRITING OF THE WARREN COURT[1]

*Is it fair?*

EARL WARREN

WARREN SET OUT in the fall of 1964 a weathered and tired man, but he cast off his problems and strode into the epic that would define the Warren Court as history remembers it. He had his votes inside the Court and his protection outside it. A Democratic president occupied the White House and used it to advance the principles that Warren trumpeted from the Court; a Democratic Congress occasionally balked but often, in the end, acquiesced. Over that time, the Court would stake out and clarify its revolutionary principles of jurisprudence and of American society, only rarely in the face of serious opposition. What emerged from the years of the middle 1960s was the clearest expression of Warren's America, the America that he had spent his life fashioning and that he now had the license and authority to recast in his terms.

In those years, Warren's insistence on racial equality evolved into a sweeping commitment to egalitarianism. His faith in voting rights grew from a belief in the franchise to a conviction that the ballot was the device by which Americans secured not just their political identity but their access to the swelling benefits of a generous government. And Warren's experiences as a prosecutor, governor, and justice now crested in a conviction that fairness required a redesigned criminal justice system. In all those areas, the Warren Court from 1964 to 1969 would forge a new America, and in every one, Warren led the way forward.

Only in one of the Court's pioneering fields of that period did it move without Warren's leadership. When it came to speech and expression, Warren's thinking was dominated by his lifelong discomfort with obscenity—an artifact of his Progressive-era deprecation of vice. Moreover, after nearly a half century of public life, Warren had seen plenty of bad, intrusive reporting, and he could not bring himself to sanction it any more than he could stomach the actions of pornographers. In the area of expression, Brennan would lead the Court, and not always well. In all others, the Warren Court was in fact Warren's Court.

No sooner had Warren gaveled the Court back into session for its 1964 term than it turned to the familiar area of racial segregation. This time, however, the Court's allies had made its burden far easier to carry. Johnson's successful pursuit of the Civil Rights Act of 1964 barred racial discrimination in places of public accommodation, and now this act, not the Court, had the lead role in striking discrimination. There would not be the confusing and bitter debate over sit-ins as in the previous term; the Court now had merely to assess the constitutionality of the act. Two cases, *Atlanta Motel v. United States* and *Katzenbach v. McClung,* came before the Court on October 5 and framed the issues. The Heart of Atlanta was a 216-room hotel along an interstate highway, and its owners preferred to serve whites. McClung was the owner of Ollie's Barbecue in Birmingham, which had sit-down dining for white customers but only take-out for Negroes. McClung too liked running a segregated establishment, even though most of his employees were black. Clark wrote for a unanimous Court in both cases and concluded that Congress's right to regulate interstate commerce gave it authority to desegregate even a Birmingham rib shack. Ollie's got forty-six percent of its meat from a local supplier who got it from out of state. That was enough.[2]

The Court dispensed with those cases easily, but the first term of Warren's post–Warren Commission service would forever be marked by one case and, at its conclusion, by a change in personnel. The case that would define the term—and that would set the rules for one of the twentieth century's most contentious Supreme Court decisions—was launched with a bit of mischief on Warren's part.

William Douglas, then sixty-five, had married twenty-three-year-old Joan Martin in the summer of 1963. By the fall of 1964, the Douglas-Martin union, barely a year old, already was suffering the fate of its predecessors.[3] And so when the Court was presented that term with a case that called for the justices to consider the sanctity and privacy of marriage, Warren gave it to Douglas to sort out.

The case before the justices arose out of an anachronistic Connecticut law. Under that 1879 statute, any person using a contraceptive to prevent conception was guilty of a crime and faced a fine of at least $50 or imprisonment of two months to a year. Any person who helped another to commit the crime of using a contraceptive was identically guilty and faced the same punishment.[4] In November 1961, Connecticut authorities arrested Estelle Griswold, director of the state's Planned Parenthood organization, and Lee Buxton, medical director of a clinic in New

Haven that dispensed contraceptives. They were fined $100 apiece. Appealing those convictions, the defendants brought their case to the United States Supreme Court, urging it to void the law as unconstitutional. It was Dr. Buxton's second trip to the Court on that issue, having tried and failed to persuade the justices to strike down the law in 1961, when the Court found that because the law was not being prosecuted, there was no issue properly before it. By forcing the state's hand and engineering their own arrests, Griswold and Buxton now had a genuine issue for the Court to consider—a "ripe" one, in the vernacular of the law.

None of the justices liked Connecticut's antiquated statute, but finding it unconstitutional was another matter. Douglas took his first crack soon after the argument, and his boredom with his work shone through his first draft. Douglas had based his rejection of the Connecticut law on the theory that it infringed a First Amendment right, in this case the right of association, which he said marriage constituted and thus deserved the same protection as political association. He showed an early draft to Brennan, who was, according to his clerks, "somewhat alarmed."[5] Brennan urged Douglas to consider that the right being violated by the Connecticut law was not that of association but of privacy. The Bill of Rights, Brennan emphasized, was full of privacy protections. *Griswold* gave Douglas an opportunity to consider these protections as a group, and Brennan urged him to try.[6] And Douglas, in a rare moment of receptivity to criticism, did agree to try again.

His second effort was hardly less controversial, but it had the creativity and the intellectual energy of which Douglas was capable. Drawing now not just on the First Amendment but on an elastic—some might say inventive—reading of the entire Bill of Rights, Douglas discovered a right of privacy that pervaded those restrictions on the government. The First Amendment, he wrote, protected not just purely political associations but social, legal, and economic ones as well; the Third Amendment prohibited the government from quartering soldiers in private homes; the Fourth Amendment, perhaps the most specific about ensuring privacy, demanded that citizens be "secure in their persons, houses, papers, and effects, against unreasonable searches and seizures"; the Fifth Amendment's protection against self-incrimination in criminal proceedings built a wall of privacy around an individual being questioned by the government; and the Ninth Amendment sought to ensure that even rights not specifically enumerated in the Constitution were retained by the people.[7] Douglas's analysis was ambitious but not without foundation. No less a conservative than Harlan recognized that the concept of "privacy" was essential to the Constitution's reliance on "ordered liberty," and found that the "Constitution protects the privacy of the home against all unreasonable intrusion of whatever character."[8]

It is thus false, as some have asserted, to say that Douglas invented privacy out of whole cloth. In *Mapp v. Ohio,* for instance, the Court had struck down the admission of illegally seized evidence in state trials. Finding that such illegal seizures violated the Fourth Amendment, the Court insisted that "the right to privacy" was "no less important than any other right carefully and particularly reserved to the people."[9] Now, however, Douglas proposed not to apply a right of privacy to an area already identified in the Constitution—protection against search and seizure, in the case of *Mapp*—but rather to marriage, an institution never named by the Framers and only sporadically honored by Douglas himself. Moreover, the right of privacy upon which Douglas relied existed not in any specific amendment but rather in his imaginative reading of all of those amendments together.

Douglas may or may not have cared what scholars would say of his work. Given what is recorded of him, it seems likely that the opprobrium of the academy would not have entered his thinking. His opinion reflected his expansive view of what the Constitution granted the nation. In Douglas's words, the "specific guarantees in the Bill of Rights have penumbras, formed by emanations from those guarantees that help give them life and substance."[10] Those emanations might be vague, but they provided real protections. And having read those shadowy zones into the hard body of the Constitution, Douglas then closed with a snorting dismissal of the police state—one where officers might root around in the bedroom for evidence of contraception—and with a herald to marriage that can only have amused his brethren:

> We deal with a right of privacy older than the Bill of Rights—older than our political parties, older than our school system. Marriage is a coming together for better or for worse, hopefully enduring, and intimate to the degree of being sacred. It is an association that promotes a way of life, not causes; a harmony in living, not political faiths; a bilateral loyalty, not commercial or social projects. Yet it is an association for as noble a purpose as any involved in our prior decisions.[11]

Warren's clerk that year, John H. Ely, would go on to an illustrious academic career. In light of that and of *Griswold*'s later significance in American politics, it is thus worthy of note that Ely strongly urged Warren not to join Douglas's opinion. None of the amendments cited by Douglas, Ely noted, "sets up a general 'right to privacy.'" Moreover, even if such a right existed, Douglas never explained how the Connecticut law violated it. "The simple answer to this is that if and when the police undertake such searches [for contraceptives, evidence that the law was being broken], courts can get rid of them under a provision which *does* appear in the Constitution—the safeguard against unreasonable searches." Ely knew that Warren liked unanimity but added that in his view, "this opinion incorporates an approach to the Constitution so dangerous that you should not join it."[12] Nevertheless, Warren joined Douglas's opinion as well as those of Goldberg and Brennan, who similarly joined Douglas but also wrote separately to give emphasis to the special language of the Ninth Amendment, with its promise that the people retained rights not specifically enumerated in the Constitution. The Ninth Amendment, rarely relied upon, was an appealing one for Warren and his fellow liberals, as it seemed to offer little restraint on what rights the justices could apply. "The Ninth Amendment shows a belief of the Constitution's authors that fundamental rights exist that are not expressly enumerated in the first eight amendments and an intent that the list of rights included there not be deemed exhaustive," Goldberg wrote.[13] Black, predictably, disagreed: If a right was not named in the Constitution or the Bill of Rights, he would not find it there. He and Stewart dissented, though even they had to admit the Connecticut law was "every bit as offensive" to them as to the others.[14]

*Griswold* was among Douglas's most consequential contributions to American law and life. It would become a foundation for *Roe v. Wade* in 1973—when the Court, under the leadership of one Nixon appointee, Warren Burger, and in an opinion written by another, Harry Blackmun, would find that, within certain medical limits, the "right of privacy . . . is broad enough to encompass a woman's decision whether or not to terminate her pregnancy."[15] Few would ever accuse the Burger Court of liberal activism, but because *Roe* depended on *Griswold*, *Griswold* would be embroiled in America's exhausting, vicious abortion debate. It came to stand as a symbol of the Warren Court's adventurism in the field of Constitutional interpretation. Forty years after Warren assigned it to his philandering colleague, *Griswold* remained a monument of the Warren Court, in fact and in image. For Douglas, it was another day at the office, and a not particularly memorable one at that. In his memoirs, the justice never mentioned the case. When the Court broke for its summer vacation, Warren teased Douglas about the ruling. "Dear Bill," he jotted in a handwritten note. "Keep our Penumbra flying all summer!"[16]

*Griswold* was the defining case of a peaceful term. Not once in the Court term beginning in October 1964 did Earl Warren dissent from the majority, a far cry from the closing years of the 1950s, when he had refused to soften his principles in the face of nervous colleagues or congressional pressure. But the term's other moment of long-standing consequence occurred after Court recessed for the year in the summer of 1965. For Warren, it was a double tragedy, though the full effects of it would not become clear to him for some time.

The first act in that sad series of events began incongruously, with Warren and three old friends out for a morning of fishing in San Francisco Bay. It was a Saturday in July, and Warren was home for his annual refreshment in The City. The friends dipped lines into the same waters that Warren had crossed upon arriving in the Bay Area in 1908. More than a half century later, Warren was far from the young boy who stared in awe at the rebuilding of San Francisco from its earthquake. With him in the boat on this Saturday morning in 1965 were Pat Brown, then at the height of his governorship; Ben Swig, the conscientious and well-connected hotelier from San Francisco; and Adlai Stevenson, the grand and respected diplomat, even then attempting to negotiate peace in Vietnam from his post as ambassador to the United Nations. The businessman, the governor, the ambassador, and the chief justice fished and talked, and then Stevenson left for a date with *Meet the Press*. Four days later, Stevenson dropped dead on a London sidewalk.[17]

"We are shocked and heartsick," Nina Warren wrote, "can't believe he's no longer with us."[18] Earl Warren and Adlai Stevenson came from different parties, and in one sense Warren owed his position to Stevenson's defeat in 1952, since Eisenhower's victory required Stevenson's loss. As Warren had drifted from Eisenhower, however, he and Stevenson had grown closer, and by 1965, whatever differences they had harbored were long behind them. Stevenson's death robbed the nation of a dignified advocate for peace, and it took from Warren a contemporary, a traveling companion, and a friend—part of the social circle that included Drew Pearson and Agnes Meyer. On July 19, Earl and Nina traveled to Illinois to honor their friend. They met the party of President Johnson in Bloomington for the service, and there heard Stevenson eulogized in the poetry of Tennyson, imagining a world of the future in which we "Hear the war-drums throb no longer, / See the battle flags all furled, / In the parliament of man, / The federation of the world."[19]

Stevenson's death was sad by itself, but it also would set off a series of events with far-reaching consequences for Warren and the Court. Suddenly without an ambassador to the United Nations, Johnson went shopping for one, and he quickly lighted upon Warren's junior colleague, Justice Arthur Goldberg. In Goldberg, Johnson had the opportunity to accomplish two objectives at once, sending to the United Nations a brilliant successor to the revered Stevenson and opening a vacancy on the Court for him to fill. Sensing the opportunity, Johnson invited Goldberg to attend the Stevenson funeral and made sure that he would accompany the president on *Air Force One*. At the funeral, Goldberg sought out Warren and told him there was talk—still apparently not from Johnson himself—of appointing Goldberg to the United Nations post. Goldberg assured Warren that he was "rather inclined against it."[20] Warren urged his younger colleague to stand fast, saying he would hate to lose him from the Court. But Goldberg had yet to face Johnson directly on the topic, and as Warren well knew, holding off a determined Johnson was something few men could do.

After the funeral, Warren returned to California, but Goldberg reboarded *Air Force One,* and Johnson gave him the treatment. Goldberg would long deny that Johnson "twisted his arm," but that is in the elbow of the beholder.[21] What Johnson did was what he did so well—find Goldberg's weak spot and exploit it. Johnson sniffed out Warren's patriotism, and Warren ended up the chairman of the Warren

Commission. In this case, Goldberg was a sophisticated and extraordinarily intelligent man, a deft negotiator and, though relatively new to the Court, already showing signs of becoming one of its great justices. But his weakness was vanity, and Johnson went for it. "I had the feeling, on the basis of what was developing, that we were going to get enmeshed in Vietnam," Goldberg said. "I also had the egotistical feeling, based on my long experience with government and private life as a person who could influence policy, that I could influence the President to not get overly involved."[22] Goldberg resigned his seat on the Court one week later.

In his place, Johnson appointed one of his closest friends and advisers, Abe Fortas, who was best known to the brethren for his argument in *Gideon* but whose career already was studded with admirers and detractors, evidence of his abiding intelligence as well as his difficult temperament. Fortas at least nominally resisted the appointment. (He had founded a Washington law firm, and felt obligated to help build it; he and his wife, the tough and bright Carol Agger, had just purchased a home and had debts to pay. Laura Kalman, Fortas's able biographer, suggests that Agger believed Fortas should spend more time with the firm and wait for a later spot on the Court.[23]) On the day of Stevenson's funeral, even as Johnson was working on Goldberg, Fortas asked not to be considered, citing his obligations to the Johnson family, whose legal interests he protected, and to his law firm.[24] But Fortas did not object to being courted, and Johnson was not in the mood for no. He lobbied and enlisted the help of others, and when Fortas still resisted, Johnson in effect tricked him, luring him to the White House on a pretext and only then telling Fortas that he was about to announce the appointment. Fortas accepted. His wife was so angry she refused to speak with the president of the United States for the next two months.[25]

On the surface, the switch meant little—a trade of one liberal justice for another. And indeed, the immediate consequences of Goldberg's departure and Fortas's arrival were muted. In the area of business and economic regulation, Fortas, the corporate lawyer, was more forgiving of financial interests than Goldberg, the labor attorney. Beyond that, the new justice largely picked up where the departing one had left off. What neither Johnson nor Warren could have guessed was that the fuse that would detonate the Warren Court had just been lit.

BY THE MID-1960S, the Court was no longer moving alone, as it had in the early days of the civil rights movement. Lyndon Johnson had refused to yield until the Senate adopted the Civil Rights Act of 1964, relieving the Court of the sole burden for breaking down racist barriers in public places. The following year, too quickly for Johnson's taste, pressure built for a similar campaign against obstacles to black voting. Just as Birmingham had provided the moral and political impetus for the

Civil Rights Act, so, this time, did Selma supply the urgency for federal action on voting. As 1965 opened, Martin Luther King, now a Nobel laureate, for the Peace Prize he had received the previous year, turned his attention to Selma and to the pernicious efforts there to thwart black voter registration. And just as Birmingham had served up a thuggish cop—there, Bull Connor—so too did Selma sink to that occasion, providing the civil rights mission with its counterpart this time in the form of Jim Clark, a thick brute all too happy to resort to violence in order to preserve racism. After weeks of skirmishing, protests began in Selma on January 19 and escalated with the now familiar routine of peaceful protest followed by mass arrest. King demanded federal action to protect voting rights. Johnson agreed in principle but held back on supporting a specific bill.

King scheduled a march from Selma to the state capitol in Montgomery, and set March 7 as the day it would leave Selma. Governor George Wallace refused to allow it, and Clark massed his officers to block the demonstration. Although King himself was not present, the march proceeded on schedule. As the demonstrators came off the Edmund Pettus Bridge, marching two-by-two behind John Lewis and Hosea Williams, police swarmed upon them, "a blur of blue shirts and billy clubs and bullwhips" cloaked in billowing tear gas.[26] Choking and hysterical, the marchers fell apart under the assault by police; when residents of a nearby housing project began to throw rocks at the marauding police force, the confrontation for a moment teetered on the precipice of disaster. The assault took place directly in front of reporters and photographers, and accounts of the brutality flooded the nation that night. ABC interrupted its programming to bring the pictures, and thus many viewers learned about the Selma brutality in the midst of watching that night's special presentation, *Judgment at Nuremberg*. The juxtaposition, though unintentional, spoke for itself.[27]

March 7 became known as "Bloody Sunday," and the same nation that winced in the face of Birmingham did so again, its moral reflexes this time twitching in sympathy with the movement's demand for voting access. At the Virginia home of Hugo and Elizabeth Black, the justice and his wife mourned the death of a family friend on the battlefield of Selma. Jim Reeb, a Unitarian minister from Boston who had performed the marriage of Hugo's daughter, walked into the wrong part of town, the white part, after the march and was set upon by a group that beat him and his companion. One thug struck Reeb with a club; he died en route to a Birmingham hospital after a Selma hospital refused to let one of its ambulances take him there.[28] "My poor Alabama!" Elizabeth Black groaned to her diary.[29]

Johnson, cautious at first in the face of King's insistence on federal action, now rose to the occasion. On March 15, 1965, Johnson appeared before his old colleagues in the Congress and delivered the most memorable speech of his life. "I speak tonight for the dignity of man and the destiny of democracy," Johnson began. He compared Selma to Lexington and Concord, to Appomattox. Congress and its invited guests listened silently, expectantly, as did the "great, rich, restless country" beyond the chambers on that late-winter night. In Selma, Johnson said, "long-suffering men and women peacefully protested the denial of their rights as Americans. Many were brutally assaulted. One good man, a man of God, was killed."[30]

Johnson that night drew upon his own life and summoned the best of his rhetoric. He well knew that the realities of voter registration were such that there was only one way to qualify to cast a ballot in many states. Literacy tests and registration requirements were a sham; "the only way to pass these barriers is to show a white skin," Johnson said. He was plain and eloquent, beseeching Congress to join him, not merely to follow. But he was uncompromising on the underlying principle: Negroes were going to be allowed to vote, and no obstacle to that right was going to be allowed. "This time, on this issue, there must be no delay, no hesitation and no compromise with our purpose," he commanded. The members applauded long and hard.

Johnson's speech was a masterpiece with an unusual structure. Its apex came not at its conclusion but near the middle. After reviewing the situation in Selma and outlining the bill he intended to send to Congress, he asked that body's members to join him in long nights and deliberations, to absorb the "outraged conscience of a nation" and pass a law to eliminate all illegal restrictions against voting. But, he warned:

> Even if we pass this bill, the battle will not be over. What happened in Selma is part of a far larger movement which reaches into every section and state of America. It is the effort of American Negroes to secure for themselves the full blessings of American life.
>
> Their cause must be our cause, too. Because it's not just Negroes, but really it's all of us, who must overcome the crippling legacy of bigotry and injustice.

Johnson had not always accepted the cause of civil rights. He'd used the word "nigger" and disparaged the lot of American blacks. He'd shuffled on the Southern Manifesto and dodged on *Brown*. But now, moved by Selma and determined to bring his Great Society to all of America, Johnson delivered his signature line. Yes, all Americans suffered under the heavy weight of bigotry and injustice. But the time had come to end that suffering. The time had come for men such as himself to join the great cause of freedom urged by blacks. Yes, said the president of the United States, leader of his divided and heartfelt people, "We shall overcome." Watching in Selma, Martin Luther King shed a tear.[31] The Congress sat stunned. But moments later, when Johnson pledged to put the power of his office behind the cause of civil rights, members of Congress jumped to their feet and thundered with applause.

They were not alone. Four members of the Court attended that night's speech. Whatever proprieties are expected in the relationship between the branches of American government were, in that moment, forgotten by the nation's chief justice. Earl Warren rose along with the Congress and cascaded Johnson with a standing ovation.[32]

Prodded by Congress and shamed by Selma, Congress moved quickly to give Johnson his act, and a delighted Johnson signed it in August of that same year.[33] As with the Civil Rights Act, the Court leapt at the chance to rule on a challenge to it. In this case, it came from South Carolina, which protested the act's provisions that allowed the attorney general to intervene in states where voting registration or turnout were suspiciously low—fewer than half of South Carolina voters had cast ballots in the 1964 presidential elections—and where tests impeded some voters from registering. The Fifteenth Amendment barred discrimination in voting by race and gave Congress the right to "enforce this article by appropriate legislation."[34] In this case, however, South Carolina argued that its literacy test was racially neutral and that the act went beyond enforcement of the Fifteenth Amendment, giving the government the authority to regulate, not merely enforce. The justices allowed South Carolina to bring its case directly to the Court, bypassing the normal route of appeal and accepting the state's bill of complaint. Other states were invited to weigh in, and Warren set arguments for January 17 and 18, 1966, less than six months after the act was adopted.

None of those who assembled can have had much doubt about where Warren himself would end up in the case. He was in his twelfth year of a campaign against Southern racism, and his impulsive leap to his feet at Johnson's introduction of the Voting Rights Bill telegraphed his feelings. The Court was another matter, however, and when the lawyers gathered in January, there were, in Warren's words, "emotional overtones" to the arguments.[35] South Carolina's lawyers tried to persuade the Court to ignore what it knew to be true—that state and local officials there would use any means at their disposal to repress its Negro population. Johnson knew it, Warren knew it, and one suspects that South Carolina's lawyers and leaders knew it, too, however much they tried to insist otherwise. Once the case was argued, Warren assigned it to himself, and turned around his opinion for the Court in under three months. In it, Warren made clear that he valued voting, that he was offended by those who had spent decades stripping citizens of their right to engage in it, and that he specifically knew who was guilty of it and why:

> Beginning in 1890, the States of Alabama, Georgia, Louisiana, Mississippi, North Carolina, South Carolina, and Virginia enacted tests still in use which were specifically designed to prevent Negroes from voting. Typically, they made the ability to read and write a registration qualification and also required completion of a registration form. These

laws were based on the fact that as of 1890 in each of the named States, more than two-thirds of the adult Negroes were illiterate while less than one-quarter of the adult whites were unable to read or write. At the same time, alternate tests were prescribed in all of the named States to assure that white illiterates would not be deprived of the franchise. These included grandfather clauses, property qualifications, "good character" tests, and the requirement that registrants "understand" or "interpret" certain matter.[36]

The Voting Rights Act, Warren wrote, was a legitimate response to devious attempts to perpetuate that discrimination. When that opinion was handed down in March, all the brethren joined except Black, who by then had slipped into a reflexive defense of the South. His opinion accepted most of Warren's analysis, but he broke in order to express the offense he took at a law that so blatantly challenged his home, Elizabeth Black's "poor Alabama." The Voting Rights Act required any state whose elections failed its tests to suspend registration tests—in this case, the literacy test—and then seek preapproval of any other tests from the federal government. Known as "pre-clearance," that requirement struck Black as patronizing and offended his sudden regard for states' rights.[37] Warren once looked to Black for guidance and counsel. No more.

One week after the argument in the South Carolina case, the justices considered another popular method of controlling voting, the poll tax. The poll tax was well on its way to oblivion by 1966, already having been struck in federal elections and disappearing from state elections as well.[38] But Warren had written that "the right to exercise the franchise in a free and unimpaired manner is preservative of other basic civil and political rights."[39] Given that, any impairment was an offense, and one he was committed to eradicating. The Fifteenth Amendment made it illegal to prevent Negroes from voting. The poll tax worked its mischief against the poor (though, often, they were Negroes as well). In theory, there were at least two problems with defending the poor from discrimination at the polling place: the Court already had upheld it, and no constitutional provision or amendment prevented states from enacting such a tax. That might have slowed a different Court, but not Warren's, not at the height of its power and in the face of such an easily understood discrimination. Warren assigned the case to Douglas, who had long opposed the tax. He delivered as expected. "We conclude that a State violates the Equal Protection Clause of the Fourteenth Amendment whenever it makes affluence of the voter or payment of any fee an electoral standard," he wrote in an opinion that Warren naturally joined. "Voter qualifications have no relation to wealth nor to paying or not paying this or any other tax."[40] Harlan, joined by Stewart, dissented to renew his objections to the Court's adventurism in rectifying bad voting laws—objections he stated in *Reynolds* and restated in this case. Black sputtered another dissent. But Warren and Douglas had their votes.

The Court's rulings in *South Carolina v. Katzenbach* and *Harper v. Virginia Board of Elections* upheld the Voting Rights Act against relatively easy challenges—brought by Southern states in defense of discredited practices. The third of the Court's three major voting cases that term turned on a more novel question and arose from outside the South. In 1922, the State of New York imposed a requirement for voting—namely, that any voter must be able to read and write English.[41] Section 4(e) of the Voting Rights Act, however, stated that any person who had completed the sixth grade in any American state, territory, District of Columbia, or Puerto Rico was entitled to vote even if he or she was not literate in English. That language was written specifically to extend the franchise to the hundreds of thousands of Puerto Ricans who had immigrated to the United States—largely to New York—many of whom were literate but not in English. It was not the result of extensive congressional analysis but rather a floor amendment introduced by Senator Robert Kennedy and accepted into the act without hearings.[42]

For the Court, the difficulty in striking New York's law in favor of the Voting Rights Act requirement was that the Court itself had upheld racially neutral literacy tests as a valid condition for voting. "The ability to read and write," the Court unanimously ruled in 1959, ". . . has some relation to standards designed to promote intelligent use of the ballot. . . . We do not sit in judgment on the wisdom of that policy. We cannot say, however, that it is not an allowable one measured by constitutional standards."[43] In a footnote to that opinion, the Court specifically recognized that of the nineteen states that required literacy among voters, some went further and required a demonstration of English literacy and aptitude.[44]

So if literacy was an acceptable condition of voting and states were allowed to make command of English a requirement, how could Congress now undo the work of the Court? And if Congress could undo that work, what would prevent it from trying its hand at other areas of constitutional doctrine? It was one thing to extend the vote, another to open the door to congressional meddling in the Court's constitutional domain.

Black had dissented from the two voting cases coming from the South, but he was more sympathetic now that the challenged state was New York. Seeing the opportunity to bring Black home to the liberal majority, Warren asked him to take the case. Black declined, saying he feared his view of the disputed section of the act would not command a majority of the Court.[45] Faced then with the doctrinal challenge posed by the complexity of the case, Warren instead assigned the opinion to Brennan, who undertook that assignment with substantial help from Black. Brennan managed to protect both the Court and Puerto Rican voters by emphasizing the vote as an instrument of civic authority. Voters have power, and power secures for those voters the blessings of their government; without power, those blessings would fall elsewhere, and for that to happen to an ethnic group was intolerable and unconstitutional—well within the power of Congress to eliminate. "This enhanced political power will be helpful in gaining nondiscriminatory treatment in public services for the entire Puerto Rican community," Brennan wrote. The disputed section of the act thus "enables the Puerto Rican minority better to obtain 'perfect equality of civil rights and the equal protection of the laws.'"[46] That satisfied half the Court's mission—extending the vote. But could Congress, using its power to enforce the equal protection clause, pass other legislation that the Court would disapprove of? Harlan raised that question in dissent, and Brennan answered with a footnote stressing that Congress had the right only to "enforce the guarantees of the Amendment." It had no comparable right to "restrict, abrogate, or dilute these guarantees."[47] If that was half a gift—permitting Congress to expand rights but not to contract them—it nevertheless was a reminder that the Warren Court was not bent on preserving for itself the entire domain of civil liberties; it openly invited Congress to come along, just not to impede.

The three voting rights cases, combined with *Baker v. Carr* and *Reynolds v. Sims*, completed the Warren Court's treatise on the centrality of the franchise in modern America. States were not to block voters from casting ballots—not because of race, illiteracy, language deficiency, or poverty. Once those votes were cast, they were to be counted equally; states were not to create districts that gave some votes more weight than others. Voters were to have power. They were to share it equally with one another, and they were expected to use it to secure the benefits of the Great Society even then taking shape in the White House and in the halls of Congress. Congress could help that process along but could not stand in its way. Warren, who won seven elections himself and lost only when hooked to doomed Tom Dewey, now placed his full faith in the ballot to extend democracy and spread its benefits across the land. Together, the three voting cases also demonstrated the extent to which Warren commanded his Court and worked the subtleties of his position. When the nation needed an affirmation of the Voting Rights Act, Warren assigned the opinion to himself, ensuring that the case would bear the signature of the Chief Justice of the United States. When the poll tax required summary burial, he assigned it to Douglas, whose brusque intolerance of the tax was conveyed in his writing. And when the issues out of New York posed the opportunity to reunite the old liberal majority, he reached first to Black; failing there, he knew he needed doctrinal subtlety, and he found it where he usually did, in Brennan.

Egalitarianism underlay Warren's belief in the power of voting and the extension of the franchise. But the idea of equality, as Cox perceived, "is not easily cabined." The insistence on equality started for Warren's Court with schools before it moved to voting. Then, even as he imposed his notions of fairness and equality into state and local elections, Warren was moving to other areas as well. As far back as 1956, the Warren Court had held that indigent defendants were entitled to a free transcript of their cases on appeal.[48] *Mapp v. Ohio* in 1961 had barred the states from admitting illegally seized evidence; *Gideon v. Wainwright* in 1963 had required all states to provide indigent defendants with lawyers; *Douglas v. California,* decided even before *Gideon* but held over in order to allow then lawyer, now Justice Fortas to make his famous argument, required the states to provide counsel for appeal in addition to trial; and, most recently, *Escobedo v. Illinois,* decided in 1964 and written by the newly departed Goldberg, had barred the use of confessions when extracted from a suspect who asked for a lawyer and was denied one. Some of those cases had been decided by close votes, but not once had Warren dissented.

In August 1965, when Warren's new clerks assembled in the Court, he told them he had a special assignment for them that year. *Escobedo,* the chief said, had laid down new law on confessions, but he wanted now to clarify that ruling. So he instructed his clerks to scour any cases coming to the Court for ones that might help the Court spell out its principles on the admissibility of confessions taken by police of suspects in custody. There were, one of Warren's clerks, Kenneth Ziffren, recalled, 200 to 300 that touched on some aspect of that issue, but the clerks were seeking cases that were uncontaminated by other factors, such as searches and seizures that introduced side elements into the confession itself. In the end, they settled on four, and suggested as the lead case *Miranda v. Arizona.*[49]

Ernesto Miranda was not a sympathetic defendant. Twenty-three years old and of limited intelligence, he tried three times in late 1962 and early 1963 to rape young women in Phoenix, twice giving up after they struggled and then succeeding on the third attempt. One victim described the car of her assailant, and a few days after the attack, her cousin spotted a vehicle that seemed similar. She hastily jotted down the license plate as the car drove off, then gave it to the detective handling the rape case. The detective found a car similar to the description and with a license plate number that was close. He called the owner, who said her boyfriend occasionally borrowed it. Her boyfriend, she added, was named Ernesto Miranda. The detective brought Miranda in for questioning, and put him in a lineup. The witnesses could not be sure, but when Miranda asked, "How'd I do?" the detective told him they had picked him as the assailant. "Well," Miranda replied, "I guess I'd better tell you about it then."[50] His confession was admitted against him at trial, and he was convicted in two separate trials of robbery, kidnapping, and rape. He was sentenced to 20–30 years for kidnapping and rape, and to 20–25 years for stealing $8 from one of his victims.

During Miranda's questioning by police, no lawyer had been present, not because he had asked for one and been refused—the case in *Escobedo*—but because he did not know he could have one if he asked, and thus did not think to request one. For the Court, the question was whether Miranda had a right to know his rights and, if so, whether the police had the obligation to tell him.

In essence, the Court was asked to consider the interaction between the Sixth Amendment's right to counsel—a right this same Court had required of all states—and the Fifth Amendment's protection against self-incrimination. If a suspect could be cajoled by police into confessing before he ever saw a lawyer or knew that he had a right to meet with one, the later appointment of counsel was meaningless—the case already was lost. Warren knew that well from two angles: As a prosecutor, he had put the *Point Lobos* defendants away after extracting a confession from a suspect unrepresented by counsel; as a justice, he had seen rough police tactics rewarded with convictions and had grown increasingly unsympathetic. He had, by his reckoning, voted the wrong way in *Irvine,* condoning invasive police misconduct in a state case. A decade later, the fullness of his change of heart had come in *Mapp* and then *Escobedo.* Now he was prepared to go further still. At the conference following the argument in *Miranda,* Warren read a long statement outlining his views and then assigned the opinion to himself.[51]

Warren rarely drafted in his own hand. After *Brown,* he had come to rely more heavily on his clerks, generally dictating to them his views of a case and the basis upon which he wanted the decision to rest. He then turned over the writing to them, and though he closely reviewed their work, he largely left drafting to them. *Miranda* was different. Warren wrote an extensive outline himself, drafting by hand in pencil on yellow legal tablets, just as he had in *Brown.* Although rough, it included the principal elements of what would become the final decision—the requirement that police warn suspects of their right to remain silent, of their right to consult with a lawyer, of their right to have a lawyer provided them if they could not afford one. The document was far from polished—Warren misspelled "Escobedo," putting it down as "Escobido"—but it was a solid start.

All three of his clerks that year contributed their thoughts in memos, and then in typewritten drafts circulated among themselves but not yet to the brethren. On May 9, their work was sufficiently developed that Warren and his clerks took one copy, still not to the conference but just to Brennan, in order to sound him out on the developing opinion.[52] What they showed Brennan reflected Warren's initial impression of the case, which is that it turned on the Sixth Amendment and concluded that Miranda's right to a lawyer was violated by the police refusal to tell him he had such a right and building that ruling largely as an extension of Goldberg's work in *Escobedo.* Clerk Kenneth Ziffren had some misgivings about that approach, as did Brennan.[53] For them, the right of Miranda's that was violated was not so much his right to a lawyer—he had been represented at trial—but his right not to be forced to be a witness against himself. By the time Miranda got his lawyer, he had signed a confession. There was little left to do to save him. Miranda's casual and unknowing abdication of his Fifth Amendment rights thus made the effective exercise of his Sixth Amendment rights impossible. Brennan expressed his thoughts to Warren in a memo on May 11, and Warren agreed to rewrite portions of his opinion.[54]

A smarter criminal would have known that he had a right to a lawyer, and, important from Warren's perspective, a wealthier one probably would have as well. What thus prevented Miranda from enjoying his constitutional rights was ignorance—ignorance closely related to poverty. That was the key, as it offended Warren's sense of egalitarianism; if a Southern state could not deny a poor voter access to the polls with a poll tax, how could police deny a suspect knowledge of his rights because the suspect was too poor and ignorant to protest? Prodded by his clerks and his colleague to focus on the Fifth Amendment basis for the opinion, Warren returned to work on it. What he produced was an opinion that seemed nearly as much the work of a governor as that of a justice—a ruling notable mainly for the extent to which it moved beyond constitutional analysis to the drawing of clear rules for police.

Warren tried at the outset of his opinion to deny its novelty—"our holding is not an innovation in our jurisprudence, but is an application of the principles long recognized and applied in other settings," he professed.[55] And in one sense, he was right, as the ruling attempted to make *Escobedo* a workable doctrine in the context of real-life police interrogation. Warren's opinion explored the atmosphere of the interrogation room, its isolation from the world, the oppressive psychological advantage that it conferred on the police officer, its encouragement of deceit and withholding by authorities eager to extract from the suspect the words that would convict him. Warren summarized police manuals and cited their encouragement of officers to use psychological advantage. "Even if he fails to do so," one police text advised, "the inconsistency between the subject's original denial of the shooting and his present admission of at least doing the shooting will serve to deprive him of a self-defense 'out' at the time of trial."[56] Such overt reliance on trickery depressed and offended Warren. If Warren's irritation with the police was evident, however, his constitutional basis for curbing them was less clear.

In doctrinal terms, *Miranda* was a bit hard to decipher. In one passage, Warren argued that the rules he was propounding were directed at restricting evidence that could be admitted at trial—a traditional role for the Supreme Court and certainly not "an innovation in our jurisprudence." "The prosecution may not use statements, whether exculpatory or inculpatory, stemming from custodial interrogation of the defendant unless it demonstrates the use of procedural safeguards effective to secure the privilege against self-incrimination," Warren wrote.[57] That suggested *Miranda* was a rule of admissibility, one commanded by the Fifth Amendment's protection against the use of compelled statements to implicate a defendant in a criminal trial. But barely had he completed that sentence before he created a different rule, not that improperly elicited testimony was merely inadmissible but rather that the Court was announcing specific rules for police conduct itself, in effect regulating not just courtrooms but police stations, too. "Prior to any questioning, the person must be warned that he has a right to remain silent, that any statement he does make may be used as evidence against him, and that he has a right to the presence of an attorney, either retained or appointed," Warren wrote. "The defendant may waive effectuation of these rights, provided the waiver is made voluntarily, knowingly and intelligently."[58]

That specific rejoinder—telling police precisely what they must inform a suspect—was in Warren's first thoughts on the case and it came perilously close to legislating. No words in the Constitution commanded such a specific warning, but Warren had tried in *Irvine, Mapp,* and *Escobedo* to nudge police conduct first by urging prosecutions of wayward police—to no avail—then, with more success, by limiting evidence acquired through misconduct. Now he resorted simply to asserting what police must do. Harlan had objected to Warren's approach from the first conference on *Miranda,* when he rejected the "radical changes" proposed by Warren.[59] The final opinion had only made Harlan more concerned, and he replied with a forceful dissent, emotionally delivered. Harlan, by that time in his life nearly blind, flushed as he addressed his brethren and the audience. *Miranda* was handed down a year after the Watts riots had stunned the nation, and at a time when lawlessness was on the rise. The Court, Harlan warned in a quavering voice, was engaged in "dangerous experimentation" in the face of a "high crime rate that is a matter of growing concern."[60]

In his written dissent, Harlan was no less determined and not much less impassioned. "One is entitled to feel astonished that the Constitution can be read to produce this result," Harlan said of Warren's conclusion that Miranda's oral and written confessions were ruled inadmissible under the new doctrine. "These confessions were obtained during brief, daytime questioning conducted by two officers and unmarked by any of the traditional indicia of coercion. They assured a conviction for a brutal and unsettling crime. . . . There was, in sum, a legitimate purpose, not perceptible unfairness, and certainly little risk of injustice in the interrogation."[61] Harlan, usually so restrained in manner and speech, called the ruling "heavy-handed and one-sided" and warned of grave consequences to society. "The social costs of crime are too great," Harlan wrote, "to call the new rules anything but a hazardous experimentation."[62]

So powerful was his argument that Brennan, having helped push Warren toward the opinion as written, drafted a concurrence to respond directly to Harlan, specifically rebutting Harlan's contention that the new rules laid down by the Court precluded states from developing their own safeguards on police interrogations. "Nothing we hold today prevents the States from devising and applying similar prophylactic means for avoiding the dangers of interrogation which at the same time eliminate the possibility of such contests of veracity between the police and the accused," Brennan wrote.[63] He neglected to note, naturally, that any such alternative would need to satisfy the Court that it was at least as effective as the warning that Warren had written for the police to deliver. Brennan showed his concurrence to Warren, who received it badly. In a relatively rare moment of disagreement between the two, they argued over its necessity and desirability. Warren was wary of suggesting to states that they could tinker with the warning, and worried, as always, about signaling a fractured Court. Brennan yielded and withdrew his concurrence.[64]

That was lucky for Warren, because he fought to hold his Court on *Miranda* until the day it was announced. Up until that morning, Warren had assumed he had the votes of Brennan, Black, Douglas, Fortas, and Clark. But Clark, who was often prone to second thoughts, bolted at the last minute. Kenneth Ziffren, Warren's clerk, was in a hallway downstairs at the Court that morning when one of Clark's clerks handed him a document. "He's dissenting and concurring," the clerk warned Ziffren. "He's what?" Ziffren responded. Ziffren knew Warren would be furious, and so he ran back to the chief justice's chambers to inform him. Warren was not there, but Margaret McHugh told Ziffren he could find the chief down in the Court's barbershop. Ziffren bolted from the chambers and headed downstairs. Warren looked up, annoyed, as Ziffren burst inside. The news of Clark's defection irritated Warren even further, and he directed Ziffren to go dig up an opinion of Clark's that he could cite from the bench to embarrass the justice over his change of heart. Ziffren unearthed Clark's writing in *Mapp v. Ohio* and hastily put together a statement for Warren to use in order to remind Clark that he had drifted from his position in that case. Warren, his irritation with Ziffren now forgotten, praised him for finding just the right citation to punish Clark for stranding Warren and leaving him with a bare 5–4 majority. Warren read the statement as written, and a seething Clark then sent his clerks back to draft a more elaborate dissent to include in the formal record. That afternoon, the other justices and clerks had a picnic to celebrate the approaching end of the session. Clark and his clerks skipped the event. As word circulated of the last-minute fireworks, the other chambers were reminded that it was dangerous to cross Warren—and with that lesson, his leadership over the Court was reconfirmed. Leading the Court, as Warren well understood, involved more than grace and cajoling. It never hurts in politics for potential opponents to know that they are allowed no free shots at the leader.[65]

Police were thunderstruck. Bernard C. Parks was a rookie police officer in the LAPD when *Miranda* came down. "The word in the locker room," he said, "was that we were done with effective policing."[66] North Carolina senator Sam Ervin similarly saw the ruling as emboldening criminals and curtailing police, both at the expense of victims. "Enough has been done for those who murder and rape and rob," he harrumphed. "It is time to do something for those who do not wish to be murdered or raped or robbed."[67]

In the political torrent that *Miranda* opened, it was easy to see Warren as pushing the vanguard of liberal judicial activism and to deplore him for handcuffing the nation's police. In fact, the decision was more correctly thought of as a melding of his deeper instincts—his unwillingness to shrink from action once convinced that action was called for and yet also his lifelong search for a middle where others saw no room for compromise. For *Miranda* was, in fact, a compromise, as was evidenced by some of the civil libertarian response to it. John de J. Pemberton, Jr., executive director of the American Civil Liberties Union, did not endorse *Miranda*. To the contrary, he expressed "regret that the Court did not take the final step of stating that the privilege against self-incrimination cannot be fully assured unless a suspect's lawyer is present during police station interrogation. Only by such an affirmative step can the abuses of police station interrogation actually and finally be eliminated."[68] That contention was not limited to the civil liberties Left. In the months leading up to *Miranda*, Attorney General Nicholas Katzenbach and Judge David Bazelon had exchanged public letters on the question of when a suspect was entitled to a lawyer, with Bazelon arguing that a poor suspect should be able to have an attorney present at any stage of an investigation where a rich suspect could call on one—including, obviously, interrogation.[69] Caught between those who demanded that only confessions given in the presence of a lawyer be admissible and those who argued any further restraints on police would only exacerbate crime, Warren chose—as he so often did—the middle, though undeniably a middle closer to the liberals than the conservatives. The ruling in *Miranda*, Warren wrote,

> does not mean, as some have suggested, that each police station must have a "station house lawyer" present at all times to advise prisoners. It does mean, however, that if police propose to interrogate a person they must make known to him that he is entitled to a lawyer and that if he cannot afford one, a lawyer will be provided for him prior to any interrogation.[70]

That was too far for Harlan and Katzenbach, not far enough for the ACLU or Bazelon. And yet if the centrist cast of *Miranda* was misunderstood at the time, so too did contemporary responses overimagine its impact. It did not flood the nation with murderers. In part because the Court, a week after its decision, took the practical and novel view that the rights secured by *Miranda* were to be applied only prospectively (except in the four instances that it actually decided with the ruling itself), the doors to jails were not thrown open. Through television and the movies,

*Miranda* rights became embedded in American culture, their gruff recitation by detectives a staple of crime drama. Young Bernard Parks went on to become chief of the Los Angeles police department and then a member of that city's city council. Over the years he and his colleagues learned to live with the decision that so offended them in 1966. "The fears about *Miranda*," he says now, "did not come true."[71]

Indeed, *Miranda* did not even have the effect one might have anticipated for Miranda himself. Sent back for retrials on both the robbery and rape/kidnapping cases, Miranda was ably represented. His confessions to police were barred from evidence, and in the rape trial, the testimony of his victim also was limited, since she had positively identified him after he had confessed. Still, Miranda while in custody had admitted the rape to his girlfriend, and she now took the stand against him—that confession having not been "compelled." Miranda was convicted again. He was sent to prison and remained there until paroled in December 1972. He promptly violated his parole and was returned to prison, finally emerging in late 1975. He was free for less than two months before he got into a barroom fight and was stabbed to death. Two men were brought in for questioning in connection with Miranda's murder. They were read their *Miranda* rights and waived them, but neither confessed. They were let go, and by the time police had collected enough evidence to charge them with the murder, both had fled. The murder of Ernesto Miranda remains unsolved.[72]

Warren's work in *Miranda* has been vindicated by time. Though the Court in the years since has carved out significant exceptions to Warren's opinion, it remains binding on the states, and its warnings have become a ubiquitous part of American culture. In 2000, Chief Justice William H. Rehnquist, not one to be accused of coddling criminals, wrote for his Court in explicitly affirming *Miranda* and overturning a congressional attempt to circumscribe it. By then, it had become so embedded in American law enforcement that some police groups urged the Court to uphold it. Though its reach has been curbed since Warren first wrote it in 1966, *Miranda* remains settled constitutional law.[73]

That is the long view, however. In its more immediate aftermath, *Miranda* threatened to reinvigorate the Warren Court's opponents. A less sympathetic president or Congress might have doomed the decision and threatened the Court that issued it. But by 1966, the Court was moving without those threats. Indeed, in September 1965, Johnson was sufficiently emboldened to insist that a historic alignment within American government was under way. "You can perform a great service," he told one interviewer, "if you say that never before have the three independent branches been so productive. Never has the American system worked so effectively in producing quality legislation—and at a time when our system is under attack all over the world."[74]

RALPH GINZBURG was a sleazy character, an inventive purveyor of dirty books, merrily preying on the frailties and weaknesses of his customers. Warren had seen his type before—in Bakersfield's saloons and whorehouses, where railroad men squandered a month's earnings in a single binge, on the *Rex* in Santa Monica Bay, where working men and women succumbed to the lure of gambling. Warren's Progressivism was solidified by those experiences, and none since had ever shaken those early convictions. When Ginzburg's business came before the United States Supreme Court, it mattered little to Warren that the works were of a marginal literary type. To Warren, Ginzburg was a smut peddler and deserved to be treated as one.

By the time Ginzburg brought his obscenity conviction to the Court, Warren had been attempting for a decade to construct a viable theory of obscenity that would achieve his basic aims—protecting the works themselves under the First Amendment while still finding a way to lock up those who trafficked in them. That was no small matter, for it required a way to make it a crime to sell or mail material that was constitutionally protected. But Warren was nothing if not stubborn, and he hammered away at the notion. Warren's first attempt came in 1957, when he tried out his doctrine in a concurrence to a Brennan opinion. In that case, a New York publisher and bookseller named Samuel Roth was convicted on four counts of mailing obscene material; he was sentenced to five years in prison and fined $5,000. Brennan's opinion for the Court insisted that the First Amendment did not "protect every utterance" and that obscenity, which he defined as material "appealing to prurient interest," fell outside the Constitution's protections. Warren agreed in that result, but reached it differently. He wrote:

> The line dividing the salacious or pornographic from literature or science is not straight and unwavering. Present laws depend largely upon the effect that the materials may have upon those who receive them. It is manifest that the same object may have a different impact, varying according to the part of the community it reached. But there is more to these cases. It is not the book that is on trial; it is a person. The conduct of the defendant is the central issue, not the obscenity of a book or picture.[75]

In Ginzburg's case, there was plenty about his conduct to find, if not exactly repellent, at least tawdry. He had been convicted of violating federal law by selling three publications through the mail: *Eros,* a coffee-table-style magazine with a hard cover and relatively mild sexual pictures and articles; *Liaison,* a cheap newsletter on sex replete with dirty jokes and poems; and *The Housewife's Handbook on Selective Promiscuity,* which Brennan described as a book that "purports to be a sexual autobiography detailing with complete candor the author's sexual experiences from

age 3 to age 36."[76] To hawk his publications, Ginzburg turned to cheap stunts, trying to get mailing privileges in Intercourse and Blue Ball, Pennsylvania, before settling on Middlesex, New Jersey. The Court was offended, and Brennan's opinion,
joined by Warren, chastised Ginzburg for maintaining "the leer of the sensualist."

Leering is not unconstitutional, and sleaziness is not against the law. Neither of
those facts dissuaded Warren, who joined the majority opinion that upheld
Ginzburg's conviction and five-year prison sentence. Ziffren, Warren's clerk, tried
to turn his boss away from that conclusion but could not. "This filthy piece of
garbage," Warren said of one of the many publications that littered the Court that
term. "If my daughters saw this . . ."[77]

*Ginzburg* was one of three obscenity decisions decided on that same March day
in 1966, and the decisions in the three cases came after elaborate negotiations
among the justices. In the end, the Court upheld Ginzburg's conviction, while overturning one that found the eighteenth-century novel *Memoirs of a Woman of Pleasure* was obscene,[78] and upholding a conviction in a third case in which a New York
man was found guilty of selling fifty books that "portray[ed] sexuality in many
guises."[79] As such, the trilogy expressed Warren's view of how to control obscenity:
punish purveyors but don't ban books. But between them, the cases attracted fourteen separate opinions by the justices, evidence of their inability to settle on a standard
and of Warren's incapacity to bring along his colleagues in his too-clever-by-half approach. For Black, his bedrock commitment to the First Amendment made the cases
far simpler, and his dissent in *Ginzburg* had all the clarity and persuasiveness that
the work of Brennan, speaking for Warren, lacked:

> My conclusion is that certainly after the fourteen separate opinions handed down in
> these three cases today no person, not even the most learned judge much less a layman,
> is capable of knowing in advance of an ultimate decision in his particular case by this
> Court whether certain material comes within the area of "obscenity" as that term is con-
> fused by the Court today.[80]

The Court's ruling in Ginzburg was excoriated—Alexander Bickel, never a
friend of the Warren Court, called it "an unforgivable injustice. . . . The law is
shamed."[81] Anthony Lewis at the *New York Times,* a fair-minded and incisive observer of the Warren Court, also wrote critically. Warren did not care. When
lawyers for Ginzburg asked for rehearing, they were joined by eminent legal scholars and notables, among them Whitney North Seymour, then the head of the
American Bar Association, from which Warren had bitterly resigned in the late
1950s. In Warren's office one Monday morning, the chief justice was dictating to
the Court clerk the justices' dispositions of various motions. When he reached the
petition for rehearing in the *Ginzburg* case, he paused, and Ziffren interjected. That

motion, he reminded Warren, was signed by a number of important legal figures, including Seymour. Warren flushed. "That son-of-a-bitch, Whitney North Seymour," he growled. "Where was he when we were being attacked after *Brown*?" After an awkward silence, Warren added, "That petition is denied."[82]

Neither Warren's Court nor his country would ever quite adopt his view of obscenity—that its control was a predicate of a decent liberal society. Indeed, from today's perspective, it can seem quaint or stodgy. But it is a reminder that for all the conservative opprobrium heaped upon Warren, he was in fact personally conservative. Though he failed, he tried long after most had given up to strike a social balance that would allow speech but restrain smut. He never stopped lobbying. In 1969, after leaving the Court, he continued to grouse about pornography to journalist Morrie Landsberg. "[S]ome of the things that are sent to my home are just unspeakable," Warren said.[83]

Warren's ambivalence about free expression in the area of obscenity extended to more traditional speech as well, though not with the same ferocity. He was wary of an aggressive, fault-prone press, and no case better illustrated his strong feelings there than one that was argued in 1966 but held over to 1967. Not only would it offer a template for Warren's concerns about an aggressive press; it also would reunite him in the fourth act of his enduring rivalry with Richard Nixon.

After their tense disagreements in the 1940s and 1950s, Warren savored Nixon's close loss to John Kennedy in 1960 and, even more satisfyingly, his humiliating defeat in 1962 at the hands of Pat Brown, the race that ended with Nixon's snarling promise to the press that it would not have "Nixon to kick around anymore." Flushed out of politics, Nixon had returned to private legal practice, hoping time would help to resurrect him politically. By 1966, four years had passed since his self-proclaimed "final press conference," and Nixon was confident enough that he had begun laying plans for another presidential run in 1968. The oral argument before the Supreme Court thus offered an appealing stage to launch his return to public prominence, but it did so in the chambers of his old, unforgiving rival.[84]

Nixon came to Court to argue the case of James and Elizabeth Hill, whose suburban Philadelphia home was invaded on September 9, 1952, by three armed escaped convicts. Along with their three daughters, the Hills were held for nineteen hours before the convicts left them, unharmed though deeply shaken. The convicts fled to New York, where a shoot-out left two of them dead. The terrifying sequence of events drew widespread publicity, and the Hills were briefly thrust to national attention, against their will. Once the incident had died down, they moved from Philadelphia to Connecticut and refused all interviews about it. Life gradually returned to normal in their new home, far from the memories of the old.

That was upended by the February 28, 1955, issue of *Life* magazine, which contained a six-photograph spread highlighting a new play, then onstage in Philadelphia.

Titled *The Desperate Hours,* it told the story of a hostage drama that bore passing resemblance to the experience of the Hill family. For its pictorial spread, *Life* took members of the cast of the play to the Hills' old Philadelphia home and posed them to suggest that the events in the play—specifically, acts of violence by the hostage takers against the family, the father beating his son, the wounding of a boyfriend—had in fact occurred. They had not. "*Life* magazine lied," was Nixon's blunt characterization. "And ... *Life* magazine knew that it lied."[85] The Hills felt doubly wounded—by the exposure of a case they had tried to put behind them and by the falsification of the details of that story to make it seem more violent than it had been.

The Hills sued *Life* magazine under a 1903 New York privacy law that that state's courts had interpreted to offer a way to punish "the press and other communications media which publish the names, pictures, or portraits of people without their consent."[86] The New York courts ruled in favor of the Hills, who were awarded $50,000 in compensatory judgments as well as $25,000 in punitive damages. Time, Inc., owners of *Life,* appealed, and though the verdict was upheld, the appellate court ordered a review of the damages. They were lowered to $30,000, but Time, Inc. continued its appeals, bringing the case to the United States Supreme Court in 1966, eleven years after the original suit was filed.

On April 27, 1966, Nixon arrived in Warren's Court for his return to the national stage. Staring up at his old rival, reflecting on the indignities each had served on the other over the years, Nixon had to blanch at how thoroughly Warren once again controlled his destiny. But this time proved different: Warren's comments from the bench that day clearly signaled his sympathy with Nixon. As Nixon reflected on the session afterward, he told his friend and cocounsel Leonard Garment that he suspected Warren, like he, understood well the lash of an irresponsible press. "[F]or private persons," Garment wrote years later, "unwanted and false public exposure could be, in Nixon's words, 'as traumatic as a physical blow.'"[87]

In conference, Warren led what appeared to be a solid, six-member majority inclined to uphold the New York court judgment against *Life* magazine.[88] He assigned the case to Fortas, trusting that Fortas's skepticism of bad journalism would lead him to write similarly to Warren's views. His initial draft opinion succeeded in that, but with unintended consequences. "Needless, heedless wanton and deliberate injury of the sort inflicted by *Life*'s picture story is not an essential instrument of responsible journalism," the opinion noted in one typically vitriolic passage.[89] (Reading that, Warren drew a line along the side of the passage.) Confronted with Fortas's invective, the opinion became a dividing one for the Court, not a uniting one. Members of the majority began to slip away, encouraged especially by Black, who unloaded on Fortas's work.

Precisely when Hugo Black lost his patience with Abe Fortas is not clear. In 1963, Fortas had argued *Gideon,* which had given Black one of his greatest opinions. And when Fortas was named to the Court in 1965, Black lobbied Fortas to take the job. Black's wife, Elizabeth, welcomed "the tremendous news" of Fortas's appointment and exclaimed, "We are all glad!"[90] But Fortas rankled his fellow justices with his open ties to the White House—he had a red light on the phone in his chambers that came on whenever he was speaking with Lyndon Johnson—and Black by the mid-1960s had begun his slide away from the Warren Court's majority, a majority that Fortas was happy to join.

Whatever the reason or moment, others at the Court began to pick up friction in their relationship soon after Fortas arrived. By the beginning of 1966, still in Fortas's first term, he and Black were edgy with each other. One early clash was over a difficult breach-of-the-peace case out of Louisiana, where Fortas wrote for himself, Warren, Brennan, Douglas, and White to overturn the convictions of five black men who refused to leave a segregated library in the parish of Clinton.[91] Fortas's opinion drew a dissent—a "high-pitched" one, in the words of Brennan's clerks. "Certain statements in that dissent, such as those accusing the majority of being distrustful of the ways of the Deep South, apparently distressed Justice Fortas, and they did not soothe an already strained personal relationship between Justices Black and Fortas."[92] In the aftermath of the case, Black stayed mad at the impudence he saw in Fortas; Fortas seethed over what he believed to be Black's dismissive and mean-spirited treatment. Their breach widened steadily over time.

So when Fortas circulated his opinion in *Time, Inc. v. Hill,* there were at least two reasons to suspect that he would have trouble with Black. For one thing, Fortas was proposing to clip the range of constitutionally protected speech. For another, Black did not like him, and by then, Fortas knew it. Thus, Black's dissent was not a surprise, but its vehemence was, as was its effect on the Warren-Fortas majority. It collapsed. Fortas had structured his opinion around the Court's still-evolving theory of privacy. His mentor, Douglas, was the architect of that idea, but in *Griswold,* Douglas had invoked privacy as a shield against government action, a position derived from but consistent with the structure and purpose of the Bill of Rights. In *Time, Inc.,* Fortas proposed to define privacy as a broader right to be left alone, and said the Hills' right of privacy was violated not by the government, as it was in *Griswold,* but by a private news organization, which invaded their privacy when it reported falsely about them. "The opinion," Brennan's clerks recalled with obvious horror, "never once mentioned a First Amendment standard."[93]

Black demolished that reasoning. He already had vented on Douglas over the right of privacy; he certainly was not going to accept its extension into an area he saw as sacrosanct, the right of free speech. With the end of the term approaching, Fortas was at sea. In a memo to the brethren, he admitted that he had been forced to rewrite the entire draft, and expressed regret at the burden he was placing on the rest of them.[94] The case was put over and reargued, but Black continued to cast derision on his colleague's "balancing test." That fall, as the conference met to discuss Nixon's reargument, the justices went around the table and saw just how much damage Fortas had done to his own position. Where the vote last time had been 6–3 to affirm the damages for the Hills, this time it was 7–2 against. Only Warren stood by Fortas (Clark eventually would join them), stern believers in the idea that privacy violated by the press was no less hurtful than privacy violated by the government.

The outcome was deep in irony. Lyndon Johnson's close adviser and Richard Nixon's old rival had come to Nixon's aid and cast their votes with him. The case's central dispute was not between Warren and Nixon, whose long-running animus made that seem likely, but rather between Black and Fortas, two men of similar upbringings whose temperaments by then had made them adversaries. Leonard Garment reflected on it decades later, with Nixon and Warren long gone from office. He credited Warren, Fortas, and Harlan, who wrote a concurrence, with seeing "the case as one of nontechnical justice—two ordinary American parents touched by near-tragedy and trying to shield themselves and their five young children from the cheapening effects of unwanted and distorted publicity."[95] Rarely has Warren been so well described. He was, as Garment intuited, always in search of "nontechnical justice," always touched by the real lives of those whose conflicts brought them to his Court, the real struggles of parents, the real consequences of law; his strong intuition for people, honed in his years of politics, allowed Warren to appreciate the underlying human consequences of the Hills' struggle against *Life* magazine, and it even permitted him to overcome his bias against Nixon. The Court handed down its decision in *Time, Inc. v. Hill* on January 9, 1967. Four and a half years later, Mrs. Hill committed suicide.[96]


THE WARREN FAMILY had always been healthy. Honey Bear's polio was staggering, but her recovery was complete. And though the Warren children had had their scrapes—Jim broke an arm playing football, there were minor car crashes now and again—the children and grandchildren had been largely charmed. It was thus especially crushing to discover in the early 1960s that Dorothy suffered from multiple sclerosis. It was only part of a sad turn in Dorothy's life, as her marriage to a professor at UCLA also was failing. Married in 1956, the two divorced in the 1960s, and Dorothy suddenly felt far from home. She came to live with her parents and recover from her dual disappointments. In those years, Dorothy often substituted for her mother at occasions when Warren was expected to be accompanied by a woman, and Dorothy cut her usual swath through Washington society despite her illness. After recovering her footing from her divorce, she found a place not far from her parents and stayed in Washington through the mid-1960s, until she met architect

Harry Knight, whom she would marry on November 27, 1968. The two then moved to Maryland.

In the meantime, Earl Warren lost the last living member of his childhood family. It was the summer of 1966, and his older sister Ethel was in the final stages of a hard life. Her husband had dropped dead on the golf course as a young man, and her daughter had died of tuberculosis. When Ethel Plank died on June 17, 1966, only her son, Bud, survived her. Her brother, so many years removed from the Bakersfield where they had grown up, had been a good sibling to her. In her waning years, Ethel battled cancer and had trouble making ends meet, as her husband had died so young. Earl supplemented her income by sending her $500 a month. He marked her passing with quiet solemnity. "She went peacefully and without prolonged suffering," he told Douglas when the latter expressed his sympathies. "For that at least we are grateful."[97]

TIME, INC. represented a failure by Warren, at least in his terms. He could not persuade the Court to follow him then or in many of his other attempts to draw a free-expression standard subject to his views of restraint. Elsewhere, he was more attuned to his colleagues and a more confident leader of the Court. Nowhere was that more true than in the area of race, and the 1966 term gave him a chance to right one of the Court's wrongs of his tenure. A decade had passed since the Court turned its back on the Naims when the state of Virginia annulled their interracial marriage and the Court had been afraid to take the issue up in the midst of school desegregation. The issue returned in 1967 in the poetically captioned case of *Loving v. Virginia*. Richard Loving, a white man, married Mildred Jeter, a black woman, in the District of Columbia in 1958. When they returned home to Virginia, they were indicted for miscegenation and sentenced to a year in prison; the judge agreed to suspend their sentence if they would leave the state for twenty-five years. They did, and settled again in Washington, D.C., but in 1963 they sued to overturn their convictions.[98]

In 1956, the Court had been unwilling to invalidate Virginia's ban on interracial marriage. In 1967, it was ready. Just two months after the case was argued, Warren delivered a unanimous Court for the Lovings and struck similar laws in sixteen states. "Under our Constitution," Warren wrote, "the freedom to marry, or not marry, a person of another race resides with the individual and cannot be infringed by the State."[99] Fortas, who occasionally displayed a light touch, treated the matter whimsically, penning a poem:

For a Negro to marry a White
Results in serious Blight.

So argues the state of Virginia

But science is all agin' ya.[100]


WARREN WOULD never admire Johnson the way he had Kennedy—Johnson was too crude for Warren's tastes.[101] But Johnson flattered Warren in the way he did so many older men, and Warren was not immune—either to the presidency or the president. In early 1964, with the Kennedy assassination still fresh and the nation desperate to rally behind Johnson, Warren wrote to LBJ to praise him on his first State of the Union address, which Warren called "magnificent in every respect." "Your great challenge comes under the most tragic circumstances that one could imagine," Warren wrote. "I thank God you were prepared for it."[102] Johnson promptly replied, and his note set the tone for their friendship. "I would so like to be worthy of your guidance and your friendship which I have had through the years," the new president wrote. "I will try very hard."[103]

For Johnson, trying hard often meant the brazen use of flattery. When Warren turned seventy-five in March 1966, Johnson used the occasion to lavish gifts and attention on the chief justice. First was a surprise visit to the Warren apartment on March 19, Warren's birthday. The Warrens were preparing to leave for dinner when the White House operator called to say that Johnson was on his way over. Johnson was weighted down with presents—flowers for Nina had arrived before him, and he came bearing the Oxford History of the American People, a bottle of thirty-year-old scotch, and, of course, pictures of himself and his family. One photo was inscribed to Warren, "the greatest Chief Justice of them all."[104] Seeing that the family was preparing to leave for dinner, Johnson teasingly complained about having not been invited, then hosted a celebration of his own for the Warren family at the White House four days later.[105] Warren was so taken aback by the attention that, in his thank-you note to the president, he dropped his normal care to avoid explicitly political remarks in writing. Warren thanked Johnson for the gifts and said he was saving the scotch for "election night of 1968, when I will drink it to your health and continued success."[106]

Contact between a president and a justice can be complicated—as Johnson was soon to discover, tragically, in his relationship with Abe Fortas. With Johnson, Warren was friendly but guarded, and sometimes the two communicated through intermediaries, either Fortas or their mutual friend Drew Pearson. In early 1966, Pearson returned from two weeks in Barbados with Warren and reported to the president on their conversations. Knowing of Johnson's manic insistence on loyalty, Pearson began by assuring the president that he had a friend in Warren: "You probably know that he is a booster of yours, but I'm sure you do not know how sincere and vigorous he is in supporting you regarding Vietnam and almost everything else, with the exception of your enforcement of the antitrust laws."[107] Pearson then went on to suggest three ways that Johnson might win Warren's favor: White House dinners for the Court should be reinitiated, rather than lumping those gatherings with larger dinners for the federal judiciary; Warren's place on the White House protocol, downgraded to below the speaker of the House during the Kennedy administration (and, Warren believed, at Johnson's suggestion), should be restored; and the justices should be given their overdue pay raise, scuttled when a petulant Congress could find no other way to retaliate for the voting rights decision in *Reynolds v. Sims*. Johnson's reply was typical: He denied having anything to do with downgrading Warren's protocol status, but he pledged to seek a pay raise and to hold more dinners for the Court. Johnson wanted Warren's friendship, and if it could be bought at so low a price, he certainly would pay it.

That summer brought still another chance for Johnson to solicit Warren's appreciation. The two men chatted one night early that summer, and Warren happened to mention that he was leaving soon for Heidelberg, where he was scheduled to deliver a commencement address. Johnson asked how he was traveling, and Warren replied that he was flying commercially. Johnson insisted that would not do, and he arranged for Warren to have the use of *Air Force One*. Warren at first protested but then warmed to the idea. He invited Brennan and Black to join him, as well as his clerks. The entire entourage made the trip.[108]

By the mid-1960s, Warren had to work harder to stay healthy. He recovered from his depletion during the Warren Commission months, but remained more fragile than usual. Now in his seventies, he fought with his weight, and his regular checkups at Walter Reed, where he received free medical care, became more frequent and exhaustive. There were also occasional scares. During his annual Christmas trip to San Francisco at the end of 1964, Warren experienced chest pains. He consulted with an Army doctor, and upon returning home in January, he underwent further tests at Walter Reed Army hospital. Walter Reed may have been free, but it also reported to a commander in chief, and it was not long before Johnson knew of Warren's troubled heart.[109] The pains passed, but Warren redoubled his health regimen, trying to swim as often as possible. That was easy during the warm parts of the Washington year, but harder in the winter, when cold closed outdoor pools and indoor ones used more chlorine than Warren was comfortable with. He griped about the problem to Pearson, who again passed along the information to Johnson.

"Our kind and mutual friend," Johnson wrote to Warren, "has written me of your difficulties in finding a pool fit for winter dips. By coincidence, I happen to have one—warm, wet and absolutely snoop proof." Johnson, clearly enjoying himself, added, "Bring your suit the first time and leave it on the peg. I will try to float free and join you from time to time."[110] Warren did not take up Johnson's offer of a running pool date, but did accept one swim, in December 1967. Johnson, as promised, "floated free," and joined the chief justice and Fortas for a dip in the White House pool.[111]

Johnson's personal overtures could sometimes be awkward—Warren simply did not know what to do with some of the gifts that Johnson gave him. Once, when Johnson presented him with a bust of himself, Warren turned it over to Nina, who confessed that she later stashed it in a closet. But their professional relationship was solid and strengthened by the quality of Johnson's appointments to the Court. In the summer of 1967, Johnson, who had given himself his first appointment by pushing out Goldberg, now secured a second vacancy by promoting Ramsey Clark to attorney general. Tom Clark, Ramsey's father, saw that it would be inappropriate for him to remain on the Court that would review so much of his son's work. And so, unwilling to stand in the way of his own son, Clark retired. Warren was sad to see Clark go. Despite their differences, they had always been friendly.[112]

But Johnson's next move pleased Warren no end. At 11:45 A.M. on June 13, 1967, after a morning of meetings and a graduation ceremony for the Capitol pages, Johnson rejoined the guests in his office, including the nation's solicitor general, Thurgood Marshall. Kennedy had put Marshall on the bench, and Johnson had convinced him to leave it to become the first African-American ever to serve as the government's top lawyer. Now Johnson had another job for Marshall. "I believe it is the right thing to do, the right time to do it, the right man and the right place," Johnson announced to the White House press corps that noon in the Rose Garden.[113] He did not mention that Marshall would become the nation's first black member of the United States Supreme Court. He did not need to.

For years, Warren had sat across the bench from Marshall, favoring his causes during the NAACP years and usually backing him during his time as the government's lawyer as well. Warren did not always have high regard for Marshall as solicitor general, but those reservations had not diminished his admiration for the lawyer's work on behalf of desegregation.[114] Now Marshall's appointment offered the chance for two men who had traveled so many of the same roads to travel them together for the first time. It was, Warren told the president, "an excellent appointment. Few men come to the court with better experience."[115] The Senate was less enthusiastic. It took all summer to overcome Southern resistance to the appointment of a black associate justice, but eventually Marshall got his vote. He joined the Warren Court that fall.

Marshall trod over racial barriers with nonchalance, but there is no overstating how dramatic his arrival at the Court was. Every one of Marshall's predecessors on the bench was a white man. When Hugo and Elizabeth Black hosted Marshall and his wife Cissy that fall for dinner along with the Warrens and Douglas, the Marshalls were the first blacks whom Elizabeth had ever entertained in her home.[116] Marshall accepted his singularity with rough, easy humor—his wry delight at the periodic showings of dirty movies for the Court to consider, his happy consumption of Jack Daniel's, his bemused earthiness exaggerated against the backdrop of the staid Court.[117] The bond with the chief was immediate. "He's just one of the greatest people who ever lived," Marshall said of his new colleague.[118] Warren and Marshall had adjoining chambers, and the Court's senior justice made it a practice to drop in on its newest member. Marshall recognized that he was far junior to the chief and tried to dissuade Warren from dropping by. It felt too informal, even for Marshall, who proposed that Warren have his secretary call over to Marshall's chambers to summon him to meetings. But Warren would hear none of it. "I don't operate that way," he said.[119] Marshall quickly fell into Warren's column, so closely associating himself with the voting of the chief justice that clerks called him "Brennan-Chief."[120]

Marshall's arrival lightened the Court and contributed to its happy relations. Its civility, however, masked troubling portents. Warren, Douglas, and Black all were aging. Douglas had a pacemaker. As the Court's 1967 term drew toward its conclusion in the summer of 1968, Elizabeth Black feared that all three might soon leave, ending in one dash their historic collaboration.[121] Outside, the nation was rumbling with rising crime and the Vietnam War, whose ramifications were rapidly overtaking the Johnson administration's domestic agenda.

Vietnam had become Johnson's singular preoccupation—it was the "center of our concerns," he announced during his 1966 State of the Union address.[122] Over the next year, public support for the conflict wobbled, then plummeted as America's entanglement deepened in lives as well as treasure. A July 1967 Gallup poll found that only one third of Americans believed that the nation was making progress in fighting the war. More than half disapproved of Johnson's handling of it, the worst rating he had yet received on the war.[123] By the end of 1967, an increase of 100,000 American soldiers in Vietnam brought the overall American presence to nearly half a million; nearly 20,000 had died on Vietnam's battlefields—and 1968 would produce more American casualties than any other year of the war—lives lost in a struggle that many Americans, perhaps even most, did not understand.[124]

Warren was not among those who had lost faith. A patriot, he was as convinced in 1967 as he was in 1925 that Communism was cruel and dangerous. He did not, to be sure, accept that legislative hunts were the way to protect America, but he readily believed that American interests abroad were real and worth defending against ideological enemies. Moreover, Warren had confidence in Johnson: "He's working hard on Viet Nam and has been for a long time, and he knows the answers for it," Warren told Pearson in 1966. "He will find some way out."[125]

As that year ground on and with it the war, Warren had hoped for a peace to be struck in the fall, in time to influence that year's national elections. Such a victory, Warren told Pearson, "would be wonderful."[126] When that did not occur, when the casualties continued to mount and the stakes for the Johnson administration rose, Warren, along with many other supporters of the war, began to lose patience with those who protested against it. Twelve years earlier, Warren had expressed his concern for the rights of protest in wartime—"Periods of domestic dissension and of foreign war are especially liable to produce tendencies to disregard established rights in the name of national safety," he warned in 1955.[127] But by the fall of 1967, his tolerance for dissent against the war was exhausted. He vented his frustration on a young man named David Paul O'Brien.

O'Brien, then nineteen years old, had mounted the steps of the South Boston courthouse with three companions—David Reed, David Benson, and John Phillips—on a March day in 1966.[128] They burned their draft cards in front of a crowd. FBI agents were among those who watched, and when the crowd turned on the protesters, the agents pulled them inside. Once there, they were informed of their rights, and O'Brien admitted burning his card as a protest. He handed an FBI agent an envelope containing the charred remains of his card. The agent took four pictures of the burned card as evidence.[129]

O'Brien was charged with violating an amendment to the Universal Military Training and Service Act of 1948, an amendment that was passed in 1965 with little discussion by a nearly unanimous Congress, whose members were infuriated by the outbreak of draft-card burning as a form of protest. Tried in federal court, O'Brien was convicted and sentenced to an extraordinary six years in prison. His conviction was overturned on appeal, where the circuit court ruled that the amendment unconstitutionally abridged O'Brien's right of free speech, though it also, in what the solicitor general would later describe as an act of "Yankee ingenuity," held that O'Brien was guilty of failing to keep the card in his possession as required by the same law.[130] Both sides appealed, the government to urge upholding of the amendment, O'Brien to contest his conviction for a crime he had never been charged with committing.[131]

O'Brien's conviction put before the Court yet again the question of where speech left off and conduct began—and whether the Court was willing to defend forms of protest that went beyond words. Indeed, as a style of protest, O'Brien's act seemed hard to distinguish from that of the black students who sat down in a Louisiana library in order to protest its refusal to serve Negro patrons. Neither was an act of pure speech. In the case of the Negro demonstrators, their message had been communicated by sitting down; in O'Brien's, by striking the match to the two-by-three-inch piece of paper that the government required him to carry and forbade him to destroy. Warren's clerk Larry Simon warned him that to declare O'Brien's act something other than speech was problematic—"there are several cases in the books where this Court has held that 'conduct' is speech within the

First Amendment," he wrote, specifically citing the Louisiana library sit-in ruling, which Warren had joined. Like the Negro protesters, O'Brien was engaged in conduct "to express an idea."[132] All of that was true and well stated. What was clearly different, however, was the target of those protests: the Negro students aimed at segregation, and the Court shared their views; O'Brien and his colleagues were challenging the war, and the Court did not agree.

That is hardly the basis for a constitutional distinction, and Warren's style of judging—his reliance on his own instincts for society's well-being—failed him here as it had in his futile attempts to create a workable obscenity doctrine.

O'Brien's lawyer, Marvin Karpatkin, tried to emphasize to the Court the character of O'Brien's act—it was public and intended to convey a political message; as such, it deserved to be treated as speech. Warren was skeptical from the start. "Suppose a soldier over in Vietnam in front of a large crowd of soldiers, broke his weapon, and said it was a protest against the war and the foreign policy of the government," Warren asked. "Would that be symbolic speech?"

Karpatkin, who would go on to represent Muhammad Ali in his draft litigation several years later, conceded that he did not know the answer to Warren's hypothetical. Karpatkin acknowledged, however, that not all political action was speech; assassination, for one thing, clearly was not protected. Fortas then pressed the question, asking whether a person could object to the tax code by destroying tax records, and whether the government could prosecute such a person for failure to maintain such records. Karpatkin fell back on the argument that in order to regulate symbolic speech, the government must demonstrate a valid purpose. That was all Warren needed. As he wrote in the final opinion:

> We think it clear that a government regulation is sufficiently justified if it is within the constitutional power of the Government; if it furthers an important or substantial governmental interest; if the governmental interest is unrelated to the suppression of free expression; and if the incidental restriction on alleged First Amendment freedoms is no greater than is essential to the furtherance of that interest. We find that the 1965 Amendment to 12 (b) (3) of the Universal Military Training and Service Act meets all of these requirements, and consequently that O'Brien can be constitutionally convicted for violating it.[133]

In one sense, that approach was a vast improvement over Warren's initial tack—the exasperating attempt to distinguish between the "speech" and the "conduct" of draft-card burning. Instead, he and the Court substituted the idea that Congress may not regulate speech by virtue of its content—a principle that has outlived the specifics of *O'Brien* and continues to define speech regulation in contemporary America under the aptly named "O'Brien test." Whether that test was applied correctly to O'Brien himself is another matter, as the Court's determination to snuff out draft-card burning, a determination adamantly shared by Warren himself, seemed to overwhelm its cool application of its new principle. That was further illustrated by another aspect of the Court's opinion, one that entailed a bit of sophistry. Congress's purpose in passing the act itself was to raise and maintain an army, but its "purpose" in passing the amendment was to prohibit draft-card desecration, which barely, if at all, helped its job of defending the nation. The real purpose of the amendment was to punish those who protested the war. But rather than admit that, Warren pretended that the Court could not examine Congress's motives. Calling such an inquiry "hazardous," Warren wrote, "What motivates one legislator to make a speech about a statute is not necessarily what motivates scores of others to enact it, and the stakes are sufficiently high for us to eschew guesswork."[134] That had not stopped the Court before—Warren had been willing to examine the motives of the legislators who adopted the Fourteenth Amendment, and, more recently, the Court had overruled the gerrymandered city limits in Tuskegee, Alabama, because the legislature there had adopted them with the intent to "despoil colored citizens, and only colored citizens, of their theretofore enjoyed voting rights."[135] But now, confronted with a form of protest it deplored against a war it accepted, Warren led the Court to uphold O'Brien's conviction and reinstate his prison sentence.

Warren's opinion was unpopular among his clerks and those of the other justices, most of them draft-age men whose sympathies ran against the war. After *O'Brien* was announced, a group of women from Connecticut attempted to hold a "burn-in" on the Court steps but were rained out. "Perhaps," Brennan's clerks noted hopefully at the term's end, "*O'Brien* as a legal precedent will likewise be confined and fizzle."[136]

O'Brien got no sympathy from Warren, and he felt the sting of offending Warren's principles. By contrast, a Florida inmate named Bennie Brooks, convicted of participating in a 1965 prison riot, touched Warren's sense of injustice. And just as Warren could be hard in opposition, so could he be effective in support. There did not, at first, seem much that Warren could do in Brooks's case. Brooks was one of more than a dozen Florida inmates at Raiford State Prison who had been convicted of participating in the riot. His conviction added time to his sentence and was obtained partly on the basis of his confession, which he had given after spending two weeks in a disciplinary "hole." All the justices but Warren voted not to hear the case; it seemed to them a matter of internal prison discipline. Warren rarely dissented from such denials, but this time he was angered by the prison officials. His clerk Tyrone Brown wrote up a simple dissent, but Warren sent him back to work on it again. Brown, the only African-American to serve as a Warren clerk, added more detail on prison discipline in order to demonstrate why this was not an internal matter but rather one for the Court. Warren still was not satisfied, and called Brown in again.

"Let's tell them what really happened," Warren said. "Tell them that the authorities placed these men in threes in tiny sweat boxes for two weeks, naked on a starvation diet with just a hole in the floor to defecate in! Tell them that they brought these men out, still naked, and forced written confessions from them! Tell them that these confessions were used to convict these men of new crimes, that many years were added to the terms they already were serving. Tell them what really happened in plain language . . . and let posterity decide who was right."[137] Brown did as directed, and Warren closed his dissent with an angry sign-off: "The record in this case documents a shocking display of barbarism which should not escape the remedial action of this Court."[138]

Warren circulated his dissent on November 9, 1967. The following day, Fortas joined him. Over the next few weeks came identical changes of heart by White, Stewart, Black, Brennan, Marshall, Douglas, and, on December 13, Harlan. Warren's lone dissent was transformed into a unanimous, per curiam, opinion of the Supreme Court. Bennie Brooks's conviction was reversed. *Brooks v. Florida* will not stand shoulder to shoulder in history with *Brown v. Board of Education* or *Baker v. Carr* or *Miranda,* but as insight into Warren it is just as profound—Bennie Brooks got justice from the United States Supreme Court because Warren was practical and professional, stubborn on principle, and committed to fairness, no matter how small the case.

Irritation with antiwar protest caused Warren to retreat from protecting symbolic speech in *O'Brien.* Similarly, the nation's rising crime troubles edged Warren and the Court away from its protection of criminal suspects. Urban riots had become an annual summer feature of American life by the mid-1960s, and crime was alarmingly on the rise. Johnson himself proposed the Omnibus Crime Control and Safe Streets Act in 1967, and though it failed that year, he came back at it in 1968, doubling the appropriation and declaring in his 1968 State of the Union Address that there was "no more urgent business before this Congress" than passage of the bill intended to spend $100 million of federal money fighting urban crime.[139] National alarm about crime metastasized in some quarters into anger at the Warren Court, where judicial rulings such as *Miranda* caused critics of the Court to blame it for coddling criminals.

The case of *Terry v. Ohio,* argued just a month before Johnson's 1968 State of the Union Address, allowed the Court to clarify how far it intended to go in proscribing police action.[140] The arc of cases from *Gideon* through *Miranda* suggested that the Court was intent on holding back police and prosecutorial advantage, but those cases generally arose in safer times. Now the Court took stock of the changing criminal landscape and reaffirmed the validity of police "hunches" in the maintenance of a safe society.

The case began on the streets of Cleveland on the afternoon of Halloween in 1963. Detective Martin McFadden of the Cleveland police department was at work that afternoon when he spotted John Terry and Richard Chilton, two black men, standing on a corner in a neighborhood known for pickpockets and thieves. McFadden was a veteran police officer, with thirty years' experience and knowledge of the neighborhood in downtown Cleveland. He couldn't say precisely what bothered him about Terry and Chilton, except to say that "they didn't look right to me at the time." As he watched from a few hundred feet away, the two men paced along a sidewalk, gazed into store windows, and then conferred with each other. They repeated this several times, and McFadden, by now very suspicious, concluded that they were casing the stores, planning a robbery.[141] The detective approached the two men. He asked their names, and when they "mumbled" a reply, he spun Terry around and patted down the outside of his clothing. McFadden found a gun and then found one on Chilton as well. They were arrested, charged with carrying concealed weapons, convicted, and sentenced to prison. Their convictions were upheld on appeal, and the Court then accepted their case for review.

At their December 13, 1967, conference, Brennan suggested that the case depended on a finding of probable cause—"probable cause to investigate suspicious behavior and ask the person to give an account of himself, and probable cause to believe that a suspect might be armed and dangerous." The other justices agreed and unanimously voted to uphold Terry's conviction (Chilton, though also convicted, had died before the case reached the Supreme Court), though Warren warned that he believed that unless the police had sufficient cause to arrest the suspect, the suspect could simply walk away without answering the officer.[142] Since Brennan had first articulated the "probable cause" approach, he expected to be given the opinion; Warren instead took it himself, disappointing his colleague. Warren's first attempts illuminated how affected he was by the charge that the rise in crime was somehow his fault or that of his Court. The first draft was "almost embarrassingly sympathetic to the plight of the policeman."[143] The second was much better. "The opinion," Brennan's clerks wrote, "read dangerously much like an apology for past decisions which have been charged with having overly restricted the police."[144] In a memo to Warren, Brennan gently suggested that the opinion would be read against the "alarums being sounded in this election year in the Congress, the White House and every Governor's office." Given that, Brennan implored Warren to modulate his tone and not appear to give too much license to police. "It will not take much of this [increased police aggressiveness] to aggravate the already white heat resentment of ghetto Negroes against the police—and this Court will become the scapegoat."[145]

With his memo and private meetings, Brennan went to work on Warren, trying to tone down the apologia and straighten out the logical flaws that flowed from Warren's attempt to back away stylistically from *Miranda* without substantively undermining it. All of that was time-consuming, and deliberations among the justices over *Terry* continued through the spring.

Then came the cataclysmic series of events of 1968. The first erupted in a faraway jungle at the end of January, when 70,000 Communist troops launched simultaneous attacks on more than a hundred South Vietnamese cities, including the capital, Saigon. The Tet offensive was repelled, and the enemy suffered heavy casualties, but the breadth of the assault showed that the North Vietnamese were far from folding. Johnson teetered toward exhaustion as he paced the White House halls at night awaiting updates from the combat theater. Meeting privately with his old friend Richard Russell, Johnson broke down in tears.[146] Anguished by the war and stunned by Eugene McCarthy's surprisingly strong showing in the New Hampshire primary, Johnson on March 31 astonished the nation and even his own advisers by concluding a speech on Vietnam with a self-inflicted end to his life in politics. "I shall not seek, and I will not accept, the nomination of my party for another term as your President," Johnson announced that night.

Hugo and Elizabeth Black opposed the war, but applauded the president's speech. It would, Hugo said, "make LBJ a hero."[147] Warren, then still a supporter of the Vietnam War, was moved as well. "Your burden has been great but your reward will be greater," Warren wrote to the president whose reelection the chief justice had hoped for.[148] Johnson worked hard on his reply, uncharacteristically fiddling with several drafts. In the words he finally settled on, the president called Warren "the kindest as well as the wisest man I have ever known. Your recent letter," Johnson added, "confirms my judgment and adds to my great debt of the heart."[149]

Barely had the nation absorbed Johnson's news before it was confronted with another, far more tragic loss. Martin Luther King had come to Memphis, Tennessee, in the spring of 1968 to support that city's sanitation workers in their tense negotiations with City Hall over union representation and over efforts to settle a strike begun in February. King led a march on March 28, but it degenerated into violence and police reprisal before the National Guard was called out to restore order. On April 3, King returned to Memphis and appeared before the group supporting the sanitation workers. Near the end of his speech that night, King reflected on the threats made against his life by "some of our sick white brothers." "Well, I don't know what will happen now. We've got some difficult days ahead," he conceded. But, he added in strong and melodic voice,

> It really doesn't matter with me now because I've been to the mountaintop. And I don't mind. Like anybody, I would like to live a long life—longevity has its place. But I'm not

concerned about that now. I just want to do God's will. And He's allowed me to go up to the mountain. And I've looked over, and I've seen the Promised Land. I may not get there with you. But I want you to know tonight that we, as a people, will get to the Promised Land. And I'm so happy tonight; I'm not worried about anything; I'm not fearing any man. Mine eyes have seen the glory of the coming of the Lord.[150]

The following day, King was dead. America's cities exploded. "All hell has broken loose in Washington," Elizabeth Black wrote in her diary. "Phones are jammed and it is incredible that the Nation's Capital is in the hands of lawless mobs."[151]

Johnson dispatched federal authorities to Memphis to search for the assassin—James Earl Ray would elude police for weeks. In Washington, the president summoned advisers and surrounded himself with icons of the struggle for civil rights. Fortas, who had argued *Gideon,* was there. Marshall, who had argued *Brown,* was there. And of course, Warren, who had led the Court in those and so many other cases advancing the cause of American blacks, was there as well. Marshall and Warren accompanied Johnson to a memorial service for King even as large chunks of Washington were set afire. So edgy were those hours that Floyd McKissick, a leader of the Congress of Racial Equality, demanded to know the guest list before agreeing to attend a White House meeting with civil rights leaders, then, hiding in fear for his life, showed up at the White House gate "with two other Negroes." Told he could join the meeting but that his companions would have to wait, McKissick disappeared into the afternoon.[152]

The president's withdrawal from the 1968 campaign and King's assassination occurred within a single week. Just as the nation absorbed those events and the riots in April, it was struck again. Bobby Kennedy, Johnson's longtime nemesis, had entered the presidential campaign late but had come on strong. By June, he had momentum building toward a likely Democratic nomination for president and thus a Kennedy rematch of sorts with Nixon, who was making headway toward his party's nomination that spring as well. On June 4, California Democrats selected Kennedy as their candidate for president. At the Ambassador Hotel in Los Angeles, he accepted the victory just after midnight on June 5, then headed for the exit through the kitchen. There, Sirhan Sirhan, a twenty-four-year-old Arab immigrant infuriated by Kennedy's support for Israel, confronted him with a .22 pistol and fired it over and over into the senator's head and body. Surgeons at Los Angeles's Good Samaritan Hospital attempted to save him but could not. Kennedy, forty-two years old, died on June 6. His younger brother, Ted, eulogized him and put him in the ground that Saturday night, buried by candlelight near his brother the president.

It was against that backdrop and in the face of that violence that Warren put the final touches on *Terry v. Ohio*. The opinion reflected the strains on Warren. One cannot read it without being struck by its caveats, its revealing "howevers" and "on the other hands." In the end, it upheld the search and deferred to Detective McFadden's experience in order to allow him and other police officers to act to protect themselves and the public from harm, even if it meant patting down suspects based on little more than a hunch. As Lucas Powe notes, it is difficult to imagine Warren's writing such a decision only two or three years earlier. The same chief justice who had outraged police with *Miranda* handed them wide latitude and power with *Terry*. In light of the events of 1968, however, it is difficult to imagine such a practical, political man writing otherwise. Indeed, left to his own devices, Warren almost certainly would have gone further to defend the police. Brennan pulled him back, and only Douglas, who had commended Brennan for his influence on Warren's opinion, nonetheless dissented. With gravity and eloquence, Douglas warned the Court to ignore its critics and exclaimed his individualism:

> There have been powerful hydraulic pressures throughout our history that bear heavily on the Court to water down constitutional guarantees and give the police the upper hand. That hydraulic pressure has probably never been greater than it is today.
>
> Yet if the individual is no longer to be sovereign, if the police can pick him up whenever they do not like the cut of his jib, if they can "seize" and "search" him in their discretion, we enter a new regime. The decision to enter it should be made only after a full debate by the people of this country.[153]

*Terry v. Ohio* was handed down on June 10, 1968. The following morning, Warren made up his mind about a matter that he had been considering for some time. At the Court, Warren pulled Fortas aside and asked him to make a call for him; the chief justice said he needed to speak with the president. Fortas, with his direct line to the White House, agreed. Johnson asked Warren to come by the next day.[154]

As long as Bobby Kennedy was in the race, the Democrats had a chance to hold on to the White House—Bobby would never be Warren's favorite, but he promised continuity on racial justice and progress elsewhere. In April, with Bobby in the race, Black urged Warren to hang on; Warren gave no indication that he would leave.[155] But now Bobby Kennedy was dead, and the Democratic Party was in confusion. Nixon—always Nixon—was in line to win the Republican nomination and thus stood the real chance of becoming president. Warren was seventy-seven years old, and had battled occasional heart troubles. Though his health was fine again in mid-1968, he could not go on indefinitely. And the prospect of a Nixon presidency meant that he would have to hold on for at least four years—perhaps eight—if he were not to hand over his seat to his old enemy. The sand was running from the glass of the Johnson administration. Soon Congress would be gone for the summer and then the fall session would be overshadowed by the campaigns. Warren knew he needed to act quickly. That Thursday morning, Warren met privately with Johnson for twenty minutes, two aging men bound by the political imperatives of the moment. The time had come, Warren said, for him to retire as Chief Justice of the United States.

Chapter 24

# THE END

*I like to think that the spirit of Earl Warren is abroad in this land,*
*quickening the conscience of our people.*

WILLIAM O. DOUGLAS[1]

WARREN'S RETIREMENT from the United States Supreme Court took the form of two letters, both delivered to Johnson at their June meeting and then held by the president as he considered his response. The first consisted of a single sentence, in which Warren advised Johnson of "my intention to retire as Chief Justice of the United States effective at your pleasure."[2] The second was more expansive. It detailed Warren's reasons for leaving, or at least those reasons that he felt comfortable disclosing. He began by asserting that he was leaving at a time of his choosing. He was not sick, Warren stressed, nor was he unhappy in his job. "My associations on the Court," he wrote, "have been cordial and satisfying in every respect, and I have enjoyed each day of the fifteen years I have been here." The only issue, Warren insisted, was age, and it was "one that no man can combat. . . . I have been continually in the public service for more than fifty years. When I entered the public service, 150 million of our 200 million people were not yet born. I, therefore, conceive it to be my duty to give way to someone who will have more years ahead of him to cope with the problems which will come to the Court."[3]

Warren's letter was true as far as it went, but it stopped well short of candor. Warren had given no sign of wanting to leave so long as Lyndon Johnson or Robert Kennedy might be there to replace him in the coming term. Only when Johnson was out of the race and Kennedy was murdered did retirement seem so appealing. And only when Richard Nixon was the probable next president of the United States did Warren submit his retirement—even then agreeing to leave at the pleasure of the incumbent and thus implicitly threatening to stay if the Congress would not move quickly to appoint his successor. Warren would always deny that he timed his retirement to keep his vacancy out of Nixon's hands, but those close to him knew better. Drew Pearson, in a piece submitted to *Look* magazine, wrote that it was "unquestionably" the case that the timing was "strongly influenced by the fact that Nixon may win his campaign for the presidency." Pearson sent that story to Warren for his approval before publishing; at Warren's request, he withdrew it.[4]

At the Court, Warren's announcement was, naturally, a sobering and sad one. The chief justice took his clerks to lunch that Saturday, as was their custom, and broke the news to them at the University Club. "I felt that I was bearing witness to the end of an era, not only in the life of the Supreme Court, but in the life of the country as well," Tyrone Brown recalled.[5] The brethren took the news hard as well. Warren told Brennan he hoped the president would pick Brennan as the new chief justice, but neither Brennan nor Warren believed that would happen—Brennan was never especially close to Johnson.[6] Black, meanwhile, was concerned that Warren would cite his age as his reason for leaving, which would put pressure on Black to step down as well. When Warren's letter was released, confirming Black's fear, he slipped into a funk, laboring over his memoirs late into the night and interpreting Warren's letter and explanation of it as "a dig" at him.[7]

There was nothing improper about Warren's attempt to structure his own succession—or about Johnson's desire to fill a vacancy late in his final term of office. But Johnson's next moves were to nominate his close friend Abe Fortas to succeed Warren as chief justice and to tap a Texas judge, Homer Thornberry, to fill Fortas's vacancy. Together, those were provocative steps by a president whose influence was precipitously on the wane. Johnson was warned against trying to do too much—no less than Clark Clifford, the Washington counselor then serving as secretary of defense, advised the president to soften the political impact by looking for a moderate Republican to fill Fortas's seat[8]—but Johnson believed that no man knew the Senate better than he. Before putting forward the nominations, he secured the support of Richard Russell and Everett Dirksen and relied upon them to neutralize his most obvious opponents, Republicans and Southern Democrats. By the old rules, the rules Johnson had learned as a senator and practiced ever since, that was enough to ensure victory.

But Johnson's opponents were of a different generation and a different outlook. They were not content to let the leadership impose on the nation two lifetime appointments by a lame-duck president. Even before Warren's resignation was officially announced—but amid furious Washington rumors that it was imminent—Senator Robert Griffin of Michigan maneuvered to delay action in order to preserve the vacancies for Nixon's expected victory in the fall. Joined by other Senate Republicans and some Southern Democrats, Griffin made the most of the taint of cronyism. In that context, Warren's letter was not wrong because it used an improper device—linking the resignation to the confirmation of a successor—but rather because it reinforced the impression that he and Johnson were collaborating to deny the next president, presumably Nixon, his opportunity to affect the Court's makeup.

Warren's actions in the days after the announcement also suggested that politics was very much on his mind, no matter how much he sought to deny it. On July 5, after Johnson had accepted his resignation and announced the Fortas and Thornberry nominations, Warren hosted the rarest of Washington rarities, a press conference by a sitting justice of the Supreme Court. He appeared fine and fit—"robust in a dark suit, green tie and California tan," Fred Graham of the *New York Times* reported—and he invited reporters to question him in the justices' conference room.[9] He opened by noting that he would not take questions about Court business, but he broke his own rule and commented on his legacy as well as contemporary politics and culture. "We have swept under the rug a number of problems that are basic to American life," he said. "They have piled up. There must be great adjustment of some kind." Asked about his Court's legacy, Warren ranked its most important decisions, starting with *Baker v. Carr,* then *Brown,* then *Gideon.* Warren defended Johnson's right to nominate his successor and warned conservatives that if Fortas were not confirmed, he would return to his seat. At one point, Warren was asked to identify his most frustrating moments as chief justice. He paused, then smiled and confessed he could not think of one. "It has not been a frustrating experience."[10]

The content of the press conference aside, its mere occurrence emphasized Warren's willingness to engage in the politics of his judicial succession. Justices, even chief justices drawn from the world of politics, do not meet with reporters to discuss matters before the Congress.

Once the nominations were formally placed in the Senate, Fortas's opponents went to work. There, Fortas became the victim of the Senate's weariness with Johnson and of the public's mounting concern about crime and licentiousness, two trends pervasively though tenuously attached to the Warren Court. Those were heavy burdens to bear, but it is possible that Fortas could have succeeded had he not contributed so mightily to his own downfall by the egocentricity that drove him to act as Johnson's adviser while serving on the Court and by an abiding personal greed that made it hard for him to turn down money. The first attack on Fortas's nomination was the least convincing: Griffin and other critics of the appointment claimed that by making his retirement effective at the president's pleasure—and by Johnson's accepting his retirement upon the confirmation of his successor—Warren had not actually left and therefore no vacancy existed.

Johnson enlisted Warren Christopher, an incisive young lawyer in the Justice Department then in the early years of a momentous career, to take charge of the nomination. Christopher smoothly demonstrated the baselessness of the no-vacancy charge. In fact, there was a long tradition of judges and justices retiring effective at the president's pleasure, and thus both history and common sense supported the practice.[11]

Nevertheless, the vacancy argument served its purpose, which at that point was merely to stall for time. Weeks passed, and senators began to peel away from Fortas. Finally, in desperation, Fortas accepted the Senate Judiciary Committee's invitation to testify—the same invitation that Warren had declined in 1954 on the theory that a sitting justice should not be interrogated by members of a coequal branch of government. Fortas, however, was confident in his abilities, and his nomination was in trouble. He elected to appear.[12] On July 16, Fortas took his seat. Beginning that first day, he adopted a strategy that was to prove disastrous. Fortas attempted, with mixed success, to contain questions about the Court and to deflect inquiries about his relationship with Johnson. When pressed on those areas, particularly on topics regarding advice he had given Johnson, Fortas made his most fateful choice: He elected, under oath, to lie.[13]

Fortas denied that while sitting as a justice, he had proposed candidates for presidential appointments, a lie. He denied helping draft presidential statements, including one on riots in Detroit, another lie. Asked what role the Court should play in leading social change, he answered, "Zero, absolutely zero." That was a request for an opinion, but Laura Kalman notes that "in the context of Fortas's other answers, this one seemed symptomatic of his dishonesty."[14] Perhaps nowhere was Fortas more consistently mendacious than over the question of his participation in the inner councils of the Johnson administration's Vietnam War apparatus. The White House Daily Diary, unavailable to the Judiciary Committee, logged dozens of contacts between Johnson and Fortas, and showed many meetings where Fortas joined the president's war group, which included Clifford, Dean Rusk, Walt Rostow, and General Wheeler. Just six weeks before his July testimony, Fortas participated in Johnson's weekly Vietnam luncheon, part of his routine consultation on matters involving Johnson's management of the war.[15] Before the committee, Fortas insisted that he played no meaningful part in the formulation of war planning. That, too, was a lie.

For the moment, Fortas got away with some of his worst deceptions. The only ones who knew the full extent of them were unwilling to speak up. But other details of his testimony came under scrutiny—Fortas was forced to admit, for instance, that he had lobbied a friend and client to tone down his criticism of the war—and deepened suspicions about Fortas's truthfulness. Moreover, the hearings took time, and time decidedly was not on Fortas's side. Charges of cronyism shifted to attacks on the Warren Court, particularly its criminal justice and obscenity rulings. Fortas again tried to deflect, arguing that he could not answer specific questions about the Court's rulings without violating the separation of powers between the government branches. But Fortas was inconsistent—he answered enough questions to encourage senators to keep prying, then retreated when he realized he'd gone too far. The nadir was reached when Senator Strom Thurmond blamed Fortas for a decision that the Court had handed down in 1957, eight years before Fortas joined the Court. That case, *Mallory v. United States,* was an early exemplar of the Warren Court's criminal justice jurisprudence, and in it the Court overturned the conviction of a nineteen-year-old rapist because he had been detained and questioned for more than five hours, and subjected to a polygraph, without being told he had the right to refuse and without formal arraignment, where he would have received a lawyer. The rape occurred in the District of Columbia, so *Mallory* was uncomplicated by issues surrounding the Fourteenth Amendment, and Frankfurter wrote for the unanimous Court that overturned Mallory's conviction.[16] By any reasonable standard, *Mallory* was irrelevant to the Fortas confirmation: The facts were so clear that even the Court's conservatives joined the opinion, and Fortas had absolutely nothing to do with it. Thurmond was not playing by the rules, however. *"Mallory,"* the senator screeched at the shell-shocked Fortas, "I want that word to ring in your ears."[17]

Fortas spent four inglorious days on the witness stand. When he was dismissed, his nomination was in serious trouble. Congress adjourned for the summer without taking a vote, a sure sign that the president's supporters were not in control. And then, before it reconvened, Fortas's greed gave further fuel to his opponents. Fortas had been teaching a seminar at American University during the summer, and arrangements for his appearances there were made by his old law partners. What emerged during the break in his nomination proceedings was that Fortas was paid $15,000 for those lectures—a significant sum at a time when associate justices received only $39,000 a year—and that the money to pay him had been raised from clients of the old Fortas law firm. Fortas replied that he had not known the source of the money, but that charge added to the others and completed a picture of an unscrupulous man, willing to bend rules to suit his interests. By September, Fortas's great opportunity had turned to torment. When the president invited Fortas and his wife to dinner at the White House, Lady Bird thought they might refuse. "I wondered if they could stand to see us, the unwitting architects of all the agony they have been going through," she confided to her diary. "Lyndon's only thought—months ago when he nominated Abe to be Chief Justice—had been to find the best Chief Justice the country could provide and to accord Abe an honor he so magnificently deserves." One can question that, but not Lady Bird's concluding thought. "Well," she added, "it hasn't turned out that way."[18] The vote finally was called on October 1, and 45 senators voted to end debate. Though that was a majority of those voting—43 voted the other way—it was far short of the two-thirds needed to end the filibuster that had delayed a vote all summer. Fortas knew it was over. He asked Johnson to withdraw the nomination.

For Johnson, the vote was an excruciating defeat. In the end, Russell abandoned him (administration debate and foot-dragging by Attorney General Ramsey Clark over a judicial nominee favored by Russell had complicated the Fortas nomination, as Russell became convinced that Johnson was holding the other nomination hostage to force Russell's support for Fortas). Their friendship, one of the defining relationships in late-twentieth-century American politics, came to an abrupt and unhappy end. Everett Dirksen, as Johnson had warned, bailed out when the nomination threatened to expose his fading influence over his own party. The elders, the great masters of the Senate, had lost, their defeat evidence of a passing era. The principal victim, of course, was Fortas, though he had done much to bring about his own demise. Others suffered as well. Warren Christopher visited Johnson along with other administration deputies during those weeks, and was struck by how old and tired Johnson appeared. Rarely, Christopher said many years later, had he ever seen a man so depleted and still on his feet.[19] Thornberry returned home to Texas, denied even a vote by the politics, interests, and lies of others.

Warren was left in an embarrassing limbo. He had promised to retire at the pleasure of the president, but now it was no longer the president's pleasure that he leave. And yet he could, by his own terms, hardly stay: Warren had blamed his advancing age for his decision, and he was only getting older. On October 7, Warren gaveled a new term of the Supreme Court to order, and Fortas retook his place on the bench. Neither took his seat comfortably. Three days later, Johnson announced that ordinarily he would have felt bound to submit another name to replace Warren's. "These are not ordinary times," he wrote. "Under the circumstances, the foundations of government would be better served by the present Chief Justice remaining until emotionalism subsides, reason and fairness prevail."[20]

So Warren pushed on. The early days of the Court's term were overshadowed by the national political campaigns, and Nixon made no secret of his antipathy toward the Court headed by a man he frankly disliked. Speaking at that year's Republican Convention, Nixon identified the Court with crime and disorder. "[L]et us . . . recognize," Nixon said, "that some of our courts in their decisions have gone too far in weakening the peace forces as against the criminal forces in this country, and we must act to restore that balance."[21] There was no question about whose Court Nixon was speaking of. On Election Night, the night that Warren had hoped to crack his thirty-year-old scotch and toast the reelection of Lyndon Johnson, he instead joined his daughter and son-in-law Virginia and John Daly as the returns rolled in across the country and Richard Nixon squeaked out a narrow victory over Hubert Humphrey.[22] Humphrey closed the gap so fast at the end that many observers believed he would have won had the campaign gone on another week. Still, close victories are victories nevertheless. The consensus period that had protected Warren and his Court and allowed its achievements to be the nation's was over.

The election of Richard Nixon culminated Warren's long dread, and it permanently ended Warren's friendly access to the White House. At the same time, it shifted Warren's place in the gathering political and cultural currents of the nation, particularly with respect to Vietnam. As long as Johnson was president, Warren supported his efforts to manage the Vietnam War. Now, however, Vietnam was not Johnson's war but Nixon's.

Warren soon began to see protesters of the war as more sympathetic. Just one week after Nixon's election, the Court heard arguments in *Tinker v. Des Moines School District.* The Tinker children and a few other students wore black armbands to school in late 1965 in order to express their sympathy for those who had died in Vietnam and to support Robert Kennedy's proposed bombing halt for that Christmas. The school authorities in Des Moines had been warned that such a demonstration might take place and had put in place rules to suspend the students if they did so. The students wore them anyway, and were suspended.

Those actions occurred in 1965, fifteen months before David O'Brien burned his draft card. Warren and all but Douglas had signaled their impatience with dissent when they upheld O'Brien's conviction and sentence. Arguably, the authorities had more discretion to control the Tinkers' protest than that of O'Brien: The Tinkers, like O'Brien, had engaged in symbolic speech—the Tinkers in violation of school orders, O'Brien in defiance of federal law. The Tinkers' actions occurred in a public school, where all sides agreed that officials had the right to preserve decorum in order to allow children to learn. Now, however, the same justices who took such offense at O'Brien's draft-card protest showed a new tolerance for the protest by the Des Moines children. Allan Herrick, the lawyer for the Des Moines school district, argued before the Court that wearing the armbands was an "explosive" act because it occurred before an "inflamed" community, its anger stirred by an exploitative press. Warren arched an eyebrow. The recently decided presidential election had included passionate debate about Vietnam, Warren noted. Could the students have been suspended for wearing Humphrey buttons? Or Nixon buttons? Perhaps, the lawyer responded, if they arrived for school with a "whole row of buttons . . . it could prove disruptive."[23] That was too much for Warren, who, joined by Marshall, pressed Herrick for evidence that the school board could reasonably have anticipated disruption from the students wearing armbands. Herrick flailed for an answer, eventually coming close to admitting that the school board had no evidence that the armbands would disrupt the city's schools.[24]

Fortas, like Warren a supporter of Johnson's Vietnam War and a critic of its critics, wrote for the Court. "It can hardly be argued that either students or teachers shed their constitutional rights to freedom of expression at the schoolhouse gate," the Court concluded. Harking back to one of Justice Jackson's great rulings, the Court reminded that the Jehovah's Witnesses were permitted to refuse to salute the flag, an expression of their deeply held beliefs in defiance of school rules. The actions of the Tinkers and the others in Des Moines were plainly intended to express their protected views—opposition to the war. While school authorities had the right to maintain order, the wearing of armbands had done nothing to impair learning and thus the state had no right to impinge the Tinkers' speech. Indeed, it had allowed other emblems to be displayed—some students had even donned iron crosses, symbols of Nazi Germany, without repercussion. Yes, there was risk of disruption, "but our Constitution says we must take this risk . . . and our history says that it is this sort of hazardous freedom—this kind of openness—that is the basis of our national strength and of the independence and vigor of Americans who grow up and live in this relatively permissive, often disputatious, society."[25] Why that same reasoning did not apply to O'Brien and his draft card was not explained.

Harlan dissented gently.[26] Black showed no such restraint. He sarcastically allowed that the armbands might constitute "'symbolic speech,' which is akin to 'pure speech,'" and then moved to other, more emotional grounds to state his case. "If the time has come when pupils of state-supported schools, kindergartens, grammar schools, or high schools, can defy and flout orders of school officials to keep their minds on their own schoolwork, it is the beginning of a new revolutionary era of permissiveness in this country fostered by the judiciary." Black once welcomed a "revolutionary era"—indeed, more than one. He had heralded the New Deal, led the cause of racial equality, pioneered the law of equal protection. He had, in fact, joined Jackson in defending the rights of schoolchildren to refuse to salute the American flag during World War II. No more. Revolution was satisfying to the young Hugo Black, alarming to the aging one. "Change has been said to be truly the law of life," Black said near his conclusion, "but sometimes the old and the tried and true are worth holding. . . . Uncontrolled and uncontrollable liberty is an enemy to domestic peace."[27] In his copy of Black's dissent, Fortas came to the passage about the threat of "uncontrollable liberty," and wrote in the margins, "Hugo Black!!"[28] Black, Warren confided sadly to his clerks, had simply stayed too long.[29]

Black and Warren would remain civil for the rest of their lives, but *Tinker* demonstrated how far apart those two friends had drifted. Black found his succor in order and old values. Warren lived by those values. He was still stern, still a patriot. But the same voices of dissent that alarmed him just months earlier now seemed less shrill. They seemed, in fact, persuasive. When, in April 1969, the son of Warren's driver, Jean Clemencia, was killed in action, Warren asked his clerks and fellow justices to accompany him to the funeral. Warren himself wrote to Clemencia and his wife, expressing his grief and honor to attend the service for the fallen young man.[30] The death affected Warren deeply, as personal matters so often did. He had supported the Vietnam War—or at least Johnson's efforts to win that war— as late as 1968; by the fall of 1969, he would publicly proclaim his opposition to its continuance.[31]

As Warren moved toward acceptance of protest, his grandson, Jeffrey Warren, dared to give him a copy of Eldridge Cleaver's *Soul on Ice,* not sure whether his grandfather would bother to read it. Others in the family were shocked at Jeffrey's presumption, but Warren read the book and absorbed it in generational terms. "I understand the man's anger," he told his grandson. "What a shame that our generation and past generations have created a world that promotes such rage." Still, Warren added, in case his grandson were to assume that the Chief Justice of the United States was ready to endorse the fuming rage of an ex-convict and leader of the Black Panthers, "How can you respect a man who uses such bad language?"[32]

Warren's appreciation of radical literature and leftist politics had its foundations in his own young life, but in the decades since, his rise and influence had all been through the most establishment causes and organizations. The Masons were his friends, not the Students for a Democratic Society. Nixon's rise to power did not suddenly drive Warren to radicalism, but it alienated him from much of the Washington establishment, the same establishment that had embraced and exalted him for nearly a decade. He knew the time had come to leave. For him, then, the challenge was how to extricate himself from the predicament of his own bungled retirement. So as 1968, the terrible year of 1968, drew to a close, Warren sought out his old rival to cut a deal.

Fearing that a personal meeting would draw too much attention to itself or, perhaps, unwilling to bring himself personally to Nixon's door, Warren asked his son-in-law John Daly to deliver the message that he was willing to step down but hoped to serve out the term. Daly did as asked, telling Nixon associate William Rogers of Warren's wishes over a round of golf.[33] Rogers, who was to become Nixon's secretary of state, passed along the message to Nixon in New York, where the White House-in-waiting was assembled at the Pierre Hotel. On December 4, the president-elect announced a version of the communication tailored to make Nixon appear to be the initiator of the talks. In that version, Nixon "called Mr. Warren in Washington . . . and told him that he wanted to avoid any disruption of the Court's work." Warren played along for the sake of protocol, releasing his own statement after the president-elect had issued his. "The statement released by the President-elect is in accordance with our conversation of yesterday, and I will be happy, at his request, to serve until the end of the present Term of Court," Warren said.[34] This time, there were no conditions attached. Warren then administered to Nixon the oath of office on January

20, 1969. Nixon was the fourth president to take the oath from Warren; it was surely Warren's least pleasant trip to that podium.

The bitter pill was swallowed. That done, Warren then returned to the Court to end his historic tenure. The term's signature case, which Warren took for himself, brought the Warren Court to its conclusion in symmetrical fashion. Adam Clayton Powell was a United States congressman, elected to represent the Eighteenth District in New York and one of few blacks to hold such a position in the late 1960s. After his reelection in 1966, when Powell arrived with his colleagues to take the oath of office and begin that session of Congress, they were asked to step forward and he was directed to step aside. The other members took the oath and assumed their seats, where they voted to appoint a special committee to investigate allegations that Powell and members of his staff had improperly billed the Congress for travel and that Powell's wife had drawn a salary from the Committee on Education and Labor, which Powell had chaired in previous Congresses. Once formed, the Select Committee invited Powell to appear, and he did, though he provided only basic biographical information, refusing to answer other questions. The committee concluded that Powell had stolen House money and filed false reports, and after other motions and debates, Congress adopted a resolution declaring his seat vacant. Powell then sued for his seat and for his back pay.[35]

Powell was a cad and a bit of a con man. Few doubted that the House could have voted to censure him. It could perhaps even have voted to expel him, though that would have been made more difficult by House traditions that suggested it could not expel a member for conduct that occurred in a previous session (each Congress, in theory, is an entirely new body). In any case, the House chose not to censure or expel but rather to exclude Powell from the seat that his constituents elected him to occupy. That raised the constitutional claim because the Constitution establishes the qualifications that members of the House must meet in order to serve. Members must be at least twenty-five years old, seven years a citizen of the United States, and an inhabitant of the state from which they are chosen.[36] Powell met all those criteria.

As with *Baker v. Carr* seven years earlier, the principal issue for Warren's Court to consider was not the substance of the claim but rather the reach of the Court to resolve it. In *Baker v. Carr*, Frankfurter had issued his final, ringing warning against the Court entering the "thicket" of politics—in that case, the politics of drawing legislative lines. Warren had prevailed. To refuse to adjudicate matters where the Constitution required fairness was to Warren then—and always—something akin to shirking his own responsibility. With Powell's lawsuit, the matter returned to the Court in new form—this time, the question of whether the Court could interfere with the organization of a coequal branch of government in an instance where the branch was accused of acting unconstitutionally in making and carrying out its internal rules. Not coincidentally, the victims, both in *Baker* and in *Powell,* were black. Powell's lawyer, Arthur Kinoy, knew well to emphasize that point:

> The reaffirmation that this is a government of laws and not men, that representative government means that ultimate power remains with the people is particularly necessary when the crisis arises in a context in which black citizens are denied the right to elect their own black representative who had risen to great heights of legislative leadership. It is difficult indeed to demand law and order of American citizens if the legislative branch itself denies the first assumptions of an ordered society, the right of people to govern themselves.[37]

That argument spoke so clearly to Warren's legacy at the Court that he could hardly have refused to accept it. The lawyer for the House of Representatives countered that under the Constitution, only the House could set its rules, that its right to govern itself was not subject to review by the courts. What, then, Warren asked, would happen if one political party someday captured a two-thirds or three-fourths majority in the Congress and, one by one, removed members of the other party from the House, finding that their views posed a threat to the nation? That would be wrong, the lawyer conceded, but reviewable only if the actions constituted "utter perversions."[38] When the lawyer argued that the House could go so far as to exclude any member by reason of his race, Warren could not disguise his indignation: "What," he asked, "could be more perverse than that?" The audience laughed. After a break, the lawyer reconsidered and admitted that perhaps such an exclusion would be so perverse that it would justify the Court's intervention. Warren's point was made.[39]

Knowing that the case turned on an issue no less grave than the relationship between the Court and the Congress, Warren assigned the opinion to himself. For its eighty-six footnotes alone, *Powell v. McCormack* was a departure from Warren's characteristic terseness. But in its conclusions, it fulfilled the important mandates of Warren's tenure. It defended democratic principles. It upheld the Court's power to act as protector of the Constitution. And it found in favor of black voters and their right to pick their representatives, however flawed those representatives might be. "It is the responsibility of this Court to act as the ultimate interpreter of the Constitution," Warren wrote. That was a duty Warren had claimed in *Baker v. Carr.* He demanded that others yield to it in *Cooper v. Aaron.* He embraced it in a long line of criminal procedure cases—from *Mapp v. Ohio* to *Miranda.* He would not stop now, not at the end. In this case, the Constitution was clear and the Court's duty was as well. Before circulating the opinion to the brethren, Warren took it to Brennan to read. Brennan approved. Warren was elated. "OK, boys," he told his clerks. "We got it."[40] When the Court handed down its ruling, Congress bent to its order, just as so many others had been forced to during Warren's service.

While Warren was at work on the *Powell* opinion, the Nixon White House settled into place, and soon was at odds with the Court. On March 12, Jack Landau,
whom Brennan had known for some time because Landau covered the Supreme
Court for the Newhouse newspaper chain, called Brennan's chambers and told his
secretary that he had an urgent matter to discuss with the justice. Brennan invited
him over and only then realized that Landau was no longer a reporter but was
working as public information director at the Justice Department. Once he arrived,
Landau nervously explained to Brennan that Attorney General John Mitchell had
sent him to express concern over a pair of wiretapping cases decided a few days earlier by the Court. Those cases required the government to turn over to defendants
evidence seized through illegal wiretaps in order to make clear that the defendant
was not being tried with illegally obtained evidence.[41]

The ruling had triggered alarm at the Justice Department, Landau told Brennan, because officials there were concerned that it would force the government to
reveal its extensive wiretapping operations directed against foreign embassies in
Washington. All of this was understandably perplexing to Brennan, who told Landau he had never heard of such wiretapping and who asked what Landau expected
the Court to do about it. When Brennan told Landau he would have to share the information with Warren, Landau expressed terror at the idea of confronting the
chief justice. Brennan insisted, and when they entered Warren's chambers, Landau
was so nervous he could not sit down. The two relayed for Warren the scenario, and
Landau awkwardly emphasized that the Department of Justice recognized its responsibility for the situation and would "do anything within reason to avoid congressional reaction against the Court."[42] That sounded suspiciously like a threat,
but Warren did not bite. Instead, Warren told Landau that if Justice wanted to address the problem, it could file a motion for rehearing or otherwise petition the
Court officially. Landau then retreated back to his office, leaving Warren to brood
on what he called "this outrageous attempt to influence a Court action."[43] Warren
contemplated a public response to upbraid the administration for its attempt to influence the Court's approach to wiretapping cases, but worried that it would backfire and be seen as "vindictiveness and reprisal" against a president who had so
prominently allied the Court with the "criminal forces" in American life. In later
years, Warren wondered whether he had been right to stay quiet as the Nixon administration became increasingly infatuated with wiretaps. Only in his memoirs
did Warren disclose the incident, noting edgily that it might be of public interest in
light of "the Watergate episode and related cases."[44]

Nixon knew he would be replacing Warren at the end of the term, but when
Mitchell saw an opportunity to turn one vacancy into two, he took it. The object
this time was Fortas, whose confirmation hearings had opened the door to questions about his integrity, and whose withdrawal from the contest had not closed it.

Reporters continued to dig, encouraged by the Nixon White House. The forces pressing on Fortas crested in May with the publication in *Life* magazine of a story exposing some aspects of a deal the justice had entered into with Louis Wolfson, a businessman whose activities had drawn the interest of the SEC and who ultimately would serve a prison sentence for assorted stock manipulation charges.[45] Wolfson had befriended Fortas, and, unbeknownst to Warren or the other justices, had agreed to pay Fortas $20,000 a year to act as an adviser to his family foundation. That was potentially problem enough, but to make matters worse, the contract with Fortas was for life and specified that should Fortas die, the payments would continue to be made to his wife, Carol Agger.

After agreeing to the deal, Fortas had reconsidered it and had returned the initial $20,000 check. Because he had done so in the same year he took it, Fortas owed no taxes on the money. Moreover, Wolfson later insisted that Fortas had never intervened with any government official on his behalf during his criminal trials. If true, that too would have meant that Fortas did nothing illegal. In political terms, however, the disclosure was devastating, especially coming on the heels of the hearings that highlighted questions about Fortas's ethics and his personal greed. *Life* magazine published its story about Fortas's relationship with Wolfson on May 4 (the magazine was dated May 9, but it was available five days earlier). The story did not disclose the lifetime contract, but the IRS subpoenaed that document the same day. By midnight, it was in the hands of Attorney General Mitchell, who recognized what he had and set out to use it to force Fortas from the Court.

Mitchell's next step was a curious one, but it proved effective. He asked to meet with Warren, and Warren, who just weeks earlier had been so offended by the White House's attempt to reach the Court informally regarding the wiretapping case, strangely agreed. Warren may have been merely curious, or he may have seen little danger in the contact, since it involved no pending case before the Court; still, it was a puzzling lapse of judgment for a justice so wary of Nixon and so committed to the form as well as the substance of propriety. Whatever drew Warren to the meeting, he left it with the sure knowledge that his Court was about to unravel. The two met in Warren's chambers on May 7, and Mitchell presented him with a copy of Fortas's contract, one that bound him for life to a criminal. After Mitchell left, Warren turned to Margaret McHugh and uttered the obvious: "He can't stay."[46]

Warren went directly to Brennan's chambers after Mitchell left and consulted with Brennan and Stewart before meeting with Fortas that afternoon.[47] Over a tense weekend, the clamor for Fortas's resignation grew, and with Douglas out of town, Fortas oddly sought guidance from Black.[48] By Monday, reporters had learned of the lifetime contract—Mitchell undoubtedly was the source. The justices met in conference that Tuesday, and Warren told them the details of the contract that Mitchell had given him. They sat, stunned. Fortas said little.[49] He resigned the following day.

SECURITY AND FREEDOM require each other and yet pull against each other. They are intertwined and inextricable, and for Warren, they stood as markers in his principled quest for a good nation. As a young man, Warren opted for safety, first in the IWW prosecutions in upholding California's syndicalism laws, and later, more tragically, in the internment of Japanese-Americans during the early, confused days of World War II. But as he moved to end his service to his nation, Warren was given a rare luxury, the opportunity to reconsider his youth in the full light of his life.

This time, the defendant convicted of violating a criminal syndicalism law came from Ohio, whose statute was virtually identical to the California law under which Warren had won a conviction against Taylor and had sustained it against Whitney. This time, the defendant was a Ku Klux Klan leader. He and like-minded figures had gathered on an Ohio farm to proclaim their hatred of blacks and Jews and to announce plans for a march on Congress. Addressing his fellow Klansmen with cameras rolling, the defendant, Clarence Brandenburg, spoke from beneath a red hood and issued a vaguely threatening, illiterate promise: "We're not a revengent organization, but if our President, our Congress, our Supreme Court, continues to suppress the white, Caucasian race, it's possible that there might have to be some revengeance taken."[50]

John Taylor had said and done far less to warrant his criminal conviction in 1920, but now the man who prosecuted Taylor for threatening security rose to the call of freedom. "We are here confronted with a statute which, by its own words and as applied, purports to punish mere advocacy and to forbid, on pain of criminal punishment, assembly with others merely to advocate the described type of action," the Warren Court ruled. "Such a statute falls within the condemnation of the First and Fourteenth Amendments. The contrary teaching of Whitney v. California . . . cannot be supported, and that decision is therefore overruled."[51] Douglas and Black chimed in with their harder-line defenses of the First Amendment, but in this case there were no dissents. *Brandenburg,* like so much of the Warren Court's best work, was unanimous, though this time its unanimity was tinged with sadness. Fortas was the author of *Brandenburg,* but he was gone by the time it was decided. The Court decided *Brandenburg* by a vote of 8–0.

*Brandenburg* completed the Court's long journey toward the embrace of radical speech: from *Dennis,* where Douglas sputtered his disapproval of the Smith Act but lost to a majority willing to punish the teachers of Communism; to *Whitney,* where Brandeis scolded men who had "feared witches and burnt women" but where the Court had upheld Whitney's criminal conviction, a conviction won by Warren's colleagues in the Alameda district attorney's office; and now, at last, to *Brandenburg,* where the Court declared that speech triumphed over fear.

*Brandenburg* and *Powell* were handed down a week apart. With them, Warren's work as chief justice was finished. He did not give any sign of unhappiness about his impending retirement, but as the date had drawn closer, his grandson Jeffrey urged him to reconsider. Jeffrey, then a college student at Warren's alma mater, was growing up in a nation at war and at an enraged university. He begged his grandfather to stay with the Court, not to yield his position at such an urgent moment. Warren's mind was made up, but with just a week left in his tenure, he paused to write a note in his own hand to explain himself to his grandson. "We are passing through one of the most troublesome times of human history," the chief justice wrote his grandson:

> The world is disjointed, fragmented, embittered, cynical, and dominated by wars and threatened wars. It is beset by poverty in some segments of society while others are more affluent than ever before in history. Discrimination is rampant and opportunities for the good life are grossly unequal.
>
> Of course, I can understand the feelings of youth. . . . I can appreciate the anxieties about their future—the Vietnam War, the draft, the arms race, the exhaustion of our resources on military expenditures to the starvation of our domestic problems of poverty, slums, education, environmental pollution, etc. Often I ask myself why all of these problems should surface in my lifetime. Is it because we who are living today have brought them into existence or is it because they are of ancient origin and we like other generations before us have not been able to measure up to them?

Slavery, he reminded Jeffrey, had been abolished more than a hundred years earlier, but "the badge of it is still on millions of our citizens, poor souls." Without crediting himself, Warren noted that there, at least, the conscience of the nation had awakened. "Now they can vote everywhere in the nation, they can attend non-segregated schools as fast as law can push human prejudice, the Jim Crow vehicles of travel are of the past, they can be served in all hotels, restaurants, theaters and other places of public accommodation such as parks, beaches and other places of recreation."

"So, Jeff," Warren continued, "we now ask ourselves, what should we do about all of this?" For Warren, the answer fused his lifetime of patient, deliberate action with his increasingly deep faith in young people. "I really believe, Jeff, that what our country needs now is the youth of America—not to destroy what is but to build—to insist on righting the wrongs of society and during its years of stewardship implement the ideal of Lincoln for 'a government of the people, by the people and for the people' so that it will not 'perish from this earth.'"[52] Warren closed by thanking Jeffrey for the faith and confidence that spurred his request that his grandfather stay on. No, Warren said, he would not stay at the Court. But as Warren prepared to go, he understood that he left his values imprinted on his nation, in its laws, and in its young people. Nixon and the war might threaten those values, but Warren re-

tired with the conviction that they were consistent with the nation's past and worthy of its future. He left the Court as he had arrived—a patient optimist, conscious
of his country's failings, confident in its ability to right them.

On June 23, 1969, Warren handed down the final decisions of the Warren
Court. Fittingly, they prohibited police from ransacking homes during searches,
protected defendants against double jeopardy, and restricted courts from handing
out stiffer sentences to defendants who were ordered retrials. Then Warren gazed
down from the bench to the counsel table, where a lawyer with little experience in
the High Court patiently waited his turn. The lawyer, President Richard Nixon,
then rose to the podium and spoke, becoming the first sitting president ever to address the United States Supreme Court. "Mr. Chief Justice," Nixon began, "may it
please the Court."

Nixon wore a cutaway coat and tails, the traditional dress of government
lawyers appearing at the Supreme Court bar. Speaking without notes, he recalled
his two arguments in the Supreme Court—both in the *Hill* case—and joked that
the only ordeal more challenging than a presidential press conference was a
Supreme Court argument. Nixon paid tribute to Warren's long service, a gracious
act toward an old foe. "Will Rogers, in commenting upon one of the predecessors
of the Chief Justice, Chief Justice William Howard Taft, said that 'It is great to be
great. It is greater to be human,'" Nixon recalled. "I think that comment could well
apply to the Chief Justice as we look at his 52 years of service." Nixon then remarked on the continuity and change that tug in opposing directions across the
history of the Court and nation—that the Warren Court gives way to the Burger
Court, that the demand for progress pulls against the dignity of order. "It was always that way; may it always be that way," Nixon concluded. "And to the extent that
it is, this nation owes a debt of gratitude to the Chief Justice of the United States for
his example."[53]

Warren thanked Nixon for his grace. "[Y]our words," he said, "are most generous and are greatly appreciated, I assure you." Both men knew of their many feuds
and disagreements, and they knew that those around them knew them as well. For
a moment, they put them aside to honor together the traditions they jointly admired. But old habits are hard to break, and the chief justice took a moment to
point out to Nixon, "because you might not have looked into the matter," that the
Court is different from Congress or the presidency. Presidents, members of the
House, and senators sit for terms, and each presidency, each new Congress, is a distinct entity. The Court, by contrast, is a continuing body, its membership developing over time, rooted in "the eternal principles of our Constitution," but changing
as well. "We, of course, venerate the past," Warren said, "but our focus is on the
problems of the day and of the future as far as we can foresee it."[54] Warren hailed
the Court's devotion to service, its fractious virility, its embrace of controversy.

"So," he concluded, "I leave in a happy vein." He then called for Warren Burger, who joined the chief justice on the bench and took the oath. There was no applause. None is permitted inside the Court. Warren left to silence.

His departure was a national event and an intimate parting. The nation celebrated his service with a tribute on the Mall. The event was held at the Lincoln Memorial, a fitting reminder of the course of freedom that Lincoln had launched and Warren had steered to triumph, and the same spot where Martin Luther King had electrified America in 1963. The brethren marked Warren's retirement with a reunion of the Court's extended family. The widow of Justice Jackson attended; the Whittakers could not, but chipped in for the gifts. Arthur Goldberg, then a private lawyer but always a member of the brethren, decided at the last minute to come, and arrived from New York. On the evening of June 6, just before the term ended, the justices, current and retired, and their wives merrily boarded the S.S. *Sequoia*, the presidential yacht, for an evening to toast their departing chief. All rose to their traditional roles—Black, the differences with Warren of recent years put aside for the night, acted as the MC, the Court's voice. Elizabeth Black, the lovely wife of the senior justice, presented Nina with a gold bracelet the justices had engraved to the "First Lady of the Judiciary, 1953–1969." Bill Douglas gave the chief his gift, an elaborate Winchester shotgun, a muscular reminder that Warren's liberalism, like Douglas's, was never at the expense of his forcefulness. Brennan, of course, was responsible for pulling together the majority—he solicited the contributions for the gifts and oversaw planning for the party.[55]

Warren's move to retirement was not an easy one. He had been in active, public life for more than half a century, moving from courtroom prosecutor to district attorney to attorney general to governor to chief justice with almost no interruption. For fifty years, every change of job had expanded the range of his intellect and influence. Now, for the first time in his life, Warren stepped back from power. And as he did, he lost a friend. Drew Pearson had been a confidant and traveling companion, a liaison to the White House and a shipmate on cruises. Warren admired Pearson's pluck and sophistication. Pearson, in turn, revered Warren, and in 1967, Warren agreed to a long series of interviews in which he was unusually candid with Pearson. Pearson had hoped to write a biography of Warren, and had prepared preliminary drafts of early chapters. That Warren would entrust Pearson with such a job was evidence of their closeness. But Pearson would not live to see the book finished. He was in and out of the hospital that August, and Warren visited him on August 21. Four days later, Warren left for a conference in Bangkok. While there, he learned that Pearson had died.[56]

When he returned home, Warren was given an office at the Court and allowed to hire one clerk a year, but that seemed, at least at first, more than he could use. He kept a light schedule for the most part, continuing to come to the Court every morning, arriving usually around nine-thirty, eating lunch there and then going home in the early evening. He spoke often to groups, and pressed his clerk into speechwriting service. And he and Nina traveled frequently, leaving his clerk with little to do in his absence.[57] Although Warren had made use of the clerks assigned to retired justices, he himself would not allow his annual clerk to work with Burger, whom Warren distrusted. As a result, some of his clerks in retirement found the experience trying—they were assigned to a great man, but had little to do.[58]

The principal focus of Warren's retirement, it seemed when he left the Court, was to produce a memoir. Warren had announced his intention to write such a book and had contracted with Doubleday to produce one, but as he tried to settle into the work, it became less an opportunity than a source of sullen obligation. Warren was not a natural memoirist. His view of the Court's sanctity prevented him from revealing the deliberations behind important decisions, and his reticence to examine his past made him an unlikely source of new insights into his own life. And so he found diversions. Rather than focus on his autobiography, Warren produced an extended essay on the state of American liberty. Titled *A Republic, If You Can Keep It,* it included a few thoughtful passages, but the best that can be said of it is that it was short. Indeed, it added little to his note to Jeffrey Warren, though at least it provided a dignified venue for Warren to contribute his ideas on the state of the country and allowed him the opportunity to attach two appendixes: the Constitution and the Declaration of Independence.

In his latter years as a justice, Warren had become taken with an organization promoting the cause of World Peace Through Law, whose ideals first captivated Warren when he met with the group at an Athens conference in 1965. Its advocacy of civil rights appealed to Warren's sense of purpose and its international reach broadened his vision of the law. He spoke at the group's regular conferences— Geneva in 1967 and 1968, Bangkok in 1969. Those appearances only solidified the far right's distrust of Warren. The *Biographical Dictionary of the Left* sneered at the "pacifist cause of 'world peace through world law'" along with Warren's other internationalist interests, which the dictionary lumped together under the headings of disarmament and "so-called civil rights."[59]

World Peace Through Law drew Earl and Nina Warren overseas, and their travel schedule in his early retirement remained busy. He and Nina visited friends and relatives, often traveling to California, where they would make their base at Ben Swig's Fairmont Hotel but work in trips to Jim in St. Helena, Earl Jr. in Sacramento, Bobby in Davis, and Honey Bear in Los Angeles. Warren's love of sports never flagged. He pulled for the Miracle Mets in 1969 and happily saw them capture the World Series. When the Redskins made it to the Super Bowl in 1973, Warren flew to Los Angeles with Edward Bennett Williams and his journalistic-politico entourage; that time, they watched in disappointment as the Redskins lost to the Miami Dolphins.[60]

WARREN CHAFED at his exclusion from the center of national life. He displayed a yearning for politics, as well as a sharpening testiness for opponents, real and sometimes imagined. In 1971, Burger convened a study group to examine the workload of the Supreme Court and to recommend ways to lighten it. Warren, smelling a rat and perhaps a bit overeager for a fight, lit into the proposal. One recommendation of the study group was the creation of a new National Court of Appeals that would screen petitions for the Supreme Court, denying those that appeared frivolous and passing along only those that, in its judgment, warranted consideration by the nation's highest Court. Warren deplored the idea, and his doubts were fueled by his belief, which Brennan encouraged, that Burger was carrying the proposal for Nixon.[61] Warren stewed for months as the panel worked, and took offense that rather than invite him to appear before it as a whole, it sent Peter Ehrenhaft, a former Warren clerk, to interview him one-on-one.[62] Warren had seen his share of attacks on the Court and had seen jurisdictional debates mask deeper challenges to its autonomy and authority. This proposal was more innocently crafted, but even the proposed court's name, the National Court of Appeals, recalled the National Court proposal that Warren had helped squelch in 1963. This time, once Warren concluded that Nixon was behind it, he could not see it as anything other than subterfuge. Warren sent a letter to his clerks—clearly intended to find its way to the press—denouncing the proposal and Ehrenhaft's involvement in it. Then, when Warren at last spoke out publicly about the proposal, he rejected it with unmistakable force: "I believe it is obligatory not only to speak out to advance the efficiency of the Supreme Court's processes but also to warn against those proposals that, under the guise of procedural reform, would cause irreparable harm to the prestige, the power and the function of the Court."[63]

Substantively, Warren was right. The National Court of Appeals envisioned by Burger was never approved, and still, in the years after Burger left, complaints about the Court's workload subsided—the result of the replacement of the dithering Burger by Rehnquist, a respected and efficient manager of the Court's business. Yet Warren's vehemence exceeded the issue. A few months after first unloading his anger against the proposal, he gathered with his clerks for their annual toast to him in Washington. Those had always been happy occasions, a reuniting of the fraternity of young men—now many growing old themselves—to share their devotion to their chief, who had launched and inspired their careers. Always in black tie, with strong cocktails and a good meal, the event was infused with the male camaraderie that Warren had cherished his whole life. He often spoke at length, good-naturedly fielding questions with the assurance that these were his men, that no breach of loyalty or confidence was even imaginable. This year, however, Warren stood before the clerks and turned on a tape recorder. It played a recording of a recent speech he had made in which he ringingly opposed the Court reform proposal. When the screed was over, Warren turned off the machine and asked Ehrenhaft whether he cared to reply. The younger man stammered out a few words, declining as the rest of the room sat quietly, embarrassed for Ehrenhaft, mystified by Warren.[64]

Warren's attack on the Court reform package doomed it, and it stood as a reminder to Burger that his own prestige was infinitesimal in contrast to that of his predecessor. And indeed, the early 1970s were full of reminders of Warren's esteem, as the Warren Court pivoted from its place as object of controversy to one of lionization and nostalgia. Warren himself was regularly included in any short list of great justices, sometimes joined only by Marshall and Charles Evans Hughes when ranked against history's other chief justices. Warren's eightieth birthday, in 1971, brought another round of praise and good wishes. Douglas dropped his old friend a line, and Warren replied with good cheer, recalling from decades earlier a talk that Herbert Hoover had given at the Bohemian Grove on the occasion of his eightieth birthday. "How does it happen that everyone now says such nice things about you when a few years ago they were throwing rocks at you?" one guest asked the former president, Warren recalled. "He answered, 'I just outlived the bastards.'"[65] One can easily imagine the cackle in Douglas's chambers.

Warren kept his place in the life of the nation with his speaking schedule. He spoke most often to students, though also to assemblages of lawyers or judges and occasionally on behalf of environmental protection—he joined the effort to protect California's redwoods, a cause spearheaded by his old classmate, Newton Drury. But Warren's abiding political preoccupation was, as it never ceased to be, Nixon. Warren's reverence for the American presidency prevented him from engaging in personal attacks on Nixon, but after 1972, the gathering storm of Watergate was more than Warren could resist. For twenty years, he had warned those closest to him that Nixon was not trustworthy, that he had crossed Warren at the 1952 convention and had more than earned the nickname "Tricky Dick." Now Warren was riveted by the disclosures of burglaries, of misuse of government agencies to persecute critics, of secret bombings in Cambodia, and of the compilation of an "enemies list."

In October 1973, soon after Earl and Nina returned from a Hawaiian vacation with Ben Swig, Swig was hospitalized, and Warren tried to lighten his friend's spirits with regular updates from Washington. To such a trusted and ailing friend, Warren indulged in passing along gossip, though of a decidedly political nature. Spiro Agnew was under investigation, and Warren predicted on October 3 that with so much talk of grand jury inquiry, "it is about time we hear of some action one way or the other."[66] By October 15, Agnew was gone, and Warren told Swig there was brief rumor that Chief Justice Burger would become the vice president in Agnew's place. Agnew's farewell address, an attack against the press rather than an admission that his tax evasion conviction had brought him down, only annoyed Warren, who described it as a "great polemic," and said it "left everyone here cold."[67] On October 20, Nixon ordered his attorney general, Elliot Richardson to fire Archibald Cox, the special prosecutor then seeking access to the White House tapes. Richardson refused and instead resigned himself. Nixon then ordered Deputy Attorney General William Ruckelshaus to fire Cox. He too refused. Finally, Robert Bork, the solicitor general but then acting attorney general, carried out Nixon's orders. Warren was amazed. "Washington is seething again with the events of last weekend," he wrote to Swig, "and conditions are far more chaotic than they have ever been in my experience."[68] By month's end, Warren could genuinely report, "There is no news here except Watergate."[69]

In public, Warren was far more circumspect, but he occasionally found it impossible to hold his tongue. In April of 1973, Warren traveled to Independence, Missouri, to pay homage to President Truman—an old adversary but really more of a friend—who had died the day after Christmas in 1972. Speaking at the library of a president he admired, Warren could not conceal his disdain for Nixon. Although he did not name him, Warren contrasted Truman's presidency with his successors', and added: "I sometimes wonder if that wholesome approach has departed permanently from the American scene."[70]

Three months later, Warren presided over a happier fulfillment of his own legacy. In Los Angeles, voters elected that city's first black mayor, Tom Bradley, and Warren, whose contributions to the cause of racial equality were without many peers, was invited to administer the oath. It was a satisfying moment for the chief justice, who had sworn in Presidents Eisenhower, Kennedy, Johnson, and, lamentably, Nixon, but who now came home to guide a black mayor through his oath of allegiance to the Constitution. When Warren, without introduction, stepped to the podium to administer the oath, Bradley began to applaud, and with him, the thousands who had gathered in Warren's home state on a sunny July morning joined in paying their respects to the former governor. Unable to stay seated, the guests rose and gave Warren a standing ovation. Some wept. One hardened newsman confessed to Bradley that even he wiped tears from his eyes.[71] Then Warren turned to the completion of what he had started in 1954 with *Brown*. He made a black man the mayor of his own birthplace. It was, Warren said, a "heart-warming event for me."[72]

By the end of 1973, Warren's health was beginning to fail, but he remained unwilling to succumb to it. On January 26, 1974, he was hospitalized in Los Angeles while doctors worked to relieve a fluid buildup around his heart and lungs. He was treated and released after a week, and then recuperated a few more days at Honey Bear's home in Beverly Hills. By March, he was sufficiently recovered to celebrate his eighty-third birthday with a dinner at Virginia and John Daly's home in Washington, and on April 5 he took in Opening Day in Baltimore. His law clerks toasted him later that month, and Warren accepted a number of speaking engagements for April and May. The last of those was to be in Atlanta, where Warren agreed to deliver a commencement address at that city's great all-black college, Morehouse. Speaking to those new graduates, Warren reflected on Watergate and urged students not to abandon their history. "The scandal, compendiously referred to as Watergate, has shaken the faith of people, not only in the individuals involved, but also in the procedures which brought them to their high stations," Warren said. "Many people are so shocked by the disclosures that they are distrustful of all persons in public life and, what is even worse, they are becoming doubtful about the institutions upon which we have relied for so long to bring about the freedom which was promulgated in the Declaration of Independence two centuries ago."[73] That would not do for Warren. Even with Nixon in the White House and the nation torn by his presidency, Warren kept his belief in those institutions, if not in those individuals who occupied them. "The great virtue of our Government," he said, "is that people can do something about it."[74]

That was Warren's final public appearance. Three days later he suffered a heart attack and was hospitalized in Washington. The last weeks of Warren's life were spent between hospital and home. During that time, he welcomed to his side the people of his lengthy career, each bringing memories that gave him comfort. On June 27 came Pat Patterson, who as a young California highway patrolman had chauffeured Governor Warren through a vast and varied state.[75] Warren was weak but cheerful, and eager to reminisce about their early days together, when the governor and his black driver struck up their friendship. They talked of the governorship, of their rides, of friends they had in common, of their long bond with each other. Patterson immodestly asked whether he was right in assuming that Warren had been writing about him in *Brown v. Board of Education* when he described the plight of black children in segregated schools. Even sick, Warren knew better than to take that belief away from Patterson. "He laughed," Patterson recalled, "and indicated many factors and much evidence were taken under consideration in making that decision." After talking for a while, Patterson reluctantly broke away. Warren encouraged him to write a book. Patterson left their final meeting vowing to try.[76]

Warren reentered the hospital on the afternoon of July 2. And soon after being admitted came the representatives of a deeper, older, more cherished memory. The University of California, Berkeley, had held a place in Warren's heart from first sight, and now to his bedside it returned, carried by two men who shared his love of it. His oldest son, Jim, whom Warren had adopted as his own when he married Nina, came with his own son, Jeffrey, who had presumed to introduce his grandfather to the writing of Eldridge Cleaver and who had begged him to stay on the Court. All three Warrens were members of the Order of the Golden Bear and were fraternity brothers across their three generations. Together, they loved poetry, and Jim and Jeffrey read to the old man as he lay in bed. Then Warren spoke up. There was one poem he wanted to read to them, he said. It was "The Explorer," by Rudyard Kipling, precisely the type of narrative, eventful poem that Warren always liked. Determined to read it aloud in accordance with the traditions of their society, Warren pulled the poem close and gravely sounded out its lines. It told the story of a man, driven to discover the "land behind the ranges" by a voice compelling him forward. It told of the man's patience and his vision. It had tinges of bitterness, the lack of appreciation that those who would come later would have for the man who blazed ahead. Warren read it slowly, his son and grandson by his side. And then, Warren came to the poem's final verses, three stanzas written as if for him:

Have I named one single river? Have I claimed one single acre?
Have I kept one single nugget (barring samples)? No, not I!
Because my price was paid me ten times over by my Maker.
But you wouldn't understand it. You go up and occupy.

Ores you'll find there; wood and cattle; water transit sure and steady
(That should keep the railway-rates down), coal and iron at your doors.
God took care to hide this country till He judged his people ready,
Then he chose me for His Whisper, and I've found it, and it's yours!

Yes, your "Never-never country"—yes, your "edge of cultivation,"
And "no sense in going further"—till I crossed the range to see.
God forgive me! No, *I* didn't. It's God's present to our nation.
Anybody might have found it, but—His Whisper came to me!

Earl Warren tossed up his hands in triumph. "We'll see ya, fellas," he exclaimed. Jim and Jeffrey left believing he might bounce back.[77]

On July 9 came greetings from the Court, delivered by Warren's two enduring friends from his era—the elfin William Brennan and the irascible William Douglas. Along with Marshall, those two colleagues were all that remained of the once dominant liberal bloc. Black had died in 1971, just eight days after retiring his seat. Goldberg and Fortas preceded Warren from the bench. Now Warren Burger sat in

Warren's chair, and Harry Blackmun in the one that Goldberg and Fortas had occupied. The Nixon appointees had not done much to roll back Warren's work, but
his legacy was under attack, and it seemed only a matter of time until it would fall
beneath the weight of conservative appointments. And yet there were other currents coursing through politics in those days, particularly as the stain of Watergate
and its associated deceptions spread through the Nixon White House. Unable to
squelch demands for his tapes by firing Archibald Cox—or, rather, by persuading
Bork to fire Cox—Nixon now turned to the Supreme Court for relief. Nixon's
lawyers argued that they should not be forced to surrender secretly made tapes of
Oval Office conversations, that executive privilege protected that material. On
July 8, prosecutor Leon Jaworski came to the United States Supreme Court—four
of whose members had been placed there by Nixon—to demand that the president
yield to the law and surrender the tapes. The Court heard three hours of argument
that day, then retreated to its conference room on July 9 to debate the emergency
matter.

When they arrived at Room 6103 that afternoon, Brennan and Douglas joined
their old chief on the seventh floor of the Georgetown hospital.[78] Outside was the
Watergate complex, where an alert security guard had caught the five burglars
whose case tugged apart the web of deceit and cover-up that now was unraveling the
Nixon presidency. They entered, and Warren took Douglas by the hand: "If Nixon
is not forced to turn over tapes of his conversation with the ring of men who were
conversing on their violations of the law, then liberty will soon be dead in this nation. If Nixon gets away with that, then Nixon makes the law as he goes along—not
the Congress nor the courts. The old Court you and I served so long will not be
worthy of its traditions if Nixon can twist, turn, and fashion the law as he sees fit."[79]
Warren was tired, but Brennan assured him that he would not be disappointed in
the Court, that it had met that day and that it would vindicate itself in its ruling on
*United States v. Nixon*.[80] Warren smiled and asked his friends to stay longer. Fearing they would tire him, they left after about an hour.

That night, Warren was joined at his bed by his wife and Honey Bear. They were
by his side when, just after eight P.M., he seized up. Honey Bear dashed into the hall
for help. Returning with a doctor, she found her mother holding her father in her
arms. At 8:10 P.M., Earl Warren died. More than thirty years earlier, Earl Warren
had wept in the hallway, shrugging off his own Election Night, at the news that his
little girl had polio. Now she was grown and healthy, there with her mother and
namesake, whom Warren had cherished since their chance meeting at an Oakland
pool party fifty-three years earlier. As her father died, Nina "Honey Bear" Warren
staggered into another hospital hallway. She wept, comforted by her mother yet as
bereft as her father had been at her illness so many years before.[81]

At Warren Burger's suggestion, Earl Warren lay in repose at the United States Supreme Court from July 11 until his funeral the next day. His clerks stood guard over the bier through that night into the warm summer day that followed, silently paying vigil as thousands of everyday men and women filed past. Warren's family converged on Washington. On July 12, Nixon accompanied Nina Warren to the funeral at the National Cathedral. Warren's clerks, one pew behind the family, winced at that, but they kept their peace.[82]

Nina Warren considered bringing her husband home to California for his burial, but his connections to California were scattered—from his birthplace in Los Angeles, to his boyhood home in Bakersfield, to the Bay Area he loved, to Sacramento where he governed. Instead, she elected to return him to his nation. Warren had served in World War I and honored his country in the decades since. Nina laid his body at Arlington National Cemetery, where he was buried at the crest of a hill overlooking the Tomb of the Unknown Soldier.

Earl Warren died hours after learning that the Court he loved would force justice on the man who had bedeviled him much of his life. On August 5, President Nixon, Warren's nemesis, bowed to the Supreme Court, Warren's seat of power for sixteen years. As ordered, Nixon turned over the tapes. Four days later, on August 9, 1974, Richard Nixon resigned the presidency of the United States.

# EPILOGUE

*It is the spirit and not the form of law that keeps justice alive.*

EARL WARREN

EARL WARREN left a great and voluminous legacy that modern America has not known quite how to absorb. In personal terms, his family bore him testament. Nina lived to celebrate her hundredth birthday and spent her remaining years as she had her life, happily consumed by her family, by then a full complement of her own children and their children—sixteen grandchildren in all. Although not a public person, Nina did occasionally visit the Court, where the staff and justices welcomed her with familial kindness. She was there, for instance, in hat and gloves, when the Court heard arguments in the *Bakke* case, which challenged affirmative action laws and grew out of California. As her husband always had, she refused to comment on what she'd heard. Through the 1970s, '80s, and early '90s, Nina resided modestly in the apartment she and Earl had shared, surrounded by memories and memorabilia of their life. "It's all right to be sad," she confided to the *Sacramento Bee* in a rare 1977 interview. "But one must not be dismal." Today, Nina Warren is buried with her husband at Arlington National Cemetery. They lie together on a sunny hilltop, surrounded by the dignified white crosses and stars that blanket Arlington's slopes. Their bodies rest beneath a tombstone inscribed with a passage from Warren's book, *A Republic, If You Can Keep It*:

Where there is injustice, we should correct it; where there is poverty, we should eliminate it; where there is corruption, we should stamp it out; where there is violence we should punish it; where there is neglect, we should provide care; where there is war, we should restore peace; and wherever corrections are achieved we should add them permanently to our storehouse of treasures.

The Warren children and grandchildren, meanwhile, scattered across the American landscape, most but not all settling in California, growing up and growing older in the state that had fashioned Warren and that he, in turn, remade for them. Today the Warrens prosper in all walks of life. They work in real estate and the law, in education and politics. They are the living memory of Earl and Nina, blond and buoyant, exuberant and successful. They uphold their family's legacy with grace.

But while Warren survives through his family, his place in the politics of the nation is more complex. The decisions he authored and orchestrated at the Supreme Court continue to set the parameters of modern American life, and most have become more settled over time. The decisions that launched the movement to impeach Earl Warren—the desegregation of schools, the insistence on free and fair elections at all levels of government, the curbs on prosecutions of Communists, the end to government-sponsored prayer in public schools—are such settled facts of American society that they barely stir dispute. No serious person today suggests that the poor be denied lawyers in state trials, as they were before *Gideon*. Few argue that illegally seized evidence should be admissible in trials, as it was before *Mapp*. Even *Miranda*, the source of fury in its time, has embedded itself so firmly in the law that police have learned to live with it and conservatives are loath to disturb it. The great exception, of course, is *Griswold*, an opinion that continues to roil the American landscape by providing the philosophical underpinnings for a right of privacy and thus for constitutionally protected abortion. Still, given the range and depth of the decisions of the Warren Court, one cannot help but be struck at the endurance of its work.

Warren, by contrast, has defied easy appreciation, as perceptions of him vary widely, according to the vantage point from which he is seen. In Sacramento, Warren's images are dusted off periodically by politicians eager to associate themselves with his moderation. When Arnold Schwarzenegger signed compacts with California's Indians in 2004, he pulled Warren's old desk out of storage for the event, and when voters rebuked Schwarzenegger in the state's 2005 special elections, he returned with a State of the State address in which he cited Warren, along with Pat Brown, Ronald Reagan, and Goodwin Knight, as the "governors who built the foundation of California's prosperity." For Schwarzenegger, Warren's legacy is an attractive association, a reminder of a bipartisan and productive past.

But the same Warren who stands for centrism and bipartisanship in California is the punching bag in the nation's fratricidal Supreme Court confirmation battles, where he has come to symbolize reckless, liberal judicial activism, against whose jurisprudence justices like Samuel Alito boast of having sharpened their skills.

When Republicans fret about the possibility of conservative justices abandoning the faith on the bench and heading off into unpredictable terrain, it is Warren who strikes that fear. Substantively, Warren's work also courses through modern legal debate in topic after topic, nowhere more so than in the nation's unwinnable argument between the forces of security and those of liberty. Warren started out a prosecutor, and his first case took aim at those whose advocacy challenged the state. Over the course of his life, he came to value freedom more highly and to see security not as undermined by freedom but rather as its product. Today's challenge to American liberty is terrorism, not Communism or the IWW, and the methods that the government chooses to defend itself have changed as well—from congressional hearings that tested loyalty to wiretaps with and without court sanction. If methods have changed, however, the question fundamentally has not: Must liberty be curtailed in order to preserve the nation, or is the nation better understood as an expression of its freedoms?

Liberty is not a partisan value, nor is it one of special interests. It is, after all—along with life and the pursuit of happiness—one of the founding values of the nation itself. Warren's belief in it thus hardly stamped him politically, and little about him fit the strictures of a runaway liberal. His manner was too conservative, his rhetoric too restrained, his devotion to nineteenth-century values too sincere for Warren ever to be a liberal in the modern sense. He was a veteran, married his whole life to one woman, a father to six children, appalled by pornography, and deeply patriotic. He was a Grand Master of the Masons. He appreciated power and those who had it. He liked to summer at the Bohemian Grove. Earl Warren was no Eldridge Cleaver.

And so Warren's legacy is a perplexing one. To a polarized society whose leading cultural and political figures seem in constant search of affirmation, Warren offers both sides a little and neither side all it wants. Too straight and too Establishment to fit a liberal model, too devoted to an expansive civil libertarianism for conservatives to honor him, Warren falls between our modern cracks. He is a reminder that centrism today is a lonely idea, honored mostly in the breach.

That is illustrated by a strange fact of Sacramento. In a city where plaques and monuments are ubiquitous—where there is a statue to Junípero Serra, a museum to its railroads, and another to its Indian heritage, where the county courthouse is named for Gordon D. Schaber and its Federal Building for Congressman Robert Matsui—there is scant mention of the man who governed California the longest. No building bears his name. There have been proposals now and again, but they fail because neither side claims Warren and because his legacy is so large that it must inevitably contain something for everyone to disapprove of. No man who desegregated schools, who prosecuted some criminals and then ordered others freed, who lobbied for the internment of Japanese-Americans, and who insisted that a lone as-sassin killed John Kennedy can avoid detractors. When, in 2003, a bill was intro-duced in the legislature to install a pair of memorials along the walk that Warren used to take from the mansion to his office, it made some headway. But like previ-ous proposals to honor Warren, it died. In this case, it was the legislature's Asian caucus that doomed the bill, retribution for Warren's advocacy of the internment.

Jim Gaither, one of the perceptive and learned men who clerked for Warren, wistfully observed in our interview that the Supreme Court could not function with nine Earl Warrens. It would be too conscious of delivering individual justice and perhaps too heedless of the need to construct an architecture of law. But nor, Gaither added, can the Court survive without one Warren. Someone needs to look after the law, as Warren did, to see not only that it is faithful to its principles but also that it is effective in action, that it serves society and does not merely bind it, that it delivers not just abstract justice but actual fairness.

In the decades since Warren left the Court, America has never suffered from too many men or women like him. It is equally true that the nation today—certainly the Court—is less fortunate not to have one of him.

# Acknowledgments

TOO MANY FRIENDS, old and new, have contributed to this book for me to thank them all. There are some, however, to whom I am so clearly in debt that they bear special recognition.

There is no question but to whom my first acknowledgment is due: Tina Bennett read my early attempt at a book proposal and guided me—with kindness, patience, and literary excellence—toward a book. Without her, this book would not exist. I am grateful to her for her work on every aspect of this project as well as for her unending good cheer, imaginative encouragement, and unsurpassed intelligence. No author could ask for more. Tina's effectiveness is magnified by that of her able and cheerful assistant, Svetlana Katz.

At Riverhead Books, Susan Lehman saw early promise in the work and helped launch it. Jake Morrissey brought it to a conclusion with deft editing and devotion. I am happy to end this project not only as his writer but also as his friend. Thanks, too, to Jake's assistant, David Moldawer.

Beyond them, there are three sets of people to whom I owe thanks: those who helped me research this book, those who read drafts or parts of drafts, and those who supplied comfort and cheer throughout. Of the first group, I am indebted especially to courteous and intelligent librarians from Berkeley to Washington, D.C., who have helped track down the far-flung records and recollections of Earl Warren's California and Washington lives. Genevieve Troka at the California State Archives in Sacramento; Paul Wormser, Director of Archival Operations, National Archives, Pacific Region; and Greg Cumming of the Richard Nixon Library and Birthplace all helped me to locate material relating to Warren's time as governor and his relationship with Richard Nixon. Mike Lange at the *Los Angeles Times* opened the paper's History Center for my use, and Richard Beene, an old friend and the distinguished president and CEO of the *Bakersfield Californian*, made his paper's archives available to me, as did the equally eminent Jerry Roberts, former editor of the *Santa Barbara News-Press*. Susan Fukushima of the Japanese American National Museum unearthed rare material in that museum's collection on the World War II internments and Warren's role in advocating them. Octavio Olvera of the UCLA Department of Special Collections guided me to materials in that library, especially the papers of Carey McWilliams, that helped illuminate the views of others regarding Warren's rise through California politics.

Throughout, Charles Faulhaber and his exemplary staff at UC Berkeley's Bancroft Library provided wisdom for understanding Warren's life in California and the broader history of the state during that period. There, one person in particular deserves special thanks: Laura McCreery is a gifted historian who was compiling her important oral history of Warren's clerks at the same time that I was at work on this book; I thank her for her many contributions to my work and to the Regional Oral History Office, where she and her colleagues for years have compiled the record of Warren's friends and intimates. Because of Laura and others at Berkeley, my months there were among the most pleasurable of this project, and were aided by support from the Institute of Governmental Studies, which generously named me as its John Jacobs Fellow for 2004 and 2005.

Records relating to Warren and his Court years are scattered in libraries across the country, and I am grateful thus to many researchers in many places. Mary Wolfskill was a gracious host at the Library of Congress; the staff of the Manuscript Division there is superb in every respect. At the National Archives, Kristen Wilhelm located and unsealed the records relating to Warren's 1954 confirmation by the Senate. Those records were supplemented by the files of Senator William Langer, whose papers Sandy Slater kindly culled for me in Grand Rapids, North Dakota. At the Court itself, Brian A. Stiglmeier found transcripts and other vital documents and managed to get them to me with much-appreciated alacrity. In Princeton, New Jersey, Dan Linke and Ben Primer steered me through the papers of Justice Harlan, an exquisitely maintained and underappreciated resource on the Warren Court. In Austin, Texas, Mary Knill went beyond all bounds of courtesy with her help navigating the holdings of the LBJ Library, including papers relating to the Warren Commission as well as the personal papers of Warren Christopher, Drew Pearson, and others. Other librarians—too many to mention but all appreciated nonetheless— helped me locate records and papers at the National Archives in College Park (main repository of the Warren Commission's files) and documents among the presidential papers of Presidents Hoover, Eisenhower, Truman, and Kennedy. Finally, Alexander Charns, whose *Cloak and Gavel* is a fascinating study of the relationship between the FBI and the Court, guided me to his extensive FBI files at the University of North Carolina during a stressful period when the FBI was not responding to my own Freedom of Information Act requests. I thank Alexander for his work and for his help.

This book is constructed largely around the original materials in the aforementioned libraries and from dozens of interviews, but it rests also on many secondary sources, which are cited in the bibliography and in footnotes accompanying the text. A few were so important that they deserve special mention. Richard Kluger's *Simple Justice* is the definitive work on the school desegregation cases; no book before or since compares. Lucas "Scot" Powe similarly commands the field on the jurisprudence of the Warren Court; his *The Warren Court and American Politics* is the best of its kind, and Powe's help to me only amplifies my gratitude to him. G. Edward White's *Earl Warren: A Public Life* is a learned legal analysis of Warren, as one would expect from White, given his own brilliance and time as Warren's clerk. Kevin Starr is California's preeminent historian; his work is cited often in these pages, and his advice along the way has been very much appreciated as well. Taylor Branch's writing on Martin Luther King is both inspiration and source. It too is cited through this work, but I owe my larger thanks to him for supplying awe.

I am not the first author to take the measure of Earl Warren. This biography builds on the hard work of others. Leo Katcher's *Earl Warren: A Political Biography* and Jack Harrison Pollack's *Earl Warren: The Judge Who Changed America* are helpful works. A lesser but still appealing book is *Mr. Chief Justice: Earl Warren, A Biography* by Bill Severn. More comprehensive are *Chief Justice: A Biography of Earl Warren* by Ed Cray, who graciously fielded questions from me, and John D. Weaver's *Warren: The Man, the Court, the Era*, a lovingly composed study made with Warren's cooperation. The history of Warren in his Court years is best captured in Bernard Schwartz's exhaustive *Super Chief: Earl Warren and His Supreme Court—A Judicial Biography* and White's *Earl Warren: A Public Life*. I am grateful to all of the above, but especially Cray and White, for their work, support, and assistance.

Undertaking a task such as this is demanding, and not just on an author. My friends and family have lived with Earl Warren these past five years almost as surely as I have. Among those whose forbearance and good humor have helped me and thus this project—and who have supplied meals and shelter and mountains of friendship—are my parents, to whom I owe more than I can articulate; Carol Stogsdill and Steve Stroud (Carol is a long-standing source of kindness and strategic wisdom, and Steve deserves an extra measure of appreciation for supervising the selection of pictures for the book and taking the author photograph); Brad Hall and Julia Louis-Dreyfus (and Henry and Charlie); Paul and Victoria Barosse (and Emilia and Eva); Whitney Ellerman and Kelly Baker (and Casey, Carter, and Charlie); Keith and Marianne Powell (and Scotty and Jackson); Mark Z. and Marianne Barabak (and Amelia and Rachel); Chris and Sarah Capel (and Elizabeth, Blair, and Anna); and last but never least, my dear and old friend Bill McIntyre, whose Mill Valley apartment is one of my favorite homes away from home. All my research trips—to Sacramento, Berkeley, Washington, Austin, Dallas, New York, Princeton,

Palo Alto, and Chapel Hill—were delightful voyages of learning, made comfortable and happy by these people. I thank them all.

To those who read the manuscript, I owe special thanks—for their time and insights and for the extraordinary depth and range of expertise they brought to bear on my behalf. Brad Hall read early drafts and was consistently a source of writerly insight. My brother John, the brains of our family, gave an early draft of the manuscript a thorough and much-appreciated edit; he and his partner, my brother-in-law Christopher Brescia, were also gracious hosts on my several trips to New York. Henry Weinstein, whose command of the law is surpassed only by his knowledge of baseball and his breath-taking decency, stole time from his important duties at the *Los Angeles Times* to give an insightful reading to a complete draft; Max Holland, the finest and most clearheaded of all scholars on the Warren Commission, generously agreed to read that chapter and significantly improved my understanding of that terrible year. Duke law professor Erwin Chemerinsky, who manages more commitments with better humor than anyone I know, read the entire manuscript and offered important insights, especially in the chapters relating to the Court. Scot Powe gave me a delightful evening in Austin, and a deeply appreciated read of the manuscript. Jeffrey Warren, who has treasured the memory and history of his grandfather, graciously devoted many, many hours to looking over my work for details of his family. And J. R. Moehringer, my friend of some twenty years, read many drafts and counseled me throughout. This is a more thoughtful and stylish book, and I am a more capable writer, because of him.

It should be emphasized that while I am deeply grateful to all of the above, any mistakes in this book are mine and mine alone.

I am especially thankful to members of the Warren family, who have shared many hours and memories in more than a dozen interviews, follow-up conversations, and e-mails. Alas, this book comes too late for me to have met Jim or Dorothy Warren (though Jim's recollections were captured, along with so many others, by Berkeley's Oral History Project). But Virginia Daly, Robert Warren, and Earl Warren, Jr., each sat down time and again, in person and over the telephone, to discuss their mother and father with me. If anything, Nina "Honey Bear" Brien was even more generous, as I called on her many times to fill in missing details. She is as lovely as she is giving. I am grateful to all four children for their generosity to me.

Beyond those who lent homes, evenings, time, and intelligence to the book itself, there are those to whom I am forever in debt for other lessons. Here again, there are indeed too many to count, much less list. My colleagues at the *Los Angeles Times* are a source of wonder; they do difficult, honest, and diligent work every day. Editor Dean Baquet manages that noble enterprise and encouraged my work on this book, even when it kept me from the newsroom. In addition, two *Times* colleagues, Dan Morain and Cathleen Decker, deserve special note, as Dan corralled Sacramento materials for me when he had better things to do, and Cathy weighed in over many lunches with her unfailingly insightful views on California politics. Mark Barabak, noted above, was likewise a font of knowledge and a good friend.

As lucky as I am to work for the *Times*, I am especially blessed to have had the great fortune to work over the years for four of America's finest journalists. Bill Kovach, Sonny Rawls, John Carroll, and James Reston taught me—or at least tried to teach me—about integrity, determination, precision, and commitment to quality, mixed in among many other lessons about life and journalism. Few reporters—indeed, few people—are so lucky as to be able to draw upon such a group of mentors. I am mindful every day of my debt to all four. I reserve a special measure of gratitude for Mr. Reston, who launched me on a career in journalism and whose gentle, joyful excellence stands as the example for which I strive.

Still, at the end of this project as at the beginning, there are two unrivaled recipients of my appreciation and love.

Karlene Goller is my wife and the source of much of this book's wisdom, as well as the great currents of its feeling. On more occasions than I can recall, she engaged in our running conversation about Warren and his life. Intuitively and with her perfect pitch of precision and grace, Karlene taught me about Warren; her patience with my need to think out loud allowed me to learn more. Beyond that, Karlene is a fine lawyer—she spearheaded the long and ultimately successful effort to obtain FBI files relating to Warren from the Bureau through the Freedom of Information Act—and a gifted reader. She was, among other things, the first to suggest the title. And still beyond that, she is the font of so much love that her influence is manifested across this entire book, as it is through every aspect of my life.

My son Jack, meanwhile, cheerfully coordinated the filing of my papers and supplied inspiration throughout. I am glad to have made Earl Warren a part of his young life, and I marvel at the ways this story has penetrated his upbringing. Early in the writing, I overheard Jack describe Warren to a friend. Warren, my six-year-old son explained, was the man who helped Martin Luther King make it so the two of them could go to school with their friends who are African-American. I've never forgotten Jack's elemental observation, and it was one of many that helped clarify my work. Over the long labor of a work such as this, a subject's essence can slip beneath the seas of detail. Time and again, Jack has been there to rescue me with the clear vision. I admire, appreciate, and love my son very much, and I am grateful to him for his many insights.

In the end, a book is a story you tell to those you love, and it is Jack and Karlene to whom I have been telling it for many years now. It is thus fitting that this book is lovingly dedicated to them.

# Notes

**ABBREVIATIONS USED IN NOTES**

BL—Bancroft Library

HI—Hoover Institution Archives

LBJ Library—Lyndon Baines Johnson Library and Museum

LOC—Library of Congress

MD—Manuscript Division

NARA—National Archives and Records Administration

PU—Princeton University

RNLB—Richard Nixon Library and Birthplace

All references to *Memoirs* are to Earl Warren's memoirs. "State archives" indicates the California State Archives.

### PROLOGUE: FIRST VACANCY

1. Oral history interview with Bartley Cavanaugh, *Hunting and Fishing with Earl Warren*, p. 33.
2. *Santa Barbara News-Press* (AP report), Jan. 19, 1939.
3. Oral history interview with Bartley Cavanaugh, *Hunting and Fishing with Earl Warren*, p. 3.
4. Ibid., p. 33.
5. Ibid., p. 34. Cavanaugh's account is unclear on some details. He refers, for instance, to a matter of days between these phone calls and Warren's nomination, when in fact weeks transpired. Still, his conversations with Warren appear correctly rendered, and Warren himself, while disputing other accounts of the confirmation, did not take issue with Cavanaugh's version.
6. Justice Tom C. Clark, quoted in the *New York Times*, Sept. 9, 1953.
7. *New York Times*, Sept. 9, 1953.
8. This remark has been recounted in various renderings, perhaps first by Joseph L. Rauh in a *New Republic* article titled "The Chief" (Aug. 9, 1982, p. 31). It has been included subsequently in many volumes, including Henry J. Abraham's *Justices and Presidents: A Political History of Appointments to the Supreme Court* (New York: Oxford University Press, 1992), p. 254.
9. *New York Times*, Sept. 9, 1953.
10. Stephen Ambrose, *Eisenhower: Soldier and President*, p. 337.
11. Herbert Brownell, *Advising Ike: The Memoirs of Attorney General Herbert Brownell*, p. 166.
12. Roger K. Newman, *Hugo Black: A Biography*, pp. 345–47.

13. John Aubrey Douglas, "Earl Warren's New Deal: Economic Transition, Postwar Planning, and Higher Education in California," *Journal of Policy History*, vol. 1.2, no. 4 (2000).

14. Dwight D. Eisenhower, *Mandate for Change: The White House Years, 1953–1956*, p. 228.

15. *Memoirs*, p. 260.

16. Brownell, *Advising Ike*, p. 166.

17. *Los Angeles Times*, Sept. 4, 1953.

18. Oral history interview with Warren, *Conversations with Earl Warren on California Government*, p. 285.

19. Eisenhower, *Mandate for Change*, p. 227. See also Brownell, *Advising Ike*, p. 166.

20. Oral history interview with Warren, *Conversations with Earl Warren on California Government*, p. 285.

21. Oral history interview with Warren Olney III, *Law Enforcement and Judicial Administration in the Earl Warren Era*, p. 386.

22. Author interviews with Earl Warren, Jr., Nov. 25, 2003, and Robert Warren, Dec. 12, 2003. Warren recalled being fetched from the island by plane not boat, but both his sons dispute that, and their recollection seems more convincing, as there is no airstrip on Santa Rosa Island.

23. Oral history interview with Merrell Small, *The Office of the Governor Under Earl Warren*, p. 209.

24. Oral history interview with Bartley Cavanaugh, *Hunting and Fishing with Earl Warren*, p. 34.

25. Pat Nixon, personal diary entry for Oct. 5, 1953, RNLB.

26. *New York Times* editorial, Oct. 1, 1953.

27. *Los Angeles Times* editorial, Oct. 1, 1953.

28. Eisenhower, *Mandate for Change*, p. 230.

29. John Lewis, *Walking with the Wind*, p. 54.

## CHAPTER 1. YOUNG MAN OF CALIFORNIA

1. David Starr Jordan, *California and the Californians*, p. 46.

2. *Memoirs*, p. 14.

3. This description is drawn largely from *Memoirs*, pp. 14–16.

4. J. A. Alexander, *Life of George Chaffey*, p. 33.

5. Charles Fletcher Lummis, "One of the Old Guard," 1900, Los Angeles Times History Center, Lummis Papers.

6. T. H. Watkins, *California: An Illustrated History*, p. 299.

7. Ray Ginger, *The Bending Cross*, p. 127.

8. Lummis, "One of the Old Guard."

9. John D. Weaver, *Warren: The Man, the Court, the Era*, p. 21.

10. *Memoirs*, p. 13.

11. William Henry Bishop, "Southern California," Beale Library, Local History collection, Bakersfield folder.

12. Oral history interview with Francis E. Vaughn, *Earl Warren's Bakersfield*, p. 21.

13. *Daily Californian*, Feb. 27, 1900.

14. *Daily Californian*, March 27, 1900.

15. *Daily Californian*, Feb. 2, 1900.

16. *Daily Californian*, Feb. 14, 1900.

17. Author interview with Robert Warren, Dec. 11, 2003.

18. Warren's childhood books are kept by his grandson, Jeffrey Warren, who shared them with the author.

19. This description comes from books collected by Warren's family, particularly those kept by Jeffrey Warren. Warren's right-handedness was relayed to the author by Robert Warren.

20. Jack Harrison Pollack, *Earl Warren: The Judge Who Changed America*, p. 24.

21. *Memoirs*, p. 21. See also oral history interview and letter from Ruth Smith Henley, *Earl Warren's Bakersfield*.

22. Bill Severn, *Mr. Chief Justice*, p. 6.

23. Author interview with Jeffrey Warren, Aug. 26, 2003.

24. As chief justice, Warren would often be asked by schoolchildren and others to name his early influences. In a speech he delivered at Temple University on March 4, 1954, Warren recalled the impact that "Acres of Diamonds" had on him. LOC, MD, Warren papers, Speeches file.

25. Russell H. Conwell, "Acres of Diamonds," p. 64.

26. Warren speech at Temple University, March 4, 1954, LOC, MD, Warren papers, Speeches file. Warren often referred correspondents, particularly students, to "Acres of Diamonds" when they inquired about his boyhood influences.

27. Journalist John Gunther in 1947 predicted that Warren would "never set the world on fire."

28. *Memoirs*, p. 23.

29. *Daily Californian*, April 16, 1903.

30. Headlines and story references all drawn from the *Daily Californian*, week of April 10, 1903.

31. Oral history interview with Maryann Ashe, *Earl Warren's Bakersfield*, p. 29.

32. High school transcript, June 1908, LOC, MD, Warren papers, family file.

33. *From Milton to Tennyson, Masterpieces of English Poetry*. Warren's copy, signed and dated April 6, 1904, is in the collection of the Bancroft Library, University of California, Berkeley.

34. *The Oracle*, commencement issue, 1908.

35. Ibid.

36. Warren speech at Sailors Union Building, San Francisco, Nov. 3, 1950, state archives, Warren administrative papers, Speeches, Alpha Files "P."

37. Ibid.

38. See, for instance, the undated tribute to Warren prepared by Douglas after Warren's death in 1974, LOC, MD, William O. Douglas papers, Part 1, Subject files, Earl Warren.

39. *Memoirs*, p. 22.

40. Certificate of the Musicians' Mutual Protection Union, June 22, 1926, LOC, MD, Warren papers, family file.

41. *Memoirs*, p. 28. See also oral history interviews, *Earl Warren's Bakersfield*, and John Weaver, *Warren: The Man, the Court, the Era*, p. 29.

42. Hubert Howe Bancroft, *History of California*, vol. 7, *1860–1890*, p. 698.

43. Ibid., pp. 698–99.

44. Ibid., p. 699.

45. Michael W. Donley, Stuart Allan, Patricia Caro, and Clyde P. Patton, *Atlas of California*, pp. 22–23.

46. For this and other details of California's labor history, I am indebted to several studies, most notably Ira B. Cross's *A History of the Labor Movement in California*.

47. Given the rudimentary seismology of the period, estimates differ on the precise length of the initial shock. Contemporary accounts placed it at forty-seven seconds, though witnesses and equipment across the Bay, in Oakland, suggested that it lasted longer than a minute. Aftershocks were recorded at 5:18 A.M., 5:20 A.M., 5:25 A.M., 5:42 A.M., 8:13 A.M. (a particularly severe one), 9:13 A.M., 9:25 A.M., 10:49 A.M., 11:05 A.M., 12:03 P.M., 12:10 P.M., 2:23 P.M., 2:27 P.M., 4:50 P.M., 6:49 P.M., and 7 P.M. (See *San Francisco Chronicle*, April 24, 1906, courtesy Museum of the City of San Francisco.)

48. Gordon Thomas and Max Morgan Witts, *The San Francisco Earthquake*, p. 70.

49. *Memoirs*, p. 34.

50. Walton Bean, *Boss Ruef's San Francisco*, pp. 93–94.

51. Fremont Older, *My Own Story*.

52. Ibid., p. 80.

53. The description of Schmitz during the earthquake is widely shared. See, for instance, the works on this period by Kevin Starr and David Lavender.

54. David Lavender, *California: Land of New Beginnings*, p. 340.

55. George E. Mowry, *The California Progressives*, p. 60.

56. Kevin Starr, *Inventing the Dream*, p. 204.

57. *Eradicating Plague from San Francisco: Report of the Citizens' Health Committee and an Account of Its Work*, prepared by Frank Morton Todd, historian for the Committee, March 31, 1909, p. 30.

58. Ibid., pp. 9, 40.

59. Older, *My Own Story*, p. 143.

60. *Memoirs*, p. 39.

61. Spencer C. Olin, *California's Prodigal Sons*, p. 179.

62. *California Weekly*, Dec. 18, 1908, quoted in George E. Mowry, *The California Progressives*, p. 97.

63. G. Edward White, *Earl Warren: A Public Life*, p. 19.

64. *Memoirs*, p. 39.

65. Warren telegram to Johnson, Nov. 7, 1934, Warren papers, state archives, Sacramento, Republican State Central Committee file.

## Chapter 2. Away from Home

1. Oral history interview with Newton Drury, *Parks and Redwoods*, p. 67.

2. Grace Noble scrapbook, Class of 1912, Bancroft Library.

3. *Memoirs*, p. 35.

4. Oral history interview with Newton Drury, *Parks and Redwoods*, p. 67.

5. Bill Severn, *Mr. Chief Justice*, p. 21.

6. Oral history interview with Robert Warren, *The Governor's Family*, p. 7.

7. Oral history interview with Newton Drury, *Parks and Redwoods*, pp. 67–68.

8. A copy of the sophomore hop dance card is included in the Boalt Law School archival collection, University of California, Berkeley.

9. John Weaver, *Warren: The Man, the Court, the Era*, p. 31.

10. Ibid.

11. *Memoirs*, p. 36.

12. Ibid., pp. 36–37.

13. Oral history interview with Newton Drury, *Parks and Redwoods*, p. 68.

14. Undated Jeffrey Warren speech honoring Earl Warren after Warren's death.

15. *Blue and Gold*, vol. 41 (1915). The entry for U.N.X., listing Warren as a graduate, appears on p. 339.

16. Poem and history supplied to the author by Charles Faulhaber, curator of the Bancroft Library, University of California, Berkeley.

17. William Sweigert, "The Legend of the Earl of Warren," included in oral history interview with Sweigert, *Administration and Ethics in the Governor's Office and the Courts, California, 1939–1975*.

18. Weaver, *Warren: The Man, the Court, the Era*, p. 30.

19. George E. Mowry, *The California Progressives*, p. 11.

20. Frank Norris, *The Octopus, A Story of California* (first published by Doubleday, Page, 1901; edition cited here, New York: Penguin, 1994), pp. 179–80.

21. Ibid., p. 502.

22. Forty-ninth Commencement program, May 15, 1912, Grace Noble scrapbook, BL.

23. Weaver, *Warren: The Man, the Court, the Era*, p. 32.

24. Author interview with James Gaither, June 2, 2002.

25. The thesis is on file at the University of California, Berkeley's Doe Library.

26. *Memoirs*, p. 45.

27. Memo, State of Military Service of Earl Warren, 0 111 042, Department of the Army, April 28, 1958, LOC, MD, Warren family file.

28. Severn, *Mr. Chief Justice*, p. 32.

29. Jack Harrison Pollack, *The Judge Who Changed America*, p. 34.

30. Ibid.

31. Warren's letter, of Oct. 13, 1918, was saved by her nephew George Perham, and shared with Jeffrey Warren, who supplied a copy to the author.

32. Pollack, *The Judge Who Changed America*, p. 35.

33. Oral history interview with Maryann Ashe, *Earl Warren's Bakersfield*, p. 31.

34. Oral history interview with Horace Albright, *The Warrens: Four Personal Views*, p. 2a.

35. Irving Stone, *Earl Warren, A Great American Story*, p. 32.

CHAPTER 3. PROSECUTOR, FATHER

1. Oral history interview with Clarence A. Severin, *Perspectives on the Alameda County District Attorney's Office*, vol. 2, p. 13s.

2. Oral history interview with Jim Warren, *The Governor's Family*, p. 7.

3. Numerous sources, including Warren papers, state archives, DA files; also LOC, MD, Warren family file, memorandum of Biographical Material for Masonic Trestle Board.

4. Undated speech of Norman Chandler, Los Angeles Times History Center, folder identified as "Norman Chandler Speeches, 1950–1959."

5. Estolv E. Ward, *The Gentle Dynamiter*, p. 69.

6. Kevin Starr, *Endangered Dreams*, p. 216–17.

7. Ibid., p. 217.

8. Ibid., p. 30.

9. *Whitney v. People of State of California*, 274 U.S. 357 (1927).

10. *Oakland Tribune*, June 17, 1920.

11. *To the Beasts*, Industrial Workers of the World pamphlet published by the California Branch of the General Defense Committee, San Francisco, April 1924, p. 22. For descriptions of Warren's argument, see the *Oakland Tribune* trial coverage, April 15–20, 1920.

12. *Memoirs*, p. 62.

13. Amazingly, neither violence nor criminalization of advocacy brought the IWW to a halt. The apotheosis of mob response to the IWW occurred in 1924 in San Pedro, when a group set upon a Wobbly evening memorial service for two dead workers. The evening was planned as a celebration, with singing and dancing, for workers and their wives and children. As the entertainment unfolded inside a local hall, hundreds of armed men ringed the building. Then, on receiving a signal, they stormed inside, beating men and women and destroying the premises. Children were dipped in urns of hot coffee and scalded with IWW initials. Once the children had been tortured and the adults beaten, many of the Wobblies were hauled out of town, tarred and feathered, and forced to walk more than forty miles home. Kevin Starr, *Endangered Dreams*, p. 53.

14. Woodrow Carlton Whitten, "Criminal Syndicalism and the Law in California, 1919–1927," Ph.D. dissertation, University of California, Berkeley. The information here comes from chapter 9.

15. *Whitney v. People of State of California*, 274 U.S. 357 (1927) (Brandeis concurrence).

16. *Oakland Tribune*, June 18, 1920.

17. *To the Beasts*, p. 23.

18. Oral history interview with Helen MacGregor, *A Career in Public Service with Earl Warren*, p. 3.

19. John Weaver, *Warren: The Man, the Court, the Era*, p. 37.

20. Oral history interview with Mary Shaw, *Perspectives on the Alameda County District Attorney's Office*, vol. 1, p. 11s.

21. Affidavit of Nina Warren in support of passport application, copy provided to author by Jeffrey Warren.

22. Author interview with Robert Warren, Dec. 11, 2003.

23. To Warren biographer Jack Harrison Pollack, Nina apparently described her stepmother favorably, as he says Nina had "warm memories" of her. To her children and grandchildren, Nina was more forthcoming.

24. Author interview with Judge James Lee Warren, Nov. 24, 2003. Also Robert Warren.

25. Affidavit of Nina Warren in support of passport application.

26. Nina Palmquist Warren's letter to Amelia Fry, Feb. 13, 1979, oral history archives, Regional Oral History Office, BL (included in Jim Warren, *The Governor's Family*).

27. Oral history interview with Jim Warren, *The Governor's Family*, pp. 4–5.

28. John Weaver, *Warren: The Man, the Court, the Era*, p. 39.

29. Bill Severn, *Mr. Chief Justice*, p. 43.

30. Oral history interview with Jim Warren, *The Governor's Family*, p. 6.

31. *Memoirs*, p. 68. See also oral history interviews with William Knowland, in which he notes that the *Tribune* supported Warren in every one of his campaigns.

32. Oral history interview with John Mullins, *Perspectives on the Alameda County District Attorney's Office*, vol. 1, p. 2.

33. *Oakland Tribune*, Jan. 12, 1925.

34. Even decades later, Warren made a point of visiting Mullins when he returned to the Alameda area, and would introduce him to audiences as the man who had given him his first break.

35. Oral history interview with Frank J. Coakley, *Perspectives on the Alameda County District Attorney's Office*, vol. 3, p. 30.

36. Decoto and Warren correspondence, April 6, 1926, and Feb. 20, 1930, state archives, Warren pregubernatorial papers, correspondence files.

37. *Memoirs*, p. 65.

38. Author interview with Earl Warren, Jr., Nov. 25, 2003.

39. Interview with Drew Pearson, Aug. 23, 1967, Pearson papers, LBJ Library.

40. Undated Warren note, LOC, MD, family file.

41. Ibid. interview with Drew Pearson, Aug. 23, 1967, Pearson papers, LBJ Library.

42. Author interview with Robert Warren, Dec. 12, 2003. See also oral history interview with Nina "Honey Bear" Brien, *The Governor's Family*, p. 25.

43. Undated Warren note, LOC, MD, family file.

44. Author interview with Robert Warren, Dec. 12, 2003.

45. Undated Warren note, LOC, MD, Warren papers, family file.

46. Ibid.

47. Oral history interview with Jim Warren, *The Governor's Family*, p. 7.

48. Author interview with Earl Warren, Jr., Nov. 25, 2003. See also undated Warren note, LOC, MD, Warren papers, family file.

49. See, for instance, oral history interview with Adrian Kragen, *Earl Warren: Views and Episodes*, p. 29. Kragen's observations are from Warren's time as attorney general, but they are consistent with the impressions of those who worked for Warren as district attorney.

50. Oral history interview with Arthur Sherry, *Arthur H. Sherry*, p. 23.

51. Oral history interview with Clarence A. Severin, *Perspectives on the Alameda County District Attorney's Office*, vol. 2, p. 13s.

52. See, for instance, oral history interview with Warren, *Conversations with Earl Warren on California Government.*

53. See oral history interviews with Lloyd Jester and Helen MacGregor.

54. Personal papers of Cecil Mosbacher, BL. Original copy of acceptance speech (undated, but accompanying newspaper clips place appointment at Jan. 19, 1951).

55. Oral history interview with Mildred Lillie, Nov. 20, 1989, Committee on the History of the Law in California of the California State Bar.

56. Oral history interview with Warren Olney III, *Law Enforcement and Judicial Administration in the Earl Warren Era.*

57. Letters from Oakland Baseball Club to Warren and Warren to Buddy Plank, April 14, 1933, state archives, Warren personal papers, correspondence files.

58. See, for instance, Jack Harrison Pollack, *Earl Warren: The Judge Who Changed America*, p. 50; also oral history interview with Warren, *Conversations with Earl Warren on California Government*, pp. 55–57.

59. *Memoirs*, p. 86.

60. Pollack, *Earl Warren: The Judge Who Changed America*, p. 50.

61. Franklin Hichborn, *The System, As Uncovered by the San Francisco Graft Prosecution*, p. 462.

62. *Memoirs*, p. 90.

63. Ibid., p. 91.

64. Ibid., p. 93. See also oral history interview with Frank J. Coakley, *Perspectives on the Alameda County District Attorney's Office*, vol. 2, p. 36.

65. Oral history interview with Warren, *Conversations with Earl Warren on California Government*, p. 55.

66. Ibid., p. 56.

67. Lloyd Ray Henderson, "Earl Warren and California Politics" (unpublished dissertation), p. 13.

68. *Memoirs*, p. 98.

69. See *Memoirs*, as well as oral history interview with Coakley, *Perspectives on the Alameda County District Attorney's Office*, and Henderson, "Earl Warren and California Politics," p. 14.

70. Letters cited here are from the Earl Warren papers at the state archives, correspondence file. Welfare League letter dated March 13, 1930; Boosters' Club dated March 4, 1930; Klan letter dated March 18, 1930. The pastor's note was signed by R. H. Moon and dated Feb. 26, 1930.

71. Earl Warren papers, state archives, Sacramento, Alameda County District Attorney campaign papers file.

72. Higgins letter to the Rev. R. E. Brown, Aug. 2, 1926, state archives, Warren papers, Alameda County District Attorney campaign papers file.

73. Warren letter, unaddressed but responding to Higgins, Aug. 20, 1926.

74. Oral history interview with Jim Warren, *The Governor's Family*, p. 25.

75. See Nina Warren's letter to Miriam Feingold, included in *The Governor's Family*. In fact, Nina did make some appearances for Earl, especially during the war, when she christened a number of ships. But her obligations were overwhelmingly domestic and her public appearances generally limited to nonspeaking roles.

76. Drew Pearson diary entry, Feb. 7, 1966, LBJ Library, Drew Pearson papers, diaries.

77. *New York Times*, Aug. 30, 1931.

78. E. P. Guinane to Hoover, May 29, 1934, FBI document 62-31548-2, Charns, Warren files, Folder 85.

79. San Francisco Special Agent in Charge to Hoover, May 18, 1937, FBI document 62-35380-3, Charns, Warren files, Folder 85.

80. For the account of the *Point Lobos* case and trial, I am indebted to Miriam Feingold Stein, whose interviews through the oral history project on this topic are particularly pointed and well informed.

81. *San Francisco Chronicle*, Sept. 1, 1936 (quoted in Henderson, "Earl Warren and California Politics," p. 26).

82. Oral history interview with Aubrey Grossman, *The Shipboard Murder Case: Labor, Radicalism and Earl Warren, 1936–1941*, p. 20.

83. *Los Angeles Times*, Oct. 31, 1936.

84. Ibid.

85. Ed Cray, *Chief Justice*, pp. 88–89 (quoting Miriam Feingold, "The King-Ramsay-Connor Case," p. 488).

86. Ibid., p. 89 (quoting Feingold, "The King-Ramsay-Connor Case," pp. 489–90).

87. *Los Angeles Times*, Jan. 6, 1937.

88. Oral history interview with Beverly R. Heinrichs, *Perspectives on the Alameda County District Attorney's Office*, vol. 2, p. 13b.

89. Oral history interview with Oscar Jahnsen, *Enforcing the Law Against Gambling, Bootlegging, Graft, Fraud and Subversion, 1922–1942*, pp. 106–8.

90. Ibid., p. 110.

91. Warren's personal calendar, entries for Jan. 27, April 8, and May 20, 1937, state archives, Warren papers.

92. Oral history interview with Aubrey Grossman, *The Shipboard Murder Case: Labor, Radicalism and Earl Warren, 1936–1941*, p. 26.

93. G. Edward White, *Earl Warren: A Public Life*, p. 40 (attributed to *San Francisco Examiner*, Nov. 28, 1941).

94. *Life*, May 10, 1948.

95. White, *Earl Warren*, p. 43.

96. Oral history interview with Myron Harris, *The Shipboard Murder Case: Labor, Radicalism and Earl Warren, 1936–1941*, p. 6.

## Chapter 4. Politician

1. *Memoirs*, p. 123.

2. Author interview with Ira Michael Heyman, Oct. 21, 2003.

3. *New York Times* obituary of Warren, July 10, 1974.

4. Warren statement, Oct. 16, 1934, state archives, Warren papers, Republican State Central Committee files, news releases.

5. "Suggestions of Earl Warren, District Attorney of Alameda County, California," Aug. 18, 1933, Hoover Institution Archives, Moley papers, FDR file, Schedule B, Box 214, Folder 4.

6. Ibid.

7. Decoto letter to Warren, June 10, 1930, state archives, Warren personal papers, correspondence files.

8. Warren speech to American Legion, Aug. 12, 1940, state archives, gubernatorial papers, speeches file.

9. Leo Katcher, *Earl Warren: A Political Biography*, p. 66.

10. Masons' official biography of Earl Warren, Grand Master, provided to the author by Al Donnici, executive assistant to the Grand Secretary, on Nov. 17, 2003.

11. *Memoirs*, p. 123.

12. Jim Riley, Grand Secretary of the Native Sons of the Golden West, e-mail to the author, Oct. 15, 2003.

13. G. Edward White, *Earl Warren: A Public Life*, p. 19.

14. Carey McWilliams, *Prejudice: Japanese-Americans, Symbol of Racial Intolerance*, p. 59.

15. Ibid.

16. *Grizzly Bear*, May 1926.

17. *Grizzly Bear*, May 1942.

18. *Grizzly Bear*, June 1942.

19. *Oakland Tribune*, May 20, 1942.

20. Knowland letter to Warren, May 20, 1942, state archives, William Knowland file.

21. *Oakland Tribune*, May 20, 1942 (at state archives, copy of story attached to Knowland's letter to Warren of same date).
22. *Grizzly Bear*, October 1942.
23. Oral history interview with Joseph R. Knowland, *Conservation and Politics*, p. 13.
24. Warren letter to Joseph Knowland, Feb. 15, 1927, state archives, pregubernatorial papers, Joseph Knowland file.
25. Warren letter and file to Joseph Knowland, Feb. 17, 1927, state archives, pregubernatorial papers, Joseph Knowland file.
26. Warren letter Joseph Knowland, Feb. 20, 1933, state archives, pregubernatorial papers, Joseph Knowland file.
27. Warren letter Joseph Knowland, March 26, 1935, state archives, pregubernatorial papers, Joseph Knowland file.
28. Oral history interview with Warren, *Conversations with Earl Warren on California Government*, p. 58.
29. Upton Sinclair, *I, Candidate for Governor: And How I Got Licked* (originally published by Upton Sinclair in 1934; edition used here is University of California Press).
30. Background for the Sinclair campaign comes from a number of sources, most notably Sinclair's own account of the race and Gregg Mitchell's *Campaign of the Century*, a superb reconstruction of the closing week of the campaign.
31. Sinclair, *I, Governor of California*, cover.
32. Walton Bean, *California: An Interpretive History*, p. 409.
33. John Steinbeck, *The Grapes of Wrath*, p. 363.
34. Kevin Starr, *Endangered Dreams*, p. 96.
35. Bean, *California: An Interpretive History*, p. 415.
36. Starr, *Endangered Dreams*, p. 108.
37. Ibid., p. 114.
38. *San Francisco Call-Bulletin*, July 20, 1934.
39. Lorena Hickok, *One Third of a Nation*, p. 298.
40. Ibid., p. 302.
41. Ibid., pp. 312–13.
42. Upton Sinclair, *Upton Sinclair Presents William Fox*.
43. Ibid., p. 146.
44. Oliver Carlson, *A Mirror for Californians*, p. 299.
45. Sinclair, *I, Governor of California*, p. 139.
46. *Los Angeles Times*, Sept. 27, 1934.
47. Greg Mitchell, *The Campaign of the Century*, p. 238.
48. Ibid., p. 306 (cited to *Los Angeles Times*, Oct. 6, 1934).
49. Republican Party press release, Oct. 15, 1934, state archives, pregubernatorial papers, 1934 campaign files.
50. Warren radio address, Oct. 21, 1934, state archives, pregubernatorial papers, 1934 campaign file.
51. Wilson telegram to Warren telegram, Nov. 6, 1934, state archives, pregubernatorial papers, 1934 campaign file.
52. Republican State Central Committee statement, Oct. 25, 1934, state archives, pregubernatorial papers, 1934 campaign file.
53. Republican State Central Committee statement, Oct. 26, 1934, state archives, pregubernatorial papers, 1934 campaign file.
54. Warren telegram to Henry Fletcher, National Republican Committee, Oct. 29, 1934, state archives, pregubernatorial papers, 1934 campaign files.

55. Mitchell, *The Campaign of the Century*, pp. 533–34.

56. Statement of Nov. 7, 1934, state archives, pregubernatorial papers, Republican State Central Committee file, news releases.

57. Katcher, *Earl Warren: A Political Biography*, p. 86.

58. Drew Pearson diary, entry for Feb. 6, 1966, LBJ Library, Pearson papers, diaries.

59. *Memoirs*, p. 112.

60. Undated campaign flyer from the personal collection of Justice Richard Mosk, Los Angeles.

61. Oral history interview with Warren Olney III, *Law Enforcement and Judicial Administration in the Earl Warren Era*, pp. 150–52.

62. *Los Angeles Times*, Feb. 18, 1938.

## CHAPTER 5. MURDER

1. Reed telegram to Warren, May 15, 1938, quoted in *Bakersfield Californian*, May 17, 1938.

2. Earl Warren's personal calendar, state archives, pregubernatorial papers, daily calendars for those days.

3. Newspaper accounts placed the watch under the bed. Oscar Jahnsen recalled it being next to the body, on the bed.

4. This re-creation of the scene is drawn largely from the press accounts at the time, especially those carried in the *Bakersfield Californian*. Some details come from author interviews with Robert Warren, and oral history interviews with Oscar Jahnsen and Robert Powers.

5. *Bakersfield Californian*, May 17, 1938.

6. Leo Katcher, *Earl Warren: A Political Biography*, p. 101.

7. In its initial story on the murder, the *Californian* noted, without explanation, that the Warrens had lived apart for twelve years. Although he cannot confirm those dates, Robert Warren, in an interview with the author, said the separation was a long one and had become permanent by the time of Methias's murder. After that early mention, stories about the murder omitted reference to the separation between the Warrens.

8. *Memoirs*, p. 125; John Weaver, *Warren: The Man, the Court, the Era*, p. 49.

9. *Bakersfield Californian*, May 16, 1938.

10. Ibid.

11. Ibid.

12. Hoover letter to Warren, May 21, 1938, FBI document 62-51247-2. (The early correspondence between Hoover and Warren was formal, and this letter was addressed to "Dear Mr. Warren." Later they would move to "Earl" and "Edgar" in addressing each another.) In 1943, with authorities still searching for Methias's killer, the FBI agreed to run a fingerprint check on a suspect.

13. Oral history interview with Ralph Kreiser, *Earl Warren's Bakersfield*, pp. 27–28.

14. Oral history interview with Robert B. Powers, *Law Enforcement, Race Relations: 1930–1960*, p. 4.

15. Ibid., pp. 11–12.

16. Ibid., p. 12.

17. Ibid., p. 16.

18. Oral history interview with Oscar Jahnsen, *Enforcing the Law Against Gambling, Bootlegging, Graft, Fraud, and Subversion, 1922–1942*, pp. 150–58. The *Californian* reported Regan's name as "Reagan," but Jahnsen corrected that in his oral history interview.

19. Ibid., p. 165.

20. Oral history interview with Robert B. Powers, *Law Enforcement, Race Relations: 1930–1960*, p. 20.

21. Powers letter to Warren, May 28, 1938, state archives, pregubernatorial papers, correspondence files.

22. Various notes, state archives, pregubernatorial papers, letters of condolence file.

23. Author interview with Earl Warren, Jr., Jan. 25, 2004 (by telephone).

24. Robert Kenny, "My First Forty Years in California Politics" (unpublished manuscript, on file at BL, University of California, Berkeley).

25. Undated note, state archives, attorney general campaign files (original draft in file 286); see also Leo Katcher, *Earl Warren: A Political Biography*, p. 109.

26. Kenny, "My First Forty Years in California Politics."

27. *Memoirs*, p. 126.

CHAPTER 6. PROGRESSIVE

1. William T. Sweigert, "The Legend of the Earl of Warren," included in oral history interview with Sweigert, *Administration and Ethics in the Governor's Office and the Courts, California, 1939–1975*.

2. *Memoirs*, p. 128. Also oral history interview with Walter P. Jones, *Bee Perspectives of the Warren Era*, pp. 43–44.

3. *Memoirs*, p. 128.

4. *Santa Barbara News-Press*, Jan. 4, 1939.

5. *Memoirs*, p. 166.

6. *Los Angeles Times*, Jan. 6, 1939.

7. *Santa Barbara News-Press*, Jan. 5, 1939.

8. Warren daily calendar, state archives, pregubernatorial papers, calendars.

9. Ibid.

10. *Los Angeles Times* editorial, Jan. 4, 1939.

11. Robert Burke, *Olson's New Deal for California*, p. 50.

12. Burke, *Olson's New Deal*, p. 54.

13. *Santa Barbara News-Press*, Jan. 7, 1939.

14. *Los Angeles Times*, Jan. 8, 1939; see also AP reports.

15. Burke, *Olson's New Deal for California*, p. 55.

16. *Los Angeles Times*, Jan. 9, 1939.

17. *Santa Barbara News-Press* and *Los Angeles Times*, Jan. 8, 1939.

18. Mooney statement from St. Luke's Hospital, Feb. 24, 1939, state archives, attorney general papers, William Knowland file.

19. *Los Angeles Times*, Jan. 8, 1939.

20. *Santa Barbara News-Press*, Jan. 8, 1939.

21. *Santa Barbara News-Press*, Jan. 10, 1939.

22. *Los Angeles Times*, Jan. 10, 1939.

23. *Santa Barbara News-Press*, Jan. 24, 1939.

24. Executive session of the Warren Commission, Dec. 5, 1963, p. 44.

25. "The Iconography of Hope: The 1939–1940 New York World's Fair" (tape-recorded message), April 30, 1939.

26. Warren letter to California district attorneys and sheriffs, July 6, 1939, state archives, attorney general papers, gambling file.

27. Warren letter to S. M. Haskins, Dec. 27, 1938, state archives, attorney general papers, gambling file.

28. Warren letter to John J. Jerome, March 14, 1939, state archives, attorney general papers, gambling file.

29. *Memoirs*, p. 131.

30. Oral history interview with Warren Olney III, *Law Enforcement and Judicial Administration in the Earl Warren Era*, p. 173.

31. *Santa Barbara News-Press*, July 29, 1939.

32. Oral history interview with Warren Olney III, *Law Enforcement and Judicial Administration in the Earl Warren Era*, p. 180.

33. Undated gambling ships' memo, state archives, attorney general papers, gambling file.

34. Ibid.

35. *Santa Barbara News-Press*, Aug. 3, 1939.

36. *Memoirs*, pp. 136–37.

37. Warren telegram to Carl F. Rayburn, sheriff of Riverside County, Jan. 3, 1941, state archives, attorney general office papers, gambling file.

38. David M. Kennedy, *Freedom from Fear*, p. 425.

CHAPTER 7. DUEL FOR POWER

1. William Sweigert, "The Legend of the Earl of Warren," included in oral history interview with Sweigert, *Administration and Ethics in the Governor's Office and the Courts, California, 1939–1975*.

2. Author interview with Virginia Warren, May 31, 2004.

3. This reconstruction of events that day comes from clips and correspondence in the state archives, Warren personal papers, letters of condolence (1940) file.

4. Helen MacGregor telegram to Everett Mattoon, May 2, 1940, state archives, Warren attorney general papers, memoranda file.

5. Mattoon letter to MacGregor, May 3, 1940, state archives, Warren attorney general papers, memoranda file.

6. Decoto letter to Warren, May 3, 1940, state archives, Warren personal papers, letters of condolence file.

7. Warren personal papers, letters of condolence file, state archives.

8. Author interview with Robert Warren, Dec. 11, 2003.

9. Warren speech to Temple Sinai, Oct. 31, 1941, original draft prepared by Herbert Wenig. These comments are included in Warren's revisions, state archives, attorney general papers, Brandeis file.

10. Derek Shearer, "A True Homegrown Radical," included in "Carey McWilliams, The Great Exception," a collection of tributes to McWilliams. "Front-man" comes from Carey McWilliams, "Warren of California," *New Republic*, Oct. 18, 1943.

11. Lloyd Ray Henderson, "Earl Warren and California Politics," p. 114.

12. Associated Press reports, June 14–26, 1940.

13. Warren letter declining to endorse another candidate for judicial position, April 29, 1935, state archives, Warren personal papers, "A" file.

14. Warren appointment books, July 2, 1940, state archives, Warren attorney general office papers, calendars.

15. Radin letter to McWilliams, July 24, 1940, UCLA, McWilliams papers, Warren file.

16. G. Edward White, *Earl Warren: A Public Life*, pp. 63–65.

17. Warren calendars, March 26–July 22, 1940, state archives, attorney general papers, appointment books.

18. *Santa Barbara News-Press*, July 23, 1940.

19. Warren Olney III, *Law Enforcement and Judicial Administration in the Earl Warren Era*, p. 78.

20. Citizens' letter to Commission on Qualifications, July 25, 1940, UCLA, McWilliams papers, Warren file.

21. Robert Gordon Sproul, memo to file, Dec. 31, 1940, BL, Sproul papers, Special Problems file.

22. Warren manuscript on file at BL.

23. Mrs. George Alberts letter to Warren, Nov. 3, 1939, state archives, attorney general papers, King-Ramsay-Conner file.

24. Warren letter to Mrs. George Alberts, Nov. 13, 1939, state archives, attorney general papers, King-Ramsay-Conner file.

25. Minutes of the Advisory Pardon Board meeting, April 30, 1940, state archives, attorney general office papers, King-Ramsay-Conner file.

26. Warren statement, Oct. 16, 1940, state archives, attorney general office papers, King-Ramsay-Conner file.

27. Olson letter to Warren, Oct. 17, 1940, state archives, attorney general papers, King-Ramsay-Conner file.

28. Warren letter to Olson, Oct. 18, 1940, state archives, attorney general papers, King-Ramsay-Conner file.

29. *Los Angeles Times*, Nov. 28, 1941.

30. Warren statement, Nov. 27, 1941, state archives, attorney general office papers, King-Ramsay-Conner file.

31. *Los Angeles Times*, Jan. 17, 1941.

32. See, for instance, the transcript of the Sept. 11, 1941, meeting of the office's Board for Civil Protection, state archives, attorney general papers, Office of Civilian Defense file.

33. Robert E. Burke, *Olson's New Deal for California*, pp. 193–94. See also coverage in the *Los Angeles Times*, the *Santa Barbara News-Press*, and other papers from January 1942.

34. Warren letter to Farnham Griffiths, April 7, 1941, state archives, Warren personal papers, Bohemian Club, 1941–53 file.

35. Knowland letter to Warren, Sept. 26, 1941, state archives, personal papers, William Knowland file.

## CHAPTER 8. "THE BEST PEOPLE OF CALIFORNIA"

1. *Ex Parte Mitsuye Endo*, 323 U.S. 283 (1944).

2. *Toyosaburo Korematsu v. United States*, 323 U.S. 214 (1944).

3. Author interviews with Earl Warren, Jr., and Robert Warren.

4. Author interview with Robert Warren, March 12, 2004.

5. "Civilians Urged to Keep Calm," *Los Angeles Times*, Dec. 8, 1941.

6. Interview with Earl Warren, Jr., Feb. 19, 2004.

7. Greg Robinson, *By Order of the President*, p. 75.

8. *Oakland Tribune*, Dec. 8, 1942.

9. Oral history interview with Helen MacGregor, *A Career in Public Service with Earl Warren*, p. 136.

10. Ibid., p. 138.

11. Author interview with Robert Warren, March 12, 2004.

12. See National Archives letter to Amelia Fry, Earl Warren Oral History Project, Nov. 30, 1971, contained in *Japanese-American Relocation Reviewed*, vol. 1, *Exodus*.

13. See, among others, Morton Grodzins, *Americans Betrayed*, p. 19.

14. *Santa Barbara News-Press*, Jan. 4, 1942, quoting Taki Asakura.

15. *Los Angeles Times*, Jan. 3, 1942.

16. *Sacramento Bee*, Jan. 5, 1942 (excerpted in Lawson Fusao Inada, ed., *Only What We Could Carry*, p. 15).

17. Quoted in *Wartime Exile*, p. 105.

18. *Los Angeles Times* editorial, Jan. 23, 1942.

19. *Los Angeles Times*, Jan. 22, 1942.

20. Grodzins, *Americans Betrayed*, p. 39.

21. *Los Angeles Times*, Jan. 25, 1942. The *Times* ran the full text of the report in its Sunday paper that morning.

22. *Los Angeles Times* editorial, Jan. 28, 1942.

23. *Los Angeles Times*, Jan. 29, 1942. Brackets indicate language that was printed in McLemore's column in other papers but edited from it in the *Times*.

24. Associated Press report, Jan. 28, 1942.

25. Grodzins, *Americans Betrayed*, p. 124.

26. Ibid., p. 125.

27. Dillon Myer, *Uprooted Americans*, p. 17.

28. Oral history interview with Herbert Wenig, *Japanese-American Relocation Reviewed*, p. 10; also oral history interview with Warren Olney III, *Law Enforcement and Judicial Administration in the Earl Warren Era*, pp. 223–25.

29. *Memoirs*, p. 145.

30. Arlington National Cemetery records, entries for John DeWitt, Calvin DeWitt, Calvin DeWitt, Jr., and Wallace DeWitt.

31. See, for instance, John Hersey, *Manzanar*, p. 16.

32. Roger Daniels, *The Decision to Relocate the Japanese Americans*, p. 14.

33. Stetson Conn, "The Decision of Evacuate the Japanese from the West Coast" (included in *Command Decisions*, p. 91).

34. Hersey, *Manzanar*, p. 30.

35. *Final Report, Japanese Evacuation from the West Coast, 1942*, p. 18.

36. Oral history interview with Tom Clark, *Japanese-American Relocation Revisited*, p. 3.

37. Hersey, *Manzanar*, p. 39.

38. Conn, "The Decision to Evacuate the Japanese from the West Coast" (*Command Decisions*, p. 95). It is not clear from DeWitt's retelling of the conversation whether that characterization was his or Olson's. In either case, DeWitt adopted it after speaking with Olson.

39. Greg Robinson, *By Order of the President*, p. 97. In keeping with DeWitt's tendency to vacillate, even as he told Defense Department officials that he favored the evacuation he reported to the FBI that he supported removal of only male Japanese from the restricted areas. San Francisco Special Agent in Charge to Hoover, Feb. 3, 1942, FBI document number 62-65880-14x, Charns, Warren file, Folder 85.

40. Associated Press report, Jan. 30, 1942. The *Los Angeles Times*, on January 31, rendered this comment in slightly different words, though substantively the remarks were identical.

41. *Los Angeles Times*, Jan. 31, 1942.

42. *Los Angeles Times*, Feb. 3, 1942.

43. *Los Angeles Times*, Feb. 4, 1942.

44. Ibid.

45. FBI report 62-65880-14x, Charns, Warren file, Folder 85.

46. Warren testimony to Tolan Committee, report prepared by the Grower-Shipper Vegetable Association and submitted to Warren's office, p. 11002.

47. Carey McWilliams, *Prejudice*, p. 87; also p. 127. In testimony before the Tolan Committee, some agricultural representatives estimated the Japanese significance in these markets more modestly, but their testimony seems suspect, as their mission was to convince the committee that exclusion would not much affect California's agricultural output.

48. Grodzins, *Americans Betrayed*, p. 23.

49. Associated Press report, Jan. 22, 1942.

50. McWilliams, *Prejudice*, p. 127. Also Grodzins, *Americans Betrayed*, pp. 27–28.

51. The Associated Farmers courted Warren through the early years of his attorney general service, inviting him to speak at their annual conference a year before Pearl Harbor. When he accepted, the organization billed the speech as a major address by a friend who shared the association's antagonism toward Olson. Warren, the announcement read, "is widely known for his leadership in fighting subversive activities. He has become nationally known as a fighter for law and order and clean government. Recently, he led the protest against the announced intention of Governor Olson to pardon the three communists who committed the brutal murder in the infamous Point Lobos case." Associated Farmer newsletter, Nov. 25, 1940.

52. Warren speech to Associated Farmers, Dec. 2, 1940, state archives, attorney general papers, Associated Farmers file.

53. Warren testimony to Tolan Committee, Feb. 21, 1942, p. 10973 (Exhibit A).

54. Ibid., p. 10974 (Exhibit A).

55. *Los Angeles Times*, Feb. 3, 1942.

56. Oral history interview with Percy Heckendorft, *Decision and Exodus*, p. 5.

57. *Los Angeles Times* editorial, Feb. 13, 1942.

58. Biddle memo to FDR, Feb. 17, 1942, excerpted in Daniels, *The Decision to Relocate the Japanese Americans*, p. 49.

59. Grodzins, *Americans Betrayed*, p. 100.

60. Ibid., p. 97.

61. Leo Katcher, *Earl Warren: A Political Biography*, p. 144.

62. Warren Olney to John H. Keith, Feb. 3, 1942. Letter is contained in collection on preevacuation location of Japanese-Americans, BL.

63. *Final Report, Japanese Evacuation from the West Coast, 1942*, p. 9.

64. Ibid., p. 34 (from DeWitt's Final Recommendation of the Commanding General, Western Defense Command and Fourth Army, Submitted to the Secretary of War, Feb. 14, 1942).

65. Warren testimony, p. 11009.

66. Ibid., p. 11012.

67. Ibid., p. 11011–12.

68. Halbert memo to Warren Olney, preevacuation location of Japanese-Americans, Feb. 18, 1942, Olney-Warren correspondence folder, BL.

69. Warren testimony, p. 11015.

70. Ibid., p. 11014.

71. McWilliams, *Prejudice*, p. 118.

72. Nellie Wang Balch and Donald Cruz, "Topaz: A Remembrance" (unpublished research paper), UCLA special collections, Edison Uno papers, Topaz file.

73. Lawson Fusao Inada, ed., *Only What We Could Carry* (testimony of Elaine Black Yoneda to the Commission on Wartime Relocation and Internment of Civilians, 1981), pp. 154–72.

74. Michi Nishimura Weglyn, *Years of Infamy*, p. 77.

75. McWilliams, *Prejudice*, p. 133.

76. *Kiyoshi Hirabayashi v. United States*, 320 U.S. 81 (1943).

77. Undated notes from Pearson interviews with Warren during a 1967 trip to Hawaii, Pearson papers, LBJ Library. This note can be dated to 1967, as it is written on the stationery of the Hotel Hana-Maui, where the Pearsons and Warrens stayed on their trip that summer.

78. *Pacific Citizen*, June 23, 1967 (reprint of Uno letter to *Life*, dated May 19, 1967).

79. Jerry Enomoto letter to Warren, May 18, 1969, UCLA special collections, Edison Uno papers, Warren file.

80. *Pacific Citizen*, April 25, 1969.

81. Ibid.

82. Author interview with Jesse Choper, Sept. 9, 2003.

83. *San Francisco Examiner*, April 23, 1970, one of many sources for the text of the letter.

84. *Memoirs*, p. 148.

85. Ibid., p. 149.

86. Oral history interview with Warren Olney III, *Law Enforcement and Judicial Administration in the Earl Warren Era*, p. 235.

87. Oral history interview with Carey McWilliams, *Warren: Views and Episodes*, p. 29d.

88. Warren letter to Jeffrey Warren, March 31, 1968, private collection.

## Chapter 9. Victory

1. Warren speech to the Commonwealth Club, San Francisco, Jan. 29, 1943, state archives, gubernatorial papers, Speeches, Alpha File "C."

2. Copy of proclamation in state archives, attorney general papers, civil defense file. Also included is Warren staff analysis concluding that the proclamation was unconstitutional.

3. Oral history interview with Warren, *Conversations with Earl Warren on California Government*, p. 103.

4. See, for instance, Sweigert memo to Warren, Dec. 19, 1941, state archives, attorney general papers, civil defense file.

5. Oral history interview with Richard Perrin Graves, *Theoretician, Advocate and Candidate in California State Government*, p. 69.

6. Ibid., p. 70.

7. Robert E. Burke, *Olson's New Deal for California*, p. 198.

8. Olson letter to DeWitt, Feb. 10, 1942, BL, Olson papers, DeWitt correspondence file.

9. Author interview with Virginia Warren, May 31, 2004.

10. Oral history interview with Jim Warren, *The Governor's Family*, p. 31.

11. Author interview with Virginia Warren, May 31, 2004. The other children all echo this observation.

12. Oral history interview with Jim Warren, *The Governor's Family*, p. 28.

13. Author interview with Earl Warren, Jr., Nov. 24, 2003.

14. Oral history interview with Adrian Kragen, *Earl Warren: Views and Episodes*, pp. 20–21b.

15. Appointment book for 1942, state archives, attorney general papers, daily calendars file.

16. Knowland letter to Warren, Sept. 26, 1941, state archives, attorney general papers, William Knowland file, 1941–1953.

17. Oral history interview with William Knowland, *Earl Warren's Campaigns*, vol. 2 (this comment from the appended interview with James Bassett included in that volume).

18. See Knowland letters to Warren in March 1942, state archives, Warren personal papers, William Knowland file, 1941–53.

19. Oral history interview with Joseph B. Feigenbaum, *Earl Warren's Campaigns*, vol. 2, p. 42a.

20. Appointment book, entry for April 4, 1942, state archives, attorney general papers, Warren calendars file.

21. *Memoirs*, p. 156.

22. Ibid.

23. Ibid.

24. Author interview with Robert Warren, March 12, 2004.

25. Oral history interview with Kragen, *Earl Warren: Views and Episodes*, p. 20b.

26. Curiously, Warren misremembered this date in his memoirs, saying he announced on April 10. Newspapers from the period make clear, however, that the actual date was April 9.

27. Associated Press report, April 9, 1942, carried in the *Los Angeles Times*, April 10, 1942.

28. "Earl Warren for Governor," *Los Angeles Times*, April 11, 1942.

29. Sweigert, for instance, compiled an extensive memorandum on Olson and how best to challenge his record. The memo was shared with Whitaker and Baxter, and many of its points were made part of the campaign.

30. Warren daily schedule, April 14, 1942, state archives, attorney general files.

31. Merrell Small, *The Country Editor and Earl Warren*, p. 272.

32. John D. Weaver, *Warren: The Man, the Court, the Era*, p. 100.

33. Small, *The Country Editor and Earl Warren*, p. 234. The episode described here occurred after Warren was elected, but Small presents it as one of many in which Warren was rough on staff members.

34. Ibid.

35. Oral history interview with Betty Foot Henderson, *The Warrens: Four Personal Views*, p. 8.

36. Oral history interview with William T. Sweigert, Sr., *Administration and Ethics in the Governor's Office and the Courts, California, 1939–1975*, p. 126.

37. Oral history interview with Betty Foot Henderson, *The Warrens: Four Personal Views*, p. 10.

38. Oral history interview with Leone Baxter, part of an incomplete oral history transcript, p. 72, BL (interviewed June 23, 1972).

39. Oral history interview with William T. Sweigert, Sr., *Administration and Ethics in the Governor's Office and the Courts, California, 1939–1975*, pp. 52–53.

40. Ibid., p. 43.

41. Sweigert memo to Warren, originally written sometime in the late spring or early summer 1942, revised at least once as of Aug. 11, 1942, contained as Appendix to oral history interview with William T. Sweigert, Sr., *Administration and Ethics in the Governor's Office and the Courts, California, 1939–1975*.

42. Speech to Council of Republican Women of Visalia, June 17, 1942, state archives, attorney general files, speeches file.

43. Burke, *Olson's New Deal for California*, p. 226.

44. Kevin Starr, *Endangered Dreams*, p. 205.

45. Warren pension address to Eagles Convention, Sacramento, June 21, 1942, state archives, attorney general papers, Speeches file.

46. Radio address delivered in Oakland and broadcast statewide on Aug. 24, 1942, at 7:15 P.M., state archives, attorney general papers, Speeches file.

47. Undated address on education, state archives, attorney general papers, Speeches file.

48. Stockton Independence Day address, July 3, 1942, state archives, attorney general papers, Speeches file.

49. *California Indicts Governor Olson, The Truth About California's Home Defense*, private collection of Stanley Mosk, held by Judge Richard Mosk.

50. Whitaker letter to Charles Blyth, Aug. 12, 1942, state archives, Whitaker and Baxter papers, Campaign Issues file.

51. Whitaker telegram to Palmer, Aug. 10, 1942, state archives, Whitaker and Baxter papers, Surveys file.

52. Palmer telegram to Whitaker, Aug. 12, 1942, state archives, Whitaker and Baxter papers, Surveys file.

53. Warren letter to Knowland, Sept. 4, 1942, state archives, Warren personal papers, William Knowland file, 1941–53.

54. *Memoirs*, p. 161.

55. *San Francisco Chronicle*, Oct. 12, 1942.

56. Burke, *Olson's New Deal for California*, p. 226.

57. *San Francisco Chronicle*, Oct. 12, 1942.

58. *Memoirs*, pp. 158–59.

59. Ibid., p. 158.

60. Burke, *Olson's New Deal for California*, p. 216.

61. Oral history interview of Leone Baxter, BL (incomplete transcript on file), p. 76.

62. *Memoirs*, p. 162.

63. Ibid., p. 165. The misspelling was Warren's own, as is reflected in the unedited copy of his manuscript, on file at the Bancroft Library.

64. Warren speech to the Commonwealth Club, San Francisco, Jan. 29, 1943, state archives, gubernatorial papers, Speeches, Alpha File "C."

65. *Memoirs*, p. 166.

66. Warren daily schedule, Nov. 5, 1942, state archives, attorney general files.

## Chapter 10. Assumption of Power

1. Richard B. Harvey, *Earl Warren, Governor of California*, p. 20.

2. Details of the speech and ceremony come from the Assembly *Daily Journal*, Jan. 4, 1943.

3. *Los Angeles Times*, Jan. 5, 1943.

4. *Los Angeles Times*, Jan. 5, 1943 ("Governor Warren's Inaugural Address").

5. Oral history interview with Helen MacGregor, *A Career in Public Service with Earl Warren*, p. 165.

6. *Memoirs*, p. 172.

7. Sweigert memo to Warren, Jan. 11, 1943, state archives, gubernatorial papers, Administrative Memoranda file, January 1943.

8. *Memoirs*, p. 168. See also oral history interview with Nina "Honey Bear" Brien, *Earl Warren: The Governor's Family*. Details about the history of the home come from the museum on the mansion grounds today.

9. Author interview with Nina "Honey Bear" Brien, May 7, 2004.

10. Oral history interview with Betty Foot Henderson, *The Warrens: Four Personal Views*, pp. 36–37.

11. Oral history interview with Irving and Jean Stone, *The Warrens: Four Personal Views*, p. 20b.

12. In Warren letter to Frank Snyder, June 26, 1947, state archives, Warren personal papers, Warren family file.

13. Author interviews with Robert Warren and Nina "Honey Bear" Brien.

14. Author interview with Nina "Honey Bear" Brien, May 6, 2004.

15. The identification of the Warren family with California is perhaps best captured by Kevin Starr in *Embattled Dreams*, where he describes a British student dancing with Honey Bear in 1953. It was, as Starr writes, "as if he were dancing with California herself" (p. 280).

16. Author interview with Earl Warren, Jr., Nov. 25, 2003.

17. Author interview with Robert Warren, March 12, 2004.

18. John Weaver, *Warren: The Man, the Court, the Era*, p. 125.

19. Author interview with Nina "Honey Bear" Brien, Jan. 28, 2004.

20. Ibid.

21. MacGregor "confidential" memo to Warren, Jan. 11, 1943, state archives, administrative files, administrative memoranda, Jan. 1943 folder.

22. Author interview with William Allen, Nov. 14, 2005.

23. Author interview with Otis Chandler, Feb. 5, 2004.

24. Oral history interview with Walter Jones, *Bee Perspectives on the Warren Era*, p. 6.

25. Author interview with William Allen, Nov. 14, 2005. Allen went on to know Warren better: He clerked for the chief justice in 1956–57, the only former reporter ever to do so.

26. *Memoirs*, p. 210.

27. *Los Angeles Times*, Jan. 6, 1942.

28. Starr, *Embattled Dreams*, p. 66.

29. Ibid., p. 74.

30. Author interview with Jeffrey Warren, Aug. 26, 2003.

31. David Lavender, *California: Land of New Beginnings*, p. 395.

32. California State Department of Finance report, *Adversity Begets Prosperity, 1930–1945*.

33. Ibid.

34. Starr, *Embattled Dreams*, pp. 105–11.

35. Robert Kenny, "My First Forty Years in California Politics," p. 185.

36. Warren speech to the Commonwealth Club, San Francisco, Jan. 29, 1943, state archives, gubernatorial papers, Speeches, Alpha File "C."

37. Warren speech to Commonwealth Club, San Francisco, Jan. 7, 1944, state archives, gubernatorial papers, Speeches, Alpha File "C."

38. See Warren's proposed California State Budget, July 1, 1949–June 30, 1950. Copies available through state archives, Los Angeles Public Library.

39. State budget, 1943–1945, governor's budget message.

40. *New Republic*, Oct. 18, 1943.

41. Ibid.

42. On the issue of the cut in pay, see Warren speech to the Commonwealth Club, San Francisco, Jan. 29, 1943, state archives, gubernatorial papers, Speeches, Alpha File "C."

43. *Memoirs*, p. 225. See also Papers of Charles H. Purcell, California State Library, Sacramento; and Drew Pearson notes of Aug. 16, 1967, interview with Warren, in Pearson papers, LBJ Library.

44. Weaver, *Warren: The Man, the Court, the Era*, p. 128.

45. *Memoirs*, p. 180.

46. California State Budget, July 1, 1949–June 30, 1950. See also budget for 1947–1948.

47. Warren address to National Convention of the American Bar Association, Section on Criminal Law, Oct. 29, 1946, reprinted in *The Public Papers of Chief Justice Earl Warren*, p. 24.

48. Oral history interview with Warren, *Conversations with Earl Warren on California Government*, p. 129.

49. *Memoirs*, p. 192.

50. Oral history interview with Helen MacGregor, *A Career in Public Service with Earl Warren*, pp. 15–17.

51. Oral history interview with Warren, *Conversations with Earl Warren on California Government*, p. 130. Also *Memoirs*, p. 194. Slight variations on this exchange have been reported over the years, but none differs substantively from this account.

52. Harvey, *Earl Warren, Governor of California*, p. 73.

53. Warren address to Conference on Aging, Oct. 15, 1951, state archives, gubernatorial papers, Speeches, Alpha File "A."

54. Ibid.

55. Harvey, *Earl Warren, Governor of California*, p. 77.

56. Ibid., p. 76.

57. *Memoirs*, p. 207.

58. Harvey, *Earl Warren, Governor of California*, p. 72.

59. Author interview with Ira Michael Heyman, Oct. 21, 2003.

60. *Time*, Jan. 31, 1944.

61. Leo Katcher, *Earl Warren: A Political Biography*, pp. 180–81.

62. Moley letter to Warren, April 24, 1944, HI, Moley papers, Warren correspondence, Box 57, Folder 62.

63. Warren address to the Republican National Convention, Chicago, June 26, 1944, state archives, gubernatorial papers, Speeches, Alpha Files, "Political, 1944."

64. Warren daily calendar, Oct. 14, 1944, state archives, gubernatorial papers, 1944 appointment books.

65. *Los Angeles Times*, Oct. 15, 1944.

66. Oral history interview with William T. Sweigert, Sr., *Administration and Ethics in the Governor's Office and the Courts, California, 1939–1975*, p. 92.

67. *Los Angeles Times*, Nov. 4, 1944.

68. Weaver, *Warren: The Man, the Court, the Era*, pp. 139–40. Weaver attributes this comment merely to "a state official," but other sources, including Katcher, *Earl Warren: A Political Biography* and later interviews with Kenny, make clear that he was the source.

CHAPTER 11.  CALIFORNIA'S FAIL DEAL GOVERNOR

1. Richard B. Harvey, *Earl Warren, Governor of California*, p. 20.

2. Leo Katcher, *Earl Warren: A Political Biography*, p. 187.

3. Confidential memo by William Sweigert comparing health plans, state archives, gubernatorial papers, health insurance files, March 8, 1945. These files were not yet indexed at the time of this research; they are contained in two boxes of material within the Warren gubernatorial papers.

4. Confidential memo by William Sweigert comparing health plans, state archives, gubernatorial papers, health insurance files, March 8, 1945.

5. Undated memo, "Governor Warren's Recommendation to the Legislature for Prepaid Medical Care," state archives, gubernatorial papers, health insurance files.

6. The date is from Warren's calendar, state archives; the place from oral history interview with William T. Sweigert, Sr., *Administration and Ethics in the Governor's Office and the Courts, California, 1939–1975*, p. 74.

7. Oral history interview with John Cline, *Earl Warren and Health Insurance, 1943–49*, pp. 15f.

8. Oral history interview with William T. Sweigert, Sr., *Administration and Ethics in the Governor's Office and the Courts, California, 1939–1975*, p. 74.

9. *Los Angeles Times*, Dec. 30, 1944.

10. Biennial Message of Earl Warren, Governor of the State of California, Jan. 8, 1945, state archives, gubernatorial papers, health insurance file.

11. *Los Angeles Times*, Dec. 28, 1944.

12. Lloyd Ray Henderson, "Earl Warren and California Politics," p. 181 (citing Los Angeles Medical Association Bulletin of Jan. 18, 1945).

13. John Weaver, *Warren: The Man, the Court, the Era*, p. 137.

14. See Merrell Small, *The Country Editor and Earl Warren*, for a discussion of the governor's messages to the legislature and the effort to compose them.

15. Biennial Message of Earl Warren, Governor of the State of California, Jan. 8, 1945, state archives, gubernatorial papers, health insurance file, p. 4.

16. Ibid., pp. 6–7.

17. Ibid., p. 9.

18. Stanley Kelley, *Professional Public Relations and Political Power*, p. 48.

19. Katcher, *Earl Warren: A Political Biography*, p. 188.

20. Kelley, *Professional Public Relations and Political Power*, p. 57.

21. Clem Whitaker, "Political Parade," Feb. 5, 1945, state archives, gubernatorial papers, health insurance file, clippings, 1945.

22. Weaver, *Warren: The Man, the Court, the Era*, pp. 137–38.

23. Author interview with Virginia Daly, May 31, 2004.

24. Radio address, Feb. 21, 1945, state archives, gubernatorial papers, health insurance file.

25. Radio address, Feb. 28, 1945, state archives, gubernatorial papers, health insurance file.

26. Ibid.

27. Sweigert memo to Warren, March 12, 1945, state archives, gubernatorial papers, health insurance file, March–April 1945.

28. *Memoirs*, p. 188.

29. Small, *The Country Editor and Earl Warren*, p. 126.

30. Oral history interview with William T. Sweigert, Sr., *Administration and Ethics in the Governor's Office and the Courts, California, 1939–1975*, p. 82.

31. David Kennedy, *Freedom from Fear*, p. 809.

32. Ibid., p. 857.

33. These casualty figures are derived from two documents: "State Summary of War Casualties," prepared by the Navy Department, lists 6,446 Navy, Marine, and Coast Guard combat deaths, as well as 266 prison camp deaths. It also notes that 70 men were considered missing. "World War II, Honor List of Dead and Missing, State of California," published by the War Department, tabulates Army and Air Force casualties. It cites 16,916 California fatalities (killed in action, died of wounds, died of injuries, etc.), and 106 missing, for a total of 17,022 presumed fatalities. Both documents are available through the National Archives' online holdings: http://www.archives.gov/research/arc/ww2/.

34. Kevin Starr, *Embattled Dreams*, p. 194.

35. *Life*, Jan. 10, 1946.

36. Ibid.

37. *Biographical Directory of the United States Congress*.

38. Oral history interview with Richard Rodda, *Bee Perspectives on the Warren Era*, p. 13r.

39. *Memoirs*, p. 187.

40. *Los Angeles Times*, Dec. 18, 1944 (Associated Press transcript of Warren statement). The FBI, whose director, Hoover, had opposed the internment, commented on Warren's defense of the returning Japanese with a notable lack of charity. Warren, a bureau memo signed by Agent R. B. Hood observed, "saw it was politically expedient to stand behind the Army and was quoted in the Los Angeles press as addressing an appeal to the people of California to respect and comply with the Army's orders." Hood memo to Hoover, Dec. 8, 1948, FBI document 100-202315, Charns, Warren papers, Folder 78.

41. Robert W. Kenny, "My First Forty Years in California Politics, 1922–1962," p. 222.

42. Oral history interview with Robert Kenny, *Earl Warren: Fellow Constitutional Officers*, p. 478.

43. Henderson, "Earl Warren and California Politics," p. 236.

44. California State Archives, election returns.

45. Weaver, *Warren: The Man, the Court, the Era*, p. 149.

46. San Francisco Special Agent in Charge to Hoover, Aug. 6, 1946, FBI document 100-3-72-86, Charns, Warren papers, Folder 87.

47. William Sweigert, "The Legend of the Earl of Warren," included in *Administration and Ethics in the Governor's Office and the Courts, California, 1939–1975*.

## CHAPTER 12. IN COMMAND

1. Herman Perry letter to Bernard C. Brennan, March 10, 1952, National Archives, Laguna Niguel branch office, Nixon pre-presidential papers, correspondence, Perry file.

2. Perry letter to Lance D. Smith, Oct. 3, 1945, reprinted in interview with Roy Day, *Richard M. Nixon in the Warren Era*, p. 6.

3. Irwin F. Gellman, *The Contender*, p. 44 (cited to *Monrovia News-Post*, March 11, 1946).

4. Gellman, *The Contender*, p. 77.

5. Oral history interview with Earl Adams, *Richard M. Nixon in the Warren Era*, p. 30.

6. Gellman, *The Contender*, p. 70.

7. Kevin Starr, *Embattled Dreams*, p. 285.

8. Gellman, *The Contender*, p. 71.

9. See, for instance, letter to Major General Curtis O'Sullivan from Warren's appointment secretary, July 14, 1948, state archives, administrative files, governor's office, administrative memoranda file. Warren refers to the plane on p. 215 of his *Memoirs*.

10. Inaugural Address, Jan. 6, 1947, from "Governors of California," courtesy California Secretary of State's office.

11. Ibid.

12. Russell H. Conwell, "Acres of Diamonds," p. 64.

13. Lloyd Ray Henderson, "Earl Warren and California Politics," p. 277.

14. *Memoirs*, p. 208.

15. *Los Angeles Times*, March 20, 1947. Quoted also in John Weaver, *Warren: The Man, the Court, the Era*, pp. 141–42.

16. Henderson, "Earl Warren and California Politics," p. 302.

17. *Memoirs*, p. 209

18. Oral history interview with Warren, *Conversations with Earl Warren on California Government*, p. 173. Warren also complained about Keck to Drew Pearson during an Aug. 17, 1967, interview, see Pearson notes from that day, Pearson papers, LBJ Library.

19. California State Budget, July 1, 1947–June 30, 1948, governor's message.

20. *Mendez v. Westminster* (1946), 64 F. Supp. 544.

21. Ibid.

22. Sections 8003 and 8004 of the California Education Code.

23. Oral history interview with Bartley Cavanaugh, *Hunting and Fishing with Earl Warren*, pp. 5–6.

24. Swig letter to Warren, April 11, 1961, LOC, MD, Warren papers, personal papers, Ben Swig file.

25. Undated manuscript of a Warren biography that Pearson began in the late 1960s. Pearson died without finishing the book; a copy of the unfinished draft is with his papers at the LBJ Library.

26. Those recollections are taken from Pearson's manuscript, which does not have page numbers; all the quotations come from chapter 2. Pearson papers, LBJ Library.

27. Oral history interview with Betty Foot Henderson, *The Warrens: Four Personal Views*, p. 25.

28. Ibid., p. 27.

29. Oral history interview with Nina "Honey Bear" Brien, *The Governor's Family*, p. 7.

30. Oral history interview with Betty Foot Henderson, *The Warrens: Four Personal Views*, p. 28.

31. Author interviews with Robert Warren, March 12, 2004, and Jan. 11, 2005.

32. Oral history interview with Betty Foot Henderson, *The Warrens: Four Personal Views*, p. 47.

33. Ibid., p. 52.

34. Ibid., p. 32.

35. Ibid., p. 53.

36. Sproul speech to Republican National Convention, June 23, 1948, state archives, gubernatorial papers, Speeches Alpha File, "Political."

37. Ibid.

38. Ibid.

39. Warren appointment-book entry, June 25, 1948, state archives, gubernatorial papers, appointment files, 1948.

40. Diary of Drew Pearson, entry for Aug. 15, 1963, LBJ Library.

41. *Memoirs*, p. 241.

42. Ibid. Also author interview with Robert Warren, Dec. 11, 2003; Robert Warren does not remember speaking those words, but says he's often been told that he did.

43. Weaver, *Warren: The Man, the Court, the Era*, p. 154.

44. Associated Press photograph.

45. *Time*, Sept. 27, 1948.

46. *Memoirs*, p. 242.

47. Oral history interview with William T. Sweigert, Sr., *Administration and Ethics in the Governor's Office and the Courts, California, 1939–1975*, p. 106.

48. *Time*, Sept. 27, 1948.

49. Warren speech in Reno, Sept. 15, 1948, state archives, gubernatorial papers, Speeches, Alpha File "Political, 1948."

50. Warren speech in Cincinnati, Sept. 23, 1948, state archives, gubernatorial papers, Speeches, Alpha File "Political, 1948."

51. Author interview with Virginia Daly, May 31, 2004.

52. Gary A. Donaldson, *Truman Defeats Dewey*, p. 179.

53. Ibid., p. 180.

54. *Memoirs*, p. 248.

55. Warren speech in Wenatchu, Washington, Oct. 14, 1948, state archives, gubernatorial papers, Speeches, Alpha file "Political, 1948."

56. Warren speech in Sacramento, Oct. 18, 1948, state archives, gubernatorial papers, Speeches, Alpha file "Political, 1948."

57. Donaldson, *Truman Defeats Dewey*, p. 209.

58. R. B. Hood to Hoover, Dec. 8, 1948, FBI document 100-202315, Charns, Warren files, Folder 78.

59. See, for example, the Nov. 15, 1951, Bureau memo replying to Warren's request of Nov. 9, 1951. In that instance, the FBI found no derogatory information on seventeen of nineteen names submitted by Warren, but did raise issues with two. FBI document 94-1-5619-113.

60. San Francisco Special Agent in Charge to Hoover, Oct. 16, 1950, FBI document 61-10149-1466, Charns, Warren files, Folder 89. Interestingly, the alleged Communist identified by the FBI was Aubrey Grossman, one of the defense lawyers from the *Point Lobos* case.

61. L. B. Nichols to Tolson, May 7, 1953, FBI document 94-1-5619-178.

62. See, for instance, Tracy to Hoover, Sept. 23, 1951, FBI document 94-1-5619-107, noting Warren's speech to the American Bar Association, and Hoover's Sept. 25 note to Warren (same document number).

63. Warren telegram to Cabell Phillips, *New York Times*, March 4, 1948.

CHAPTER 13. LOYALTY

1. David P. Gardner, *The California Oath Controversy*, p. 145.

2. Arthur H. Samish, *The Secret Boss of California*, p. 131. Tenney thought he smelled Communists in Warren's camp as well. Not knowing of Hoover's affection for Warren, Tenney alerted the FBI's Los Angeles office that he suspected "Hollywood Communist screenwriters" of helping draft Warren speeches. There is no evidence of Bureau action. FBI document 100-273526-3, Charns, Warren files, Folder 78.

3. The Sproul–Warren correspondence stretches across Warren's entire professional life, from his days as Alameda district attorney through his time on the United States Supreme Court. In those later years, Sproul often called on Warren when business brought him to Washington.

4. Truman announcement that the Soviets had exploded an atomic bomb, Sept. 23, 1949. Yale Law School archives, Avalon Project.

5. Gardner, *The California Oath Controversy*, pp. 24–29, 126. I am particularly indebted in this chapter to Gardner's meticulous history of the oath controversy. Although others have written about the events of those years, Gardner's work remains the definitive account. Gardner went on to serve as chancellor of the university.

6. Minutes of the California Board of Regents meeting, March 25, 1949.

7. Gardner, *The California Oath Controversy*, p. 26.

8. Ibid., p. 30.

9. *Memoirs*, pp. 84–85.

10. Letter from Neylan to Warren, Feb. 9, 1943, and Warren reply, state archives, gubernatorial papers, correspondence file "N."

11. *Memoirs*, p. 218.

12. Gardner, *The California Oath Controversy*, p. 105.

13. Ibid., p. 107.

14. Warren letter to Griffiths, April 7, 1941; Griffiths letter to Warren, April 24, 1941; Warren Horner letter to Warren, June 5, 1941, state archives, personal papers, Bohemian Club file, 1941–53.

15. *Los Angeles Times*, March 1, 1950 (from Chronicle News Bureau).

16. *Los Angeles Times*, March 2, 1950.

17. *Los Angeles Times*, March 3, 1950.

18. Oral history interview with John Francis Neylan, *Politics, Law, and University of California*, p. 188.

19. *Los Angeles Times*, March 9, 1950, one of many references to this resolution in news coverage in March.

20. Gardner, *The California Oath Controversy*, p. 143.

21. Ibid., p. 145.

22. *Los Angeles Times*, April 1, 1950.

23. Robert Leckie, *Conflict: The History of the Korean War*, p. 54.

24. Ibid.

25. Text of Truman speech of July 19, 1950, contained in the papers of George M. Elsey, Truman Presidential Museum and Library.

26. *Memoirs*, p. 221.

27. The precise date of the conversation between Warren and Chandler is not preserved, but the context of the conversation makes clear that it was in 1950, and the Grove's annual encampment that year was from July 14 to July 30. Since the regents met on July 21, it seems likely that Warren and Chandler spoke sometime between July 14 and July 21, 1950.

28. *Los Angeles Times*, July 22, 1950.

29. *Los Angeles Times*, Sept. 21, 1950. In October 1950, the State of California distributed *Survival Under Atomic Attack*, a thirty-two-page pamphlet with tips for surviving such an attack. The pamphlet was distributed by the California Office of Civil Defense; on the cover was the state seal over the words "Earl Warren, Governor."

30. Undated memo, LOC, MD, Warren personal papers, confirmation file. The memo was prepared at the request of Deputy Attorney General William Rogers and included in the FBI's background report prepared in connection with Warren's confirmation to the Supreme Court. A copy of the memo is included in that file as well.

31. *Memoirs*, p. 198.

32. Los Angeles Special Agent in Charge to Hoover, Sept. 16, 1947, FBI document 62-75147-26-205, Charns, Warren files, Folder 85.

33. *Fortnight*, Nov. 5, 1948.

34. Final Report of The Special Crime Study Commission on Organized Crime, p. 17.

35. *Collier's*, Aug. 13, 1949.

36. Ibid.

37. Samish, *The Secret Boss of California*, p. 173.

38. Warren daily schedules for May 1950, state archives, attorney general files.

39. "Report to the People" (1950), published by Friends of Earl Warren as campaign material.

40. Richard B. Harvey, *Earl Warren, Governor of California*, pp. 114–16.

41. Ibid., pp. 134–36.

42. NBC broadcast, Oct. 20, 1950, transcript in state archives, gubernatorial papers, Speeches, Alpha File "Political," May 24, 1950–1952.

43. Roosevelt statement Aug. 6, 1950, and Warren response, state archives, gubernatorial papers, Speeches, Alpha File "Political," May 24, 1950–1952.

44. *Los Angeles Times*, Feb. 23, 1950.

45. William Sweigert, "The Legend of the Earl of Warren," included in *Administration and Ethics in the Governor's Office and the Courts, California, 1939–1975*.

46. *Los Angeles Times*, Sept. 13, 1950.

47. Undated Douglas–Marcantonio Voting Record flyer, distributed in 1950 campaign.

48. Oral history interview with Frank Jorgensen, *Richard M. Nixon in the Warren Era*, p. 47.

49. Ibid.

50. Leo Katcher, *Earl Warren: A Political Biography*, p. 261.

51. *Los Angeles Times*, May 28, 1950.

52. Warren speech to Sailors Union, Nov. 3, 1950, state archives, gubernatorial papers, Speeches, Alpha File "Political."

53. Ibid.

54. Warren daily schedule, Nov. 7, 1950, state archives, attorney general files.

55. Author interview with Nina "Honey Bear" Brien, Jan. 28, 2004.

56. *Sacramento Bee*, Oct. 30, 1977 (profile of Nina Warren).

57. Associated Press report Nov. 8, 1950 (as carried in the *Santa Barbara News-Press*).

58. *Sacramento Bee*, Oct. 30, 1977 (profile of Nina Warren).

59. *Santa Barbara News-Press*, Nov. 7, 1950. The quotation is from Warren's driver, Pat Patterson.

60. Author interview with Nina "Honey Bear" Brien, Jan. 28, 2004. See also Weaver, p. 162, and news reports from AP, *Sacramento Bee*, and others.

61. Associated Press report, Nov. 8, 1950.

62. Appointment book for 1950, California State Archives, attorney general papers, daily calendars file.

63. Oral history interview with Betty Foot Henderson, *The Warrens: Four Personal Views*, p. 20.

64. Daily calendar, March 6, 1951, state archives, governor's administrative file. See also letters of condolence file.

65. Warren letter to C. E. Bates, Feb. 26, 1951, state archives, personal papers, Nina Warren file, 1950–52.

66. Author interview with Bill Boyarsky.

67. A sampling of the mail to Honey Bear is preserved at the state archives in Sacramento, personal papers, Nina Warren file, 1950–52.

68. Warren letter to Ray Brown, May 16, 1951, state archives, personal papers, Nina Warren file, 1950–52.

69. Author interview with Warren Olney IV, Feb. 10, 2004.

70. Earl Warren, *A Republic, If You Can Keep It*, p. 2.

71. Warren to Sproul, Jan. 16, 1956, BL, Sproul personal papers, Warren correspondence.

72. Kenny to Warren, Nov. 5, 1952, state archives, gubernatorial papers, administrative files, Elections—General, 1952.

CHAPTER 14. "TRAITOR IN OUR DELEGATION"

1. *Los Angeles Times*, June 20, 1952.

2. *Los Angeles Times*, July 4, 1952.

3. Oral history interview with Frank Jorgensen, *Richard M. Nixon in the Warren Era*, p. 69.

4. Author interview with Virginia Daly, May 31, 2004.

5. Calendars, Jan. 17–19, 1952, state archives, Governor's Administrative Files, Daily Calendars, 1952.

6. M. F. Small memo to James Oakley, Feb. 28, 1952, state archives, 1952 Presidential Campaign files, Finance/General, Jan.–May 31, 1952.

7. "The Washington Merry-Go-Round," Feb. 21, 1952, copy of the column in Pearson's papers, LBJ Library.

8. Reporters' Roundup, Warren interview, Feb. 14, 1952, state archives, Warren papers, Administrative files, Alpha File "Political," 1950–1952.

9. *Memoirs*, p. 250.

10. *New York Times*, May 19, 1952.

11. *Memoirs*, p. 252.

12. Stephen E. Ambrose, *Eisenhower, Soldier and President*, pp. 238–50.

13. Ibid., p. 248.

14. Undated memorandum titled "Republican National Convention, July 1952, Chicago, Ill.," HI, Box 3, Political Parties, Republican Party folder. This memo is signed by the author, but use of it is conditioned on not divulging the author's name.

15. Ambrose, *Eisenhower, Soldier and President*, p. 265 (taken from interview with Jacqueline Cochran, Eisenhower Library).

16. Associated Press poll, July 4, 1952, reported in the *Los Angeles Times*.

17. Reporters' Roundup, Feb. 14, 1952, state archives, Warren speeches, Alpha File "Political," 1950–1952.

18. Neylan statewide radio address, May 7, 1952, clip of the speech at National Archives, Warren confirmation files, Box 53.

19. Oral history interview with Victor Hansen, *Earl Warren's Campaigns*, vol. 2, p. 68w.

20. John Weaver, *Warren: The Man, the Court, the Era*, p. 179.

21. Helyn E. Noid to Nixon, June 9, 1952, National Archives (Laguna Niguel), Nixon pre-presidential papers, Herman Perry correspondence file.

22. Oral history interview with Keith McCormac, *Earl Warren's Campaigns*, vol. 3, p. 112.

23. Undated "Declaration of Policy," Free Werdel G.O.P. Delegation, excerpted in oral history interview with Keith McCormac, *Earl Warren's Campaigns*, vol. 3, p. 97.

24. The poll and its results are held at RNLB. Weaver (*Warren: The Man, the Court, the Era*, pp. 180–83), among others, discusses the poll and Nixon's preconvention moves.

25. *Memoirs*, p. 251.

26. *Los Angeles Times*, June 20, 1952.

27. Perry to Brennan, April 21, 1952, RNLB, correspondence files.

28. Perry to Brennan, May 12, 1952, National Archives (Laguna Niguel), Nixon pre-presidential papers, Perry correspondence file.

29. Nixon to Brennan, June 9, 1952, National Archives (Laguna Niguel), Nixon pre-presidential papers, Brennan correspondence file.

30. Perry to Nixon, June 12, 1952, National Archives (Laguna Niguel), Nixon pre-presidential papers, Perry correspondence file.

31. Nixon to Perry, June 16, 1952, National Archives (Laguna Niguel), Nixon pre-presidential papers, Perry correspondence file.

32. *Los Angeles Times*, July 6, 1952.

33. Roger Morris, *Richard Milhous Nixon*, p. 693; see also Leo Katcher, *Earl Warren: A Political Biography*, pp. 288–89.

34. Oral history interview with Frank Jorgensen, *Richard M. Nixon in the Warren Era*, p. 69.

35. Katcher, *Earl Warren: A Political Biography*, p. 291.

36. *Memoirs*, p. 252.

37. The exchange with Taft is recounted ibid., pp. 252–53.

38. Undated memorandum titled "Republican National Convention, July 1952, Chicago, Ill.," HI, Box 3, Political Parties, Republican Party folder. (See note 14 above.)

39. Given the importance of the vote on the Fair Play Amendment, it seems likely that this was the matter that Warren was referring to when he threatened to hurt Eisenhower's candidacy if Nixon was not reined in.

40. Oral history interview with Thomas Mellon, *Earl Warren's Campaigns*, vol. 2, p. 9q.

41. *Los Angeles Times*, July 11, 1952.

42. *Memoirs*, p. 254.

43. Oral history interview with Victor Hansen, *Earl Warren's Campaigns*, vol. 2, p. 89w.

44. *Memoirs*, p. 251–52.

45. Small to Warren, Aug. 25, 1972, Warren memoirs file, BL.

46. *Los Angeles Times*, Aug. 4, 1952.

47. *Los Angeles Times*, Aug. 6, 1952.

48. *Memoirs*, p. 255.

49. Warren telegram to Nixon, Sept. 11, 1952, RNLB, correspondence files.

50. Oral history interview with Keith McCormac, *Earl Warren's Campaigns*, vol. 3, pp. 190–92.

51. Morris, *Richard Milhous Nixon*, pp. 759–61.

52. *New York Post*, Sept. 18, 1952 (quoted in Morris, *Richard Milhous Nixon*, p. 762).

53. *New York Post*, Sept. 22, 1952.

54. Nixon memorandum of telephone conversation, Sept. 20, 1952, RNLB.

55. Ibid.

56. Stassen telegram to Nixon, Sept. 21, 1952, RNLB, correspondence files.

57. "Warren Silent on Nixon Fund," Sept. 23, 1952, RNLB, fund files.

58. Nixon address, Sept. 23, 1952, copy from *Los Angeles Times* History Center, Jim Bassett files.

59. Ibid.

60. Author interview with Herb Klein, March 23, 2004.

61. Ambrose, *Eisenhower, Soldier and President*, p. 280.

62. Ibid., p. 282.

63. Warren memorandum to the conference, May 15, 1965, Princeton University, Mudd Library, John Marshall Harlan papers, Correspondence, Earl Warren file.

64. Katcher, *Earl Warren: A Political Biography*, p. 294.

65. Ronald Humphreys telegram to Murray Chotiner, Sept. 23, 1952, RNLB, fund file.

66. *Los Angeles Times*, Nov. 1, 1952.

67. *Memoirs*, p. 215.

68. Farewell message to the people of California, Oct. 2, 1953, state archives, administrative files, speeches, Alpha file "F."

69. Oral history interview with Royce D. Delmatier, *The Rumble of California Politics, 1848–1970*, p. 317.

70. "Earnings and House, by Industry, California," annual reports from 1940 to 1953, State Department of Industrial Relations.

71. Farewell message to the people of California, Oct. 2, 1953, state archives, administrative files, speeches, Alpha file "F."

72. Interviewed about the case by the Earl Warren Oral History Project in 1971 and 1972, Warren grew agitated. "Nobody," he insisted, "came to court and testified to anything of that kind [meaning mistreatment of the suspects]." Warren, the transcript notes, banged his hand on the table as he spoke. Oral history interview with Warren, *Conversations with Earl Warren on California Government*, p. 76.

73. Ibid., p. 142.

74. Oral history interview with Ernest O. Ramsay, *The Shipboard Murder Case*, p. 38.

CHAPTER 15. THE CHIEF AND HIS COURT

1. For the judicial profiles of Warren's colleagues in this chapter, I have drawn from a wide variety of sources, intermingling them in such a way that makes specific attribution at times difficult. These sketches owe much to Henry Abraham's *Justices and Presidents*, Lucas Powe's *The Warren Court and American Politics*, and Edward G. White's *The American Judicial Tradition* (expanded edition) and to

leading biographies on the major justices—namely, Roger K. Newman's *Hugo Black*, Eugene Gerhart's *America's Advocate: Robert Jackson*, Urofsky's *Felix Frankfurter*, and Bruce Murphy's *Wild Bill* (Douglas). Those extraordinarily capable secondary sources are supplemented by the personal papers of Douglas, Harlan, Brennan, Burton, Black, Warren, and Frankfurter, as well as the relevant cases, cited separately.

2. Earl Warren, *A Republic, If You Can Keep It*, p. 6.

3. William O. Douglas, *The Autobiography of William O. Douglas: The Court Years, 1939–1975*, p. 81.

4. Robert and Michael Meeropol, *We Are Your Sons*, pp. 236–38.

5. Richard Kluger, *Simple Justice*, p. 585.

6. *Youngstown Co. v. Sawyer*, 343 U.S. 579 (1952).

7. See, for instance, Roger Newman, *Hugo Black: A Biography*, p. 367.

8. Henry J. Abraham, *Justices and Presidents: A Political History of Appointments to the Supreme Court*, p. 243.

9. Douglas, *The Autobiography of William O. Douglas*, p. 243.

10. Felix Frankfurter, *From the Diaries of Felix Frankfurter*, p. 336.

11. Bernard Schwartz, ed., *The Warren Court: A Retrospective*, p. 9.

12. Drew Pearson, *Diaries 1949–1959*, entry for March 17, 1950, p. 112.

13. Abraham, *Justices and Presidents*, pp. 247–48.

14. Jeffrey D. Hockett, *New Deal Justice*, p. 143.

15. Ibid., p. 160.

16. G. Edward White, *The American Judicial Tradition*, p. 192.

17. Eugene Gerhart, *America's Advocate: Robert H. Jackson*, p. 191.

18. Ibid., p. 175 (quoting *Time*).

19. *Minersville School District v. Gobitis*, 310 U.S. 586 (1940).

20. *West Virginia State Board of Education v. Barnette*, 319 U.S. 624 (1943).

21. Ibid.

22. Ibid.

23. Ibid. (dissent).

24. Roger Newman, *Hugo Black: A Biography*, p. 3.

25. Ibid., p. 195.

26. Joseph Alsop and Turner Catledge, *The 168 Days*, p. 301.

27. Newman, *Hugo Black*, p. 251.

28. *Jewell Ridge Coal Corp. v. Local 6167, United Mine Workers of America*, U.S. 161 (1945).

29. Gerhart, *America's Advocate*, p. 251.

30. Newman, *Hugo Black*, p. 337.

31. Ibid., p. 345.

32. *Rochin v. California*, 342 U.S. 165 (1952).

33. *Adamson v. People of State of California*, 332 U.S. 46 (1947) (dissent).

34. Newman, *Hugo Black*, p. 354.

35. One thing that Douglas had in common with Frankfurter, Black, and Jackson was that he arrived at the Supreme Court with no significant judicial background. That was true also, of course, for Warren.

36. *Dennis v. United States*, 341 U.S. 494 (1951).

37. Ibid.

38. Ibid. (dissent).

39. *Memoirs*, p. 276.

40. Warren letter to Douglas, Dec. 1, 1950, LOC, MD, William O. Douglas papers, Part 1, Earl and Nina Warren correspondence file.

41. Undated tribute written after Warren's death in 1974, LOC, MD, William O. Douglas papers, Part 1, Earl Warren subject file.

42. *Memoirs*, p. 279.

43. Ibid., p. 280.

44. Burton diary entry, Oct. 5, 1953, LOC, MD, Harold H. Burton papers, Diaries, 1953.

45. Newman, *Hugo Black*, p. 427.

46. Burton letter to Warren with monograph enclosed, Oct. 12, 1953, LOC, MD, Warren papers, correspondence, Harold Burton file, 1952–57.

47. Warren letter to Douglas, Nov. 4, 1953, LOC, MD, Warren papers, correspondence, William O. Douglas, 1955–56.

48. Clark letter to Warren, Oct. 12, 1953, LOC, MD, Warren papers, correspondence, Tom C. Clark, 1953–1961.

49. Joseph P. Lash, *From the Diaries of Felix Frankfurter* (biographical introduction), p. 84.

50. Black to Hugo and Sterling Black, Oct. 15, 1953, LOC, MD, Black family papers, Hugo Black, Jr., file, 1953–54.

CHAPTER 16. SMEAR

1. Public hearings of the Subcommittee of the Committee on the Judiciary, Feb. 19, 1954, as quoted in *New York Times*, Feb. 20, 1954.

2. *Memoirs*, p. 274, note.

3. Ibid., p. 272.

4. *Sacramento Bee*, Oct. 30, 1977 (profile of Nina Warren).

5. See calendar entries for March 30 and April 30, 1954, LOC, MD, calendars for 1953–54.

6. Author interview with Warren Olney IV, Feb. 10, 2004. See also Warren Olney, *Law Enforcement and Judicial Administration in the Earl Warren Era*, p. 393.

7. Warren speech to Columbia University, Jan. 14, 1954, LOC, MD, Warren papers, speeches file. Also quoted in *New York Times*, Jan. 15, 1954.

8. Although it is impossible to determine the extent or cause, Langer's life was characterized by distinct and abrupt shifts from euphoria to inactivity. His sympathetic biographer, Agnes Geelan, identified diabetes as a likely culprit; see *The Dakota Maverick*, p. 57.

9. Glenn Smith, *Langer of North Dakota: A Study in Isolationism*, p. 112.

10. *New York Times*, Feb. 18, 1954.

11. Two letters regarding Warren's nomination that never found their way to the committee actually were among the more interesting. Loyd Wright, part of California's disaffected right wing and soon to head the American Bar Association, urged Brownell not to pick Warren, whom Wright described as "not a Republican . . . [not] a lawyer nor an executive in the sense of the judiciary" (Wright telegram to Brownell, Sept. 28, 1953, HI, Loyd Wright papers, Political file, Earl Warren folder). Another letter was sent to Justice Jackson by a former clerk, one William H. Rehnquist. In it, Rehnquist reported that among his colleagues in Phoenix, "most everyone . . . was quite disappointed by the nomination of Warren. . . . The few opinions of Warren I have seen have not been very good" (undated but sent apparently in early 1954; Jackson's chambers estimated it to have been written on April 24, 1954; LOC, MD, Jackson papers, General correspondence, William H. Rehnquist folder).

12. Testimony of William Rogers before the Subcommittee of the Committee on the Judiciary, Feb. 19, 1954, p. 84.

13. INS wire story, Feb. 2, 1954, carried in *Los Angeles Evening Herald Express*, copy in Judiciary Committee files on Warren nomination, Box 55.

14. Babcoke letter to committee, Dec. 2, 1953, Judiciary Committee files on Warren nomination, Box 53, file labeled "Protests, Arranged Alphabetically, from 97 Individuals."

15. Undated letter signed "Mr. and Mrs. Fulton," Glendale, California, Judiciary Committee files on Warren nomination, Box 53, file labeled "Protests, Arranged Alphabetically, from 97 Individuals."

16. Gorke letter to committee, Jan. 2, 1954, Judiciary Committee files on Warren nomination, Box 53, file labeled "Protests, Arranged Alphabetically, from 97 Individuals."

17. The numbers do not square with Langer's "97 protests" because letters continued to arrive at the committee throughout the proceedings. As such, it is difficult to tell which ninety-seven Langer had in hand when he made his public comments. Although the file labeled "Protests, Arranged Alphabetically, from 97 Individuals" contains fewer than that many letters, other letters from the same time period are scattered throughout the six boxes of material.

18. A. F. Levy letter to Judiciary Committee, Jan. 8, 1954, Judiciary Committee files on Warren nomination, Box 53.

19. Wain O. Waco letter to Judiciary Committee, Feb. 20, 1954, Judiciary Committee files on Warren nomination, Box 52.

20. Undated statement by McCloskey, presented in writing to the Judiciary Committee, Judiciary Committee files on Warren nomination, Box 53.

21. Oral history interview with Warren Olney, *Law Enforcement and Judicial Administration in the Earl Warren Era*, p. 392.

22. Oral history interview with Warren, LBJ Library, p. 3 (Internet copy).

23. Undated statement by McCloskey, presented in writing to the Judiciary Committee, Judiciary Committee files on Warren nomination, Box 53.

24. *Chicago Sun-Times*, Feb. 22, 1954, reprinted by *Washington Post*.

25. University records confirm that McCloskey attended during that period but did not graduate.

26. McCloskey to Langer, March 27, 1953, Langer papers, Chester Fritz Library, University of North Dakota, McCloskey file.

27. McCloskey "Statement to the Senate" included in letter to Langer, July 1, 1957, Langer papers, Chester Fritz Library, University of North Dakota, McCloskey file.

28. Testimony of Warren Olney to the Subcommittee of the Committee on the Judiciary, Feb. 20, 1954, p. 13, Judiciary Committee files on Warren nomination, Box 51.

29. Letter to American Rally members, May 1954, William Langer papers, Chester Fritz Library, University of North Dakota, McCloskey file.

30. *Chicago Sun-Times*, Feb. 22, 1954, reprinted by *Washington Post*.

31. Memorandum from Judiciary Counsel to Langer, Judiciary Committee, Feb. 11, 1954, Judiciary Committee files on Warren nomination, Box 51.

32. Undated letter to Judiciary Committee, Judiciary Committee files on Warren nomination, Box 51. The letter is stamped "Rec'd Feb. 19, 1954," but that is inaccurate, for the charge from the note appears in the counsel's Feb. 11 memorandum; as such, it is impossible to know precisely when it was sent and received.

33. Rogers testimony before the Subcommittee of the Committee on the Judiciary, Feb. 19, 1954, p. 83, Judiciary Committee files on Warren nomination, Box 51.

34. L. B. Nichols to Tolson, Feb. 9, 1954, FBI document 77-61323-7.

35. Judge James Oakley letter to Warren, Feb. 12, 1954, LOC, MD, Warren papers, personal file, correspondence (confirmation file).

36. Warren investigation, Feb. 16, 1954, FBI document 77-6123-1.

37. Ibid.

38. Nichols to Tolson, Feb. 16, 1954, FBI document 77-6123-13.

39. Knowland appearance before Subcommittee of the Committee on the Judiciary, Feb. 19, 1954, p. 80.

40. *New York Times*, Feb. 20, 1954.

41. Ibid.

42. *New York Times*, Feb. 21, 1954.

43. *Santa Monica Evening Outlook* editorial, Feb. 23, 1954, copy in Judiciary Committee files on Warren nomination, Box 53.

44. Anne M. Fisher letter to Langer, Feb. 3, 1954, Judiciary Committee files on Warren nomination, Box 52.

45. Warren's position on the loyalty oath was noted by the committee, and one clipping about the oath contained in the committee's files bears a handwritten note suggesting that the committee subpoena Neylan to testify against Warren. During the FBI investigation, Warren, at William Rogers's request, drew up a memo explaining his actions in that debate, and the FBI included it in its background report. The "charge" of opposing the oath, however, was placed on a list of those beyond the committee's purview, and never engaged its interest.

46. McCloskey letter to Langer, March 27, 1953, William Langer papers, Chester Fritz Library, University of North Dakota, McCloskey file.

47. Langer letter to McCloskey, April 3, 1953, William Langer papers, Chester Fritz Library, University of North Dakota, McCloskey file.

48. McCloskey letter to Langer, Nov. 24, 1953, William Langer papers, Chester Fritz Library, University of North Dakota, McCloskey file.

49. Hearing of the Subcommittee of the Committee on the Judiciary, Executive Session, Feb. 20, 1954, p. 9, Judiciary Committee files on Warren nomination, Box 51.

50. Ibid., p. 21.

51. Only once in the Judiciary Committee records is there reference to a past association between McCloskey and Langer. It came in a *Chicago Sun-Times* story that ran after the February 19 hearing. In that story, which also appeared in the February 22 edition of the *Washington Post*, McCloskey described himself as a "disciple" of Langer. Langer demurred, acknowledging that he had known McCloskey for years and respected his judgment but noting that he did not consider him a "political disciple."

52. Oral history interview with Warren Olney, *Law Enforcement and Judicial Administration in the Earl Warren Era*, p. 392.

53. Hearing of the Judiciary Committee, Executive Session, Feb. 24, 1954, p. 100, Judiciary Committee files on Warren nomination, Box 51.

54. Ibid., p. 147

55. This page of notes is included in the Judiciary Committee files. It is undated and unsigned, but its contents—references to Warren as "chief magistrate" and to "organized crime"—make it clear that it is a haphazard record of the Wilson testimony.

56. *American Rally*, January 1955.

57. Burton Crane letter to Warren, Feb. 21, 1954, LOC, MD, Warren papers, personal file, correspondence (confirmation file).

## CHAPTER 17. ALL MEN ARE CREATED EQUAL

1. I have not attempted a complete history of the segregation cases. For those interested in such an analysis, Richard Kluger's *Simple Justice* remains the definitive work, arrestingly written and meticulously accurate. I have relied on it extensively, as have all serious students of the period.

2. Vernon Parrington, *Main Currents in American Thought*, vol. 3, *The Beginnings of Critical Realism in America, 1860–1920*, p. 410. Quoted from Gunnar Myrdal, *An American Dilemma*, pp. 6–7.

3. *Plessy v. Ferguson*, 163 U.S. 537 (1896).

4. Ibid.

5. Ibid.

6. Ibid. (dissent).

7. Mark V. Tushnet, *Making Civil Rights Law*, p. 8.

8. Ibid., pp. 121–22.

9. *State of Missouri ex rel. Gaines v. Canada*, 305, U.S. 337 (1938). "Negro" does not have a capital N in the opinion; the stylistic decision rankled Marshall, who always capitalized it in his briefs and resented it when others did not.

10. Ibid. (separate opinion).

11. *Sipuel v. Board of Regents of the University of Oklahoma*, 332 U.S. 631 (1948).

12. *Sweatt v. Painter*, 339 U.S. 629 (1950).

13. Ibid.

14. Ibid.

15. *McLaurin v. Oklahoma State Regents*, 339 U.S. 637 (1950).

16. Ibid.

17. Ibid.

18. *Sweatt v. Painter*, 339 U.S. 629 (1950).

19. Executive Order 9981, "Establishing the President's Committee on Equality of Treatment and Opportunity in the Armed Services," signed by Truman, July 26, 1948. The document is contained in the desegregation collection of the Truman Presidential Library.

20. Richard Kluger, *Simple Justice*, p. 327.

21. William Faulkner, *Essays, Speeches and Public Letters*, p. 107 (from "A Letter to the Leaders in the Negro Race," first published in *Ebony*, Sept. 1956).

22. Kluger, *Simple Justice*, p. 291.

23. Ibid., p. 294.

24. Ibid., p. 395.

25. *Brown v. Board of Education of Topeka*, 347 U.S. 483 (1954).

26. Kluger, *Simple Justice*, p. 447.

27. *Brown v. Board of Education of Topeka*, 347 U.S. 483 (1954), footnote 10.

28. Kluger, *Simple Justice*, p. 349.

29. Ibid. See also Peter Irons, *A People's History of the Supreme Court*, pp. 385–86.

30. Taylor Branch, *Parting the Waters*, p. 20.

31. Kluger, *Simple Justice*, p. 478.

32. Mark V. Tushnet, *Making Civil Rights Law*, pp. 162–63.

33. Ibid., p. 165.

34. Kluger, *Simple Justice*, p. 572.

35. Ibid., p. 573.

36. Ibid., p. 581.

37. Conference notes of Robert Jackson, Dec. 12, 1952, LOC, MD, Jackson papers, Legal file, Supreme Court, October term 1953, Segregation case file.

38. Douglas, "Memorandum for the File in re Segregation Cases," May 17, 1954, LOC, MD, William O. Douglas papers, Part II, Segregation Cases file. Included in the file are Douglas's notes from the December 12, 1952, conference, mislabeled "Dec. 13, 1952." Jackson's notes support most of Douglas's observations of the conference.

39. Conference notes of Robert Jackson, Dec. 12, 1952, LOC, MD, Jackson papers, Legal file, Supreme Court, October term 1953, Segregation case file.

40. Douglas conference notes, Dec. 12, 1952, LOC, MD, Douglas papers, Supreme Court file, Case file, Segregation cases folder.

41. Jackson conference notes, Dec. 12, 1952, LOC, MD, Jackson papers, Legal file, Supreme Court, October term 1953, Segregation case file.

42. Douglas "Memorandum for the File, in re Segregation Cases," May 17, 1954, LOC, MD, Douglas papers, Supreme Court file, Case file, Segregation cases folder.

43. Ibid.

44. Douglas conference notes, Dec. 12, 1952, LOC, MD, Douglas papers, Supreme Court file, Case file, Segregation cases folder.

45. As he contemplated the cases, Jackson appears to have solicited the input of his clerks. One of their memos deserves special note because its author was William H. Rehnquist, later to join the Court himself and to ascend to the chief justiceship. In 1952, young William Rehnquist took the position that *Plessy* was correctly decided and should be upheld. "I realize that is an unpopular and unhumanitarian position, for which I have been excoriated by 'liberal' colleagues, but I think *Plessy* was right," Rehnquist wrote. Fourteen years later, when his own appointment to the Court was presented to the Senate for its consideration, Rehnquist said those words had been written for Jackson to present to the other justices at conference and were not Rehnquist's own views. That argument is almost certainly false, however, as the language and approach of the memo strongly suggest Rehnquist was speaking for himself. It is inconceivable, for instance, that Jackson would have so patronized his colleagues of long standing as to address them in conference by complaining that they had "excoriated" him; Rehnquist, by contrast, did in fact complain of the influence of liberal clerks on the Court over their justices and after leaving the Court wrote an article to that effect. And even should Jackson have complained of "excoriation," would he have identified his critics as "liberal colleagues"? Jackson was a proponent of judicial restraint, but he was a lifelong Democrat, a friend and ally of FDR, and that president's solicitor general and attorney general. Perhaps most tellingly, Rehnquist's memo derided previous Court rulings that attempted to protect minorities and singled out the Jehovah's Witness flag case as one in which the Court overreached. It is ludicrous to think Jackson would cite that case for that proposition. The Jehovah's Witness opinion was written by Jackson himself, and it was one of his most celebrated opinions.

46. William O. Douglas, *The Court Years*, p. 113.

47. Douglas "Memorandum for the File in re Segregation Cases," May 17, 1954, LOC, MD, William O. Douglas papers, Part II, Segregation Cases file.

48. Frankfurter memorandum for the conference, June 4, 1953, LOC, MD, William O. Douglas papers, Part II, Segregation Cases file.

## CHAPTER 18. JUSTICE

1. Thomas Jefferson, *Autobiography*, included in *Jefferson, Writings*, p. 44 (quoted in Gunnar, Myrdal, *An American Dilemma*, p. 85).

2. *Newsweek*, Oct. 19, 1953.

3. Burton diary entry, Dec. 8, 1953, LOC, MD, Harold H. Burton papers, Diaries, 1953.

4. Michael J. Klarman, *From Jim Crow to Civil Rights*, p. 311.

5. William O. Douglas and Harold Burton notes on conference, Dec. 12, 1953, LOC, MD, William O. Douglas papers (Segregation Cases file) and Harold F. Burton papers. See also Del Dickson, *The Supreme Court in Conference*, p. 654.

6. William O. Douglas and Harold Burton notes on conference, Dec. 12, 1953, LOC, MD, William O. Douglas papers (Segregation Cases file) and Harold F. Burton papers.

7. William O. Douglas notes on conference, Dec. 12, 1953, LOC, MD, William O. Douglas papers, Segregation Cases file. Douglas's notes list Black as "absent."

8. *Memoirs*, p. 2.

9. Interviewed by Drew Pearson in 1967, Warren gave a truer account. Although that interview never was published, Pearson's notes indicate the lineup as Warren saw it. "Minton, Burton, no trouble . . ." Pearson wrote. "Clark a little trouble. Stanley Reed lot of trouble." Pearson interview notes, Aug. 21, 1967, Pearson papers, LBJ Library.

10. William O. Douglas notes on conference, Dec. 12, 1953, LOC, MD, William O. Douglas papers, Segregation Cases file.

11. Ibid.

12. Mark V. Tushnet, *Making Civil Rights Law*, p. 211.

13. Douglas, "Memorandum for the File in re Segregation Cases," May 17, 1954, LOC, MD, William O. Douglas papers, Segregation Cases file.

14. Douglas conference notes, Dec. 12, 1953, LOC, MD, William O. Douglas papers, Segregation Cases file.

15. *Memoirs*, p. 285. See also Burton diary and Douglas notes.

16. Warren's calendars, as maintained by the LOC, MD, begin in early 1954; Burton's diaries, however, cover late 1953 as well.

17. Burton diary entries for Dec. 12, 14, 15, 16, 17, and 18, 1953, LOC, MD, Harold H. Burton papers, 1953 Diaries.

18. Burton diary entry, Jan. 15, 1954, LOC, MD, Harold H. Burton papers, 1954 Diaries.

19. Burton diary entry, Jan. 16, 1954, LOC, MD, Harold H. Burton papers, 1954 Diaries.

20. Eisenhower invitation to Warren, Jan. 12, 1954, LOC, MD, Warren papers, Personal File, Presidents' Correspondence, 1953–1963.

21. *Memoirs*, p. 291. Some others, in relating this exchange, have recorded that Eisenhower used the term "bucks," rather than "Negroes," supporting that claim by noting that Eisenhower on other occasions did resort to that slur. In this case, however, only Eisenhower and Warren were parties to the remark, and since Eisenhower never acknowledged it and Warren recorded it this way, there is no credible evidence that Eisenhower used the slur.

22. Jack Slater, "1954 Revisited," *Ebony*, May 1974, p. 126. The exact date of this trip is unknown, as it does not appear on Warren's schedules for early 1954. Warren's weekends were often left open, however, so it could have taken place then, or in the fall of 1953, before the period in which his schedules were saved.

23. Author interview with Judge James Lee Warren, Nov. 24, 2003.

24. "Supreme Court Law Clerks' Recollections of *Brown v. Board of Education*," *St. John's Law Review*, volume 78 (Summer 2004), p. 529. Some analysts have surmised that Jackson drafted his memo in early 1954, but his clerk E. Barrett Prettyman, Jr., recalls that he began on December 11, 1953. An uncirculated memo among Jackson's papers is dated December 7, 1953, just a few days before the December 12 conference.

25. Jackson memo on segregation cases, Dec. 7, 1953, LOC, MD, Jackson papers, Legal file, Supreme Court, Segregation cases. Subsequent drafts in January, February and March are also in the file.

26. Undated Prettyman memorandum to Jackson, "Re Nos. 1–4," LOC, MD, Jackson papers, Legal file, Supreme Court, Segregation cases.

27. "Supreme Court Law Clerks' Recollections of *Brown v. Board of Education*," p. 545.

28. Ibid., p. 543.

29. Undated memorandum. This draft, written in Warren's hand, is contained with his papers at the LOC, MD, Warren papers, segregation case file.

30. Author interview with Earl Pollock, Jan. 10, 2005. The date comes from "Supreme Court Law Clerks' Recollections of *Brown v. Board of Education*," p. 551.

31. Author interview with Earl Pollock, Jan. 10, 2005.

32. Ibid.

33. "Supreme Court Law Clerks' Recollections of *Brown v. Board of Education*," p. 550.

34. *Bolling v. Sharpe*, 347 U.S. 497 (1954). Also author interview with Earl Pollock, Jan. 10, 2005.

35. *Bolling v. Sharpe*, 347 U.S. 497 (1954).

36. "Supreme Court Law Clerks' Recollections of *Brown v. Board of Education*," p. 552.

37. Burton diary entry, May 8, 1954. LOC, MD, Harold H. Burton papers, 1954 Diaries.

38. Warren letter to Jackson, April 2, 1954, LOC, MD, Robert Jackson papers, General correspondence file, Warren folder.

39. Warren schedule, May 13, 1954, LOC, MD, Earl Warren papers, Personal file, 1954 Calendars.

40. "Supreme Court Law Clerks' Recollections of *Brown v. Board of Education*," pp. 553–55.

41. Ibid., p. 553.

42. Richard Kluger, *Simple Justice*, p. 698.

43. Burton diary entry, May 8, 1954, LOC, MD, Harold H. Burton papers, 1954 Diaries. Burton's diary reflects his observations before the final vote was taken, on May 15, but after Burton had concluded that the draft was likely to win a united Court.

44. Ibid.

45. Chief Justice calendars, May 16, 1954, LOC, MD, Warren papers, Personal file, Warren's schedule lists their hike as along the "B & O Canal," but that is undoubtedly a typo.

46. Bruce Allen Murphy, *Wild Bill*, p. 331.

47. *New York Times*, May 18, 1954. The *Times* recorded Nina's presence but not Helen MacGregor's. Her recollection comes from the oral history interview with her in *A Career in Public Service with Earl Warren*, p. 129.

48. *Memoirs*, p. 286.

49. "Supreme Court Law Clerks' Recollections of *Brown v. Board of Education*," p. 559.

50. *New York Times*, May 18, 1954.

51. *Memoirs*, p. 3.

52. Cheryl Brown Henderson, *The College Board Review*, issue 200 (Fall 2003), pp. 6–11.

53. Taylor Branch, *Parting the Waters*, p. 112.

54. Martin Luther King, Jr., *The Papers of Martin Luther King, Jr.*, vol. 3, pp. 471–79.

### CHAPTER 19.  RESISTANCE

1. Wallace's speech of June 11, 1963, is preserved at the Alabama Department of Archives and History and is available through its website: http://www.archives.state.al.us/index.html.

2. *New York Times*, March 4, 1954.

3. *New York Times*, May 18, 1954.

4. Ibid. Reston did, however, misspell his name, writing it as "Cardoza"; the mistake slipped by the *Times*'s copy desk. Although Reston did not disclose the source of his insight into the Court, it likely was Frankfurter, with whom he was close. Frankfurter spoke frequently with the columnist and once suggested that he emulate the justices and hire a clerk. Reston took that advice and for more than three decades hired one young college graduate a year as his assistant. I held that position for one year, beginning in the fall of 1985.

5. *Brown v. Board of Education*, 347 U.S. 483 (1954) (footnote 11).

6. Elmo Richardson, *The Presidency of Dwight D. Eisenhower*, p. 110.

7. Eisenhower to Hazlett, Oct. 23, 1954, Eisenhower Library, Civil Rights file.

8. *Memoirs*, p. 292.

9. Reed memo to conference, March 28, 1955, Harold Burton copy, LOC, MD, Harold H. Burton papers, Warren correspondence file, 1954–1955.

10. Bernard Schwartz, *Super Chief*, pp. 113–14. This exchange took place in open court and has been widely documented; Tushnet and Powe, for instance, each include accounts of it in their works. For the specific language and nonverbal responses of the participants, I have drawn principally from Schwartz.

11. Frankfurter conference notes (typewritten), April 16, 1955, LOC, MD, Felix Frankfurter papers, Legal File, Segregation case file, 1955. These thoughts are reflected also in Douglas's conference notes for the same session, which are mistakenly dated April 16, 1954, when the conference actually took place in 1955.

12. Ibid.

13. Ibid.

14. Ibid.

15. Douglas conference notes, April 16, [1955], LOC, MD, Douglas papers, Supreme Court file, Segregation case file.

16. Ibid.

17. Ibid.

18. Frankfurter letter to Philip Elman, June 4, 1947, LOC, MD, Felix Frankfurter papers, General Correspondence, Elman file (Reel 32).

19. *Brown v. Board of Education*, 349 U.S. 294 (1955).

20. Lucas A. Powe, Jr., *The Warren Court and American Politics*, p. 55.

21. Warren schedules, Sept. 30 and Oct. 1, 1955, LOC, MD, Warren papers, Personal file.

22. Warren handwritten note and typewritten statement, April 15, 1955, LOC, MD, Personal files, Presidential Ambitions Disavowed, 1955–56.

23. Drew Pearson, *Diaries 1949–1959*, entry for Feb. 19, 1949, p. 23.

24. Ibid., entry for Oct. 27, 1953, p. 280.

25. Shirley S. Johnson letter to Warren, Oct. 6, 1955, LOC, MD, Personal files, Presidential Ambitions Disavowed, 1955–1956.

26. Schwartz, *Super Chief*, p. 126.

27. *Han Say Naim v. Ruby Elaine Naim*, 197 Va. 80; 87 S.E. 2d 749 (1955).

28. *Naim v. Naim*, 350 U.S. 985 (1956).

29. Author interview with Sam Stern, May 10, 2005.

30. *Irvine v. California*, 347 U.S. 128 (1954). Details not included in the opinion come from Jackson's case file, LOC, MD, Jackson papers, Legal file, Supreme Court, *Irvine* file.

31. *Irvine v. California*, 347 U.S. 128 (1954).

32. Ibid.

33. Hoover to Tolson, Ladd, and Nichols, Feb. 8, 1954, FBI document 44-7129-1, Charns, Warren files, Folder 90.

34. G. Edward White, *Earl Warren: A Public Life*, p. 266.

35. Nichols to Tolson, Sept. 2, 1954, FBI document 94-1-5619-217 (and follow-up memos documenting the effort).

36. Los Angeles Special Agent in Charge to Hoover, Jan. 26, 1954, FBI document 94-1-5619-196. Also Nichols to Tolson, Feb. 1, 1954, same document number.

37. Nichols to Tolson, Nov. 1, 1955, FBI document 94-5619-224. This favor also is noted in a November 6, 1978, memo from McCreight to Bassett, alerting Bureau officials that a request for information from the *New York Times* might cause the FBI's providing "background information regarding competence and reputation of future sons-in-law" to Warren to become known publicly. It did not at that time, as the *New*

*York Times* apparently did not pursue the request. While the 1978 memo uses the plural "sons-in-law," there is no evidence in the FBI files as released that the Bureau performed such a task other than in the case of Dr. Brien. Finally, it is worth adding that when the FBI released its files to Charns, enough information was included in this file to make its context clear. In 2006, when the same documents were released to me, they were so heavily redacted as to be incomprehensible without access to Charns's papers.

38. The Southern Manifesto, March 1956, copy at Carl Vinson Institute of Government, University of Georgia (taken from Vinson Institute website).

39. *Pennsylvania v. Nelson*, 350 U.S. 497 (1956).

40. Although many analysts, historians, and commentators have reviewed this period, none has ever capsulated it more carefully or persuasively than Lucas Powe in *The Warren Court and American Politics*. My account relies on many sources, but Powe in particular.

41. Resolution Requesting Impeachment of Six Members of the United States Supreme Court, adopted by the General Assembly of Georgia, Feb. 22, 1957.

42. Undated pamphlet produced by the Cinema Educational Guild, Inc., Hollywood, California, copy in author's possession.

43. *Griffin v. Illinois*, 351 U.S. 12 (1956).

44. *New York Times*, May 18, 1956. See also Schwartz, *Super Chief*, p. 183, and Powe, *The Warren Court and American Politics*, p. 88.

45. Associated Press, June 27, 1956.

46. Field report, July 15, 1956, FBI document 89-816-2.

47. *Washington Post*, July 26, 1956, FBI document 89-816-A.

48. Powe, *The Warren Court and American Politics*, p. 62.

49. Warren schedule, July 7, 1956, LOC, MD, Earl Warren papers, Personal file, 1956 Calendars.

50. Although Warren did not publicly reveal his vote, his son Earl Jr. is among many who recalled his fondness and support for Stevenson. The elder Warren told Pat Brown in 1960 that he believed the Democrats should select Stevenson as well. See oral history interview with Brown, *Years of Growth*, p. 250.

51. Herbert Brownell, *Advising Ike*, p. 180.

52. Ibid.

53. William Brennan, included in *The Warren Court, A Retrospective*, p. 10.

54. Brennan letter to Bernard Schwartz, Oct. 15, 1980, LOC, MD, Brennan papers, Part II, Correspondence, Bernard Schwartz file. Brennan described the scene to Schwartz after Schwartz had incorrectly written up an account of it for his book *Super Chief*. The above reflects Brennan's recollection.

55. Oral history interview with Bartley Cavanaugh, *Hunting and Fishing with Earl Warren*, p. 30.

## Chapter 20. "Dumb Swede"

1. Peter Irons, *The Courage of Their Convictions*, p. 104.

2. Roger K. Newman, "The Warren Court and American Politics: An Impressionistic Appreciation," p. 673. See also *New York Times Magazine*. Oct. 5, 1986.

3. *U.S. v. E. I. DuPont*, 351 U.S. 377 (1956).

4. Bernard Schwartz, *Super Chief*, p. 222.

5. *United States v. DuPont*, 353 U.S. 586 (1957) (dissent).

6. Undated tribute to Warren prepared by Douglas after Warren's death in 1974, LOC, MD, William O. Douglas papers, Part 1, Subject files, Earl Warren.

7. Frankfurter note to Harlan, April 26, 1957, PU, ML, Harlan papers, *Konigsberg v. the State Bar of California* file.

8. Hand letter to Frankfurter, Jan. 1, 1956, LOC, MD, Felix Frankfurter papers, General correspondence, Learned Hand (Reels 39–40).

9. Hand letter to Frankfurter, Oct. 25, 1956, LOC, MD, Felix Frankfurter papers, General correspondence, Learned Hand (Reels 39–40).

10. Ibid.

11. Undated memo in papers of Drew Pearson, LBJ Library, Personal Papers of Drew Pearson, File #2. In the memo, Pearson notes that Frankfurter used the term with his then clerk Phil Graham, later publisher of the *Washington Post.*

12. Frankfurter letter to Harlan, Dec. 26, 1960, PU, ML, Harlan papers, Frankfurter correspondence file for 1960.

13. Author interview with Sam Stern, May 10, 2005. See also Roger K. Newman, "The Warren Court and American Politics: An Impressionistic Appreciation," p. 676, note 82.

14. Schwartz, *Super Chief*, p. 257.

15. Del Dickson, *The Supreme Court in Conference*, p. 560. The excerpt is taken from Douglas's notes from a 1962 conference discussion over *Machiboda v. United States.*

16. Warren schedule, Nov. 25, 1954, LOC, MD, Earl Warren papers, Personal file, 1954 Calendars.

17. Author interview with Virginia Daly, May 31, 2004.

18. Roger K. Newman, "The Warren Court and American Politics: An Impressionistic Appreciation," p. 686.

19. Oral history interview with Jim Warren. Eve Dillingham, Harlan's daughter, confirms that her father had an extra clerk to assist him when his eyesight was failing.

20. Author interview with Douglas Kranwinkle, Jan. 21, 2005.

21. Author interview with Peter Ehrenhaft, Jan. 31, 2005.

22. Note in file, May 14, 1958, RNLB, Warren file, 1956–1962.

23. Author interview with William Brennan III, July 2003.

24. *Mesarosh v. United States*, 352 U.S. 1 (1956).

25. *Jencks v. United States*, 353 U.S. 657 (1957). *Jencks* was first argued on October 17, 1956.

26. Ibid.

27. Dickson, *The Supreme Court in Conference*, p. 557.

28. *Jencks v. United States*, 353 U.S. 657 (1957) (dissent).

29. *Sweezy v. New Hampshire*, 354 U.S. 234 (1957).

30. Lucas Powe, *The Warren Court and American Politics*, p. 96.

31. *Watkins v. United States*, 354 U.S. 178 (1957).

32. Ibid.

33. Undated note from Frankfurter to Harlan, PU, ML, Harlan papers, *Watkins v. U.S.* file.

34. *Watkins v. United States*, 354 U.S. 178 (1957).

35. Ibid.

36. Burton Crane letter to Warren, Feb. 21, 1954, LOC, MD, Warren papers, personal file, correspondence (confirmation file).

37. *Watkins v. United States*, 354 U.S. 178 (1957).

38. *Service v. Dulles et al*, 354 U.S. 363 (1957).

39. *Yates v. United States*, 354 U.S. 298 (1957).

40. Mohr to Tolson, May 9, 1958, FBI document 62-40772-400, Charns, Warren files, Folder 77.

41. Eisenhower letter to Warren, June 21, 1957, LOC, MD, Warren papers, Personal file, Presidents' correspondence, 1953–1963. The specific quote "never been as mad" comes from *The Papers of Dwight David Eisenhower*, vol. 28, document 211, bibliographic note 1.

42. Eisenhower letter to Warren, June 21, 1957, LOC, MD, Warren papers, Personal file, Presidents' correspondence, 1953–1963.

43. Warren schedule, June 21–24, 1957, LOC, MD, Earl Warren papers, Personal file, 1957 Calendars.

44. Warren letter to Eisenhower, July 15, 1957, LOC, MD, Warren papers, Personal file, Presidents' correspondence, 1953–1963.

45. Jack Harrison Pollack, *Earl Warren: The Judge Who Changed America*, p. 192.

46. Author interview with Peter Ehrenhaft, Jan. 31, 2005.

47. *Memoirs*, p. 322.

48. Ibid.

49. Warren schedule, Sept. 4, 1957, LOC, MD, Earl Warren papers, Personal file, 1957 Calendars.

50. *Memoirs*, p. 329.

51. Stephen Ambrose, *Eisenhower: Soldier and President*, pp. 443–44.

52. *Cooper v. Aaron*, 358 U.S. 1 (1958).

53. Ibid.

54. Statement by Orval Faubus, Sept. 14, 1957, released after meeting with Eisenhower, Eisenhower Library, Little Rock school integration crisis file (available in online holdings).

55. Mark V. Tushnet, *Making Civil Rights Law*, p. 258. Also Ambrose, *Eisenhower: Soldier and President*, p. 446; and Woodrow Wilson Mann telegram to Eisenhower, Sept. 23, 1957, Eisenhower Library, Little Rock School integration crisis file (available in online holdings).

56. Woodrow Wilson Mann telegram to Eisenhower, Sept. 24, 1957, Eisenhower Library, Little Rock school integration crisis file (available in online holdings).

57. Presidential Address from the White House, delivered Sept. 24, 1957, at nine P.M. Text from Eisenhower Library, Little Rock school integration crisis file (available in online holdings).

58. Ibid.

59. Undated handwritten note by Eisenhower on use of troops in Little Rock, Eisenhower Library, Little Rock school integration crisis file (available in online holdings).

60. Telephone call log for Eisenhower's day, Sept. 25, 1957, Eisenhower Library, Little Rock school integration crisis file (available in online holdings).

61. Ambrose, *Eisenhower: Soldier and President*, p. 447.

62. Warren schedule, Sept. 20, 1957, LOC, MD, Earl Warren papers, Personal file, 1957 Calendars.

63. *Cooper v. Aaron*, 358 U.S. 1 (1958). See also Marshall's oral argument from Aug. 28, 1958, and Tushnet, *Making Civil Rights Law*, and Powe, *The Warren Court and American Politics*, p. 159.

64. Burton, still in the habit of rating the oral arguments in his diary, gave Butler an "excellent."

65. *Cooper v. Aaron* oral argument, Aug. 28, 1957. This exchange is taken from the tape of the argument, made available by the Oyez Project, Northwestern University (Oyez.com).

66. See, for instance, Ed Cray, *Chief Justice*, p. 346. Relying on Heyman's recollection, Cray places the exchange at the August 28 argument, though neither transcript nor tape of that day supports the version presented. Heyman relayed the same account to me in our interview on October 21, 2003. Even if Warren's comment to Butler was made out of earshot of the court reporter, it eluded the press covering the argument and appears to have made little impression on Butler, as he did not repeat it to friends and colleagues with whom he argued the case and who later spoke with me.

67. Tushnet, *Making Civil Rights Law*, p. 260.

68. Transcript of oral argument in *Cooper v. Aaron*, Sept. 11, 1958, provided by the Librarian of the Supreme Court.

69. Harlan draft to conference, Sept. 18, 1958, PU, ML, Harlan papers, *Cooper v. Aaron* file.

70. *Cooper v. Aaron*, 358 U.S. 1 (1958).

71. Ibid.

72. *Memoirs*, pp. 298–99.

73. The analysis of the 1958 attack on the Court is contained in Powe, *The Warren Court and American Politics*. Powe's quotation is from his conversation with me on January 19, 2005.

74. Frankfurter letter to Hand, Nov. 27, 1956, LOC, MD, Frankfurter papers, General correspondence, Learned Hand (Reels 39–40).

75. Learned Hand, *The Bill of Rights*, p. 71.

76. *Trop v. Dulles*, 356 U.S. 86 (1958).

77. The circulation of drafts and dates comes from Harlan's case file, PU, ML, Harlan papers, *Trop v. Dulles* file.

78. *Trop v. Dulles*, 356 U.S. 86 (1958).

79. That language has found contemporary purchase in the assessment of capital punishment. It was used in 2002 by the Court majority to strike the executions of mentally retarded defendants (*Atkins v. Virginia*), and used again in 2005 to banish the executions of minors (*Roper v. Simmons*).

80. Burton diary entry, July 17, 1958, LOC, MD, Burton papers, diary. After Eisenhower's retirement, the former president was said to have remarked that the Warren and Brennan appointments were his two biggest mistakes, "damn-fool mistakes," in some retellings. Although the evidence of that statement is indirect—Brownell, for one, doubted that Eisenhower would say such a thing—the president's comment to Burton makes clear that Eisenhower did indeed regret those appointments, whether or not he said so colorfully.

81. Gerald Gunther, *Learned Hand*, p. 661.

82. Robert Caro, *Master of the Senate*, p. 1033. See also Powe, *The Warren Court and American Politics*, p. 133.

83. *Memoirs*, p. 313.

84. *Bartkus v. Illinois*, 359 U.S. 121 (1959).

85. *Bartkus v. Illinois*, 355 U.S. 281 (1958).

86. End-of-term memo, 1958, Chambers of William J. Brennan, Jr., LOC, MD, Brennan papers, Part II.

87. Ibid.

88. Ibid.

89. Author interview with Jim Adler, Jan. 14, 2005.

90. *Bartkus v. Illinois*, 329 U.S. 121 (1959).

91. The decision in *Bartkus* remains the law today. After two Los Angeles police officers were convicted in 1993 for violating the civil rights of Rodney G. King, they argued that their previous trial in state court on assault charges arising from the same beating should invalidate the federal prosecution. The Supreme Court upheld their convictions in 1996 (*Koon v. United States*).

92. *New York Times*, March 21, 1961.

93. Ibid.

94. *Barenblatt v. United States*, 360 U.S. 109 (1959).

95. Ibid.

96. Ibid. (dissent).

97. Ibid.

98. Stephen Ells, "Willard Uphaus: A Prisoner in Thoreau County Becomes One of New Hampshire's Men of the Century," Internet article, Aug. 4, 2001.

99. *Uphaus v. Wyman*, 360 U.S. 72 (1959).

100. Ibid. (dissent).

101. Ells, "Willard Uphaus."

102. *Washington Post* editorial, Sept. 7, 1959.

103. *New York Times*, June 14, 1959.

104. *Memoirs*, p. 343.

105. Warren schedule, Oct. 28 and 30, 1959, LOC, MD, Earl Warren papers, Personal file, 1959 Calendars.

106. *Greensboro Record*, Feb. 2, 1960.

107. Author interview with Earl Warren, Jr., Nov. 25, 2003. See also interviews with Jesse Choper, Ira Michael Heyman, and Jeffrey Warren.

108. Theodore H. White, *The Making of the President, 1960*, pp. 203–16.

109. Johnson letter to Judge H. R. Wilson, May 28, 1954, LBJ Library, Johnson Senate papers, Legislative files, Social welfare (Segregation) folder.

110. Taylor Branch, *Parting the Waters*, pp. 360–61.

111. Ibid., p. 375.

112. Ibid., pp. 375–76. See also White, *The Making of the President, 1960*, p. 315. White's account implies that Walsh drafted his statement just hours after King was imprisoned. Branch makes clear that it was later, and completed at a time when it had become superseded by events.

113. Branch, *Parting the Waters*, p. 362.

114. Ibid., p. 370.

115. Author interview with Virginia Warren, May 31, 2004.

116. Swig letter to Warren, Feb. 1, 1961, LOC, MD, Warren papers, personal papers, Ben Swig file.

117. Author interview with Bruce Boynton, Dec. 27, 2005.

118. *Boynton v. Virginia*, 364 U.S. 454 (1960).

119. Author interview with Jesse Choper, Oct. 20, 2003.

120. *Boynton v. Virginia*, 364 U.S. 454 (1960).

121. Warren's insistence that the case not interrupt Boynton's law career was vindicated by Boynton's life thereafter. He passed the bar examination and applied for admission to the Alabama bar. The association informed him that it was inquiring into conviction in the bus terminal case, notwithstanding that it had been overturned by the Court. Matters thus stood for years while Boynton instead practiced in Tennessee. Finally, in 1966, Boynton was allowed to practice law in Alabama. Thirty years later, the same bar association that had blocked his admission for nearly a decade named him one of its "Living Legends."

122. Robert Frost, 1942 (dated, handwritten copy included in the collection of the LOC).

123. Thurston Clarke, *Ask Not*, p. 188.

CHAPTER 21. KENNEDY, KING, AND A NEW ERA

1. Kennedy telegram to Warren, March 23, 1963, LOC, MD, Warren papers, Presidents' correspondence, 1953–1963.

2. Jacqueline Kennedy letter to Warren, Dec. 20, 1963, LOC, MD, Warren papers, Presidents' correspondence, 1953–1963.

3. Kennedy letter to Warren, Jan. 25, 1961, LOC, MD, Warren papers, Presidents' correspondence, 1953–1963.

4. Kennedy letter to Warren, Jan. 28, 1961, LOC, MD, Warren papers, Presidents' correspondence, 1953–1963.

5. Author interview with Flannery, Feb. 2, 2005.

6. Author interview with Ziffren, Jan. 12, 2005.

7. Leo Katcher, *Earl Warren: A Political Biography*, p. 426.

8. *Mapp v. Ohio*, 367 U.S. 643 (1961).

9. *Irvine v. California*, 347 U.S. 128 (1954; concurrence).

10. Harlan letter to Clark, May 1, 1961, PU, ML, Harlan papers, *Mapp v. Ohio* case file.

11. *Mapp v. Ohio*, 367 U.S. 643 (1961).

12. Lucas Powe, *The Warren Court and American Politics*, pp. 198–99.

13. *Bulletin of the John Birch Society*, January 1961, copy supplied to author by the Birch Society's public affairs office.

14. For background on the John Birch Society, see its *Blue Book* and *White Book*, official publications of the organization published annually in the late 1950s and early 1960s.

15. *New York Times*, July 30, 1963.

16. *Bulletin of the John Birch Society*, January 1961.

17. Ibid.

18. *New York Times*, June 18, 1964 (AP report from Boston, dated June 17); also *New York Times*, July 30, 1963.

19. "Twelfth Report of the Senate Fact-Finding Subcommittee on Un-American Activities," Report of the California Legislature, 1963.

20. See, for instance, FBI memos of Feb. 28 and Oct. 25, 1963, and Feb. 6, 1964 (FBI documents 94-1-5619-272, 273, 275, and 287).

21. Letter writer to FBI, June 17, 1964, FBI document 94-1-5619-290.

22. Rosen to Belmont, Sept. 17, 1962, FBI document 157-6-53-94.

23. Author interview with Douglas Kranwinkle, April 2003.

24. *Memoirs*, p. 304.

25. Ibid., p. 305.

26. Ibid., p. 304.

27. *Los Angeles Times* editorial, March 12, 1961. See also Robert Gottlieb and Irene Wolt, *Thinking Big*, p. 337.

28. Philip Chandler letter to Norman Chandler, May 5, 1963, Los Angeles Times History Center, Norman Chandler files. At the time of my research, the complete files of Norman Chandler were in transition from the *Times* to the Huntington Library. I requested copies of those files from their interim curator, Bill Stinehart. He denied that request without explanation, first orally and then in writing.

29. Norman Chandler letter Philip Chandler, June 19, 1963, Los Angeles Times History Center, Norman Chandler files.

30. *Memoirs*, p. 305.

31. Francis X. Gannon, *Biographical Dictionary of the American Left*, pp. 574–75.

32. *Memoirs*, p. 310.

33. End-of-term memo, 1961, Chambers of William J. Brennan, Jr., LOC, MD, Brennan papers, Part II.

34. *Colegrove v. Green*, 328 U.S. 549 (1946).

35. Ibid.

36. *Gomillion v. Lightfoot*, 364 U.S. 339 (1960).

37. *Memoirs*, p. 307.

38. End-of-term memo, 1961, Chambers of William J. Brennan, Jr., LOC, MD, Brennan papers, Part II.

39. Author interview with Peter Ehrenhaft, Jan. 31, 2005. See also end-of-term memo, 1961, Chambers of William J. Brennan, Jr., LOC, MD, Brennan papers, Part II.

40. Harlan letter to Whittaker and Stewart, Oct. 11, 1961, PU, ML, Harlan papers, *Baker v. Carr* file.

41. Frankfurter note to Harlan, Oct. 11, 1961, PU, ML, Harlan papers, *Baker v. Carr* file.

42. End-of-term memo, 1961, Chambers of William J. Brennan, Jr., LOC, MD, Brennan papers, Part II.

43. Ibid.

44. Bernard Schwartz, *Super Chief*, p. 424.

45. Craig Alan Smith, *Failing Justice*, p. 219. Also author interview with Jim Adler, Jan. 14, 2005.

46. Author interview with Jim Adler, Jan. 14, 2005.

47. Schwartz, *Super Chief*, p. 428.

48. Robert Dallek, *An Unfinished Life*, p. 493.

49. It is ironic, given that Warren helped scotch the Hastie nomination on the grounds of his conservatism, that White ended up being one of the most conservative members of the Warren Court.

50. Frankfurter letter to Kennedy, Aug. 28, 1962, LOC, MD, Brennan correspondence file, 1961–1964.

51. Author interview with Jim Adler, Jan. 14, 2005.

52. *New York Times*, March 28, 1962.

53. Ibid.

54. *New York Times* transcript of Kennedy press conference, March 30, 1962.

55. *Engel et al. v. Vitale et al.*, 370 U.S. 421 (1962).

56. Ibid.

57. *New York Times*, June 26, 1962.

58. *New York Times*, June 28, 1962.

59. Brown letter to McWilliams, Aug. 2, 1974, UCLA, Charles E. Young Research Library, Special Collections, Carey McWilliams papers. See also Edmund Brown, Sr., *Earl Warren: Fellow Constitutional Officers*.

60. Ibid.

61. Author interview with Earl Warren, Jr., Nov. 25, 2003.

62. Ibid.

63. *Oakland Tribune*, Sept. 15, 1962.

64. Ibid.

65. Jack Harrison Pollack, *Earl Warren: The Judge Who Changed America*, p. 215.

66. Tape of press conference accessed at www.historyplace.com.

67. Richard Reeves, *President Kennedy, Profile of Power*, p. 435. McGrory's comment comes from a 1964 Press Panel oral history prepared by the Kennedy Library.

68. Oral argument in *Gideon v. Wainwright*, 372 U.S. 335 (1963). Argument accessed at Oyez.com.

69. Abe Fortas's oral argument in *Gideon v. Wainwright*, 372 U.S. 335 (1963), Jan. 15, 1963. Argument accessed at Oyez.org.

70. *Carnley v. Cochran*, 369 U.S. 506 (1962).

71. Powe, *The Warren Court and American Politics*, pp. 382–83.

72. *Douglas v. California*, 372 U.S. 353 (1963).

73. Powe was the first to discover the intertwined history of *Douglas* and *Gideon*, and he notes that the justices held *Douglas* over because they already had secured Fortas to argue *Gideon* as the landmark case. Having done so, they did not then want to steal his thunder by announcing *Douglas* first.

74. *Gideon v. Wainwright*, 372 U.S. 335 (1963).

75. Ibid. (concurrence).

76. Taylor Branch, *Parting the Waters*, p. 705.

77. King's case challenging his arrest eventually found its way to the Supreme Court and posed one of the Court's most difficult problems of the civil rights era. It reluctantly upheld the conviction, concluding that while the "breadth and vagueness of the injunction itself would also unquestionably be subject to substantial constitutional question," the protesters should have challenged it legally rather than simply violate it. Stewart wrote for the majority in that case. Warren dissented, joined by Brennan and Fortas (*Walker v. City of Birmingham*, 388 U.S. 307 [1967]). When King learned of the ruling, he remarked, "Now even the Supreme Court has turned against us." Taylor Branch, *At Canaan's Edge*, p. 623.

78. Branch, *Parting the Waters*, p. 761.

79. Martin Luther King, Jr., *The Autobiography of Martin Luther King, Jr.*, chapter 19.

80. Andrew Young, *An Easy Burden*, p. 250.

81. End-of-term memo, 1962, Chambers of William J. Brennan, Jr., LOC, MD, Brennan papers, Part II.

82. Ibid.

83. *NAACP v. Button*, 371 U.S. 415 (1963).

84. Dallek, *An Unfinished Life*, pp. 603–5.

85. Kennedy Address to the Nation, June 11, 1963, Public Papers of the President, 237—Radio and Television Report to the American People on Civil Rights. Obtained courtesy John Woolley and Gerhard

Peters of The American Presidency Project, University of California at Santa Barbara; http://www
.presidency.ucsb.edu.

86. Branch, *Parting the Waters*, p. 882.

87. Drew Pearson diary entry, Aug. 29, 1963, LBJ Library, Drew Pearson papers, Earl Warren #2 file.

88. Branch, *Parting the Waters*, p. 883.

89. Pollack, *Earl Warren: The Judge Who Changed America*, p. 219.

90. Kennedy telegram to Warren, March 23, 1963, LOC, MD, Warren papers, personal file, Presidents' correspondence, 1953–1963.

91. Kennedy letter to Warren, Sept. 23, 1963, LOC, MD, Warren papers, personal file, Presidents' correspondence, 1953–1963.

92. Various letters, 1953–1954, LOC, MD, Warren papers, personal papers, real estate file.

93. Katharine Graham, *Personal History*, p. 257.

94. Drew Pearson diary entry for Aug. 4, 1963, LBJ Library, Pearson papers, diaries.

95. Evan Thomas, *The Man to See*, p. 239.

96. Author interview with Jeffrey Warren, Aug. 26, 2003.

97. Proceedings of the Bar and Officers of the Supreme Court of the United States, Proceedings Before the Supreme Court of the United States, May 27, 1975.

98. Author interview with Warren Olney IV, Feb. 10, 2004.

99. Author interview with Judge James Lee Warren, Nov. 23, 2003.

100. This event is captured in news photographs of the evening. Other details, including Warren's reaction to the Kennedys, were supplied by papers and recollections of Jeffrey Warren, interviewed by the author on Aug. 26, 2003.

101. Pollack, *Earl Warren: The Judge Who Changed America*, p. 221.

## Chapter 22. The Longest Year

1. John Weaver, *Warren: The Man, the Court, the Era*, p. 300.

2. Author interview with Beytagh, April 8, 2005. See also McHugh letter to John Weaver, Oct. 12, 1965, LOC, MD, Warren papers, Kennedy file.

3. Jack Harrison Pollack, *Earl Warren: The Judge Who Changed America*, p. 222.

4. McHugh letter to John Weaver, Oct. 12, 1965, LOC, MD, Warren papers, Kennedy file.

5. Warren handwritten and typewritten statements, Nov. 22, 1963, LOC, MD, Warren papers, Personal file, Presidents' correspondence, 1953–1963.

6. Author interview with Beytagh, April 8, 2005. Johnson's inquiry was made to Robert Kennedy, who forwarded it to Nicholas Katzenbach. He eventually read the oath to the Johnson party, by then on *Air Force One* on the Love Field tarmac in Dallas. The oath was administered by Sarah Hughes, a Texas federal judge whose appointment had been a source of tension between Johnson and the Kennedy administration to which he was uncomfortably appended. In the aftermath of that day, the questions about the administration of the oath—whether Robert Kennedy or Johnson had suggested it, whether it was even necessary at all—would widen the already broad rift between Johnson and Kennedy. See William Manchester, *The Death of a President, 1960*, and Max Holland, *The Kennedy Assassination Tapes*.

7. Manchester, *The Death of a President, 1960*, p. 10.

8. Manchester places Nina Warren at home at the time of the assassination. Beytagh insists she was at a luncheon and returning that afternoon. Because Beytagh's memory of that day is clear—and because Manchester garbles some other small details regarding Warren (his secretary's name, for instance, appears in Manchester as Dorothy not Margaret McHugh)—I have relied on Beytagh. Beytagh's account also explains why Warren drove with him, not with Clemencia and Nina, to Andrews Air Force Base that evening.

9. Author interview with Beytagh, April 8, 2005.

10. Manchester, *The Death of a President, 1960*, p. 401.

11. Oral history interview with Warren, Sept. 21, 1971, by Joe B. Frantz, LBJ Library (Internet copy). Also author interview with Beytagh, April 8, 2005, and follow-up interview. In his memoirs, Warren wrote that he was accompanied by Nina at Andrews that evening, and his daily schedule for November 22 suggests her presence as well. That does not agree with Manchester's account or Beytagh's memory, though it is possible that she joined the chief justice after Beytagh dropped him off, since she still had access to the chief justice's car.

12. Warren Commission Report, p. 157.

13. Warren did not record his reaction to the press conferences as they took place, but the Warren Commission report reflects his dismay at the pretrial publicity orchestrated by Dallas authorities. See Warren Commission Report, pp. 231–40.

14. *Memoirs*, p. 352. Manchester maintains that Jackie Kennedy did not call Warren directly, but it is difficult to imagine that Warren misremembered that conversation, which he recalled not only in his memoirs but also in conversations with friends, clerks, and family members for years afterward.

15. *Memoirs*, p. 353.

16. Copies of Warren's remarks are in his memoirs, as well as in the files of the various brethren. Warren stumbled slightly in the penultimate paragraph, hence the ellipsis.

17. Author interview with Beytagh, April 8, 2005.

18. Public Papers of the President, Nov. 27, 1963. The American Presidency Project, UC Santa Barbara, Johnson Papers, 11.

19. Warren schedule, Nov. 28, 1963, LOC, MD, Earl Warren papers, Personal file, 1963 Calendars.

20. Author interview with Beytagh, April 8, 2005.

21. Presidential daily diary, Nov. 29, 1964, LBJ Library.

22. Oral history interview with Warren, LBJ Library, p. 15. Johnson recalled the conversation somewhat differently, saying, for instance, that the number of potential fatalities was 40 million, but he acknowledged, indeed boasted, of using the threat of war to induce Warren's participation. See Holland, *The Kennedy Assassination Tapes*, p. 205.

23. Oral history interview with Warren, LBJ Library, p. 15.

24. Holland, *The Kennedy Assassination Tapes*, p. 206.

25. Warren was, Beytagh said in our interview, "the opposite of upbeat." Author interview with Beytagh, April 8, 2005.

26. Author interview with Jesse Choper, Sept. 9, 2003.

27. Holland, *The Kennedy Assassination Tapes*, p. 173.

28. Oral history interview with Jacqueline Kennedy Onassis, May 13, 1981, University of Kentucky, Lexington.

29. This conversation is related, in context, in Holland, *The Kennedy Assassination Tapes*, pp. 195–206. The Miller Center for Public Affairs at the University of Virginia offers the unedited tape through its website, http://millercenter.virginia.edu.

30. I have adopted Holland's punctuation and rendering of the tape. While others have rendered the tape more formally, Holland better captures Johnson's manner and language. As noted above, the tape is publicly available through the Miller Center.

31. To Specter, Ford said he "was resisting as strongly as I could." But Johnson's call to Ford lasted all of 1:32 minutes, and Ford's response to Johnson consisted entirely of "Well, you know very well I would be honored to do it, and I'll do the very best I can" (Miller Center tape; Holland transcript, p. 186).

32. Author interview with confidential source.

33. Executive session transcript, Dec. 5, 1963, NARA, College Park, Records of the Presidential Commission to Investigate the Assassination of President Kennedy, p. 1.

34. Ibid., p. 39.

35. Olney's duties and communications with Warren are reflected in papers at the LOC, MD, Warren papers, Lower courts file, Administrative Office of the Courts papers.

36. FBI interview with Olney, Oct. 12, 1978, NARA, College Park, House Select Committee on Assassinations, Numbered files.

37. Executive session, Dec. 5, 1963, NARA, College Park, Records of the Presidential Commission to Investigate the Assassination of President Kennedy, p. 47.

38. Executive session, Dec. 6, 1963, NARA, College Park, Records of the Presidential Commission to Investigate the Assassination of President Kennedy, p. 21.

39. Ibid., p. 6.

40. Executive session, Dec. 16, 1963, NARA, College Park, Records of the Presidential Commission to Investigate the Assassination of President Kennedy, pp. 1–9.

41. Ibid., p. 11.

42. Ibid., p. 18.

43. Ibid., p. 20.

44. Hoover to Tolson, Belmont, DeLoach, Evans, and Rosen, Dec. 14, 1963, FBI document 94-1-5619.

45. See, for instance, *Time*, Dec. 13, 1963.

46. Author interview with Mosk, April 20, 2005.

47. DeLoach memo to Mohr, Dec. 17, 1963, NARA, College Park, House Select Committee on Assassination records, FBI Investigative file on Lee Harvey Oswald.

48. Ibid. When the DeLoach memo became public years later, then President Ford insisted that his contacts had not continued during the rest of the Commission's service. No other documentation has surfaced to challenge Ford's denial.

49. *Reynolds v. Sims*, 377 U.S. 533 (1964).

50. Ibid.

51. Ibid.

52. End-of-term memo, 1963, Chambers of William J. Brennan, Jr., LOC, MD, Brennan papers, Part II.

53. Author interview with Beytagh, April 8, 2005.

54. *Reynolds v. Sims*, 377 U.S. 533 (1964).

55. Ibid.

56. Warren often made this point to confidants and interviewers. See, for example, his interviews with Morrie Landsberg and Tony Lewis after his retirement.

57. *Memoirs*, p. 308.

58. *Lucas v. Colorado General Assembly*, 377 U.S. 713 (1964).

59. See Brennan correspondence with Arthur Freund, LOC, MD, Brennan papers, Part II, Correspondence files, Freund folders.

60. Warren speech at Duke University, April 27, 1963, LOC, MD, Warren papers, Speeches file.

61. End-of-term memo, 1963, Chambers of William J. Brennan, Jr., LOC, MD, Brennan papers, Part II.

62. Elizabeth Black, *Mr. Justice and Mrs. Black: The Memoirs of Hugo L. Black and Elizabeth Black*, diary entry for May 11, 1964, p. 92.

63. End-of-term memo, 1963, Chambers of William J. Brennan, Jr., LOC, MD, Brennan papers, Part II.

64. Harlan note to Warren, Oct. 26, 1963, PU, ML, Harlan papers, *Griffin v. Maryland* file.

65. Archibald Cox letter to Chief and Justices, Nov. 21, 1963, PU, ML, Harlan papers, *Griffin v. Maryland* file.

66. End-of-term memo, 1963, Chambers of William J. Brennan, Jr., LOC, MD, Brennan papers, Part II.

67. Black, *Mr. Justice and Mrs. Black*, diary entry for May 11, 1964, p. 92.

68. End-of-term memo, 1963, Chambers of William J. Brennan, Jr., LOC, MD, Brennan papers, Part II. See also Roger Newman, *Hugo Black*, pp. 540–48.

69. End-of-term memo, 1963, Chambers of William J. Brennan, Jr., LOC, MD, Brennan papers, Part II.
70. *New York Times v. Sullivan*, 376 U.S. 254 (1964).
71. Ibid.
72. Ibid.
73. Ibid. (Black concurrence).
74. Lucas Powe, *The Warren Court and American Politics*, p. 306.
75. Memos and drafts contained in Harlan papers, PU, ML, Harlan papers, *New York Times v. Sullivan* file.
76. *New York Times v. Sullivan*, 376 U.S. 254 (1964).
77. Ibid.
78. Harry Kalven, "The New York Times Case: A Note on 'The Central Meaning' of the First Amendment," *Supreme Court Review*, 1964, p. 191.
79. Evan Thomas, *The Man to See*, p. 314.
80. Melvin Eisenberg memo to file, Feb. 17, 1964, NARA, College Park, Records of the Presidential Commission to Investigate the Assassination of President Kennedy. Arlen Specter, *Passion for Truth*, pp. 53–56. Some have attributed the remark to Rankin, who may well have repeated it on other occasions.
81. Redlich testimony to the House Select Committee on Assassinations.
82. Author interview with Sam Stern, May 10, 2005.
83. Executive session, Jan. 22, 1964, NARA, College Park, Records of the Presidential Commission to Investigate the Assassination of President Kennedy, p. 1.
84. Executive session, Feb. 24, 1964, NARA, College Park, Records of the Presidential Commission to Investigate the Assassination of President Kennedy.
85. Warren letter to Arlen Specter, Feb. 23, 1967, LOC, MD, Warren papers, Organizations file, Kennedy Assassination Commission file, Correspondence, 1963–1967.
86. Ibid.
87. *Hearings Before the President's Commission on the Assassination of President Kennedy*, vol. 1, p. 2.
88. Ibid., p. 13.
89. Ibid., p. 119.
90. Ibid., p. 72.
91. Ibid., p. 76.
92. Pearson notes, LBJ Library, Aug. 21, 1967.
93. *New York Times*, Feb. 5, 1964.
94. Warren Commission Report, p. xiii.
95. *Hearings Before the President's Commission on the Assassination of President Kennedy*, vol. 2, pp. 189–90.
96. David W. Belin, *November 22, 1963: You Are the Jury*, p. 454.
97. Jack Harrison Pollack, *Earl Warren: The Judge Who Changed America*, p. 243. Pollack misreports some of Rowland's testimony, but this exchange appears in substantially similar form elsewhere. It is not in the hearing's official transcript, as it occurred during the recess that Warren called in order to comfort Rowland.
98. Author interview with Mosk, April 20, 2005.
99. Belin, *November 22, 1963: You Are the Jury*, pp. 345–49. Also Specter, *Passion for Truth*, p. 86.
100. Executive session, May 19, 1964, NARA, College Park, Records of the Presidential Commission to Investigate the Assassination of President Kennedy, pp. 6601–2.
101. A copy of Ford's notes is included with his pre-presidential papers housed among the Kennedy-related material at NARA, College Park. Warren appears also to have done background work before the meeting, as his personal schedule records a lunch with J. Edgar Hoover less than a week before the hearing over Redlich. Warren schedule, May 13, 1964, LOC, MD, Earl Warren papers, Personal file, 1964 Calendars.

102. Executive session, May 19, 1964, NARA, College Park, Records of the Presidential Commission to Investigate the Assassination of President Kennedy, p. 6608.

103. Ibid., pp. 6612–16.

104. Author interview with Ford, Dec. 8, 2004.

105. Warren schedule, May 19, 1964, LOC, MD, Earl Warren papers, Personal file, 1964 Calendars.

106. Oral history interview, Bartley Cavanaugh, *Hunting and Fishing with Earl Warren*, p. 9.

107. Author interview with Ford, Dec. 8, 2004. Also Specter, *Passion for Truth*, p. 108.

108. Warren Commission Report, pp. 92–110. That conclusion was further strengthened by the House Select Committee on Assassinations, which subjected the bullet to neuron activation analysis and concluded that the fragments recovered from Connally were "highly likely" to have come from the same bullet that was found on the governor's stretcher and that the shot to Kennedy's head came from a different bullet. The Committee supported the single-bullet theory, and it too concluded that it was consistent with the film and other evidence. See Committee report, pp. 42–48 (Internet copy).

109. Specter, *Passion for Truth*, p. 112.

110. Specter remembers the interrogation taking place in the afternoon, but the transcript of the session indicates that it began at 11:45 A.M. *Hearings Before the President's Commission on the Assassination of President Kennedy*, vol. 5, p. 181.

111. Specter, *Passion for Truth*, p. 113. Also oral history interview with Warren, Sept. 21, 1971, by Joe B. Frantz, transcript on file at LBJ, p. 15 (Internet copy).

112. *Hearings Before the President's Commission on the Assassination of President Kennedy*, vol. 5, p. 182. Warren would later regret having agreed to the test, as his acquiescence was interpreted as an endorsement of the machines. As for the test itself, the examiner concluded that Ruby told the truth on the relevant questions, while J. Edgar Hoover expressed doubt about whether the results were reliable, especially given Ruby's mental state. The Commission elected to attach the transcript and analysis to its report but did not rely on either to reach its conclusions. Warren Commission report, Appendix 17, pp. 807–16.

113. *Hearings Before the President's Commission on the Assassination of President Kennedy*, vol. 5, p. 198–99, cited in Warren Commission report, p. 354. The citation in the official report contains an incor-rect note, suggesting that the testimony here came from another source; that appears to be merely a typographical error, for the note given as 1084 in fact corresponds to footnote 1094).

114. Warren Commission exhibit 2421, vol. 25, p. 523.

115. Among Ruby's possessions when he was arrested were Polaroid photographs taken the previous morning of a sign that disturbed him. It was a billboard in Dallas. On it were the words "Impeach Earl Warren." Warren Commission hearings, testimony of George Senator, vol. 14, pp. 220–21.

116. *U.S. News & World Report*, Aug. 12, 1992.

117. Ibid. To DeLoach in their December conversation, Ford also indicated that Warren was mindful of the political calendar; Ford said Warren hoped to finish by July.

118. Warren schedule, July 6 and Aug. 1, 1964, LOC, MD, Earl Warren papers, Personal file, 1964 Calendars.

119. Pearson notes, Aug. 21, 1967, Pearson papers, LBJ Library.

120. Specter, *Passion for Truth*, p. 120. Specter quotes Ford, who does not name the Commission member who objected; in his recollections during his oral history interview for the Johnson Library, Warren downplayed the seriousness of the objection but identified Russell as the person who protested.

121. Warren Commission Report, p. 21.

122. Holland, *The Kennedy Assassination Tapes*, p. 251. Also Miller Center tape of conversation from Sept. 18, 1964.

123. Warren Commission Report (*New York Times* edition), p. xxxviii.

124. Max Holland, *American Heritage*, Nov. 1995.

125. Hoover to Warren, June 16, 1968. FBI document 94-1-5619-318.

126. *Hearings Before the President's Commission on the Assassination of President Kennedy*, vol. 1, p. 187.

127. Ibid., vol. 2, p. 51.

128. Ibid., vol. 5, p. 552. When Lane eventually did supply the tape, it did not support his version of the conversation but rather showed him attempting to lead the witness and her resisting his attempts to put words in her mouth.

129. Ibid., vol. 5, p. 553.

130. Mark Lane, *Rush to Judgment*, p. 83.

131. Ibid., p. 105.

132. Belin, *November 22, 1963, You Are the Jury*, p. 150.

133. To Drew Pearson, Warren said Lane had "got into some trouble for molesting children," ending Lane's political career. In public, Warren was never so crass. Pearson diaries, entry for Oct. 26, 1966, LBJ Library, Pearson papers, Earl Warren folder.

134. *Memoirs*, p. 367.

135. Patricia Lambert, *False Witness*, p. 182 (citing New Orleans *Times-Picayune*, Dec. 27, 1967).

136. FBI urgent teletype to Director from New Orleans, Sept. 5, 1967 NARA, College Park, House Select Committee on Assassinations, Records of the Federal Bureau of Investigation, HQ.

137. Note filed under Domestic Intelligence Division, Sept. 5, 1967, NARA, College Park, House Select Committee on Assassinations, Records of the Federal Bureau of Investigation, HQ. As a former chairman of the Warren Commission, Warren might well have had to recuse himself from any such case. It is possible that he used the potential for conflict as a pretext for avoiding Garrison, whom Warren wanted to avoid dignifying by debate.

138. This short summary of Garrison's case is distilled primarily from Lambert, *False Witness*.

139. *U.S. News & World Report*, Aug. 17, 1992. See also Warren correspondence with Redlich, Belin in LOC, MD, Warren papers, Organizations file, Kennedy Assassination Commission folders. When Warren learned that Commission staff member Wesley Liebeler had set to work on a book, Warren alerted the FBI's DeLoach and said Liebeler was a "beatnick" and not to be trusted. DeLoach to Tolson, Nov. 25, 1966, FBI document 94-1-5619.

140. There was an obvious and innocent explanation for the entry. Hosty interviewed Marina Oswald after their return from Russia. Lee Oswald, who was not present for the interview, was furious when he learned of it, and in all likelihood had made a note in his book in case he sought to communicate directly with Hosty.

141. House Select Committee on Assassinations, final report, p. 190 (Internet copy).

142. Ibid., p. 43.

143. Holland, *American Heritage*, Nov. 1995.

144. Deposition of J. Lee Rankin, Aug. 17, 1978, NARA, College Park, House Select Committee on Assassinations.

145. The most thorough study of that "evidence" was presented in late 2005. The authors rejected it entirely. See R. Linsker, R. L. Garwin, H. Chernoff, P. Horowitz, and N. F. Ramsey, "Synchronization of Acoustic Evidence in the Kennedy Assassination," *Science & Justice*, vol. 45, no. 4 (2005).

146. Peter Dale Scott, *Deep Politics and the Death of JFK*, p. 4.

147. Gerald D. McKnight, *Breach of Trust*: "McCormick" references, pp. 32, 74; Kennedy meeting, p. 40; various bullet-grain/postage-stamp comparisons, pp. 120, 182, 222.

## CHAPTER 23. AN ENFORCED CODE OF DECENCY

1. Archibald Cox, *The Warren Court: Constitutional Decision as an Instrument of Reform*, p. 6. This title's chapter is taken from an observation regarding Warren and the Court by Arlen Specter, who described the Chief Justice's "code of decency" in *Passion for Truth*.

2. *Katzenbach v. McClung*, 379 U.S. 294 (1964), and *Atlanta Motel v. United States*, 379 U.S. 241 (1964).

3. Bruce Allen Murphy, *Wild Bill*, pp. 374–77.

4. *Griswold v. Connecticut*, 381 U.S. 479 (1965).

5. End-of-term memo, 1964, Chambers of William J. Brennan, Jr., LOC, MD, Brennan papers, Part II.

6. Brennan note to Douglas, April 24, 1965, LOC, MD, Douglas papers, Supreme Court file, Case file, *Griswold* miscellaneous folder.

7. *Griswold v. Connecticut*, 381 U.S. 479 (1965).

8. *Poe v. Ullman* 367 U.S. 497 (1961) (dissent).

9. *Mapp v. Ohio*, 367 U.S. 643, (1961).

10. *Griswold v. Connecticut*, 381 U.S. 479 (1965).

11. Ibid.

12. Undated memo, Ely to Warren, LOC, MD, Warren papers, Supreme Court file, Opinions of the Associate Justices, *Griswold v. Connecticut*.

13. *Griswold v. Connecticut*, 381 U.S. 479 (1965; concurrence).

14. Ibid. (dissent).

15. *Roe v. Wade*, 410 U.S. 113 (1973).

16. Warren to Douglas, June 14, 1965, LOC, MD, Douglas papers, correspondence files, Earl and Nina Warren, 1960–1976.

17. The fishing trip appears to have taken place on Saturday, July 10, 1965, as Nina Warren wrote to Drew Pearson on Monday, July 19, 1965, and noted details of the trip, which she said occurred on "Saturday morning." Stevenson died on July 14, 1965, a Wednesday.

18. Nina Warren letter to Drew Pearson, July 19, 1965, LBJ Library, Pearson papers, Warren file.

19. President's Daily Diary, diary backup, July 19, 1965, LBJ Library.

20. Oral history interview with Warren, Sept. 21, 1971, by Joe B. Frantz, LBJ Library, p. 20 (Internet copy).

21. Oral history interview with Goldberg, March 23, 1983, by Ted Gittinger, LBJ Library, Interview I, p. 1.

22. Ibid.

23. Laura Kalman, *Abe Fortas*, pp. 242–45.

24. Fortas letter to Johnson, July 19, 1965, LBJ Library, Presidential papers, Confidential file, Supreme Court folder.

25. Kalman, *Abe Fortas*, p. 245.

26. John Lewis, *Walking with the Wind*, p. 327.

27. Andrew Young, *An Easy Burden*, pp. 353–58.

28. Ibid., p. 361.

29. Elizabeth Black, *Mr. Justice and Mrs. Black: The Memoirs of Hugo L. Black and Elizabeth Black*, diary entry for March 12, 1965, p. 105.

30. Lyndon Johnson, *Special Message to the Congress: The American Promise*, March 15, 1965, Presidential Papers, 1965, p. 107.

31. Taylor Branch, *At Canaan's Edge*, p. 115.

32. Lucas Powe, *The Warren Court and American Politics*, p. 259.

33. Robert Dallek, *Flawed Giant*, p. 220

34. United States Constitution, Fifteenth Amendment.

35. *South Carolina v. Katzenbach*, 383 U.S. 301 (1966).

36. Ibid.

37. Ibid. (concurrence; dissent).

38. *Harper v. Virginia Board of Elections*, 383 U.S. 663 (1966) (Harlan dissent). Only four states imposed a poll tax in 1996: Alabama, Mississippi, Texas, and Virginia.

39. *Reynolds v. Sims*, 377 U.S. 533 (1964).

40. *Harper v. Virginia Board of Elections*, 383 U.S. 663 (1966).

41. *Katzenbach v. Morgan*, 384 U.S. 641 (1966).

42. Powe, *The Warren Court and American Politics*, p. 262.

43. *Lassiter v. Northampton Election Board*, 360 U.S. 45 (1959).

44. Ibid., footnote 7.

45. End-of-term memo, 1965, Chambers of William J. Brennan, Jr., LOC, MD, Brennan papers, Part II.

46. *Katzenbach v. Morgan*, 384 U.S. 641 (1966).

47. Ibid., footnote 10. See also end-of-term memo, 1965, Chambers of William J. Brennan, Jr., LOC, MD, Brennan papers, Part II. Powe provides a particularly lucid explanation of this case and the accompanying 1966 voting decisions in chapter 10 of *The Warren Court and American Politics*.

48. *Griffin v. Illinois*, 351 U.S. 12 (1956).

49. Author interviews with Kenneth Ziffren, Jan. 12, 2005, and Michael Smith, July 8, 2005.

50. Gary L. Stuart, *Miranda: The Story of America's Right to Remain Silent*, p. 6.

51. Del Dickson, *The Supreme Court in Conference*, pp. 515–16.

52. These drafts, including Warren's outline, are at the LOC, MD, Warren papers, Supreme Court file, Opinions of the Chief Justice, *Miranda v. Arizona*, Folder 1.

53. End-of-term memo, 1965, Chambers of William J. Brennan, Jr., LOC, MD, Brennan papers, Part II. Also author interview with Kenneth Ziffren, Jan. 12, 2005.

54. Brennan memo to Warren, May 11, 1966, LOC, MD, Warren papers, Supreme Court file, Opinions of the Chief Justice, *Miranda v. Arizona*, Folder 1.

55. *Miranda v. Arizona*, 384 U.S. 436 (1966).

56. Inbau and Reed, *Criminal Interrogation and Confessions*, 1962, cited in *Miranda v. Arizona*, 384 U.S. 436 (1966), footnote 16.

57. *Miranda v. Arizona*, 384 U.S. 436 (1966).

58. Ibid. The question of whether *Miranda* constitutes a direct restraint of police or a doctrine of admissibility is a hotly contested one, and one that the Supreme Court has made more difficult with the passage of time. See, for instance, Steven D. Clymer, "Are Police Free to Disregard *Miranda*?" *Yale Law Journal*, vol. 112, pp. 447–552. What seems clear is that Warren, at least, viewed it as both and deliberately wrote it that way.

59. Dickson, *The Supreme Court in Conference*, p. 517.

60. *New York Times*, June 14, 1966.

61. *Miranda v. Arizona*, 384 U.S. 436 (1966) (Harlan dissent).

62. Ibid.

63. End-of-term memo, 1965, Chambers of William J. Brennan, Jr., LOC, MD, Brennan papers, Part II.

64. Ibid.

65. Author interview with Kenneth Ziffren, Jan. 12, 2005.

66. Author interview with Bernard Parks, June 22, 2005.

67. *New York Times*, July 23, 1966, cited in Powe, *The Warren Court and American Politics*, p. 399.

68. *New York Times*, June 14, 1966.

69. Their letters can be found at the LOC, MD, Warren papers, Supreme Court file, Subject file, Katzenbach-Bazelon correspondence folder.

70. *Miranda v. Arizona*, 384 U.S. 436 (1966).

71. Author interview with Bernard Parks, June 22, 2005.

72. Stuart, *Miranda: The Story of America's Right to Remain Silent*, pp. 95–99.

73. *Dickerson v. United States*, 530 U.S. 428 (2000).

74. Dallek, *Flawed Giant*, p. 278. The conversation quoted was between Johnson and historian William E. Leuchtenburg.

75. *Roth v. United States*, 354 U.S. 476 (1957) (concurrence).

76. *Ginzburg v. United States*, 383 U.S. 463 (1966).

77. Author interview with Kenneth Ziffren, Jan. 12, 2005.

78. *Memoirs v. Massachusetts*, 383 U.S. 413 (1966).

79. *Mishkin v. New York*, 383 U.S. 502 (1966).

80. *Ginzburg v. United States*, 383 U.S. 463 (1966) (dissent).

81. Ralph Ginzburg, *Castrated*, p. 11.

82. Author interview with Michael Smith, July 8, 2005.

83. Landsberg interview with Warren, June 23, 1969, transcript provided to the author by Mitchell Landsberg, Morrie's son.

84. Leonard Garment, *The New Yorker*, April 17, 1989. Garment, who worked with Nixon on the *Hill* case, described their discussions and preparations in this piece.

85. Richard Nixon's reargument in *Time, Inc. v. Hill*, Oct. 19, 1966 (accessed at Oyez.org).

86. *Time, Inc. v. Hill*, 385 U.S. 374 (1967).

87. Garment, *The New Yorker*.

88. End-of-term memo, 1966, Chambers of William J. Brennan, Jr., LOC, MD, Brennan papers, Part II.

89. Fortas draft opinion, April 14, 1966, LOC, MD, Warren papers, Supreme Court file, Opinions of the Associate Justices, *Time, Inc. v. Hill*.

90. Elizabeth Black, *Mr. Justice and Mrs. Black*, diary entry for July 28, 1965, p. 119.

91. *Brown v. Louisiana*, 383 U.S. 181 (1966).

92. End-of-term memo, 1965, Chambers of William J. Brennan, Jr., LOC, MD, Brennan papers, Part II.

93. End-of-term memo, 1966, Chambers of William J. Brennan, Jr., LOC, MD, Brennan papers, Part II.

94. Fortas memorandum to the conference, June 14, 1966, PU, ML, Harlan papers, *Time, Inc. v. Hill* file.

95. Garment, *The New Yorker*.

96. Ibid.

97. Warren note to Douglas, June 24, 1999, LOC, MD, Douglas papers, correspondence files, Earl and Nina Warren folder.

98. *Loving v. Virginia*, 388 U.S. 1 (1967).

99. Ibid. That language today stands at the center of the nation's gratuitous debate over gay marriage. Should that matter reach the United States Supreme Court—and there seems little likelihood that it will not—the above sentence will surely be cited in defense of the principle that invidious discrimination in the regulation of marriage has no place under the Constitution.

100. Kalman, *Abe Fortas*, p. 320.

101. Author interviews with Jesse Choper and Kenneth Ziffren.

102. Handwritten note from Warren to Johnson, Jan. 11, 1964, LOC, MD, Earl Warren papers, Personal file, Presidents Correspondence, 1964–1973.

103. Johnson letter to Warren, Jan. 14, 1964, LOC, MD, Earl Warren papers, Personal file, Presidents Correspondence, 1964–1973.

104. Warren letter to Johnson, April 6, 1966, LOC, MD, Earl Warren papers, Personal file, Presidents Correspondence, 1964–1973. Detail of the inscription comes from John Weaver, *Warren: The Man, the Court, the Era*, p. 336.

105. President's Daily Diary, diary backup, March 23, 1966, LBJ Library.

106. Warren letter to Johnson, April 6, 1965, LOC, MD, Earl Warren papers, Personal file, Presidents Correspondence, 1964–1973.

107. Pearson letter to Johnson, Feb. 21, 1966, LBJ Library, Office files of White House aides, files of Henry McPherson, Supreme Court decisions folder.

108. Author interviews with Kenneth Ziffren and Michael Smith.

109. Dr. Buckley memo to Jack Valenti, Jan. 13, 1965, LBJ Library, Presidential papers, Confidential file, Supreme Court folder.

110. Johnson letter to Warren, Nov. 8, 1967, LOC, MD, Earl Warren papers, personal papers, Presidents' correspondence, 1964–1973.

111. President's Daily Diary, diary backup, Dec. 4, 1967, LBJ Library.

112. Author interview with Earl Warren, Jr., Nov. 25, 2003.

113. President's Daily Diary, diary backup, June 13, 1967, LBJ Library.

114. Drew Pearson diary entry, Feb. 5, 1966, LBJ Library, Pearson papers, Warren #2 file.

115. Warren to Johnson, June 19, 1967, LBJ Library, Presidential papers, Name file, Warren, Earl.

116. Elizabeth Black, *Mr. Justice and Mrs. Black*, diary entry for Oct. 20, 1967, p. 178.

117. Author interviews with Lucas Powe, June 6, 2005, and Jeffrey Warren, Aug. 26, 2003.

118. Oral history interview with Thurgood Marshall, by T. H. Baker, LBJ Library, p. 18.

119. Ibid.

120. Author interview with Scott Bice, July 11, 2005.

121. Black, *Mr. Justice and Mrs. Black*, diary entry for June 17, 1968, p. 196.

122. Stanley Karnow, *Vietnam: A History*, p. 479.

123. Dallek, *Flawed Giant*, p. 474.

124. Karnow, *Vietnam: A History*, p. 512. Casualty figures courtesy National Archives, Combat Area Casualties Current File (CACCF).

125. Drew Pearson diary entry, Feb. 7, 1966, LBJ Library, Drew Pearson papers, Warren #2 file.

126. Drew Pearson diary entry, Oct. 26, 1966, LBJ Library, Drew Pearson papers, Warren #2 file.

127. Address delivered at Washington University, St. Louis, Missouri, Feb. 19, 1955, LOC, MD, Warren papers, Speech file.

128. *Firing Line* (publication of the American Legion), June 1966, included in PU, ML, Harlan papers, *United States. v. O'Brien* file. For this analysis of *O'Brien*, I am indebted to Larry Simon, who drafted the opinion at Warren's instruction. The conclusions are mine, but Professor Simon helped explain the case's history and theory. Author interview, June 10, 2006.

129. *United States v. O'Brien*, 391 U.S. 367 (1968). Also oral argument in *United States v. O'Brien* (accessed at Oyez.com).

130. Ibid. (both sources).

131. Ibid. (both sources).

132. Undated memo to Warren, LOC, MD, Warren papers, Supreme Court files, Opinions of the Chief Justice, *United States v. O'Brien* file.

133. *United States v. O'Brien*, 391 U.S. 367 (1968).

134. Ibid.

135. *Gomillion v. Lightfoot*, 364 U.S. 339 (1960) See also Powe, *The Warren Court and American Politics*, p. 325.

136. End-of-term memo, 1967, Chambers of William J. Brennan, Jr., LOC, MD, Brennan papers, Part II.

137. Tyrone Brown, "Clerking for the Chief Justice," from *The Warren Court: A Retrospective*, p. 278.

138. *Brooks v. Florida*, 389 U.S. 413 (1967).

139. Dallek, *Flawed Giant*, pp. 516–517.

140. *Terry v. Ohio*, 392 U.S. 1 (1968).

141. Ibid.

142. End-of-term memo, 1967, Chambers of William J. Brennan, Jr., LOC, MD, Brennan papers, Part II.

143. Ibid.

144. Ibid.

145. Brennan memo to Warren, March 14, 1968, LOC, MD, Warren papers, Supreme Court file, Opinions of the Chief Justice, *Terry v. Ohio*.

146. Dallek, *Flawed Giant*, p. 527.

147. Elizabeth Black, *Mr. Justice and Mrs. Black*, diary entry, March 31, 1968, p. 190.

148. Warren letter to Johnson, April 2, 1968, LBJ Library, White House Central Files, Name File, Warren, Earl (Chief Justice).

149. Johnson letter to Warren, April 30, 1968, LBJ Library, White House Central Files, Name File, Warren, Earl (Chief Justice).

150. Martin Luther King, Jr., "I've Been to the Mountaintop," April 3, 1968, Martin Luther King, Jr., Papers Project, Speeches.

151. Elizabeth Black, *Mr. Justice and Mrs. Black*, diary entry, April 5, 1968, p. 191.

152. President's Daily Diary, diary backup, April 5, 1968, LBJ Library.

153. *Terry v. Ohio*, 392 U.S. 1 (1968) (Douglas dissent).

154. Jim Jones memo to Johnson, June 11, 1968, LBJ Library, White House Central Files, Name File, Warren, Earl. Johnson's reply is indicated by the notation: "Bring him in tomorrow." In fact, the White House schedule shows that Warren came the day after that, June 13.

155. Elizabeth Black, *Mr. Justice and Mrs. Black*, diary entry, April 8, 1966, p. 191.

CHAPTER 24. THE END

1. William O. Douglas, *The Court Years*, p. 241.

2. Warren letter to Johnson, June 13, 1968, LOC, MD, Warren papers, Supreme Court file, Subject files, Retirement.

3. Second Warren letter to Johnson, June 13, 1968, LOC, MD, Warren Papers, Supreme Court file, Subject files, Retirement.

4. Memo, Aug. 19, 1968, LOC, MD, Warren papers, Articles file. If that article had run in 1968, it would have contributed to the controversy surrounding the confirmation of Warren's successor. It is no wonder that Warren asked Pearson to pull it back. Warren also confided to his clerks that he was leaving so that Nixon would not have the chance to replace him. Author interview with Larry Simon, June 12, 2006.

5. Tyrone Brown, "Clerking for the Chief Justice," from *The Warren Court: A Retrospective*, p. 277.

6. Author interview with William Brennan III, July 2003.

7. Elizabeth Black, *Mr. Justice and Mrs. Black*, diary entries for June 13–July 6, 1968, pp. 195–98.

8. Laura Kalman, *Abe Fortas*, p. 328.

9. *New York Times*, July 6, 1968.

10. Ibid.

11. The practice has continued since the Warren–Fortas episode in 1968. When she submitted her retirement in 2005, Justice Sandra Day O'Connor specified that her departure was contingent upon the confirmation of her successor, a condition that attracted scarcely any notice at all.

12. Author interview with Warren Christopher, June 2005.

13. Kalman, *Abe Fortas*, p. 337. Also author interview with Warren Christopher, June 2005.

14. Kalman, *Abe Fortas*, p. 338.

15. Memo to the President, June 3, 1968, LBJ Library, Subject files, Supreme Court folder.

16. *Mallory v. United States*, 354 U.S. 449 (1957).

17. Kalman, *Abe Fortas*, p. 340.

18. Lady Bird Johnson, *A White House Diary*, entry for Sept. 28, 1968, p. 712.

19. Author interview with Warren Christopher, June 2005.

20. Statement by President Johnson, Oct. 10, 1968, Public Papers of the President, Document 527. Obtained courtesy John Woolley and Gerhard Peter of The American Presidency Project, University of California at Santa Barbara, http://www.presidency.ucsp.edu.

21. Nixon to Republican National Convention, August 8, 1968. American Presidency Project.

22. Warren schedule, Nov. 5, 1968, LOC, MD, Warren papers, schedules, 1968 folder.

23. Oral argument in *Tinker v. Des Moines*, Nov. 12, 1968 (accessed at Oyez.com).

24. Ibid.

25. *Tinker v. Des Moines School District*, 393 U.S. 503 (1969).

26. Ibid. (Harlan dissent).

27. Ibid. (Black dissent).

28. Kalman, *Abe Fortas*, p. 290.

29. Author interview with Scott Bice, July 11, 2005.

30. Warren letter to Mr. and Mrs. Clemencia, April 5, 1969, LOC, MD, Warren papers, Supreme Court file, Subject files, Personnel.

31. *New York Times Magazine*, Oct. 19, 1969 (interview conducted in September by Anthony Lewis).

32. Author interview with Jeffrey Warren, Aug. 26, 2003. Also undated speech by Jeffrey Warren, who provided a copy to the author.

33. Jack Harrison Pollack, *Earl Warren: The Judge Who Changed America*, p. 284. This meeting was confirmed for the author by Virginia Daly.

34. Warren statement to press, Dec. 4, 1968, LOC, MD, Warren papers, Supreme Court file, Subject files, Retirement.

35. *Powell v. McCormack*, 395 U.S. 486 (1969).

36. United States Constitution, Article 1, Section 2.

37. Oral argument in *Powell v. McCormack*, April 21, 1969 (accessed at Oyez.com).

38. Ibid.

39. Ibid.

40. Author interview with Scott Bice, July 11, 2005.

41. *Alderman v. United States*, 394 U.S. 165 (1969). The decision in *Alderman* was applied to two other pending cases, *Ivanov v. United States* and *Butenko v. United States*, both espionage prosecutions.

42. Brennan memo to Warren, March 18, 1969, LOC, MD, Warren papers, Correspondence files, Brennan folder, 1967–1974.

43. *Memoirs*, p. 340.

44. Ibid., p. 342.

45. *Life*, May 9, 1969. The story, written by William Lambert, ran beneath the headline "Fortas of the Supreme Court: A Question of Ethics. The Justice . . . and the Stock Manipulator," and featured nearly full-page pictures of Fortas and Wolfson.

46. Bernard Schwartz, *Super Chief*, p. 762.

47. Warren schedule, May 7, 1969, LOC, MD, Warren schedules for 1969.

48. Elizabeth Black, *Mr. Justice and Mrs. Black*, diary entry for May 10, 1969, p. 220.

49. Kalman, *Abe Fortas*, p. 373.

50. *Brandenburg v. Ohio*, 395 U.S. 444 (1969).

51. Ibid.

52. Warren letter to Jeffrey Warren, June 15, 1969, supplied to the author by Jeffrey Warren.

53. *New York Times*, June 24, 1969.

54. Ibid.

55. Brennan memo to the justices, May 29, 1969, LOC, MD, Brennan papers, Part II, Correspondence files, Earl Warren 1956–1967 folder. Other memos in the same file spell out the arrangements and guest list.

56. Warren schedules, Aug. 21–Sept. 20, 1969, LOC, MD, Warren papers, schedules for 1969.

57. G. Edward White, *Earl Warren: A Public Life*, pp. 315–16.

58. Author interviews.

59. Francis X. Gannon, *The Biographical Dictionary of the Left*, p. 574.

60. Evan Thomas, *The Man to See*, pp. 290–91.

61. Author interview with Peter Ehrenhaft, Jan. 31, 2005.

62. Ibid.

63. *American Bar Association Journal*, July 1973, p. 724.

64. Author interview with Peter Ehrenhaft, Jan. 31, 2005.

65. Warren letter to Douglas, March 26, 1971, LOC, MD, William Douglas papers, Part I, Correspondence files, Earl and Nina Warren folder.

66. Warren letter to Swig, Oct. 3, 1973, LOC, MD, Warren papers, personal papers, Ben Swig file.

67. Warren letter to Swig, Oct. 16, 1973, LOC, MD, Warren papers, personal papers, Ben Swig file.

68. Warren letter to Swig, Oct. 24, 1973, LOC, MD, Warren papers, personal papers, Ben Swig file.

69. Warren letter to Swig, Oct. 31, 1973, LOC, MD, Warren papers, personal papers, Ben Swig file.

70. Pollack, *Earl Warren: The Judge Who Changed America*, p. 315.

71. Bradley letter to Warren, Aug. 1, 1973, LOC, MD, Warren papers, personal papers, Bradley swearing-in file.

72. Warren letter to Bradley, Aug. 17, 1973, LOC, MD, Warren papers, personal papers, Bradley swearing-in file.

73. Warren speech at Morehouse College, May 21, 1974, LOC, MD, Speeches and Statements file, Morehouse folder.

74. Ibid.

75. Handwritten note attached as appendix to oral history interview with Edgar James Patterson, *Governor's Mansion Aide to Prison Counselor*, 1975.

76. Ibid.

77. Author interview with Jeffrey Warren, Aug. 26, 2003.

78. Warren was at Georgetown rather than Walter Reed either because of misunderstanding or because of an act of brutish insensitivity on Nixon's part. Supreme Court justices are entitled to free medical care at military facilities, and Warren had availed himself of that privilege throughout his Court career. A policy change in the Nixon years, however, required retired military personnel to seek White House authorization before receiving treatment. That policy apparently was applied by mistake to Warren, who then moved to Georgetown. Members of the Warren family and others believed that Nixon had intentionally forced Warren to seek care elsewhere. Author interview with Nina "Honey Bear" Brien, May 6, 2004.

79. William Douglas, *The Court Years*, p. 238. Douglas, whose autobiography is notoriously riddled with errors, writes that he visited Warren alone. That is contradicted by members of the Warren and Brennan families, who say that Brennan accompanied Douglas on that final visit.

80. Author interview with William Brennan III, July 2003.

81. Author interview with Nina "Honey Bear" Brien, May 6, 2004.

82. Author interviews with Jesse Choper, Peter Ehrenhaft, and Dennis Flannery.

# Bibliography

NOTES ON SOURCES

Most of the sources for this book are self-explanatory and are listed below. A few of them require brief explication:

The FBI files cited in this book were delivered to the author in response to requests made under the Freedom of Information Act. They consist of 2,206 pages. In addition, the FBI released Warren material to author Alexander Charns during the preparation of his 1992 book *Cloak and Gavel*. In most cases, the material given to me and to Charns is identical, or what I have received is slightly more expansive, since it was released more than a decade later. Where I have drawn on the material released to me, I have cited it merely by official document number. In the few instances where, inexplicably, the FBI released material to Charns but did not include those same files in complying with my request or where it redacted those files more heavily, I have cited the document numbers as well as Charns's papers, which are housed at the University of North Carolina.

In addition, previous studies of Warren have been made without access to two vitally important sets of records, held out of public view for different reasons. Congressional files related to Supreme Court nominations are sealed for fifty years, and thus the story of Warren's nomination was locked away until 2004. Those files, opened at my request, are housed at the National Archives in Washington, D.C.

Also, large portions of the papers of William J. Brennan, Jr., Warren's great friend and colleague, have been restricted over the years by a biographer working through Brennan's large and important legacy. Brennan's son, William J. Brennan III, intervened on my behalf to release his father's records for the Warren years, and thus this book is the first of its type to rest on the revelations in those papers, particularly the annual memos composed by the Brennan clerks and summing up each term. Those memos and the rest of the Brennan papers reside at the Manuscript Division of the Library of Congress, where a restricted-access agreement controls their availability. I am grateful to Bill Brennan for his efforts on my behalf and sad to report that he did not live to see this book published.

ORAL HISTORIES

Unless otherwise noted, oral histories are from the Regional Oral History Office of the University of California, Berkeley.

*Single-Interview Volumes*

Amerson, A. Wayne. *Northern California and Its Challenges to a Negro in the Mid-1900s*, with an introduction by Henry Ziesenbenne, 1974.

Baxter, Leone. Interviewed June 23, 1972, transcript on file with the Bancroft Library, University of California, Berkeley.

Boggs, Hale. Interviewed March 13, 1969, by T. H. Baker, Hale Boggs Oral History interview I, transcript on file with the Lyndon Baines Johnson Library, Austin, Texas (Internet copy).

Boggs, Hale. Interviewed March 27, 1969, by T. H. Baker, Hale Boggs Oral History interview II, transcript on file with the Lyndon Baines Johnson Library, Austin, Texas (Internet copy).

Breed, Arthur H. Jr. *Alameda County and the California Legislature, 1935–1958*, interviews conducted in 1973 by Gabrielle Morris, 1977.

Brown, Edmund G., Sr. *Years of Growth, 1939–1966: Law Enforcement, Politics, and the Governor's Office*, interviews conducted by Malca Chall, Amelia R. Fry, Gabrielle Morris, and James Rowland, 1977–1981.

Call, Asa. *Notes for Oral History*, Bancroft Library, University of California, Berkeley. (This interview was intended for inclusion in *Richard Nixon in the Warren Era*, but Call died before the interview could be edited; the interview transcript and notes are on deposit with the Bancroft).

Carty, Edwin L. *Hunting, Politics, and the Fish and Game Commission*, interviews conducted by Amelia R. Fry, 1976.

Christopher, Warren. Interviewed Oct. 31, 1968, by Thomas H. Baker, Lyndon Baines Johnson Library, Austin, Texas.

Clark, Tom. Interviewed Oct. 7, 1969, by Joe B. Frantz, Lyndon Baines Johnson Library, Austin, Texas.

Drury, Newton Bishop. *Parks and Redwoods, 1919–1971*, interviews conducted between 1960 and 1970 by Amelia Roberts Fry and Susan Schrepfer, Regional Oral History Office, Bancroft Library, University of California, Berkeley, 1972.

Graves, Richard Perrin. *Theoretician, Advocate and Candidate in California State Government*, interviewed by Gabrielle Morris, 1973.

Jahnsen, Oscar J. *Enforcing the Law Against Gambling, Bootlegging, Graft, Fraud and Subversion, 1922–1942*. Interview conducted in 1970 by Alice King and Miriam Feingold Stein, 1976.

Katzenbach, Nicholas. Interview conducted on Nov. 12, 1968, by Paige E. Mulhollan, Lyndon Baines Johnson Library, Austin, Texas.

Lillie, Mildred L. Interviews conducted Nov. 20, 1989, and July 26, 1990, by the Committee on the History of Law in California of the California State Bar.

MacGregor, Helen S. *A Career in Public Service with Earl Warren*, with an introduction by Earl Warren, interviews conducted in 1971 and 1973 by Amelia Fry, June Hogan, and Gabrielle Morris, 1973.

McCormac, Keith. *Earl Warren's Campaigns*, vol. 3, *The Conservative Republicans of 1952*, interviews conducted by Amelia Fry, 1976. (Volumes 1 and 2 of this series are listed below, with the multiple-interview oral histories.)

Marshall, Thurgood. Interview conducted on July 10, 1969, by T. H. Baker, Lyndon Baines Johnson Library, Austin, Texas.

Neylan, John Francis. *Politics, Law, and the University of California*, interview conducted by Dr. Corinne L. Gilb and Professor Walton E. Bean, 1961.

Olney, Warren, III. *Law Enforcement and Judicial Administration in the Earl Warren Era*, 1981, interviews conducted by Miriam F. Stein and Amelia R. Fry, 1970–1977.

Onassis, Jaqueline Kennedy. Interviewed on May 13, 1981, University of Kentucky, Lexington.

Patterson, Edgar James. *Governor's Mansion Aide to Prison Counselor*, with an introduction by Merrell F. Small, 1975.

Powers, Robert B. *Law Enforcement, Race Relations, 1930–1960*, interviews conducted in 1969 by Amelia R. Fry, 1976.

Sherry, Arthur H. *The Alameda County District Attorney's Office and the California Crime Commission*, interviews conducted in 1971 and 1973 by Amelia Fry and Miriam Feingold, 1976.

Small, Merrell Farnham. *The Office of the Governor Under Earl Warren*, interviews conducted in 1970 and 1971 by Amelia R. Fry and Gabrielle S. Morris, 1976.

Sweigert, William T. *Administration and Ethics in the Governor's Office and the Courts, California, 1939–1975*, interviews conducted by Amelia Fry, 1987.

Temple, Larry. Interviews conducted by Joe B. Frantz on June 11 and August 11, 1970, Lyndon Baines Johnson Library, Austin, Texas.

Warren, Earl. *Conversations with Earl Warren on California Government*, interviews conducted in 1971 and 1972 by Amelia R. Fry and members of the Regional Oral History Staff, 1982.

Warren, Earl. Interview conducted on September 21, 1971, by Joe B. Frantz, Lyndon Baines Johnson Library, Austin, Texas (Internet copy).

Waters, Laughlin E. Interviewed 1987 by Carlos Vasquez, California State Archives, State Government Oral History Program.

Young, Andrew. Interviewed June 18, 1970, by Thomas H. Baker, Lyndon Baines Johnson Library, Austin Texas (Internet copy).

*Multiple-Interview Volumes*

*Bee Perspectives of the Warren Era*, 1975. Interviews by Amelia R. Fry and June C. Hogan with:
Walter P. Jones, "An Editor's Long Friendship with Earl Warren."
Herbert L. Phillips, "Perspectives of a Political Reporter."
Richard Rodda, "From the Capitol Press Room."

*California Democrats in the Earl Warren Era*, 1976. Interviews by Amelia R. Fry with:
Florence Clifton, "California Democrats, 1934–1950."
Robert Clifton, "The Democratic Party, Culbert L. Olson, and the Legislature."
Roger Kent, "A Democratic Leader Looks at the Warren Era."
George Outland, "James Roosevelt's Primary Campaign."
Langdon Post, "James Roosevelt's Northern California Campaign, 1950."
James Roosevelt, "Campaigning for Governor Against Earl Warren 1950."

*Earl Warren and Health Insurance: 1943–1949*, 1971. Interviews by Gabrielle Morris with:
Gordon Claycombe, "The Making of a Legislative Committee Study."
John W. Cline, M.D., "California Medical Association Crusade Against Compulsory State Health Insurance."
Russel VanArsdale Lee, M.D., "Pioneering in Prepaid Group Medicine."
Byrl R. Salsman, "Shepherding Health Insurance Bills Through the California Legislature."

*Earl Warren as Executive: Social Welfare and State Parks*, 1977. Interviews by Rosemary Levenson and Amelia R. Fry with:
Newton B. Drury, "A Conservationist Comments on Earl Warren and Harold Ickes."
Charles Irwin Schottland, "State Director of Social Welfare, 1950–54."

*Earl Warren: Fellow Constitutional Officers*, 1979. Interviews with:
Edmund G. Brown, Sr., "The Governor's Lawyer."
Robert Kenny, "Attorney General for California and the 1946 Gubernatorial Campaign."
Thomas H. Kuchel, "California State Controller."

*Earl Warren's Bakersfield*, 1971. One volume. Interviews with:
Maryann Ashe and Ruth Smith Henley, "Earl Warren's Bakersfield."
Omar Cavins, "Coming of Age in Bakersfield."
Ralph Kreiser, "A Reporter Recollects the Warren Case."
Martin Manford and Ernest McMillan, "On Methias Warren."
Francis Vaughan, "Schooldays in Bakersfield."

*Earl Warren's Campaigns*, first of two volumes. (This volume contains Nina Palmquist Warren's letter to the history project staff.) Interviews with:

Stanley N. Barnes, "Experiences in Grass Roots Organization."

Thomas J. Cunningham, "Southern California Campaign Chairman for Earl Warren, 1946."

Murray Draper, "Warren's 1946 Campaign in Northern California."

William S. Mailliard, "Earl Warren in the Governor's Office."

Rollin Lee McNitt, "A Democrat for Warren."

Archibald M. Mull, Jr., "Warren Fund-Raiser; Bar Association Leader."

*Earl Warren's Campaigns*, second of two volumes. Interviews with:

B. Joseph Feigenbaum, "Legislator, Partner of Jesse Steinhart, Warren Aide."

Victor Hansen, "West Coast Defense During World War II; The California Gubernatorial Campaign of 1960."

William F. Knowland, "California Republican Politics in the 1980s."

Samuel Ladar, "Jesse Steinhart, Race Relations and Earl Warren."

Thomas J. Mellon, "Republican Campaign of 1950 and 1952."

John H. Steinhart, "Jesse and Amy Steinhart."

*Earl Warren's Campaigns*, third of three volumes. Interviews with:

McCormac, Keith, "The Conservative Republicans of 1952."

*The Governor's Family*, 1980. Interviews with:

Earl Warren, Jr., "California Politics."

James Warren, "Recollections of the Eldest Warren Son."

Nina Warren (Honey Bear), "Growing Up in the Warren Family."

Robert Warren, "Playing, Hunting, Talking."

*Hunting and Fishing with Earl Warren*, 1976. Interviews with:

Bartley Cavanaugh, "A Mutual Interest in Government, Politics and Sports."

Wallace Lynn, "Hunting and Baseball Companion."

*Perspectives on the Alameda County District Attorney's Office*, with an introduction by Arthur Sherry. Three volumes.

Volume 1, 1972. Interviews with:

Edith Balaban, "Reminiscences About Nathan Harry Miller, Deputy District Attorney, Alameda County."

Judge Oliver D. Hamlin, "Reminiscences About the Alameda County District Attorney's Office in the 1920s and '30s."

John F. Mullins, "How Earl Warren Became District Attorney."

Mary Shaw, "Perspectives of a Newspaperwoman."

Willard W. Shea, "Recollections of Alameda County's First Public Defender."

Volume 2, 1973. Interviews with:

John Bruce, "A Reporter Remembers Earl Warren."

Richard H. Chamberlain, "Reminiscences About the Alameda County District Attorney's Office."

E. A. Daly, "Alameda County Political Leader and Journalist."

Beverly Heinrichs, "Reminiscences of a Secretary in the District Attorney's Office."

Lloyd Jester, "Reminiscences of an Inspector in the District Attorney's Office."

Clarence E. Severin, "Chief Clerk in the Alameda County District Attorney's Office."

Homer R. Spence, "Attorney, Legislator, and Judge."

Volume 3, 1974. Interviews with:

J. Frank Coakley, "A Career in the Alameda County District Attorney's Office."

Albert E. Hederman, Jr., "From Office Boy to Assistant District Attorney."

Lowell Jensen, "Reflections of the Alameda County District Attorney."

James H. Oakley, "Early Life of a Warren Assistant."

*The Warrens: Four Personal Views*, 1976. Interviews by Amelia Fry, Miriam Feingold, and Wendy Won with:

Horace Albright, "Earl Warren Job Hunting at the Legislature."

Betty Foot Henderson, "Secretary to Two Warrens."

Irving and Jean Stone, "Earl Warren's Friends and Biographers."

Benjamin H. Swig, "Shared Social Concerns."

*The Japanese-American Relocation Reviewed*, with an introduction by Mike M. Masoka. Two volumes.

Volume 1, *Decision and Exodus*, 1976. Interviews by Amelia Fry and Miriam Feingold Stein with:

Tom Clark, "Comments on the Japanese-American Relocation."

Edward Ennis, "A Justice Department Attorney Comments on the Japanese-American Relocation."

Percy C. Heckendorf, "Planning for the Japanese Evacuation: Reforming Regulatory Agency Procedures."

James Rowe, "The Japanese Evacuation Decision."

Herbert Wenig, "The California Attorney General's Office, the Judge Advocate General Corps, and Japanese-American Relocation."

Volume 2, *The Internment*, 1974. Interviews by Rosemary Levenson, Amelia R. Fry and Miriam Feingold Stein with:

Robert Cozzens, "Assistant National Director of the War Relocation Authority."

Hisako Hibi, painting of Tanforan and Topaz camps.

Ruth W. Kingman, "The Fair Play Committee and Citizen Participation."

Dillon S. Myer, "War Relocation Authority: The Director's Account."

*Earl Warren, the Chief Justiceship*, 1977. One volume. Interviews with:

Herbert Brownell, "Earl Warren's Appointment to the Supreme Court."

Louis Finkelstein, "Earl Warren's Inquiry into Talmudic Law."

James Hagerty, "Campaigns Revisited: Earl Warren, Thomas Dewey and Dwight Eisenhower."

William Oliver, "Inside the Warren Court, 1953–1954."

Martin F. Richman, "Law Clerk for Chief Justice Warren, 1956–1957."

Harold Stassen, "Eisenhower, the 1952 Republican Convention and Earl Warren."

*Labor Looks at Earl Warren*, 1970. One volume. Interviews with:

Germain Bulke, "A Longshoreman's Observations."

Joseph W. Chaudet, "A Printer's View."

Paul Heide, "A Warhouseman's Reminiscences."

U. S. Simonds, "A Carpenter's Comments."

Ernest H. Vernon, "A Machinist's Recollection."

*Labor Leaders View the Warren Era*, 1976. Interviews by Miriam Feingold Stein and Amelia R. Fry with:

Robert S. Ash, "Alameda County Labor Council During the Warren Years."

Cornelius J. Haggerty, "Labor, Los Angeles, and the Legislature."

*Richard M. Nixon in the Warren Era*, 1980. One volume. Interviews with:

Earl Adams, "Financing Richard Nixon's Campaigns from 1946 to 1960."

Roy P. Crocker, "Gathering Southern California Support for Richard Nixon in the 1950 Senate Race."

Roy O. Day, "Campaigning with Richard Nixon, 1946–1952."

John Walton Dinkelspiel, "Recollections of Richard Nixon's 1950 Senatorial Campaign in Northern California."

Frank E. Jorgensen, "The Organization of Richard Nixon's Congressional Campaigns, 1946–1952."

*The Shipboard Murder Case: Labor, Radicalism and Earl Warren, 1936–1947*, 1976. Interviews with:

Aubrey Grossman, "A Defense Attorney Assesses the King, Ramsay, Conner Case."

Myron Harris, "A Defense Attorney Reminiscences."

Miriam Dinkin Johnson, "The King-Ramsay-Conner Defense Committee: 1938–1941."
Peter Odeen, "Captain of the Point Lobos."
Ernest G. Ramsay, "Reminiscences of a Defendant in the Shipboard Murder Case."
Herbert Resner, "The Recollections of the Attorney for Frank Conner."


*Interviews with the Author*
Steven D. Clymer, interviews throughout 2003, 2004, and 2005.
Warren Christopher, Los Angeles, April 2003 and June 2005.
Raymond Fisher, Pasadena, California, April 2003.
Douglas Kranwinkle, Los Angeles, Century City, April 2003 and Jan. 21, 2005.
William J. Brennan III, Princeton, New Jersey, July 2003.
Jeffrey Warren, St. Helena, California, Aug. 26, 2003, and Feb. 29, 2004.
Jesse Choper, Berkeley, California, Sept. 9 and Oct. 20, 2003.
Erwin Chemerinsky, Pasadena, California, Sept. 12, 2003; follow-up interviews 2004–2006.
Jim Riley, Oct. 15, 2003 (by telephone).
Ira Michael Heyman, Oct. 21, 2003.
Al Donnici, Nov. 15, 2003.
James Lee Warren, San Francisco, Nov. 24, 2003.
Earl Warren, Jr., Sacramento, Nov. 25, 2003, and Jan. 25, 2004 (by telephone); Feb. 19, 2004.
Robert Warren, Sacramento, Dec. 11, 2003, and March 12, 2004.
Nina "Honey Bear" Brien, Beverly Hills, California, Jan. 28 and May 6, 2004.
Richard Mosk, Beverly Hills, California, Jan. 28, 2004, and April 20, 2005.
Otis Chandler, Oxnard, California, Feb. 5, 2004.
Warren Olney IV, Santa Monica, California, Feb. 10, 2004.
G. Edward White, March 9, 2004 (by telephone).
Herb Klein, March 23, 2004 (by telephone).
Virginia Daly, Century City, California, May 31, 2004.
Jim Gaither, June 2, 2004 (by telephone).
Edward Kamin, Dec. 8, 2004 (by e-mail).
President Gerald Ford, Dec. 8, 2004 (by telephone).
Earl E. Pollock, Jan. 10, 2005 (by telephone).
Peter Taft, Los Angeles, Jan. 11, 2005.
Kenneth Ziffren, Century City, California, Jan. 12, 2005.
Jim Adler, Century City, California, Jan. 14, 2005.
Lucas "Scot" Powe, Jan. 19, 2005 (by telephone); Austin, June 6, 2005.
Peter Ehrenhaft, Washington, D.C., Jan. 31, 2005.
Dennis Flannery, Washington, D.C., Feb. 2, 2005.
Francis X. Beytagh, April 8, 2005 (by telephone).
Bill Beebe, Santa Monica, California, April 20, 2005.
Sam Stern, Washington, D.C., May 10, 2005.
Bernard C. Parks, Los Angeles, June 22, 2005.
Gabrielle Morris, Berkeley, California, July 6, 2005.
Michael Smith, Berkeley, California, July 8, 2005.
Scott Bice, Pasadena, California, July 11, 2005.
Eve Dillingham, Oct. 22, 2005 (by telephone).
William Allen, Nov. 14, 2005 (by telephone).
Robert M. O'Neil, Dec. 2, 2005 (by telephone).

Richard Posner, Dec. 2, 2005 (by telephone).

Bruce Carver Boynton, Dec. 27, 2005 (by telephone).

George Perham, Jan. 24, 2006 (by telephone).

Larry Simon, June 12, 2006.


*Books*

Abraham, Henry J. *Justices and Presidents, A Political History of Appointments to the Supreme Court*, Third
    edition. New York: Oxford University Press, 1992.

Alexander, J. A. *Life of George Chaffey.* London: Macmillan, 1928.

Alsop, Joseph, and Turner Catledge. *The 168 Days.* New York: Doubleday, 1938.

Ambrose, Stephen E. *Eisenhower, Soldier and President: The Renowned One-Volume Life.* New York: Simon
    & Schuster /Touchstone, 1990.

Armor, John, and Peter Wright (commentary by John Hersey, photographs by Ansel Adams). *Manzanar*
    New York: Random House, 1988.

Baker, Liva. *Felix Frankfurter: A Biography.* New York: Coward-McCann, 1969.

Bancroft, Hubert Howe. *The Works of Hubert Howe Bancroft, History of California.* San Francisco: The His-
    tory Company, 1890.

Bass, Jack. *Unlikely Heroes.* Tuscaloosa: University of Alabama Press, 1981.

Bean, Walton. *Boss Ruef's San Francisco: The Story of the Union Labor Party, Big Business and the Graft Pros-
    ecution.* Berkeley: University of California Press, 1967.

Bean, Walton. *California: An Interpretive History.* New York: McGraw-Hill, 1968.

Beebe, Lucius, and Charles Clegg. *San Francisco's Golden Era.* Berkeley, CA: Howell-North, 1960.

Black, Hugo L. and Elizabeth. *Mr. Justice and Mrs. Black: The Memoirs of Hugo L. Black and Elizabeth Black.*
    New York: Random House, 1986.

Bozell, L. Brent. *The Warren Revolution: Reflections on the Consensus Society.* New Rochelle, NY: Arlington
    House, 1966.

Branch, Taylor. *At Canaan's Edge: America in the King Years, 1965–68.* New York: Simon & Schuster, 2006.

Branch, Taylor. *Parting the Waters: America in the King Years, 1954–1963.* New York: Simon & Schuster, 1988.

Branch, Taylor. *Pillar of Fire: America in the King Years, 1963–65.* New York: Simon & Schuster, 1998.

Brechin, Gary. *Imperial San Francisco: Urban Power, Earthly Ruin.* Berkeley: University of California Press, 1999.

Brownell, Herbert. *Advising Ike, The Memoirs of Attorney General Herbert Brownell.* Lawrence: University
    Press of Kansas, 1993.

Burke, Robert E. *Olson's New Deal for California: The Story of California's Transition from Depression to
    Wartime Prosperity and of a Governor Whose New Deal Never Came to Pass.* Berkeley: University of Cal-
    ifornia Press, 1953.

Burns, James MacGregor, and Stewart Burns. *A People's Charter: The Pursuit of Rights in America.* New York:
    Vintage, 1993.

Camp, William Martin. *San Francisco: Port of Gold.* New York: Doubleday, 1947.

Cardozo, Benjamin. *The Nature of the Judicial Process: The Storrs Lectures at Yale University.* New Haven, CT:
    Yale University Press, 1921.

Carlson, Oliver. *A Mirror for Californians.* Indianapolis: Bobbs-Merrill, 1941.

Carrillo, Leo. *The California I Love.* Englewood Cliffs, NJ: Prentice-Hall, 1961.

Charns, Alexander. *Cloak and Gavel: FBI Wiretaps, Bugs, Informers, and the Supreme Court.* Urbana and
    Chicago: University of Illinois Press, 1992.

Christopher, Warren M. *Chances of a Lifetime.* New York: Scribner, 2001.

Clark, Sydney A. *Golden Tapestry of California.* New York: Robert M. McBride, 1937.

Compston, Christine. *Earl Warren: Justice for All.* New York: Oxford University Press, 2001.

Cooper, Erwin. *Aqueduct Empire, A Guide to Water in California: Its Turbulent History, Its Management Today*. Glendale, CA: Arthur H. Clark, 1968.

Cray, Ed. *Chief Justice: A Biography of Earl Warren*. New York: Simon & Schuster, 1997.

Cross, Ira B. *A History of the Labor Movement in California*. Berkeley: University of California Press, 1935.

Dallek, Robert. *An Unfinished Life: John F. Kennedy, 1917–1963*. Boston: Little, Brown, 2003.

Daniels, Roger. *The Decision to Relocate the Japanese Americans*. Malabar, FL: Krieger, 1975, repr. 1986.

Donley, Michael W., Stuart Allan, Patricia Caro, and Clyde P. Patton. *Atlas of California*. Culver City, CA: Pacific Book Center, 1979.

Douglas, William O. *The Autobiography of William O. Douglas: The Court Years, 1939–1975*. New York: Random House, 1980.

Dubofsky, Melvyn. *We Shall Be All: A History of the Industrial Workers of the World*. New York: Quadrangle, 1969.

Eisen, Jonathan, and David Fine, with Kim Eisen, eds. *Unknown California, Classic and Contemporary Writing on California Culture, Society, and Politics*. New York: Macmillan, 1985.

Eisenhower, Dwight D. *The Eisenhower Diaries*, edited by Robert H. Ferrell. New York: W. W. Norton,1981.

Eisenhower, Dwight D. *Mandate for Change: The White House Years, 1953–56*. New York: Doubleday, 1963.

Felton, Ernest L. *California's Many Climates*. Palo Alto, CA: Pacific Books, 1965.

Federal Writers' Project of the Works Progress Administration for the State of California. *California: A Guide to the Golden State, American Guide Series*. New York: Hastings House, 1939, repr. 1942, 1943.

Frank, John P. *The Warren Court*. New York: Macmillan, 1964.

Frankfurter, Felix. *From the Diaries of Felix Frankfurter*. Ed. Joseph P. Lash. New York: W. W. Norton, 1974.

Gardner, David P. *The California Oath Controversy*. Berkeley: University of California Press, 1967.

Garrow, David J. *Bearing the Cross: Martin Luther King, Jr., and the Southern Christian Leadership Conference*. New York: William Morrow, 1986.

Garrow, David J. *Liberty and Sexuality: The Right to Privacy and the Making of Roe v. Wade*. New York: Lisa Drew/Macmillan, 1994.

Geelan, Agnes. *The Dakota Maverick: The Political Life of William Langer, Also Known as "Wild Bill."* Bismarck, ND: Prairie House, 1975.

Gentry, Curt. *Frame-up: The Incredible Case of Tom Mooney and Warren Billings*. New York: W. W. Norton, 1967.

Gerhart, Eugene C. *America's Advocate: Robert H. Jackson*. Indianapolis: Bobbs-Merrill, 1958.

Ginger, Ray. *The Bending Cross: A Biography of Eugene Victor Debs*. New Brunswick, NJ: Rutgers University Press, 1949.

Goodwin, Doris Kearns. *No Ordinary Time, Franklin and Eleanor Roosevelt: The Home Front in World War II*. New York: Simon & Schuster, 1994.

Graham, Katharine. *Personal History*. New York: Alfred A. Knopf, 1997.

Grodzins, Morton. *Americans Betrayed: Politics and the Japanese Evacuation*. Chicago: University of Chicago Press, 1949.

Hand, Learned. *The Bill of Rights: The Oliver Wendell Holmes Lectures, 1958*. New York: Atheneum, 1968 (originally pub. Harvard University Press, 1958).

Harvey, Richard B. *Earl Warren, Governor of California*. New York: Exposition Press, 1969.

Hichborn, Franklin. *The System, As Uncovered by the San Francisco Graft Prosecution*, San Francisco: James H. Barry, 1915.

Hickok, Lorena. *One Third of a Nation*. Ed. Richard Lowitt and Maurine Beasley. Urbana and Chicago: University of Illinois Press, 1983 (originally pub. 1981).

Hill, Gladwin. *Dancing Bear: An Inside Look at California Politics*. Cleveland: World, 1968.

Hockett, Jeffrey D. *New Deal Justice: The Constitutional Jurisprudence of Hugo L. Black, Felix Frankfurter and Robert H. Jackson*. Lanham, MD: Rowman & Littlefield, 1996.

Horwitz, Morton J. *The Warren Court and the Pursuit of Justice*. New York: Hill and Wang, 1998.

Irons, Peter. *The Courage of Their Convictions: Sixteen Americans Who Fought Their Way to the Supreme Court*. New York: Penguin, 1988.

Irons, Peter. *Justice at War: The Story of the Japanese-American Internment Cases*. New York: Oxford University Press, 1983.

Irons, Peter, and Stephanie Guitton, eds. *May It Please the Court*. New York: New Press, 1993.

Inada, Lawson Fusao, ed. *Only What We Could Carry: The Japanese American Internment Experience*. Berkeley, CA: Heyday, 2000.

Jackson, Joseph Henry, ed. *Continent's End: A Collection of California Writing*. New York: McGraw-Hill, 1944.

Jefferson, Thomas. *Writings*. Ed. Merrill D. Patterson. New York: Library of America, 1984.

Johnson, Lady Bird. *A White House Diary*. New York: Holt, Rinehart and Winston, 1970.

Jordan, David Starr. *California and the Californians*. San Francisco: A. M. Robertson, 1967.

Kalman, Laura. *Abe Fortas: A Biography*. New Haven, CT: Yale University Press, 1990.

Karnow, Stanley. *Vietnam: A History*. New York: Viking 1983.

Katcher, Leo. *Earl Warren: A Political Biography*. New York: McGraw-Hill, 1967.

Kelley, Stanley Jr. *Professional Public Relations and Political Power*. Baltimore: Johns Hopkins University Press, 1966 (originally pub. 1956).

Kennedy, David M. *Freedom from Fear: The American People in Depression and War, 1929–1945*. New York: Oxford University Press, 1999.

Kennedy, John Castillo. *The Great Earthquake and Fire: San Francisco, 1906*. New York: William Morrow, 1963.

Klarman, Michael J. *From Jim Crow to Civil Rights: The Supreme Court and the Struggle for Racial Equity*. New York: Oxford University Press, 2004.

Klurfeld, Herman. *Behind the Lines: The World of Drew Pearson*. Englewood Cliffs, NJ: Prentice-Hall, 1968.

Lambert, Patricia. *False Witness: The Real Story of Jim Garrison's Investigation and Oliver Stone's Film JFK*. New York: M. Evans, 1998.

Lane, Mark. *Plausible Denial: Was the CIA Involved in the Assassination of JFK?* New York: Thunder's Mouth Press, 1991.

Lane, Mark. *Rush to Judgment*. New York: Thunder's Mouth Press, 1992 (originally pub. 1966).

Lavender, David. *California, Land of New Beginnings*. New York: Harper & Row, 1972.

Leckie, Robert. *Conflict: The History of the Korean War*. New York: G. P. Putnam's Sons, 1962.

Lewis, Anthony. *Gideon's Trumpet*. New York: Vintage, 1989 (originally pub. 1964).

Lewis, Frederick P. *The Context of Judicial Activism: The Endurance of the Warren Court Legacy in a Conservative Age*. Lanham, MD: Rowman & Littlefield, 1999.

Lewis, John, with Michael D'Orso. *Walking with the Wind: A Memoir of the Movement*. New York: Simon & Schuster, 1998.

Los Angeles County Museum of Art. *Made in California: Art, Image and Identity, 1900–2000*. Berkeley: University of California Press, 2000.

Lower, Richard Coke. *A Bloc of One, The Political Career of Hiram Johnson*. Stanford, CA: Stanford University Press, 1993.

Manchester, William. *The Death of a President*. New York: Harper & Row, 1967.

Mazo, Earl. *Richard Nixon: A Political and Personal Portrait*. New York: Harper & Brothers, 1959.

McGroarty, John S. *California, Its History and Romance*. Los Angeles: Grafton, 1911.

McWilliams, Carey. *Factories in the Field: The Story of Migratory Farm Labor in California*. Berkeley: University of California Press, 1935, repr. 1999.

McWilliams, Carey. *Fool's Paradise: A Carey McWilliams Reader*. Berkeley, CA: Heyday, 2001.

McWilliams, Carey. *Ill Fares the Land: Migrants and Migratory Labor in the United States*. Boston: Little, Brown, 1942.

McWilliams, Carey. *Prejudice: Japanese-Americans, Symbol of Racial Intolerance*. Boston: Little, Brown, 1944.

Mitchell, Greg. *The Campaign of the Century: Upton Sinclair's Race for Governor of California and the Birth of Media Politics*. New York: Random House, 1992.

Morgan, H. Wayne. *Eugene V. Debs: Socialist for President*. Syracuse, NY: Syracuse University Press, 1962.

Morris, Roger. *Richard Milhous Nixon: The Rise of an American Politician*. New York: Henry Holt, 1991.

Mowry, George E. *The California Progressives*. Chicago: Quadrangle Books, 1963.

Muir, John. *The Mountains of California*. Century, 1904.

Murphy, Bruce Allen. *Fortas: The Rise and Ruin of a Supreme Court Justice*. New York: William Morrow, 1988.

Murphy, Bruce Allen. *Wild Bill: The Legend and Life of William O. Douglas, America's Most Controversial Supreme Court Justice*. New York: Random House, 2003.

Myrdal, Gunnar. *An American Dilemma: The Negro Problem and Modern Democracy*, 2 vols. Somerset, NJ: Transaction, 2002 (originally pub. 1944).

Newman, Roger K. *Hugo Black, A Biography*. New York: Pantheon, 1994.

Norris, Frank. *The Octopus*. New York: Penguin, 1994.

Ogletree, Charles J., Jr. *All Deliberate Speed*. New York: W. W. Norton, 2004.

Older, Fremont. *My Own Story*. San Francisco: Call Publishing, 1919. (Edition cited here is New York: Macmillan, 1926.)

Olin, Spencer C. *California's Prodigal Sons: Hiram Johnson and the Progressives, 1911–1917*. Berkeley: University of California Press, 1968.

Patterson, James T. *Brown v. Board of Education: A Civil Rights Milestone and Its Troubled Legacy*. New York: Oxford University Press, 2001.

Pearson, Drew. *Diaries 1949–1959*. Ed. Tyler Abell. New York: Holt, Rinehart and Winston, 1974.

Phillips, Herbert L. *Big Wayward Girl: An Informal Political History of California*. New York: Doubleday, 1968.

Pollack, Jack Harrison. *Earl Warren: The Judge Who Changed America*. Englewood Cliffs, NJ: Prentice-Hall, 1979.

Powe, Lucas A., Jr. *The Warren Court and American Politics*. Cambridge, MA: Belknap Press of Harvard University Press, 2000.

Reeves, Richard. *President Kennedy: Profile of Power*. New York: Simon & Schuster, 1993.

Rice, Arnold S. *The Warren Court, 1953–1969*, vol. 8 of *The Supreme Court in American Life*. Millwood, NY: Associated Faculty Press, 1987.

Richardson, Elmo. *The Presidency of Dwight D. Eisenhower*. Lawrence: Regents Press of Kansas, 1979.

Robinson, Greg. *By Order of the President, FDR and the Internment of Japanese Americans*. Cambridge, MA: Harvard University Press, 2001.

Rogin, Michael Paul, and John L. Shover. *Political Change in California: Critical Elections and Social Movements, 1890–1966*. Westport, CT: Greenwood, 1970.

Roosevelt, Franklin Delano. *F.D.R. His Personal Letters*, 4 vols. Ed. Elliott Roosevelt. New York: Duell, Sloan and Pearce, 1930.

Rush, Philip S. *The Californias, 1846–1957*. San Diego, CA: Neyenesch, 1957.

Samish, Arthur H., and Bob Thomas. *The Secret Boss of California: The Life and High Times of Art Samish*. New York: Crown, 1971.

Schwartz, Bernard. *Super Chief: Earl Warren and His Supreme Court—A Judicial Biography*. New York: New York University Press, 1983.

Schwartz, Bernard. *The Warren Court: A Retrospective*. New York: Oxford University Press, 1996.

Scott, Peter Dale. *Deep Politics and the Death of JFK*. Berkeley: University of California Press, 1993.

Sinclair, Upton. *I, Candidate for Governor: And How I Got Licked*. Berkeley: University of California Press, 1994 (originally pub. 1934).

Sinclair, Upton. *Upton Sinclair Presents William Fox.* Pasadena, CA: Self-published, 1933.

Smith, Glenn H. *Langer of North Dakota: A Study in Isolationism, 1940–1959.* New York: Garland, 1979.

Specter, Arlen, with Charles Robbins. *Passion for Truth: From Finding JFK's Single Bullet to Questioning Anita Hill to Impeaching Clinton.* New York: William Morrow, 2000.

Starr, Kevin. *Embattled Dreams: California in War and Peace, 1940–1950.* New York: Oxford University Press, 2002.

Starr, Kevin. *Endangered Dreams: The Great Depression in California.* New York: Oxford University Press, 1996.

Starr, Kevin. *Inventing the Dream: California Through the Progressive Era.* New York: Oxford University Press, 1985.

Starr, Kevin. *Material Dreams: Southern California Through the 1920s.* New York: Oxford University Press, 1990.

St. Clair, James E., and Linda C. Gugin. *Chief Justice Fred M. Vinson of Kentucky, A Political Biography.* Lexington: The University Press of Kentucky, 2002.

Stone, Irving. *Earl Warren, A Great American Story.* Englewood Cliffs, NJ: Prentice-Hall, 1948.

Storke, Thomas M. *California Editor.* Foreword by Earl Warren. Los Angeles: Westernlore, 1958.

Stuart, Gary L. *Miranda: The Story of America's Right to Remain Silent.* Tucson: University of Arizona Press, 2004

Thomas, Gordon, and Max Morgan Witts. *The San Francisco Earthquake.* New York: Stein and Day, 1971.

Thompson, Fred, compiler. *The I.W.W., Its First Fifty Years: The History of an Effort to Organize the Working Class.* Chicago: Industrial Workers of the World, 1955.

Tushnet, Mark V. *Making Civil Rights Law: Thurgood Marshall and the Supreme Court, 1936–1961.* New York: Oxford University Press, 1994.

Tushnet, Mark V. *The Warren Court in Historical and Political Perspective.* Charlottesville: University Press of Virginia, 1973.

Tussey, Jean Y., ed. *Eugene V. Debs Speaks.* New York: Pathfinder, 1970.

Warren, Earl. "All Men Are Created Equal," Twenty-seventh Annual Benjamin Cardozo Lecture, delivered before the Association of the Bar of the City of New York, 1970. Introduction by Mendes Hershman. New York: New York Bar Association, 1970.

Warren, Earl. *The Memoirs of Chief Justice Earl Warren.* Lanham, MD: Madison, 1977.

Warren, Earl. *The Public Papers of Chief Justice Earl Warren.* Ed. Henry M. Christman. New York: Simon Schuster, 1959.

Warren, Earl. *A Republic, If You Can Keep It.* New York: The New York Times Company, 1972.

Watkins, T. H. *California: An Illustrated History.* Palo Alto, CA: American West, 1973.

Weaver, John D. *Warren: The Man, The Court, The Era.* Boston: Little, Brown, 1967.

Welch, Robert. *The Politician.* Belmont, MA: Belmont, 1964.

Weglyn, Michi Nishimura. *Years of Infamy: The Untold Story of America's Concentration Camps.* Seattle: University of Washington Press, 1976, 1996.

White, G. Edward. *The American Judicial Tradition,* New York: Oxford University Press, 1976.

White, G. Edward. *Earl Warren, A Public Life.* New York: Oxford University Press, 1982.

White, Theodore H. *The Making of the President, 1960.* New York: Atheneum, 1962.

Young, Andrew. *An Easy Burden: The Civil Rights Movement and the Transformation of America.* New York: HarperCollins, 1996.

### Periodicals

*American Bar Association Journal,* Chicago

*American Rally*

*Bakersfield Californian,* Bakersfield, California

*Collier's: The National Weekly,* Springfield, Ohio

*Ebony*, Chicago

*Fortnight*, Los Angeles

*Fortune*, New York

*Greensboro Record*, Greensboro, North Carolina

*Grizzly Bear* (magazine of the Native Sons and Daughters of the Golden West)

*Harvard Law Review*, Cambridge, Massachusetts

*Holiday*, Philadelphia

*Journal of Policy History*, St. Louis

*Life*, New York

*Los Angeles Times*, Los Angeles

*Minnesota Journal of Global Trade*, Minneapolis

*New York Times*, New York

*Newsweek*, New York

*Oakland Tribune*, Oakland, California

*Pacific Citizen*, Los Angeles

*Playboy*, Chicago

*Rafo Shimpo*, Los Angeles

*Reviews in American History*, The Johns Hopkins University Press, Baltimore

*Sacramento Bee*, Sacramento

*San Francisco Chronicle*, San Francisco

*San Francisco Examiner*, San Francisco

*Santa Barbara News-Press*, Santa Barbara, California

*Saturday Evening Post*

*Science & Justice*, North Yorkshire, UK

*Studies in Intelligence*, Washington, D.C.

*Time*, New York

*U.C. Davis Law Review*

*Other Written Sources—Government Reports, Articles, Dissertations, Pamphlets*

Biennial messages of Governor Earl Warren to the State Legislature (including inaugural addresses), 1943–53, state archives, Sacramento.

California State Department of Finance reports, including annual state budgets, 1935–1955 (available through Los Angeles County Public Library and Los Angeles County Law Library).

Cho, Sumi, "Redeeming Whiteness in the Shadow of Internment: Earl Warren, Brown and a Theory of Racial Redemption," *Boston College Law Review*, December 1998.

Conwell, Russell H., "Acres of Diamonds" (bound copy of the speech as delivered many times in the early 1900s).

*The Evacuated People, A Quantitative Description*, United States Department of the Interior, J. A. Krug, Secretary; War Relocation Authority, D.S. Myer, Director, prepared at the closing of the Authority, June 30, 1946.

*Final Report, Japanese Evacuation from the West Coast, 1942*, United States of America War Office, prepared by Lt. Gen. John L. DeWitt, transmitted to Chief of Staff, United States Army, War Department, Washington, D.C., on June 5, 1943.

*Final Report of the Special Crime Study Commission on Organized Crime*, May 11, 1953.

Hearings and Exhibits of the President's Commission on the Assassination of President John F. Kennedy, Volumes I–XXVI, United States Government Printing Office, 1964.

Henderson, Lloyd Ray, "Earl Warren and California Politics," unpublished Ph.D. dissertation, University of California, Berkeley, June 1965 (copy on file at Doe Library, Berkeley).

International Labor Defense Pamphlets, 22 pamphlets by various organizations and publishers, collected in a single volume and housed at the Main Library, University of California, Berkeley.

John Birch Society, official records of the Society, including Blue and White books for early 1960s and January 1961 bulletin "So Let's Impeach Earl Warren," supplied by Jaclyn Strelka, public affairs officer for the Society.

Kenny, Robert W. "My First Forty Years in California Politics," unpublished manuscript, at the Bancroft Library, University of California, Berkeley.

King-Ramsay-Conner Defense Committee, *The King-Ramsay-Conner Frame-Up: Earl Warren's "Murder" Case, 1936* (pamphlet). Other materials also from the committee.

The Official Report of the President's Commission on the Assassination of President John F. Kennedy (edition cited here is by Longmeadow Press, 1992), reprinted from the original Warren Commission Report, October 1964.

*The Oracle*, student publication of Kern Co. High School, Commencement Issue, 1908 (copies at Bakersfield High School and Law History Center of Boalt Hall, University of California, Berkeley).

Scoggins, Verne. *It Happened in California* (pamphlet published by Friends of Earl Warren), 1953.

Sinclair, Upton. *EPIC Answers, How to End Poverty in California* (End Poverty League, pamphlet), 1934.

Sinclair, Upton. *I, Governor of California And How I Ended Poverty: A True Story of the Future* (self-published pamphlet), 1933.

Sinclair, Upton. *The Lie Factory Starts* (End Poverty League, Inc., pamphlet), July 1934.

Small, Merrell, "The Country Editor and Earl Warren" (unpublished manuscript, at the Bancroft Library, University of California, Berkeley).

*State Summary of War Casualties [California]*, United States Navy, 1946.

"Supreme Court Law Clerks' Recollections of Brown v. Board of Education," *St. John's Law Review*, vol. 78 no. 3 (Summer 2004).

*To the Beasts*, Industrial Workers of the World (California Branch of the General Defense Committee, San Francisco, California), April 1924 (pamphlet).

*Tule Lake Relocation/Segregation Center, 1942–1946*, War Relocation Authority (TelCom Productions), 1987.

United States Congress, Records of the Judiciary Committee into Earl Warren's confirmation as Chief Justice of the United States. Six boxes, 51–56, held at the National Archives, Washington, DC.

*Wartime Exile, The Exclusion of the Japanese Americans from the West Coast*, United States Department of the Interior, J. A. Krug, Secretary; War Relocation Authority, D. S. Myer, Director; report prepared by Ruth E. McKee, historian (U.S. Government Printing Office), undated.

Whitten, Woodrow Carlton. "Criminal Syndicalism and the Law in California, 1919–1927," Ph.D. dissertation, University of California, Berkeley, 1946.

*World War II, Honor List of Dead and Missing, State of California*, United States War Department, June 1946.

### Collections of Papers

American Civil Liberties Union papers, Seeley G. Mudd Manuscript Library, Princeton University, Princeton, New Jersey.

Bakersfield History documents, Beale Library Local History Collection, Bakersfield, California.

Hugo Lafayette Black papers, Library of Congress, Manuscript Division, Washington, D.C.

William J. Brennan, Jr., papers, Library of Congress, Manuscript Division, Washington, D.C. The Brennan papers are divided into Parts I and II; the end-of-term memos quoted at length in this book are included in Part II, to which access is controlled but was granted to the author by William J. Brennan III in 2003.

Harold H. Burton papers, Library of Congress, Manuscript Division, Washington, D.C.

Alexander Charns papers, Southern Historical Collection, University of North Carolina, Chapel Hill.

Warren M. Christopher papers, Lyndon Baines Johnson Library and Museum, Austin, Texas.

William O. Douglas papers, Library of Congress, Manuscript Division, Washington, D.C.

Allen Dulles papers, Seeley G. Mudd Manuscript Library, Princeton University, Princeton, New Jersey.

Felix Frankfurter papers, Library of Congress, Manuscript Division, Washington, D.C.

John Marshall Harlan papers, Seeley G. Mudd Manuscript Library, Princeton University, Princeton, New Jersey.

Harry Honda (editor of *Pacific Citizen*) papers, Japanese American National Museum, Los Angeles.

Herbert Hoover papers, Hoover Institution Archives, Stanford, California.

Robert H. Jackson papers, Library of Congress, Manuscript Division, Washington, D.C.

Lyndon Baines Johnson papers, Lyndon Baines Johnson Library and Museum, Austin, Texas.

Robert W. Kenny papers, Bancroft Library, University of California, Berkeley.

William Langer papers, Elwyn B. Robinson Department of Special Collections, Chester Fritz Library, University of North Dakota, Grand Forks.

Carey McWilliams papers, Charles E. Young Research Library (Special Collections), UCLA, Los Angeles.

Raymond Moley papers, Hoover Institution Archives, Stanford, California.

Cecil Mosbacher papers, Bancroft Library, University of California, Berkeley.

Stanley Mosk personal papers, privately held by Justice Richard Mosk, Los Angeles.

Richard Nixon Pre-Presidential papers, National Archives, Laguna Niguel, California.

Richard and Pat Nixon papers, Richard Nixon Library and Birthplace, Yorba Linda, California.

Culbert L. Olson personal papers, Bancroft Library, University of California, Berkeley.

Drew Pearson papers, Lyndon Baines Johnson Library and Museum, Austin, Texas.

Robert Gordon Sproul papers, Bancroft Library, University of California, Berkeley. Sproul's papers also include official records of the university, filed separately but also maintained by the Bancroft.

Edison Uno papers, Charles E. Young Research Library (Special Collections), UCLA, Los Angeles.

Earl Warren papers, California State Archives, Sacramento. Papers at the archives include Warren's years as district attorney, attorney general and governor. Some Warren personal papers also held by the Bancroft Library, University of California, Berkeley.

Earl Warren papers, Library of Congress, Manuscript Division, Washington, D.C. Papers here cover Warren's years as chief justice, 1953–1969, and the years from his retirement until his death in 1974.

Earl Warren confirmation records, Senate Judiciary Committee files, National Archives, Washington, D.C. These six boxes of confirmation materials, including closed hearings and correspondence of the committee, were sealed until 2004, when they were opened to the public on the fiftieth anniversary of Warren's confirmation to the Supreme Court.

Albert C. Wedermeyer papers, Hoover Institution Archives, Stanford, California.

Loyd Wright papers, Hoover Institution Archives, Stanford, California.

# Index